IN THE CLOSET
OF THE
VATICAN

'Sensational ... This is much, much more than an exposé of some taffeta-clad hypocrites ... Fascinating'

Sunday Times

'A remarkable feat of investigation. Any friend of the Roman Catholic Church needs to take this book's message seriously.'

Sir Diarmaid MacCulloch, Professor of the History of the Church at the University of Oxford, writing in *The Times*

'The carnival is over ... I would love to be able to dismiss Martel's book as mere gossip. It will anger and sadden vast numbers of Catholics. For many this may be the last straw and they will be off. But it would be a mistake to rubbish this book. It is based on years of research. [Martel] is a highly intelligent and honest journalist and the Church will need courage to respond to his revelations fruitfully.'

Timothy Radcliffe OP, internationally renowned theologian and former Master of the Dominican Order, writing in *The Tablet*

'[An] earth-shaking exposé of clerical corruption ... What Martel does, quite masterfully, is to connect the dots that reveal an ecclesial system in profound decay ... *In the Closet of the Vatican* examines in impressive detail the double lives led by many of the church's prelates ... A truly remarkable publishing event.'

National Catholic Reporter

'I urge every Catholic to read it, however difficult that may be ... The book did not surprise me, as such, but it still stunned, shocked, and disgusted me. You simply cannot unread it, or banish what is quite obviously true from your mind ... This may seem like hyperbole, but in my view, the last drops of moral authority the Vatican might hope to have evaporate with this book. It is difficult to express the heartbroken rage so many of us in the pews now feel.'

Andrew Sullivan, *New York Magazine*

'The first global account of the dishonesty about homosexuality which is endemic in the structures of the modern Roman Catholic Church.'

James Alison, International theologian and priest

'A glimpse of the poisonous world that Frédéric Martel ... has spent five years researching for this book.'

Andrew Brown, *Guardian*

'A captivating story.'

Catholic Herald

'An important revelation.'

Daily Telegraph

'A "bombshell" of a book.'

Spectator

'It is not often that someone attempts to break the wall of silence that surrounds the Vatican. There is no doubt that Martel's book is a brilliant exception. Homosexuality is still the most obscure and unexplored area in the world today, and discussion largely taboo and forbidden. Martel brings to light, as never before and with admirable objectivity, a world of secrecy, blackmail and power, far beyond anything imagined hitherto.'

Gianluigi Nuzzi, journalist who exposed the 'Vatileaks' scandal

'A truly shocking theory about the Vatican; the largest gay community in the world.'

Il Giornale [Italy]

'Probably one of the best books by a journalist ever written.'

Gazeta Wyborcza [Poland]

'Masterful and spine-chilling ... Everybody must read this astonishing piece of investigative journalism.'

Washington Book Review

IN THE CLOSET OF THE VATICAN

Power, Homosexuality, Hypocrisy

Revised and Expanded Edition

FRÉDÉRIC MARTEL

Translated by
Shaun Whiteside

BLOOMSBURY CONTINUUM
LONDON · OXFORD · NEW YORK · NEW DELHI · SYDNEY

BLOOMSBURY CONTINUUM
Bloomsbury Publishing Plc
50 Bedford Square, London, WC1B 3DP, UK

BLOOMSBURY, BLOOMSBURY CONTINUUM and the Diana logo are trademarks of
Bloomsbury Publishing Plc

Published in France as *Sodoma* by Éditions Robert Laffont
© Éditions Robert Laffont, S.A.S, Paris, 2019
First published in Great Britain 2019
Paperback, 2019

A catalogue record for this book is available from the British Library

Library of Congress Cataloguing-in-Publication data has been applied for

ISBN: PB: 978-1-4729-6618-6; HB: 978-1-4729-6614-8; TPB: 978-1-4729-6624-7;
EPDF: 978-1-4729-6616-2; EPUB: 978-1-4729-6615-5

2 4 6 8 10 9 7 5 3 1

Typeset by Integra Software Services Pvt. Ltd.
Printed and bound in Great Britain by CPI Group (UK) Ltd, Croydon CR0 4YY

To find out more about our authors and books visit www.bloomsbury.com
and sign up for our newsletters

CONTENTS

CONTENTS

THE POPE IS

AGAINST CHRISTIAN

TEACHING

THE CHURCH HAS

BEEN DRASTICALLY

CHANGED AFTER

(2ND VATICAN

COUNCIL)

PREFACE TO THE REVISED AND EXPANDED EDITION

In response to the French Catholic philosopher Jacques Maritain, a 'homophile' who had come to beg him not to publish his book on homosexuality, the renowned writer André Gide, a Protestant, said: 'Catholics don't like the truth.' And the Nobel laureate in Literature nevertheless courageously published his little treatise, *Corydon*. That was in 1923.

A century later and it seems that some Catholics still don't like the truth! Theologians, priests and 'Vaticanologist' journalists have deemed that I should not have published *In the Closet of the Vatican*, either. And, like Gide, I persist and affirm my decision. Not only did this book need to be written, it needed to be written in the form of a major report, a work of 'narrative non-fiction' with exactly the sources and writing style that I employed – these provided the only way to describe a reality that has been hidden for too long.

The book's considerable and unprecedented success in over fifty countries confirms the opportuneness of its publication. *In the Closet of the Vatican* has been translated into over twenty languages; it has been the subject of several thousand articles; and the book, a *New York Times* bestseller, topped the sales lists in some fifteen countries. All of this goes to show that it came at the right time.

The reader of this new English-language paperback edition will find an update of the original version. The initial translation has been carefully revised by the American editor Jacob Bromberg. Corrections to details have also been made, as well as updates to certain parts of the book, to take new events into account. But the book itself remains true to what it was in the first place – as I will explain.

In the Closet of the Vatican is a vast, counter-intuitive puzzle: over the course of the book, I carefully accumulate pieces of information, fit them together and patiently describe all that I have seen until the 'code' appears clearly at its end – and, finally, the puzzle is complete. One chapter, one story, one situation would not be enough to understand the system; it is the accumulation of facts, the multiple new sources, the cumulative effect and the high-spirited, subversive style that make this book what it is and reveal the secret of the Vatican. This is why, if I had to rewrite the book, I would keep its *gayissimo* style. As I understand it, the Vatican is a predominantly gay organization, and so it was necessary to use the very terms of 'gay subculture' to describe it.

In doing so, my sole motivation has been the necessity of truth. It never ceased to guide me throughout the writing of *In the Closet of the Vatican*. And it is this unstinting pursuit of the truth – so rare in the Church, unfortunately – that has captivated hundreds of thousands of readers, countless Catholics and even bishops and cardinals (who have passed word or written to me confidentially). Pope Francis confided to his entourage, 'I read the book. It's good. I knew it all,' according to the indiscretions of the American, French and Italian press.

Of course, some priests, commentators and Vaticanologists (sometimes 'in the closet' themselves) judged that my book is based on 'insinuations' or 'rumours' and that it 'caricatured' certain prelates. How predictable!

There are two kinds of readers or critics who are liable not to understand this book: those who are completely unfamiliar with the gay world and thus appear helpless or incredulous when faced with the reality I describe; and those who, like the Vaticanologists, know this reality all too well and are perfectly aware of the truth of the 'Closet', but who, for various reasons, prefer to deny it or keep it a secret. For many of them, the book is full of information that can be shared in conversation but never written. It will take time for them to understand – but that time will come.

It is nevertheless the case that this book is not based on a single rumour, insinuation, 'innuendo' or piece of gossip. There are only facts. In addition to the hundreds of interviews I conducted with cardinals, bishops, nuncios and priests, I have published over three hundred pages of sources online. These include over two thousand archival documents gathered with the help of my team of eighty researchers, thousands of declassified documents from the American State Department, confidential diplomatic telegrams, police reports and court records, testimonies from doctors and prostitutes, duly cited press articles and the list of books consulted. The slightest fact presented in this book is thus corroborated by dozens of notes in what I believe to be a modern editorial method in this digital age, which is to publish sources online in order to have enough space to lay them out in detail.

Since when have such sources and recorded interviews, the latter largely carried out before a witness, not been considered reliable? If that were the case, there would be no more journalism, no more sociology, no more investigations, police or systems of justice. Each page of this book is thus based on countless precise, cross-checked sources – even if, of course, I cannot write or reveal everything, due to legal or moral reasons.

Beyond the facts, it is of course possible to debate my interpretations. But even if I am mistaken in one case or another, I am unequivocally certain of my analysis of the whole, of the structurally homosexualized nature of the Church.

As the English theologian James Alison suggested, 'Labelling something "mere gossip" can also contribute to cover-up. All those who dismissed those tales as "mere gossip" were, as a matter of fact, contributing to their cover-up.' Indeed, following his return from Chile in 2018, Pope Francis invited us to 'find the roots and the structures that have enabled these events to occur and to perpetuate themselves'. In my own way, I am answering his call.

To my eyes, one cannot understand the Vatican and the Catholic Church without taking into consideration the homosexual element. Those who pretend to speak about the Church while neglecting its intrinsically homosexual aspect are doomed to continue misunderstanding how it functions. I sincerely pity them, because they will continue to fail to understand the scandals for a long time, proceeding from disillusionment to disillusionment. This matter, you see, is not a question of black sheep, but a structural problem – a system.

If not for bringing this system to light, how else should we understand the impact that *In the Closet of the Vatican* has had around the world since its publication in February 2019, in dozens of countries? If the analysis was wrong or caricatural, why has the book created such an unprecedentedly huge explosion within the Church? Why has it been so very widely read by bishops and priests? Why has it changed the terms of debate in the media worldwide, to the point where, according to the influential theologian James Alison, it has 'reshuffled the cards and changed the rules of the game forever'? Why, if not because it confirms what all the witnesses, all the priests and cardinals of the Curia, all the Vaticanologists and sufficiently well-informed people knew (and told me 'off the record')? Since the book's publication, I have received thousands of letters and emails, sometimes desperate and very moving, that contain testimonies confirming my thesis. And this is not to count the numerous scandals and other affairs that have continued to erupt since the arrival of *In the Closet of the Vatican*, and that confirm the structural nature of the problem.

This is why I am happy to have contributed to changing the conversation about Catholicism. From now on, the question is not to try to understand why so many cardinals and priests are homophobic, but rather to understand why they are so very frequently homosexual. It is no longer a matter of denouncing the gay presence in the Church, but one of understanding why the Church predominantly attracts, recruits and promotes homosexuals due to this 'clerical homosexuality'. This is why we must no longer confuse homosexuality with sexual abuse – on the contrary, we must understand why the illusion of chastity and the culture of secrecy concerning the sexuality of priests are the true template for the system of cover-ups. And if there were only one rule to take away from this book, it is the following: the more homophobic a cardinal is in public, the more likely he is homosexual in private.

We should not forget – I have repeated it several times in the book and in hundreds of interviews – that, personally, I have no problem with the fact of a cardinal, bishop or priest being actively gay. I even think that this reality, widespread as it is, should be recognized by the Church and that living as such should be an option for priests, among others, since it is already very often the case. The celibacy and chastity of priests, which are profoundly unnatural, have failed: that is the truth. The assessment is the same in Rome today, including within the pope's entourage. Moreover, the abstinence of priests, like the refusal to ordain women, is a late invention that has nothing to do with the Bible or the Gospels. In practice, and especially since the sexual 'liberation' of the 1970s, chastity is no longer humanly sustainable over time; it is generally the sign of acute emotional immaturity or the source of serious pathological problems. Moreover, we should never forget that now, and no matter what the Church thinks of it, homosexuality and same-sex marriage are legal in the majority of democratic countries. Homophobia, however, has become a crime. In fifty years, we have gone from the criminalization of homosexuality to the penalization of homophobia. The Church should now draw the logical conclusions from this. And undertake a comprehensive *aggiornamento*.

I have also been accused of promoting an 'LGBT agenda'. This is incorrect: I have always been transparent regarding my project and I do not believe that it is the job of researchers or journalists to reform the Church or to change it. Our job is simply to describe reality and, making use of the facts, to try to write a good book. And while I have already written books and articles on homosexuality (which is a well-known fact), I have always done so with the utmost autonomy, without militancy, and I have even offered severe critiques of the gay community when it was necessary. Having *the right to criticize one's own* seems to me a primordial rule for all researchers and journalists. In writing this book, moreover, I did not attack the Church so much as a very particular gay community that has become a majority within the College of Cardinals and in the Vatican. An 'LGBTP' ('P' for 'priest') community!

Could *In the Closet of the Vatican* have been written differently? Could it have made use of other sources or a different style? It's possible. But the fact that nobody had ever successfully dealt with such a crucial subject before would seem to prove that it was necessary to first find a new way of writing, new sources and an original style to bring to light one of the most important secrets of the past fifty years.

Such a book could not, therefore, have been written by a simple Vaticanologist, since they are generally reluctant, on principle, to describe the truth of the system. Furthermore, if a Vaticanologist had attempted to write something of the sort, they would have lost their job. An Italian, too, would have encountered problems with their publisher or the owner of their newspaper, since the subject remains taboo in Italy. A heterosexual would not have had the necessary codes or the networks to conduct the investigation. This explains why the book was written by a secular, non-Vaticanologist Frenchman who understands the 'codes'. A kind Catholic American critic summarized it thus: 'This is a book that could only be written by a relative outsider of the Catholic Church, precisely because it refuses some of the euphemisms and discretion that would come naturally to one inside the Church.' This is exactly the case. I am outside the system even though I lived inside the Vatican and have a deep respect for priests and believers. Anyone who reads the epilogue of this book will have no doubt about the respect, and sometimes even affection, that I have for the Church. Still, I did not write this book just for believers, theologians and Vaticanologists. I am a journalist who seeks to address everyone, and a researcher driven solely by the love of what the philosopher Hannah Arendt called 'the truth of the facts'.

This is why I sincerely believe that I have done the Church a service by publishing *In the Closet of the Vatican*, which I am sure will be recognized in the medium to long term. It is a book whose need for truth ultimately meets Pope Francis's demand for truth.

Frédéric Martel, Autumn 2019
(*Translated by Jacob Bromberg*)

NOTE FROM THE AUTHOR
AND THE PUBLISHERS

In the Closet of the Vatican has been published in more than twenty languages and fifty countries. The initial publishing houses and groups were: Robert Laffont in France; Feltrinelli in Italy; Bloomsbury in the United Kingdom, the United States and Australia. It was also published by Agora in Poland, Roca Editorial in Spain and Latin America, Balans in the Netherlands, Porto Editora in Portugal, Kawade Shobo Shin-Sha in Japan, Fischer in Germany, Fokus Na Hit in Croatia, Book Travel in Bulgaria, Dar Al Farabi in the Arabic-speaking territories, Rao Distributie in Romania and Companhia das Letras in Brazil. In France, where the book is published under the title *Sodoma*, the editor is Jean-Luc Barré. The English language editor is Robin Baird-Smith.

This book is based on a large number of sources. In the course of the investigation on the ground over a period of four years, almost 1,500 people have been questioned at the Vatican and in 30 countries: among them, 41 cardinals, 52 bishops and monsignori, 45 apostolic nuncios and foreign ambassadors. All of these interviews took place in person, none by telephone or email. To these first-hand sources we may add a vast bibliography of over a thousand references, books and articles. Finally, a team of 80 researchers, correspondents, advisers, fixers and translators was mobilized to complete research carried out in 30 countries.

All the sources and notes, the bibliography, the team of researchers, and three unpublished chapters too long to be included here, are collected in a 300-page document that can be accessed on the internet. This codex is available online at: www.sodoma.fr; updates will also be published with the hashtag #sodoma on the author's Facebook page: @fredericmartel; on the Instagram account: @martelfrederic and on the Twitter thread: @martelf

PROLOGUE

'He's of the parish,' the priest whispers conspiratorially in my ear.

The first person who used that coded expression in front of me was an archbishop from the Roman Curia.

'You know, he's very practising. He's of the parish,' he stressed in a low voice, talking to me about the morals of a famous Vatican cardinal, a former 'minister' of John Paul II, who both of us knew well.

He added: 'And if I told you all the things I know, you wouldn't believe it!'

And, of course, he talked.

We will come across this archbishop several times again in the course of this book, the first in a long series of priests who described the reality of which I was already aware, but which many people will see as a fiction. A fairy tale.

'The problem is that if you tell the truth about the "closet" and the special friendships in the Vatican, people won't believe you. They'll say it's made up. Because here reality goes beyond fiction,' I am told by a Franciscan friar, a man who has also worked and lived inside the Vatican for over thirty years.

But lots of people described this 'closet' to me. Some of them were worried about what I was going to reveal. Others disclosed secrets to me, first in a whisper, then shortly afterwards, in a loud voice: actual scandals. Others, last of all, proved to be loquacious, excessively so, as if they had been waiting for so many years to come out of their silence. About forty cardinals and hundreds of bishops, monsignori, priests and 'nuncios' (the pope's ambassadors) agreed to meet me. Among them, avowed homosexuals, who were present in the Vatican every day, introduced me to their world of initiates.

Open secrets? Rumours? Evil gossip? I'm like St Thomas: I need to check to believe. So I had to spend a long time investigating and living immersed in the Church. I installed myself in Rome, one week every month, regularly inside the Vatican, thanks to the hospitality of senior prelates who sometimes revealed that they too were 'part of the parish'. And then I travelled across the world, through more than thirty countries, among the clergies of Latin America, Asia, the United States and the Middle East, to collect over a thousand statements. During that long investigation I spent more than a hundred and fifty nights a year reporting, away from home, away from Paris.

During the four years of that investigation, I never concealed my identity as a writer, a journalist and a researcher when approaching cardinals and priests, who sometimes proved to be unapproachable. All interviews were conducted under my real name, and my interlocutors had only to do a quick search on Google, Wikipedia, Facebook or Twitter to discover the details of my biography as a writer and reporter. Often, those priests, influential or otherwise, came on to me discreetly and some, with very little reluctance, more intensely. It's an occupational hazard!

Why did these men, who were used to being silent, agree to break the *omertà*? That is one of the mysteries of this book and my reason for writing it.

What they told me was unsayable for a long time. It would have been difficult to publish a book like this twenty or even only ten years ago. For a long time, the ways of the Lord remained, if I may say so, impenetrable. They are less so today because the resignation of Benedict XVI and Pope Francis's desire for reform have freed people's tongues. Social networks, more courage on the part of the press, and countless ecclesiastical sex scandals have made it possible, and necessary, to reveal this secret today. So this book criticizes not the Church overall, but a very particular 'genre' within the gay community; it tells the story of the majority of those in the College of Cardinals and the Vatican.

Many cardinals and priests who officiate at the Roman Curia, most of those who meet up in conclave beneath the frescoes of the Sistine Chapel painted by Michelangelo – one of the most grandiose scenes of gay culture, peopled with virile bodies, surrounded by the *Ignudi*, those robust and beautiful naked young men – share the same 'inclinations'. They have a 'family resemblance'. In fact, in an aside that had something of the disco-queen about it, another priest whispered to me in English: 'We are family!'

Most of the monsignori who have spoken at the balcony of the Loggia of St Peter's, between the pontificate of Paul VI and that of Francis, to deliver the sad announcement of the death of the pope or, with frank gaiety, to say *Habemus papam*!, share the same secret. *È Bianca!*

Whether they are 'practising', 'homophile', 'initiates', 'unstraights', 'wordly', 'versatile', 'questioning', or simply 'in the closet', the world I am discovering, with its 50 shades of gay, is beyond comprehension. The intimate stories of these men who give an image of piety in public and lead a quite different life in private, so different from one another, present us with a complex intrigue to unravel. Never, perhaps, have the appearances of an institution been so deceptive; and equally deceptive are the pronouncements about celibacy and the vows of chastity that conceal a completely different reality.

The best-kept secret of the Vatican is no secret to Pope Francis. He knows his 'parish'. Since arriving in Rome he has known that he is dealing with an organisation that is quite extraordinary in its way, and that isn't restricted, as people believed for a long time, to a few lost sheep. It's a system; and a huge herd. How many are there? It doesn't matter. Let's just say: they represent the great majority.

At first, of course, the pope was surprised by the extent of that 'malicious colony', its 'charming qualities' and its 'unbearable shortcomings' of which the French writer Marcel Proust wrote in his celebrated book *Sodom and Gomorrah*. But what Francis is unable to bear is not so much the homophilia that is so widespread, as the dizzying hypocrisy of those who advocate a rigid morality while at the same time having a companion, affairs and sometimes escorts. That's why he spends so much time denouncing fake devotees, whited sepulchres and hypocrites. Francis has often denounced this duplicity in his morning homilies from Santa Marta. His phrase should be placed as an epigram at the start of this book: 'Behind rigidity something always lies hidden; in many cases, a double life.'

Double life? The phrase has been uttered, and this time the evidence cannot be challenged. Francis has often repeated his criticisms of the

Roman Curia: he has pointed his finger at the 'hypocrites' who live 'hidden and often dissolute lives'; the ones who 'put make-up on their souls and live off make-up'; the 'lie' erected into a system that does 'a lot of harm, hypocrisy does a lot of harm: it's a way of life'. Do as I say, not as I do!

Do I need to say that Francis knows the people he addresses in this way without naming them: cardinals, papal masters of ceremonies, former secretaries of state, deputies, minor assistants or chamberlains? In most cases it isn't simply a general inclination, of a certain fluidity, homophilia or 'tendencies', as people once said, nor even repressed or sublimated sexuality, all equally prevalent in the Church of Rome. Many of these cardinals who 'have not loved women, for all the blood that flows in their veins!', as the Poet says, are practising. What detours I am taking to say such simple things – things which, so shocking yesterday, are so banal today!

Practising, certainly, but still 'in the closet'. I don't need to introduce you to this cardinal who appears in public on the balcony of the Loggia, and who was caught up in a quickly suppressed case of prostitution; this other French cardinal who for a long time had an Anglican lover in America; or this other one who, in his youth, had a chain of adventures like the beads on a nun's rosary; not forgetting those who live with their boyfriends in the palaces of the Vatican, where I have met them; they introduced their companions as their assistants, their *minutante*, their deputy, their chauffeur, their valet, their factotum, even their bodyguard!

The Vatican has one of the biggest gay communities in the world, and I doubt whether, even in San Francisco's Castro, the emblematic gay quarter, though more mixed today, there are quite as many gays!

The reason for this, among the older cardinals, should be sought in the past: their stormy youths and roguish years before gay liberation explain their double lives and their homophobia in the old style. I've often had a sense during my investigation that I've gone back in time and found myself in the 1930s or 1950s, years that I haven't known myself, with the dual mentality of the chosen people and the cursed people, which led one of the priests that I met often to say: 'Welcome to *Sodoma!*'

I'm not the first to discuss this phenomenon. A number of journalists have already revealed scandals and affairs within the Roman Curia. But that isn't my subject. Unlike those Vaticanologists, who denounce individual 'excesses' but in such a way as to conceal the 'system', I am less concerned with exposing these affairs than with revealing the very banal double life of most of the dignitaries of the Church. Not the exceptions but the system and the model, what American sociologists call 'the pattern'. The details, certainly, but also the great laws – and there are, as we will see, 14 general rules in this book. The subject is: the intimate society of priests, their fragility, and the suffering bound up with forced celibacy, which has become a system. So it is not a matter of judging these homosexuals, even the closeted ones – I like them! – but of understanding their secret and collective way of life. It is not a matter of denouncing these men, nor of 'outing' them while they are alive. My project isn't about 'naming and shaming', the American practice of making names public in order to expose them. Let it be clear that for me a priest or a cardinal should not be ashamed about being homosexual; I even think it should be one possible social status among others.

But one becomes aware of the need to expose a system built, from the smallest seminaries to the holy of holies – the cardinals' college – both on the homosexual double life and on the most dizzying homophobia. Fifty years after Stonewall, the gay revolution in the United States, the Vatican is the last bastion still to be liberated! Many Catholics now have a sense of this lie without yet having been able to read the revelations in this book.

Without this key for understanding, the recent history of the Vatican and the Roman Church remains opaque. By failing to recognize the broadly homosexual dimension, we deprive ourselves of one of the keys to a greater understanding of most of the facts that have stained the history of the Vatican for decades: the secret motivations that led Paul VI to confirm the prohibition on artificial contraception, the rejection of condoms and the strict obligation of celibacy on the priesthood; the war against 'liberation theology'; the scandals of the Vatican Bank in the time of the famous Archbishop Marcinkus (he too was a homosexual); the decision to forbid condoms as a way of battling AIDS, even when the pandemic would lead to more than thirty-five million deaths; the

VatiLeaks I and II affairs; the recurrent and often unfathomable misogyny of many cardinals and bishops; the resignation of Benedict XVI; the current rebellion against Pope Francis … Every time, homosexuality plays a central part that many people can only guess at, and the truth of which has never really been told.

The gay dimension doesn't explain everything, of course, but it is key for anyone wishing to understand the Vatican and its moral postures. We might also put forward the hypothesis, even though it isn't the subject of this book, that lesbianism is a major key to an understanding of convent life, whether that of cloistered orders or not. Lastly – alas! – homosexuality is also one of the keys that explain the institutionalized cover-up of sexual crimes and misdemeanours, of which there are now tens of thousands. Why? How? Because the 'culture of secrecy', which was necessary to maintain silence about the huge presence of homosexuality inside the Church, has made it possible to hide sexual abuse, and for predators to benefit from this system of protection within the institution – even though paedophilia is not the subject of this book.

'How much filth there is in the Church,' said Cardinal Ratzinger, who also discovered the extent of the 'closet' through a secret report by three cardinals, the content of which was described to me and that was one of the major reasons for his resignation. This report is said to reveal not so much the existence of a 'gay lobby', as was said, as the omnipresence of homosexuals in the Vatican, blackmail and harassment built into the system. There is, as Hamlet might have said, something rotten in the state of the Vatican.

The homosexual sociology of Catholicism also helps us to explain another reality: the end of vocations in Europe. For a long time, as we will see, young Italians who discovered that they were homosexual, or who had doubts about their inclinations, chose the priesthood. So these pariahs became initiates and made a strength of a weakness. With the homosexual liberation of the 1970s, and particularly since the gay socialization of the 1980s, Catholic vocations, especially in European countries, have naturally fallen. A gay adolescent today has other options, even in Italy, apart from entering holy orders. The lack of vocations has multiple causes, but the homosexual revolution is paradoxically one of the main forces behind it.

This pattern explains the war against Francis. Here we will have to be counter-intuitive in order to understand it. This Latino pope is the first to have used the word 'gay' rather than just 'homosexual' – and if we compare him with his predecessors, we may see him as the most 'gay-friendly' of modern pontiffs. There have been carefully chosen words about homosexuality: 'Who am I to judge?' And we might assume that this pope probably doesn't have the tendencies or inclination attributed to four of his recent predecessors. However, Francis today is the object of a violent campaign, precisely because of his supposed liberalism on questions of sexual morality, by conservative cardinals who are very homophobic – and, most of them, secretly homosexual.

The world turned upside down, in some respects! We might even say that there is an unwritten rule that always proves true in this book: the more homophobic a priest is, the greater the chance that he himself is homosexual. Those conservatives, those traditionalists, those *'dubias'*, are in many cases the famous 'rigid people leading a double life' of whom Francis speaks so often.

'The carnival is over,' the pope is reported to have said to his master of ceremonies at the very moment when he was elected. Since then, the Argentinian has overturned the little games of connivance and the homosexual fraternity that developed clandestinely after Paul VI, were amplified under John Paul II, before becoming ungovernable under Benedict XVI, leading eventually to his downfall. With his calm ego and relaxed attitude towards sexuality, Francis is an anomaly. He isn't part of the parish!

Have the pope and his liberal theologians realized that priestly celibacy was a failure? Did they guess that the battle launched against gays by the Vatican of John Paul II and Benedict XVI was a war that was lost in advance? One that would be turned against the Church as soon as everyone became aware of its real motivations: a war waged between closeted homosexuals and gays who had come out! War between gays, in short.

In this gossiping society, Francis is well-informed. His assistants, his closest collaborators, his masters of ceremony and masters of liturgy, his theologians and his cardinals, where gays are also in the majority, know that in the Vatican many of the called and many of the chosen are in fact homosexuals. They even suggest, when questioned, that by forbidding priests to marry, the Church has become sociologically homosexual; and that by imposing a continence that is against nature, and a secretive culture, it is partly responsible for the tens of thousands of instances of sexual abuse that are undermining it from within. They also know that sexual desire, and homosexual desire first and foremost, is one of the main engines and wellsprings of Vatican life.

Francis knows that he has to move on the Church's stance, and that he will only be able to do this at the cost of a ruthless battle against all those who use sexual morality and homophobia to conceal their own hypocrisies and double lives. But there we have it: these secret homosexuals are in the majority, powerful and influential and, in terms of the most 'rigid' among them, very noisy in their homophobic utterances.

Here is the pope: threatened and attacked on all sides and generally criticized, Francis is said to be 'among the wolves'.

It's not quite true: he's among the queens.

Part I

Francis

FRANCIS

Since 2013

GERHARD LUDWIG MÜLLER
LUIS LADARIA FERRER
Congregation for the Doctrine of Faith

FABIÁN PEDACCHIO
Personal Secretary

PIETRO PAROLIN
Secretary of State

GIOVANNI ANGELO BECCIU
EDGAR PEÑA PARRA
Secretary for Internal Affairs

PAUL GALLAGHER
Secretary for Relations with States

PETER WELLS
PAOLO BORGIA
Assessor

ANTOINE CAMILLERI
Under Secretary

1

Domus Sanctae Marthae

'Good evening,' the voice says. 'I wanted to thank you.'

With thumb and little finger brought close to his ear, Francesco Lepore mimes the telephone conversation for me. He has just picked up, and his body language now seems as important as the words that his mysterious interlocutor is saying in Italian, with a strong accent. Lepore remembers the tiniest details of the call.

'It was 15 October 2013, about a quarter to five, I remember very clearly. My father had just died, a few days earlier, and I felt alone and abandoned. That was when my mobile phone rang. No number came up. I answered a bit mechanically.

'*Pronto.*'

The voice goes on: '*Buona sera!* Pope Francis here. I received your letter. Cardinal Farina passed it on to me and I'm calling you to tell you that I'm very touched by your courage and the coherence and sincerity of your letter.

'Holy father, it's me who is touched by your call, and that you made the effort to call me. It wasn't necessary. I just felt a need to write to you.'

'No, really, I was touched by your sincerity, by your courage. I don't know what I can do to help you now, but I'd like to do something.'

The trembling voice, that of Francesco Lepore, startled by such an unexpected message, hesitates. After a moment's silence, the pope resumes.

'Can I ask you a favour?'

'What favour?'

'Would you pray for me?'

Francesco Lepore says nothing.

'In the end I told him I'd stopped praying. But if the pope wanted to, he could pray for me,' he says to me.

Francis explained to him that he was 'already praying' for him, before asking him: 'Can I bless you?'

'I answered in the affirmative to this question from Pope Francis, of course. There was a certain silence, he thanked me again and the conversation ended like that.'

After a moment Francesco Lepore says to me: 'You know, I'm not very much in favour of this pope. I don't defend Francis a lot, but I was very touched by his gesture. I've never spoken about it, I've kept it to myself, like a personal secret. It's the first time I've told anybody that.' (Cardinal Farina, whom I interviewed twice in his Vatican apartment, confirmed to me that he had passed on Lepore's letter to the pope, and the authenticity of Francis's phone call.)

When he received the call, Francesco Lepore was at odds with the Church. He had just resigned and was now, in the time-honoured phrase, 'reduced to the state of a layman'. The intellectual priest who was the pride of the cardinals in the Vatican had hung up his cassock. He had just written a letter to Pope Francis, a message in a bottle hurled into the sea with the force that comes from grief, an epistle in which he set out his story as a homosexual priest who had become the pope's Latin translator. To get it over with. To regain his coherence and leave hypocrisy behind. With his gesture, Lepore was burning his boats.

But that blessed call returned him inexorably to a past that he wanted to forget, a page he had wanted to turn: his love of Latin and the priesthood; his religious conversion; his ordination as a priest; his life in the residence at Santa Marta; his special friendships with so many bishops and cardinals; his interminable conversations about Christ and homosexuality, under the cassock, at times in Latin.

Lost illusions? Yes, of course. His rise was swift: a young priest attached to the most prestigious cardinals, and soon to the personal service of three popes. They had ambitions for him; he was promised a career in the apostolic palace, perhaps even the episcopate or, who knows, the scarlet robe and red hat!

That was before he made his choice. Francesco had had to arbitrate between the Vatican and homosexuality – and, unlike many priests who prefer to lead a double life, he opted for coherence and freedom. Pope Francis didn't address the gay issue directly in that brief conversation, but it was clear that it was the priest's honesty that led him to phone Francesco Lepore personally.

'He seemed touched by my story, and perhaps also by the fact that I had revealed certain Vatican practices to him: how inhumanely my superiors had treated me – there are a lot of protectors, a lot of *droits du seigneur* in the Vatican – and how they had abandoned me immediately after I'd stopped being a priest,' he adds.

More importantly, Pope Francis explicitly thanked Francesco Lepore for privileging 'discretion' about his homosexuality, a form of 'humility' and 'secrecy' rather than a deafening public coming out.

A short time afterwards, Mgr Krzysztof Charamsa, a priest who was close to Cardinal Ratzinger, would be more vocal, and his highly public coming out would prompt a violent reaction from the Vatican. The pope wouldn't call him!

Here we understand the unwritten rule of *The Closet*. If you want to integrate with the Vatican, adhere to a code, which consists of tolerating the homosexuality of priests and bishops, enjoying it if appropriate, but keeping it secret in all cases. Tolerance went with discretion. And like Al Pacino in *The Godfather*, you must never criticize or leave your 'family'. 'Don't ever take sides against the family.'

As I would discover in the course of this long inquiry, being gay in the clergy means being part of a kind of norm. Being homosexual is possible in the Vatican, easy, ordinary, and even encouraged; but the word 'visibility' is forbidden. Being discreetly homosexual means being part 'of the parish'; to be one who brings down scandal upon it is to exclude oneself from the family.

In line with this 'code', Pope Francis's call to Francesco Lepore now assumes its full significance.

I first met Lepore at the start of this investigation, a few months before his letter and the call from the pope. This man who was professionally silent, the holy father's discreet translator, agreed to talk to me openly. I had just started this book and had few contacts within the Vatican: Francesco Lepore was one of my first gay priests, before dozens of others. I would never have thought that the priests of the holy see, and even members of the Swiss Guard, would have confessed to me in such numbers.

Why do they talk? Everyone confides in Rome: the priests, the Swiss Guard, the bishops, the countless 'monsignori' and, even more than the others, the cardinals. Real canary birds! All those excellencies and eminences are very chatty if you know how to approach them, sometimes almost overly loquacious and frequently imprudent. Each of them has his reasons: for some it's conviction, to take part in the fierce ideological battle now being fought inside the Vatican, between traditionalists and liberals; for others it's a hunger for influence and, we might even say, vanity. Some talk because they are homosexual and want to tell all, about the others, for want of talking about themselves. Last of all, some are expansive out of bitterness, out of a taste for scandal and malicious gossip. Old cardinals live only on tittle-tattle and denigration. They make me think of the regulars at those shady homophilic clubs in the 1950s who cruelly mocked everyone, worldly and poisonous, because they didn't accept their own nature. The 'closet' is the place of the most incredible cruelty. And the Vatican is one huge 'closet'.

Francesco Lepore wanted to leave it. He immediately told me his real name, agreeing to have our conversations recorded and made public.

At our first meeting, organized by a mutual friend, Pasquale Quaranta, a journalist with *La Repubblica*, Lepore arrived a little late on the second floor of the Eataly restaurant in Piazza della Repubblica, Rome, where we had agreed to meet, because of the umpteenth transport strike. I chose Eataly, which surfs on the wave of 'slow food', fair-trade suppliers and 'made in Italy', because it's a relatively discreet location far from the Vatican, where one can converse freely. The menu offers 10 kinds of (rather disappointing) pasta, and 73 types of pizza. Lepore and I met there often, for long discussions, almost every month, over spaghetti all'amatriciana – my favourite, although hardly compatible with my 'low carb' diet. And, every time, the former priest would suddenly grow animated.

Many have told me that they found the Church to be 'like a second mother': and we know the importance of the cult – always irrational and self-selecting – of the holy virgin to this fraternity. *Mamma!* Many homosexual writers, from Marcel Proust to Pasolini, via Julien Green or Roland Barthes, and even Jacques Maritain, have sung their passionate love of their mothers, an emotional effusion that was not only essential but often constitutes one of the keys to their self-censorship (many writers and priests only accepted their homosexuality after the death of their mother). *Mamma*, who always remained true to her little boy, giving him that love and watching over her son as if he were her own flesh, understood everything – and she absolves!

Francesco Lepore, on the other hand, wants to follow in the footsteps of his father. On the slightly yellowed photograph that he shows me, the dog-collar is dazzling, chalky white under the black cassock: Francesco Lepore had just been ordained as a priest. His short hair is well-combed and his face close-shaven; by contrast with today, when he has a generous beard and a completely smooth head. Is it the same man? The repressed priest and the alleged homosexual are two sides of a single reality.

'I was born in Benevento, a town in Campania, a little to the north of Naples,' Lepore tells me. 'My parents were Catholic, although they weren't practising. Very soon I came to feel a deep attraction to religion. I loved churches.'

Many homosexual priests I have interviewed have described that 'attraction' to me. A mysterious quest for grace. The fascination with the sacraments, the splendour of the tabernacle, its double curtain, the ciborium and the monstrance. The magic of the confessional, toll booths rendered fantastical by the promises attached to them. The processions, the recollections, the banners. The robes of light as well, the vestments, the cassock, the alb, the stole. The desire to penetrate the secret of the sacristies. And then the music: the sung vespers, the men's voices and the sonority of the organ. Not forgetting the prie-dieux!

'My father was a Latin teacher and I wanted to learn the language to approach that world,' Lepore goes on. 'Learn Latin perfectly. And from the age of 10 or 11 I wanted to join the seminary.'

Which he did, contrary to his parents' advice: by 15 he already wanted to 'embrace', as the saying goes, the ecclesiastical career.

A classic path for young priests in general: the seminary in a Catholic grammar school, then five years of higher education in philosophy and theology, followed by 'ministries', still known in Italy as 'minor orders', with their readers and acolytes, before the diaconate and ordination.

'I became a priest at the age of 24, on 13 May 2000, at the time of the Jubilee and World Gay Pride,' Franceso Lepore says, in a gripping résumé.

The young man understood very quickly that the connection between the priesthood and homosexuality was not contradictory, or even contingent, as he had originally thought.

'I've always known that I was homosexual. At the same time, I had a kind of attraction–repulsion for that kind of desire. Growing up in a milieu that considered homosexuality to be intrinsically bad, and reading theology books that defined it as a sin, for a long time I experienced it as guilt. The path that I chose to leave that guilt was to deny that sexual attraction by transferring it to religious attraction: I made the choice of chastity and the seminary. For me, becoming a priest was a kind of solution to expiate an error that I had not committed. During those years of training at the University of Opus Dei in Rome, I devoted myself very intensely to prayer, I was ascetic, going so far as to accept corporal punishment, even trying to become a Franciscan to experience my religion even more intensely, and managing, in any case, to remain chaste for five years, without even masturbating.'

The journey of Francesco Lepore, between sin and mortification, with that searing need to escape desires at the cost of the most trying constraints, was almost normal in twentieth-century Italy. For a long time, the ecclesiastical career was the ideal solution for many homosexuals who found it difficult to accept their private orientation. Tens of thousands of Italian priests sincerely believed that the religious vocation was 'the' solution to their 'problem'. That is the first rule of *The Closet: For a long time the priesthood was the ideal escape-route for young homosexuals. Homosexuality is one of the keys to their vocation.*

Let's dwell on that pattern for a moment. To understand the journey of most of the cardinals and countless priests that we will meet in this book, we have to start out with the almost Darwinian selection process that is explained sociologically. In Italy, it was even a rule for a long time. These effeminate young men who were worried about their desires;

those boys who felt an inclination towards their best friends, who were teased for the affectation of their voices; those homosexuals who sought to find themselves without wishing to declare themselves; those seminarians who weren't on the right path – they had few options in Italy in the 1930s, 40s and 50s. Some of them understood precociously, almost atavistically, how to turn homosexuality into a strength, to turn a weakness into an advantage: by becoming a priest. This allowed them to regain power over their own lives, imagining that they were answering the twofold call of Christ and their desires.

Did they have any other options? In a little Italian town in Lombardy, or a village in Piedmont, where many cardinals came from, homosexuality was still considered at the time to be absolutely evil. People could barely comprehend this 'dark misfortune'; they feared this promise of a 'multiple and complex love', to use the words of the Poet; they dreaded that 'unspeakable, even unbearable happiness'! To yield to it, even while remaining discreet, meant choosing a life of lies or of exile becoming a priest, on the other hand, appeared like a form of escape. By joining the clergy, everything became simpler for the homosexual who admitted nothing: he went and lived among boys and wore dresses; he stopped being asked questions about his girlfriends; his school-mates, who were already making unpleasant jokes, were impressed; having been mocked, he now enjoyed great honour; he had joined a race of the elect, having belonged to an accursed race; and *Mamma*, I repeat, who had understood everything without saying a word, encouraged this miraculous vocation. Most importantly, this chastity with women and the promise of celibacy weren't frightening; quite the contrary: he joyfully embraced them both! In Italy between 1930 and 1960, the fact that a young homosexual should have chosen ordination and this kind of 'vow of celibacy among men' was in the order of things, and indeed decreed by circumstances.

An Italian Benedictine monk, who was one of the senior officials at the Sant'Anselmo University in Rome, explained the logic to me: 'For me the choice of the priesthood was at first the product of a deep and vital faith. But retrospectively I also analyse it as a way of keeping my sexuality under control. I've always known that I was gay, but it was only later, after the age of 40, that I accepted this fundamental aspect of my identity.'

All careers are unique, of course. Many Italian priests told me that they had only discovered their homosexuality after their ordination or when they started working at the Vatican. Many of them, in fact, crossed the line only later, after the age of 40, or during the 1970s.

To this sociological selection of priests we might add the selection of bishops, which amplifies the phenomenon still further. Homophilic cardinals privilege prelates who have homosexual inclinations and who, in turn, choose gay priests. Nuncios, those ambassadors of the pope who are given the task of selecting bishops and among whom the percentage of homosexuals reaches record levels, in turn perform a 'natural' selection. According to all the statements that I have collected, the priests who have such inclinations are thought to be favoured when their homosexuality is guessed. More prosaically, it is not rare for a nuncio or a bishop to promote a priest who is also part of 'the parish' because the former expects some favours in return.

That is the second rule of *The Closet*: *Homosexuality spreads the closer one gets to the holy of holies; there are more and more homosexuals as one rises through the Catholic hierarchy. In the College of Cardinals and at the Vatican, the preferential selection process is said to be perfected; homosexuality becomes the rule, heterosexuality the exception.*

I really began this book in April 2015. One evening my Italian editor, Carlo Feltrinelli, invited me for dinner at the Rovelli restaurant on Via Tivoli in Milan. We knew each other already, because he had published three of my books, and I had wanted to talk to him about this one. For over a year I had been investigating the question of homosexuality in the Catholic Church, carrying out many interviews in Rome and in various different countries, reading lots of books on the subject, but my project still remained hypothetical. I had the subject, but not the way of writing it.

At public lectures in Naples and Rome that year talking about gay Catholics, I said: 'One day this history of the Vatican will have to be told.' A young Neapolitan writer reminded me of that phrase, and the journalist with *La Repubblica*, Pasquale Quaranta, a friend who has accompanied me since then in the preparation of this book, also reminded me of my words. But my subject still remained unutterable.

Before dinner, I had imagined that Carlo Feltrinelli would turn down such a project; I would have abandoned it had that been so, and *In the*

Closet of the Vatican would never have seen the light of day. The opposite happened. The publisher of Boris Pasternak, of Günter Grass and, more recently, of Roberto Saviano, bombarded me with questions and asked me about my ideas before saying, to encourage me to work while putting me on my guard: 'This book should be published in Italy and, at the same time, in France, the UK and the United States, to give it greater weight. Will you have photographs? At the same time, you're going to have to show me that you know more about it than you're letting on.'

He topped up his vintage wine and went on thinking out loud. And all of a sudden he added, stressing the letter 's': 'But they will try to assassssssinate you!'

I had been given the green light. I hurled myself into the adventure and started living in Rome every month. But I still didn't know that I was going to carry out my investigation in more than thirty countries and over a period of four years. *In the Closet of the Vatican* was launched. Come what may!

At number 178 Via Ostiense, in the south of Rome, Al Biondo Tevere is a working-class trattoria. The Tiber flows at the foot of the terrace – hence the name of the restaurant. It's nothing special, it's far from the centre, it doesn't attract many customers and, that January, it was terribly cold. Why on earth had Francesco Gnerre arranged to meet me in such a remote spot?

A retired professor of literature, Gnerre devoted a significant part of his research to gay Italian literature. He had also written, over more than forty years, hundreds of book reviews in different homosexual journals.

'Thousands of gays like me built their libraries on the basis of articles by Francesco Gnerre in *Babilonia* and *Pride*,' I am told by the journalist Pasquale Quaranta, who organized the dinner.

Gnerre had chosen the place deliberately. It was at Al Biondo Tevere that the Italian film-maker Pier Paolo Pasolini had dinner on the night of 1 November 1975, with Giuseppe Pelosi, the young prostitute who would murder him a few hours later on a beach in Ostia. This 'last supper', just before one of the most horrible and famous crimes in Italian history, is strangely commemorated on the walls of the restaurant. Press clippings, photographs from shoots, still pictures, the whole of Pasolini's universe comes to life on the enamel-painted walls of the restaurant.

'The biggest gay association is the Vatican,' Francesco Gnerre says by way of antipasto.

And the literary critic launches off on a long story of the intricate relationships between Italian priests and homosexuality, and, among them, genuine meeting points; he reveals the homosexuality of several Catholic novelists and also talks to me about Dante: 'Dante wasn't homophobic,' Gnerre explains. 'There are four references to homosexuality in *The Divine Comedy* in the parts called 'Inferno' and 'Purgatory', even if there are none in 'Paradise'! Dante has sympathy for his gay character, Brunetto Latini, who is also his old teacher of rhetoric. And even if he puts him in the third ring of the seventh circle of hell, he has respect for the homosexual condition.'

Taking the route of literature, Latin and culture to attempt to resolve his own dilemma, the priest Francesco Lepore also spent years trying to decode the hidden messages in literature or cinema – the poems of Pasolini, Leopardi, Carlo Coccioli, the *Memoirs of Hadrian* by Marguerite Yourcenar, the films of Visconti, not to mention the homosexual figures in Dante's *Divine Comedy*. As for many Italian priests and homosexuals who were uncomfortable in their own skin, literature played a major role in their lives: 'the safest of refuges', as they say.

'It was through literature that I started understanding things,' Lepore adds. 'I was looking for codes and passwords.'

To try and decipher those codes, we might take an interest in another key figure about whom the academic Francesco Gnerre and I spoke: Marco Bisceglia. Bisceglia had three lives. He was the co-founder of Arcigay, the main Italian homosexual association of the last 40 years. Even today it has several hundred thousand members, scattered around local committees in over fifty towns in the country. Before that, and first of all, Bisceglia was a priest.

'Marco went to the seminary because he was convinced that he had had a calling from God. He told me he believed, in good faith, in his religious vocation, but he discovered his true vocation once he was over 50: it was homosexuality. For a long time he repressed his sexual orientation. I think that trajectory is very typical in Italy. A boy who prefers reading to football; a boy who doesn't feel attracted to girls and who doesn't really understand the nature of his desires; a boy who doesn't want to admit his thwarted desires to his family and his mother: all of that led young Italian homosexuals quite naturally towards the seminaries. But what was fundamental in Marco Bisceglia was that he wasn't a hypocrite. For several decades, while he remained in the Church, he didn't experience gay life; it was only afterwards that he lived out his homosexuality with the excess of the freshly converted.'

This warm portrait drawn for me by Gnerre, who knew Bisceglia, probably conceals the torments and psychological crises of this Jesuit priest. He then turned towards liberation theology, and apparently had some disagreements with the Catholic hierarchy, which probably led him towards gay militancy. Having become a priest again at the end of his life, after his years of gay activism, he died of AIDS in 2001.

Three lives, then: the priest; the gay militant opposed to the priest; last of all the man dying of AIDS who reconciles himself with the Church. His biographer, Rocco Pezzano, whom I interview, is still amazed by this 'loser's life', in which Marco Bisceglia moved from failure to failure without ever really finding his path. Francesco Gnerre is more generous: he stresses Marco's 'coherence' and the movement of a 'painful but magnificent life'.

Priests and homosexuals: two sides of the same coin? Another figure from the Italian gay movement, Gianni Delle Foglie, the founder of the first gay bookshop in Milan, who was interested in homosexual Catholic writers, made this remark: 'The gays are almost alone in the face of the Vatican. But maybe that's good: leave us together! The battle between the gays and the Vatican is a war among poofs!'

It was in Rome that Francesco Lepore experienced his first sexual adventures, when, as for many Italian priests, the capital – the city of Hadrian and Michelangelo – revealed its unique attractions. It was there that he discovered that the vow of chastity was not greatly respected, and that the majority of priests are homosexual.

'I found myself alone in Rome, and it was there that I discovered the secret: priests often led licentious lives. It was a completely new world for me. I began a relationship with a priest that lasted for five months. When we split up I went through a deep crisis. My first spiritual crisis. How could I be a priest and, at the same time, live out my homosexuality?'

Lepore talked about the subject with his confessors, as well as with a Jesuit priest (to whom he told all the details) and then with a bishop (who was spared them). They all encouraged him to persevere in the priesthood, to stop talking about homosexuality and not to feel guilty. He was very directly given to understand that he could live out his sexuality as long as he remained discreet and didn't turn it into a militant identity.

It was then that his name was put forward for a prestigious position within the Secretariat of State at the apostolic palace of the Vatican, an equivalent of the position of prime minister to the pope.

'They were looking for a priest who spoke perfect Latin, and since the rumour had circulated that I was going through a crisis, someone put forward my name. Mgr Leonardo Sandri, who has since then become a cardinal, contacted my bishop and invited me to meet the people in the Latin section. They made me take a Latin test and I passed. I remember that they still put me on my guard, which proves that they knew I was gay: with a formula full of innuendos, they told me that "if I had reached the right level to qualify for the post", I would have to start "dedicating my life to the pope and forgetting everything else".

On 30 November 2003, the Neapolitan priest joined Domus Sanctae Marthae, the official residence of the cardinals at the Vatican – and the current home of Pope Francis.

You can only visit Domus Sanctae Marthae with special permission, and only on Wednesday and Thursday mornings, between 10 o'clock and midday, when the pope is at St Peter's. Mgr Battista Ricca, the famous director of the residence, who has an office there, granted me the necessary permit. He explained to me in minute detail how to pass through the police checks, and then the checks of the Swiss Guard. I would often bump into this prelate with the liquid eyes, an outsider close to Francis, who has known both triumphs and failures, and who would end up, as we will see, giving me permission to stay in one of the Vatican residences.

With 5 floors and 120 bedrooms, Domus Sanctae Marthae could be an ordinary motel in the suburbs of Atlanta or Houston if the pope didn't live there. Modern, impersonal and Spartan, the residence contrasts with the beauty of the apostolic palace.

When, with the diplomat Fabrice Rivet, I visit the famous Third Loggia of the apostolic palace, I am amazed by the mappae mundi painted on the walls, Raphael-style wild animals, and the painted ceilings reflected in the costumes of the Swiss Guard. Nothing of the kind in Saint Martha's.

'It's a bit cold, that's true,' agrees Harmony, a young woman of Sicilian origins who's been given the task of showing me around.

On a panel by the entrance I note: 'suitable dress required'. And a little further on: 'no shorts or skirts'. I also notice a number of Gammarelli-brand bags – the luxury trademark of pontifical clothing, waiting at Saint Martha's reception. The linked audience hall and press room are quite Spartan too, and everything is bland: the triumph of bad taste.

In the pope's meeting room I find a huge painting representing the Virgin of Guadalupe, which symbolizes all the superstitious religiosity of Latin America: a present given to the pope by the Cardinal Archbishop of Mexico, Norberto Rivera Carrera, who might have been seeking forgiveness for his associations and his sins. (The cardinal has been criticized for his response to allegations of sexual abuse against priests, including those against the famous Marcial Maciel. He was retired by Francis in 2017.)

A few metres away there is a chapel reserved for the pope: he celebrates mass there with a small congregation at seven o'clock every morning. It is very plain, like the dining room, much bigger, but like a works canteen. Harmony shows me the table, a little apart from the others, where Francis takes his meals, with six people at the most.

On the second floor is the holy father's private apartment, which one is not allowed to visit; I am shown an exact replica of it in the opposite wing: it's a modest suite consisting of a little sitting room and a bedroom and a single bed. One of the Swiss Guard who protects the pope, and who frequently spends the night outside his bedroom door, will confirm this information. I will see him often in Rome, and we will even have regular visits to the Makasar Café in the Borgo, a wine bar not far from the Vatican, where I will meet everyone who wants to see me discreetly. Over the months, as we will see, this young man will become one of my informants about gay life in the Vatican.

Now we're in the laundry. Anna is a small, gentle woman, highly devout, and Harmony introduces her to me as 'the pope's laundress'. In two rooms to the left of the papal chapel, this nun devotedly looks after Francis's outfits. With painstaking care, she unfolds, as if they were the holy shroud, chasubles and albs to show them to me (unlike his predecessors, Francis refuses to wear the rochet or the red mozzetta).

'You can see the different habits that his holiness wears. White in general; green for an ordinary mass; red and violet for special occasions; and silver last of all, but the holy father doesn't use that colour,' Anna tells me.

As I'm getting ready to leave Domus Sanctae Marthae, I bump into Gilberto Bianchi, the pope's gardener, a jovial Italian, devoted servant of the holy father, and clearly concerned about his holiness's citrus fruit trees, which have been planted outside, just in front of the pontifical chapel.

'Rome isn't Buenos Aires,' a worried Gilberto tells me with a knowing air.

As he waters the orchids, the holy father's gardener adds: 'It was too cold last night for the orange trees, the lemon trees, the mandarin trees; I don't know if they'll survive.'

Now worried myself, I observe the trees lined up against a wall, hoping that they will get through the winter. Indeed, we're not in Buenos Aires!

'That wall that you see there, next to the chapel, where the orange trees are, marks the border,' Harmony suddenly says to me.

'What border?'

'The border of the Vatican! On the other side there's Italy.'

On my way out of Domus Sanctae Marthae, right by the front door, I find myself face to face with an umbrella stand containing, quite visibly, a big umbrella with the colours of the rainbow: a rainbow flag!

'It's not the pope's umbrella,' Harmony is quick to point out, as if she suspected a blunder.

And while the Swiss Guards salute me and the policemen lower their eyes as I leave, I start dreaming. Who could this lovely umbrella with the unnatural colours belong to? Mgr Battista Ricca, the *direttore* of Santa Marta, who very kindly invited me to visit the residence of which he was in charge? Was it left there by one of the pope's assistants? Or by a cardinal whose cappa magna went so well with the rainbow umbrella?

In any case, I imagine the scene: its lucky owner, perhaps a cardinal or a monsignore, takes his stroll in the gardens of the Vatican with his rainbow flag in his hand! Who is he? How dare he? Or is he perhaps not aware of it? I imagine him taking the Via delle Fondamenta and then the Rampa dell'Archeologia, to visit Benedict XVI, who lives cloistered in the monastery of Mater Ecclesiae. Unless, beneath that multicoloured umbrella, he takes a little tour to the Palace of the Holy Office, the base of the Congregation for the Doctrine of the Faith, the old Inquisition. Perhaps this rainbow umbrella has no known owner, and he too is in the closet. It lies about. People borrow it, put it back, take it away again, use it. Then I imagine the priests passing it around, swapping it according to circumstances and bad weather. Some 'to say a prayer to the rainbow'; some to go strolling near the Triton Fountain or Saint John's Tower; some to go and pay homage to the most venerated statue in the Vatican gardens, the one of Bernard of Clairvaux, the great reformer and doctor of the Church, known for his homophilic poems and his love for the Irish archbishop Malachy of Armagh. Is the placement of this stiff statue, which evokes a double life at the very heart of Roman Catholicism, a symbol in itself?

How I would like to have been a discreet observer, a Swiss Guard on duty, a receptionist at Santae Marthae, to follow the life of that umbrella, that 'drunken boat', lighter than a cork dancing in the Vatican gardens? Might this rainbow flag – 'damned by the rainbow', in the Poet's words – be the secret code of a 'savage parade'? Unless, in fact, its sole purpose is to protect people from the rain?

'I came to Saint Martha's late in 2003,' Francesco Lepore continues.

Although he was the youngest priest working in the holy see, he began living among the cardinals, bishops and old nuncios of the Vatican. He knows them all, has been an assistant to several of them, measures the breadth of their gifts and little foibles, and has guessed their secrets.

'The people who worked with me lived there, and even Mgr Georg Gänswein, who would become private secretary to Pope Benedict XVI, lived there too, with us.'

Lepore spent a year in this famous residence, which proved to be a hotbed of startling homo-eroticism. 'Saint Martha's is a place of power,' he explains. 'It is a big crossroads of ambitions and intrigues, a place filled with competition and envy. A significant number of priests who live there are homosexual, and I remember, during meals, that there were constant jokes on the subject. Nicknames were given to the gay cardinals, feminizing them, and that made the whole table laugh. We knew the names of the ones who had a partner or who brought young men to Saint Martha's to spend the night with them. A lot of them led a double life: priest at the Vatican by day; homosexual in bars and clubs at night. Often those prelates were in the habit of making advances on younger priests like me, seminarians, the Swiss Guard, or laypeople who worked at the Vatican.'

Several of them have told me about those 'scandal-mongering meals' at which priests told stories of the papal court out loud and stories of the young men very quietly. Ah, those quips at Domus Sanctae Marthae! The whispering I encountered at Domus Internationalis Paulus VI, Domus Romana Sacerdotalis and in the Vatican apartments, when I was staying and lunching there too.

Francesco Lepore goes on: 'One of the priests in Saint Martha's worked at the Secretariat of State. He was close to Cardinal Giovanni Battista Re. At that time he had a young Slavic friend, and in the evenings he often brought him to the residence to sleep with him. Then he presented him to us as a member of his family: his nephew. Of course no one fell for it! One day, when the priest was promoted, the rumours started flying. Then a public declaration was made by Cardinal Giovanni Battista Re and Bishop Fernando Filoni to confirm that the young Slav was indeed a member of his family and the case was closed!'

So the omnipresence of homosexuals in the Vatican isn't just a matter of a few black sheep, or the 'net that caught the bad fish', as Josef Ratzinger put it. It isn't a 'lobby' or a dissident movement; neither is it a sect of a Freemasonry inside the holy see: it's a system. It isn't a tiny minority; it's a big majority.

At this point in the conversation, I ask Francesco Lepore to estimate the size of this community, all tendencies included.

'I think the percentage is very high. I'd put it at around 80 per cent.'

During a discussion with a non-Italian archbishop, whom I met several times, he confirmed to me: 'Three of the last five popes are said to have been homophilic, some of their assistants and secretaries of state too, as well as most cardinals and bishops in the Curia. But it isn't a matter of knowing whether those Vatican priests have this kind of inclination: they do. It's a matter of knowing – and this, in fact, is the true debate – whether they are practising or non-practising homosexuals. That's where things get complicated. Some prelates who have inclinations do not practise homosexuality. They might be homophilic in their life and culture, but without having a homosexual identity.'

Over the course of about a dozen interviews, Francesco Lepore told me about the mad gaiety of the Vatican. His testimony is incontestable. He has had several lovers among archbishops and prelates; he has been propositioned by a number of cardinals, whom we discuss: an endless list. I have scrupulously checked all of those stories, making contact myself with those cardinals, archbishops, monsignori, nuncios, assistants, ordinary priests and confessors at St Peter's, all essentially homosexual.

For a long time Lepore was inside the machine. And yet it is easy, when a cardinal discreetly hits on you, or when a monsignore shamelessly propositions you, it's easy to spot the 'closeted', the practising gays and other members of the 'parish'. I've experienced that myself. The game's too easy! Because even when you're a confirmed bachelor, locked away in a closet that could easily be a safe, and you've taken a vow of heterosexual celibacy, there's always a moment when you give yourself away.

Thanks to Lepore, and soon, by a process of networking, thanks to 28 other informants, priests and laymen, within the Vatican – and openly gay with me – I knew from the beginning of my investigation where to go. I had identified the ones who were 'of the parish' before I'd even met them; I knew the assistants to approach and the names of the monsignori whom I would have to befriend. There was no shortage.

I will never forget the endless conversations with Lepore in the Roman night during which, when I mentioned the name of a particular cardinal or archbishop, I would immediately see him growing animated, exploding with joy and finally exclaiming, waving his hands in the air: '*Gayissimo!*'

For a long time Francesco Lepore was one of the favourite priests in the Vatican. He was young and charming – even sexy. He was also a highly literate intellectual. He charmed both physically and intellectually. During the day he translated the pope's official documents into Latin and answered the letters addressed to the holy father. He also wrote cultural articles for *l'Osservatore romano*, the official Vatican newspaper.

Cardinal Ratzinger, the future Pope Benedict XVI, at the time prefect of the Congregation for the Doctrine of the Faith, agreed to write a preface to a collection of Lepore's erudite essays, and praised the young priest.

'I have a very pleasant memory of that time,' Lepore told me, 'but the homosexual problem remained, more pressing than ever. I had a sense that my own life no longer belonged to me. And then I was very quickly drawn to the gay culture of Rome: I started attending sports clubs, heterosexual at first, but people knew about it. I started celebrating mass less and less often, going out in plain clothes, without my cassock or dog-collar; I soon stopped sleeping at Saint Martha's. My superiors were informed of it. They wanted me to change jobs, perhaps remove me from the Vatican, and it was then that Mgr Stanisław Dziwisz, the personal secretary to Pope John Paul II, and the director of the *Osservatore Romano*, for which I was writing, intervened in my favour. They managed to allow me to stay in the Vatican.'

In this book we will often bump into Stanisław Dziwisz, now a retired cardinal in Poland, where I met him. For a long time he was one of the most powerful men in the Vatican, effectively running it with the Cardinal Secretary of State Angelo Sodano, as John Paul II's health deteriorated. It would be a euphemism to say that a dark legend surrounds this enterprising Polish cleric. But let's not get ahead of ourselves; readers will have all the time in the world to understand the system.

So thanks to Dziwisz, Francesco Lepore was appointed private secretary to Cardinal Jean-Louis Tauran, a very influential Frenchman, a seasoned diplomat and 'minister' of foreign affairs for John Paul II. I would meet Tauran four times, and he would become one of my regular informants and contacts at the Vatican. In spite of his fathomless split personality, I developed an affection for this extraordinary cardinal, who suffered terribly from Parkinson's for a long time before he finally succumbed to it in the summer of 2018, just as I was revising the final version of this book.

Thanks to Tauran, who was well-aware of his homosexuality, Lepore pursued his life as an intellectual in the Vatican. Then he worked for the Italian cardinal Raffaele Farina, who ran the Vatican library and the secret archives, and then for his successor, Archbishop Jean-Louis Bruguès. He was in charge of the publication of rare manuscripts; he edited collections of theological colloquia published by the official presses of the holy see.

'My double life, that searing hypocrisy, weighed upon me terribly,' Lepore continues. 'But I hadn't the courage to chuck it all in and abandon the priesthood.'

Finally, though, he revoked his calling, carefully working out the best way to do so without causing a scandal.

'I was too cowardly to resign. Out of weakness, I ensured that the decision didn't come from me.'

According to the version he gives me (which is confirmed by Cardinals Jean-Louis Tauran and Farina), he 'deliberately' chose to consult numerous online gay sites, accessing these on his computer from the Vatican, and to leave his session open, with compromising articles and websites.

'I knew very well that all the Vatican computers were under tight control, and that I would be spotted quickly. And that's what happened. I was called in and things happened very quickly: there was no trial, and no punishment. It was suggested that I return to my diocese, where I would take up an important position. Which I refused.'

The incident was taken seriously; it deserved to be, in the eyes of the Vatican. Then Francesco Lepore was received by Cardinal Tauran, 'who was extremely sad about what had just happened'.

'Tauran kindly rebuked me for having been naïve, for not having known that "the Vatican had eyes everywhere", and that I would have to be more cautious. He didn't blame me for being gay, just for having been spotted! And that's how things came to an end. A few days later I left the Vatican; and I stopped being a priest once and for all.'

2

Gender theory

An ante-room? A study? A boudoir? I'm in the sitting room of the private apartment of the American cardinal Raymond Leo Burke, an official residence in the Vatican, Via Rusticucci in Rome. It's a strange and mysterious room, which I observe minutely. I'm on my own. The cardinal hasn't arrived yet.

'His Eminence is held up outside. He will be here soon,' I am told by Don Adriano, a Canadian priest, elegant and slightly uptight: Burke's assistant. 'Are you up to date with current events?'

On the day of my visit the American cardinal had been summoned by Pope Francis to receive a talking-to. I should add that Burke had launched countless provocations and protests against the holy father, so much so that he was considered his number-one opponent. For Francis, Burke was a Pharisee – hardly a compliment coming from a Jesuit.

Within the pope's entourage, the cardinals and monsignori I've interrogated are amused: '*Son Éminence Burke est folle!* [His Eminence Burke is insane!]' one of them says to me, insisting with French grammatical logic on the feminine adjective.

This feminization of men's titles is surprising, and it took me a lot of time to get used to hearing the cardinals and bishops of the Vatican being talked about in this way. If Paul VI was in the habit of expressing himself in the first person plural ('We say …'), I learn that Burke likes to be spoken of in the feminine: '*Votre Éminence peut être fière*'; '*Votre Éminence est grande*'; '*Votre Éminence est trop bonne*' ('Your Eminence can be proud'; 'Your Eminence is great'; 'Your Eminence is too kind').

More cautious, Cardinal Walter Kasper, an intimate of Pope Francis, merely shook his head in consternation and disbelief when I mentioned Burke's name, even calling him mad – but '*fou*', in the masculine.

More rational in his criticism, Father Antonio Spadaro, a Jesuit considered to be one of the men behind the pope, with whom I have often chatted at the offices of the journal *La Civiltà Cattolica*, which he edits, explains: 'Cardinal Burke led the opposition to the pope. Those opponents are very vehement and sometimes very wealthy, but there aren't many of them.'

One Vaticanologist told me the nickname by which the American cardinal was known in the Curia: 'The Wicked Witch of the Midwest'. And yet when faced with this rebellious Eminence who had assumed the task of defending tradition, Pope Francis didn't mince his words. Beneath the façade of a smiling and jovial man, he is in reality a hard nut. 'A sectarian', say his detractors, of whom there are now many in the Vatican.

The holy father sanctioned Cardinal Burke, stripping him without warning of his post of prefect in charge of the supreme court of the Apostolic Signatura, the Vatican's appeal tribunal. By way of consolation, he was then appointed *promoveatur ut amoveatur* (kicked upstairs), the pope's representative at the Order of Malta. With the grand title of 'Cardinalis Patronus' – the cardinal patron of the order – Burke went on defying the successor of Peter; this brought him a new warning from the ruling pontiff on the day of my arrival.

The origin of this new confrontation is something you couldn't make up: a distribution of contraceptives! The Order of Malta, a sovereign religious order, carries out charitable work in lots of countries around the world. In Burma, some of its members were said to have distributed contraceptives to HIV-positive people to avoid spreading the disease. After a knockabout internal inquiry, the 'Grand Master' accused his number two, the 'Grand Chancellor', of authorizing the condom campaign. Then, in a Pasolinian scene, the Grand Master dismissed the Grand Chancellor from his duties in the presence of the pope's representative: Cardinal Burke.

Ite, missa est? Hardly. Things cranked up another notch when the pope learned that the settling of scores between rivals had contributed to this argument and that he understood exactly who and what was involved (control over the way in which a fund of 110 million euros, sheltered in a bank account in Geneva, would be distributed) and summoned Burke to ask him to explain himself. The Order of Malta is indeed like many religious congregations, a mad den of gaiety.

Greatly displeased, Francis decided to reinstall the Grand Chancellor by force, in spite of the opposition of the Grand Master, who invoked the sovereignty of his organization and the support of Burke. This tug of war, which held the Curia in suspense, came to an end with the resignation of the Grand Master and the placing of the order under trusteeship. As for Burke, severely repudiated though he had kept his title he had been stripped of power, which was transferred to the pope's 'substitute'. 'The holy father left me the title of Cardinalis Patronus, but now I don't have a single function. I'm no longer kept informed either by the Order of Malta or by the pope,' Burke would go on to lament.

It was during one of the episodes of this rollicking TV mini-series, while Burke had been summoned by the pope's entourage, that I had a meeting with him. And while Burke was being taught his lesson, I waited for the cardinal at his home, alone, in his ante-room.

In fact I wasn't really alone. Daniele Particelli had joined me in the end. This young Italian journalist had been recommended to me a few months before by seasoned colleagues, and he frequently came with me when I did my interviews. Researcher and translator, dogged fixer, Daniele, whom we will encounter frequently throughout this book, would be my chief colleague in Rome for almost four years. I still remember our first conversation.

'I'm not a believer,' he told me, 'which allows me to be freer and more open-minded. I'm interested in everything to do with the LGBTQ community here in Rome, the parties, the apps and the gay underground scene. I'm also very into computers; very much a geek, very digital. I'd like to be a better journalist and learn to tell stories.'

That was the start of our professional collaboration. Daniele's boyfriend cultivated species of exotic plants; he himself was supposed to spend every evening looking after Argo, a pedigree Pembroke Welsh

Corgi, which required special treatment. The rest of the time he was free to help me with my investigations.

Before Daniele, I approached other Roman journalists to help me, but they all proved to be careless or distracted; too militant or not militant enough. Daniele liked my subject. He didn't want to take revenge on the Church, and he wasn't indulgent towards it either. He just wanted to do some neutral journalistic work, following the model of the excellent articles in the *New Yorker* and what is known as 'narrative non-fiction'; and that corresponded to my project. He aspired to do 'straight journalism', as they call it in the States: factual journalism with facts, nothing but the facts, and 'fact-checking'. He would never have imagined that the world he was going to discover with me would be so unlikely and so 'unstraight'.

'I'm sorry. His Eminence has informed me that he will be a little late,' Burke's assistant, a visibly embarrassed Don Adriano, comes to tell us again.

To fill the silence, I ask him if we are in the cardinal's apartment or in his office.

'His Eminence has no office,' the young priest tells me. '*Elle travaille chez elle*. [Her Eminence works at home.] You can go on waiting here.'

Cardinal Burke's ante-room, a vast place that will stay in my memory for ever, is a kind of huge drawing room, at once classical, luxurious and Spartan. 'Bland', you might say. In the middle of the room is a dark wooden table, a modern copy of an antique model, placed on a rug that matches the furniture; we are surrounded by a set of red, yellow and beige carved wood armchairs whose curved armrests are decorated with the heads of sphinxes or maned lions. On a chest of drawers is a Bible open on a lectern; on the table, an arrangement of dried pine cones, braided and glued together – the ornamental art of elderly dandies. A complicated lampshade. Some precious stones and dreadful religious statues. And table mats! On the walls, a library with well-filled shelves and a huge portrait of a cleric. A portrait of Burke? No – but the idea crosses my mind.

I surmise that Burke is a hero to his young assistant, who must lionize him. I try to strike up a conversation about the sex of angels, but Don Adriano turns out to be shy and far from talkative, before he leaves us alone again.

When waiting becomes awkward, I leave the drawing room at last. I take the liberty of wandering about the cardinal's apartment. All of a sudden I happen upon a private altar in a fake iceberg setting, an altarpiece in the form of a colourful triptych, like a little open chapel, embellished with a garland of blinking lights, with the cardinal's famous red hat in the middle. A hat? What am I saying: a headdress!

Then I find myself remembering the extravagant photographs of Raymond Leo Burke, so often mocked on the internet: the diva cardinal; the dandy cardinal; the drama-queen cardinal. They must be seen to be believed. Looking at them, you start imagining the Vatican in a different light. Laughing at Burke is almost too easy!

My favourite picture of the American prelate isn't the most spectacular. It shows the 70-year-old cardinal sitting on an asparagus-green throne twice as large as he is, surrounded by silvery drapery. He wears a fluorescent yellow mitre in the shape of a tall Tower of Pisa, and long turquoise gloves that look like iron hands; his mozzetta is cabbage-green, embroidered with yellow, lined with a leek-green hood revealing a bow of crimson and pomegranate lace. The colours are unexpected; the accoutrements unimaginable; the overall image eccentric and very camp. It is easy to caricature a caricature.

Don Adriano surprises me as I meditate on the cardinal's red hat, and guides me with the gentleness of a chamberlain towards the toilets, which I tell him I'm looking for.

'This way,' he murmurs, with a tender glance.

While His Eminence Burke is being told off by Francis, here I am in his bathroom, the place where he performs his ablutions. A strange wet room worthy of a deluxe spa resort, and heated like a sauna. The luxury soaps, with their subtle perfumes, are arranged in the Japanese style, and the little towels folded on medium-sized ones, which are in turn arranged on large ones, and the large ones on very large. The toilet paper is new, and set in a protective cover that guarantees its immaculate purity. As I am leaving, in the corridor, I find dozens of bottles of champagne. High-class champagne! But why on earth would a cardinal need so much alcohol? Isn't frugality commanded by the Gospels?

Not far off I spot a mirrored wardrobe, or perhaps a 'psyche', one of those tilting mirrors that lets you see yourself all at once, which I find enchanting. If I had performed the experiment of opening the three doors at the same time I would have seen myself as the cardinal did every morning: from all sides, surrounded by his image, enwrapped in himself.

In front of the wardrobe: impressive red bags, fresh from the shop – was it Gammarelli again, tailor to the popes? Inside the hatboxes: the cardinal's headdresses, his fake fur coats and his red trapezoid outfits. I feel as if I'm behind the scenes of the film *Fellini's Roma* when they're preparing the extravagant ecclesiastical fashion parade. Soon some priests on roller-skates will appear (to get to paradise faster); priests in wedding dresses; bishops in blinking lights; cardinals disguised as standard lamps; and, the chief attraction, the Sun King in his full splendour, garlanded in mirror and lights. (The Vatican demanded that the film be banned in 1972, even though it's been confirmed to me that it was shown on loops in the gay-friendly dormitories of certain seminaries.)

The wardrobe of the American Eminence did not reveal all its secrets to me. Don Adriano, the superintendent in charge of the cardinal's outfits, led me back to the drawing room, cutting short my exploration and depriving me of the opportunity to see the cardinal's famous cappa magna.

Burke is well-known for wearing this garb from another era. The photographs of him wearing this big ceremonial altar-boy outfit are famous. He's a big man; in his cappa magna he becomes a giant – he looks like a Viking bride! Performance. Happening. In his long robe (he could be wearing a curtain), Burke shows himself in his full plumage.

This billowing jacket is a cape of red moiré silk, with a hood buttoned by the neck and fastened at the front (the hands emerge from a slit) and involving a train which is said to vary according to the solemnity of the occasion. Burke's train can reach a length of 12 metres. Is this 'larger-than-life' cardinal trying to enlarge himself at the same time as the pope is trying to shrink him?

Francis, who isn't worried about confronting the Vatican's Nobility of the Robe, is said to have told Burke, repeatedly and in vain, that wearing the cappa magna in Rome is out of the question. 'The carnival is over!' he is supposed to have said (according to a phrase reported by the media). Unlike his predecessor, the pope is not keen on the frills and furbelows of the 'traditional' cardinals. He wants to shorten their robes. To tell the truth, it would be a shame if Burke obeyed him: his portraits are so unorthodox.

On the internet, the photographs of his extraordinary outfits have caused a stir. Here we see him wearing the *galero cardinalice*, a big red hat with tassels that was abandoned by almost all prelates after 1965, but Burke still wears it, even if, at the age of almost seventy, it makes him look like a vindictive old woman. At the Order, a ritualistic sect that has its own capes, crosses and regalia, he isn't considered quite so shocking and can dress in the medieval style without troubling its members.

There, His Eminence wears farthingale robes that give him breadth while concealing his rolls of flesh. In this other photograph, he clashes with his cape and a thick white ermine stole around his neck, giving him a triple chin. Here he is again, smiling with braces above his knees and stockings below them, looking like the King of France waiting to go to the guillotine. Often we see him surrounded by young seminarians kissing his hand – also magnificent in that our Hadrian seems to follow the cult of Greek beauty, which, as we know, was always more male than female. Winning both the admiration and the laughter of Rome, Burke always appears surrounded by obsequious chaperones, Antinous-like figures kneeling in front of him or page boys carrying the long red train of his cappa magna, as choirboys might for a bride. What a spectacle! The skirted cardinal playfully slaps his young men, and they in turn adjust his rolled-up robes. He makes me think of the Infanta Margarita in Velázquez's *Las Meninas*.

To be perfectly honest, I've never seen anything quite so fantastical. At the sight of this man disguised to display his virility, one is utterly lost for words. There are no adjectives to describe this cardinal draped in his female attire. And there you have your gender theory! As reviled by Burke himself, of course: 'Gender theory is an invention, an artificial creation. It is a madness that will cause immense damage in society and in the lives of those who support this theory … Some men [in the United States] insist on going into women's rest rooms. That is inhuman', the cardinal was bold enough to explain in an interview.

Burke is a mass of contradictions. In fact he sets the bar remarkably high. He can stroll about in full sail, in his cappa magna, in an unthinkably long robe, in a forest of white lace or dressed in a long coat shaped like a dressing gown, while at the same time, in the course of an interview, denouncing in the name of tradition a 'Church that has become too feminized'.

'Cardinal Burke is the very thing he denounces,' a cleric close to Francis states starkly. The same man believes that the pope might have had him in mind in 2017 when he denounced 'hypocritical' priests with 'made-up souls'.

'It's a fact, these days Burke feels isolated within the Vatican. But he's unique rather than alone,' disagrees the Englishman Benjamin Harnwell, one of Burke's loyal colleagues, whom I have interviewed five times.

The prelate can probably still count on a few friends who try and match him in terms of their bright-red, goose-poop or marron glacé outfits: the Spanish cardinal Antonio Cañizares, the Italian cardinal Angelo Bagnasco, the Sri Lankan cardinal Albert Patabendige, the patriarch and Archbishop of Venice Francesco Moraglia, the Argentinian archbishop Héctor Aguer, the late American bishop Robert Morlino, or the Swiss Vitus Huonder, all of whom compete with him in terms of the cappa magna. These 'self-caricatures' could still try their chances in *Drag Race*, the TV reality show that chooses the prettiest drag queen in the United States, but in Rome they have all been marginalized or relieved of their functions by the pope.

His partisans at the holy see claim that Burke 'gives spirituality back to our era', but they avoid appearing with him; Pope Benedict XVI, who brought him to Rome because he thought he was a good canon lawyer, remained silent when he was punished by Francis; Burke's detractors, who don't want to be quoted, whisper to me that he's 'a bit mad', and circulate rumours, but none of them has yet delivered the slightest proof of real ambiguity. Let's just say that, like all men of the Church, Burke is 'unstraight' (a nice neologism invented by the hero of the Beat Generation, Neal Cassady, in a letter to his friend Jack Kerouac to describe a non-heterosexual or one who is sexually abstinent).

What makes Burke stand out is his appearance. Unlike most of his fellow Catholics, who think they can hide their homosexuality by issuing one homophobic declaration after another, he practises a kind of sincerity. He is anti-gay and rages against homosexuality in broad daylight. He makes no attempt to conceal his tastes: he displays them with provocative affectation. There's nothing effeminate about Burke: it is a matter of respecting tradition, he says. Still: his accoutrements and his unusual drag-queen appearance tell another story.

Julian Fricker, a German drag artist who aims to achieve a high artistic standard, explained to me during an interview in Berlin: 'What strikes me when I look at Cardinal Burke's cappa magna, robes or hats topped by floral ornaments, is its overstatement. The biggest, the longest, the tallest: it's all very typical of drag-queen codes. He has this sense of "extravagance", this boundless artificiality – the rejection of "realness" as it's called in drag jargon, to refer to those who want to parody themselves. There's a certain "camp" irony, too, in the choice of robes by these cardinals, which the androgynous Grace Jones or Lady Gaga could have worn. These clerics are playing with gender theory and gender identities that are not fixed, but fluid and queer.'

Burke isn't ordinary. He's not run-of-the-mill, or common-or-garden. He's complex and unusual – and therefore fascinating. It's very strange. A masterpiece. Oscar Wilde would have loved him.

Cardinal Burke is the spokesman for the 'traditionalists', and the front-runner in terms of homophobia within the Roman Curia. On this question he has issued no end of resounding declarations, collecting the beads of a genuine anti-gay rosary. 'You shouldn't,' he said in 2014, 'invite gay couples to family gatherings when children are present.' A year later, he considered that homosexuals who live in stable couples are like 'the person who murders someone and yet is kind to other people'. He has denounced 'the pope, who is not free to change the Church's teaching with regard to the immorality of homosexual acts and the indissolubility of marriage'. In a book of interviews, he even theorized about the impossibility of love between people of the same sex: 'When homosexual love is spoken of as a conjugal love, it is impossible, because two men or two women cannot experience the characteristics of conjugal union.' For him, homosexuality is a 'grave sin' because it is, in a classic formula of the Catholic Catechism, 'intrinsically disordered'.

'Burke falls within the traditionalist line of Pope Benedict XVI,' the former priest Francesco Lepore tells me. 'I am very hostile to his positions, but I must acknowledge that I appreciate his sincerity. I don't like cardinals who practise double-speak. Burke is one of the few with the courage of his convictions. He is a radical opponent of Pope Francis, and has been sanctioned by Francis for that reason.'

Obsessed with the 'homosexual agenda' and gender theory, Cardinal Burke has condemned the 'gay days' in Disneyland in the United States, and the permission granted to men to dance together at Disney World. As for 'same-sex marriage', he clearly sees it as 'an act of defiance against God'. In an interview, he says of gay marriage that 'there is only one place these types of lies come from, namely Satan'.

The cardinal is leading his own crusade. In Ireland in 2015, at the time of the gay marriage referendum, his remarks during the debates were so violent that they forced the president of the Irish episcopal conference to break with him (the 'yes' vote won by 62 per cent against 38 per cent).

In Rome, Burke is like a bull in a china shop: his homophobia is so intense that it even disturbs the most homophobic Italian cardinals. His legendary 'hetero-panic', the characteristic of a heterosexual who exaggerates his fear of homosexuality to such an extent that he arouses doubts about his own inclinations, raises smiles. His misogyny is unsettling. The Italian press mocks his blue-stocking pretensions, his crocus-coloured dresses and his lacy Catholicism.

During Francis's visit to Fátima, in Portugal, Cardinal Burke went so far as to provoke the pope by ostentatiously reciting his rosary, clutching the beads in his hands, flicking through the Vulgate, while the pope pronounced his homily: the photograph of this disdainful gesture was on the front pages of the Portuguese press.

'With a pope who doesn't wear red shoes or eccentric outfits, Burke goes literally mad,' one priest in the Vatican told me, hardly containing his mirth.

'Why are there so many homosexuals here in the Vatican, among the most conservative and traditionalist cardinals?'

I put that question directly to Benjamin Harnwell, that close associate of Cardinal Burke's, after talking to him for less than an hour. At the time, Harnwell was busy explaining the difference between 'traditionalist' and 'conservative' cardinals within the right wing of the Church. For him, Burke, like Cardinal Sarah, is a traditionalist, while Müller and Pell are conservatives. The former reject the Second Vatican Council, while the latter accept it.

My question catches him off guard. Harnwell looks at me beadily. And, at last, he says: 'That's a good question.'

Harnwell, in his fifties, is English, and speaks with a strong accent. An enthusiastic celibate, slightly esoteric and close to the far right, he has a complicated CV. He takes me back in time, and along with his conservatism I have a sense of dealing less with a subject of Elizabeth II than with one of Queen Victoria. He is a minor character in this book, not even a priest; but I very quickly learned to take an interest in these secondary characters, who allow the reader to understand what is going on through the prism of complex logics. Most importantly, I learned to like this radical and fragile Catholic convert.

'I support Burke, I defend him,' Harnwell warns me from the outset. I am already aware that he is one of the confidants and close advisers to the 'traditionalist' cardinal (not 'conservative', he insists).

I met Harnwell for almost four hours one evening in 2017, first on the first floor of a sad little trattoria near Roma Termini station, where he had cautiously arranged to meet me, before pursuing our discussion in a more bohemian restaurant in the centre of Rome.

With a black Panizza hat in his hand, Benjamin Harnwell is the head of the Dignitatis Humanae Institute, an ultra-conservative association, and a political lobby of which Cardinal Burke is president among a dozen cardinals. The administrative council of this 'traditionalist' sect brings together the most extremist prelates of the Vatican, and includes the most obscure orders and groupuscules of Catholicism: legitimist monarchists, the extremists of the Order of Malta and the Equestrian Order of the Holy Sepulchre, the partisans of the ancient rite, and certain European fundamentalist Catholic parliamentarians (for a long time, Harnwell was assistant to a British Member of the European Parliament).

A spearhead for the conservatives in the Vatican, this lobby is openly homophobic and viscerally opposed to gay marriage. According to my sources (and the '*Testimonianza*' of Mgr Viganò, which we will come to speak of shortly), some of the members of the Dignitatis Humanae Institute in Rome and the United States are homophilic or practising. Hence my direct question to Benjamin Harnwell, which I repeat now.

'Why are there so many homosexuals here in the Vatican, among the most conservative and traditionalist cardinals?'

That was how the conversation branched off and continued. Strangely, my question freed our man to speak. Previously we were having a polite and tedious conversation, but now he looks at me differently. What does this soldier of Cardinal Burke think? He must have investigated me. It would only have taken him two clicks on the internet to know that I have already written three books on the gay question and am an ardent supporter of civil partnerships and gay marriage. Is it possible that those details would have escaped him? Or is it the attraction of the forbidden, a kind of paradoxical dandyism, that led him to see me? Or was it the sense that he was untouchable (the source of so many lapses)?

The Englishman makes a point of distinguishing, as if establishing a hierarchy of sins, the 'practising' homosexuals from those who abstain.

'If there is no act, there is no sin. And besides, if there is no choice, there are no sins either.'

Benjamin Harnwell, who was in a hurry at first, and had little time to devote to me between two trains, now appears not to want to leave me. He invites me to join him for a drink. He wants to talk to me about Marine Le Pen, the far-right French politician with whom he strongly sympathizes; and also about Donald Trump, whose politics he approves of. He also wants to discuss the gay question. And here we are in the midst of my topic, which Harnwell is now reluctant to let go of. He suggests that we go for dinner.

'The lady doth protest too much, methinks.' I only discovered the deeper meaning of this phrase of Shakespeare's, which I was going to use as the epigraph for this book, later on, after that first conversation with Benjamin Harnwell and my visit to Cardinal Burke. I wasn't able to interrogate these two Anglo-Saxons about the famous line from *Hamlet*.

Haunted by the ghost of his father, Hamlet is convinced that his uncle has murdered the king before marrying the queen, his mother, so that his stepfather could ascend the throne in place of his father. Should he take his revenge? How can he be sure of this crime? Hamlet hesitates. How can one know?

It is here that Shakespeare invents his famous dumb show, a real play within a play: Hamlet will try to trap the usurping king. To do so he resorts to the theatre, asking some travelling players to act out a scene in front of the real characters. This shadow-play, with a comical king and queen at the heart of the tragedy, allows Hamlet to discover the truth. His actors, under borrowed names, manage to penetrate the real characters psychologically in such a way as to bring out the most secret aspects of their personalities. And when Hamlet asks his mother, who is watching the scene, 'Madam, what think you of this play?' she replies, speaking of her own character: 'The lady doth protest too much, methinks.'

The phrase, which reveals hypocrisy, means that when one protests too violently against something there is a strong likelihood that one is being insincere. That excess gives you away. Hamlet understands by her reaction, and the king's, mirrored in the king and queen in the play, that the couple probably poisoned his father.

Here is a new rule of *The Closet*, the third one: *The more vehemently opposed a cleric is to gays, the stronger his homophobic obsession, the more likely it is that he is insincere, and that his vehemence conceals something.*

That was how I found the solution to the problem of my inquiry: by basing it on the dumb show in *Hamlet*. The objective is not to 'out' any living homosexuals on principle, however homophobic they might be. I don't want to implicate anybody, certainly not to add to the problems of priests, monks or cardinals whose experience of their homosexuality – as almost a hundred of them confessed to me – was one of suffering and fear. My approach is what one might call 'non-judgemental': I'm not a judge, so I'm not concerned with judging gay priests. Their sheer numbers will be a revelation to many readers, but in my eyes that is not a scandal.

If we are right to denounce their hypocrisy – which is the subject of this book – it is not with a view to rebuking them for their homosexuality, and there is no point giving out too many names. Instead, the intention is to 'inspect the invisible and hear the unheard', as the Poet has it. So it's through the theatre of those who 'protest too much' and the 'fantasies' of a system built almost entirely on the secret of homosexuality that I would like to explain matters. But at this stage, as the Poet has said, 'I alone hold the key to this wild parade'!

Almost a year after my first meeting with Benjamin Harnwell, which was followed by several other lunches and dinners, I was invited to spend the weekend with him in the abbey of Trisulti in Collepardo, where he now lives, far away from Rome.

The Dignitatis Humanae Institute, which he runs with Burke, was put in charge of this Cistercian abbey by the Italian government, on condition that they maintained this heritage site, classified as a national monument. Two monks still live there, and on the evening of my arrival I am surprised to see them sitting at either end of the U-shaped table, eating in silence.

'They are the last two brothers of a much larger religious community, all of whose members are dead. Each one had his seat and the last two still sit where they have always sat, as the seats between them have gradually emptied,' Harnwell explains to me.

Why have these two old men stayed in this isolated monastery, still saying mass at dawn every morning for the rare parishioners of their congregation? I wonder about the disturbing and magnificent intention of these clerics. One can be a non-believer – as I am – and still admire this devotion, this piety, this asceticism, this humility. These two monks, whom I deeply respect, represent the mystery of faith as far as I am concerned.

At the end of the meal, clearing the plates and cutlery in the kitchen, austere but vast, I notice a calendar on the wall to the glory of Il Duce. Every month, a different photograph of Mussolini.

'Here in the South of Italy you will very often find pictures of Mussolini,' says Harnwell in a bid for self-justification, visibly embarrassed by my discovery.

Harnwell and Burke's plan is to transform the monastery into the Italian headquarters of ultra-conservative Catholics and a seminary. In his plans, which he describes to me at length, Harnwell suggests opening a 'retreat' for hundreds of seminarists and American believers. By staying in the abbey of Trisulti for several weeks or several months, these new kind of missionaries will take courses, learn Latin, recharge their batteries and play together. Over time, Harnwell wants to create a huge mobilization movement to set the Church back 'in the right direction', and I understand that the plan is to fight against the ideas of Pope Francis.

To bring this battle to its conclusion, Burke's association, the Dignitatis Humanae Institute, has received the support of Donald Trump and his famous far-right former adviser Steve Bannon. As I am informed by Harnwell, who organized the meeting between Burke and the Catholic Bannon, in that same ante-room in which I found myself in Rome, the understanding between the two men was 'instant'. Their closeness grew as their meetings turned into colloquia. Harnwell speaks of Bannon as if the latter were his mentor, and he is part of the close Roman entourage of the American strategist every time he plots at the Vatican.

The 'fundraising' being the nerve end of the activities, Harnwell set out to raise money in order to finance his ultra-conservative project. He appealed to Bannon and right wing foundations in the USA to help him. He even had to pass his driving test in order to reach the Carthusian monastery at Trisulti on his own initiative. During a lunch with me in Rome, he announced with a beaming smile that he had finally passed his driving test after trying for 43 years.

Trump has sent another emissary to the holy see in the person of Callista Gingrich, the third wife of the Republican former speaker of the House of Representatives, who was appointed ambassador. Harnwell has wooed her as well since her arrival in Rome. An objective alliance has formed between the American ultra-right and the ultra-right of the Vatican. (Burke has likewise multiplied his overtures to Europeans, receiving in his ante-room the Italian Deputy Prime Minister and Minister of the Interior Matteo Salvini, as well as the homophobic, right-wing Minister of European Affairs and former Minister of Family and Disability Lorenzo Fontana).

Pursuing this idea, I take advantage of my time with Harnwell to ask him again about the gay question in the Church. The fact that the close entourage of John Paul II, Benedict XVI and Francis consisted, and continues to consist, of many homosexuals is an open secret well known to Harnwell. But when I tell him that a former cardinal and secretary of state was gay, the Englishman doesn't believe it.

Sitting opposite me, he says over and over again: 'The cardinal secretary of state was gay! The cardinal secretary of state was gay!' And the assistant to a particular pope was gay too! And another one, gay as well! Harnwell seems to be filled with wonder at our conversation.

Then, during another lunch with him in Rome, he will tell me that he has carried out a little inquiry of his own. And he will confirm that, according to his own sources, I was well-informed: 'Yes, you're right, the cardinal secretary of state was in fact gay!'

Benjamin Harnwell stops talking for a moment; in this stuffy Christian restaurant, he crosses himself and prays out loud before eating. The gesture is anachronistic here, slightly out of place in this secular part of Rome, but no one pays him any attention, and he goes on politely eating his lasagne, washed down with a glass of (very good) Italian white wine.

Our conversation takes a strange turn now. But each time he protects 'his' Cardinal Raymond Burke: 'he isn't a politician', 'he is very humble', even though he wears the cappa magna.

Harnwell is a kindly man, and on the sensitive subject of the cappa magna he stubbornly defends the tradition, and not the transvestism. On other subjects and other church figures he opens up, he takes risks. Now he shows me his true face.

I could give a lengthier account of our conversations and our five lunches and dinners; could pass on the rumours spread by the conservatives. Let's save that one for later, because the reader certainly wouldn't want me to reveal everything right now. At this stage I need only say that if I had been given an outline of the unimaginable story that I am about to tell in all its details, I confess that I wouldn't have believed it. Truth is definitely stranger than fiction. The lady doth protest too much!

Still sitting in the drawing room of Cardinal Burke, who's yet to arrive, cheered by his absence because observing an apartment is sometimes better than a long interview, I start gauging the extent of the problem. Is it possible that Cardinal Burke and his co-religionist Benjamin Harnwell are unaware that the Vatican is populated by gay clerics? The American cardinal is both a clever hunter of homosexuals and a passionate scholar of medieval history. More than anyone, he knows the dark side of the Vatican. It's a long story.

As early as the Middle Ages, Popes John XII and Benedict IX committed the 'abominable sin', and everyone in the Vatican knows the name of the boyfriend of Pope Adrian IV (the famous John of Salisbury), and of the lovers of Pope Boniface VIII. The marvellously scandalous life of Pope Paul II is equally famous: he is said to have died of a heart attack in the arms of a page. As for Pope Sixtus IV, he appointed several of his lovers cardinal, including his nephew Raphael, who was made cardinal at the age of 17 (the expression 'cardinal-nephew' has been passed down to posterity). Julius II and Leo X, both patrons of Michelangelo, and Julius III, are also generally presented as bisexual popes. Sometimes, as Oscar Wilde observed, some popes were called Innocent by antiphrasis!

Closer to our own time, Cardinal Burke is aware, like everyone else, of the recurring rumours about the morals of Pope Pius XII, John XXIII and Paul VI. Pamphlets and booklets exist, the film director Pasolini, for example, having dedicated a poem to Pius XII in which he mentions an alleged lover (*A un Papa*). It is possible that these rumours are based on curial grudges, to which the Vatican and its gossiping cardinals hold the secret.

But there is no need for Burke to go back so far. To assess these close friendships fully, he would need only to look towards his own country, the United States. Having stayed there for so long, he knows his co-religionists by heart, and the endless list of scandals surrounding a large number of American cardinals and bishops. Contrary to what one might expect, sometimes it has been the most conservative clerics, the most homophobic, who have been 'outed' in the United States by a vengeful harassed seminarian, an overly chatty rent boy, or the publication of a risqué photograph.

A two-tier morality? In America, where everything is bigger, more extreme, more hypocritical, I found a ten-tier morality. I was living in Boston when the first revelations of the huge 'Spotlight' paedophilia scandal came out, and I was startled, as everyone was, by what had happened. The investigation in the *Boston Globe* freed the tongues of people all over the country, bringing to light a systematic network of sexual abuse: 8,948 priests were accused, and over 15,000 victims identified (85 per cent of them boys between the ages of 11 and 17). The Archbishop of Boston, Cardinal Bernard Francis Law, became the symbol of the scandal: his cover-up campaign, and his protection of numerous paedophile priests, finally forced him to resign (with an exfiltration to Rome, handily organized by Cardinal Secretary of State Angelo Sodano, which allowed him to enjoy diplomatic immunity and thus escape American justice).

A fine connoisseur of the American episcopate, Burke could not have been unaware of the fact that most of the Catholic hierarchy in his country – the cardinals, the bishops – are homosexual: the famous and powerful cardinal and Archbishop of New York, Francis Spellman, was a 'sexually voracious homosexual', if we are to believe his biographers, the testimony of Gore Vidal and confidential remarks by the former head of the FBI, J. Edgar Hoover. Similarly, Cardinal Wakefield Baum of Washington, recently deceased, lived for many years with his personal assistant – a classic of the genre.

Cardinal Theodore McCarrick, former Archbishop of Washington, was also a practising homosexual: he was well-known for his 'sleeping arrangements' with seminarians and young priests whom he called his 'nephews' (finally accused of sexual abuse, he was forbidden to hold public office by the pope in 2018). Archbishop Rembert Weakland was 'outed' by a former boyfriend (he has since described his journey as a homophile in his memoirs). One American cardinal has been banned from the Vatican and sent back to the United States for his improper conduct with a Swiss Guard.

Another American cardinal, the bishop of a large city in the United States, 'has lived for years with his boyfriend, a former priest', while an archbishop of another city, a devotee of the Latin mass and a man much given to cruising, 'lives surrounded by a flock of young seminarians', a fact confirmed to me by Robert Carl Mickens, an American Vaticanologist familiar with the gay lifestyle of the senior Catholic hierarchy in the United States. The Archbishop of St Paul and Minneapolis, John Clayton Nienstedt, is also a homophile, and was investigated by his Archdiocese in connection with allegations that he had inappropriate sexual contact with adult men (allegations he categorically denies). He subsequently resigned when criminal charges were brought against the Archdiocese concerning its handling of allegations of inappropriate behaviour by a priest who was later convicted of molesting two boys; another resignation that was accepted by Pope Francis.

The private lives of the American cardinals, in a country where Catholicism is a minority religion and has long had bad press, is often the subject of probes in the media, which have fewer scruples than in Italy, Spain or France about revealing the double life of the clergy. Sometimes, as in Baltimore, it was the cardinal's entourage that came under fire for its bad habits and wild behaviour. The cardinal in question, Edwin Frederick

O'Brien, the former archbishop, was unwilling to answer my questions about the special friendships in his diocese. He now lives in Rome, where he bears the title and attributes of the Grand Master of the Equestrian Order of the Holy Sepulchre of Jerusalem – one could hardly make it up. He had me received by his deputy, Agostino Borromeo, then his spokesman, François Vayne, a pleasant Frenchman who was careful, over three meetings that I had with him, to deny all rumours.

According to my information, however, as gathered by my researchers across 30 countries, a significant number of 'lieutenants', of 'grand priors', 'grand officers' and 'chancellors' of the Equestrian Order, in the countries where they are represented, are 'closeted' and 'practising'. So much so that some people are amused by this Equestrian Order, whose hierarchy is said to be 'an army of horse-riding queens'.

'The presence of many practising homosexuals in the hierarchical structures of the Equestrian Order is no secret to anyone,' I am assured by a grand officer of the order, himself openly homosexual.

The American cardinal James M. Harvey, appointed prefect of the Pontifical House in the Vatican, a sensitive post, was subjected to a fast-tracked removal process, 'promoveatur ut amoveatur', by Benedict XVI, who was said to have rebuked him for recruiting Paolo Gabriele, the pope's butler and the one from whom the stories put out by VatiLeaks originated. Might Harvey have played a part in this scandal?

What does Cardinal Burke make of these repeated scandals, these strange coincidences and the large number of cardinals who are part 'of the parish'? How can he put himself forward as a defender of morals when the American episcopate has been so discredited?

Let us also remember that about a dozen American cardinals were implicated in sexual abuse scandals – whether they were responsible for them, like Theodore McCarrick, who was dismissed; whether they protected the predatory priests by switching them from parish to parish, like Bernard Law and Donald Wuerl; or whether they were insensitive to the fate of the victims, playing down their suffering to protect the institution (Cardinals Roger Mahony of Los Angeles, Timothy Dolan of New York, William Levada of San Francisco, Justin Rigali of Philadelphia, Edwin Frederick O'Brien of Baltimore or Kevin Farrell of Dallas.) All were criticized by the press or by victims' associations, or by Mgr Viganò in his 'Testimonianza'. Cardinal Burke himself was referenced by the important American association Bishop Accountability for his inadequate management of paedophile questions in the dioceses of Wisconsin and Missouri when he was bishop and then archbishop: he was said to have tended to play down the facts, and to have been somewhat 'insensitive' to the fate of the plaintiffs.

Pope Francis, keeping the American cardinals specifically in mind, had harsh words on the plane coming back from his trip to the United States in September 2015: 'Those who have covered these things [paedophilia] up are also guilty, including certain bishops who have covered them up.'

Francis, exasperated by the American situation, also appointed three replacement cardinals: Blase Cupich in Chicago, Joseph Tobin in Newark, and Kevin Farrell, called to Rome as prefect to deal with the ministry in charge of laity and the family. Polar opposites to Burke's reactionary homophobia, these new cardinals are pastors who are inclined to be sensitive to the cause of migrants or LGBT people, and partisans of zero tolerance on the question of sexual abuse. If one of them were homosexual (Mgr Viganò accuses all three of espousing a 'pro-gay' ideology), apparently the two others aren't part 'of the parish', which would tend to confirm the fourth rule of *The Closet*: *The more pro-gay a cleric is, the less likely he is to be gay; the more homophobic a cleric is, the more likely he is to be homosexual.*

And then there's Mychal Judge. In the United States, this Franciscan friar was the anti-Burke par excellence. He had an exemplary career marked by simplicity and poverty, often in contact with those excluded from society. A former alcoholic, Judge managed to kick the habit and then dedicated his life as a friar to helping the poor, drug addicts, the homeless and even AIDS patients, whom he went so far as to hold in his arms – an image that was still rare in the early 1980s. Appointed chaplain to New York City Fire Department, he attended fires with the firefighters and, on the morning of 11 September 2001, he was among the first to hurry to the twin towers of the World Trade Center. It was there that he died, at 9.59 in the morning, struck by falling masonry.

His body was carried by four firefighters, as is shown by one of the most famous photographs from 9/11, immortalized by Shannon

Stapleton for Reuters – a true 'modern *pietà*'. Immediately identified in hospital, the priest Mychal Judge was the first official victim of the 11 September attacks: No. 0001.

Since then, Mychal Judge has become one of the heroes of the story of the attacks: 3,000 people attended his funeral in St Francis of Assisi Church in Manhattan, in the presence of Bill and Hillary Clinton and the Republican mayor of New York, Rudolph Giuliani, who declared that his friend was 'a saint'. A block of a New York Street was rechristened in his name; his fireman's helmet was given to Pope John Paul II in Rome; and France posthumously made him a member of the Légion d'Honneur. During an investigation in New York in 2018, when I spoke to several 'firefighters' and came into contact with the spokesman for the city Fire Service, I noted that his memory is still alive.

Shortly after his death, his friends and work colleagues revealed, despite this, that Mychal Judge was a gay priest. His biographers confirmed his sexual orientation, as did the former commander of the New York Fire Department. Judge was a member of Dignity, an association that brought gay Catholics together. In 2002, a law granted social rights to the homosexual companions of firefighters and police officers killed on 11 September. It was called the Mychal Judge Act.

The homophobic cardinal Raymond Burke and the gay-friendly priest-chaplain Mychal Judge: two opposing sides of the Catholic Church in the United States.

When I deliver the initial results of my inquiry and these raw data to the American cardinal James Francis Stafford, former Archbishop of Denver, at two interviews in his private apartment in Rome, he is stunned. He listens to me religiously and takes all the blows. I knew immediately, the first impression is always good: my 'gaydar' works quite well; his attitude and sincerity convince me that Stafford is probably not homosexual himself – in itself a rare thing in the Roman Curia. His reaction is no less scathing for that: 'No, Frédéric, it's not true. It's false. You are mistaken.'

I mention the name of an important American cardinal whom he knows well, and Stafford categorically denies his homosexuality. I have wounded him. And yet I know that I'm not mistaken, because I have first-hand testimony, since confirmed; I also discover that the cardinal has never really asked himself the question concerning his friend's possible double life.

Now he seems to reflect and hesitate. His curiosity wins out over his legendary prudence. In a silent interior monologue I make a note to myself that the cardinal 'has eyes but he doesn't see'. He himself will tell me later that he was sometimes 'a little naïve', and that he often learned only belatedly of things that the whole world knew.

To defuse the atmosphere, I take the cardinal aside, obliquely mention other names, precise cases, and Stafford admits that he has heard certain rumours. We talk quite openly about homosexuality, about the countless cases that have tarnished the image of the Church in the United States and in Rome. Stafford seems genuinely appalled, horrified by what I tell him, things that he can now barely deny.

Now I speak to him about some great Catholic literary figures, like the writer François Mauriac, who was such an influence on him in his youth. The publication of Jean-Luc Barré's biography of Mauriac, as is well-documented, definitively confirmed Mauriac's homosexuality.

'You see, sometimes it's only in retrospect that we understand people's true motivations, their well-protected secrets,' I tell him.

Stafford is shattered. 'Even Mauriac,' he seems to say, as if I had delivered a shocking revelation, although the writer's homosexuality is no longer a matter for debate. Stafford seems a little lost. He is no longer sure of anything. I see in his eyes his unfathomable distress, his fear, his grief. His eyes cloud over, now full of tears.

'I don't weep often,' Stafford tells me. 'I don't cry easily.'

Along with the Frenchman Jean-Louis Tauran, James Francis Stafford will certainly remain my favourite cardinal in this long investigation. He is gentleness personified, and I find myself very drawn to this frail, elderly man whom I cherish for his very frailty. I know that his mysticism isn't feigned.

'I hope you're wrong, Frédéric. I really hope so.'

We talk about our shared passion for America, for its apple pies and ice creams, which, as in *On the Road*, become better and creamier the further one drives towards the American West.

I hesitate to tell him about my trip through Colorado (he was the Archbishop of Denver) and my visits to the most traditional churches of

Colorado Springs, the bastion of the evangelical American right. I would like to talk to him about those priests, and those violently homophobic pastors whom I interviewed at Focus on the Family or in the New Life Church. The founder of the latter, Ted Haggard, finally revealed himself to be homosexual after being denounced by an escort shocked by his hypocrisy. But do I need to provoke him? He isn't responsible for these religious madmen.

I know that Stafford is conservative, pro-life and anti-Obama, but if he can appear hard-line and puritanical, he has never been sectarian. He isn't a polemicist, and he doesn't approve of the cardinals who have taken charge of the ultra-conservative Dignitatis Humanae Institute. I know he expects nothing from Burke, even if he has a nice word, a polite one, about him.

'He is a very good man,' Stafford tells me.

Was our conversation – in the autumn of his life; he is 86 – the end of his illusions?

'Soon I am going to return to the United States for good,' Stafford confides in me as we walk through the different libraries, arranged in a long line, in his vast apartment on Piazza di San Calisto.

I promised I would send him a little present, a book I'm fond of. In the course of my investigation, this same little white book would become, as we shall see, a code of which I would rather remain silent. Once I was hooked, month after month I would give it to about twenty cardinals, including Paul Poupard, Leonardo Sandri, Tarcisio Bertone, Robert Sarah, Giovanni Battista Re, Jean-Louis Tauran, Christoph Schönborn, Gerhard Ludwig Müller, Achille Silvestrini, Camillo Ruini, and of course Stanisław Dziwisz and Angelo Sodano. Not to mention the archbishops Rino Fisichella and Jean-Louis Bruguès, or indeed Mgr Battista Ricca. I also gave it to other eminences and excellencies who will have to remain anonymous.

Most of the priests appreciated the double-edged gift. Some of them talked to me about it again afterwards, others wrote to thank me for giving them this book of sinners. Perhaps the only one who really read it, Jean-Louis Tauran – one of the few genuinely cultured cardinals at the Vatican – told me he had been very inspired by that little white book, and that he quoted it often in his homilies.

As for old Cardinal Francis Stafford, he talked to me affectionately about the little alabaster-coloured book when I saw him again a few months later. And added, staring at me: 'Frédéric, I will pray for you.'

The daydream that had taken me so far away was suddenly interrupted by Don Adriano. Cardinal Burke's assistant poked his head into the drawing room once more. He apologized again, even before passing on his latest bit of information. The cardinal wouldn't arrive in time for the meeting.

'His Eminence apologizes. He ('*Elle*') is genuinely sorry. I'm very embarrassed, I'm sorry,' Don Adriano repeats helplessly, sweating deferentially and staring at the floor as he speaks to me.

I would learn from the papers shortly afterwards that the cardinal had been sanctioned again by Francis. I am sorry to leave the apartment without being able to shake His Eminence's hand. We'll make another date, Don Adriano promises. *Urbi* or *Orbi*.

In August 2018, when I once again spent several weeks living peacefully in an apartment inside the Vatican, and at the same time as I was finishing this book, the surprise publication of the '*Testimonianza*' of Archbishop Carlo Maria Viganò caused a veritable conflagration inside the Roman Curia. To say that this document 'was like a bomb going off' would be a euphemism crossed with a litotes! There were immediate suspicions raised in the press that Cardinal Raymond Burke and his American networks (including Steve Bannon, Donald Trump's former political strategist) might have had some involvement. Even in his worst nightmares, old Cardinal Stafford could never have imagined such a letter. As for Benjamin Harnwell and the members of his Dignitatis Humanae Institute, they had a moment of joy ... before becoming disillusioned.

'You were the first to talk to me about this secretary of state and those cardinals being homosexual and you were right,' Harnwell tells me during a fifth lunch in Rome, the day after the outbreak of hostilities.

In an eleven-page letter published in two languages by ultra-conservative websites and newspapers, the former nuncio in

Washington, Carlo Maria Viganò, wrote a pamphlet that was a vitriolic attack on Pope Francis. Deliberately published on the day of the pope's trip to Ireland, a country where Catholicism was ravaged by cases of paedophilia, the prelate accused the pope of personally covering up the cases of homosexual abuse by the former American cardinal Theodore McCarrick, now aged 88. McCarrick, a former president of the American Bishops' Conference a powerful prelate, a great collector of money – and lovers – was stripped of his status as cardinal and dismissed by Pope Francis. However, Viganò saw the McCarrick affair as the moment to settle his scores, uninhibited by any super-ego. Supplying a large amount of information, notes and dates to back up his thesis, the nuncio inelegantly took advantage of the situation to call for the pope's resignation. Even more cunningly, he named the cardinals and bishops of the Roman Curia and the American episcopate who, according to him, took part in this huge 'cover-up': it's an endless list of names of prelates, among the most important in the Vatican, who were thus 'outed', whether for right or wrong. (When the pope dismissed the allegations, his entourage indicated to me that Francis 'was initially informed by Viganò that Cardinal McCarrick had had homosexual relations with over-age seminarians, which was not enough in his eyes to condemn him'. In 2018, when he learned for certain that he had also, apart from his homosexual relations, sexually abused minors, 'he immediately punished the cardinal'. The same source doubts that Benedict XVI took serious measures against McCarrick, and if they ever existed they were never applied.)

A real 'VatiLeaks III', the publication of the '*Testimonianza*' of Mgr Viganò enjoyed an unprecedented international resonance in the late summer of 2018: thousands of articles were published around the world, the faithful were dumbfounded and the image of Pope Francis was dented. Consciously or not, Viganò had just given arguments to everyone who had long thought that there was complicity within the Vatican itself over crimes and sexual abuse. And even though the *Osservatore Romano* only devoted a single line to the report ('a new episode of internal opposition' was all that the official organ of the holy see had to say on the matter), the frenzied conservative and far-right press demanded an internal inquiry, and in some instances the resignation of the pope.

Cardinal Raymond Burke – who had already stated a few days before: 'I think it's high time to acknowledge that we have a very serious problem with homosexuality in the Church' – was one of the first to claim a kill: 'The corruption and filth which have entered into the life of the Church must be purified at their roots,' the prelate thundered, demanding an 'investigation' into Viganò's '*Testimonianza*', taking into account the serious pedigree of the accuser, of whose authority there was, in his view, no doubt.

'Cardinal Burke is a friend of Mgr Viganò,' Benjamin Harnwell confirmed to me just after the publication of the vexatious letter. (Harnwell also told me he had a meeting with Burke that day 'to exchange ideas'.)

Subsequently, several ultra-conservative prelates dived into the open breach to weaken Francis. The reactionary Archbishop of San Francisco, Salvatore Cordileone, for example, put his head over the parapet to accredit and legitimize Viganò's 'serious' and 'disinterested' text, and violently to denounce the homosexualization of the Church – which is amusing in itself, in a way.

The right wing of the Curia had just declared war on Francis; there is nothing to stop us thinking that this war had been declared by one gay faction of the Curia against another one, the former being on the left and pro-Francis, the latter on the far-right and anti-Francis. A remarkable split that the priest and theologian James Alison would sum up for me, during an interview in Madrid, in a significant couple of sentences: 'It's an intra-closet war! The Viganò affair is the war of the old closet against the new closet!'

This gesture of Archbishop Carlo Maria Viganò, whose seriousness was generally acknowledged, was not above suspicion. Certainly, the nuncio knew by heart the situation of the Church in the United States, where he spent five years as ambassador for the holy see. Before that he was secretary general of the governorate of the Vatican City, which enabled him to point to countless dossiers and to be informed about all internal affairs, including those concerning the contradictory morals of the most senior prelates. It's even possible that he kept sensitive files on a large number of them. (In this post, Viganò succeeded Mgr Renato Boccardo, now Archbishop of Spoleto, whom I interviewed: he told me some interesting secrets.)

Having also been placed in charge of the appointment of diplomats of the holy see, an elite body that produced a large number of cardinals in the Roman Curia, Viganò still appears to be a reliable witness, and his letter is irrefutable.

Many people have said that this 'Testimonianza' was an operation conducted by the hard wing of the Church to destabilize Francis, since Viganò was closely linked to the networks of the Catholic far right. According to my information, this point is far from proven. In fact it is less a 'plot' or an attempted 'putsch', as some have claimed, than an isolated and slightly fanatical act. For a conservative, Viganò is primarily a 'Curial', a man of the Curia and a pure product of the Vatican. According to one witness who knows him well, he is 'the kind of man who is generally loyal to the pope: pro-Wojtyła under John Paul II, pro-Ratzinger under Benedict XVI and pro-Bergoglio under Francis'.

'Mgr Viganò is a conservative, let's say in the line of Benedict XVI, but first and foremost he is a great professional. He backs himself with dates and facts, he is very precise in his attacks,' the famous Italian Vatican specialist Marco Politi tells me over lunch in Rome.

Cardinal Giovanni Battista Re, one of the few people quoted positively in the document, was still harsh in his judgement when I spoke to him at his apartment in the Vatican in October 2018.

'Sad! How sad it is! How could Viganò have done such a thing? There's something going wrong in his head … [He gestures to indicate a lunatic.] It's unbelievable!'

For his part, Father Federico Lombardi, former spokesman for Popes Benedict XVI and Francis, suggested to me at one of our regular discussions, after the publication of the letter: 'Mgr Viganò has always tended to be rigorous and brave. At the same time, in each of the posts that he has held, he was a very divisive figure. He was always somewhat at war. By appealing to well-known reactionary journalists, he therefore put himself at the service of an anti-Francis operation.'

There is no doubt that the Viganò affair was made possible thanks to the help of the media and ultra-conservative journalists opposed to Pope Francis's position (the Italians Marco Tosatti and Aldo Maria Valli, the *National Catholic Register*, LifeSiteNews.com or the extremely wealthy American Timothy Busch of the Catholic television network EWTN).

'This text was immediately instrumentalized by the reactionary Catholic press,' the Italian Benedictine monk Luigi Gioia, who knows the Church extremely well, tells me during an interview in London. 'The conservatives frantically attempted to deny the cases of sexual abuse and the cover-up by the Church: clericalism. That is, an oligarchic and condescending system devoted to the preservation of its own power regardless of the price. To refuse to acknowledge that it is the very structure of the Church that is at stake, they look for scapegoats: gays who have infiltrated the institution and compromised it because of their dark inability to rein in their sexual appetites. That is Viganò's thesis. The right had no trouble in grasping that unexpected opportunity to impose his homophobic agenda.'

If that anti-Francis campaign is confirmed it nonetheless seems to me that Viganò's gesture is more irrational and isolated than has been imagined: it is a desperate act, a personal revenge, and first and foremost the fruit of a deep and intimate wound. Viganò is a wolf – but a solitary wolf.

So why did he suddenly break with the pope? An influential monsignore in the immediate entourage of Mgr Becciu, who was at the time a 'substitute', or the pope's 'minister' of the interior, gave his hypothesis to me during a meeting at the Vatican shortly after the publication of the letter (this conversation, like most of my interviews, was recorded with the agreement of the *minutante*): 'Archbishop Carlo Maria Viganò, who has always been vain and slightly megalomaniacal, dreamed of being created cardinal. It was his ultimate dream, in fact. The dream of his life. It is true that his predecessors were generally elevated to the rank of cardinal. But not him! First of all Francis dismissed him from Washington, then he deprived him of his superb apartment here in the Vatican, and he had to move to a residence where he was surrounded by retired nuncios. During all this time, Viganò was champing at the bit. But he went on hoping! Once past the consistory of June 2018, when he was not created cardinal, his last hopes had foundered: he was about to turn 78 and he realized that he had missed his chance. He was desperate and decided to take his revenge. It was as simple as that. His letter has little to do with sexual abuse and everything to do with that disappointment.'

For a long time Viganò was criticized for his infatuation, his gossiping, his paranoia, and he was even suspected of feeding stories to the press, which led to his being fired from Rome and sent to Washington on the order of the then Cardinal Secretary of State Tarcisio Bertone under Benedict XVI (the VatiLeaks notes are explicit on these different points). There are also rumours about his inclinations: his anti-gay obsession is so irrational that it could conceal repression and 'internalized homophobia'. That is, incidentally, the thesis of the American Catholic journalist Michael Sean Winters, who 'outed' Viganò: his 'self-hatred' led him to hate homosexuals; he had become the very thing he denounced.

The pope, who refused to comment on this controversial pamphlet, suggested a similar analysis. In a coded homily of 11 September 2018, he let it be understood that the 'Great Accuser speaking out against the bishops', who 'was trying to reveal sins', would be better off, rather than accusing others, 'accusing himself'.

A few days later, Francis repeated his attack: once again he took issue with Viganò, without naming him, in another homily directed at 'hypocrites', a word that he would repeat a dozen times. 'The hypocrites within and without,' he insisted, adding: 'the devil is using hypocrites [...] to destroy the Church'. The lady doth protest too much!

Whether or not it was written by a 'drama queen' betraying his internalized homophobia, the most interesting aspect of the '*Testimonianza*' lies elsewhere. Not only in the secret motivations of Mgr Viganò, which were probably multiple, but in the veracity of the facts that he revealed. And it is here that his letter becomes a unique document, a major and for the most part incontestable testimony concerning the 'culture of secrecy', the 'conspiracy of silence' and the homosexualization of the Church. In spite of the opacity of his text, a mixture of facts and insinuations, Viganò eschews double-speak: he deems it necessary to 'confess publicly the truths that we have kept hidden', and thinks that 'the homosexual networks present in the Church must be eradicated'. To this end, the nuncio names the three last cardinal secretaries of state – Angelo Sodano under John Paul II, Tarcisio Bertone under Benedict XVI and Pietro Parolin under Francis – as being suspected, according to him, of being guilty of covering up sexual abuse or belonging to the '*corrento filo-omosessuale*', the 'pro-homosexual trend' in the Vatican. Good heavens!

For the first time, a senior Vatican diplomat reveals the secrets of cases of paedophilia and the major presence of homosexuality in the Vatican. But I would suggest, following the analysis of several seasoned Vatican experts, that the monsignore is less interested in the issue of sexual abuse (he himself has been accused in the press of seeking to close the investigation into Archbishop John Nienstedt – allegations Viganò strongly denies) than in the gay question: 'outing' appears to be the sole true motivation of his letter.

In this the nuncio committed two major errors. First of all, in a single critique, he lumped together several categories of prelate that were largely unconnected, namely priests who were suspected of committing acts of sexual abuse (the Cardinal of Washington Theodore McCarrick); prelates who he claims had covered up these predators (for example, according to his letter, Cardinals Angelo Sodano and Donald Wuerl); prelates he claims 'belong to the homosexual current' (without any evidence, he mentions the American cardinal Edwin Frederick O'Brien and the Italian, Renato Raffaele Martino); and prelates who he claims are 'blinded by their pro-gay ideology' (the American cardinals Blase Cupich and Joseph Tobin). Overall, nearly forty cardinals and bishops were singled out or 'outed'. (Mgr Cupich and Mgr Tobin firmly denied the nuncio's allegations; Donald Wuerl offered the pope his resignation, which was accepted; the others did not comment.)

What is shocking in the Viganò testimony is the great confusion between priests capable of crimes or a cover-up on the one hand, and homosexual or simply gay-friendly priests on the other. This serious intellectual dishonesty, which mixes up abusers, those who failed to intervene and those who were simply homosexual or homophile, can only be the product of a muddled mind. Viganò has remained stuck in the homophilia and homophobia of the 1960s, when he himself was 20: he hasn't understood that the times have changed and that in Europe and America, since the 1990s, we have moved from the criminalization of homosexuality to the criminalization of homophobia! His thoughts from another era also recall the writings of homophobic homosexuals like the French priest Tony Anatrella or the Colombian cardinal Alfonso López Trujillo, whom we will discuss in due course. This inadmissible confusion between culprit and victim remains at the heart of the question of sexual abuse: Viganò is the caricature of the very thing he denounces.

Aside from this serious generalized intellectual confusion, Viganò's second error, the more serious in strategic terms for the durability of his 'testimony', was that of 'outing' major cardinals who were close to Francis (Parolin, Becciu), but also those who helped to lead the pontificates of John Paul II (Sodano, Sandri, Martino) and Benedict XVI (Bertone, Mamberti). Certainly, anyone familiar with the history of the Vatican knew that the source of the McCarrick affair lay in disturbances orchestrated under the pontificate of John Paul II: by writing it down, however the nuncio deprived himself of much of his support among conservatives. More impulsive than strategic, Viganò blindly took his revenge by 'outing' everybody he didn't like, without a plan or a tactic, while his word alone was sufficient proof to denounce the homosexuality of his colleagues – for example the Jesuits, who were considered largely to be 'deviants' (meaning homosexuals)! In accusing everyone except himself, Viganò magnificently, and inadvertently, revealed that the theology of fundamentalists can also be a sublimation of homosexuality. That was how Viganò managed to lose his allies: however critical it might have been, the right wing of the Vatican could not allow doubt to be cast on the previous pontificates of John Paul II and Benedict XVI. By targeting Angelo Sodano and Leonardo Sandri (even though, strangely, he spared Cardinals Giovanni Battista Re, Jean-Louis Tauran and, most importantly, Stanisław Dziwisz), Viganò committed a major strategic mistake, whether his accusations were true or not.

The far right of the Church, which initially supported the nuncio and defended his credibility, quickly understood the trap. After an initial thunderous outburst, Cardinal Burke fell silent, outraged in the end that the name of his close friend, the ultra-conservative Renato Martino, appeared in the letter (Burke validated a press communiqué written by Benjamin Harnwell, which firmly contested the idea that Martino might be part of the 'homosexual current' – without supplying evidence, of course). Likewise, Georg Gänswein, the closest collaborator of the retired pope Benedict XVI, was careful not to confirm the letter, whatever the cost. For conservatives, lending credence to Viganò's testament meant shooting themselves in the foot, while at the same time risking involvement in a civil war where any means were permitted. There are probably more closeted homosexuals on the right than on the left of the Church, and the boomerang effect would be devastating.

In Francis's entourage, a curial archbishop whom I met when the letter was published justified the pope's prudence with these words: 'How do you expect the pope to respond to a letter that voices suspicions about several former Vatican secretaries of state and dozens of cardinals of being gay or complicit in homosexual abuses? Confirm? Deny? Deny sexual abuse? Deny homosexuality in the Vatican? You can see that he didn't have much room for manoeuvre. If Benedict XVI didn't react either, it was for the same reasons. Neither wanted to talk after such a perverse text.'

Lies, double life, 'cover-up', the *'Testimonianza'* of Mgr Viganò shows one thing at least: everyone is connected and everyone lies in the Vatican. Which echoes Hannah Arendt's analyses of lies in *The Origins of Totalitarianism* or in her famous article 'Truth and Politics', in which she suggested that 'when a community has embarked upon organized lying', 'when everyone lies about everything of importance', and when there is a 'tendency to turn fact into opinion', to reject 'factual truths', the result is not so much that one believes in lies, as that one destroys 'the reality of the common world'.

The curial archbishop concluded: 'Viganò is barely interested in the question of sexual abuse, and his memo is of little use where this first point is concerned. On the other hand, what he wants to do is to list the homosexuals of the Vatican; it is to denounce the infiltration of gays in the holy see. That is his objective. Let's say that, on this second point, his letter is probably closer to the truth than it is on the first.' (In this book I will use Viganò's *'Testimonianza'* prudently, because it mixed verified or probable facts with pure slander. And even if that letter was judged credible by dozens of ultra-conservative cardinals and bishops, it should neither be taken literally nor under-estimated.)

So here we are in *The Closet*. This time, the witness is irrefutable: an eminent nuncio and emeritus archbishop has just bluntly revealed the massive presence of homosexuals in the Vatican. He has given us a well-kept secret. He has opened Pandora's box. Francis is indeed among queens!

3

Who am I to judge?

'Who am I to judge?' Giovanni Maria Vian repeats this phrase, still apparently trying to find its deeper meaning. 'Who am I to judge?' Is it a new doctrine? A phrase improvized more or less at random? Vian doesn't really know what to think. Who is he to judge?

The phrase, in the interrogative form, was uttered by Pope Francis on the night of 28 July 2013 in the plane bringing him back from Brazil. Broadcast around the world, it immediately became the most famous phrase of the pontificate. In its empathy, it is very like Francis, the 'gay-friendly' pope who wants to break with the homophobia of his predecessors.

Giovanni Maria Vian, whose job consists not so much of commenting on the pope's words as relaying them, remains cautious. He gives me the official transcript of the improvised talk in the course of which Francis delivered his line. Once it's put back in the context of Francis's reply, it's not absolutely certain, he tells me, that it can be read in a 'gay-friendly' way.

A layman, Vian is an academic who likes to be called '*professore*', and the director of the *Osservatore Romano*, the newspaper of the holy see. This official daily paper is published in five languages, and its offices are located in the very heart of the Vatican.

'The pope talked a lot this morning,' Vian explains when I arrive.

His newspaper publishes all the interventions by the holy father, his messages, his writings. It's the Vatican's *Pravda*.

'We're an official newspaper, that's obvious, but we also have a freer part, with editorials, articles on culture, more independent writing,' Vian adds, knowing that his room for manoeuvre is very small.

Perhaps to free himself from the constraints of the Vatican, and to show a spirit of mischief, he is surrounded by Tintin figurines. His office is filled with posters of *The Black Island, King Ottokar's Sceptre*, miniatures of Tintin, Snowy and Captain Haddock. A strange invasion of pagan objects in the heart of the holy see! And to think that it never occurred to Hergé to do a *Tintin in the Vatican*!

I spoke too fast. Vian picks me up on it, telling me about a long article in the *Osservatore Romano* about Tintin which is said to prove that, in spite of his miscreant characters and memorable expletives, the young Belgian reporter is a 'Catholic hero' inspired by 'Christian humanism'.

'The *Osservatore Romano* is as pro-Bergoglio under Francis as it was pro-Ratzinger under Benedict XVI,' explains a diplomat based in the holy see.

Another colleague on the *Osservatore Romano* confirms that the paper exists to 'defuse all scandals'.

'The silences of the *Osservatore Romano* also speak', Vian tells me, not without humour. In the course of my investigation I would often visit the paper's offices. *Professore* Vian would agree to be interviewed on the record five times, and off the record even more often, as would six of his colleagues in charge of the Spanish, English and French editions.

It was a Brazilian journalist, Ilze Scamparini, Vatican correspondent for the TV channel Globo, who dared to confront the pope head-on with the question about the 'gay lobby'. The scene played out on the plane on the way back from Rio to Rome. It was the end of the improvised press conference and the pope was tired, always flanked by Federico Lombardi, his spokesman. 'One last question?' Lombardi asks, in a hurry to bring the session to an end. It's then that Ilze Scamparini raises her hand. Here I will quote at length the dialogue that followed, from the original transcript given to me by Giovanni Maria Vian.

'I would like to request permission to ask a slightly delicate question. Another picture has gone around the world: that of Mgr Ricca, as well as information on his private life. Holy Father, I would like to know what you plan to do about this. How would Your Holiness expect to approach this problem, and how do you plan to confront the question of the gay lobby?'

'Where Mgr Ricca is concerned,' the pope replies, 'I have done what canon law recommends doing: an *investigatio praevia* [preliminary inquiry]. This investigation has not thrown up anything that he is being accused of. We have found nothing. That's my answer. But there's something I would like to add: I see that often in the Church, beyond this case, but in this case as well, people look, for example, for "the sins of youth" and publish them. No crimes, then? Crimes are something, the abuse of minors is a crime. No, sins. But if a layperson, or a priest, or a nun, has committed a sin and then converted, the Lord forgives ... But let's come back to your more concrete question: you were talking about the gay lobby. Well! A lot is written about the gay lobby. I haven't yet found anyone in the Vatican who has given me his identity card with "gay" written on it. They say there are some. I believe that when you find yourself with such a person you must distinguish the fact of being "gay" from that of constituting a lobby. Because not all lobbies are good. This one is bad. If a person is gay and seeks the Lord, if they demonstrate goodwill, who am I to judge? The problem isn't having this tendency, it's turning that tendency into a lobby. That's the more serious problem as far as I'm concerned. Many thanks for asking that question. Thank you very much!'

Dressed entirely in black, and with a slight cold, the day I meet him for the first time, Father Federico Lombardi remembers that press conference very clearly. As a good Jesuit, he admired the new pope's phrase. Who am I to judge? Never, perhaps, had a phrase of Francis's been such a perfect masterpiece of Jesuit dialectics. The pope answers a question ... with a question!

We are at the headquarters of the Ratzinger Foundation, of which Lombardi is now president, on the ground floor of a building of the Vatican on Via della Conciliazione in Rome. I will interview him at length several times in his offices about the three popes he has served – John Paul II, Benedict XVI and Francis. He was head of the press service of the first of these, and spokesman for his successors.

Lombardi is a gentle, simple man who ignores the glamorous, worldly style of many Vatican priests. I am struck by his humility, which has often impressed many of those who have worked with him. While Giovanni Maria Vian, for example, lives all on his own in a magnificent little tower in the Vatican gardens, Lombardi prefers to share his life with his Jesuit colleagues in a modest room in their community. We are a long way from the vast cardinals' apartments that I have visited in Rome so often, like those of Raymond Burke, Camillo Ruini Paul Poupard, Giovanni Battista Re, Roger Etchegaray, Renato Raffaele Martino and many others. Not to mention the palace of Cardinal Betori, which I visited in Florence, or of Carlo Caffarra in Bologna, or of Cardinal Carlos Osoro in Madrid. Neither is it in any respect like the apartments, which I haven't visited, of the former Secretaries of State Angelo Sodano and Tarcisio Bertone, which shocked people with their outrageous luxury and extravagant size.

'When Pope Francis spoke those words, "Who am I to judge?", I was beside the holy father. My reaction was a bit mixed, you might say. You know, Francis is very spontaneous, he speaks very freely. He accepted the questions without knowing them in advance, without preparation. When Francis speaks freely, for an hour and a half in a plane, without notes, with 70 journalists, it's spontaneous, it's very honest. But what he says isn't necessarily part of doctrine; it's a conversation and should be taken as such. It's a problem of hermeneutics.'

At the word 'hermeneutics', uttered by Lombardi, whose job has always been one of interpreting texts, establishing a hierarchy for them and giving a meaning to the phrases of the popes whose spokesman he has been, I have a sense that the Jesuit father wants to diminish the significance of Francis's pro-gay catchphrase.

He adds: 'What I mean is that this phrase is not evidence of a choice or a change of doctrine. But it did have a very positive aspect: it is about personal situations. It is an approach based on proximity, accompaniment, pastoral care. But that isn't to say that that [being gay] is good. It means that the pope doesn't feel it is his place to judge.'

'Is it a Jesuit formula? Is it Jesuitical?'

'Yes, if you like, it's a Jesuit phrase. It's the choice of mercy, the pastoral way with personal dilemmas. It is a phrase of discernment. [Francis] is looking for a path. In a way he is saying: "I am with you to go on a journey." But Francis replies to an individual situation [the case of Mgr Ricca] with a pastoral response; on matters of doctrine, he remains faithful.'

On another day, when I'm questioning Cardinal Paul Poupard about the same semantic debate, during one of our regular meetings at his home, this expert of the Roman Curia, who was 'close to five popes' as he put it himself, observes: 'Don't forget that Francis is an Argentinian Jesuit pope. As I say: Jesuit *and* Argentinian. Both words are important. Which means that when he says the phrase "Who am I to judge?", what matters isn't necessarily what he says but how it is received. It's a bit like St Thomas Aquinas's theory of understanding: each thing is received according to what one wishes to understand.'

Francesco Lepore was hardly convinced by Pope Francis's explanation. And neither does he share the 'hermeneutics' of its exegetes.

For this former priest, who knows Mgr Ricca well, this reply by the pope is a typical instance of double-speak.

'If we follow his reasoning, the pope is suggesting that Mgr Ricca was gay in his youth, but that he ceased to be so since he was ordained as a priest. So what the Lord forgave would be a youthful sin. And yet the pope must have known that the facts in question occurred recently.'

A lie? A half-lie? For a Jesuit, they say, telling half-lies is the same as telling half-truths! Lepore adds: 'There is an unwritten rule at the Vatican, which is that a cleric must be supported in all circumstances. Francis has protected Battista Ricca despite all opposition, just as John Paul II covered for Stanisław Dziwisz and Angelo Sodano, or as Benedict XVI defended Georg Gänswein and Tarcisio Bertone to the end, in the face of all criticisms. The pope is a monarch. He can protect the people he likes in all circumstances, without anyone being able to stop him.'

At the start of the affair there was a detailed investigation by the Italian magazine *L'Espresso*, in July 2013, the front page being devoted entirely to the Vatican and audaciously titled: 'The gay lobby'. In this article, Mgr Ricca is presented under his real name as having had a relationship with a Swiss soldier when he was working at the embassy of the holy see in Switzerland and then in Uruguay.

The night-life of Battista Ricca in Montevideo is particularly detailed: he was said to have been beaten up one night at a public meeting place, and to have come back to the nunciature with his face swollen after appealing to some priests for assistance. *L'Espresso* reported that another time, he was found stuck in the middle of the night in a lift, which had unfortunately broken down, in the offices of the Vatican embassy, not being freed by the firemen until the early hours of the morning, when he was found with a 'handsome young man' who had been stuck with him. Rotten luck!

The magazine, which cites a nuncio as a source, also mentions the suitcases of the Swiss soldier, Ricca's alleged lover, in which 'a pistol, a huge quantity of condoms and pornographic material' were said to have been found. Pope Francis's spokesman, Federico Lombardi, as always, denied the facts, which were not, in his view, 'trustworthy'.

'The way the affair was managed by the Vatican was quite comical. So was the pope's response. It was a venial sin! It was in the past! It's a bit like when President Bill Clinton was accused of taking drugs and apologized, adding that he had smoked marijuana but without inhaling!' chuckles a Rome-based diplomat who knows the Vatican very well.

The press was greatly amused by the tribulations of the cleric, his alleged double life and his lift misadventures. At the same time, we shouldn't forget that the attack came from Sandro Magister, a formidable 75-year-old pro-Ratzinger Vaticanologist. Why, all of a sudden and 12 years after the events in question, did he denounce Mgr Ricca?

The Ricca case was in fact a settling of scores between the conservative wing of the Vatican, let's call it the pro-Ratzinger faction, and the moderate wing that Francis represents, and, particularly, between two homosexual camps. A diplomat without having been a nuncio, and a '*Prelato d'Onore di Sua Santità*' (honorary prelate of the pope) who was not elected bishop, Battista Ricca is one of the holy father's closest colleagues. He is in charge of the Domus Sanctae Marthae, the pope's official residence, and also runs two other pontifical residences. Last of all, he is one of the representatives of the supreme pontiff at the highly controversial Vatican Bank (IOR). Which is to say that the cleric was quite exposed.

So his alleged homosexuality was only a pretext for weakening Francis. The assault of which he was victim was exploited to 'out' him, when it would have been more Catholic to defend him against his aggressors, given the violence to which he was subjected. As for the young man with whom he was found in the lift, should we point out here that he was a consenting adult? Let us add that one of Ricca's accusers was known, according to my sources, to have been homophobic and homosexual! A double game that is fairly typical of the Vatican way of operating.

So the Ricca affair falls within a long sequence of score-settling between different gay factions within the Roman Curia – whose victims include Dino Boffo, Cesare Burgazzi, Francesco Camaldo and even the former secretary general of the Vatican City, Carlo Maria Viganò – and we will have the opportunity to tell their story. Each time, priests or laypeople were denounced by clerics, most of whom had themselves been financially corrupted or demoted for sexually inappropriate behaviour. And here we have yet another rule of *The Closet*, the fifth: *Rumours, gossip, settling of scores, revenge and sexual harassment are rife in the holy see. The gay question is one of the mainsprings of these plots.*

'You didn't know that the pope is surrounded by homosexuals?' I am asked by a disingenuous archbishop whose nickname in the Roman Curia is 'la Païva', in tribute to a famous marquess and courtesan. So that is what I will call him in this book.

His Excellency La Païva, with whom I have regularly enjoyed lunch and dinner, knows all the secrets of the Vatican. I act naïve: 'By definition, no one practises heterosexuality in the Vatican do they?'

'There are many gays,' La Païva goes on, 'very many.'

'I knew there were homosexuals in the entourage of John Paul II and Benedict XVI's entourage, but I didn't know about Francis.'

'Yes, lots of people in Santa Marta are part of *the parish*,' La Païva says, using and abusing this esoteric formula. 'Of the parish,' he repeats, laughing. He is proud of his expression, a little as if he had invented sliced bread. I guess that he has used it hundreds of times in the course of his long career, but on this occasion, reserved for the initiated, it still has the intended effect.

'Being of the parish' could even be this book's subtitle. The expression is an old one in both French and Italian: I have found it in the homosexual slang of the 1950s and 1960s. It may pre-date those years, so similar is it to a phrase in Marcel Proust's *Sodom and Gomorrah* and Jean Genet's *Notre Dame des Fleurs* – even though I don't think it appears in either of those books. Was it more of a vernacular phrase, from the gay bars of the 1920s and 30s? Not impossible. In any case, it heroically combines the ecclesiastical universe with the homosexual world.

'You know I like you,' La Païva announces suddenly. 'But I'm cross with you for not telling me if you prefer men or women. Why won't you tell me? Are you at least a sympathizer?'

I'm fascinated by La Païva's indiscretion. The archbishop is thinking out loud, and even enjoying himself in letting me have a glimpse of his world, in the belief that it will allow him to win my friendship. He starts revealing the mysteries of Francis's Vatican, where homosexuality is a hermetic secret, an impenetrable freemasonry. The truculent La Païva shares his secret: curious man that he is! Twice as curious as the average on the subject: bi-curious, in fact. Here he is itemizing the names and titles of 'practitioners' and 'non-practitioners', while at the same time acknowledging that homophiles added to homosexuals together constitute the great majority in the cardinals' college!

The most interesting thing, of course, is 'the system'. According to La Païva, the homosexual presence within the Curia is broadly constant from one pope to the next. So the majority of the entourage of Popes John XXIII, Paul VI, John Paul I, John Paul II, Benedict XVI and Francis are said to be 'of the parish'.

Sentenced to live with this peculiar fauna, Pope Francis does what he can. With his phrase 'Who am I to judge?' he tried to change the basic deal. To go further would be to touch upon doctrine, and immediately start a war within the College of Cardinals. So ambiguity remains preferable, which suits this Jesuit pope, who is quite capable of saying a thing and its opposite within a single sentence. Being both gay-friendly and anti-gay – what a gift! His public words are sometimes at odds with his private actions. So Francis is constantly defending migrants but, as an opponent of gay marriage, he prevents undocumented gay immigrants from enjoying regularization when they have a stable partner. Francis also calls himself a 'feminist', but deprives women who are unable to have children of choice by refusing the option of medically assisted fertility treatment. Mgr Viganò accused him in his 2018 '*Testimonianza*' of being surrounded by homosexuals and appearing too gay-friendly; at the same time, Francis has suggested young homosexuals resort to 'psychiatry' (statements that he says he regrets).

In a speech before the conclave and his election, Jorge Bergolio established his priority: the 'peripheries'. In his eyes this concept, which would serve him well, encompasses the 'geographical' peripheries, the Christians of Asia, South America and Africa, which are a long way from westernized Roman Catholicism, and the 'existential' peripheries, bringing together everyone that the Church has left by the roadside. Notably among them, according to the interview that he would go on to give to the Jesuit Antonio Spadaro, are divorced couples, minorities and homosexuals.

Beyond ideas there are symbols. That was how Francis publicly met Yayo Grassi, aged 67, one of his former gay students, in the company of his Indonesian boyfriend, Iwan at the embassy of the holy see in Washington. Selfies and a video show the couple hugging the holy father.

According to a number of sources, the broadcast of this meeting between the pope and the gay couple was not a matter of chance. Initially presented as a 'strictly private', almost fortuitous encounter, by the pope's spokesman, Federico Lombardi, it was promoted a little later into a real 'audience', also by Lombardi.

In the meantime, it should be said that a controversy had broken out. The pope, on that same trip to the United States, met – under pressure from the very homophobic apostolic nuncio Mgr Viganò – a local politician from Kentucky, Kim Davis, who refused to authorize gay marriages in her region, even though she herself was twice divorced. In the face of the outcry provoked by this favour granted to a high-profile homophobic figure, the pope went into reverse and denied that he supported Ms Davis's position (the politician was arrested and briefly imprisoned for refusing to obey American law). To show that he had no intention of allowing himself to be trapped in this debate, and while regretting the damage caused behind his back by Viganò (whom he would soon exfiltrate from Washington), the pope therefore counter-balanced his initial homophobic gesture by publicly receiving his gay former pupil and his companion. A twofold process with all the trappings of a very Jesuit irenicism.

The example of the chaotic appointment of a French ambassador to the holy see reveals the same ambiguity, and also a certain Machiavellianism, on the part of Pope Francis. The man in question is Laurent Stéfanini: he is a high-ranking diplomat, a practising Catholic, held to be rather right-wing and a lay member of the Order of Malta. A highly esteemed professional, he was chief of protocol at the Élysée Palace under Nicolas Sarkozy, and was in the past the no. 2 in the same embassy. President François Hollande chose to appoint him French ambassador to the Vatican in January 2015, and his appointment was officially presented to the pope. Was the public announcement, which appeared in the satirical journal *Le Canard Enchaîné*, premature? It remains the case that the pope withheld his agreement. Motive: the diplomat was gay!

It isn't the first time that a French ambassador has been questioned by Rome because of his homosexuality: it was true in 2008 for the candidacy of Jean-Loup Kuhn-Delforge, openly homosexual and in a civil partnership with his companion, a diplomat whom Nicolas Sarkozy wanted to move to the Vatican. Pope Benedict XVI refused to give his agreement for a year, imposing a change of candidate. On the other hand, it should also be pointed out that in the past several French ambassadors to the holy see have been openly homosexual, proof that this rule may sometimes be broken.

This time the Stéfanini case was blocked at a high level. Pope Francis vetoed it. Was he wounded that other people had tried to force his hand? Did he think that an attempt was being made to manipulate him by imposing a gay ambassador on him? Was the process of agreement via the apostolic nuncio to Paris bypassed? Was Stéfanini the victim of a campaign hatched against him in France (we know that ambassador Bertrand Besancenot, close to the Order of Malta, had his eye on the job)? Should we instead seek the intrigue within the right wing of the Curia, which sought to use the affair to trap the pope?

The imbroglio assumed the appearance of an acute diplomatic crisis between Francis and François when President Hollande lent forceful support to Stéfanini's candidacy, a nomination refused once again by the pope. There would be no French ambassador to the Vatican, Hollande insisted, if they refused to accept M. Stéfanini!

In this case, the plotters were barely concerned with the consequences for the party in question, whose private life was now put on public view. As for defending the Church, as they imagined, they were in fact weakening it by putting the pope in a highly awkward situation. Francis was obliged to receive Stéfanini with all due honours, and by way of apology, with one of those ironies of Jesuit diplomacy, he told him that he had nothing against him in person!

The Archbishop of Paris was mobilized in turn to try and sort out the affair, as was the French Cardinal Jean-Louis Tauran, a man close to the pope, who found nothing unusual in the nomination of a gay ambassador – quite the contrary! On the Roman side, Cardinal Pietro Parolin, no. 2 at the Vatican, even had to go to Paris to meet François Hollande, who, in the course of a tense discussion, asked him straight out whether the problem might be 'Stéfanini's homosexuality'. According to the story that the president told one of his advisers, Parolin, who was visibly very uneasy about the matter, and personally affected, crimson with shame, terrified, stammered that the problem had nothing to do with his homosexuality …

Pope Francis's ignorance of France came to light as a result of this affair. Francis, who had not appointed a single French cardinal and, unlike all his predecessors, does not speak French, and who – alas! – seems to confuse *laïcité* with atheism, seems to be the victim of a manipulation whose codes he does not understand.

A collateral victim, Laurent Stéfanini was caught in the cross-fire of criticisms, in a battle that was beyond him, and of which he was no longer the focus. In Rome, it was an offensive by the Ratzinger wing, itself broadly homosexualized, which was moving its pawns around the board to embarrass Pope Francis. The Order of Malta, of which the diplomat is a member, divided between a rigid 'closeted' trend and a flexible 'un-closeted' trend, clashed around his case (Cardinal Raymond Burke, a patron of the sovereign order, was said to have 'atomized' Stéfanini's candidacy). The nuncio in Paris, Mgr Luigi Ventura, a former nuncio in Chile (who was close to Cardinal Angelo Sodano and the Legion of Christ led by Marcial Maciel) himself currently under fire from the press for failing to denounce the paedophile crimes of Father Fernando Karadima and who is now suspected of harassing and sexually assaulting several young men, played a double game that would take interested parties in Paris and Rome a long time to decode, by opposing the appointment of Stefanini. In France, the affair was an opportunity for the right and left to settle their scores against a background of the debate surrounding the law on gay marriage: François Hollande against Nicolas Sarkozy; 'La Manif pour tous', an anti-gay-marriage organization, against Hollande; and the extreme right against the moderate right. President Hollande, who sincerely supported Stéfanini's candidacy, was amused at the end of the day to see the right tearing itself apart over the fate of this senior Sarkozyist diplomat, a practising Catholic … and a homosexual. He taught the right a sound lesson about their hypocrisy! (Here, I am using my interviews with several advisers to President Hollande and French prime minister Manuel Valls, as well as a meeting with the first adviser to the apostolic nunciature in Paris, Mgr Rubén Darío Ruiz Mainardi.)

In a more Machiavellian bit of manoeuvring, one of François Hollande's advisers suggested that, if Stéfanini's candidacy was torpedoed, the Paris-based nuncio Luigi Ventura would be summoned to the Élysée and dismissed, because his homosexuality was well-known in the Quai d'Orsay (which is the address of the French Ministry of Foreign Affairs, where there are just as many homosexuals, so much so that it is sometimes referred to as the 'Gay d'Orsay').

'You know the Vatican diplomats in Paris, Madrid, Lisbon, London! Rejecting Stéfanini because of his homosexuality is the funniest decision that this pontificate has made! If the gay nuncios of the holy see were rejected, what would become of any apostolic representation left anywhere in the world?' smiled a French ambassador who had once held the post in the holy see.

The French Foreign Affairs Minister Bernard Kouchner confirmed during a discussion at his home in Paris: 'The Vatican strikes me as poorly placed to reject homosexual candidacies! I had the same problem when we wanted to appoint Jean-Loup Kuhn-Delforge as French ambassador to the Vatican, when he had a civil partnership with his partner. We came up against the same rejection. It was absolutely inadmissible to discriminate against a senior diplomat on the grounds of his homosexuality. We couldn't accept it! So, I can reveal to you today that I called my counterpart, Mgr Jean-Louis Tauran, who was the equivalent of the Minister of Foreign Affairs at the Vatican, and asked him to withdraw his apostolic nuncio from Paris, which he did. I said to him: "It's tit for tat!"' (Two Vatican diplomats that I have spoken to contest this version of events, and maintain that the nuncio left at the end of his normal five-year term of office.)

One piece of testimony is significant here: the Argentinian Eduardo Valdés is close to the pope, and he was ambassador to the holy see during the Stéfanini affair.

'I'm certain', he explains to me during a conversation in Buenos Aires, 'that everyone opposed to Stefanini's appointment as ambassador was just as [homosexual] as he was. It's always the same hypocrisy! Always the same double standard! It's the most practising ones who are quickest to condemn homosexuals.'

For over 14 months the post remained vacant, until François Hollande yielded and appointed a mutually agreed-upon diplomat coming to the end of his career, married with children. For his part, Stéfanini would good-humouredly declare that this diplomatic appointment no longer belonged to him, any more than he had chosen his homosexuality! (My sources on this 'Stéfanini dossier' are, apart from the names mentioned above, Cardinal Tauran, Archbishop François Bacqué and a dozen other Vatican diplomats; four French ambassadors to the holy see: Jean Guéguinou, Pierre Morel, Bruno Joubert and Philippe Zeller; and of course the ambassadors Bertrand Besancenot and Laurent Stéfanini.)

So is Francis as gay-friendly as they say? Some people think so, and tell me this next story to back up their thesis. During an audience between the pope and the German Cardinal Gerhard Müller, the then-prefect of the important Congregation for the Doctrine of the Faith, the latter arrived with a file on an old theologian who was said to have been denounced for his homophilia. He questioned the pope about the sanction he expected to take. The pope was said to have answered (according to the story I was told by two witnesses inside the Congregation, who heard it from the lips of Müller): 'Wouldn't it be better to invite him for a beer, talk to him like a brother and find a solution to the problem?'

Cardinal Müller, who made no secret of his hostility against gays, was caught utterly off guard by Francis's answer. Back in his office, he hurried to tell the anecdote to his colleagues and his personal assistant. He was said to have criticized the pope harshly for his ignorance of the Vatican, his error of judgement concerning homosexuality and in managing case files. These criticisms reached the ears of Francis, who would go on to punish Müller methodically, first of all by depriving him of his colleagues one after the other, then by publicly humiliating him, before failing to renew his post a few years later and making him take early retirement. (I asked Müller about his relationship with the pope during an interview at his home, and I'm partially basing this account on his testimony.)

Might the pope have been thinking about conservative cardinals like Müller or Burke when he denounced the gossip of the Curia? In a solemn mass at the Vatican on 22 December 2014, not much more than a year after his election, the holy father launched his attack. That day, facing the cardinals and bishops assembled for the Christmas blessings, Francis let them have it: he drew up the catalogue of the 15 'diseases' of the Roman Curia, including 'spiritual Alzheimer's' and 'existential schizophrenia'. He particularly targeted the hypocrisy of the cardinals and bishops who led 'a hidden and often dissolute life', and he criticized their 'gossip', a genuine 'terrorism of loose talk'.

The charges were severe, but the pope had not yet found his killer phrase. He would do so the following year, in one of his morning homilies at Santa Marta, on 24 October 2016 (according to the official transcript of Radio Vatican, which I shall quote here at some length, given the importance of his words): 'Behind the rigidity there is something hidden in a person's life. Rigidity is not a gift from God. Gentleness, yes, goodness, yes, benevolence, yes, forgiveness, yes. But rigidity, no! Behind rigidity there is always something hidden, in many cases a double life, but there is also something like an illness. How the rigid suffer: when they are sincere and realize that, they suffer! And how much they suffer!'

In the end, Francis had found his formula: 'Behind the rigidity, there is always something hidden, in many cases a double life.' The phrase, shortened to make it more effective, would often be repeated by his entourage: 'The rigid who lead a double life.' And while he has never mentioned names, it isn't hard to imagine which cardinals and prelates he has had in mind.

A few months later, on 5 May 2017, the pope resumed his attack, almost in the same terms: 'There are those who are rigid with the double life: they appear handsome and honest, but when no one can see them they do bad things … They use rigidity to cover up weaknesses, sins, personality disorders … The rigid hypocrites, the ones with the double life.'

Again, on 20 October 2017, Francis attacked the cardinals of the Curia whom he described as 'hypocrites', 'living on appearance': 'Like soap bubbles, [these hypocrites] hide the truth from God, from other people and from themselves, showing a face with a pious image to assume the appearance of holiness … On the outside, they present themselves as righteous, as good: they like to be seen when they pray and when they fast, when they give alms. [But] it is all appearance and in their hearts there is nothing … They put make-up on their souls, they live on make-up: holiness is make-up for them … Lies do a lot of harm, hypocrisy does a lot of harm: it is a way of life.'

Francis would go on repeating these ideas, as in October 2018: 'They are rigid. And Jesus knows their souls. And we are shocked by that … They are rigid, but behind rigidity there are always problems, serious problems … Be careful around those who are rigid. Be careful around Christians, whether they are lay people, priests or bishops, who present themselves to you as "perfect". They are rigid. Be careful. They lack the spirit of God.'

Francis has repeated these formulations, severe if not accusatory, so frequently since the beginning of his pontificate that we must admit that the pope is attempting to pass a message to us. Is he attacking his conservative opponents by denouncing their double game concerning sexual morality and money? That much is certain. We can go further: the pope is warning certain conservative or traditionalist cardinals who reject his reforms, by making them aware that he knows about their hidden life. (This interpretation is not mine: several Bergoglian cardinals, archbishops, nuncios and priests have confirmed this strategy on the part of the pope.)

Meanwhile, the mischievous Francis has gone on talking about the gay question in his own way, which is to say the Jesuit way. He has taken a step forward, then a step back. His small-step policy is ambiguous and often contradictory. Francis doesn't always seem to have singleness of purpose.

Is it a simple matter of communication? A perverse strategy for playing with the opposition, sometimes stirring it up and other times soft-soaping it, since he knows that for his opponents the acceptance of homosexuality is a fundamental problem and a private question? Are we dealing with a weak-willed pope who blows hot and cold out of intellectual weakness and a lack of conviction, as his detractors have said to me? Even the keenest Vaticanologists are a bit lost. Pro-gay or anti-gay, it's hard to tell. 'Why not have a beer with a gay?' Francis suggested. In essence that is what he has done, several times, at his private residence in Santa Marta or during his travels. For example, he unofficially received Diego Neria Lejarraga, a transsexual, born a woman, accompanied by his girlfriend. On another occasion, in 2017, Francis officially received at the Vatican Xavier Bettel, the Prime Minister of Luxembourg with his husband, Gauthier Destenay, a Belgian architect.

Most of these visits were organized by Fabián Pedacchio, the pope's private secretary, and Georg Gänswein, the prefect of the pontifical house. In photographs, we see Georg warmly greeting his LGBT guests, which has a certain piquancy when we bear in mind Gänswein's frequent criticisms of homosexuals.

As for the Argentinian Pedacchio, who is less well-known to the wider public, he has become the pope's closest collaborator since 2013 and lives with him in Santa Marta, in one of the rooms beside Francis's, number 201, on the second floor (according to a Swiss Guard I interviewed, and to Viganò in his '*Testimonianza*'). Pedacchio is a mysterious figure: his interviews are rare, or have been deleted from the internet; he doesn't talk much; his official biography is minimal. He is also the subject of below-the-belt attacks from the right wing of the Roman Curia.

'He's a hard man. He's something like the bad guy that every good and generous man needs by his side,' I am told by Eduardo Valdés, the former Argentinian ambassador to the holy see.

In this classical dialectic of 'bad cop' and 'good cop', Pedacchio was criticized by those who didn't have the courage to attack the pope directly. So the cardinals and bishops in the Curia denounced Pedacchio's turbulent life and dug up an account that he's said to have opened on the social dating network Badoo to 'look for friends' (that page was closed down when its existence was revealed by the Italian press, but it remains accessible in the memory of the web and what is known as the 'deep web'). On this Badoo account, and in his few interviews, Mgr Pedacchio states that he loves opera and 'adores' the cinema of the Spanish director Pedro Almódovar, having seen 'all of his films' which, as he acknowledges, contain 'hot sexual scenes'. His vocation is supposed to have come from 'quite a special' priest who changed his life. Concerning Badoo, Pedacchio denounced a cabal against him and swore that it was a fake account.

Deaf to the criticisms addressed to his most immediate entourage, Pope Francis continued his small-step policy. After the massacre of 49 people in a gay club in Orlando, Florida, the pope said, closing his eyes in a sign of grief: 'I think that the Church must apologize to the gay people that it has offended [just as it must also] apologize to the poor, to women who have been exploited, to the young who have been deprived of work, and for having given its blessing to so many [military] weapons.'

In parallel with these merciful words, Francis has been inflexible on the subject of 'gender theory'. Eight times between 2015 and 2017 he expressed opinions against the ideology of 'gender', which he calls 'demonic'. Sometimes he does so superficially, without knowing about the subject, as he did in October 2016 when he denounced the French school textbooks that propagate 'a sly indoctrination of gender theory', before the French publishers and the Ministry of National Education confirmed that 'these textbooks contain no mention of or reference to this gender theory'. The pope's error apparently has its source in genuine 'fake news' passed on by the Catholic associations close to the French far right, and that the sovereign pontiff took as references without checking.

One of Francis's secretaries is a discreet monsignore who replies each week to about fifty of the pope's letters, among the most sensitive. He agrees to meet me, under cover of anonymity.

'The holy father doesn't know that one of his secretaries is a gay priest!' he confesses to me proudly.

This priest has access to all parts of the Vatican, given the function that he holds with the pope, and over the past few years we have made a habit of meeting up regularly. At one of these meals, in the restaurant Coso on Via Lucina, my source tells me a secret that no one knows, and that shows yet another facet of Francis.

Since his memorable phrase 'Who am I to judge?' the pope has started receiving a large number of letters from homosexuals thanking him for his words and asking him for advice. This huge correspondence is managed at the Vatican by the services of the Secretariat of State, and more particularly by the section of Mgr Cesare Burgazzi, who is in charge of the holy father's correspondence. According to Burgazzi's entourage, whom I have also interviewed, these letters are 'often desperate'. They come from seminarians or priests who are sometimes 'close to suicide' because they can't reconcile their homosexuality with their faith.

'For a long time we replied to those letters very conscientiously, and they bore the holy father's signature,' my source tells me. 'The letters from homosexuals were always treated with a great deal of consideration and skill, given the considerable number of gay monsignori at the Secretariat of State.'

But one day Pope Francis decided that he was dissatisfied with the management of his correspondence, and demanded that the service be reorganized. Adding one disturbing instruction, according to his secretary: 'Suddenly, the pope asked us to stop replying to letters from homosexuals. We had to classify them as "unanswered". That decision surprised and astonished us. Contrary to what one might imagine, this pope is not gay-friendly.' (Two other priests in the Secretariat of State confirmed the existence of this instruction, but it is not certain that it came from the pope himself; it may have been suggested by one of his aides.)

From the information at my disposal, the monsignori of the Secretariat of State still went on 'doing resistance work', as one of them put it: when homosexuals or gay priests express their intention to kill themselves in their letters, the pope's secretaries get together to put the holy father's signature to a comprehensive reply, but using subtle euphemisms. Without intending to do so, Pope Francis therefore continues to send merciful letters to homosexuals.

4

Buenos Aires

The picture is known as the 'photograph of the three Jorges'. It's in black and white. The future pope, Jorge Bergoglio, on the left, dressed as a clergyman, is in seventh heaven. On the right we recognize Jorge Luis Borges, the greatest Argentinian writer, almost blind now, with his big glasses and a serious expression. Between these two men is a young seminarian in a dog-collar, lanky and disturbingly handsome: he is trying to dodge the camera and lower his eyes. It's August 1965.

This photograph, discovered only a few years ago, has prompted a number of rumours. The young seminarian in question is over 80 today, the same age as Francis. His name is Jorge González Manent. He lives in a town about thirty kilometres west of the Argentinian capital, not far from the Jesuit college where he studied with the future pope. They took their first religious vows together at 23. Close friends for almost ten years, they explored deepest Argentina and travelled within Latin America, particularly to Chile, where they studied together in Valparaiso. One of their famous compatriots had made the same journey a few years before: Che Guevara.

In 1965, Jorge Bergoglio and Jorge González Manent, always inseparable, were working in a different establishment, the College of the Immaculate Conception. There, at the age of 29, they invited Borges to join their literature course. The famous photograph is said to have been taken after the class.

In 1969, the two Jorges went their separate ways: Bergoglio was ordained a priest and González Manent left the Society of Jesus.

Defrocked even before being frocked! 'When I started studying theology, I saw the priesthood from very close quarters, and felt uneasy. [And] when I left, I told my mother I'd rather be a good layman than a bad priest,' Jorge González Manent said. Contrary to rumours, González Manent doesn't seem to have abandoned the priesthood because of his inclinations; in fact, he left to marry a woman. Recently, he published his private memoirs of his years with the future pope in a little book entitled *Yo y Bergoglio: Jesuitas en formación*. Does this book contain a secret?

Strangely, the book was withdrawn from bookshops and made unavailable even in the shop of the publishing house that issued it in the first place, where – I checked on the spot – it is listed as having been 'withdrawn at the request of the author'. Neither was *Yo y Bergoglio* deposited by the publisher in Argentina's national library (I looked), which is a legal obligation. A mystery!

Rumours about Pope Francis are far from rare. Some of them are true: the pope did indeed work in a stocking factory; he was also a bouncer in a nightclub. On the other hand, certain pieces of gossip dreamed up by his opponents are fake, like his alleged illness and the notion that he 'lacks a lung' (whereas, in fact, only a small part of one, on the right, was removed).

An hour's drive west from Buenos Aires: the Jesuit seminary El Colegio Máximo de San Miguel. There I meet the priest and theologian Juan Carlos Scannone, one of the pope's closest friends. I'm accompanied by Andrés Herrera, my main 'researcher' in Latin America, an Argentinian, who organized the meeting.

Scannone, who receives us in a little sitting room, is over 86, but he has a perfect recollection of his years with Bergoglio and Manent. On the other hand, he has completely forgotten the photograph of the three Jorges and the vanished book.

'I think Jorge lived here for 17 years, first as a student of philosophy and theology, then as a Jesuit provincial, and finally as the rector of the college,' Scannone tells me.

The theologian is direct and sincere, and unafraid of any question. We discuss very openly the homosexuality of a number of influential Argentinian prelates with whom Bergoglio has been in open conflict, and Scannone makes some comments. On gay marriage, he is equally clear: 'Jorge [Bergoglio] wanted to give some rights to homosexual couples; that was really his idea. But he wasn't in favour of marriage, because of the sacrament. The Roman Curia, on the other hand, was hostile to civil partnerships. Cardinal Sodano was particularly inflexible. And the nuncio in Argentina was also very hostile to civil partnerships.' (The nuncio at the time was Adriano Bernardini, a comrade of arms with Angelo Sodano, who has had appalling relations with Bergoglio.)

We talk about Francis's intellectual and psychological moulding, in which his Jesuit past and his journey as the son of Italian migrants hold a special place. The stereotype that 'Argentinians are basically Italians who speak Spanish' is not mistaken in his case!

On the question of 'liberation theology' Scannone repeats rather mechanically what he has written in a number of books. 'The pope has always been favourable to what is called the preferential option for the poor. So he does not reject liberation theology as such, but he is opposed to its Marxist origins and opposed to any use of violence. He has privileged what we in Argentina call a "people's theology".'

Liberation theology is a major intellectual trend in the Catholic Church, particularly in Latin America, and, as we will see, an essential point in this book. I have to describe it, because it will assume central importance in the big battle between the homosexual clans at the Vatican under John Paul II, Benedict XVI and Francis.

This post-Marxist ideology defends the figure of Christ by radicalizing him: it argues for a church of the poor and the excluded, and for solidarity. First popularized at the Latin American Bishops' Conference in Medellín, Colombia, in 1968, it was only given its name later in the writings of the Peruvian theologian Gustavo Gutiérrez, who asks ceaselessly how to tell the poor that God loves them.

During the 1970s, this composite trend, based on a heterogeneous collection of thinkers and texts, spread throughout Latin America. In spite of their divergences, the liberation theologians shared the idea that the causes of poverty and misery are economic and social (they still ignore factors related to race, identity or gender). They also argue for a 'preferential option for the poor', against the grain of the Church's classical language about charity and compassion: liberation theologians see the poor not as 'subjects' to be helped, but as 'actors' who are masters of their own narrative and their liberation. Finally, this intellectual movement is essentially communitarian: its starting point is in the land and the base, particularly in church communities, 'popular pastorals' and favelas, and in this it also breaks both with a 'Eurocentric' vision and with the centralism of the Roman Curia.

'Originally, liberation theology comes from the streets, the favelas, the base communities,' I am told during a meeting in Rio de Janeiro by the Brazilian Dominican Frei Betto, one of the major figures of this current of thought. 'It was not created in universities, but in the heart of ecclesial or base communities, the famous CEBs. Theologians like Gustavo Gutiérrez and Leonardo Boff went on to systematize these ideas. First of all, the fact that sin is not a personal but a social question. By and large we should be less interested in individual masturbation than in the exploitation of the masses! Then, this theology feeds off the example of Jesus Christ, who modelled his action on that of the poor.'

Some liberation theologians were communists, supporters of Che Guevara, close to the guerrilla movements of Latin America, or sympathetic to Fidel Castro. Others, following the fall of the Berlin Wall, would be able to shift their attitudes, taking into account the defence of the environment, identity issues among the Latin American indigenous peoples, women or people of African descent, and opening themselves up to questions of 'gender'. In the 1990s and 2000s, the most famous theologians, Leonardo Boff and Gustavo Gutiérrez, would start taking an interest in questions of sexual identity and gender, contrary to the official positions of Popes John Paul II and Benedict XVI.

Was Jorge Bergoglio close to liberation theology? That question has provoked intense discussions, all the more so in that the holy see launched a violent campaign against this trend in the 1980s, and reduced many of its thinkers to silence. At the Vatican, Francis's 'liberationist' past, and his association with these turbulent priests, was emphasized by his enemies and played down by his supporters. In an instruction manual and work of propaganda, *Francis, the American Pope*, two journalists from the *Osservatore Romano* firmly rejected any connection between the pope and this way of thinking.

The people close to Francis that I interviewed in Argentina are less categorical. They are aware that Jesuits in general, and Francis in particular, have been influenced by these left-wing ideas.

'I have distinguished four currents within liberation theology, one of which, the people's theology, is a better reflection of Jorge Bergoglio's thought. We didn't use the category of class struggle taken from Marxism, and we clearly rejected violence,' Juan Carlos Scannone explains.

However, this friend of the pope's insists that in Argentina, and today in Rome, Francis has always enjoyed good relations with the two main liberation theologians, Gustavo Gutiérrez and Leonardo Boff, both sanctioned by Joseph Ratzinger.

To find out more, I travelled to Uruguay, taking a boat across the Rio de la Plata – a three-hour crossing from Buenos Aires, one of the ferries bearing the name *Papa Francisco*. In Montevideo, I had a meeting with Cardinal Daniel Sturla, a young, warm and friendly priest who embodies the modern line of Pope Francis's Church. Sturla welcomes Andrés and me in a short-sleeved black shirt, and I notice a Swatch watch on his wrist, unlike the luxury watches worn by so many Italian cardinals. The interview, planned for 20 minutes, lasts for over an hour.

'The pope adheres to what we call "*la teología del pueblo*". It's a theology of the people, the poor,' Sturla says to me, taking another sip of his maté.

In the image of Che Guevara, who shared it with his soldiers, Sturla insists on giving me a taste of this bitter, stimulant traditional drink in its gourd, making me suck it up through the *bombilla*.

In the eyes of Cardinal Sturla, the question of violence represents the fundamental difference between 'liberation theology' and 'the people's theology'. In his view, it was even legitimate for the Church to reject Guevarist priests who took up arms and joined the Latin American guerrillas.

In Buenos Aires, the Lutheran pastor Lisandro Orlov still identifies the subtle differences: 'Liberation theology and the people's theology are similar. I would say that the latter is the Argentinian version of the former. It remains very populist, let's say Peronist [from the former Argentinian president Juan Péron]. It is very typical of Bergoglio, who was never on the left but who was a Peronist!'

Last of all, Marcelo Figueroa, a Protestant who co-presented a well-known television programme with Bergoglio on the subject of inter-religious tolerance, and whom I interviewed at the famous Café Tortoni in Buenos Aires, commented: 'We might say that Bergoglio is on the left even if in theological terms he is quite conservative. Peronist? I don't think so. And he isn't really a liberation theologian either. A Guevarist? He might agree with some of Che Guevara's ideas, but not with his prac-tices. You can't put him in any particular box. Most of all he's a Jesuit.'

Figueroa is the first to have used a comparison with Che Guevara, and other Argentinian priests that I've interviewed also present the same image. It's an interesting one. Not, of course, the picture of the warlike, criminal Che Guevara of Havana, the sectarian revolution-ary *compañero* with blood on his hands, or the indoctrinated guerrilla fighter of Bolivia. Che's theoretical and practical violence isn't Francis's style. But the future pope was not indifferent to this 'people's poetry', that sort of slightly naïve romanticism, and he was fascinated by the myth of Che, like so many Argentinians and so many young rebels around the world (Bergoglio was 23 at the time of the Cuban revo-lution). And in any case, how could he not have been seduced by his compatriot: the young Buenos Aires doctor who left his country by motorbike in search of the 'peripheries' of Latin America; who went on the road to discover poverty, misery, exploited workers, Indians and all the 'wretched of the earth'? That's what the pope likes: the 'first' Guevara, still compassionate, generous and relatively unideological, sensitive rebellion and social asceticism, the one who rejects privi-leges and, always holding a book in his hands, reads poems. If Francis's thought leans to some extent towards Guevarism (and not Castrism or Marxism), it is less because of his Leninist catechism than due to his slightly naïve romanticism, and the legend that is ultimately discon-nected from any kind of reality.

We can see it: we're a long way from the image that the Catholic extreme right tries to attach to Francis – that of a 'communist' or 'Marxist' Pope, as several bishops and nuncios in Rome had no compunction in saying to me. They accuse him at random of bringing Muslim migrants back from the island of Lesbos (and no Christians); of siding with the displaced people; of wanting to sell churches to help the poor; and of course of using gay-friendly speech. These criticisms point to a political agenda rather than a strictly Catholic position.

Francis a communist? Does that even mean anything? Figueroa is amazed by the bad faith of the anti-Bergoglio opposition, which, with its far-right cardinals, the Raymond Burkes and Robert Sarahs, looks like an American-style Tea Party movement!

Before they were Roman, Pope Francis's chief enemies were Argentinian. It's interesting to go back to the source of the anti-Bergoglio opposition, since it's so revealing in terms of our subject. Let's now focus on three major figures in the very special context of the Argentinian dictatorship: the nuncio Pio Laghi, the Archbishop of La Plata, Héctor Aguer, and the future cardinal, Leonardo Sandri.

The first of these, a nuncio to Buenos Aires from 1974 until 1980, only clashed with Jorge Bergoglio much later, when he became a cardinal and ran the Congregation for Catholic Education. During his years in Argentina, Laghi was still close to the military junta, who were responsible for at least fifteen thousand deaths by firing squad, around thirty thousand '*desaparecidos*' (disappeared) and a million exiles. His attitude has long been subject to criticism, not least because the nuncio liked playing tennis with one of the dictators. However, a number of people I have interviewed, such as the theologian and friend of the pope, Juan Carlos Scannone, or Argentina's former ambassador to the Vatican, Eduardo Valdés, put this friendship and his collaboration with the dictatorship into perspective.

As for Archbishop Claudio Maria Celli, who was Pio Laghi's deputy in Argentina in the late 1980s, he said to me during an interview in Rome: 'It's true that Laghi engaged in dialogue with Videla [one of the dictators], but it was a more subtle form of politics than is admitted today. He was trying to persuade him to change tack.'

The archives declassified by the American government and several witness statements that I collected in Buenos Aires and Rome show, on the contrary, that Pio Laghi was an accomplice of the military, a CIA informer and an introverted homosexual. On the other hand – and no surprise here – the Vatican archives, which have also been partly declassified, tend to exonerate him.

The main thing that emerges from the reading of 4,600 declassified secret notes and documents from the CIA and the State Department, which we have been able to consult in detail, is the nuncio's closeness to the United States Embassy. In a series of memos from 1975 and 1976 that I have at my disposal, Laghi tells the American ambassador and his collaborators everything. He constantly pleads the case of the dictators Videla and Viola, who he says are 'good men' who want to 'correct the abuses' of the dictatorship. The nuncio clears the military of their crimes, the violence coming as much from the government, he says, as from the 'Marxist' opposition. He also denies, to the American agents, that priests might be persecuted in Argentina. (At least a dozen were murdered.)

According to my sources, Pio Laghi's homosexuality might explain his positions, and might have played a part in his closeness to the dictatorship – a template that we will encounter many times. Of course, that did not predispose him to cooperation, but by making him vulnerable in the eyes of the military, who knew his predilections, it could have forced him to remain silent. However, Laghi went further: he chose to socialize actively with the fascistoid gay mafia surrounding the regime.

'Pio Laghi was an ally of the dictatorship,' says Lisandro Orlov, a Lutheran pastor who was a genuine opponent of the military junta, and one of the men best acquainted with the Argentinian Catholic Church, whom I interviewed several times at his home in Buenos Aires and then in Paris.

One of the '*madres de la Plaza de Mayo*', the famous group of mothers of the *desaparecidos* whose public demonstrations every Thursday, at 3.30 p.m. in the Plaza de Mayo in Buenos Aires I was able to witness, also testified against Laghi in court.

Finally, several investigative journalists that I have met are currently investigating the links between Laghi and the dictatorship, and the nuncio's double life. They talked to me particularly about his 'taxi boys', an Argentinian euphemism for escorts. New revelations will be made public in the coming years.

Under the dictatorship, Héctor Aguer and Leonardo Sandri were still young Argentinian priests, certainly influential, but without any major responsibility. Much later, the former would become Archbishop of La

Plata, while the latter, a future nuncio and cardinal, would be appointed Vatican 'substitute' in 2000, or 'minister' of the interior of the holy see, and one of the most influential prelates of the Catholic Church under John Paul II and Benedict XVI. Both have been long-term enemies of Jorge Bergoglio, who, once he was made pope, would force Aguer to retire just a week after his seventy-fifth birthday, and would always keep his distance from Sandri.

According to several witness statements, the two Argentinians, having become friends, were particularly 'understanding' towards the dictatorship. Close to the most reactionary currents of Catholicism (Opus Dei for Aguer, later the Legion of Christ for Sandri), they were both violent opponents of liberation theology. They liked the regime's slogan '*Dios y Patria*', a mixture of national revolution and Catholic faith.

Even today, Héctor Aguer is seen by the press as an 'ultra-conservative', a 'right-wing fascist' (*la derecha fascista*), a 'crusader', an 'accomplice of the dictatorship', or a 'fundamentalist'. In spite of his affected voice – when we meet, he quotes *Madama Butterfly* by heart, in Italian – he is also reputed to be an extreme homophobe, and he acknowledged having been in the front line against gay marriage in Argentina. While he denies any ideological kinship with the dictatorship, he is antagonistic towards liberation theology, 'which has always carried the Marxist virus'.

'Aguer is on the far right of the Argentinian Church,' explains Miriam Lewin, an Argentinian journalist for Channel 13 who was imprisoned during the dictatorship. (I wasn't able to meet Aguer during my trips to Buenos Aires, but my Argentinian and Chilean researcher, Andrés Herrera, interviewed him at his summer residence in Tandil, a town 360 kilometres from Buenos Aires. Aguer spent his holidays there with about thirty seminarians, and Andrés was invited to lunch with the elderly archbishop surrounded by '*los muchachos*' (the boys), as he calls them, several of whom seemed to him to 'embody all the stereotypes of homosexuality'.)

As for Sandri, whom I was able to interview in Rome, and whom we will encounter once again when he becomes unavoidable in the Vatican, he already appears, during his Argentinean years, on the far right of the Catholic political spectrum. A friend of the nuncio Pio Laghi and an enemy of Jorge Bergoglio, his failure to condemn the dictatorship was offensive and rumours abounded concerning his behaviour, his contacts, his bromances and his political severity. According to the testimony of a Jesuit who studied with him at the Metropolitan Seminary in Buenos Aires, his youth was stormy, and his trouble-making well-known even at the seminary. Even as a teenager 'he surprised us with his desire to charm his superiors intellectually, and he reported all the rumours circulating about the seminarians to them,' my source tells me.

Several other people, like the theologian Juan Carlos Scannone and the biblical scholar Lisandro Orlov, described Sandri's Argentinian years to me and supplied me with first-hand information. Their testimonies concur. Because of his anti-conformist image, was Sandri forced by rumours to leave Argentina after the end of the dictatorship? Feeling frail, did he need to get away? It's one hypothesis. The fact remains that having become right-hand man to Juan Carlos Aramburu, the Archbishop of Buenos Aires, Sandri was sent to Rome to become a diplomat. He would never return to live in his country. Appointed to Madagascar and then to the United States, where he became deputy to Pio Laghi in Washington and kept company with the ultra-conservatives of the American Christian far right, he went on to be appointed apostolic nuncio to Venezuela and then Mexico – where he was pursued by rumours about his 'worldliness' and extremism, according to several witness statements that I gathered in Caracas and Mexico. (In his '*Testimonianza*', Archbishop Viganò would, without supplying any proof, suspect Sandri of covering up for sexual abuse in the exercise of his functions in Venezuela and Rome, and 'having been ready to hide them'.) In 2000 he settled in Rome, where he would effectively become 'Interior Minister' to John Paul II.

In this overall context, Jorge Bergoglio's attitude under the dictatorship seems braver than has generally been admitted. With regard to Pio Laghi, Héctor Aguer, Leonardo Sandri and an episcopacy whose prudence bordered on connivance, and many priests who got involved with fascism, the future pope demonstrated an undeniable spirit of resistance. He wasn't a hero, certainly, but he didn't collaborate with the regime.

The lawyer Eduardo Valdés, who was Argentinian ambassador to the holy see in the 2010s, and who was close to the president, Cristina Kirchner, receives Andrés and me in his private 'Peronist' café in the centre of Buenos Aires. He's a chatty character, which suits me, and I let him talk, with a voice recorder in plain sight. He sums up what he sees as Francis's ideology (liberation theology in an Argentinian Peronist sauce), and tells me about the ecclesiastical complicities with the military junta. We also talk about the nuncio Pio Laghi, the Archbishop of La Plata, Héctor Aguer, Cardinal Leonardo Sandri, and several other clerics who were notorious opponents of Cardinal Bergoglio. The ambassador, now throwing caution to the wind, tells us amid great explosions of Peronist laughter about the outlandish lifestyles and frolics of members of the Argentinian Bishops' Conference or their entourage. If he is to be believed, these clergy included countless 'rigid' individuals who are in fact leading a double life. (This information would be confirmed by other bishops and priests that I met in Buenos Aires, and by the militant LGBT campaigner Marcelo Ferreyra, who has very complete files, drawn up with his lawyers, about the most homophobic and most outspoken prelates in Argentina.)

Soon, in Chile, Mexico, Colombia, Peru, Cuba and the 11 countries of Latin America where I carried out investigations for this book, I would discover similar behaviour. And always there is this well-established rule of *The Closet*, which the future pope fully grasped during his Argentinian years: the most homophobic clergy are often the most enthusiastic practitioners.

There is one last point that allows us to explain the positions of Cardinal Bergoglio once he was made pope: the debate around civil unions (2002–7) and gay marriage (2009–10). Against all expectations, in July 2010 Argentina actually became the first Latin American country to recognize marriage for same-sex couples.

Much has been written on the equivocal attitude of the future pope, who never demonstrated any great clarity on the subject when he was in Buenos Aires. To sum up his position, we may consider that Francis has been relatively moderate with regard to civil unions, refusing to incite bishops to take to the streets, but he has opposed homosexual marriage with all his strength. It should be said that the first civil partnerships occurred only slowly in Argentina, on the basis of local decisions, making large-scale mobilization difficult, and it was only same-sex marriage, which was debated in parliament and which President Kirchner was keen to instigate, that prompted a national debate.

Bergoglio's detractors point out that he was ambiguous even on civil unions, saying everything and its opposite when these were introduced in the district of Buenos Aires – but in fact he said little on the subject. We are reduced to interpreting his silences!

'I think that Jorge [Bergoglio] was in favour of civil unions; for him it was a law that echoed the civil rights movement. He would have accepted them if [the Vatican] hadn't been hostile to them,' Marcelo Figueroa comments.

The close friends of the future pope that I have met stress the difficulties Bergoglio faced from Rome when acting in favour of gay rights in Argentina. In private, Bergoglio had supported the proposed law as a good compromise for avoiding marriage. 'He was very isolated,' his friends remark, however. In their view, an extremely violent battle took place between the Vatican and the future pope on the subject, locally relayed by ambiguous priests who finally made him renounce his most open-minded ideas.

The prominent man in Argentina was, in fact, the Archbishop of La Plata, Héctor Aguer. This visceral homophobe was close to Benedict XVI, an important fact when it came to countering Bergoglio's too 'violently moderate' ideas. Wishing to get rid of the Cardinal of Buenos Aires as quickly as possible, Benedict XVI was said to have promised Aguer that he would appoint him in Bergoglio's place as soon as the latter reached the maximum age of 75. Knowing that he had support in high places. Aguer, who was usually more effeminate, went into macho overkill. Surrounded by seminarians, the prelate launched a violent campaign against civil unions and gay marriage.

'Cardinals Sodano and Sandri, then Bertone, had been managing Argentina from Rome, with Archbishop Héctor Aguer and the nuncio Adriano Bernardino on the ground, against Bergoglio,' Lisandro Orlov explains to me. (On the day of Francis's election, Aguer's nose was so out of joint that he refused to ring the bells of the archbishopric of La Plata, as tradition demands; as for Nuncio Bernardini, who was equally shocked, he would fall ill …)

So the future pope had no room to manoeuvre with regard to Rome. Witnesses confirm, for example, that all the names of priests put forward by Cardinal Bergoglio to be consecrated as bishops – generally progressives – were rejected by the Vatican, which appointed conservative candidates in their place.

'Héctor Aguer wanted to trap Bergoglio. He radicalized the positions of the Catholic Church on gay marriage to force him out of his silence on the subject. In order to understand Bergoglio you must listen to his silences about civil unions and his words against gay marriage!' Lisandro Orlov adds.

This point is confirmed by Father Guillermo Marcó, who was at the time Bergoglio's personal assistant and spokesman. Marcó received us, Andres and me, in his office, a former nunciature and now university chaplaincy in the centre of Buenos Aires. 'Since the Vatican was hostile to civil unions, Bergoglio had to follow that line as an archbishop. As his spokesman, I recommended avoiding the subject and not saying anything about it, to avoid having to criticize them. After all, it was a union without a sacrament, and not a marriage: why talk about it at all? Jorge validated that strategy. I told the homosexual organizations in Buenos Aires that we wouldn't express an opinion on the subject, and asked them not to involve us in that battle; that was our objective,' Marcó tells me.

Father Marcó, young and friendly, is a good professional. We talk for a long time in front of a very visible Nagra recording device, the kind used by professional radio journalists. Talking about a classical battle, he speaks of the inevitable conflict between city priests and country priests: 'Cardinal Bergoglio lived in Buenos Aires, an urban area, unlike other provincial bishops in rural regions. In contact with the big city, he developed a lot. He understood issues of drugs, prostitution, the problems of the favelas, homosexuality. He became an urban bishop.'

According to two different sources, Cardinal Bergoglio had shown understanding with regard to Argentinian priests who blessed homosexual unions. And yet, when the debate on same-sex marriage began in 2009, Archbishop Jorge Bergoglio's attitude changed.

Bergoglio hurled himself into battle. He had very harsh words on the subject of gay marriage ('an attack designed to destroy God's plans') and even summoned politicians, including the mayor of Buenos Aires, to give them a lecture on the subject. He publicly opposed the president, Cristina Kirchner, engaging with her in a tug of war that would turn into a settling of scores – and that he would lose in the end. The future pope also tried to silence priests who expressed opinions in favour of gay marriage, and punished them; he encouraged Catholic schools to take to the streets. This image of harshness contrasts, at the very least, with that of the pope who uttered his famous line, 'Who am I to judge?'

'Bergoglio isn't Francis,' the journalist Miriam Lewin commented acidly.

The Argentinian Lutheran pastor Lisandro Orlov adds: 'That's what explains why everyone was anti-Bergoglio in Buenos Aires! Even though they've all become pro-Francis since he's been pope!'

However, the militant homosexuals who fought Bergoglio on the question of gay marriage agree that they have to take account of the situation. This is true of Osvaldo Bazan, the author of a key work on the history of homosexuality: 'We must remember that Cardinal Antonio Quarracino, the Archbishop of Buenos Aires, wanted to deport homosexuals to an island! Héctor Aguer is such a caricature that it's better not to mention him! Bergoglio had to position himself in relation to this viscerally homophobic milieu,' he tells me.

Cardinal Bergoglio is supposed to have been equally understanding in his response to the Bishop of Santiago del Estero, Juan Carlos Maccarone, when Maccarone was denounced as a homosexual. This highly respected prelate, close to liberation theology, had to resign after a video cassette showing him with a 23-year-old man was passed to the Vatican and the media. Convinced that this was a settling of political scores and an act of blackmail, Bergoglio gave his spokesman, Guillermo Marcó, the task of defending and expressing 'his affection and understanding' for the priest. Pope Benedict XVI, on the other hand, demanded that he be dismissed from his functions. (Here I am not going to turn to the case of the priest Julio Grassi, which is outside the scope of this book. According to some in the media, the Argentinian priest suspected of acts of sexual abuse against 17 minors was protected by Cardinal Bergoglio, who went so far as to ask the episcopal conference of which he was president to finance the defence of the abuser, by launching a counter-inquiry to try and have the accusations against him dropped. In 2009, Father Grassi was given 15 years in prison, a sentence confirmed by the Argentinian supreme court in 2017.)

One of the specialists in Argentinian Catholicism, an influential adviser to the current government, sums up the debate more or less as follows: 'What do you expect of Francis? He's an 82-year-old Peronist priest. How do you expect him to be modern and progressive at his age? He's rather left-wing on social issues and rather right-wing on moral matters and sexuality. It's a bit naïve to expect an old Peronist to be progressive!'

So it's in this overall context that we need to locate the positions of Cardinal Bergoglio. According to one person within his circle, he has been 'conservative about marriage, but not homophobic'. The same person adds, saying out loud what everyone is thinking: 'If Jorge Bergoglio had been in favour of gay marriage, he would never have been elected pope.'

5

The Synod

'There has been a reaction.'

Lorenzo Baldisseri is a calm and thoughtful man. And at this stage in our conversation the cardinal chooses his words even more carefully, with extreme prudence. He takes his time before saying about the Synod on the Family: 'There has been a reaction.'

I listen to Baldisseri playing the piano. He takes his time in that as well, unlike so many pianists, who can't stop racing about. He is calm when he interprets the composers he particularly likes: Vittorio Monti, Erik Satie, Claude Debussy or Frédéric Chopin. And I like his rhythm, particularly in the pieces he excels at, such as the *danzas españolas* by Enrique Granados or 'Ave Maria' by Giulio Caccini.

In his huge office in the Vatican, the cardinal has installed his baby grand piano, which has gone with him everywhere since Miami, where he bought it when he was the nuncio to Haiti. It's a well-travelled piano, which has visited Paraguay, India and Nepal, and lived for nine years in Brazil!

'I play the piano from eight till eleven every evening in this office. I can't do without it. Here, in the Vatican, they call me God's pianist!' he adds with a chuckle.

A cardinal playing the piano on his own, at night, in this deserted palace in the Vatican: it's an enchanting image. Baldisseri hands me three CDs brought out by the Libreria Editrice Vaticana. His own.

'I also do concerts. I played for Pope Benedict XVI in his summer residence at Castel Gandolfo. But he's German, he likes Mozart! I'm Italian: I'm romantic!'

At 78, the musician cardinal, to preserve his touch and dexterity, plays every day, wherever he is, at the office, at home or on holiday.

'I've even played for Pope Francis. That was a challenge. He doesn't really like music!'

Baldisseri is one of Francis's right-hand men. Since Francis's election, to which Baldisseri contributed as conclave secretary, the new pope has given the Italian bishop the task of preparing an extraordinary Synod on the Family, in 2014–15, and then one on youth in 2018. And he was also made cardinal, to give him the necessary authority.

A synod called by the pope is an important moment for the Church. Bringing together the cardinals and a large number of bishops in an assembly affords an opportunity to debate fundamental questions and issues of doctrine. The family is one of these, and a more sensitive issue than some others.

Francis knew from the beginning that to have ideas accepted, and not to rush the rigid cardinals, most of them appointed by John Paul II and Benedict XVI, he would have to demonstrate diplomacy. Baldisseri was a nuncio, trained at diplomatic school – the great one, the school of Casaroli and Silvestrini, not the more recent, decried one of Sodano and Bertone.

'I worked in a spirit of openness. Our model was the Second Vatican Council: bring the debate to life, appeal to laypeople and intellectuals, inaugurate a new method, a new approach. Besides, that was Francis's style: a Latin American pope, open, accessible, behaving like a simple bishop.'

Was he experienced enough? Was he incautious?

'I was very new, it's true. I learned everything putting that first synod together. Nothing was taboo, nothing was held back. All questions were open. Burning! Everything was on the table: celibacy of the priesthood, homosexuality, communion for divorced couples, the ordination of women … All the debates were opened at once.'

Surrounded by a sensitive, cheerful and smiling little team, some of whom I meet in the offices of the secretariat of the Synod – Archbishops Bruno Forte, Peter Erdö, and Fabio Fabene, all since promoted by the pope – Lorenzo Baldisseri constructed a veritable war machine at Francis's service.

From the outset, Baldisseri's gang worked with the most open and gay-friendly cardinals: the German Walter Kasper, the head of the liberals at the Vatican, who was in charge of writing the preparatory report, as well as the Austrian Christoph Schönborn and the Honduran Óscar Maradiaga, a personal friend of the pope.

'Our line was essentially Kasper's. But what was also important was the method. The pope wanted to open doors and windows. The debate had to take place everywhere, in the episcopal conferences, in the dioceses, among the faithful. The people of God had to choose,' Baldisseri tells me.

This method is unheard-of. And what a change from John Paul II, the archetype of the 'control freak', or Benedict XVI, who refused to open this kind of debate, both out of principle and out of fear. By delegating the preparation of the Synod to the base, by launching a huge consultation on 38 questions all over the world, Francis thinks he can change the deal. He wants to get the Church moving. By doing so, he seeks most of all to get round the Curia, and the existing cardinals – who are used to absolute theocracy and papal infallibility – spotted the trap immediately.

'We've changed habits, that's true. It's the method that surprised people,' the cardinal explains to me prudently.

Baldisseri's gang are fast workers, that's for sure. Confident and perhaps even foolhardy, Walter Kasper announced publicly, even before the Synod, that 'homosexual unions, if they are lived in a stable and responsible manner, are respectable'. Respectable? The very word is already a revelation.

On the basis of that huge reconnaissance mission, the secretary of the Synod had to prepare a preliminary text that the cardinals would go on to discuss. 'The text was debated. The replies came in en masse, from everywhere, in all languages. The episcopal conferences replied; experts replied; many individuals also replied,' Baldisseri rejoices.

About fifteen priests were urgently mobilized to read all these notes – these letters that had come in by the thousand, an unexpected flood, an unprecedented wave. They also had to deal with the answers from the 114 episcopal conferences and almost 800 Catholic associations, in countless languages. At the same time, several secretaries (including at least one homosexual activist who I met) were mobilized to write the first drafts of a text that would, a year later, become the famous apostolic exhortation: *Amoris laetitia*.

One statement is deliberately added to this draft document: 'Homosexuals have gifts and qualities to offer the Christian community.' Another is an explicit reference to AIDS: 'Without denying the morally problematic areas connected with homosexual unions, we note that there are cases when mutual support to the point of sacrifice constitutes precious help for the lives of partners.'

'Francis came here every week,' Baldisseri tells me. 'He personally presided over the sessions where we debated the propositions.'

Why did Francis choose to move on questions of family and sexual morality? Apart from Cardinal Baldisseri, and some of his collaborators, I went to interrogate dozens of cardinals, bishops and nuncios, in Rome and 30 countries, opponents or supporters of Francis, partisans or adversaries of the Synod. Those discussions enabled me to retrace the pope's secret plan and the unimaginable battle that would soon be fought between two homosexualized factions of the Church.

Since the start of his pontificate, the pope has put the Curia on its guard, concerning both financial and sexual affairs: 'We are all sinners, but we are not all corrupt. Sinners must be accepted, not the corrupt.' He sought to denounce double lives, and preached zero tolerance.

Even more than traditionalists and conservatives, the people that Francis hates above all, as we have seen, are rigid hypocrites. Why go on opposing the sacrament for remarried divorcees when so many of the priests themselves are living with women in Latin America and Africa? Why go on hating homosexuals when they are so much in the majority among cardinals and those around him at the Vatican? How to reform the Curia, which is tangled up in denial and lies, when an insane number of cardinals and the majority of secretaries of state since 1980 practise a contrary life (three out of four according to my information)? If it's high time to do some spring cleaning, as they say, where do we start when the Church is on the brink of the abyss because of its planned obsolescence?

When Francis hears his opponents, these inflexible cardinals who deliver conservative and homophobic speeches and publish texts against his sexual liberalism – people like Raymond Burke, Carlo Caffarra, Joachim Meisner,

Gerhard Ludwig Müller, Walter Brandmüller, Mauro Piacenza, Velasio De Paolis, Tarcisio Bertone, George Pell, Angelo Bagnasco, Antonio Cañizares, Kurt Koch, Paul Josef Cordes, Willem Eijk, Joseph Levada, Marc Ouellet, Antonio Rouco Varela, Juan Luis Cipriani, Juan Sandoval Íñiguez, Norberto Rivera, Javier Errázuriz, Angelo Scola, Camillo Ruini, Robert Sarah and many others – he can't help but be cast down.

Francis is, most importantly, exasperated by the cases of sexual abuse – thousands, in fact tens of thousands – that are infecting the Catholic Church all over the world. Every week new charges are pressed, bishops are accused or found guilty, priests are sentenced, and scandal follows scandal. In over 80 per cent of cases, these affairs concern homosexual abuse – very rarely heterosexual.

In Latin America, episcopates are highly compromised and suspected by the press and victims of playing down the facts – as much in Mexico (Norberto Rivera and Juan Sandoval Íñiguez) as in Peru (Juan Luis Cipriani). In Chile, the scandal is such that all the bishops in the country have had to resign, while most of the nuncios and prelates, starting with Cardinals Javier Errázuriz and Riccardo Ezzati, have had the finger pointed at them for ignoring sexual abuse allegations. Wherever you look, the Church has been criticized over its handling of sexual abuse, up to the highest level: in Austria (Hans Hermann Groër), in Scotland and Ireland (Keith O'Brien, Sean Brady), in France (Philippe Barbarin), in Belgium (Godfried Danneels), and so on to the United States, Germany etc. In Australia, it was the 'minister' of the economy, George Pell, who was himself charged and put on trial in Melbourne. Dozens of cardinals – when they weren't being accused of such acts themselves – were denounced by name in the press or summoned by the law for covering up, whether by inertia or hypocrisy, the sexual misdeeds committed by priests. In Italy, cases of the same kind were proliferating, implicating dozens of bishops and several cardinals, even though the press, curiously, showed a kind of reticence about revealing them. But the pope and his immediate entourage knew that the dyke would eventually yield, even in Italy.

During an informal discussion in Rome, Cardinal Marc Ouellet, the Prefect of the Congregation for Bishops, described to me the unimaginable explosion in cases of sexual abuse. The man is an expert in double-speak: he is a Ratzingerian who claims to be defending Pope

Francis. The figures that the Québécois quoted to me are terrifying. He paints a picture of a Church that is literally falling apart. In his view, all the parishes in the world, all the bishops' conferences, all the dioceses are sullied. The image is horrific: the Church seems like a *Titanic* that is sinking while the orchestra goes on playing. 'It's unstoppable,' one of Ouellet's colleagues told me, frozen with shock. (In a second 'memo', Mgr Viganò was to denounce Ouellet's gay entourage.)

Where sexual abuse is concerned, Francis therefore no longer intends, as John Paul II and his right-hand men Angelo Sodano and Stanisław Dziwisz did for too long, to close his eyes or, as Benedict XVI tended to do, to demonstrate indulgence. Yet despite affirming this position he has not acted on it publicly.

Most importantly, his analysis is different from that of Joseph Ratzinger and his right-hand man, Cardinal Tarcisio Bertone, who turned this question into an intrinsically homosexual problem. According to Vatican experts and the confidences of two of his close colleagues whom I interviewed, Pope Francis thinks, on the contrary, that the deep root of sexual abuse lies in the 'rigidity' of a façade that hides a double life and, alas, perhaps also in the celibacy of priests. The holy father is said to believe that cardinals and bishops who cover up sexual abuse do it less to support the paedophiles than because they are afraid. They fear that their homosexual inclinations would be revealed if a scandal erupted or a case came to trial. So, a new rule of *The Closet*, the sixth in this book, and one of the most important, can be put as follows: *Behind the majority of cases of sexual abuse there are priests and bishops who have protected the aggressors because of their own homosexuality and out of fear that it might be revealed in the event of a scandal. The culture of secrecy that was needed to maintain silence about the high prevalence of homosexuality in the Church has allowed sexual abuse to be hidden and predators to act.*

For all of these reasons, Francis has realized that paedophilia is not an epiphenomenon – not the 'latest gossip' that Cardinal Angelo Sodano talked about: it is the most serious crisis that the Roman Catholic Church has had to confront since the great schism. The pope even anticipates that the story is just beginning: in a time of social media and VatiLeaks, in a time of freedom of the press and a readiness in modern societies for people to resort to the law, not to mention the 'spotlight effect', the

Church is a Tower of Pisa that is threatening to fall. Everything needs to be rebuilt and changed, or there is a risk that we will witness the disappearance of a religion. That was the philosophy underlying the 2014 Synod.

So Francis chose to speak. At his morning masses in Santa Marta, in talks improvised on aeroplanes or at symbolic meetings, he began regularly denouncing the hypocrisy of the 'hidden and often dissolute lives' of the members of the Roman Curia.

He had already mentioned the 15 'Curial diseases': without naming them, he talked of the Roman cardinals and bishops who had 'spiritual Alzheimer's'; he criticized their 'existential schizophrenia', their 'scandal-mongering', their 'corruption' and the way of life of those 'airport bishops'. For the first time in the history of the Church, the criticisms didn't come from the enemies of Catholicism, the Voltairean pamphleteers and other 'Cathophobes': they came from the holy father in person. That's how we must understand the whole reach of Francis's 'revolution'.

The pope also wanted to act. He wanted to 'knock down a wall', in the phrase of one of his colleagues. And he would do so through symbols, acts and the tool of the conclave. He started, with a flourish of his pen, by crossing out from the list of future cardinals all the archbishops, nuncios and bishops compromised under John Paul II and Benedict XVI. The Palace of Castel Gandolfo, the summer residence of the pope where rumours emerged of the parties that happened there under John Paul II, would be opened to tourists and, eventually, sold.

On the matter of homosexuality, Francis undertook a long pedagogical task. The Church needed to distinguish, in a new and fundamental way, between the crimes of paedophilia – abuse and aggression directed at minors under the age of 15; acts without consent or within the context of a situation of authority (catechism, confession, seminaries etc.) – and legal homosexual practices between consenting adults. He also turned a page on the debate about condoms, stressing the 'obligation to care'.

But what was to be done in the face of the crisis of vocations, not to mention those hundreds of priests every year who asked to be reduced to lay status so that they could get married? Mightn't it be time to think of future challenges, questions that have been left hanging for too long; to leave the realm of theory and respond instead to concrete situations? That was the point of the Synod. By doing so, he was walking on eggshells.

'Francis had seen the obstacle. By virtue of his function, he was in a situation of responsibility. He was in charge. So he took his time, he listened to all points of view,' Cardinal Lorenzo Baldisseri explained to me.

The texts coming from the episcopates were astonishing. The first, made public in Germany, Switzerland and Austria, were damning for the Church. Roman Catholicism appeared disconnected from real life; doctrine no longer had any meaning for millions of families; the faithful had lost any understanding of Rome's position on contraception, condoms, cohabitation, the celibacy of the priesthood and, to some extent, homosexuality.

The 'brains' of the Synod, Cardinal Walter Kasper, who was following the German debate closely, was delighted to see his ideas validated at grass-roots level. Was he too sure of himself? Did the pope trust him too much? The fact remains that the preparatory text followed the Kasper line and suggested a loosening of the Church's position on sacraments for divorcees and on homosexuality. The Vatican was now willing to acknowledge the 'qualities' of young people living together, remarried divorcees and homosexual civil partnerships.

It was then, in Baldisseri's modest phrase, that there was 'a reaction'. Once it was made public, the text immediately came under fire from critics on the conservative wing of the College of Cardinals, with the American Raymond Burke at their head.

The traditionalists were up in arms about the documents that had been distributed, and some, like the South African cardinal Wilfrid Napier, had no hesitation in claiming that if people in 'irregular situations' were recognized, it would inevitably lead to the legitimation of polygamy. Other African or Brazilian cardinals put the pope on guard, for strategic reasons, against any relaxation of the Church's positions, because of competition from thriving, highly conservative Protestant evangelical movements.

Of course all of these priests said they were open to debate and ready to add footnotes and codicils where required. But their secret mantra was none other than the famous and much-quoted phrase of the Prince of Lampedusa in *The Leopard*: 'Everything must change so that nothing changes.' Francis would also denounce, without naming them, the 'hearts of stone' who 'wanted everything to stay as it was'.

Discreetly, five ultra-conservative cardinals (the 'usual suspects', Raymond Burke, Ludwig Müller, Carlo Caffarra, Walter Brandmüller and Velasio De Paolis) were working on a collective book in defence of traditional marriage, which would be published in the United States by the Catholic publishing house Ignatius. They planned to have it distributed to all participants in the Synod – before Baldessari had the pamphlet seized! The conservative wing cried censorship! The Synod was already turning farcical.

From the first assembly, litigious points concerning communion for remarried divorcees and homosexuality were the subject of bitter debates that forced the pope to revise his text. Within a few days, the document was modified and watered down, and the position on homosexuality greatly hardened. However, even this new 'lite' version was rejected in the final vote by the fathers of the Synod.

The attack on the text was so powerful, so hard, that it was clear that it was the pope himself who was under fire. His method, his style, his ideas were rejected by part of the College of Cardinals. The most 'rigid', the most traditional, the most misogynist rebelled. Were they also those with the strongest 'inclination'? It is significant, in fact, that this war between conservatives and liberals was being played out, in reverse, on the gay issue. So you need to be counter-intuitive to decode it. Even more significant is the fact that several of the leaders of the anti-Francis rebellion led a double life. Would these closeted homosexuals, crammed full of contradictions and internalized homophobia, revolt out of self-hatred or in order to avoid being unmasked? The holy father was so exasperated that he attacked these very cardinals on their Achilles' heel: the private lives concealed behind their excessive conservatism.

That's what James Alison, an openly gay English priest, highly respected for his theological writings on the subject, summed up in a phrase that is subtler than it seems, when I talked to him several times in Madrid: 'It's the revenge of the closet! It's the vengeance of the closet!' Alison summarizes the situation in his own way: the homosexual cardinals 'in the closet' declared war on Francis, who encouraged gays to come 'out of the closet'!

Luigi Gioia, an Italian Benedictine monk, one of the directors of the Benedictine University of Sant'Anselmo in Rome, gives me another clue to what happened in the Vatican: 'For a homosexual, the Church appears to be a stable structure. In my view, that's one of the explanations for the fact that many homosexuals chose the priesthood. And yet when you need to hide, to feel secure, you need to feel that your context doesn't move. You want the structure in which you have taken refuge to be stable and protective, and afterwards you can navigate freely within it. Yet Francis, by wanting to reform it, made the structure unstable for closeted homosexual priests. That's what explains their violent reaction and their hatred of him. They're scared.'

The chief craftsman and witness of the Synod, Cardinal Baldisseri, sums up for his part, and more factually, the state of affairs after the battle: 'There was a consensus on everything. Except on the three sensitive issues.'

In fact, a 'liberal' majority emerged from the Synod, but the quorum required for the adoption of the controversial articles, which required two-thirds of the votes, was missing. Three paragraphs out of 62 were therefore rejected – and they were the most to the point. The pope didn't get his quorum. Francis's revolutionary project on the family and homosexuality was defeated.

Francis had lost a battle, but he hadn't lost the war. To say that he was unhappy with his failure at the Synod would be a euphemism. This man, authoritarian but frank, was annoyed to have been blocked by the conservative cardinals of the Curia. Their hypocrisy, their double game, their ingratitude, revolted him. Those behind-the-scenes manoeuvres, that plotting, that method expressly contrary to the laws of the Curia – it was all too much. To his colleagues, Francis privately let it be known that he had no intention of giving up. He would fight and launch a counter-offensive.

'He's stubborn, he's hard-headed,' I am told by a monsignore who knows him well.

The pontiff's reaction would be played out over several stages. First of all, he was able to prepare a second Synod planned for the following year, which gave him time to get organized. Then he decided to mount a broad campaign in favour of his propositions, from the end of 2014, to win the battle of ideas. He wanted to turn defeat into victory.

This war would be largely secret, unlike the previous one, which was participatory and consultative. Caught in the trap of democratization, Francis intended to show his opposition what it meant to be an absolute monarch in a Caesarian theocracy!

'Francis bears grudges. He is vindictive. He is authoritarian. He is a Jesuit: he never wants to lose!' a nuncio hostile to the pope observes.

Francis had three useful mechanisms at his disposal when it came to reacting. In the short term, he could try and encourage a more modern debate around the world by means of a move on the episcopates and Catholic public opinion – that was the new mission that he entrusted to Baldisseri and his team. In the medium term: to sanction the cardinals who had humiliated him, starting with Gerhard Ludwig Müller, the man in charge of Church doctrine. And in the long term: to modify the composition of the College of Cardinals by creating bishops favourable to his reforms – this was the supreme weapon, the one that only the pontiff could use.

Sly and cunning, Francis would go on the offensive using these three techniques simultaneously, with extraordinary speed and, his opponents would say, extraordinary vehemence.

The 'preparatory' work for the second Synod, planned for October 2015, got under way. In fact, it was a veritable war machine that went into action, on five continents. The nuncios, the allies, the friendly cardinals, everyone was mobilized. It was Henry V before the Battle of Agincourt. Francis had a kingdom to play with: 'We are not a tyrant, but a Christian king, and our anger is subject to our leniency.' Leniency there was; but there was even more anger.

I was able to follow this offensive in many countries, where I could assess the extent to which the episcopates were divided into two irreconcilable camps, as for example in Argentina, Uruguay, Brazil or the United States. The battle raged on the ground.

First of all in Argentina: there the pope mobilized his friends, his support base. The theologian Víctor Manuel Fernández, a close colleague of Francis and one of his speechwriters, recently promoted as bishop, immediately came out swinging. In a long interview in the *Corriere della Sera* (May 2015), he fiercely attacked the conservative wing of the Curia and, without naming him, Cardinal Müller: 'The pope is moving slowly because he wants to be certain that there will be no going back. He is aiming at irreversible reforms ... He is absolutely not alone. The people [the faithful] are with him. His adversaries are weaker than they think ... Besides, it's impossible for a pope to please everyone. Did Benedict XVI please everyone?' It was a 'declaration of war' on the Ratzinger wing of the Curia.

Not far from Buenos Aires, the 'Bergoglian' Archbishop of Montevideo in Uruguay, Daniel Sturla, stuck his neck out just as suddenly, expressing his opinion on the question of homosexuals. He would even go on to make public a contribution to the gay question in the Synod.

'I didn't yet know Pope Francis. I mobilized myself spontaneously, because times have changed and here, in Montevideo, it had become impossible not to have compassion for homosexuals. And you know what? There was no opposition here against my pro-gay positions. I think that society is changing everywhere, which helps the Church to go forward on the question. And everyone discovers that homosexuality is a very wide phenomenon, even within the heart of the Church,' Sturla told me during a long conversation in his office in Montevideo. (Pope Francis made him a cardinal in 2015.)

Another friend of the holy father threw himself into the fray: the Cardinal of Honduras, Óscar Maradiaga. The coordinator of 'C9', the council of nine cardinals close to Francis, the archbishop travelled around all the capitals of Latin American, accumulating air miles on his Platinum card. Everywhere, he distilled Francis's thought in public, and set out his strategy in a small committee; he also recruited supporters, informed the pope about his opposition and prepared the plans for battle. (In 2017, the office of the Archbishopric of Óscar Maradiaga would be rocked by allegations of a serious case of financial corruption, one of the alleged beneficiaries of which would be his deputy and a close friend: an auxiliary bishop also suspected by the press of 'serious misconduct and homosexual connections' – who would finally resign in 2018. In his '*Testimonianza*', Mgr Viganò also delivers a severe judgement about Maradiaga on the subject of protecting those accused of homosexual abuse. At this stage, an inquiry into the events is still under way, and the suspected prelates are presumed innocent.)

In Brazil, a large Catholic country – the largest in the world, with a community estimated at 135 million faithful, and a real influence in the synod with its ten cardinals – the pope relied on his close friends: Cardinal Cláudio Hummes, Emeritus Archbishop of São Paulo, Cardinal João Bráz de Aviz, former Archbishop of Brasilia, and the new archbishop of the Brazilian capital, Sérgio da Rocha, who would be crucial to the synod, and whom Francis would thank by making him cardinal immediately afterwards. He gave them the task of marginalizing the conservative wing, which was particularly embodied by the anti-gay Cardinal Odilo Scherer, Archbishop of São Paulo, who was close to Pope Benedict XVI. The old Hummes–Scherer battle, which had for a long time defined power relations within the Brazilian episcopate, doubled in intensity. Francis would also sanction Scherer, ejecting him from the Curia without warning, while elevating Sérgio da Rocha to the cardinalship.

The recurring tension was summed up for me by Frei Betto, a famous Dominican friar and Brazilian intellectual close to former president Lula, and one of the key figures in liberation theology. 'Cardinal Hummes is a progressive cardinal who had always been close to social causes. He was a friend of Pope Francis, and was able to count on his support. Cardinal Scherer, on the other hand, was a limited man and a conservative, who had no social fibre. He was very traditional,' Betto confirms to me when we meet in Rio de Janeiro.

When I interviewed him, Cardinal Odilo Scherer made a better impression on me. Affable and a little roguish, he received me in a sky-blue shirt, with a black-and-white Montblanc pen sticking out of his pocket, in his magnificent office in the archbishop's palace in São Paulo. There, during a lengthy interview, he is careful to play down the tensions within the Brazilian Church, of which he is the highest dignitary: 'We have a pope, just one: Francis; we don't have two, even if there is a pope emeritus. Sometimes people don't like what Francis says, and then they turn towards Benedict XVI; others don't like Benedict XVI, so they are with Francis. Each pope has his own charisma, his personality. One pope complements the other. You can't set one pope against the other one.'

The United States was another crucial country, with 17 cardinals, including 10 with a vote. A strange world, all in all, with which Francis was unfamiliar, and where the rigid cardinals leading double lives were very numerous. Barely having any confidence in the president of the American Bishops' Conference, the self-styled liberal Daniel DiNardo – an opportunist who was pro-Ratzinger under Ratzinger and then became pro-Francis under Francis – the pope discovered to his alarm that he had few allies in the country. That was why he chose to rely on three little-known gay-friendly bishops: Blase Cupich, whom he had just appointed Archbishop of Chicago, and who was favourable to homosexual couples; Joseph Tobin, the Archbishop of Indianapolis and now of Newark, where he welcomed married homosexuals and LGBT activists; and last of all, Robert McElroy, a liberal, pro-gay priest from San Francisco. These three supporters of Francis in the United States would give their full support to the Synod, and the first two were rewarded by being appointed cardinals in 2016, while McElroy would be made a bishop during the debates.

In Spain, France, Germany, Austria, the Netherlands, Switzerland and Belgium, Francis also sought allies and allied himself with the most liberal cardinals, such as the German Reinhard Marx, the friendly Austrian Christoph Schönborn, or the Spaniard Juan José Omella (whom he would appoint Archbishop of Barcelona shortly afterwards, and then go on to create cardinal). Also, in an interview in the German newspaper *Die Zeit*, the pope launched an idea with a bright future: the ordination of the famous *viri probati*. Rather than suggesting the ordination of women or the end of celibacy for seminarians – a *casus belli* for conservatives – Francis wanted to ordain older married Catholic men, a way of responding to the crisis in vocations, to limit homosexuality in the Church and to try to halt cases of sexual abuse.

In launching a series of grass-roots debates on the ground, the pope put conservatives on the defensive. He 'cornered' them, to use the word of a priest who worked for the synod, and showed them that they were in a minority in their own country.

The pope had been clear since 2014: 'For most people, the family [as imagined by John Paul II in the early 1980s] no longer exists. There are divorces, rainbow families, single-parent families, the phenomenon of surrogate pregnancy, couples without children, same-sex unions … The traditional doctrine will certainly remain, but pastoral challenges require a contemporary response, which can no longer come from authoritarianism or moralism.' (These daring proposals by the pope, which have not been denied, were reported by the Cardinal of Honduras, Óscar Maradiaga, a personal friend of Francis's.)

Between the two synods of 2014 and 2015, the battle between liberals and conservatives therefore broadened, and now extended to all episcopates, while Francis continued with his small-step policy.

'We mustn't oversimplify the debate,' says Romilda Ferrauto, a journalist from Radio Vatican who took part in both synods, seeking to add some perspective. 'There were genuine debates that shook the holy see. But there weren't liberals on one side and conservatives on the other. There wasn't such a clean break between left and right; there were a lot of nuances, a lot of dialogue. Cardinals can follow the holy father on financial reform and not on morality, for example. As for Pope Francis, he was presented by the press as a progressive. That isn't precisely true: he's merciful. He has a pastoral approach: he holds his hand out to the sinner. It isn't the same thing at all.'

Apart from the cardinals mobilized all over the world, and the Curia, which was agitated and chaotic, the pope's team was also interested in intellectuals. These 'opinion-formers', Baldisseri's gang reckoned, would be vital for the success of the synod. Hence the development of a large and secret plan of communication.

Behind the scenes, an influential Jesuit, Father Antonio Spadaro, the editor of *La Civiltà Cattolica*, was active in this respect. 'We're not an official journal, but all of our articles are reread by the Secretariat of State and are "certified" by the pope. We might call it an authorized journal, semi-official,' Spadaro tells me in his office in Rome. And what an office! The Villa Malta, Via di Porta Pinciana, where the journal is based, is a magnificent location in the area around the Villa Medici and the Palazzo Borghese.

Always jet-lagged and caffeinated, Antonio Spadaro, with whom I have had six interviews and dinners, is the pope's pilot fish. He's both a theologian and an intellectual, a rare beast in today's Vatican. His closeness to Francis makes people jealous: he is said to be one of his *éminences grises*; in any case, one of his unofficial advisers. Young, dynamic and charming, Spadaro is an impressive man. His ideas fly around with obvious speed and intelligence. The Jesuit is interested in all kinds of culture, particularly literature. He already has several books to his credit, including a far-sighted essay on cyber-theology and two biographical works on Pier Vittorio Tondelli, the Catholic homosexual Italian writer who died of AIDS at the age of 36.

'I'm interested in everything, including rock music,' Spadaro says to me over dinner in Paris.

Under Francis, the Jesuit journal has become a space for experimentation in which ideas are tested and debates launched. In 2013 Spadaro published a first long interview with Pope Francis, shortly after his election. It's a milestone text. 'We spent three afternoons together for that interview. I was surprised by his openness of mind, his sense of dialogue.'

In a way, this famous text sets out the road map for the coming synod. In it, Francis puts forward his innovative ideas and his method. On the questions of sexual morality and communion for divorced couples, he argues in favour of a collegial and decentralized debate. It was also then that Francis first unveiled his ideas about homosexuality.

Spadaro won't let go of the gay question, pushing Francis on his entrenchments and leading him to sketch out a truly Christian vision of homosexuality. The pope asks that homosexuals be accompanied 'with mercy', and he imagines pastoral care for 'irregular situations' and the 'socially wounded' who feel 'condemned by the Church'. Never has a pope had so much empathy and, let's say the word, fraternity, for homosexuals. It's a genuine Galilean revolution! And this time, his words certainly weren't improvised, as they might have been for his famous phrase: 'Who am I to judge?' The interview has been minutely edited and every word carefully weighed (as Spadaro confirms to me).

For Francis, however, the crux lies elsewhere: it's time for the Church to move away from questions that divide believers and concentrate instead on the real issues: the poor, migrants, poverty. 'We can't only insist on questions bound up with abortion, homosexual marriage and the use of contraceptive methods. It's not possible … It isn't necessary to go on talking about it all the time,' the pope says.

Apart from this crucial interview, Antonio Spadaro would mobilize his international networks to support the pope's positions on the family. So, in 2015, points of view and interviews favourable to Francis's ideas flourished in the journal *La Civiltà Cattolica*. Other experts were enlisted by Spadaro or by the secretariat of the Synod, like the Italian theologians Maurizio Gronchi and Paolo Gamberini, or the Frenchmen Jean-Miguel Garrigues (who is close to Cardinal Schönborn) and Antoine Guggenheim. Guggenheim immediately began defending the recognition of homosexual unions in the French Catholic daily *La Croix*. 'The recognition of a faithful and enduring love between homosexual people,' he writes, 'whatever their degree of chastity, seems to me to be a hypothesis worth studying. It might take the form that the Church usually gives to prayer: a benediction.'

On a trip to Brazil during the same period, Spadaro also met a pro-gay priest, a Jesuit like himself, Luís Corrêa Lima. They had a long conversation, in the residence of the Society of Jesus at the Catholic University in Rio de Janeiro, about 'Bible studies in favour of homosexuals', organized by Father Lima. Charmed by this idea, Spadaro commissioned an article on the subject for *La Civiltà Cattolica*, although it would not be published in the end. (Apart from Mgr Baldisseri, Kasper and Spadaro, I interviewed Antoine Guggenheim and Jean-Miguel Garrigues, who confirmed the overall strategy. I also met Father Lima in Rio de Janeiro, and went with him to the favela of Rocinha, where he celebrates mass every Sunday, and to the space where those LGBT Bible studies are held.)

Another high-level intellectual followed the pre-Synod debates with great attention. An Italian Dominican, also a theologian – discreet and loyal – he lives in the Priory of Saint-Jacques, adjacent to the famous Saulchoir Library in Paris.

Brother Adriano Oliva is a reputed medieval historian, a seasoned Latinist and a doctor of theology. Most significantly, he is one of the world's most eminent authorities on Saint Thomas Aquinas: he presided over the famous Leonine Commission responsible for the critical edition of the works of the medieval thinker – a seminal work.

So why did Oliva unexpectedly mobilize himself at the beginning of 2015, and set about writing a risky book in favour of the remarriage of divorcees and the blessing of homosexual unions? Is it possible that the Italian Dominican was directly encouraged by the secretariat of the Synod, if not the pope, to intervene in the debate?

Saint Thomas Aquinas, as we know, is generally the guarantee on which conservatives rely to oppose all sacraments for divorcees or homosexual couples. Tackling this subject head-on is therefore hazardous and strategic at the same time. The title of the book, which was published shortly afterwards, is *Amours*.

It's rare these days to read such a courageous work. Even though it is erudite, analytic and written for specialists, *Amours* is, in only 160 pages, a minutely detailed work undermining the moralistic ideology of the Vatican, from Paul VI to Benedict XVI. Brother Oliva takes as his starting point a twofold doctrinal failure of the Church: the contradictions in its discourse on the remarriage of divorcees, and the impasse in which it has found itself over homosexuality. His project is clear: 'The aim of the present study is to show that a desirable change on the part of the Magisterium concerning homosexuality, and the exercising of sexuality by homosexuals, would correspond not only to contemporary anthropological, theological and exegetical studies, but also to developments of a theological tradition, Thomist in particular.'

The Dominican attacks the dominant interpretation of the thought of Thomas Aquinas: relating to the heart of the doctrine, not its margin. Oliva: 'We are used to considering as "against nature" not only sodomy but also the homosexual inclination. Saint Thomas, on the other hand, considered this inclination "within the nature" of the homosexual person seen as an individual.' Oliva relies on the 'brilliant intuition' of the angelic doctor: the 'natural "against nature"' through which one can explain the origin of homosexuality. And Oliva observes, in almost Darwinian fashion, that 'Saint Thomas places the origin of homosexuality on the level of the *natural principles of the species*.'

For Saint Thomas, man, with his irregularities and singularities, is therefore part of the divine plan. The homosexual inclination is not against nature, but comes from the soul. Oliva again: 'homosexuality does not bear within it any illicitness, neither in its origin, natural to the individual and rooted in what animates him as a human being, nor in its aim, loving another person, which is a good aim'. And Oliva concludes in calling for 'the welcoming of homosexual people at the heart of the Church and not on its margins'.

After reading *Amours*, cardinals, bishops and many priests have told me that their vision of Saint Thomas Aquinas has changed, and that the prohibition on homosexuality has definitely been lifted. Some, both among the faithful and among the church hierarchies, even told me that the book has had the same effect on them as André Gide's *Corydon*, and Adriano Oliva finishes his book with an allusion to Gide's novel *If It Die*.... (When I asked him, Brother Oliva refused to comment on the genesis of his book or to discuss his connections with Rome. His publisher, Jean-François Colosimo, director of Éditions du Cerf, was more forthcoming, like the team of Cardinal Baldisseri, who confirmed that they had sent 'analysis requests to experts' including Brother Oliva. In the end I received confirmation that Adriano Oliva had been welcomed at the Vatican by Baldisseri, Bruno Forte and Fabio Fabene – the chief architects of the Synod.)

As might have been expected, the book did not go unnoticed in Thomist circles, where it had the effect of a cluster bomb. The argument enflamed the most orthodox Catholic circles, all the more so since the attack came from within, signed by a priest who could not easily be rebutted, a Thomist among Thomists. Five Dominicans from the Angelicum, the pontifical University of Saint Thomas Aquinas in Rome, soon dashed off a scathing riposte, even though several of them are themselves homophiles. Identitarian militants joined in, violently attacking the priest for having the audacity to turn Thomas Aquinas into a 'gay-friendly' author! On sites and blogs, the Catholic far right blustered.

Supported by the Master of the Order of Dominicans, on whom he depended, Brother Oliva also came under fresh attacks, academic this time, in several Thomist journals, including a 47-page article. In reply, a new 48-page article signed by the Dominican Camille de Belloy (whom I also interviewed) took up the defence of Oliva in the *Revue des Sciences philosophiques et théologiques*. More salvoes have followed since then ...

As we can see, the subject is a sensitive one. For Brother Oliva, who says he acted freely, it was probably the most dangerous subject of his career. And as courageous as the Dominican might have been, it was impossible for a scholar of his calibre to embark on such a study of Saint Thomas Aquinas and the gay question without getting a green light from on high. Cardinals Baldisseri and Kasper? Without question. And perhaps Pope Francis himself?

Cardinal Walter Kasper confirmed Francis's personal intervention. 'Adriano Oliva came to see me here. We talked. He had sent me a letter that I showed to the pope: Francis was impressed. And he asked Baldisseri to order him a text to send to the bishops. I think that was the text that became *Amours*.' Kasper added: 'Adriano Oliva served the Church, without being militant.'

Amours would be distributed during the synod, on the pope's suggestion. The book was not just one more pamphlet or an isolated and slightly suicidal essay, as has been claimed: it was a weapon in an overall plan favoured by the pontiff himself.

The pope's strategy, his manoeuvre, his war machine set in motion against the conservatives in the Church, did not escape his opponents. When I questioned these anti-Francis clerics, whether they were cardinals or simple monsignori, they preferred to react off the record. By tradition, a cardinal never speaks ill of the pope outside the Vatican. The Jesuits and members of Opus Dei keep their disagreements even more quiet. Dominicans are prudent and generally progressive, like Franciscans. But *ad hominem* criticisms of Francis are quick to come once the mike is switched off. There is even a real outpouring of hatred.

One of those viper-tongued prelates is a key prelate in the Curia, with whom I had over a dozen meetings, lunches and dinners. Witty and malicious – viperine, in short – Aguisel (I have changed his name) is an uninhibited homosexual who, in spite of his considerable age, remains a great charmer. Aguisel is a Gay Pride march all by himself! He makes passes at the seminarians he invites to dinner in batches; he flirts with waiters in cafés or Roman restaurants where we're having dinner, calling them by their first names. And it turns out that Aguisel likes me.

'I'm from the Old Testament,' our prelate tells me in a funny, self-mocking and very true turn of phrase.

Aguisel hates Francis. He reproaches him for his 'communizing' tendency, his liberalism with regard to the family, and for his positions, which are too favourable to homosexuals.

'The pope is a zealot,' he tells me, and on his lips it's not a term of praise.

Another day, when we are having dinner at the Campana, a typical Roman restaurant on Vicolo della Campana (a building where Caravaggio is supposed to have pursued his habits), Mgr Aguisel lists Francis's incoherencies, his changes of direction. This pope is 'inconsistent' in his view. On homosexuality he takes one step forward, then two steps back, proof that he's playing it by ear. 'How can Francis attack gender theory and, at the same time, officially receive a Spanish transsexual in the Vatican with his or her fiancé or fiancée … you see, we don't even know how to say it! It's all incoherent, and shows that there is no doctrine, only impulsive acts of communication.'

The prelate whispers in a confidential tone: 'But you know, the pope has made lots of enemies in the Curia. He's wicked. He's firing everyone. He can't bear to be contradicted. Look at what he did to Cardinal Müller!'

I suggest that there are other reasons for Francis's animosity to Müller (whom the pope dismissed without warning in 2017). My interlocutor is aware of the matters I raise, and realizes I am well-informed. But he is wholly obsessed by the small vexations endured by Müller and his allies.

'The pope intervened from on high, and personally, to fire Müller's assistants within the Congregation for the Doctrine of the Faith. From one day to the next they were sent back to their countries! Apparently they were speaking ill of the pope. Criminals? It's not true. They were just the opposition. It's not good, when you're pope, to take it out personally on humble monsignori!'

After a pause, Aguisel goes on: 'Francis has a spy in the Congregation for the Doctrine of the Faith who reports everything to him. You know that? He has a spy! The spy is the under-secretary!'

Over lots of meals, that's more or less the kind of conversation I had with the prelate. He knows the secrets of the Curia, and of course the names of 'practising' bishops and cardinals. He enjoys giving them to me, telling me everything, even though every time he 'outs' a co-religionist he catches himself, surprised by his own daring.

'Oh, I'm talking too much. I'm talking too much. I shouldn't. You must think me terribly cheeky!'

I was fascinated by the prelate's calculated imprudence during our regular dialogues, which spread out over dozens of hours and several years. Like all the prelates I meet, he knows very well that I'm a well-known reporter and the author of several books on the gay question. If he talks to me, like so many anti-Francis cardinals and bishops, it isn't by chance or by accident, but because of this 'illness of rumour, gossip and scandal-mongering' that the pope has mocked so effectively.

'The holy father is a bit special,' Mgr Aguisel adds. 'The people, the crowds, everyone loves him all over the world, but they don't know who he is. He is brutal! He is cruel! He is crude! Here we know him, and he is loathed.'

One day when we were having lunch somewhere near the Piazza Navona in Rome, his Excellency Aguisel takes me by the arm without warning at the end of the meal and leads me towards the church of San Luigi dei Francesi.

'Here, you have three Caravaggios, and it's free. You mustn't miss them.'

The paintings – oil on canvas – are sumptuous, with their crepuscular depth and their brutal darkness. I put a euro coin in a little machine at the front of the chapel; suddenly the works are illuminated.

After greeting a 'sacristy queen' who has recognized him – as everywhere, there are large numbers of gays among the seminarians and priests of this French church – Aguisel now has a honeyed chat with a group of young tourists, stressing his prestigious curial title. After this intermezzo, we resume our dialogue about Caravaggio's homosexuality. The eroticism emanated by the *Martyrdom of Saint Matthew*, an old man on the ground being killed by a handsome naked warrior, echoes his *Saint Matthew and the Angel*, location now unknown, which was judged too homoerotic to be worthy of a chapel! For the *Lute Player*, the *Boy with the Basket of Fruit* and his *Bacchus*, Caravaggio used his lover Mario Minniti as model. Paintings like *Narcissus, Concert, Saint John the Baptist* and the strange *Amor Vincit Omnia* (*Love Victorious*, which I saw at the Gemäldegalerie in Berlin) have long confirmed the painter's attraction to boys. The writer Dominique Fernandez, a member of the Académie française, wrote: 'For me, Caravaggio is the greatest homosexual painter of all time; I mean that he has vehemently exalted the bond of desire between two men.'

Isn't it strange, then, that Caravaggio should be the favourite painter of Pope Francis, of the rigid closeted cardinals of the Curia and of the gay militants who organize LGBT City Tours in Rome, one of the stops of which consists precisely in coming to honour 'their' painter?

'Here in the church of San Luigi dei Francesi, we welcome whole busloads of visitors. There are fewer and fewer parishioners and more low-cost tourists! They only come to see Caravaggio. They behave with a vulgarity that they would never display in a museum! I have to chase them away!' explains Mgr François Bousquet, the rector of the French church, with whom I have lunch twice.

Suddenly, Mgr Aguisel has something else to show me. He takes a little detour, lights the beautiful chapel, and here it is: *Saint Sebastian*! This painting by Numa Boucoiran was added to the church in the nineteenth century, at the request of the French ambassador to the Vatican ('at least five have been homosexual since the war,' adds Aguisel, who has counted them carefully). Conventionally painted, without any great artistic genius, this *Saint Sebastian* still brings together all the codes of gay iconography: the boy is standing up, flamboyant, proud and rapturous, with a nudity exaggerated by the beauty of his muscles, his athletic body pierced by the arrow of his executioner, who may be his lover. Boucoiran is loyal to the myth, even if he doesn't have the talent of Botticelli, Il Sodoma, Titian, Veronese, Guido Reni, El Greco or Rubens, all of whom have painted this gay icon, or indeed Leonardo da Vinci, who drew it eight times.

I have seen several *Saint Sebastian*s in the Vatican museums, in particular the one by Girolamo Siciolante da Sermoneta, which is so enticing and libidinous that it could be used on the cover of an encyclopaedia of LGBT cultures. And that's not counting the *Saint Sebastian* in St Peter's Basilica in Rome, which has a chapel dedicated to it, on the right of the entrance, just after Michelangelo's *Pietà*. It is also where John Paul II's body is laid.

The Saint Sebastian myth is a veiled code, highly prized, whether consciously or not, by the men of the holy see. To strip that code away is to reveal many things in spite of the multiple readings it offers. Sebastian can be turned into an ephebophilic figure, or a sadomasochistic one; he can represent the submissive passivity of a youth or, conversely, the martial vigour of a soldier resisting whatever it takes. And especially this: Sebastian, tied to the tree, in his absolute vulnerability, seems to love his executioner, to wrap his arms around him. This 'ecstasy of pain', the executioner and his victim mixed together, caught in a single breath, is a marvellous metaphor for homosexuality in the Vatican. In *The Closet*, Sebastian is celebrated every day.

One of the few opponents of Francis who agrees to speak publicly is the Australian cardinal George Pell, the pope's 'minister' of the economy. When Pell approaches me to greet me, I'm sitting in a little waiting room in Loggia I of the apostolic palace of the Vatican. He is standing, I am seated: suddenly I have a giant in front of me. He is gangling, his gait slightly unbalanced. Flanked by his assistant – who is equally enormous, who walks nonchalantly, and who will take conscientious note of our exchanges – I have never felt so small in my life. Together, they're at least four metres tall!

'I work with the pope and meet him every two weeks,' Pell tells me with great courtesy. 'We probably have different cultural backgrounds: he comes from Argentina, I'm from Australia. I may have divergences of opinion with him, as on climate change for example. But we are a religious organization, not a political party. We must be united where faith and morality are concerned. Apart from that I would say that we are free, and as Mao Zedong said, let a hundred flowers blossom ...'

George Pell answers my questions in the Anglo-Saxon style, with professionalism, concision and humour. He is efficient; he knows his files and his music. Everything here is on the record. I am struck by the cardinal's politeness, given that his colleagues have told me he is 'brutal' and 'confrontational', if not as frightening as a 'bulldog'. His nickname at the Vatican: 'Pell Pot'.

We talk about the finances of the holy see; about his work as a minister; about the transparency that he is busy implementing where opacity prevailed for so long.

'When I arrived, I discovered almost 1.4 billion euros sleeping, forgotten by all the balance sheets! Financial reform is one of the few subjects that unite the right, the left and the centre in the Vatican, both politically and sociologically.'

'There is a right and a left in the Vatican?' I cut in.

'I think everyone here is a variation of the radical centre.'

At the Synod, George Pell, who is generally considered to be one of the representatives of the conservative right wing of the Vatican, a 'Ratzingerian', has been one of the cardinals who are critical of Francis. As I expected, the cardinal puts into perspective his disagreements, which have leaked into the press, demonstrating a certain casuistry, if not double-speak: 'I'm not an opponent of Francis. I'm a loyal servant of the pope. Francis encourages free and open discussions, and he likes to hear the truth of people who don't think like that.'

Several times, George Pell talks about the 'moral authority' of the Church, which he sees as its *raison d'être* and its main engine of influence all around the world. He thinks it must remain faithful to doctrine and tradition: you can't change the law, even if society is transformed. All of a sudden, Francis's line on the 'peripheries' and his empathy for homosexuals strike him as vain, if not erroneous.

'It's fine to take an interest in "peripheries". But still you need a critical mass of believers. Without a doubt you need to take care of the lost sheep, but you must also take an interest in the 99 other sheep who have stayed with the herd.' (Since our interview, Pell has left Rome after being questioned by the Australian courts in connection with cases of historic sexual abuse against boys, charges that he fervently denies. His highly publicized trial, with thousands of pages of transcripts, is currently under way.)

The result of nearly two years of debates and tensions around the synod has a lovely name: *Amoris laetitia* (the joy of love). This post-synodal apostolic exhortation bears the personal mark and cultural references of Francis. The pope insists on the fact that no family is a perfect reality; pastoral attention must be devoted to all families, as they are. We are a long way from talk of the ideal family as delivered by those conservatives who are opposed to gay marriage.

Some prelates think, with some justification, that Francis has gone back on his reforming ambitions, choosing a kind of status quo on the most sensitive questions. Francis's defenders, on the other hand, see *Amoris laetitia* as a major turning point.

According to one of the authors of the text, the homosexuals have lost the battle of the Synod, but on the other hand they still managed to include, by way of reprisal, three coded references to homosexuality in this apostolic exhortation: a hidden formula on 'loving friendship' (§127); a reference to the joy of the birth of Saint John the Baptist, whom we know to have been painted as effeminate by both Caravaggio and Leonardo da Vinci, who modelled him on his lover Salaï (§65); and finally, the name of a Catholic thinker who eventually acknowledged his homosexuality, Gabriel Marcel (§322) ... A slender victory!

'*Amoris laetitia* is the result of the two synods,' Cardinal Baldisseri tells me. 'If you read chapters 4 and 5, you will see that it is a magnificent text about loving relationships and love. Chapter 8, the chapter about sensitive subjects, is, it is true, a compromise.'

The conservative wing of the Vatican did not like that compromise. Five cardinals, including two of the pope's 'ministers', Gerhard Ludwig Müller and Raymond Burke, had already set out their disagreements, even before the Synod, in a book called *Remaining in the Truth of Christ* – a public disavowal as uncommon as it was noisy. Cardinal George Pell, another of Francis's ministers, and Angelo Scola, effectively joined them in the opposition. Without allying himself formally with them, Georg Gänswein, Pope Benedict XVI's famous private secretary, delivered an enigmatic public message confirming this line.

The same group picked up its pen, once the discussions of the second Synod were completed, to make their disagreement public. Calling for 'clarity' about the 'doubts' of *Amoris laetitia*, the letter is signed by four cardinals: the American Raymond Burke, the Italian Carlo Caffarra and two Germans, Walter Brandmüller and Joachim Meisner (soon nicknamed the four '*dubia*', *doubts* in Latin). Their letter was made public in September 2016. The pope didn't even take the trouble to answer them.

Let us linger for a moment on those four '*dubia*'. Two of these four have recently died. According to many sources in Germany, Switzerland, Italy and the United States, they were closeted and had multiple 'worldly' encounters and special friendships. The entourage of one of them was mocked in the German-speaking press for consisting entirely of handsome and effeminate young men; his 'homophilia' has now been attested by journalists beyond the Rhine. As for Carlo Caffarra – the former Archbishop of Bologna, made cardinal by Benedict XVI – who founded the John Paul II Institute 'for studies on marriage and the family', he was so vocal in his opposition to gay marriage that this obsession gives him away.

The '*dubia*' have a style of their own: apparent humility and extravagant vanity; obsequious explosions of laughter from their handsome young companions and book burnings; sacristy hangers-on, liturgy queens, well-combed choirboys with their straight partings from the Jesuit schools and the Inquisition; a tortuous and, indeed, tortured language and medieval positions on sexual morality. And on top of that, what a lack of enthusiasm for the fair sex! Such misogyny! Such divine gaiety, such virile rigidity – or vice versa. 'The Lady doth protest too much, methinks.'

Fully informed about the 'homophilia' of some of these '*dubia*' and the paradoxes of his opponents' lives – these paragons of moral intransigence and rigidity – the pope is deeply revolted by such a level of duplicity.

It is now that we see the third part of Francis's battle against his opposition: the Luciferian. Methodically, the pope will punish his enemies, one cardinal after the other: either by taking away their ministries (Gerhard Müller would be dismissed as prefect of the Congregation for the Doctrine of the Faith, Mauro Piacenza was unceremoniously moved, Raymond Burke ejected from his post as head of the Supreme Tribunal); by emptying their function of all substance (Robert Sarah is back at the head of a ministry, a real empty shell, deprived of all support); by dismissing their entourages (Sarah and Müller's colleagues have been ousted and replaced by supporters of Francis); or by letting the cardinals weaken themselves (the accusations of sexual abuse against George Pell, the mishandling of these matters by Gerhard Müller and Joachim Meisner, and the internal battle within the Order of Malta involving Raymond Burke). Who said Pope Francis was merciful?

The morning when I meet Cardinal Ludwig Gerhard Müller at his private residence in the Piazza della città Leonina, near the Vatican, I have a sense that I've woken him up. Was he singing matins all night? The all-powerful prefect of the Congregation for the Doctrine of the Faith, and enemy no. 1 of Pope Francis, opens the door himself ... and he's still in his nightclothes. My first cardinal in pyjamas!

In front of me I see a tall man in a crumpled tee-shirt, in loose, long and elastic leisure-wear trousers, Vittorio Rossi brand, and slippers. Slightly embarrassed, I stammer: 'We did arrange to meet at 9.00?'

'Yes, absolutely. But you didn't plan to take any photographs, did you?' asks the cardinal-prefect emeritus, who now seems to realize how incongruous his outfit is.

'No, no – no photographs.'

'So I can stay [dressed] like this,' Müller says to me.

We sit down in his vast office, where an impressive library covers each wall. The conversation is heated, and Müller seems more complex than his opponents suggest.

An intellectual who was close to Benedict XVI, he is perfectly familiar, like the pope emeritus, with the work of Hans Urs von Balthasar and Jacques Maritain, and we talk about them for a long time. Müller shows me their books in his impeccably organized library to prove to me that he has read them.

The apartment is classical, and ugly in a rather un-Catholic way. That's a trait shared by dozens of cardinals' apartments I have visited: this *demi-mondain* semi-luxury, this mixture of genres that don't match, the ersatz, and the superficial rather than depth. It is, in a word, what I will call 'middlebrow'! That's the term they use in the United States for things that are neither elitist nor working-class: it's the culture of the middle, the culture of between-the-two; the culture that is bang in the centre. A large, opulent, fake art-deco clock that has stopped working; an over-styled baroque chest of drawers; an ostentatious table all mixed up together. It's the culture of moleskin notebooks, spuriously modelled on those of Bruce Chatwin and Hemingway, apocryphal legends. That style without style, 'bland' and dull, is common to Müller, Burke, Stafford, Farina, Etchegaray, Herranz, Martino, Ruini, Dziwisz, Re, Sandoval and many cardinals in search of 'self-aggrandizement' that I have visited.

Following his dismissal, Müller is greatly diminished when I meet him. The pope fired him without ceremony from the Congregation for the Doctrine of the Faith, of which he had been 'prefect' since Benedict XVI.

'What do I make of Pope Francis?' Müller wonders. 'Let's say that Francis has his own way of doing things, his own style. [But] you will understand that the question of "pro" and "anti" Francis barely has any meaning for me. The red dress that we wear is the sign that we are ready to give our blood to Christ, and serving Christ means, for all cardinals, serving the Vicar of Christ. But the Church is not a community of robots, and the freedom of the children of God allows us to have different opinions, different ideas, other feelings than the pope. But I repeat, and I insist, that doesn't mean that we don't want to be deeply loyal to the pope. We are, because we want to be deeply loyal to the Lord.'

With Raymond Burke, Robert Sarah, Angelo Bagnasco and Mauro Piacenza, the loyal Müller joins the long list of Judases, making many sly and bitter attacks on the pope. With his quarrelsome nature, the rebellious cardinal wanted to teach the holy father a few lessons. Sanctimoniously, he violently contradicts his line on the Synod. He has given interviews on morality that contradict Francis, and that led to mounting tension and eventual rupture between them. To say that he has fallen into disgrace would be to imply that he was once in a state of grace. There had been a price on his red galero for several months. And Francis demoted him without hesitation during a discussion that, according to Müller, 'lasted a minute'. And here he was, in front of me, in his underwear!

All of a sudden a nun, filled with devotion, who had just knocked gently at the door, comes in with the cardinal's tea, which she has prepared with the clerical care befitting His Eminence, fallen though that Eminence might be. Ruffled by the nun's entry, the cardinal barely watches her setting down the cup and, without a word of thanks, dismisses her brutally. The ancient sister, who came in quite diligently, leaves in a sulk. Even a maid in a well-to-do family would be treated better! I felt sorry for her and later, when the time came to leave, I wanted to go and see her to apologize for his rudeness.

Cardinal Müller is a man of many contradictions. In Bavaria, where he was bishop, he was remembered as an 'ambiguous' prelate, and perhaps even a 'schizophrenic' one, according to over a dozen testimonies that I collected in Munich and Regensburg. Priests and journalists described his worldly associations to me, in the 'Regensburger Netzwerk'. He seemed to be under the influence of Joseph Ratzinger and Georg Gänswein.

'When Müller was Bishop of Regensburg, here in Bavaria, his personality was not very well-understood. His relationship with the famous German Cardinal Karl Lehmann, a liberal and a progressive, seemed particularly complicated where the gay question was concerned: they exchanged very harsh, very bitter letters, and not what one might have expected. Lehmann was rather gay-friendly and heterosexual, whereas Müller was very anti-gay. At the same time Müller was a regular at the parties of Princess Gloria von Thurn und Taxis at St Emmeram Castle,' I am told by a journalist from the *Süddeutsche Zeitung* in Munich, Matthias Drobinski, who has been covering the German church for 25 years.

The castle in Regensburg combines, with a certain daring and a certain felicity, a Romanesque and Gothic cloister, a Benedictine abbey, a baroque wing, and rococo and neo-rococo ballrooms. Playing with styles and eras, the palace is even known for having belonged to the sister of Empress Sissi! It is home to Princess Gloria von Thurn und Taxis, the widow of a wealthy industrialist whose family made its fortune by having the monopoly of the postal service during the days of the Holy Roman Empire, before this was expropriated by Napoleon. Her lair is the meeting place of the most conservative fringe of the German Catholic Church, which may be what won the princess her nickname of 'Gloria TNT', because of her explosive conservatism!

Freshly returned from her daily tennis lesson, the lady of the manor, in a monogrammed pink polo shirt matching her sparkling oval glasses, her Rolex watch and big rings covered with crosses, grants me an audience. What a woman! What a circus!

We have a glass of wine in the 'Café Antoinette' – named after the decapitated queen of France – and Gloria von Thurn und Taxis, previously described to me as being rigid of character and butch of appearance, proves to be strangely gentle and friendly towards me. She expresses herself in perfect French.

Gloria 'TNT' takes her time to tell me of her life as a 'queen'; the extent of her inheritance running into the billions, with the five hundred rooms of her castle to look after, not to mention 40,000 square metres of roofs: 'it's very, very expensive,' she complains, widening her eyes. She goes on to speak of her reactionary right-wing political commitment; her affection for clerics, including her 'dear friend' Cardinal Müller; and her restless life between Germany, New York and Rome (where she lives in a *pied-à-terre* with another princess, Alessandra Borghese, prompting mad rumours about their royalist inclinations). Gloria TNT is particularly insistent on her muddled version of Catholicism: 'I am of the Catholic faith. I have a personal private chapel in which my priest friends can celebrate mass when they want to. I love it when the chapels are used. I have had my own domestic priest, for over a year. He was retired, I brought him here. Now he lives with us in an apartment in the castle: he is my personal chaplain,' Gloria 'TNT' explains.

The priest in question is Mgr Wilhelm Imkamp. Even though he has the title 'monsignore', he isn't a bishop.

'Imkamp is a well-documented ultra-conservative priest. He wanted to become a bishop, but that was blocked for personal reasons. He is very close to the radical conservative wing of the German Church, particularly Cardinal Müller and Georg Gänswein,' the *Süddeutsche Zeitung* journalist Matthias Drobinski tells me in Munich.

This turbulent Imkamp is a curious priest: he appears to be well in with the Vatican, where he is a 'consultant' for several congregations. He was also assistant to one of the most delicately anti-gay German cardinals, Walter Brandmüller. Why did these active connections and his Ratzingerian friendships not enable him to become a bishop under Benedict XVI? That is a mystery that deserves explanation.

David Berger, an ex-seminarian and theologian, now a gay militant, explains during an interview in Berlin: 'Every morning, Mgr Imkamp celebrates mass in Latin according to the ancient rite in the chapel of Gloria von Thurn und Taxis. He is an ultra-conservative close to Georg Gänswein; she is a Madonna of the gays.'

The decadent aristocrat Gloria 'TNT' is not short of means, or indeed of paradoxes. She describes her collection of contemporary art, which features works by, among others, Jeff Koons, Jean-Michel Basquiat, Keith Haring and the photographer Robert Mapplethorpe, including a magnificent and famous portrait of her by the latter. Koons is still alive, while two of these artists, Haring and Mapplethorpe, were homosexual and died of AIDS; Basquiat was a drug addict; Mapplethorpe was rejected by the American Catholic far right for his work, which was judged to be homoerotic and sadomasochistic. Contradictory, at all?

The princess summed up her divided feelings about homosexuality in a debate with the Bavarian Conservative Party (CSU) in the presence of Mgr Wilhelm Imkamp: 'Everyone can do what they like in their bedroom, but it mustn't be turned into a political programme.' We understand the code: great tolerance for 'closeted' homosexuals; zero tolerance for gay visibility!

An explosive cocktail, this 'Gloria TNT': a religious devotee and an aristo-punk jetsetter; a fervent Catholic and crazed fundamentalist surrounded by a throng of gays. A 'cocotte' of the first order!

Traditionally close to the conservatives of the CSU in Bavaria, over the last few years she seems to have absorbed certain ideas from the AfD, the right-wing reactionary German party, although she has not formally joined it. She has been seen marching beside its deputies at the '*Demos für Alle*', the anti-gay-marriage demonstrations; she also declared, in an interview, her affection for Duchess Beatrix von Storch, vice-president of the AfD, while at the same time acknowledging her disagreements with her party.

'Gloria von Thurn und Taxis is typical of the grey area between the Christian Socialists of the CSU and the hard right of the AfD, who agree on their hatred of "gender theory", their fight against abortion, gay marriage or the denunciation of Chancellor Angela Merkel's immigration policy,' I am told by the German theologian Michael Brinkschröder in Munich.

Here we are at the heart of what is called the 'Regensburg network', a constellation in which the Sun-Queen Gloria 'TNT' is the bright star around which 'a thousand blue devils dance'. The prelates Ludwig Müller, Wilhelm Imkamp and Georg Gänswein have always seemed at ease in this 'friendly' coterie in which the butlers are in livery and the cakes are decorated with '60 marzipan penises' (we are told by the German press). A princess by nature, Gloria TNT also supplies an after-sales service: she promotes the anti-gay books of her friends, reactionary cardinals like Müller, or the Guinean ultra-conservative Robert Sarah, or the German Joachim Meisner, with whom she has co-written a book of interviews. Meisner was the quintessence of the hypocrisy of Catholicism: he was at once one of the enemies of Pope Francis (one of the four '*dubia*'); a committed homophobe; a bishop who knowingly ordained, both in Berlin and Cologne, practising gay priests; someone who was locked firmly in the closet since his late puberty; and an aesthete who lived with his effeminate and largely LGBT entourage. An impressive set of qualities!

Should Cardinal Müller's thought be taken seriously? Important German cardinals and theologians have been critical of his writings, which lack authority, and his thought, which is not always trustworthy. Perfidiously, they stress that he has coordinated the publication of Ratzinger's complete works, thus insinuating that the closeness between the two men might explain his elevation to cardinal and his appointment to the Congregation for the Doctrine of the Faith.

These harsh judgements need to be qualified: Müller was made cardinal by Francis and not by Benedict XVI. He was a priest in Peru and is the author of serious books, particularly on liberation theology in Latin America, which allows us if not to put his conservatism into perspective, then at least to show its complexity. During our conversation, he insists that he is a friend of Gustavo Gutíerrez, the 'founding father' of this religious movement, with whom he wrote a book.

On the other hand there is no doubt about his homophobia: when the pope showed empathy in a private conversation with Juan Carlos Cruz, a homosexual who was the victim of sexual abuse – 'The fact that you are gay is irrelevant. God made you how you are and loves you like that and it doesn't matter to me. The pope loves you like that. You must be happy as you are,' Francis would say – Cardinal Müller immediately made a series of outraged declarations, publicly insisting that 'homophobia is a hoax'.

This severity, this confidence, sits uneasily with the inaction that Cardinal Müller has demonstrated in cases of sexual abuse of which he has been informed. Under his leadership the Congregation for the Doctrine of the Faith, in charge of the paedophile dossiers at the Vatican, demonstrated negligence (which Müller has firmly denied), and little empathy with the victims. Its lack of support also contributed to the departure of the influential Irish laywoman Marie Collins, herself a victim of paedophile priests, from the commission for the protection of minors set up by the Vatican to fight against sexual abuse in the Church.

At the Synod on the Family, Müller clearly rallied opposition to Pope Francis, although he tells me today, with a hint of hypocrisy, that he didn't want to 'add confusion to confusion, bitterness to bitterness, hatred to hatred'. He led the '*dubia*' rebellion, he elevated the refusal of communion to remarried divorcees to a dogma, and he proved radically hostile to the ordination of woman and even of '*viri probati*'. To him – a man who knows by heart all the verses of the Old Testament and the epistles that mention this 'evil' – homosexual people must be respected on condition that they remain chaste. In the end the cardinal seems to be a firm opponent of 'gender ideology', which he has coarsely caricatured, without the subtlety that he showed in his analysis of liberation theology.

Pope Francis did not appreciate Müller's critiques of the Synod on the Family, and in particular of *Amoris Laetitia*. In his Christmas wishes in 2017, he singled out Müller without naming him, by denouncing those people 'who betray [his] trust [and] allow themselves to be corrupted by ambition or vainglory; and when they are delicately expelled falsely declare themselves to be martyrs to the system, rather than doing their *mea culpa*'. Even more sternly, the pope has denounced those behind 'plots', and who represent 'a cancer' in these small circles. As we can see, Francis and Müller are hardly on the best of terms.

We are suddenly interrupted, during our conversation in the cardinal's sitting room, by a phone call. Without apologizing, the priest in flip-flops gets up and answers it. Surly a moment ago, here he is, having seen the number on the display, assuming a pose and an affected voice: now he has manners. He starts talking in German, in a perfumed voice. The flowery conversation lasts only a few minutes, but I understand that it is a personal one. If I didn't have a man in front of me who had taken a vow of chastity, and if I didn't hear echoing down the line, from far away, a baritone voice, I would have understood it to be an intimate call.

The cardinal comes back and sits down close to me, vaguely worried. And all of a sudden he asks me, inquisitorially: 'Do you understand German?'

In Rome, you sometimes feel you're in a Hitchcock film. Also living in the same building where Müller lives is his great enemy: Cardinal Walter Kasper. I would even end up by getting to know the caretaker of the soulless art-deco building, to whom I would pass on messages left by the two rival cardinals, or the famous white book, which I would drop off as a present for Müller.

The two Germans have been crossing swords for a long time, and their theological jousting is memorable. They had a rematch in 2014–15: As Francis's inspiration and unofficial theologian, Kasper found himself entrusted with the task of giving the keynote speech for the Synod on the Family, and it was Müller who demolished it!

'Pope Francis backtracked, that's a fact. He had no choice. But he's always been very clear. He accepted a compromise while trying to steer his course,' Kasper tells me during an interview at his house.

The German cardinal, wearing a very smart dark suit, talks in a warm and infinitely gentle voice. He listens, meditates in silence, before throwing himself into a long philosophical explanation, which reminds me of my long conversations with the Catholics of the journal *Esprit* in Paris.

Here is Kasper, discoursing on Saint Thomas Aquinas, whom he is rereading and who was, in his view, betrayed by the neo-Thomists, those exegetes who radicalized and travestied him, as the Marxists did with Marx and the Nietzscheans with Nietzsche. He talks to me about Hegel and Aristotle and, while he is looking for a book by Emmanuel Levinas and trying to find another one by Paul Ricoeur, I realize that I am dealing with a real intellectual. His love of books isn't feigned.

Born in Germany the year Hitler came to power, Kasper studied at the University of Tübingen, whose rector was the Swiss theologian Hans Küng, and where he regularly saw Joseph Ratzinger. It was during those crucial years that these two essential friendships began, which would last until the present day in spite of the mounting disagreements he would have with the future pope, Benedict XVI.

'Francis is closer to my way of thinking. I hold him in great esteem, I have a lot of affection for him, even though in the end I don't see him very much. But I also maintained very good relations with Ratzinger, in spite of our differences.'

Those 'differences' date back to 1993, and already concerned the debate about remarried divorcees – Kasper's real concern, even more than the homosexual question. With two other bishops, and probably with the encouragement of Hans Küng, who had broken with Ratzinger, Kasper had a letter read out in the churches in his diocese to open up the debate on the communion of divorcees. He talked about mercy and the complexity of individual situations, a little like Francis today.

In the face of this act of gentle dissidence, Cardinal Ratzinger, who was then running the Congregation for the Doctrine of the Faith, halted these adventurers mid-flow. In a letter as rigid as it was severe, he warned them to return to the ranks. With that simple piece of samizdat, Kasper found himself in opposition to the future Benedict XVI, just as Müller, facing in the other direction from his next-door neighbour, would do with Francis.

Kasper–Müller is thus the dividing line of the synod, another battle refought in 2014–15 after being waged in the same terms and almost with the same warriors, 25 years earlier, between Kasper and Ratzinger! The Vatican often seems like a big ocean liner that is moving at a standstill.

'I'm pragmatic,' Kasper corrects me. 'The path set out by Francis, and the small-step strategy, is the right one. If you advance too quickly, as in the ordination of women or the celibacy of the priesthood, there will be a schism among Catholics, and I don't want that for my Church. On divorcees, on the other hand, you can go further. I've defended that idea for a long time. When it comes to recognizing homosexual couples, that's a more difficult subject: I tried to move the debate forward at the synod, but we weren't listened to. Francis found a middle way by talking about people, about individuals. And then, very gradually, he moved the lines. He's also broken with a certain kind of misogyny: he's appointing women everywhere: in the commissions, in the dicasteries, among the experts. He is moving in his own rhythm, in his own way, but he has a goal.'

Walter Kasper adopted a position, after the victory over 'same-sex marriage' in Ireland, that the Church would accept the verdict of the vote. This referendum in May 2015 was held between the two synods, and the cardinal thought at the time that the Church would have to take account of it, as he told *Corriere della Sera*: in his view, the question of marriage, which was still 'marginal' before the first Synod, became 'central' when, for the first time, marriage was opened up to same-sex couples 'by a popular vote'. And the cardinal added in that same interview: 'A democratic state must respect the will of the people. If a majority [of the citizens of a country] wants this kind of union, it is the duty of the state to recognize those rights.'

We talk about all of these subjects in his apartment, during the two interviews that he grants me. I admire the cardinal's sincerity and his probity. We talk with great freedom of tone about the homosexual question and Kasper proves open; he listens, he asks questions, and I know from several of my sources, and also by intuition – and what is known as 'gaydar' – that I am probably dealing with one of the few cardinals in the Curia who aren't homosexual. That's the seventh rule of *The Closet*, which almost always proves to be true: *The most gay-friendly cardinals, bishops and priests, the ones who talk little about the homosexual question, are generally heterosexual.*

We mention a few cardinals' names, and Kasper is actually aware of the homosexuality of several of his colleagues. Some of these are also his opponents, the most 'rigid' in the Roman Curia. We have doubts about some of the names, and agree about others. At this stage our conversation is private, and I promise to keep our little 'outing' game confidential. He simply tells me, as if he had just made a disturbing discovery: 'They hide. They dissemble. That's the key.'

Now we turn our attention to the 'anti-Kaspers' and, for the first time, I sense that the cardinal is becoming irritated. But at the age of 85, Francis's theologian no longer wants to fight against the hypocrites, the reactionaries. With a wave of his hand he closes the debate and says, in a phrase that might sound vain and smug, but which is in fact a stark warning against the pointless little games of those prelates who are cut off from reality and, worse, from their own reality: 'We will win.' And when he utters those words, I suddenly see a beautiful smile appear on the face of the cardinal, generally so austere.

On a low table is a copy of the *Frankfurter Allgemeine Zeitung*, the newspaper he reads every day. Kasper talks to me about Bach and Mozart, and I can hear his German soul resonating. On the wall of the drawing room I see a painting showing a village, and ask him about it.

'You see, that's reality. My village in Germany. I go back to my region every summer. There are bells, churches. At the same time, today, people don't go to mass very much and seem to be happy without God. That's the big question. That's what worries me. How to find the way of God? I feel it's lost. We've lost the battle.'

6

Roma Termini

Mohammed is talking to a girl, clutching a beer with one of the '*meufs*' he hopes to '*emballer*' (get off with), as he will tell me later using French-Arab slang. It's late afternoon, Happy Hour at *Twins* – 'With Your Cocktail, A Free Shot', a flyer I'm given says in English.

Mohammed is sitting on a moped, in the street, outside the little bar. The moped isn't his, but he uses it, like everyone around here, so as not to stand up all evening. Around him is a group of migrants, his gang. They call each other noisily by their first names, they whistle, are aggressive, affectionate and roguish among themselves, and their shouts mingle with the hubbub of Roma Termini.

Now I see Mohammed going into *Twins*, a marvellously louche little bar on Via Giovanni Giolitti, opposite the southern entrance of Rome's central station. He wants to take advantage of Happy Hour to buy a drink for that passing girl. In *Twins*, they welcome the most exotic clienteles – migrants, addicts, transvestites, prostitutes (boys or girls) – with the same benevolence. If necessary, you can get a sandwich at four in the morning, a cheap slice of pizza, and dance in the back room to outdated reggae. Drugs circulate freely on the surrounding pavements.

Suddenly, I see Mohammed leaving, abandoning the moped and girl after, it would seem, he received a mysterious phone call. I watch him. He's now in the Piazza dei Cinquecento, at the crossing with Via Manin and Via Giovanni Giolitti. A car has stopped on the roadside. Mohammed is talking to the driver, and now he's getting into the car and off they go. In front of *Twins* the girl continues a conversation with another boy – a young Romanian – also perched on a moped. (All the names of the migrants have been altered in this chapter.)

'I am one of the immigrants who defends Pope Francis,' Mohammed tells me with a smile a few days later. We're back in *Twins*, the headquarters of the young Tunisian, who uses it to arrange meetings with his friends: 'If you want to talk to me, you know where to find me; I'm there from 6.00 every night,' he will tell me on another occasion.

Mohammed is a Muslim. He came to Italy on a small fishing boat, without an engine, at the risk of losing his life on the open Mediterranean. I met him for the first time in Rome when I was starting this book. I followed him for almost two years, before losing sight of him. One day Mohammed's phone stopped answering. 'The number's unavailable,' the Italian operator told me. I don't know what happened to him.

In the meantime I interviewed him a dozen times, for several hours, in French, with one of my researchers, often over lunch. He knew I would tell his story.

When he came back from the Greek island of Lesbos in 2016, Pope Francis brought with him, on his plane, three families of Syrian Muslims: a symbol to assert his defence of refugees and his liberal vision of immigration.

Mohammed, who is part of this huge wave of refugees, perhaps the last still to believe in the 'European dream', did not travel with the pope. On the contrary, he was exploited in an unexpected way that he himself couldn't have imagined when he left Tunis for Naples, via Sicily. Because while this 21-year-old man is heterosexual, he's condemned to prostitute himself with *men* every evening near Roma Termini station just to survive. Mohammed is a 'sex worker'; to me he calls himself an 'escort', which is a better visiting card. And even more extraordinarily, this Muslim's clients are essentially Catholic priests and prelates connected to the churches of Rome or the Vatican.

To investigate the unnatural relations between the Muslim rent boys of Roma Termini and the Catholic priests of the Vatican, over a period of three years I interviewed about sixty migrant prostitutes in Rome (in most cases I was accompanied on these interviews by a translator or a 'researcher').

Let's say from the outset that the prostitutes' 'timetables' suited me very well: in the early morning and during the day I met priests, bishops and cardinals in the Vatican, who never offer appointments after 6.00 p.m. In the evening, on the other hand, I interviewed male prostitutes, who rarely get to work before 7.00 p.m. My interviews with the prelates took place when the prostitutes were still asleep; and my conversations with escorts when the priests had already gone to bed. So during my weeks in Rome, my diary was divided up ideally: cardinals and prelates by day, migrants in the evening. I gradually worked out that these two worlds – these two kinds of sexual poverty – were intrinsically interwoven. That the timetables of the two groups overlapped.

To explore the night-life of Roma Termini I had to work in several languages – Romanian, Arabic, Portuguese, Spanish, as well as French, English and Italian – so I appealed to friends, 'scouts' and sometimes professional translators. I investigated the streets around Roma Termini with my researchers Thalyson, a Brazilian architecture student, Antonio Martínez Velázquez, a gay Latino journalist from Mexico, and Loïc Fel, an activist who knows the sex workers and drug addicts, who had come from Paris.

Apart from these precious friends, I identified, over the course of the evenings spent around Roma Termini, a number of 'scouts'. Generally escorts, like Mohammed, they became indispensable 'informers' and 'pathfinders', agreeing to bring me information about prostitution in the area in return for a drink or lunch. I chose three regular places for our meetings, so that I could guarantee a certain discretion: the café in the garden of the Hôtel Quirinale; the bar of the hotel NH Collection on Piazza dei Cinquecento; and the second floor of the restaurant Eataly, which, only a few years ago, was a McDonald's. Outside these, the paid encounters of Rome were played out.

Mohammed tells me about crossing the Mediterranean.

'It cost me 3,000 Tunisian dinars (900 euros), he informs me. I worked like a lunatic for months to get that sum together. And my family also contributed to help me. I didn't care; I had no idea of the risks. The fishing boat wasn't very stable; I could easily have drowned.'

Two of his friends, Billal and Sami, left as he did from Tunisia for Sicily, and also became prostitutes in Roma Termini. We talk in a 'halal pizzeria' on Via Manin, over an unappetizing four-euro kebab. Billal, in an Adidas polo shirt, with his hair shaved at the side, arrived in 2011 after crossing in a small boat, a kind of motorized raft. Sami, auburn hair, tanned, landed in 2009. He took a bigger boat, with 190 people on board, and it cost 2,000 dinars: more expensive than a low-cost flight.

Why did they come?

'For an opportunity,' Mohammed says to me, using a strange phrase.

And Sami adds: 'We have to leave because of the lack of possibilities.'

In Roma Termini we find them engaging in illicit commerce with the priests of the churches of Rome and the prelates of the Vatican. Do they have a pimp? Apparently they don't have a protector, or very rarely.

On another day I have lunch with Mohammed at Il Pommidoro in San Lorenzo, in the area of Via Tiburtina, the restaurant that gained its notoriety from the fact that Pasolini dined there with his favourite actor, Ninetto Davoli, on the evening of his murder. He was due to meet – under the arcades of Roma Termini – the 17-year-old gigolo, Giuseppe Pelosi, who would kill him. As in Al Biondo Tevere, where the two men went later, victim and killer mixed up in collective memory, Italy commemorates these 'last suppers' of Pasolini. At the entrance to the restaurant, the original cheque for the meal, signed by Pasolini – and not cashed – is displayed, a strange sepulchral trophy, behind a pane of glass. If Pelosi embodied the '*ragazzo di vita*' and the Pasolini-type – jacket, tight jeans, low forehead, curly hair and a mysterious ring decorated with a red stone, with the inscription 'United States' – Mohammed, on the other hand, is the quintessence of Arab beauty. He is harder, more manly, darker; his forehead is high, his hair short. He has the blue eyes of the Berber; he barely smiles. No ring – that would be too feminine. In his way he embodies the Arab myth that 'orientalist' writers racked by male desires have liked so much.

This Arabic style, which brings with it something of the memory of Carthage and Flaubert's *Salammbô*, is highly prized in the Vatican today. It's a fact: the 'homosexual priests' adore Arabs and 'orientals'. They love this migrant sub-proletariat, as Pasolini loved the poor young men of the '*borgate*', the Roman suburbs. The same accidental lives; the same enchantments. Each one abandons part of himself when he comes to Roma Termini: the '*ragazzo*' abandons his Roman dialect; the migrant his mother tongue. Both need to speak the Italian of the arcades. The Arab boy fresh off the boat is the new Pasolinian model.

The relationship between Mohammed and the priests is already a long story. A strange trade, incidentally, abnormal, irrational, and which, on both the Catholic and the Muslim side, is not simply 'unnatural' but also sacrilegious. I soon understood that the presence of priests in search of male prostitutes in Roma Termini is a well-established business – a small industry. It involves hundreds of prelates and even some bishops and cardinals from the Roman Curia whose names we know. These relationships follow a remarkable sociological rule, the eighth in *The Closet: In prostitution in Rome between priests and Arab escorts, two sexual poverties come together: the profound sexual frustration of Catholic priests is echoed in the constraints of Islam, which make heterosexual acts outside of marriage difficult for a young Muslim.*

'With the priests, we get along quite naturally,' Mohammed says to me in a frightening phrase.

Mohammed very quickly understood that sex was the 'major issue' and 'the only true passion' – in a temporal sense – for most of the priests that he meets. And he was enchanted by this discovery, by its strangeness, its animality, the role-playing it suggests, but also, of course, because it became the key to his economic model.

Mohammed insists that he works on his own. His start-up does not depend on the presence of a pimp.

'I would be ashamed, because it would mean becoming part of a system. I don't want to become a prostitute,' he assures me very seriously.

Like all the rent boys in Roma Termini, Mohammed loves his regulars. He loves to 'make relationships' as he says, getting his clients' mobile phones in order to 'build something long-lasting'. From his own observation, priests are among his most 'loyal' customers; they 'instinctively' latch on to prostitutes that they like and want to see again. Mohammed appreciates this regularity, which, apart from the financial benefits that it offers, seems to raise his social status.

'An escort is someone with regulars. He's not a prostitute,' the young Tunisian insists.

'*Bună ziua.*'
  '*Ce faci?*'
  '*Bine! Foarte bine!*'

I'm talking to Gaby in his own language, and my rudimentary Romanian, which surprised him at first, now seems to reassure him. I once lived in Bucharest for a year and I still have a few basic expressions from those days. Gaby, 25, works in the area 'reserved' for Romanians.

Unlike Mohammed, Gaby is a legal immigrant in Italy, because Romania is part of the European Union. He found himself in Rome rather by chance; the two main migration routes, the one called 'the Balkans' – rooted in central Europe and, beyond that, in Syria and Iraq – and the 'Mediterranean' route taken by most of the migrants from Africa and the Maghreb, pass through Roma Termini, the big central station of the Italian capital. In the literal sense of the term, it is the 'terminus' of many migration routes. So everyone stops there.

Always in transit, like most prostitutes, Gaby is already thinking of leaving again. While he waits, he's looking for a little 'normal' job in Rome. Without any real training or a profession, few opportunities are open to him: unwillingly, he started selling his body.

Some journalist friends from Bucharest had already alerted me to this disconcerting phenomenon: Romania was exporting its prostitutes. Certain newspapers, like *Evenimentul zilei*, carried out the investigation, writing ironically about this Romanian 'record': becoming the first European country to export sex workers. According to TAMPEP, a Dutch NGO, almost half of the prostitutes in Europe, men and women, are migrants; one prostitute in eight is said to be Romanian.

Gaby comes from Iași in Romania. First he crossed Germany where, not understanding the language, and knowing nobody, he decided not to stay. After a 'very disappointing' time in the Netherlands, he turned up in Rome without any money, but with the address of a Romanian friend. This boy, himself a prostitute, put him up and initiated him into the 'trade'. He gave him the secret code: the best clients are the priests!

As a rule, Gaby starts his night's work in Roma Termini at about 8.00 p.m. and, depending on the number of customers, he stays there until 6.00 in the morning.

'Prime time is between 8.00 and 11.00 p.m. We leave the afternoon to the Africans. The Romanians come in the evening. The best clients prefer the white boys,' he tells me with a certain pride. Summer is better than winter, when there aren't so many clients, but August isn't good because the priests are on holiday and the Vatican is almost empty.

The ideal evening, according to Gaby, is Friday. The priests come out 'in plain clothes' – meaning without their dog-collars. Sunday afternoon is another promising time of day, according to Mohammed, who hardly has any time off on that day. No rest on the seventh day! Sunday boredom means that the area around Roma Termini is always busy, before and after vespers.

At first I barely paid attention to these discreetly exchanged glances, all the movement around Via Giovanni Giolitti, Via Gioberti and Via delle Terme di Diocleziano, but thanks to Mohammed and Gaby I can decode the signs now.

'Most of the time I tell the punters I'm Hungarian, because they aren't too keen on Romanians. They get us confused with gypsies,' Gaby explains, and I sense that the lie is a burden, since like many Romanians he hates the Hungarian neighbour and traditional enemy.

All the local rent boys invent lies and fantasies for themselves. One of them tells me he is Spanish, when I can tell by his accent that he is from Latin America. A bearded youth, with the physique of a gypsy, who likes to be called Pitbull, generally presents himself as a Bulgarian, when he is in fact a Romanian from Craiova. Another, smaller one, who refuses to tell me his first name – let's call him Shorty – explains that he's there because he's missed his train; but I'll bump into him again the next day.

The customers lie too, and invent lives for themselves.

'They say they're passing through, or travelling on business, but we're not idiots and we spot them straight away; you can see the priests coming from a long way off,' Gaby remarks.

When making advances on these young men, the priests use a formula that's very threadbare but still seems to work.

'They ask us for a cigarette even when they don't smoke! They don't generally wait for us to answer. As soon as you've swapped glances, the code has been understood, and they suddenly say, very quickly, "*Andiamo*".'

Mohammed, Gaby, Pitbull and Shorty acknowledge that they sometimes take the first step, particularly when the priests pass in front of them with 'lecherous expressions' but don't dare to approach them.

'Then I help them,' Mohammed says to me, 'and I ask them if they want to do coffee.'

'*Faire café*' – it's a lovely phrase in French, and part of the approximate vocabulary of the Arabs who are still finding their words.

During the first two years of my investigation, I lived in the area around Termini in Rome. One week a month on average, I rented a little flat on Airbnb, either from S, an architect, whose studio near the Basilica of Santa Maria Maggiore I have always loved, or, if it was booked, in the Airbnbs on Via Marsala or Via Montebello north of Termini Station.

The edges of the Esquilino, one of the seven hills of the city, have long been filthy, that's a fact; but Termini is in the middle of a process of '*gentrificazione*', as the locals say, using an Italianized Anglicism. The Romans advised me to live in Trastevere, around the Pantheon, in the Borgo, or even in Prati, to be closer to the Vatican. But I stayed loyal to Termini: it's a question of habit. When you travel, you very quickly try to create a new routine, to find some landmarks. In Roma Termini I'm right next to the express train, known as the Leonardo express, that leads to Rome's international airport; the underground trains and the buses stop there; I have my little laundry, Lavasciuga, on Via Montebello, and, most importantly, the Feltrinelli international bookshop near Piazza della Repubblica, where I supplied myself with books and notebooks for my interviews. Literature is the best travelling companion. And since I've always thought that there are three things you should never skimp on in life – books, travel and cafés for meeting friends – I took pleasure in remaining loyal to that rule in Italy.

I finally 'moved away' from Termini in 2017, when I was given permission to live in the official residences of the Vatican, thanks to a very well-connected monsignore, Battista Ricca, and Archbishop François Bacqué. Living at the time in the very official Casa del Clero, an 'extraterritorial' place near the Piazza Navona, or in other residences of the holy see and even several months inside the Vatican a few dozen metres from the pope's apartment, thanks to important prelates and cardinals, I was sorry to leave Termini.

It took me several months of careful observation and meetings to understand the subtle nocturnal geography of the boys of Roma Termini. Each group of prostitutes has its patch, its marked territory. It's a division that reflects racial hierarchies and a whole range of prices. So the Africans are usually sitting on the guardrail by the south-western entrance to the station; the Maghrebis, sometimes the Egyptians, tend to stay around Via Giovanni Giolitti, at the crossing with the Rue Manin or under the arcades on Piazza dei Cinquecento; the Romanians are close to Piazza della Repubblica, beside the naked sea-nymphs of the Naiad Fountain or around the Dogali Obelisk; the 'Latinos', last of all, cluster more towards the north of the square, on Viale Enrico de Nicola or Via Marsala. Sometimes there are territorial wars between groups, and fists fly.

This geography isn't stable; it changes with the years, the seasons or the waves of migrants. There have been 'Kurdish', 'Yugoslav', 'Eritrean' periods; more recently a wave of Syrians and Iraqis, and now we see Nigerians, Argentinians and Venezuelans arriving at Roma Termini. But there is one fairly constant element: there are few Italians on Piazza dei Cinquecento.

The legalization of homosexuality, the proliferation of bars and saunas, mobile apps, laws on same-sex marriage, and the socialization of gays tend, everywhere in Europe, to dry up the market in male street prostitution. With one exception: Rome. There's quite a simple explanation: the priests help to keep this market alive, even though it's increasingly anachronistic in the time of the internet. And for reasons of anonymity, they seek out migrants.

There's no fixed price for 'tricks' in Roma Termini. In the market of goods and services, the rate for the sexual act is currently at its lowest. There are too many available Romanians, too many undocumented Africans, too many Latino transvestites for inflation to be possible. Mohammed brings in an average of 70 euros a trick; Shorty asks for 50 euros, on condition that the punter pays for the room himself; Gaby and Pitbull rarely discuss the price in advance, partly for fear of plain-clothes policemen and partly as a sign of their poverty and economic dependence.

'When it's over, I ask for 50 euros if they don't suggest anything; if they offer 40, I ask for 10 more; and sometimes I'll take 20 if the punter is stingy. Most importantly, I don't want problems, because I come here every evening,' Gaby says to me.

He doesn't tell me that he has 'his reputation' to think about, but I get the idea.

'Having a regular customer is what everybody wants around here, but not everyone's that lucky,' says Florin, a Romanian prostitute who comes from Transylvania and speaks fluent English.

I met Florin and Christian in Rome in August 2016, with my researcher Thalyson. They're both 27 and live together, they tell me, in a makeshift little flat, in a suburb a long way out of the city.

'I grew up in Braşov,' Christian tells me. 'I'm married and I have a child. I have to feed him! I told my parents and my wife that I'm a bartender in Rome.'

Florin told his parents that he was working 'in construction', and he tells me that he is able to 'make in 15 minutes what he would make in 10 hours on a building site'.

'We work around the Piazza della Repubblica. It's a square for people from the Vatican. Everyone here knows that. The priests take us by car. They take us home or, more often, to a hotel,' Christian says.

Unlike other prostitutes I've interviewed, Christian doesn't say he has difficulties renting a room.

'I never have a problem. We pay. They can't refuse us. We have ID, we're in order. And even if the hotel people aren't happy about two men taking a room for an hour, there's nothing they can do.'

'Who pays for the hotel?'

'They do, of course,' Christian replies, surprised by my question.

Christian tells me about the dark side of the dark nights in Roma Termini. The lubriciousness of the clerics goes beyond the normal and into abuse, according to the statements I've collected.

'I had a priest who wanted me to urinate on him. They want you to dress up as a woman, as a transvestite. Others practise rather unpleasant SM acts.' (He spares me the details.) 'One priest even wanted to have a naked boxing match with me.'

'How do you know they're priests?'

'I'm a professional! I identify them straight away. Priests are among the most persistent clients. You can tell from their crosses when they undress.'

'But don't lots of people have crosses or baptismal medallions?'

'No, not crosses like these. You can recognize them from miles away, even if they're disguised as ordinary citizens. You can tell from their posture, which is a lot stiffer than that of the other customers. They're not used to living …'

'They're unhappy,' Christian goes on. 'They're not alive; they don't love. Their way of approaching you, their little game, phone to their ears to make them look normal, as if they have a social life, when they're not talking to anyone. I know it all by heart. And most importantly, I've got regulars. I know them. We talk a lot. They confess. I have a cross around my neck too, I'm a Christian. It creates a bond! They feel safer with an Orthodox Christian; it's reassuring for them! I talk to them about John Paul II, whom I like a lot, as a Romanian; no one liked that pope more than I did. And an Italian hardly ever takes us to a hotel. The only ones who take us to hotels are priests, tourists and cops!'

'Cops?'

'Yes, I've got regulars who are cops … But I prefer priests. When we go to the Vatican they pay us very well because they're rich …'

The boys of Roma Termini don't know the names of the cardinals or bishops involved, but they remember those orgies at the Vatican. Several of them have talked to me about Friday-night 'foursomes' when 'a chauffeur would turn up in a Mercedes in search of prostitutes and drive them to the Vatican', but none of them have been taken to the holy see 'by chauffeur', and I have a sense that all that information is second-hand. The collective memory of the boys of Termini repeats this story, although it is impossible to know if it ever really happened.

Christian does tell me that he went to the Vatican three times with a priest, and a Romanian friend, Razvan, who comes over and chats with us, went once.

'If you go to the Vatican and come across a big fish, you're much better paid. It's not 50–60 euros, it's more like 100–200. We all want to catch a big fish.'

Christian goes on: 'Most of the priests and the people in the Vatican want regulars. It's less visible and less risky for them: it means they don't have to come and find us here, Piazza della Repubblica, on foot or by car; they just send us a text!'

Shrewd and battle-hardened, Christian shows me the contacts list on his phone, and displays the names and numbers of priests' mobile phones. The list is infinite. When he talks about them, he calls them 'my friends', which makes Florin laugh: '"My friends", for people you met two hours ago. So they're your fast friends! A bit like fast food!'

Some of Christian's customers have probably given him fake names, but the numbers are genuine. And it occurred to me that if one were to publish this huge list of clerics' mobile numbers, you'd set fire to the Italian Bishops' Conference!

How many escorted priests come regularly to Termini? How many 'closeted' prelates and 'unstraight' monsignori come here to warm themselves up with these sons of the Orient? Social workers and police suggest figures: 'dozens' every evening, 'hundreds' every month. Boastfully, the prostitutes themselves talk about 'thousands'. But everyone underestimates and over-estimates an inestimable market. And nobody really knows.

Christian wants to stop.

'I'm one of the old ones here. I don't mean I'm old, I'm only 27, but I think I'm on the way out. Often the priests walk by; they greet me: "*Buongiorno*" ... but they don't pick me up. When a boy turns up in Termini, he's brand-new. Everyone wants him. That's the jackpot. He's very much in demand. He can really make himself a lot of money. But it's too late for me. I'm going back in September. I'm done.'

With my researchers, Thalyson, Antonio, Daniele and Loïc, I do the tour of Termini's hotels over a few evenings. It's an amazing part of the city.

In Roma Termini, we counted over a hundred small hotels around Via Principe Amedeo, Via Giovanni Amendola, Via Milazzo and Via Filippo Turati. Here the stars don't mean much: a 'two-star' hotel can be quite run down; a 'one-star' hotel is somewhere you'd hardly want to step inside. Sometimes, I discover, the short-stay hotels even advertise on Airbnb to fill their rooms when they're short of clients: privatization on the edge of legality ... We questioned several hotel managers and receptionists about prostitution, and tried several times to rent rooms 'by the hour' to see their reaction.

A Bangladeshi Muslim in his fifties who runs a small hotel on Via Principe Amedeo, thinks prostitution is the 'scourge of the district'.

'If they come and ask me for an hourly rate, I refuse them. But if they take a room for the night, I can't throw them out. The law forbids it.'

In the hotels of Roma Termini, including the filthiest of them, managers have sometimes been known to wage an actual war on male prostitutes without realizing that by doing so they're also turning away a more respectable clientele: priests! They create digicodes, recruit intransigent night porters, install surveillance cameras in lobbies and corridors, even on emergency staircases, in internal courtyards, 'which the rent boys sometimes use to bring their customers in without passing by the front desk' (according to Fabio, a Roman born and bred, in his thirties, vaguely desocialized, who works off the books in one of the hotels). Those signs that say '*Area Videosorvegliata*', which I've often seen in these small hotels, are principally there to scare off the clerics.

Migrant prostitutes are often asked for their papers in a bid to get rid of them, or else the price of the room is multiplied by two (Italy is one of those archaic countries where you sometimes pay for the night according to the number of occupants). After trying everything to make this market dry up, the landlords are sometimes reduced to shouting insults, such as '*Fanculo i froci!*', at people who have taken a client to their 'single' room.

'We get everything at night,' Fabio tells me. 'A lot of prostitutes have no papers. So they fake them, they borrow them. I saw a white guy coming in with a black guy's papers. Frankly, you don't do that! But of course you shut your eyes and you let them get on with it.'

According to Fabio, it isn't uncommon for a manager to forbid prostitution in one of his hotels and encourage it in another. In that case he gives out the card of the alternative hotel and, dropping lots of hints, recommends a better address for this fleeting couple. Sometimes the manager is even worried about the client's safety and possible dangers, so keeps the prostitute's paper behind the front desk until he comes back down with his customer, to check that there hasn't been a theft or violence. Vigilance that may well have avoided a few extra scandals at the Vatican!

At Roma Termini, the passing tourist, the visitor, the ordinary Italian, untrained in these matters, doesn't go beyond the surface of things: they will only see the Vespa-hirers and the reduced rates for tours on 'Hop

On, Hop Off' double-decker buses. But behind those tantalizing posters telling you to visit the Palatine Hill, another life exists on the upper storeys of the little hotels at Roma Termini, which is no less tantalizing.

At Piazza dei Cinquecento I observe the interplay between the boys and their clients. The merry-go-round isn't very subtle, and the clients are less than reputable. Many of them drive by in their cars, window open, hesitate, turn round, come back, and finally take their young escorts in some unknown direction. Others are on foot, lacking confidence, and finish their biblical dialogue in one of the pitiful hotels in the district. Here's one who's a bit bolder and more sure of himself: he might be a missionary in Africa! And another gives me the impression, from the way he's staring at the animals, that he's on safari!

I ask Florin, the Romanian prostitute whose name recalls the old coin of the popes in the days of Julian II, if he has visited the museums, the Pantheon, the Coliseum.

'No, I've just visited the Vatican, with some of my clients. I haven't got 12 euros to visit a … a normal museum.'

Florin has a short, 'three-day' beard, which he keeps up because, he tells me, it is part of his 'power of attraction'. He has blue eyes and his hair is perfectly combed and slicked 'with Garnier gel'. He tells me that he wants to 'get a tattoo of the Vatican on his arm, it's so beautiful'.

'Sometimes the priests pay for us to go on holiday,' Florin explains to me. 'I went away for three days with a priest. He paid for everything. Normal. There are also some clients,' he adds, 'who hire us regularly; every week, for example. They pay a kind of subscription. And they're given a discount!'

I ask Gaby, as I did with the others, what the clues are that tell him he's dealing with priests.

'They're more discreet than the others. In sexual terms, they're lone wolves. They're afraid. They never use coarse language. And of course they always want to go to hotels, because they haven't got a house: that's the sign, that's how you tell.'

He adds: 'Priests don't want Italians. They're more comfortable with people who don't speak Italian. They want migrants because it's easier, it's more discreet. Have you ever heard of a migrant reporting a bishop to the police?'

Gaby goes on: 'I've got some priests who pay just to sleep with me. They talk about love, about love stories. They are insanely tender. They're like teenage girls! They tell me off for kissing them badly, and the kisses seem important to them. There are also some who want "to save me". Priests always want to help us, to "take us off the street" ...'

I have heard this remark often enough to think it's based on real and repeated experiences. Priests fall instantly in love with their migrants, now whispering in their ear, 'I luv you' – a way of avoiding saying the word, the way people swear by saying 'Oh my gosh' rather than blaspheming by saying 'Oh my God!'

At any rate, they're all hopelessly in love, even though they refuse to admit it. And the prostitutes are often startled by the excessive tenderness on the part of the priests: their voyage across the Mediterranean is certainly full of surprises!

And, I wonder: do priests fall in love with their boys more than other men? Why do they try to 'save' the prostitutes they're exploiting? Is there a remnant of Christian morality that makes them human at the very moment when they are betraying their vow of chastity?

Florin asks me if men are allowed to marry in France. I say yes, marriage between people of the same sex is permitted. He hasn't thought about it much, but it basically strikes him as 'normal'.

'Here in Italy it's forbidden. Because of the Vatican, and because it's a communist country.'

Florin punctuates each of his sentences with the word 'normal', even though his life is anything but normal.

What strikes me during my many interviews with Christian, Florin, Gaby, Mohammed, Pitbull, Shorty, and many others, is their lack of judgementalism about the priests they're sleeping with. They don't lumber themselves with morality or guilt. If an imam was gay, the Muslims would have been shocked; if an orthodox pope was homosexual the Romanians would have thought it was strange; but it strikes them as 'normal' for Catholic priests to indulge in prostitution. And in any case, it's a windfall as far as they're concerned. Sin doesn't bother them. Mohammed insists that he is still 'active', which apparently is less of an offence against Islam.

'Is a Muslim permitted to sleep with a Catholic priest? You can always ask the question if you have the choice,' Mohammed adds. 'But I don't have the choice.'

On another evening I meet up with Gaby in Agenzia Viaggi, a cybercafé on Via Manin (now closed). There are about thirty Romanian male prostitutes there, chatting on the internet with their friends and families who are still in Bucharest, Constanţa, Timişoara or Cluj. They are talking via Skype or WhatsApp, and updating their Facebook status. In Gaby's online biography, while he's talking to his mother, I see: 'Life lover', in English. And 'Live in New York'.

'I tell her about my life here. She's happy to see that I'm visiting in Europe: Berlin, Rome, soon London. I have a sense that she envies me a little. She asks me a lot of questions and she's really happy for me. It's as if I were in a film as far as she's concerned. Of course she doesn't know what I do. I'll never tell her.' (Like the other boys, Gaby uses the word 'prostitute' as little as possible, and instead uses metaphors or images.)

Mohammed tells me more or less the same thing. He goes to a cyber-café called Internet Phone, on Via Gioberti, and I go with him. Calling his mother via the internet, as he does several times a week, costs 50 cents for 15 minutes or 2 euros an hour. He calls his mother, in front of me, via Facebook. He talks to her in Arabic for about ten minutes.

'Mostly I do Facebook. My mother is better at Facebook than Skyping. I just told her that everything's going fine, that I'm working. She was so happy. Sometimes she tells me she'd like me to come back. To be there, even just for a few minutes. She tells me: "Come back for a minute, just a minute, so that I can see you." She says to me: "You're my whole life."'

Regularly, as if apologizing for his absence, Mohammed sends his mother a bit of money, by Western Union transfer (he complains about their extravagant commission costs; I recommend PayPal, but he hasn't got a credit card).

Mohammed dreams of going home 'one day'. He remembers the old-fashioned TGM line, the little train that connects Tunis Marine with La Marsa, with its legendary stops that he lists out loud for me, remembering the name of each station in the right order: Le Bac, La Goulette, L'Aéroport, Le Kram, Carthage-Salammbô, Sidi Bousaïd, La Marsa.

'I miss Tunisia. My mother often asks me if I'm not cold. I tell her I've got a hat, and also a hood. Because it's incredibly cold here in winter. She suspects, but she has no idea how cold it is here.'

In Mohammed's Arab clique in Rome, not all of them have slipped into prostitution. Several of his friends prefer to sell hashish and cocaine (heroin, which is too expensive, doesn't seem to feature locally, according to all the prostitutes I've interviewed, and MDMA is only a marginal presence).

Drugs? Mohammed isn't interested. His argument is irreproachable: 'Drugs are illegal and they're very risky. If I went to prison, my mother would discover everything. And she would never forgive me. What I'm doing in Italy is completely legal.'

Above Giovanna Petrocca's desk, two crucifixes hang on the wall. On a nearby table, photographs show her posing with John Paul II.

'He's my pope,' she tells me with a smile.

I'm in the central police station in Roma Termini, and Giovanna Petrocca runs this important police station. She's a chief inspector; in Italian her title, as it appears on the door of her office, is '*primo dirigente, commissariato di Polizia, Questura di Roma*'.

The meeting was officially organized by the press service of the central office of Italian police, and Giovanna Petrocca answers all my questions quite honestly. She is a real professional, who knows her subject inside out. It's clear that prostitution in Roma Termini hasn't escaped the attention of the police, who know everything down to the smallest details. Petrocca confirms most of my hypotheses and, most importantly, she corroborates what the prostitutes have said to me. (In this chapter I also use information from Lieutenant Colonel Stefano Chirico, who runs the anti-discrimination office at the Direzione Centrale della Polizia Criminale, the headquarters of the national police in the south of Rome, which I visited.)

'Roma Termini has a long history of prostitution,' Inspector Giovanna Petrocca explains to me. 'It comes in waves, following migrations, wars, poverty. Each nationality is grouped together by language, it's quite spontaneous, a little wild. Italian law does not punish individual prostitution, so we just try to contain the phenomenon, to limit its expansion. And of course we make sure that it stays within limits: no obscenities or attacks on public morality in the street; no prostitution with minors; no drugs; and no pimping. That's forbidden, and severely sanctioned.'

With a law degree from La Sapienza University, Petrocca, having spent a long time working on the ground in an urban police patrol, joined a new specialist anti-prostitution unit of the criminal police, created in 2001, where she stayed for 13 years before being made one of the officers in charge of it. In the long term she was able to follow the demographic changes in prostitution: Albanian women prostituted by force by mafias; the arrival of the Moldovans and Romanians and organized pimping; the wave of Nigerians, which she calls 'medieval', since the women prostitute themselves in response to tribal rules and voodoo precepts! She keeps an eye on massage apartments with 'happy ending' – a specialism of the Chinese – prostitution that is more difficult to control, because it happens in private houses. She knows the short-stay hotels around Roma Termini and, of course, in detail the male prostitution in the area.

With the precision of a scientist, the chief inspector outlines recent cases, homicides, the cruising areas of the transvestites, which are different from those of the transsexuals. But Giovanna Petrocca, her words translated by Daniele Particelli, my Roman researcher, isn't trying to dramatize the situation. Roma Termini, in her view, is a place of prostitution like any other, the same as all the areas around the big train stations in Italy, quite similar to Naples or Milan.

'What can you do? We check the activities in public streets, and we pounce at random, about twice a week, on the hotels around Roma Termini. When a hotel officially accepts prostitutes, it's a crime; but renting a room by the hour is legal in Italy. So we intervene if we discover organized pimping, drugs, or minors.'

Giovanna Petrocca takes her time and we talk about the types of drugs circulating in the area, about the hotels I've spotted, and which she knows as well. I've rarely come across a police officer so competent, so professional and so well-informed. Roma Termini is 'under control'.

If the chief inspector didn't talk to me 'on the record' about the number of priests who make use of prostitutes around Roma Termini, other policemen have done so in a detailed and probing way, outside of the office. In this chapter, in fact – but also throughout this book – I often use a lot of information from the association Polis Aperta, a group of about a hundred LGBT soldiers, *carabinieri* and policemen. Several of its members in Rome, Castel Gandolfo, Milan, Naples, Turin, Padua and Bologna, and in particular a lieutenant colonel of the *carabinieri*, have given me accounts of the prostitution at Roma Termini and, more broadly, the commercial sex lives of ecclesiastics. (In some cases I also use anonymized information and statistics from the SDI crime database shared by the various Italian law-enforcement organizations.)

These police officers and *carabinieri* confirm that there are many incidents: priests who have been robbed, kidnapped or beaten up; priests who have been arrested; priests who have been murdered, in cruising areas off the beaten track. They tell me about the blackmail, the sex tapes, the 'Catholic revenge porn' and the countless cases of 'immorality' affairs among the clergy. These priests, even if they are victims, seldom make a complaint: the price to be paid for making a report at the police station would be too high. They only do so in the most serious cases. Most of the time they say nothing; they hide and go home in silence, weighed down with their vice and hiding their bruises.

There are also the homicides, which are rarer, but which eventually make it into the public eye. In his book *Omocidi* (*Homocides*) the journalist Andrea Pini revealed the considerable number of homosexuals killed by prostitutes in Italy, particularly after anonymous encounters that occurred in shady places. Among these, police sources agree, priests are over-represented.

Francesco Mangiacapra is a high-class Neapolitan escort. His testimony is of huge importance here because, unlike other male prostitutes, he agrees to talk to me under his real name. A law student, slightly paranoid, but level-headed, he has drawn up long lists of gay priests who used his services in the region of Naples and Rome. This unique database has been enriched over the years with photographs, videos and, most importantly, by the identity of the people in questions. When he shares this massive amount of confidential information with me, I leave the anonymous qualitative discussion that I was having in the streets around Roma Termini, to enter the quantitative. Now I had tangible proof.

Mangiacapra was recommended to me by Fabrizio Sorbara, an activist and one of the directors of the Arcigay association in Naples. I've interviewed him several times in Naples and Rome, in the presence of Daniele and the activist and translator René Buonocore.

White shirt open over his chest, fine hair a chestnut colour, slender face, carefully unshaven, he's a charming young man. If our first contact is cautious, Mangiacapra is quickly at ease with me. He knows very well who I am, because he attended a talk I gave a few months earlier at the Institut français in Naples, after the publication in Italian of my book *Global Gay*.

'I didn't start doing this job for money, but to know my value. I have a law degree from the famous Federico II University in Naples, and when I started looking for a job, all doors were closed. There's no employment here, in Southern Italy, no opportunities. My fellow students did one humiliating internship after another in lawyers' offices, or were exploited for 400 euros a month. My first client, I remember, was a lawyer: he paid me for 20 minutes what he pays his trainees for two weeks' work! Rather than sell my mind for a small amount of money, I decided to sell my body for a lot.'

Mangiacapra is an unusual sort of escort. He's an Italian prostitute who expresses himself, as I have said, under his real name, showing his face, without any sense of shame. I was immediately struck by the strength of his testimony.

'I know my value and the value of money. I don't spend much; I save as much as possible. We often think,' the young man adds, 'that prostitution is money earned quickly and easily. No. It's money earned at great cost.'

Soon Francesco Mangiacapra discovered a line of business that he would never have imagined. Prostitution with gay priests.

'At first it started quite naturally. I had priest clients who recommended me to other priests, who invited me to parties where I met still other priests. It wasn't a network; these weren't orgies like people sometimes think. They were just very ordinary priests who simply recommended me in quite a mundane way to other priest friends.'

The advantages of this kind of client appeared quickly: loyalty, regularity and security.

'Priests are the ideal clientele. They are loyal and they pay well. If I could, I would only work for priests. I always give them priority. I'm lucky, because I'm very much in demand and I'm able to choose my clients, unlike other male prostitutes who get chosen. I wouldn't say I'm happy with this job, but I look at the other prostitutes, the other students who are unemployed, and I say to myself that I'm lucky in the end. If I'd been born somewhere else or in another time I'd have used my degrees and my intelligence to do something different. But in Naples prostitution is the most accessible job that I've been able to find.'

The young man starts coughing. I sense a certain fragility. He's frail and sensitive. He tells me he has '30 regular priests' at the moment, clients who he is sure are priests, and many others about whom he has doubts. Since he took up prostitution, he tells me, there have been 'hundreds of priests'.

'Priests have become my speciality.'

According to Mangiacapra, ecclesiastics prefer prostitution because it gives them a certain security, an anonymity, while remaining compatible with their double life. The normal 'chatting up' process, even in the homosexual milieu, takes time. It implies a long discussion; you have to come out into the open and say who you are. Prostitution is quick and anonymous and doesn't expose you.

'When a priest contacts me, we don't know each other; there's no previous contact between us. They prefer that kind of situation; that's what they're looking for. I've often had very good looking priest clients. I would gladly have slept with them for free! They would easily have been able to find a lover in gay bars or clubs. But that was incompatible with their priesthood.'

The young escort doesn't work 'la strada' (the street) like the migrants in Roma Termini. He doesn't live at the rhythm of Fellini's Nights of Cabiria. He meets his clients on the internet, on specialist sites or on Grindr. He regularly exchanges messages with them on apps like WhatsApp or, for greater discretion, Telegram. Then he tries to turn them into regular clients.

'In Rome there's a lot of competition; here in Naples it's calmer. But there are priests who call me to the capital; they pay for my train and my hotel.'

From his sexual experiences with dozens if not hundreds of priests, Mangiacapra shares some sociological rules with me.

'By and large, among priests, there are two kinds of client. There are the ones who feel infallible and very strong in their position. Those clients are arrogant and stingy. Their desire is so repressed that they lose their sense of morality and any sense of humanity. They feel they're above the law. They aren't even afraid of AIDS! Often they don't hide the fact that they're priests. They're demanding and harsh, and they don't let you take power! They have no hesitation about saying that if there's a problem they're going to report you to the police as a prostitute! But they forget that, if I want, I'm the one who could report them as priests!'

The second type of clients with whom Francesco works are of a different kind.

'They're priests who are very uncomfortable in their skin. They're very attached to affection, to caresses; they want to kiss you all the time. They have a terrible need for tenderness. They're like children.'

These clients, Mangiacapra confirms, often fall in love with their prostitute, and want to 'save him'.

'Those priests never discuss the price. They're riven with guilt. They often give us money in a little envelope that they've prepared in advance. They say it's a present to help me, to let me buy something I need. They try to justify themselves.'

With me, Mangiacapra is happy to use more explicit words. He tells me he is a prostitute, and even '*marchettaro*' – literally a 'whore' (the slang term comes from '*marchetta*', the 'receipt' that made it possible to quantify the number of clients that a prostitute had had in a short-stay hotel). The escort deliberately uses this insult to invert the prejudice, like turning someone's gun on them.

'Those priests want to see their *marchettaro* again. They want a relationship. They want to stay in touch. They are often in a state of denial, and won't understand that we don't think highly of them, because they think they're good priests. Then they think that we're friends; they insist on that. They introduce you to their friends, to other priests. They take big risks. They invite you to church, take you to see the nuns in the sacristy. They trust you very quickly, a little as if you were their best pal.

Often they add a tip in kind: a piece of clothing that they've bought in advance, a bottle of after-shave. They shower you with attention.'

Francesco Mangiacapra's testimony is lucid – and terrible. It's harsh and brutal testimony, like the world he's describing.

'The price? Inevitably it's the highest price that the client is willing to pay. That's why it's about marketing. There are escorts who are more handsome, more charming, than I am; but my marketing is better. By virtue of the site or the app that they use to contact me, of what they say to me, I do my first assessment of the price. When we meet, I adapt that price by asking them what area they live in, what they do for a living, I look at their clothes, their watches. I assess their financial capacity very easily. Priests are willing to pay more than a normal client.'

I interrupt the young escort, asking him how priests, who generally have a salary of a thousand euros a month, can finance such escapades.

'*Allora* … A priest is someone who hasn't got a choice. So you're more exclusive for him. It's a more sensitive category. They are men who can't find other guys, so you hike the price. You might say it's a bit like disabled people.'

After a pause, still punctuated by a long '*Allora* …', Mangiacapra continues: 'Most priests pay well; they rarely haggle. I imagine they scrimp on their leisure activities, but never on sex. A priest has no family, no rent to pay.'

Like many rent boys I interviewed in Rome, the Neapolitan escort confirms the importance of sex in the lives of priests. Homosexuality seems to give direction to their existence, to dominate their lives: and it does so in different proportions to those of most homosexuals.

Now the young prostitute tells me some of his marketing secrets.

'The key is customer loyalty. If the priest is interesting, if he pays well, he has to come back. For that to happen, you have to do everything to make sure that he never falls back into reality; he has to stay in the fantasy. I never introduce myself as a "prostitute", because that breaks the fantasy. I never say that he's "my client"; I say he's "my friend". I always call the client by his first name, taking care never to mix up different clients' names! Because I need to show him that he's unique to me. Clients like to be remembered, and that's what they want; they don't want you to have other clients! So I've opened a list on my phone. For every client

I record everything: I note down the first name he's given me, his age, the positions he prefers, the places we've gone to together, the essential things he's told me about himself, etc. I keep a minutely detailed record of all that. And, of course, I also note the maximum price he's agreed to pay, to ask for the same, or a bit more.'

Mangiacapra shows me his 'files', and points to the surnames and first names of dozens of priests with whom he says he has had sexual relations. It's impossible for me to check his information.

In 2018 he made public the sex lives of 34 priests in a 1,200-page document that included the names of the clerics concerned, their photographs, audio recordings and screen shots of his sexual exchanges with them, from WhatsApp or Telegram. It all caused a considerable scandal, dozens of articles and television programmes appearing in Italy. (I was able to consult the 'dossier' called *Preti gay*; it reveals dozens of priests celebrating mass in their cassocks and then, stark naked, celebrating other kinds of frolic via webcam. The photographs, alternating homilies and intimate pictures, are quite extraordinary. Mangiacapra sent the whole file directly to the Archbishop of Naples, the versatile cardinal Crescenzio Sepe. This close colleague of Cardinal Sodano – like him, gregarious – is a man of many connections who is said to have hurried, once he received the file, to pass it to the Vatican. Subsequently, Crescenzio Sepe met Mangiacapra secretly, he says.)

'When I sleep with rich married lawyers, important doctors or all those priests with their double lives, I can tell that they aren't happy. Happiness doesn't go hand in hand with money or the priesthood. None of those clients have the same happiness and freedom that I do. They have been trapped by their desires; they are incredibly unhappy.'

After reflection, the young man adds, as if to put into perspective what he had just said: 'The difficulty of this job isn't sexual by nature; it isn't about having relations with somebody you don't love, or that you find ugly. The difficulty lies in having sex when you don't feel like it.'

Night has fallen on Naples now, and I have to catch my train to get back to Rome. Francesco Mangiacapra is smiling, visibly happy to have talked to me. We'll stay in touch, and I'll even agree to sign a short preface to the book that he will later publish about his experience as an 'escort'.

Thanks to this little book, Mangiacapra would have his hour of glory, recounting his experience on popular Italian television programmes. But we can only rely on his account.

As he leaves me, the young man suddenly wants to add something. 'I'm not judging anybody. I'm not judging those priests. I understand their choices and their situation. But I think it's sad. I'm transparent. I have no double life. I live in broad daylight, without hypocrisy. That isn't true of my clients. I think it's sad for them. I'm an atheist but I'm not anti-clerical. I'm not judging anybody. But what I'm doing is better than what priests do, isn't it? It's morally better, isn't it?'

René Buonocore, a social worker of Venezuelan origin, who lives and works in Rome, accompanied me to Naples to interview Mangiacapra, and he was also my guide in the homosexual places of the Roman night. Speaking five languages, he was part of the project 'Io Faccio l'attivo' (I'm active) of the Mobile Assistance Unit for sex workers in Rome. In this milieu, they use the expression 'MSM' (or Men who have Sex with Men), so as to include men who have relations with other men but don't recognize themselves as homosexual. According to Buonocore and other sources, the priests who are still in the closet tend to favour migrants or the anonymity of public parks rather than commercial establishments.

In Rome, they tend to frequent the area around the Villa Borghese, the streets surrounding the Villa Medici or the parks near the Coliseum and the Campidoglio. There, with my guide, I see people driving their cars near the National Gallery of Modern Art or walking, looking lost, on the shores of the lake of the Tempio di Esculapio. We also find the same fauna in the beautiful zigzag streets around Villa Giulia. I'm struck by the nocturnal peace of the places, the silence, the passing hours and, all of a sudden, the acceleration, an encounter, a passing car, a boy rushing to get in with a stranger. Sometimes violence.

If you go eastwards and cross the whole park, you happen on another 'corner' that is very prized by the 'MSM': the Villa Medici. Here the night-time scene is based essentially around Viale del Galoppaoio, a street as curly as the hair of young Tadzio in *Death in Venice*. It's a well-known cruising area where men generally circulate in cars.

There was a scandal that occurred in the setting of these streets, between the Villa Borghese and the Villa Medici. Several priests of the parish of the Church of Santa Teresa d'Avila were regular visitors to the area. The affair could have continued had not the lover of one of these priests, a homeless man, not recognized him saying mass. The case widened, and several other priests were also recognized by their parishioners. After a press scandal and a petition addressed by about a hundred churchgoers to the holy see, all of the priests concerned, and their superiors who had covered up the scandal, were moved to other parishes – and other parks.

The garden opposite the Coliseum, called Colle Oppio, was also an open-air cruising spot in the 1970s and 1980s (a gate has been installed in the last few years), as was the park at Via di Monte Caprino, behind the famous Piazza del Campidoglio designed by Michelangelo. One of the assistants to Jean Paul II was stopped there, according to police sources. A senior Dutch cleric who enjoyed a very high profile under John Paul II and Benedict XVI was also arrested in the little park by the Coliseum in the company of a young man – cases that were leaked anonymously to the press and later suppressed. (The names have been confirmed to me.)

One of the most influential bishops under John Paul II, a Frenchman, since made a cardinal, was also known for cruising in the parks around the Campidoglio: out of prudence, the cleric had refused to have his official car registered with Vatican diplomatic plates, to attract less attention. You never know!

Finally, one of the outside meeting places most highly prized by priests is none other than St Peter's Square: the Vatican is the only real 'gaybourhood' in Rome.

'In the 1960s and 1970s I remember that Bernini's columns in St Peter's were the cruising area for the people of the Vatican. The cardinals went out for a little walk and tried to meet *ragazzi*,' the literary specialist Francesco Gnerre tells me.

More recently, an American cardinal amused the Vatican with his attempts to stay fit: he systematically went jogging in shorts around the columns. Even today some prelates and monsignori have their habits: strolls at nightfall in a state of creative ascesis, perhaps the hope of impromptu encounters that might go further.

A phenomenon of which the wider public is largely unaware, the commercial homosexual relations in which Italian priests are involved constitute a very far-reaching system. They are one of the two options offered to practising ecclesiastics; the second being to cruise within the Church.

'A lot of people here in the Vatican have been seriously burned,' I am told in confidence by Don Julius, a confessor at St Peter's whom I meet several times in the 'Parlatorio'. (His name has been changed at his request.)

Sitting on a green velvet sofa, the priest adds: 'We often think that to talk freely about the Curia you have to go outside the Vatican. A lot of people think you have to hide. In fact, the easiest way to talk without being under surveillance is to do it here, in the very heart of the Vatican!'

Don Julius reveals the tangled lives of the inhabitants of *The Closet*, and sums up the alternative that is offered to so many priests: cruising inside or outside the Church.

In the first case, priests are among their own kind. They are interested in the co-religionists or the young seminarians who have just arrived from their Italian province. It's a cautious form of cruising, conducted in the bishops' palaces and sacristies of Rome; it shows social restraint, with priests undressing each other with their eyes. It's generally safer, since clergymen seldom run into laypeople in their chosen erotic life. This physical security has its downside: it inevitably leads to rumours, and sometimes to blackmail.

Robert Mickens, an American Vaticanologist, who is well-versed in the subtleties of gay life in the Vatican, believes that this is the option favoured by most cardinals and bishops, who would risk being recognized outside. Their rule: 'Don't fuck the flock', he tells me, a daring phrase with obviously biblical connotations (there are other variants in English: 'Don't screw the sheep' or 'Don't shag the sheep' – in other words, don't sleep with your people, the lost flock waiting for their shepherd).

So here we may talk in terms of 'extraterritorial' relations, because they take place outside of Italy, within the sovereign state of the holy see and its dependencies. This is the code of homosexuality 'on the inside'.

Homosexuality 'on the outside' is very different. It, on the contrary, is a matter of avoiding cruising within the religious world so as to escape rumours. Then gay night-life, public parks, saunas and prostitution are favoured by active gay priests. More dangerous, the homosexuality of commercial transactions, of dates with escorts and other kinds of escapades, are no less frequent. The risks are greater, but so are the benefits.

'Every evening priests have these two options,' Don Julius says, summing up the situation.

Vatican 'in', or Vatican 'out': both choices have their supporters, their practitioners and their experts, and both have their own codes. Sometimes priests hesitate for a long time – when they don't mix the two – between the dark, harsh world of external cruising, the city at night, its violence, its risks, its laws of desire, this '*Du côté de chez Swann*', the truly dark version of *The Closet*; and on the other hand there is the luminous world of interior cruising, with its worldliness, its subtleties, its games, the '*Côté de Guermantes*', which is a sunny version of *The Closet*, more dazzling and radiant, the version of caps and cassocks. In essence, whichever the path chosen, the 'way' one chooses to take in the Roman night is never that of a peaceful, orderly life.

It is in terms of this fundamental opposition that the story of the Vatican needs to be written, and that is the story I will tell in the chapters that follow, going back in time to the pontificate of Paul VI, and returning to the present day via those of John Paul II and Benedict XVI. This tension between a closet 'on the inside' and a closet 'on the outside' grants us an understanding of most of the workings of the holy see, because the rigidity of doctrine, the double lives of individuals, the atypical appointments, the countless intrigues, the moral scandals, are almost always inscribed in one or the other of these two codes.

After we had been talking for a long time in this Parlatorio inside the Vatican, only a few metres from Pope Francis's apartment, the confessor of St Peter's says to me: 'Welcome to *Sodoma*.'

Part II

Paul

PAUL VI

1963–1978

ALFREDO OTTAVIANI
Congregation for the Doctrine of Faith

JOHN MAGEE
PASQUALE MACCHI

Personal Secretary

JEAN VILLOT
Secretary of State

ANGELO DELL'ACQUA
GIOVANNI BENELLI
Secretary for Internal Affairs

ANTONIO SAMORÈ
AGOSTINO CASAROLI
Secretary for Relations with States

EDUARDO MARTÍNEZ SOMALO
Assessor

7

The Maritain Code

Cardinal Paul Poupard has one of the finest libraries in the Vatican: I counted 18 shelves on 11 levels. Made to measure, in an arc, it occupies the full length of a huge oval reception room.

'There are almost 15,000 books in all', Cardinal Poupard tells me with false modesty, receiving me in his slippers, surrounded by his folio volumes and autograph manuscripts, on one of my many visits.

The French cardinal lives on the top floor of a palace attached to the holy see, overlooking the Piazza di San Calisto, in the bobo district of Trastevere in Rome. The palace is vast; so is the apartment. Two Mexican nuns serve His Eminence, who sits in splendour like a prince in his castle.

Facing the library, the cardinal has his portrait on an easel. A large work, signed by a Russian artist, Natalia Tsarkova, for whom John Paul II and Benedict XVI have also sat. Cardinal Poupard spreads himself out magnificently, sitting on a high chair, one hand delicately stroking his chin, the other holding the pages of a handwritten speech. On his right ring finger: an episcopal ring decorated with a precious Veronese blue-green stone.

'The artist made me pose for almost two years. She wanted it to be perfect, and for my whole universe to fill the painting. You can see the books, the red biretta, it's very personal,' Poupard tells me. Before adding: 'I was a lot younger …'

Behind this Dorian Gray, whose model seems to have aged more quickly than his portrait, I notice two other paintings, hung more discreetly on the wall.

'They are two works by the French Catholic writer Jean Guitton, who gave them to me,' Poupard explains.

I look at the daubs. Interesting as the portrait on the easel is, the church-blue Guittons look like pallid Chagalls.

Using a green ladder, the cardinal is able to take down books of his choice from his panoramic library. He is showing off his own works and countless off-prints of articles from theological journals, which fill a whole shelf. We talk for a long time about the francophone authors that he likes: Jean Guitton, Jean Daniélou, François Mauriac. And when I mention the name of Jacques Maritain, the Catholic philosopher, Cardinal Poupard gets to his feet, shivering with delight. He walks towards a shelf to show me the complete works of the French philosopher.

'It was Paul VI who introduced Maritain to Poupard. It was on 6 December 1965, I remember very clearly.'

The cardinal is now talking about himself in the third person. At the start of our discussion I felt a vague unease: that I might be more interested in Maritain than in the work – oh, how significant! – of Poupard. And here he was joining in, without batting an eyelid.

We discuss at length the work of Maritain and his sometimes stormy relations with writers André Gide, Julien Green, François Mauriac and Jean Cocteau, and it occurs to me that all these French pre-war Christian writers were very gifted. They were also homosexual. All of them.

Now we've come back to stand in front of Jean Guitton's daubings, which Poupard studies as if searching them for a secret. He tells me he has kept almost two hundred letters from him: an unpublished correspondence that might itself contain plenty of secrets. Standing in front of Guitton's paintings, I ask Poupard about his mentor's sexuality. How is it that this erudite, secular and misogynist man, a member of the Académie française, essentially lived his life in chastity, on the model of Jacques Maritain, only late in life marrying a woman whom he very seldom spoke about, whom nobody saw very often, and who prematurely left him a widower, after which he never sought to remarry?

The cardinal launches into a continuous, Mephistophelian fit of the giggles, hesitates, and then says: 'Jean was made to have a wife, just as I was made to be a cobbler!' (He was in slippers.)

Then, suddenly serious, carefully weighing his words, he adds: 'We are all more complicated than we think. Behind the appearance of the straight line things are more complex.'

The cardinal, essentially so controlled and restrained, so guarded with his emotions, opens up for the first time. He adds: 'Continence, for Maritain, for Guitton, was their own way of coming to terms with things; that was how they did it. A personal matter, a long time ago.'

He won't say more than that. He guesses that he may have gone too far. And, performing a skilful pirouette, he boldly adds this quotation, which he will often repeat in the course of our regular conversations: 'As Pascal, my favourite author, would say: that's all of a different order.'

To understand the Vatican and the Catholic Church, at the time of Paul VI or today, Jacques Maritain is a good entry point. I have gradually discovered the importance of this codex, this complex and secret password, a real key to understand *The Closet*. The Maritain code.

Jacques Maritain was a French writer and philosopher who died in 1973. He is not well-known among the general public today, and his work seems dated. Nevertheless, his influence was considerable in the European religious life of the twentieth century, particularly in France and Italy, and it's a textbook example for our investigation.

This Catholic convert's books are still quoted by Popes Benedict XVI and Francis, and his closeness to two popes, John XXIII and Paul VI, is well-attested, and especially interesting for us.

'Paul VI saw himself as one of Maritain's disciples,' Poupard confirms to me.

The future pope Giovanni Montini, an enthusiastic reader of Maritain from 1925 onwards, even translated one of his books (*Three Reformers: Luther, Descartes, Rousseau*) and wrote the preface. Having become Pope Paul VI, he would remain very closely connected with the French theologian and philosopher, and even considered appointing Maritain a cardinal.

'I would like to put that rumour to bed once and for all. Paul VI was very fond of Maritain, but there was never any question of creating him a cardinal,' Poupard says, using a time-honoured phrase.

Definitely not a cardinal, then; but Maritain still charmed Paul VI. How can we explain that unusual influence? According to the witnesses I have interviewed, their relationship was not one of connivance or personal friendship, as would be the case between Paul VI and Jean Guitton: 'Maritainism' really exercised a lasting fascination on the Italian Church.

It would have to be said that Maritain's thought, focused on sin and concentrated on grace, illustrates a generous, albeit sometimes naïve Catholicism. The extreme piety of Jacques Maritain, his sincere faith, of admirable depth, set an example that impressed Rome. The political spirit of his work did the rest: in post-fascist Italy, Maritain defended the idea that democracy was the only legitimate political form. By doing so, he pointed the way towards the necessary rupture between Catholics and anti-Semitism and far-right extremism. This contributed to the reconciliation of Christians with democracy: in Italy it ushered in the way for a long companionship between the Vatican and Christian Democracy.

The former Curia priest Francesco Lepore confirms Maritain's influence on the Vatican: 'Maritain's work is sufficiently important to be studied even today in the pontifical universities. There are still "Maritain circles" in Italy. And a Maritain chair has even been recently inaugurated by the president of the Italian Republic.'

Cardinal Giovanni Battista Re, John Paul II's 'minister' of the interior, tells me of his passion for Maritain in the course of two meetings at the Vatican, echoing many other prelates who experienced something very similar: 'I have had little time in my life to read. But I have read Maritain, Daniélou, Congar, Mauriac's *Life of Christ*. When I was very young, I read all those authors. French was a second language for us. And Maritain was the point of reference.'

The same admiration is voiced by Cardinal Jean-Louis Tauran, 'minister' of foreign affairs under John Paul II, whom I interviewed four times in his office in Rome: 'Jacques Maritain and Jean Guitton had a very big influence here, at the Vatican. They were very close to Paul VI. And Maritain was quoted even more under John Paul II.'

However, an influential foreign diplomat at the holy see puts this attraction into perspective: 'Italian Catholics like the mystical side of Maritain, and appreciate his piety, but in the end they find him a bit fiery. The holy see has always been afraid of this fanatical layman!'

The Vice-Dean of the College of Cardinals, the Frenchman Roger Etchegaray, whom I will meet twice in his big apartment on Piazza di San Calisto in Rome, opens his eyes wide when I utter the code name.

'I knew Maritain well.'

The cardinal, who was for a long time John Paul II's 'flying' ambassador, pauses, offers me a chocolate and then adds, regaining his composure: 'Knowing. It's something that's impossible. You can't know someone. Only God truly knows us.'

Cardinal Etchegaray tells me he is going to take the Maritains with him to the house in the South of France to which he expects to retire, having put it off for 20 years: the Maritains, but also the books by Julien Green, François Mauriac, André Gide, Henry de Montherlant, and the works of Jean Guitton, of whom he too was a close friend. All of these authors are, without exception, homophilic or homosexual.

Suddenly Roger Etchegaray takes my hand with the pious affection of figures in a Caravaggio. 'Do you know how old I am?' the cardinal asks me.

'I think I do, yes …'

'I'm 94. You wouldn't believe it, would you? Ninety-four years old. At my age, my reading, my ambitions, my plans are rather limited.'

The enduring influence of Maritain took root with his theological and political thought, but it also fed on the example of his life. At the heart of the Maritain mystery is his marriage to Raïssa, his wife, and the secret pact that united them. The meeting between Jacques and Raïssa was built initially on a spectacular double conversion to Catholicism: he was Protestant; she was Jewish. United by a passionate love, their marriage was neither loveless nor one of convenience. It wasn't a bourgeois marriage, nor a substitute marriage, even though Maritain perhaps wanted to use it to escape loneliness, and what is sometimes called 'the sadness of men without women'.

From this point of view, the marriage recalls that of writers like Paul Verlaine, Louis Aragon or, later, Jean Guitton. It also echoes the famous marriage of André Gide to his cousin Madeleine, which he seems never to have consummated: 'Gide's wife replaced his mother as a symbol of the pole of restraint to which he always had to be able to return, and without which his other pole of joy, liberation, perversion, would have lost all meaning', wrote George Painter, Gide's biographer. The author of *The Vatican Cellars* therefore balanced freedom with constraint.

For Maritain there were also two poles: that of his wife Raïssa, and a second world, not of perversion, but of friendly 'inclinations'. Not having yielded to 'Evil', the devil would tempt him through the virtue of friendship.

Jacques and Raïssa formed an ideal couple – but one without sex for most of their lives. That *trompe-l'oeil* heterosexuality wasn't only a religious choice, as was believed for a long time. In 1912, the Maritains decided to take a vow of chastity together, one which remained secret for a long time. Is the sacrifice of bodily desire a gift to God? The price of salvation? It's possible. The Maritains talked about 'spiritual companionship'. They said they 'wanted to help one another to go towards God'. Behind this almost Catharist version of relations between the sexes one might also see a popular choice of the times: the one favoured by many homophiles. Because Maritain's entourage included an incredible number of homosexuals.

Throughout his life, Maritain was a man of great 'loving friendships' with the biggest homosexual figures of his century: he was the friend or confidant of Jean Cocteau, Julien Green, Max Jacob, René Crevel and Maurice Sachs, but also of François Mauriac, a 'closeted' writer whose true amorous inclinations, not merely sublimated, were left in no doubt after the publication of the important biography by Jean-Luc Barré.

In their house in Meudon, Jacques and Raïssa Maritain constantly received celibate Catholics, homosexual intellectuals and handsome young men with the most effusive hospitality. With the sort of air of wisdom that his effeminate entourage loved so much, the philosopher discoursed endlessly about homosexual sin, exclaiming 'I love you' to his young friends, whom he called his 'godsons' – having chosen not to have a sex life with his wife, and hence to be childless.

Homosexuality was an obsession of Maritain's. The friend of Paul VI kept returning to the subject, as is revealed by his now-published correspondence. Certainly, he did so in a detached and, we might say, 'Ratzingerian' way. Maritain wished to save the gays he invited into his coterie in Meudon to protect them from 'Evil'. Self-hatred, probably; but concern for others too, sincere and honest. *Autres temps.*

Counter-intuitively, this fanatical Catholic was barely interested in more orthodox Catholics, the ones who were more heterosexual: he certainly corresponded regularly with the Jesuit priest Henri de Lubac, a future cardinal, and less regularly with the writer Paul Claudel; he also knew Georges Bernanos professionally, but his passionate friendships with such people were rare.

On the other hand, Maritain didn't miss a single major homosexual figure of his time. What a remarkable 'gaydar' he must have had, as we would say today. It's a fact that Maritain specialized in homophilic friendships on the pretext of trying to bring some of the greatest 'introvert' writers of the twentieth century back to faith and chastity. And to keep these writers from sin and possibly hell – because in those days the homosexual condition still had a whiff of sulphur about it – Maritain set about watching over them, 'sorting out their problem', as he put it, which required him to spend an enormous amount of time with them! So it was that André Gide, Julien Green, Jean Cocteau, François Mauriac, Raymond Radiguet and Maurice Sachs engaged in dialogue with him, like almost all the great homosexuals of the day. In passing, he tried to convert them and make them chaste; and we know that conversion and continence, as a bid to repress inclinations of this kind, remained a classical attitude until the late 1960s.

The implications of this debate for our subject are considerable. We cannot understand Popes John XXIII, Paul VI or Benedict XVI, or most of the cardinals in the Roman Curia, if we do not decipher 'Maritainism' as a sublimated intimate precept. In Italy, where Maritain, as well as Catholic and homosexual literatures, have had considerable influence, the whole of the Vatican hierarchy knows the subject by heart.

One of the most important historians of gay literature in Italy, Professor Francesco Gnerre, who has published important texts about writers including Dante, Leopardi and Pasolini, explained this curious state of affairs to me during several discussions in Rome.

'Unlike France, which had Rimbaud and Verlaine, Marcel Proust, Jean Cocteau and Jean Genet, and many others, homosexual literature barely existed in Italy until 1968. The first time homosexuality appeared on the front page of the newspapers there was in the 1970s, with Pasolini, let's say. Until then, Italian homosexuals had to content themselves with reading French publications. It was a bit the same for Italian Catholics, who for a long time read the French Catholics, so influential here. But what is absolutely extraordinary is that they are exactly the same writers!'

Let's go into detail here. We have to, because the secret of *The Closet* is based on this 'Maritain code' and the battles that set Jacques Maritain against four major French writers: André Gide, Jean Cocteau, Julien Green and Maurice Sachs.

With Gide, to begin with, the debate fizzled out. Maritain's correspondence with the Protestant Gide, Gide's *Diaries*, and a long meeting between the two men late in 1923, attest that Maritain wanted to keep the great writer from publishing *Corydon*, a brave treatise in which Gide revealed himself and expounded militant views over four dialogues about homosexuality. So Maritain went to his house to beg him in the name of Christ not to publish. He was also worried about the salvation of his soul after the publication of the book, which amounted to a confession of his homosexuality. Gide saw it coming from a long way off. And since his rule for life, which was at the heart of the morality of his *Fruits of the Earth*, was to cease to resist temptation, he had no intention of losing his freedom to yield to the pleadings of this grumpy preacher.

'I hate lying,' Gide replied to him. 'That's probably where my Protestantism takes refuge. Catholics don't like the truth.'

Maritain made numerous attempts to prevent the writer from publishing his little treatise. To no avail. A few months after their encounter, André Gide, who had long accepted his homosexuality in private, published *Corydon* under his real name. Jacques Maritain, like François Mauriac, was terrified. They would never forgive Gide for 'coming out'.

The second battle was fought against Jean Cocteau, on the same subject. Maritain had been friends with Cocteau for a long time, and his grip was tighter on the young convert writer than it was on the great Protestant one. Besides, in Meudon, Cocteau still seemed well-behaved and a conscientious Catholic. But when he was far from Maritain, he had many lovers, including the young Raymond Radiguet, whom he finally introduced to Maritain. Strangely, the man from Meudon, rather than rejecting this viscerally unnatural homosexual relationship, attempted to tame Cocteau's young lover. Radiguet, a literary prodigy who had written his novella *The Devil in the Flesh* at the age of 20, and would die shortly afterwards of typhoid fever, would say of this period, in a lovely phrase: 'When you didn't marry, you converted.'

But Maritain failed again. Jean Cocteau took the big step of publishing, first anonymously and then under his real name, his *White Book*, in which he confessed his homosexuality.

'This project is diabolical,' Maritain wrote to him. 'It's the first time you have publicly declared your adherence to Evil. Remember Wilde and the degradation that lasted until his death. Jean, it's your salvation that is at stake, it's your soul that I have to defend. Between the devil and me, choose whom you love. If you love me, you will not publish this book and you will let me look after the manuscript.'

'I need love, and to make love with souls,' was Cocteau's brazen reply.

The White Book would indeed be published. The incomprehension between the two men would deepen further, but their relationship of 'loving friendship', suspended for a moment, continued in spite of everything, as their correspondence attests. During a recent visit to the Dominican monastery in Toulouse, where Jacques Maritain spent the last years of his life, Brother Jean-Miguel Garrigues confirmed to me that Jean Cocteau had continued to visit Maritain until his death.

The third battle went better for Maritain, although it too ended with his defeat by Julien Green. For almost forty-five years the two men engaged in a regular correspondence. Mystical and deeply religious, their dialogue played out at sublime heights. But here again its dynamic was based on a 'wound': that of homosexuality. Julien Green was haunted by his male desire, which he had experienced since his youth as a hazard that was difficult to reconcile with the love of God. Maritain guessed Green's secret even though he never explicitly mentioned it during the first few decades of their correspondence. Neither of them named the 'inclination', which ate away at them even as they beat diligently around the bush.

Maritain, himself a convert, admired Julien Green for his conversion in 1916, which was the result of the 'campaign' of a Dominican who believed that the priesthood was the solution to homosexuality (we have since discovered that this priest was also gay). Maritain admired the writer for his continence, which was all the more admirable in that he used faith to resist his inclination.

Over the years, however, Julien Green evolved, and in the end he took the crucial step: he began by revealing himself in his work, which became openly homosexual (I'm thinking of *South*, his greatest book), and also started living out his romances in broad daylight, as is attested by his *Diaries*, and by accounts given by his known lovers. (The unexpurgated *Journal* of Julien Green appeared in 2019: it reveals the obsessive and active homosexuality of Green, his evenings of debauchery and his use of prostitutes. His language is crude, often lewd, but always explicit. Also mentioned is his relationship with his regular 'friend' which he claimed was 'chaste', but which in fact he describes in a lascivious manner.)

The fourth battle, which he also lost – and what a defeat! – was fought with his true friend, the tetchy writer of the inter-war years, Maurice Sachs. A Jewish convert to Catholicism, Sachs was close to Maritain, whom he called 'darling Jacques'. But he was also an enthusiastic young homosexual. He prayed, but he couldn't help being a scandalous seminarian because of his poisonous special friendships. In his novel *The Sabbath* the narrator, who tells his friends that he has gone to the 'Seminary', is asked whether this is a new gay club! The literary critic Angelo Rinaldi would write of Maurice Sachs: 'An abbot by turn in a cassock and pink underwear ... takes refuge in a sauna cabin where he spends happy days as a gluttonous fellating baby.' Sachs would soon be drawn into every available moral abyss; after 1940 this protégé of Jacques Maritain would become a collaborator and Pétainist, and, even though he was Jewish, he would end up as a Nazi informer before dying, probably shot at the edge of a ditch with a bullet to the back of the neck, by an SS officer in 1944 – an unthinkable way of life, all in all.

Those four battles lost by Jacques Maritain reveal, among other facts, the philosopher's obsession with homosexuality. Maritain's relationship with the gay question is, in my eyes, more than a confession.

Here I am using the word 'gay' on purpose, as a deliberate anachronism. If we must always prefer the words specific to their own time – and for that reason I use the concepts of 'loving friendship', 'homophilia' or 'inclinations' when necessary – we must also sometimes call things by their names. For too long it was written in school textbooks that Rimbaud and Verlaine were 'friends' or 'companions', and even today I read in the Vatican museums signs describing Antinous as Emperor Hadrian's 'favourite', when in fact he was his lover. Here the anachronistic use of the word 'gay' is politically fruitful.

Apart from Christ or St Thomas Aquinas, the other great preoccupation of Jacques Maritain's life was therefore the gay question. If he probably didn't practise homosexuality, or did so very little, he experienced it with the same frantic anxiety as his Catholic faith. And that's Maritain's secret, and one of the most hidden secrets of the Catholic priesthood: the choice of celibacy and chastity as the product of sublimation or repression.

Because how did Maritain socialize with all the gay writers of his era, those 'sublime national queens' of literature (to quote another phrase of Angelo Rinaldi), when he hated homosexuality so much? Was he a homophobe? Was he a voyeur? Was he fascinated by his opposite, as has been suggested? I don't believe that these hypotheses are genuinely convincing. The truth is much simpler.

Maritain's confession is found in a letter to Julien Green from 1927. Here the terms of the dialogue appear to be reversed: while Julien Green was still tormented by the sin of homosexuality, it was Jacques Maritain who, in their correspondence, seems to have found the solution for what he called 'this mysterious evil'.

And what does he suggest to Green? Chastity. Faced with the 'sterile love' of homosexuality, 'which will always remain an evil, a profound rejection of the cross', Maritain defends the 'only solution' in his eyes, 'the love of God above all', that is: abstinence. The remedy he offered Green, already prescribed for Gide, Cocteau and Maurice Sachs, who rejected it, was the one that he and Raïssa had chosen: the sublimation of the sexual act by faith and chastity.

'Nowhere does the gospel tell us to mutilate our heart, but it advises us to make ourselves eunuchs for the kingdom of God. That is how the question appears in my eyes,' he wrote to Julien Green.

Settling the question of homosexuality through chastity, this form of castration, to give pleasure to God: Maritain's idea, with its hint of masochism, is a powerful one. It would find acceptance among a majority of post-war cardinals and bishops. 'Remaining king of one's griefs,' Louis Aragon would have said, another brilliant writer who noisily sang in public of 'the eyes' of his wife Elsa, so that he could then, in private, pursue boys.

In a letter to Cocteau, Maritain makes another clear confession: the love of God is the only one that can make us forget the earthly loves that one has known and, 'although it is hard for me to say this, I know it otherwise than through books'.

'Otherwise than through books'? We guess that the question of homosexuality was a burning one in the youth of Jacques Maritain, a man who was in any case effeminate and sensitive, devoted to his mother to the point of caricature, and that he preferred to destroy his private notebooks to ensure that his biographers 'didn't venture too far' or discover some 'old personal affair' (in the words of his biographer Jean-Luc Barré).

'I didn't want to put that word, that label of "homosexuality", in my biography of Maritain, because everyone would have boiled my book down to that,' Barré tells me over lunch in Paris. 'But I should have done. If I wrote it today, I would say things more clearly about this. With regard to Maritain one can probably speak of homosexuality that is latent if not quite real.'

The great love of Jacques Maritain's youth was named Ernest Psichari. The two young men were still teenagers when they met at the Lycée Henri IV in Paris in 1899 (Jacques was 16). It was love at first sight. A 'loving friendship' of unimaginable power blossomed between them. Unique and indestructible, their bond was a 'great wonder', as Maritain put it to his mother. To his father, Ernest confided: 'I could no longer conceive of life without Jacques' friendship; it would be to conceive of me without myself.' This passion was 'fatal', Maritain wrote in another letter.

Their passionate relationship is quite well-known today. Recently published, the correspondence between the two young boys – 175 love letters – even creates a sense of vertigo: 'I feel that our two unknowns penetrate each other gently, timidly, slowly,' Maritain writes. 'Ernest, you are my friend. You alone'; 'Your eyes are resplendent beams. Your hair is a virgin forest, full of whispering and kisses'; 'I love you, I live, I think of you'; 'It is in you, in you only that I live'; 'You are Apollo. (…) Will you leave with me for the Orient, all the way to India? We will be alone in the desert'; 'I love you, I kiss you'; 'Your letters, my jewel, give me infinite pleasure and I reread them ceaselessly. I am in love with all of your letters, your a's, your d's, your n's and your r's.' And like Rimbaud and Verlaine, these two lovers signed their poems by uniting their initials.

Was this total fusion with the loved one consummated, or did it remain chaste? We don't know. Yves Floucat, a Thomist philosopher and specialist in the work of Maritain and Julien Green and co-founder of the Centre Jacques Maritain, whom I interviewed at his house in Toulouse, thinks it was probably a 'passionate but chaste friendship'. He adds, although of course he has no proof either of their having a physical relationship or of the opposite, that it was a 'true love between people of the same sex'.

Brother Jean-Miguel Garrigues of the Dominican monastery where Maritain ended his days, and whom I also interviewed in Toulouse, explains: 'The relationship between Jacques and Ernest was deeper than simple companionship. I would say that it was *loving* rather than amorous, in the sense that it was led more by the heart's wish to help the other be happy than by emotional or carnal desire. For Jacques, it was more of the order of "loving friendship" than homophilia, if we see it as a more or less sublimated desire of the libido. Ernest, on the other hand, had an active homosexual life over the years.'

Today, in fact, there is no longer any doubt about Psichari's practising homosexuality: it is confirmed by a recent biography, by the publication of his 'travel diaries' and by the appearance of new witness statements. His homosexuality was even very active: he had countless intimate liaisons in Africa – *à la* Gide – and resorted to male prostitutes until his death.

In a correspondence that remained unpublished for a long time, between Jacques Maritain and the Catholic writer Henri Massis, Ernest Psichari's two best friends explicitly acknowledge his homosexuality. Massis was even worried that 'the terrible truth [would be] revealed one day'.

We would have to say that André Gide had no hesitation in 'outing' Psichari in an article in the *Nouvelle Revue Française* in September 1932. The Catholic writer Paul Claudel, who was very saddened by this revelation, proposed a counter-attack that he had already used in relation to Arthur Rimbaud: if Ernest converted when he was homosexual, it was a marvellous victory for God. And Claudel summed up the argument: 'God's work is all the more admirable in such a soul.'

Still, Ernest Psichari died in combat at the age of 31, killed by a German bullet to the temple on 22 August 1914. Jacques learned the news several weeks later. According to his biographer, the news of Ernest's death left him in a state of shock, stupor and grief. Jacques Maritain never got over the death of his loved one, and never managed to forget the great love of his youth – before Christ, and before Raïssa. Years later he would set off on his travels all the way to Africa, following his lover's path; he went on seeing Ernest's sister and during the Second World War he wanted to fight so that he could 'die like Psichari'. All his life, Jacques would constantly mention his love and, having lost his Eurydice, he would speak of the 'desert of life' after Ernest's death. A sorrow that he felt, in fact, 'otherwise than through books'.

In order to understand the very particular sociology of Catholicism, and particularly that of the Vatican on my subject, we must therefore rely on what I choose here to call the 'Maritain code'. Sublimated, if not repressed, homosexuality is often translated into the choice of celibacy and chastity, and, even more often, into an internalized homophobia. Indeed, most popes, cardinals and bishops who are over the age of 60 today grew up in the atmosphere and the way of thinking of the 'Maritain code'.

If the Vatican is a theocracy, it is also a gerontocracy. One cannot understand the Church from Paul VI to Benedict XVI, indeed even that of Francis, their cardinals, their morals or their intrigues in terms of contemporary gay lifestyles. In order to grasp their complexity, we must therefore return to old templates, even if they seem to us to be those of another age. An age in which one was not homosexual but 'homophilic'; in which homosexual identity was distinguished from the practices to which it could give rise; a time when bisexuality was commonplace; a secret world in which marriages of convenience were the rule and gay couples the exception. A time when continence and the heterosexual celibacy of priests were embraced with joy by the young homosexuals of the Vatican.

It is certain that the priesthood was a natural choice for men who imagined they had unnatural morals. But careers and lifestyles vary greatly between mystical chastity, spiritual crises, double lives, sometimes sublimation, fanaticism or perversions. In all cases, a general feeling of insecurity remains, well-described by homosexual French Catholic writers and their 'perpetual balance between the boys whose beauty damns them, and God whose goodness absolves them' (another phrase from Angelo Rinaldi).

That's why the context, while it might have the charm of theological and literary debates of another age, is so important to our subject. A sexless priest in the 1930s could easily become homophilic in the 1950s and actively practise homosexuality in the 1970s. Some cardinals currently working have passed through those stages, the internalization of desire, the struggle against themselves, homophilia, and then, soon, they stopped 'sublimating' or 'surmounting' their homosexuality, and they began to experience it with prudence, soon with temerity and sometimes even in a state of intoxication. Of course, these same cardinals who have by now reached a canonical age barely 'practise' at 75 or 80, but they remain intrinsically marked, branded for ever, by that complex identity. Most importantly, they have always travelled a one-way journey, contrary to the theories that some have erected: it goes from denial to defiance, or to put it in the terms used by Proust in *Sodom and Gomorrah*, the rejection of the 'cursed race' in favour of the 'chosen people'. And this is another rule of *The Closet*, the ninth: *The homophiles of the Vatican generally move from chastity towards homosexuality; homosexuals never go into reverse gear and become homophilic.*

As the theologian-psychoanalyst Eugen Drewermann observed, there is 'a kind of secret complicity between the Catholic Church and homosexuality'. I will often come across this dichotomy in the Vatican, and we might even say that it is one of its secrets: the violent rejection of homosexuality outside of the Church; its extravagant endorsement within the holy see. Hence a sort of 'gay freemasonry' that is very much present within the Vatican, but mysterious if not invisible outside it.

In the course of my investigation, countless cardinals, archbishops, monsignori and other priests insisted on telling me of their almost religious devotion to the works of François Mauriac, André Gide or Julien Green. Prudently, and being sparing with their words, they gave me the keys to their heart-rending struggle: that of the 'Maritain code'. I guess that it was their way, with infinite meekness and a certain introverted anxiety, of revealing one of the secrets that haunted them.

8

Loving friendship

The first time I met Archbishop Jean-Louis Bruguès at the Vatican, I committed an unforgivable error. It's true that the ranks and titles of the Roman Curia sometimes get muddled: they vary according to the dicasteries (ministries), the hierarchy, the orders and sometimes other criteria. Some people have to be addressed as 'Eminence' (a cardinal), others as 'Excellency' (an archbishop, a bishop), and still others as 'Monsignor' (the ones who are more than a priest but less than a bishop). Sometimes a prelate is plain father, sometimes brother, and sometimes a bishop. And how do we address the nuncios who have the title of archbishop? Not to mention the 'monsignori', an honorific title attributed to prelates but also to simple priests?

So when I prepared for an interview with Cardinal Bertone, who was Benedict XVI's 'prime minister', his personal assistant, taking the lead, explained to me by email that I would be well-advised to address him, when I saw him, with the phrase 'His Eminence Cardinal Bertone'.

For me these titles have become a code and a game. For a Frenchman, the words have a whiff of monarchy and aristocracy – and when those got too big for their boots we chopped their heads off! In my conversations at the Vatican, out of mischief, I took pleasure in oafishly adding extra ones, in a spirit of mock deference. I also stuffed my many letters to the holy see full of them, adding by hand, in beautiful gothic script, these meaningless phrases to which I would add a monogram stamp, a number, a heraldic signature at the bottom of my missives – and it seemed to me that the replies to my requests were more positive the more I used pedantic titles and brown ink stamps. And yet nothing could be more alien to me than these vain formulas, which belong to the etiquette of another time. Had I dared, I would have perfumed my dispatches!

Their replies were delicious epistles. All headed paper, fat signatures in blue ink and gushing endearments ('*Pregiatissimo Signore Martel*', Angelo Sodano wrote to me), almost always written in impeccable French, they contained obsequious formulations: 'I wish you a fine ascent towards Easter,' Mgr Battista Ricca wrote to me; 'In the hope of greeting you in Urbe in the near future,' said Mgr Fabrice Rivet; 'Assuring you of my prayers,' wrote Archbishop Rino Fisichella; 'With the assurance of my prayers in Christ,' declared Darío Castrillón Hoyos (who is now no longer with us); 'Please accept my very best wishes in Christ,' Cardinal Robert Sarah signed off. Cardinal Óscar Maradiaga, my friend after two letters, replied to me in Spanish: '*Le deseo una devota Semana Santa y una feliz Pascua de Resurrección, su amigo* [I wish you a devout Holy Week and a Happy Easter of Resurrection, my friend]'. Even more chummily, the Cardinal of Naples, Crescenzio Sepe, sent off a letter in which he addressed me with a friendly '*Gentile Signore*', before concluding with a cool '*cordiali saluti*'. Mgr Fabián Pedacchio, Francis's personal assistant, concluded his missive thus: 'Warmly recommending the pope to your prayers, please accept the assurance of my devotion in the Lord.' I have kept dozens of letters of this ilk.

Happy these letter-writers of another age! Few cardinals use email in 2019; many still prefer to use the mail, and some the fax. Sometimes their assistants print out the emails they receive for them; they reply by hand on paper; scanned and mailed instantly to their addressee!

Most of these cardinals still live in a power-play worthy of the Renaissance. Hearing myself saying 'Your Eminence' to a cardinal has always made me laugh internally; and I like the simplicity of Pope Francis, who wanted to get rid of those pretentious titles. Because isn't it strange for a bunch of simple Curia employees to be called 'monsignore'? For some poor closeted nuncios to cling to their title as 'Excellencies'? For cardinals to take people more seriously if they call them 'Your Eminence'? If I was in their place, I would prefer to be called '*signore*'. Or rather: Angelo, Tarcisio or Jean-Louis!

As we have observed, in this book I have decided, as a good son of French *laïcité*, not always to follow the Vatican conventions. I have just written 'holy see' and not 'Holy See'; and I always speak of the holy father, the holy virgin, the supreme pontiff – without capitals. I never say 'His Holiness', and I write 'the holy of holies'. When I write 'His Eminence', the irony should be obvious. Neither do I use the title 'Saint' John Paul II, particularly after shedding light on the double games of his entourage! French *laïcité*, so little understood in Rome – and even, alas, by Francis – consists in respecting all religions, but not giving any one of them a particular status. On the other hand, I do write 'the Poet' – which in this book always refers to Rimbaud – with a capital! Luckily, in France we believe more in poetry than in religion.

With Monsignor Bruguès I used the appropriate word, 'Excellency', but added, immediately afterwards, that I was happy to meet a French cardinal. A serious rookie error! Jean-Louis Bruguès let me speak without interruption and then, as he answered, he slipped in, between two minor observations, with an anodyne and falsely modest expression on his face, as if his title were of no importance, though he was clearly inwardly wounded: 'Besides, I'm not a cardinal. It's not automatic. I'm just an archbishop.' He spoke with a lovely south-west French accent, which immediately made me warm to him.

I had come to interview Bruguès, on that first occasion, for a radio programme, and I promised I would erase those words from the recording. After that, we saw each other often to chat or exchange ideas, and I never made the same mistake again. I've found out that for a long time he was on the short list to be 'created' cardinal, taking into account his closeness to Pope Benedict XVI, which was why he had coordinated the delicate passages about homosexuality in the *New Catechism of the Catholic Church*. But the pope had resigned. And his successor, Francis, never forgave Archbishop Bruguès, when Bruguès was secretary general of the Congregation for Catholic Education, for crossing swords with him over the appointment of his friend as rector of Buenos Aires University. So he missed being appointed cardinal. (In 2018, when he had reached the end of his mandate and the pope didn't reappoint him head of the library, Bruguès left Rome.)

'The holy father never forgets anything. He's rancorous; if one has upset him one day, or merely rubbed him up the wrong way, he remembers it for a long time. Bruguès won't be created cardinal as long as Bergoglio is pope,' a French archbishop gives me to understand.

For a long time Jean-Louis Bruguès ran the famous Biblioteca Apostolica Vaticana and the no less famous Secret Vatican Archives. In this library, they religiously preserve the Vatican 'codices', the old books, invaluable papyruses, incunabula, or a vellum copy of the Gutenberg Bible.

'We're one of the oldest and wealthiest libraries in the world. In total we have 54 kilometres of printed books and 87 kilometres of archives,' Bruguès tells me: he is plainly a stickler for accuracy.

Cardinal Raffaele Farina, whom I interviewed several times at his home in the Vatican, and who was Bruguès' predecessor in the secret archives, gives me to understand that the most sensitive files, on sexual abuses for example, are in fact kept at the Secretariat of State: the inoffensive secret archives are only secret in terms of their name. (In passing, Farina takes advantage of our meeting to level an accusation at the commission in charge of the fight against paedophilia in the holy see, which 'is doing nothing'.)

Father Urien, who worked for a long time in those archives, is even more categorical (his name has been altered): 'All the reports on the financial scandals at the Vatican, all the cases of paedophilia, all the files on homosexuality, including everything we know about Paul VI, are kept at the Secretariat of State. If those documents had been made public, popes, cardinals and bishops might have been troubled by the law. The archives aren't just the dark face of the Church. It's the devil!'

During our five conversations, Archbishop Bruguès is extremely cautious, although our dialogues focus essentially on literature – he is a passionate reader of Proust, François Mauriac, Jean Guitton, Henry de Montherlant, Tony Duvert, Christopher Isherwood; he's travelled to Valparaíso in the footsteps of Pierre Loti; he knew Jacques Maritain at the Dominican monastery in Toulouse; and he had a long correspondence with Julien Green.

'The recent archives aren't open,' Bruguès goes on. 'They do it chronologically, by papacy, and only the holy father can decide to make a new period public. We are currently opening up the archives of Pius XII, those of the Second World War.'

Paul VI will have to wait for a while.

Is there a secret Paul VI? Rumours about the homosexuality of the man who was pope for 15 years – between 1963 and 1978 – are countless, and I've discussed them very freely with several cardinals. Someone who had access to the secret archives of the secretary of state even assures me that there are several files on the subject. But they aren't public, and we don't know what they contain.

To grasp in all their complexity the mysteries surrounding this pope, we must therefore be counter-intuitive. For want of evidence, it's important to go through the whole body of evidence all at once: Paul VI's reading matter, the essence of the 'Code Maritain', are one such article of evidence; his friendships with Maritain, but also with Charles Journet and Jean Daniélou, are another; his spectacularly homophilic entourage at the Vatican, yet another. And then there is Jean Guitton. In the complex skein of particular inclinations, loving friendships and passions of this literate and Francophile pope, one single constant appears.

The reader, by now, knows enough already. He may even be weary of these drip-fed confessions, these encrypted codes for saying things that are ultimately banal. And yet I have to come back to them again, because everything here has its own significance and these details, as in a great treasure hunt, will soon lead us, after Paul VI, to the heart of the troubling pontificate of John Paul II and the great Ratzingerian firework display. But let's not jump ahead of ourselves …

A right-wing French Catholic writer, Jean Guitton (1901–99) was born in and died with the twentieth century. A prolific author, he was a friend of Maritain, but also of the openly homosexual Jean Cocteau. His career during the Second World War remains to be written, but we may guess that he was a close collaborator and a lackey of Marshal Pétain. His theological work is minor, like his philosophical work, and his books have been almost completely forgotten today. The only survivor of this literary shipwreck consists of a few famous interviews with President François Mitterrand, and indeed with Pope Paul VI.

'Jean Guitton has never been taken very seriously in France. He was a theologian for the Catholic middle class. His closeness to Paul VI remains something of a mystery,' the editor-in-chief of *Esprit*, Jean-Louis Schlegel, observes during an interview at the journal's offices.

An Italian cardinal completes the picture, but I can't tell whether he's talking naively or whether he is trying to convey a message to me: 'Jean Guitton's work barely exists in Italy. He was a weakness of Paul VI, a very special friendship.'

The same point of view comes from Cardinal Poupard, who was his friend for a long time.

'Jean Guitton was an excellent writer, but not really a thinker.' In spite of the superficiality of his work, the friendship that Guitton was able to form with Pope Paul VI is certainly based on a commonality of views, in particular about the subject of moral standards and sexual morality. Two historical texts reveal this connection. The first is the encyclical *Humanae vitae*, published in 1968: it concerns marriage and contraception, and has become famous under the unflattering name of the 'encyclical on the pill' because it definitively forbade its use, making it a rule that any sexual act must make the transmission of life possible.

The second text is no less famous: this is the 'declaration' *Persona humana* of 29 December 1975. This crucial text expressly set about stigmatizing 'the relaxation of morals': it advocates strict chastity before marriage (at the time, the fashion was for 'juvenile cohabitation', and the Church wanted to put an end to it), severely condemned masturbation ('an intrinsically and gravely disorderly act'), and proscribed homosexuality. 'For according to the objective moral order, homosexual relations are acts which lack an essential and indispensable finality. In Sacred Scripture they are condemned as a serious depravity and even presented as the sad consequence of rejecting God.'

Major texts and yet texts that quickly became anachronistic. Even at the time they were badly received by the scientific community, since they ignored all of its biological, medical and psychoanalytical discoveries, and even more so by public opinion. The Catholic Church suddenly appeared violently opposed to the trends in society, and from then on its distance from the real life of the faithful would constantly grow. These archaic rules would never be understood by most Catholics: they would be massively ignored or mocked by new couples and young people, and roundly rejected by the great majority of the faithful.

There was even talk, where they were concerned, of a 'silent schism' that would lead to a drop in vocations and a collapse in Catholic practice.

'The mistake was not to speak out about sexual morality,' a cardinal I interviewed in Rome says regretfully. 'It was desirable, and remains desired by the majority of Christians. The humanization of sexuality, to take up a phrase from Benedict XVI, is a theme about which the Church needed to say something. The error: setting the bar too high, if I can put it like that, and being disconnected and inaudible, the Church has put itself outside the debates on sexual morality. A hard-line position on abortion would also have been better understood had it been accompanied by a flexible position on contraception. By advocating chastity for young people, divorced couples or homosexuals, the Church stopped talking to its own people.'

Today, we know from witness statements and archive documents that the prohibition on the pill, and perhaps the other moral condemnations of masturbation, homosexuality and the celibacy of the priesthood, were discussed at length. According to historians, the hard line was held by a minority, but Paul VI took his decision alone, *ex cathedra*. He did so by rallying the conservative wing embodied by the old cardinal Ottaviani and a newcomer: Cardinal Wojtyła, the future Pope John Paul II, who played a belated but decisive role in this spectacular hardening of the Church's sexual morality. Jean Guitton, a militant advocate of heterosexual chastity, also argued for keeping celibacy among priests.

Many theologians and experts that I have met reproach Pope Paul VI, whose ideas were so non-heterodox, for 'taking a hard line' for bad reasons, whether strategic or personal. They have pointed out to me that celibacy is a value that has been historically defended in the Church by its homophilic and homosexual components. According to one of these theologians: 'Few heterosexual priests place value on heterosexual abstinence; it's essentially an idea put forward by homosexuals, or at least people who have profoundly interrogated their own sexuality.' Is Paul VI's gentle secret revealed in broad daylight by the choice of the celibacy of the priesthood? A lot of people think so today.

Such a priority, out of line with the times, teaches us about the Vatican's state of mind. It also invites us to probe a quasi-sociological observation, established since at least the Middle Ages (if we believe the historian John Boswell), and which is a new rule of *The Closet* – the tenth: *Homosexual priests and theologians are much more inclined to impose priestly celibacy than their heterosexual co-religionists. They are very concerned to have this vow of chastity respected, even though it is intrinsically against nature.*

The most fervent advocates of the vow of chastity are therefore, of course, the most suspicious. And it is here that the dialogue between Paul VI and Jean Guitton comes to the fore as a veritable contemporary drama.

The theme of chastity was a recurrent preoccupation among the homosexual writers that we have discussed, from François Mauriac to Julien Green, not to mention Jacques Maritain, but it reaches an insane level in Guitton.

Coming from a middle-class Catholic family in which 'you keep your distance', Jean Guitton never discussed his private life in public, with the result that it remained mysterious for a long time. This puritan aesthete did not display his emotions, and even though he was a layman he did not speak of his amorous experiences. The witnesses I have spoken to confirm that Jean Guitton was not greatly interested in women. He thought they were 'decorative' or 'ornamental', as the misogynist characters in *The Picture of Dorian Gray* put it.

But he did get married, late in life, to Marie-Louise Bonnet. In his autobiography, *Un siècle, une vie* (A Century, a Life), he devoted a chapter to his wife, which once again reveals a high level of misogyny: 'I had been looking for an angel to keep the house tidy and do the dusting. The angel appeared in the form of Marie-Louise, who taught art history and home economics at a lycée in Montpellier.' They lived 'like brother and sister', according to the expression he is supposed to have used, and when his wife died prematurely, Guitton remained a bachelor.

A detail that did not escape Florence Delay. The novelist, who was elected to Guitton's 'chair' at the Académie française, had to deliver, as tradition required, his 'eulogy' on the day when she entered the hallowed halls. One unusual thing: Florence Delay, even though she was praising the deceased, made multiple allusions to his legendary misogyny: 'What would he have thought about being succeeded by a woman, when he considered us incomplete!' Neither did she take his late marriage any more seriously: 'Some people are surprised or amused that M. Guitton, apparently devoted to monastic chastity, or more philosophically to

Kantian celibacy, wrote an essay on human love – even before his affectionate autumnal marriage to Marie-Louise Bonnet. It's that human love which includes the love that flows from disciple to master, and from master to disciple.' Ah! how elegantly put!

If the new academician had been more mischievous, or more ironic, she might have alluded to a famous remark by the sexologist Alfred Kinsey, a contemporary of Guitton. The author of the famous *Kinsey Report* on the sexuality of Americans stressed, scientifically for the first time, the high proportion of homosexuals in the general population. So widespread was it that homosexuality ceased to be an anomaly, a sickness and a perversion. And Kinsey added slyly that the only real remaining perversions were three in number: abstinence, celibacy and late marriage! Guitton was perverted three times over!

If he had little love for women, and never mentioned the fair sex, which was invisible to him, Guitton did love many men 'as friends'. Starting with Cardinal Poupard, who had a long correspondence with him (over two hundred handwritten letters, which have not, as I have said, been published, will perhaps bear witness to this one day). His masculine passions were also directed towards his students: notably to one of his young pupils, a certain Louis Althusser, 'so fair and handsome that he could have been his apostle' (a daring Florence Delay, once again!).

Jean Guitton's relationship with Pope John XXIII, whom he knew under the name of Roncalli when he was nuncio in Paris, also seems atypical, and 'loving friendship' may have played a part in it.

Similar to this was the relationship that he formed at a young age with Giovanni Battista Montini, the future Pope Paul VI. Their closeness was the subject of incomprehension and rumours. A theologian as influential as Father Daniélou didn't hesitate to say that 'the pope [Paul VI] committed an imprudence in putting Guitton on the [Vatican] council'. Others mocked the holy father for 'falling for a second-rate writer, a minor literary figure'. Finally, there was a recurrent joke about him in the Vatican, one of the former directors of Radio Vatican tells me: 'Guitton can't be classed among the laymen on the conclave because he has no children ...'

When one reads the very exalted *Dialogues with Paul VI*, the book of real or imagined interviews by Jean Guitton with the pope (with a preface by Cardinal Paul Poupard), one is also struck by the strangeness of the dialogue between the holy father and the layman about abstinence and about what they call the 'love plus' between Jesus and Peter, which 'includes a frightening imperative'.

Now we know this language all too well. It is the language of early Gide and late Mauriac, of Julien Green too, of Henry de Montherlant, and finally of Maritain. It is the language of guilt and hope for the 'civilization of love' (to use the famous expression of Paul VI). It is the language of Plato, whom Paul VI had made acceptable once again by abolishing his place on the Index, on which he had been placed alongside Montaigne, Machiavelli, Voltaire, André Gide and many others.

Once again, let's not exaggerate. It is possible that Jean Guitton experienced these discussions in the 'Maritain style', quite innocently and naively, without realizing the part probably played by gay inclinations and sublimation. Besides, Guitton stated that he didn't understand anything about homosexuality. That might paradoxically indicate a homophilic affective orientation, truly unconscious in this case.

Apart from Marie-Louise Bonnet, the only woman we find in Jean Guitton's entourage is 'Maréchale' de Lattre de Tassigny, the widow of a senior French military officer, about whom a persistent rumour, particularly within the army, suggests that he was bisexual (the writer Daniel Guérin stated as much in his book *Homosexualité et revolution*, and the writer Jean-Luc Barré, who published the work of Maréchale de Lattre de Tassigny, thinks so too).

Between the death of the Maréchal de France in 1952 and her own death in 2003, at the age of 96, the 'Maréchale' lived surrounded by a flock of homosexuals in her Parisian salon. Jean Guitton, mischievous and always cheerful, according to a witness, was a loyal visitor: he was 'always accompanied by handsome members of the stronger sex and effeminate cuties'. Another witness confirms that Guitton was always 'surrounded by ephebes and '*gitons de passage*''.

Here was a man who lived like a priest, who chose not to have children, married late, and, throughout his life, had intense homophilic friendships, surrounded by desirable young men. Was he a 'restrained' homosexual? It seems likely, and there has been nothing so far to indicate the opposite. Yet here we must find another word to define this kind of relationship. Guitton suggests one, imperfect though it might be: 'companionship'. Let us listen to him here, in his own words, in his book *Le Christ de ma vie*, in which he converses with Father Joseph Doré, the future Archbishop of Strasbourg: 'There's something superior to man's love of woman, and that is companionship. David's love of Jonathan, Achilles' love of Patroclus … A Jesuit can have a companionable love for another Jesuit which is superior to the love that this man would have felt had he been married … In companionship – it is often misunderstood, because of homosexuality – there is something quite unique and extraordinary.'

A magnificent confession, a game of mirrors in which the reference to David and Jonathan is chosen deliberately by a man who cannot ignore the homoerotic charge of this explicitly gay code (the main homosexual Catholic association in France already bears this name).

Jean Guitton, like Jacques Maritain, tries to invent a language to grasp masculine complicity without reducing it to sex. Here we are at the heart of what is called – the expression has been more enduring than Guitton's mediocre 'companionship' – 'loving friendship' (*'amour d'amitié'*).

It's an old concept, and it's important, just for a moment, to trace its genesis, which is so central to our theme. The idea of 'loving friendship' is rooted in the thought of classical Greece, in Socrates and Plato, later systematized by Aristotle. Via Cicero and St Augustine, it passed through late antiquity and into the Middle Ages. We find the idea of it, if not the letter, in Saint Aelred of Rievaulx, a twelfth-century Cistercian monk who became the first 'LGBT saint' (because he never hid his loving relationships). A century later, at a time when the idea of 'homosexuality' didn't yet exist (as we know, the word would not be invented until the late nineteenth century), the Middle Ages re-appropriated this concept of 'loving friendship'. Thomas Aquinas distinguishes 'concupiscent love' (*amor concupiscentiae*) from 'loving friendship' (*amor amicitiae*); the former seeks the other for personal and selfish gain; the latter, on the other hand, privileges the good of the friend, who is loved like another self. These days, even though it's imperfect, we would call it 'platonic love'.

The idea of 'loving friendship' was then used to define the relationship between Shakespeare and the young man called the 'Fair Youth' in the *Sonnets*, Leonardo da Vinci and his young pupil Salai, or Michelangelo and the young Tommaso dei Cavalieri. Love? Friendship? Specialists today think that in this precise case it was probably a matter of homosexuality. On the other hand, what are we to say of the writers Montaigne and La Boétie, for whom the expression 'loving friendship' was also used? We should guard against misrepresenting a relationship that was perhaps never sexual, and which a famous phrase of Montaigne may sum up more accurately, because it defies rational explanation: 'Because it was him, because it was me.'

The expression 'loving friendship' was also used to describe the relationship between Father Henri Lacordaire, one of the restorers of the Dominican Order in France, and his 'friend' Charles de Montalembert. For a long time the Church covered its face over this subject by insisting on calling a 'friendship' what is now known to have been homosexual (the inestimable correspondence between Lacordaire and Montalembert, recently published, reveals not only an exemplary dialogue about French liberal Catholicism, but also the explicit relationship between the two men).

The concept of 'loving friendship' therefore covers infinitely varied situations, and has been used indiscriminately through the ages for a broad continuum of relationships that run from pure manly friendship to actual homosexuality. According to the specialists in the subject, of which there are many at the Vatican, this concept should only be applied to chaste homophilia. It is not an equivocal feeling that tends to maintain the confusion between love and friendship, but an authentic and chaste love, a perfectly innocent relationship between two men. Its success in the homophilic Catholic milieu in the twentieth century is explained by the fact that it stresses the virtues of the loved one, more than carnal desire, which is carefully denied; it allows us to not sexualize affection. Finally, the most conservative – and most homophobic – cardinals like the American Raymond Burke, the German Joachim Meisner, the Italian Carlo Caffarra or the Guinean Robert Sarah, who have themselves taken a vow of chastity, firmly insist on homosexuals limiting themselves to relationships of 'loving friendship', meaning chastity, to avoid committing a sin and going to hell. In so doing they reveal themselves.

From Jacques Maritain to Jean Guitton, this world of 'loving friendship' constitutes a subterranean influence of the Second Vatican Council.

Jacques Maritain did not take part in the council himself, but had an important influence on it because of his friendship with Paul VI. It was also true of other influential theologians like the priests Yves Congar, Charles Journet, Henri de Lubac and Jean Daniélou. The last of these is the most enlightening: the French Jesuit, a renowned theologian, was called as an expert to the Second Vatican Council by John XXIII, before he was appointed cardinal by Paul VI. A friend of Jean Guitton (they co-authored a book), it was thanks to Guitton that he entered the Académie française. Rather progressive, Daniélou was one of the close friends of Paul VI.

Much has been made of Daniélou's death, as sudden as it was extraordinary, on 20 May 1974, in the arms of 'Mimi' Santoni, a (female) prostitute on the Rue Dulong in Paris. The cause of death was probably a heart attack brought on by orgasm. A version contradicted, of course, by the Jesuits, who, in response to the scandal prompted by the affair at the time, put forward their own version of the facts, which was immediately picked up by *Le Figaro*: the cardinal had come to give the prostitute money to help her, and died 'in the epektasis of the apostle meeting the living God'.

It's a version confirmed to me today by the Italian cardinal Giovanni Battista Re, who was 'minister' of the interior under John Paul II: 'We used to read Jean Daniélou a lot. We liked him a lot. His death? I think he wanted to save the prostitute's soul, that was it. To convert her, perhaps. In my view he died in the apostolate.'

Cardinal Paul Poupard, a friend of Daniélou (they also co-authored a book), confirms to me, raising his hands to heaven, that this generous cardinal, so humble-hearted, with a heart of gold, came to redeem the sins of the prostitute. Perhaps even to try, gallant man that he was, to free this loose-living girl from her sorry trade.

Apart from the laughter that these explanations provoked at the time – Daniélou was entirely naked when the ambulance arrived – for our purposes the essence of the case lies elsewhere. If Daniélou was really a practising heterosexual who was clearly not part of 'the parish', his brother, on the other hand, was clearly homosexual. Alain was a celebrated Hinduist, a specialist in the divinized eroticism of the ecstatic East, in yoga and the worship of Shiva. He was also a friend of François

Mauriac and the choreographer Maurice Béjart. His homosexuality, which had been common knowledge for a long time, was recently confirmed by his autobiography and by the publication of his brother Jean's *Carnets spirituels*. We know that Alain lived for a long time with the Swiss photographer Raymond Burnier.

The relationship between the Daniélou brothers is interesting because it allows me to state today that Jean was sympathetic to Alain's choice of lifestyle, and that he supported him in his homosexuality. He wanted to shoulder the weight of Alain's sins and take care of his soul.

Cardinal Jean Daniélou went further. From 1943, he went to celebrate a mass for homosexuals every month. This fact is well-established (in Alain's autobiography and in a detailed biography devoted to the two brothers). It appears that this mass, which also included the famous Islamic specialist Louis Massignon, a Christian who was also homosexual, continued over several years.

The key point here, then, is not the death of Jean Daniélou in the arms of a prostitute, but the organization by a high-profile cardinal, a renowned theologian close to the pope, of regular masses intended for the 'salvation' of homosexuals.

Did Paul VI know about this? It's possible but not certain. The fact remains that this largely homophilic, or pro-gay, entourage was part of the history of his pontificate – the quintessence of the 'code Maritain'.

'Anyone looking at this sequence of pictures will wonder what connection we might have with this people, with their vigorous faces ...' On the occasion of the fifth centenary of the birth of Michelangelo, an astonishing 'gay-friendly' homage was delivered on 29 February 1976 by Pope Paul VI to the Italian sculptor in St Peter's basilica in Rome. With great pomp, the holy father sang the memory of the 'incomparable artist' beneath the majestic dome that he designed, right next to the sublime *Pietà*, which this 'boy who had not yet reached the age of 25' brought out of this cold marble with the greatest 'tenderness'.

A stone's throw away are the Sistine Chapel and its vault, painted with its manly throng, of which Paul VI praises the angels – but not the Ignudi, those firm-bodied naked ephebes with their insolent physical splendour, which he passes over in silence. Also cited in the pope's speech are 'the world of Sibyls' and 'Pontiffs'; but no mention is made of Michelangelo's naked Christ, nor of the saints in their birthday suits or the 'confusion of nudes' of the *Last Judgement*. With this deliberate silence, the pope is once again censoring the pink flesh that one of his predecessors had once castrated by covering the genitals of the naked men with a modest veil.

Paul VI, now swept away by his own audacity, grows heated, moved to tears by the confusion of bodies and the play of muscles. And 'what an eye!' the pope noted. That of the 'young athlete who is the Florentine David' (entirely naked, and beautifully proportioned), and the last *Pietà*, called the 'Rondanini', 'full of sobs' and *non finito*. Clearly, Paul VI is lost in wonder at the work of this visionary of 'secret beauty', whose 'aesthetic delight' is a match for 'Hellenic perfection'. And all of a sudden, the holy father begins to read a sonnet by Michelangelo!

What connection, indeed, 'can we have with this people, with their vigorous faces'? Never in the history of the Vatican can such 'girly' praise have been bestowed in such a sacred place on such a boldly homosexual artist.

'Paul VI wrote his own speeches by hand. All the manuscripts have been preserved,' I am told by Micol Forti, a cultivated and energetic woman who is one of the directors of the Vatican museums.

Paul VI's passion for culture was to some extent part of a political strategy. In Italy at the time, culture was sliding from the right to the left; religious practice was already in decline among artists. While for centuries the Catholics had dominated culture, the codes, the art networks, that hegemony had vanished in the late 1960s and early 1970s. Paul VI still thought it wasn't too late, and that the Church could recover if it could only find out how to cruise (or woo) the Muses.

The witnesses I interviewed also confirm that Paul VI's commitment to culture was at the same time sincere, and based on his personal inclinations.

'Paul VI was a "Michelangelo addict",' I am told by a bishop who knew the holy father.

In 1964 the pope announced his plan for a big collection of modern and contemporary art. He launched himself into the great cultural battle of his life, to win back the artists.

'Paul VI began by apologizing on behalf of the Church for having paid little attention to modern art. And then he asked artists and intellectuals from all over the world to build up a collection for the Vatican museums,' Micol Forti goes on.

The cardinals and bishops I spoke to put forward several hypotheses to explain this passion of Paul VI for the arts. One of them notes the crucial influence exerted on him by a book by Jacques Maritain, his essay *Art and Scholasticism*, in which he imagines a philosophy of art that allows artists their own peculiarities.

Another fine connoisseur of the cultural life of the Vatican under Paul VI insists on the role of the pope's personal assistant, the Italian priest Pasquale Macchi, a man of letters who was passionate about art, and a proven homophile who kept the company of artists.

'Thanks to Pasquale Macchi, Paul VI brought together the intellectuals and tried to bring artists back to the Vatican. They both measured the gulf that already separated them from the world of art. And Macchi was one of the craftsmen behind the new collections,' a priest in the Pontifical Council for Culture tells me.

I've visited that modern wing of the Vatican museums. Although it is by no means a match for the old collections – how could it be? – it must be acknowledged that the Vatican curators were enlightened in their choices. I notice in particular two unorthodox artists: Salvador Dalí, a bisexual painter, with a fine painting entitled *Crucifixion* with masochist soldierly connotations. And most importantly, Francis Bacon, an artist who was openly gay!

Paul VI's homosexuality is an old rumour. In Italy it is very persistent, having been mentioned in articles and even on the pope's Wikipedia page, which goes so far as to mention the name of one of his famous alleged lovers. During my many stays in Rome, cardinals, bishops and dozens of monsignori working at the Vatican have talked to me about it. Some denied it.

'I can confirm that this rumour existed. And I can prove it. There were pamphlets, after the election of Montini [Paul VI] in 1963, denouncing his morals,' I am told by Cardinal Poupard, who was one of the pope's collaborators.

Cardinal Battista Re assures me: 'I worked with Pope Paul VI for seven years. He was a great pope and all the rumours I have heard are false.'

Paul VI is generally said to have had a relationship with Paolo Carlini, an Italian theatre and television actor 25 years his junior. They met when Giovanni Montini was Archbishop of Milan.

While that relationship is often mentioned in Italy, some of its factual elements seem anachronistic or erroneous. For example, Paul VI was said to have chosen his name in tribute to Paolo, which is denied by various sources, which put forward other, more credible explanations. Similarly, Paolo Carlini is said to have died of a heart attack 'two days after Paul VI, out of grief': and yet, while he was already ill, he didn't die until much later. Montini and Carlini were also said to have shared an apartment near the archbishop's palace, which is not confirmed by any trustworthy police source. Finally, the file kept by Milan police on the Montini–Carlini relationship, which is often cited, has never been made public and to this day there is no proof that it ever existed.

Claiming to be better informed than anyone else, the French writer Roger Peyrefitte, a militant homosexual, set about 'outing' Paul VI in a series of interviews: first in *Gay Sunshine Press*, then in the French magazine *Lui*, an article picked up in Italy by the weekly magazine *Tempo* in April 1976. In his repeated interventions, and later in his books, Peyrefitte declared that 'Paul VI was homosexual' and that he had 'proof'. 'Outing' was his speciality: the writer had already accused François Mauriac in an article in the journal *Arts* in May 1964 (rightly on that occasion), as well as King Baudouin of Belgium, the Duke of Edinburgh and the Shah of Iran – until it was discovered that some of his sources were mistaken, and that he had fallen for a journalistic hoax!

I did have the opportunity, when I was a young journalist, shortly before his death, to interview Roger Peyrefitte about the rumour concerning Paul VI's homosexuality. A repetitive gossip, the old writer didn't seem to me to be very well-informed and, in truth, was simply excited by the scent of scandal. In all these cases, he never supplied the least proof of his 'scoop'. It seems in fact that he wanted to attack Paul VI after his declaration *Persona Humana*, which was hostile to homosexuals. In any case, the mediocre and sulphurous writer, close to the extreme right and deliberately polemical, at the end of his life became a specialist in fake information, and indeed homophobic, as well as sometimes spreading anti-Semitic rumours.

The interesting point was, of course, Paul VI's public reaction. According to several of the people I interviewed (notably cardinals who worked for him), the articles about his alleged homosexuality deeply affected the holy father. Taking the rumour very seriously, he was said to have encouraged multiple political interventions to make it stop. He was believed to have asked in person for the help of the then Italian prime minister, Aldo Moro, who was among his close friends and with whom he shared a passion for Maritain. What did Moro do? We don't know. The political leader was kidnapped a few months later by the Red Brigades, who demanded a ransom. Paul VI publicly intervened to ask for his release, and was even said to have tried to assemble the necessary funds. But Moro was murdered in the end, plunging Paul VI into despair.

The pope finally chose to deny, in person, the rumour started by Roger Peyrefitte: he spoke out publicly on the subject, on 4 April 1976. I found his intervention in the Vatican press office. Here is Paul VI's official declaration: 'Beloved brothers and sons! We know that our cardinal vicar and with him the Italian Episcopal Conference have invited you to pray for our humble person, who has been the object of mockery and horrible and slanderous insinuations on the part of a certain press, in contempt of honesty and truth. We thank you for your filial demonstrations of piety, moral sensibility and affection … Thank you, thank you from the bottom of our heart … Also, since this episode and others were caused by a recent declaration by the Congregation for the Doctrine of the Faith, about certain questions of sexual ethics, we ask you to give this document your virtuous observance, and thus to strengthen you in a spirit of purity and love opposed to the licentious hedonism that is very widespread in the morals of the world today.'

Major communication error! While the rumour put about by a reactionary author with little credibility was limited to some anti-clerical homophilic milieu, Paul VI's public denial, in the solemnity of the Palm Sunday angelus, helped to spread it around the world. Hundreds of articles were published passing on this denial, particularly in Italy, and probably raising doubts. Something that had only been a rumour became a question, perhaps even a theme. The Curia learned its lesson: better to ignore rumours of the homosexuality of popes or cardinals than give them publicity by denying them.

Since then other witness statements have appeared, supporting the 'terrible' rumour: first of all that of a minor Italian poet, Biagio Arixi, a friend of Carlini's, whom the actor was said to have revealed his liaison with the pope shortly before he died. The chamberlain and master of ceremonies of John XXIII and Paul VI, Franco Bellegrandi, also mentioned the subject in a dubious book. The Polish archbishop Juliusz Paetz also expatiated at length about the pope's supposed homophilia, even distributing photographs and suggesting that he might have been in a bromance with him, as is confirmed by witnesses, journalists from *Gazeta Wyborcza* and my 'researchers' in Warsaw (Paetz's testimony is uncorroborated.) A former Swiss Guard also provided information of a similar kind, and several former lovers, whether real or self-proclaimed, of Paul VI tried to testify, often in vain, and in any case unconvincingly. On the other hand, other witness statements from cardinals and a number of serious biographers firmly rebut this claim about the pope.

A more important point: the hypothesis of Paul VI's homosexuality and his relationship with Paolo Carlini were taken seriously enough during the beatification process of Paul VI. According to two sources whom I have interviewed, the file was examined in extreme detail by the priests who had prepared for that 'trial'. If there was a debate, if there was a file, it's at least because there was doubt. The question of the alleged homosexuality of Paul VI even figures explicitly in the documents submitted to Pope Benedict XVI, which were written by Father Antonio Marrazzo. According to one first-hand source who is very familiar with the large dossier assembled by Marrazzo, and who talked to him about the morals attributed to the holy father, the question appears in numerous documents and written statements. According to that same source, however, Marrazzo concluded, after checking and cross-checking all the documents, that Paul VI probably wasn't homosexual. His position was finally taken by Pope Benedict XVI, who, after examining the file at length, decided to beatify Paul VI and to acknowledge his 'heroic virtues', bringing the controversy to a temporary close.

One mystery remains around Paul VI: his entourage, full of homophiles and practising homosexuals. Consciously or otherwise, this pope severely forbade this form of sexuality, yet surrounded himself with men almost all of whom had 'inclinations'.

This was, as we have seen, true of Paul VI's personal secretary, Pasquale Macchi, who worked with him for 23 years, first in the archbishopric of Milan and then in Rome. Aside from the part he played in the creation of the collection of modern art in the Vatican museums, this priest, with a legendary artistic bent, was a close friend of Jean Guitton and had many contacts with the creative people and intellectuals of his era, in the name of the pope. His homophilia was confirmed by more than ten witnesses.

In the same way, the priest and future Irish bishop, John Magee, who was also a close friend and assistant of Paul VI, was homosexual (as the courts made clear in the trial for scandals in his diocese of Cloyne).

Another man close to Paul VI, Loris Francesco Capovilla, who was also personal secretary to his predecessor, John XXIII, and a key participant in the council (he was appointed cardinal by Pope Francis in 2014 and died at the age of 100 in 2016), was said to have been homophilic.

'Mgr Capovilla was a very discreet man. He said his little words to the younger priests, and was very kind. He made delicate passes. He wrote to me once,' the former Curia priest Francesco Lepore confirms to me. (A cardinal and several archbishops and prelates in the Vatican also confirmed Capovilla's inclinations.)

Paul VI's official theologian, the Dominican Mario Luigi Ciappi, a Florentine with a devastating sense of humour, was also seen as an 'extrovert homophile' who lived side-by-side with his 'socius', or personal secretary, according to three convergent witness statements by Dominican priests that I have taken (Ciappi was one of the official theologians of five popes, between 1955 and 1989, and was created cardinal by Paul VI in 1977).

The same is true of Paul VI's master of pontifical ceremonies, the Italian 'monsignore' Virgilio Noè, a future cardinal. People in the Vatican were amused for a long time by this man who was straight as a die in public, and said to lead a racy life in private.

'Everyone knew that Virgilio was practising. Let's even say very practising! It was a kind of joke between us, inside the Vatican,' a priest of the Roman Curia confirms.

The pope's manservant was also a known homosexual; and the same is true of one of the main translators and bodyguards of the holy father – the famous Archbishop Paul Marcinkus, whom we will be speaking of again. As for the cardinals, many of them are 'part of the parish', beginning with Sebastiano Baggio, whom the pope entrusted with the Congregation for Bishops, after making him a cardinal. Last of all, one of the heads of the Swiss Guard under Paul VI, a close friend of the pope, still lives with his boyfriend in a suburb of Rome, where one of my sources met him.

By recruiting most of his entourage among priests who were homophile, 'questioning', 'closeted' or practising, what was Paul VI trying to tell us? I will leave that up to the reader, who has in front of them all the points of view and all the pieces of the puzzle. In any case, the 'Maritain code', a template drawn up under Paul VI, would be perpetuated under the subsequent pontificates of John Paul II, Benedict XVI and Francis. Ever astute, the pope made 'loving friendship' a rule of the Vatican fraternity. The 'Maritain code' was born under its good auspices; it still applies today.

Part III

John Paul

JOHN PAUL II

1978–2005

JOSEPH RATZINGER
Congregation for the Doctrine of Faith

STANISLAW DZIWISZ
Private Secretary

AGOSTINO CASAROLI
Secretary of State
1979–1990

**EDUARDO MARTÍNEZ SOMALO
GIOVANNI BATTISTA RE**
Secretaty for Internal Affairs

**ACHILLE SILVESTRINI
ANGELO SODANO**
Secretary for Relations with States

**GIOVANNI BATTISTA RE
CRESCENZIO SEPE**
Assessor

JEAN-LOUIS TAURAN
Under Secretary

ANGELO SODANO
Secretary of State
1990–2006

LEONARDO SANDRI
Secretary for Internal Affairs

**JEAN-LOUIS TAURAN
GIOVANNI LAJOLO**
Secretary for Relations with States

**JAMES HARVEY
GABRIELE CACCIA**
Assessor

**CLAUDIO MARÍA CELLI
CELESTINO MIGLIORE
PIETRO PAROLIN**
Under Secretary

9

Quite the Sacred College

'Under Paul VI, we were still in the days of homophilia and "inclination". With John Paul II things changed completely in their nature and breadth. In his entourage there were more practitioners – unimaginable levels of venality and corruption. Even around the holy father there was a veritable ring of lust.'

It's a priest of the Curia who talks to me like this, one of the witnesses of the pontificate. When he uses the expression 'ring of lust', this monsignore is only picking up an idea already put forward by Benedict XVI and Francis. If they were careful not to quote any particular cardinals or to criticize their Polish predecessor, the two popes were shocked by John Paul II's hybrid entourage.

Francis never speaks at random. And when he launched his scathing attack, which has often been repeated since, against the 'current of corruption' in the Curia, he obviously had names in mind. It was June 2013, the beginning of his reign – the pope was speaking in Spanish to a group of Latin American Catholic representatives. The discussion turned, just this once, to the gay lobby. And if the new pope talked about a ring of 'corruption', it was because he had the proof: he had particular cardinals in his sights. He was thinking of Italians, Germans and also Latino cardinals and nuncios.

It is a matter of public knowledge that the pontificate of John Paul II was strewn with scandals, and that several of the cardinals in his close circle were both homosexual and corrupt. But until this investigation, I hadn't been aware of the full degree of hypocrisy of the Roman Curia under Karol Wojtyła. Might his pontificate have been 'intrinsically disordered'?

John Paul II is the pope of my youth, and many of my friends and relations always respected him. Among the editors of *Esprit*, an anti-totalitarian Catholic journal to which I contributed, Wojtyła was generally considered as one of the major figures associated with the end of communism. I have read several books and biographies of this giant of the twentieth century, this global figure. It was when I met the cardinals, bishops and priests who worked with him that I discovered the hidden side – the dark side – of his very long pontificate. A pope surrounded by plotters, thugs, a majority of closeted homosexuals, who were homophobes in public, not to mention all those who protected paedophile priests.

'Paul VI had condemned homosexuality, but it was only with the arrival of John Paul II that a veritable war was waged against gays,' I was told by a Curia priest who worked at John Paul II's ministry of Foreign Affairs. 'Irony of history: most of the players in this boundless campaign against homosexuals were homosexual themselves. In making this choice of official homophobia, John Paul II and his entourage had not realized the extent of the trap that they were setting for themselves, and the risk to which they were exposing the Church by undermining it from within. They hurled themselves into a suicidal moral war that they were inevitably going to lose, because it consisted of denouncing what they were. The fall of Benedict XVI would be the final consequence of this.'

To try to understand one of the best-kept secrets of this pontificate, I interviewed numerous cardinals in Rome. Among them the main 'ministers' of the pope: Giovanni Battista Re, Achille Silvestrini, Leonardo Sandri, Jean-Louis Tauran and Paul Poupard, who were, at the time, at the heart of the Roman Curia. I visited the pope's private secretary, Stanisław Dziwisz, in Kraków; I also met about ten nuncios who worked as diplomats on his behalf, several of his press advisers, assistants and masters of ceremony and secretaries, members of the Secretariat of State between 1978 and 2005, as well as many bishops or simple monsignori. In addition, I obtained a great deal of information and confidences from cardinals, bishops and ordinary priests as I travelled abroad, pursuing

QUITE THE SACRED COLLEGE

my investigations in Latin America and, of course, in Poland. Last of all, the archives of the Chilean dictatorship, recently opened, were crucial.

One mystery survives for me today, as I begin to give an account of this descent into hell. What did John Paul II know concerning what I am about to relate? What did he know of the double lives of most of his entourage? Was he naively unaware of it; did he quietly indulge or validate the financial scandals and sexual wickedness of his close colleagues – because those two excesses, money and the flesh, combined together, as though paired and mating, in the course of his pontificate? For want of an answer to this enigma, I would like to believe that the pope, who would very soon fall ill, and become senile, knew nothing about any of it and didn't cover up the excesses that I am about to describe.

The two main players in the John Paul II years were the cardinals Agostino Casaroli and Angelo Sodano. Both Italians, both from modest families in Piedmont, they were the holy father's chief collaborators, occupying, in turn, the post of cardinal secretary of state – the most important function in the holy see: the pope's 'prime minister'.

Cardinal Casaroli, who died in 1998, was for a long time a subtle and cunning diplomat, notably when responsible for the communist countries under John XXIII and Paul VI, before becoming John Paul's right-hand man. His great and unfussy diplomacy, which consisted of dialogues, compromises and small steps, is admired even today by most of the diplomats who have talked to me about him; for example, the nuncio François Bacqué, Mgr Fabrice Rivet or the nuncio Gabriele Caccia, whom I interviewed in Beirut.

I have often heard it said at the Secretariat of State that one nuncio or another was 'in the line of the great Casaroli diplomacy'. Even today that magical name seems to be a benchmark, much as one might say of an American diplomat that he is 'Kissingerian' or of a French diplomat that he is 'neo-Gaullist'. Implicitly, it is also a subtle way of distinguishing this version from the diplomacy of his successor Angelo Sodano, who was put in place after 1991.

Casaroli's diplomacy was still based on 'patience', according to the title of his posthumous memoirs. A 'classic' diplomat, if the word has any meaning in the Vatican, he was a pragmatist who favoured realpolitik over morality and the long term over immediate effects. Human rights are important, but the Church has its traditions, which should also be respected. This supposed realism does not rule out mediation or parallel diplomacy as practised by organizations like the Sant'Egidio community or 'flying ambassadors' like Cardinal Roger Etchegaray on secret missions for John Paul II to Iran, China or Cuba.

According to Etchegaray, whom I interviewed, Agostino Casaroli 'was a great intellectual' who read a great deal, particularly the French writers Jacques Maritain and his friend Jean Guitton (who would write the preface to one of his books). Even more importantly: Casaroli was a brave, hands-on diplomat; he sometimes travelled incognito on the other side of the Iron Curtain, and was able to set up a network of local informers who proved precious after the changes in the USSR and its satellite countries.

Cardinal Paul Poupard, who worked with him, told me: 'He was a man of great nuance. He expressed disagreements in clear and courteous terms. He was the quintessence of the Vatican diplomat. And he was Italian! The previous secretary of state, Jean Villot, a Frenchman, had worked well with Paul VI, who was Italian. But with a Polish pope, Villot recommended that John Paul II take an Italian. He told him: "You need an Italian." In the end Casaroli ticked all the boxes.'

When he became the pope's 'prime minister' and was created cardinal, Casaroli's talent was deployed on the communist question. Following John Paul II, who made anti-communism his priority in speeches and travels, the secretary of state carried out subtle or secret actions which are quite well-known today. Massive sums were paid, quite opaquely, to the Polish trade union Solidarność; private offices were set up in Eastern Europe; the Vatican Bank, run by the famous archbishop Paul Marcinkus, organized counter-propaganda. (When I questioned Cardinals Giovanni Battista Re and Jean-Louis Tauran, they denied that the holy see ever directly financed Solidarność.)

This battle was the personal choice of John Paul II. The pope devised his strategy on his own, and only a very small number of collaborators were able to decrypt it as it was deployed (principally Stanisław Dziwisz, his private secretary, the Cardinal Secretaries of State state Casaroli and then Sodano, and, at the beginning of the pontificate, the Cardinal Archbishop of Warsaw, Stefan Wyszynski).

The role of Stanisław Dziwisz, in particular, was crucial, and here it is necessary to go into details – it is of great importance for our subject. This Polish prelate knew the communist world from inside: he was John Paul II's principal collaborator in Warsaw and then in Rome. Witnesses confirm that he was the key man in all the secret anti-communist missions; he knew all the sensitive files and the parallel financing. We know that Dziwisz's relations with Cardinal Ratzinger were execrable, but Ratzinger, once elected pope, perhaps in response to a promise made to the dying John Paul II, and whatever the cost to himself, appointed him Archbishop of Kraków and then created him cardinal.

'Mgr Dziwisz was a very great private secretary, very loyal, a great servant. He was constantly with saint John Paul II and told the holy father everything,' Cardinal Giovanni Battista Re tells me, summing up the situation.

John Paul II's former head of protocol, who often accompanied the pope on his travels, Renato Boccardo, confirmed the equally crucial influence of Dziwisz, during a conversation in Spoleto, 130 kilometres from Rome, where he is now archbishop. 'There was no way of avoiding private secretary Dziwisz. He was very active on all the pope's travels and, of course, when they were going to Poland, he took things even more in hand. Then it was the "gang of Poles" who managed the trip: Cardinal Grocholewski, Cardinal Deskur and Dziwisz. I remember the 2002 trip and we all guessed that it would be the pope's last trip to the country of his birth. Dziwisz, who had come with us, knew everybody. We were extraordinarily well-received.'

Without saying as much, Renato Boccardo is giving us to understand that Dziwisz, who stayed in the shadows for a long time, was revealed at the end of the pontificate to be the true master of the Vatican.

'There has been a lot of talk about a Polish "mafia" around Cardinals Stanisław Dziwisz, Andrzej Deskur, Zenon Grocholewski, Stefan Wyszynski or indeed the Primate of Poland, Mgr Józef Glemp. There was even talk of a gang! I think that was largely a myth. The only one who was truly influential where John Paul II was concerned was his private secretary: Stanisław Dziwisz,' the Polish Vaticanologist Jacek Moskwa says, putting things into perspective, when I interview him in Warsaw.

Now living in retirement in Kraków, Cardinal Dziwisz has none-theless left an ambiguous reputation in Rome. His loyalty to the pope is admired, but his hypocrisy is criticized. It is difficult to decipher his self-referential codes, his mood swings and extravagances, which came to the surface in those times he used to spend on his own near the Villa Medici, as if saying, like the Poet, 'I am hidden and I'm not.' And since his departure from the Curia, tongues have loosened.

One of the most secretive men in the recent history of the Vatican (Dziwisz has hardly ever given interviews in almost thirty years beside Karol Wojtyła) is gradually emerging into the light. So, for example, a colleague of Casaroli's who still works at the Vatican indicated to me that Dziwisz's multiple lives are one of the great secrets of Roman Catholicism.

'Dziwisz was given a nickname: "The Pope Has Said". He was John Paul II's secretary, there was no getting around him, and everything had to go through him. Obviously he often "screened" information, which is to say that he passed on to the pope what he wanted to pass on. Gradually, and as John Paul II's illness got worse, he began speaking for the pope, and it was far from clear who, the pope or Dziwisz, was giving the orders. This applied to the files on paedophilia or financial scandals: it was on these issues that tensions arose with Cardinal Ratzinger. Dziwisz was very tough. He is said to have made Ratzinger cry on several occasions.'

A Curia priest confirms this information: 'Dziwisz was very unpredictable, very aggressive. He was very enterprising, and got on with his affairs all the more serenely for being the holy father's close collaborator. He knew he was protected and out of range.'

'Wdowa'. The Polish nickname of Mgr Stanisław Dziwisz, literally 'the widow', is now one of the most recurring jokes in Poland – and it's not a very happy one. During my investigation in Warsaw and Kraków I heard this pet name so often, whether used out of irony or malice, that it is difficult to ignore it.

'I wouldn't use the expression myself. People who call him "the widow" are being slanderous. What is true, on the other hand, is that Dziwisz speaks only about John Paul II. He's the only thing that matters in his life. His only goal is John Paul II; his story and his memory. He has always been very much in the shadow of the great man. He is now the executor of his will,' I am told by the Polish Vaticanologist Jacek Moskwa, who was for a long time a correspondent in Rome, and who is the author of a four-volume biography of the pope.

I questioned dozens of priests, bishops and cardinals about the career of Stanisław Dziwisz, and a very contrasting image emerges from these conversations. In Warsaw, at the headquarters of the Polish Bishops' Conference, where I am received, they emphasize his 'major' and 'determining' role at the side of John Paul II. I hear the same kind of praise when I visit the pontifical Papieskie Dzieła Misyjne foundation, which is also based in the Polish capital.

'Here we are all orphans of Wojtyła,' I am told by Pawel Bielinski, a journalist with the Catholic information agency KAI.

The Pole Wlodzimierz Redzioch, who knows Dziwisz well, and worked with the *Osservatore Romano* in Rome for 32 years, paints a laudatory picture of John Paul II's assistant when I meet him. If he is to be believed, 'His Eminence the venerable Dziwisz' is 'one of the most honest and virtuous men of our times', 'his great heart', his 'purity' and his 'piety' are said to have been extraordinary, very close to those of a 'saint' …

A poor child, born in a small village in Poland, Stanisław Dziwisz effectively owed his career to a single man: Karol Wojtyła. It was he who ordained the young seminarian as a priest in 1963, and who also had him elected bishop in 1998. They would be inseparable for several decades: Dziwisz would be the private secretary of the Archbishop of Kraków, then of Pope John Paul II in Rome. He was by his side, and shielded him with his body, it is said, in the attempt on his life in 1981. He knew all of the pope's secrets; and he kept his private notebooks. After the pope's long illness and painful death, a universal symbol of human suffering, Dziwisz also kept as a relic a sample of the holy father's blood, a strange fluid memorial that prompted countless macabre comments.

'Cardinal Stanisław Dziwisz is a highly respected figure in the Polish Church. Bear in mind: he was the right-hand man of Pope John Paul II,' I am told during an interview in Warsaw by Krzysztof Olendski, an ambassador who now runs the Polish Institute, a state cultural agency close to the ultra-conservative right and the Catholic Church.

Other witnesses are less generous. Some speak to me about Dziwisz as an 'unimpressive hayseed' or a 'simple man who became complicated'. Some deliver harsh judgements: 'idiot', 'John Paul II's evil genius'. I am told that in Kraków they had to keep a watchful eye on the cardinal, so that he didn't commit any indiscretions or go off the rails in an interview.

'He certainly isn't an intellectual, but he made considerable progress over the years,' says the journalist Adam Szostkiewicz, an influential specialist in Catholicism in *Polityka* who knows him well.

To grasp this atypical relationship between the pope and his private secretary, some put forward another explanation: loyalty.

'It's true, he isn't a big personality; he has lived essentially in the shadow of John Paul II,' the Vaticanologist Jacek Moskwa, who was a member of Solidarność, concedes.

And he immediately adds: 'But he was the ideal secretary. I knew him when he was a young priest beside John Paul II at the Vatican. He was reliable and faithful: those are great qualities. For a long time Dziwisz was quite reserved, quite discreet. He never received journalists, even though he often talked to them on the telephone, off the record. In the end, for a priest of his origins, he had a magnificent career in the Church. The key to his relationship with the pope was loyalty.'

Sent to Kraków as an archbishop by Benedict XVI, and then created cardinal, Dziwisz lives today in an old town house on Kanonicza Street, where he grants me an audience.

'The cardinal,' I am told by his Italian assistant Andrea Nardotto, 'barely gives interviews to journalists, but he is willing to see you.'

I wait on the sunlit patio, amid the pink oleanders and the young dwarf conifers, waiting for 'the widow'. In the hall: the papal coat of arms of John Paul II in bronze, an unsettling brown; on the patio: a chalk-coloured statue of John Paul II. In the distance, I hear the nuns gargling. I see home-delivery men bringing in ready-made dishes.

Suddenly Stanisław Dziwisz wrenches open the massive wooden door of his office, and stands stiffly in the doorway, staring at me, surrounded by handsome young men in dog-collars and wimpled old women. His assistant Nardotto introduces me as a French writer and journalist; without any further formalities, Stanisław Dziwisz ushers me into his lair.

It's an enormous room with three wooden tables. A small rectangular desk covered with papers; a square, blank dining table seems to be where he is holding his meeting; a wooden desk that looks like something from a school classroom, framed by big scarlet armchairs. Having collected himself, Mgr Dziwisz gestures to me to sit down.

The cardinal asks me about the 'eldest daughter of the Church' (France) without really listening to my answers. It's my turn to question him, but he doesn't listen to my questions either. We talk about French Catholic intellectuals, about Jacques Maritain, Jean Guitton, François Mauriac ...

'And André Frossard and Jean Daniélou!' the cardinal insists, citing the names of intellectuals that he has read, or at least met.

This exchange, this list, this name-dropping, is like a confession: I am not in the presence of an intellectual. This emeritus cardinal seems to be barely interested in ideas.

I receive confirmation of this over breakfast with Olga Brzezinska, a renowned academic who runs several cultural foundations and a major literary festival in Kraków: 'Dziwisz is well-known here, and somewhat controversial, but he isn't considered as a major intellectual figure in the city. Most of his legitimacy derives from the fact that he was close to John Paul II. He keeps his notebooks, his secrets and even his blood! It's rather sinister ...'

On the wall of Dziwisz's office, I see three paintings showing John Paul II and a fine portrait of Dziwisz himself in his cardinal's robes. On one of the three tables, the cardinal's skullcap lies inside out with no regard for protocol. A grandfather clock, its pendulum still, has stopped telling the time. The frighteningly cheerful cardinal hails me.

'I find you very likeable,' the cardinal says to me suddenly, marking a pause, jovial and chummy. A man from the south of Poland, he is very likeable himself.

Mgr Dziwisz apologizes for not being able to talk to me for longer. He has to see a representative of the Order of Malta, a little crumpled man who is already waiting in the vestibule. 'What a bore,' he says to me almost confidentially. But he suggests coming back to see him the next day.

We take a selfie. Dziwisz, engagingly, seems to be in no hurry, and with a feminine gesture that doesn't detract from the dominance of his presence, he takes me by the arm so that we can look properly into the lens. A 'sentinel soul', reining in his follies, his impulses, his idylls, he employs guile with me and I play with him. Proudly, he steps back and I think of the Poet saying, 'Do you want to see the meteors gleam?' But at eighty years old, happiness is in flight.

I have studied this character in such depth that, now confronted by my subject, standing in front of me in priestly garb and with a whiff of sulphur, I am amazed. I would never have presumed to admire this creature of heaven for his 'harsh freedom', his goodness, his enchantments. I love the side of him that is – in Rimbaud's words – 'tumbler, beggar, artist, bandit – priest!' A juggler, a tightrope-walker, a nomad of travels untold. While my last doubts fade I admire, fascinated, the 'ardent patience' of this great prince of the Church sitting in front of me. Out of reach. Unconstrained. He hasn't changed. Incurable. What a life! What a man!

In Kraków, the cardinal's way of life provokes considerable astonishment. I am told of his acts of generosity; his sometimes excessive indulgence; his repeated philanthropic gifts to the village of Mszana Dolna, where he was born. Paunchy and fond of his creature comforts, our man enjoys good food and surprises – that's only human. On the evening of our first meeting, when I am in the city, I see him dining at Fiorentina, a starred restaurant where he spends almost three hours, and about which Iga, the manager, will later tell me: 'We're one of the best restaurants in the city. Cardinal Dziwisz is a friend of the manager.'

Where do his funds come from? How does this prelate, with his priest's pension, lead such a posh life? That's one of the mysteries of this book.

Another mystery lies in the unfailing support that Stanisław Dziwisz showed when he was personal secretary to Pope John Paul II towards some of the darker figures in the Church. When I was pursuing my inquiry in Poland, I worked with my 'researcher' Jerzy Sczesny, as well as a team of investigative journalists from the Polish daily *Gazeta Wyborcza* (particularly Mirosław Wlekły, Marcin Kacki and Marcin Wójci). Some harsh aspects of the dark side of John Paul II's private secretary came to light and more dizzying revelations would shortly follow. (The huge success, in autumn 2018, of the film *Kler*, about the paedophilia of priests in Poland, confirms that the debate about the hypocrisy of the Church has begun in the most Catholic country in Europe.)

The name of Stanisław Dziwisz recurs in the dozens of books and articles about cases of sexual abuse; not that he himself is accused of such acts, but because he is suspected of covering up for corrupt priests from within the Vatican. His connections with the Mexican Marcial Maciel, the Chilean Fernando Karadima, the Colombian Alfonso López Trujillo, and the Americans Bernard Law and Theodore McCarrick are well-established. His name also appears in connection with several sexual scandals in Poland, notably in the famous Juliusz Paetz affair: this bishop wooed seminarians by giving them 'ROMA' underwear, which could be read backwards, he told them, as 'AMOR' (he had to resign). Similarly, Dziwisz was personally acquainted with the priest Józef Wesolowski, ordained in Kraków: appointed nuncio to the Dominican Republic, this archbishop was at the heart of a vast scandal of homosexual abuse before being arrested in Rome, by the Vatican police, at the request of Pope Francis. What precisely did Stanisław Dziwisz know about what was in all these files? Did he pass on adequate information to Pope John Paul II, or did he 'filter' them and keep them from him? Was he, with Cardinal Angelo Sodano, guilty of failing to take appropriate action in some of these cases?

Some Polish Catholic prelates I have questioned suggest that Dziwisz could not have been connected to any of these scandals, because he knew nothing about them. Others, on the contrary, think that he 'should be in prison today' for his complicity. Apart from these diametrically opposite opinions, some even go so far as to claim, without any proof, that Dziwisz might have been 'recruited' by the Polish, Bulgarian or East German secret services because of his 'vulnerabilities' – but there isn't a shred of evidence for this Vatican 'infiltration'.

When I interview him in Warsaw, the Polish Vaticanologist Jacek Moskwa gives me a plausible explanation for this: he suggests that if John Paul II and Dziwisz committed an error of judgement about several priests suspected of sexual abuse, it wasn't deliberate, and was the result of communist propaganda: 'Don't forget the context: before 1989, rumours of homosexuality and paedophilia were constantly used by the Polish secret services to discredit opponents of the regime. Being used to blackmail and political manipulations, John Paul II and his assistant Dziwisz never wanted to believe in any of those rumours. Their mentality was that of the besieged fortress: enemies of the Church were trying to compromise the priests. So they had to show solidarity, whatever the cost.'

Adam Szostkiewicz of the newspaper *Polityka* completely agrees, but with one reservation: 'John Paul II had his precise goal and political agenda with regard to Poland and communism. He never deviated from that trajectory. And he was barely concerned with his entourage, or with the morality of his supporters.'

It is likely that the national forces of law and order who are investigating sexual abuse in the Church in dozens of countries will one day shed some light on these mysteries. For now, Stanisław Dziwisz has not been troubled by the law, no complaints or charges have ever been brought against him, and he is enjoying a very active retirement in Kraków. But if one day he was to be implicated in any investigation, the very image of John Paul II's pontificate would be sullied to its heart.

The next day I go back to Kanonicza Street, and Cardinal Dziwisz receives me for a second informal interview. He is more incautious, less controlled than his friends Cardinals Sodano, Sandri or Re. More spontaneous.

I have brought the 'little white book', and he opens the wrapping paper with delight.

'Is this your book?' he asks me, full of kindness again, now remembering that I am a journalist and writer.

'No, it's a present: a little white book that I'm very fond of,' I say.

He looks at me with a hint of surprise, amused now that a stranger should come all the way from Paris to give him a book. I am struck by his eyes, they are identical to the ones I have seen so often in photographs: the greedy and idolatrous eye is more eloquent than the tongue. It is a very reproachful look.

We resume our game. The cardinal asks me to dedicate my present to him, and he lends me his fountain pen. Meanwhile he disappears into an ante-room and I hear him opening drawers and cupboards. He comes back with four presents for me: a photograph, a lovely-looking book and two rosaries, one with black beads, one with white, bearing on their fine verdigris-coloured cases a coat of arms with his effigy. His episcopal motto is simple: 'Sursum Corda' ('Raise your hearts'). On the train back to Warsaw, I will give one of these rosaries to a passenger in a wheelchair. The man, a practising Catholic who suffers from Parkinson's, will tell me that he studied at the John Paul II University in Kraków, and knows the name of Dziwisz, whom he venerates.

The photograph I have been given shows John Paul II holding an animal in his arms.

'It's a lamb,' Dziwisz tells me, himself as gentle as a lamb.

Now the cardinal dedicates the book of photographs to me with his beautiful pen, in a prince's tiny black-ink handwriting.

'You're a writer, Frédéric: how do you spell your name in French?' he asks me.

'Frédéric, like Frédéric Chopin.'

He gives me the present and I thank him for it, even though the book is horrible, useless and vain.

'You're very likeable for a journalist. Really very likeable,' Dziwisz insists.

Since he is forbidden the 'companionship of women', I sense his Cracovian ennui, his weariness, having once been in the spotlight, at the right hand of the man who was guiding the course of the world. In Rome, he knew all the seminarians and all the Swiss Guards by their first names. Time has passed, and the old bachelor has ceased to count his widowhoods. In Kraków the old man in his holy robe, grieving, a young pensioner, questions me. Not even a companion by his side.

'No, I'm not bored here. I prefer Kraków to Rome,' Dziwisz tells me, apparently not a man given to blushing.

We're no longer alone now. A bishop has come in. He bows deeply, addressing Dziwisz with a very reverential 'Eminence'.

I tell the cardinal, with irony and a hint of shame, that I have never used the term 'Eminence'; he bursts out laughing, taking me by the hand as if bringing me into his confidence, as if saying that it isn't serious, that titles are of no use, that he really doesn't care. As if, having returned from his season in hell: 'I'm not an eminence! I'm a widow!'

To understand John Paul II's pontificate we must therefore start with the concentric circles that surround the pope. The first ring is that of those closest to him, of whom Stanisław Dziwisz is the central link. The secretary of state, Agostino Casaroli, isn't part of this group. In reality he didn't really work well with the pope. The relationship between the two men soon experienced tensions, sometimes with vehement debate, and Casaroli, who was averse to conflict, suggested resigning several times, according to a number of sources, all of which agree. These tensions didn't leak to the outside world: the relationship between the two men invariably appeared fluid since Casaroli always yielded to the pope's demands. As a good diplomat, he played from the score he was given, even if he didn't approve of it. But in private their relationship deteriorated, about fundamental principles and about the choice of men.

About communism, first of all: Cardinal Casaroli was a man of the Cold War, and barely anticipated the fall of communism, even though it was what he desired. In a book of interviews, Pope Benedict XVI would confirm this point: 'It was obvious that in spite of all his good intentions, Casaroli's policy had essentially failed ... It was clear that rather than trying to placate [the communist regime] with compromises, we had to stand up to it. That was John Paul II's point of view and I approved of it.' On this subject, it is quite plain that history proved the Polish pope right, since he is considered today as one of the chief architects of the fall of communism.

The other tension between the holy father and his 'prime minister' arose around the choice of men. Was this the tragedy of Casaroli's succession, as some have said to me? In any case, the old and powerful cardinal, condemned to retirement having reached the age limit, in December 1990 (even though the pope could have deferred it), wanted to see a close colleague and his deputy appointed in his place: Achille Silvestrini. The relationship between these two men was magnetic and long-lasting. They had often worked in tandem: Silvestrini was his private secretary before becoming his deputy; he would write the preface for his posthumous memoirs. The Italian press even mentioned legal documents about their supposed 'financial association': the two prelates were said to have been complicit in under-the-table financial dealings, which they shared. This was never proven. (I met Mgr Achille Silvestrini in his private apartment inside the Vatican, near the Piazza del Forno: we exchanged a few words, a few glances, and his team wanted us to take a selfie, but he was ill and, at 95, too old for his testimony to be of use.)

What is known, however, is how close Casaroli and Silvestrini were to one another; and when I interview cardinals and bishops about this curious relationship, my question usually provokes what we might call 'knowing smiles'. Few prelates lay their cards on the table; few will call a spade a spade. Their answers are metaphorical, sometimes poetic, and I understand that hidden behind those smiles there are secrets that no one wants to reveal. Then they resort to highly allusive images. Are they 'of the parish'? Have they 'eaten of the cursed bread'? Do they form an 'unusual household'?

Some will say that I am being bold with my hypotheses; to tell the truth, I'm not nearly bold enough. It's simply that I sometimes have to attribute to hearsay what could have been written as fact! And this is what I can state now, more boldly:

Contrary to countless rumours, Casaroli doesn't seem to have been Silvestrini's lover. Let's listen to the former Curia priest Francesco Lepore, who was assistant to several cardinals, and who is for the first time in public revealing what he knows about the Casaroli–Silvestrini household: 'First of all, Casaroli was homosexual and everyone in the Vatican knew it. He liked young men, not minors, no, but young adults. It is quite certain that Silvestrini was one of his "creatures". But they were probably never lovers, because Casaroli liked younger men.' (More than a dozen priests have confirmed these inclinations of Casaroli's, some even informing me that they had intimate relations with him.)

Father Federico Lombardi, the former spokesman of the three last popes, didn't even want to discuss the hypothesis of Casaroli's homosexuality when I questioned him on the subject during one of our five interviews: 'All of these accusations of homosexuality are a little excessive,' he tells me. 'Of course there are homosexuals [in the Church], that's obvious. There are even a few who are more obvious than the others. But I refuse to read things that way, and to believe that homosexuality is an explanatory factor.'

What is certain is that the two men in this strange household, Casaroli and Silvestrini, always helped one another, sharing friendships and hatreds. So, for example, they always remained suspicious of John Paul II's new 'minister' of foreign affairs, Angelo Sodano, who had had his eye on Casaroli's post since 1989, when he came back from Chile.

Did this plotter want the job promised to Silvestrini? They reassured themselves as best they could, remembering that John Paul II had just appointed Silvestrini as prefect of the Supreme Tribunal of the Apostolic Signatura, and created him a cardinal as a sign of his support before the promotion he dreamed of.

'I met Silvestrini just before the fateful day, and he was already behaving as if he were secretary of state,' the Slovene cardinal Franc Rodé told me during an interview in his Vatican office.

Rodé came from the communist bloc, and analysed the choice between Silvestrini and Sodano as a rational and political one: 'I was in Slovenia, and, like John Paul II, I sensed that communism was in its death throes. We might say that Casaroli represented the left wing. Some will even say that Casaroli was the soft line and Silvestrini was the soft line of the soft line. John Paul II favoured someone on the right. Sodano was an upright man, a man of wisdom and loyalty.'

Everyone understood why John Paul II hesitated. And what should only have been a formality went on for ever. But the pope reassured Casaroli, confirming that, since he was unaccustomed to Roman intrigues and not greatly interested in Italian affairs, he wanted to take an Italian as his deputy.

Casaroli showed considerable mettle in defence of his young protégé. Some first-hand witnesses of his campaign testify to this: they describe it in terms of a Shakespearian epic, one which was prepared for like the Battle of Agincourt by Henri V: others – more French – prefer to describe it as a Napoleonic conquest, which started with Austerlitz but ended in Waterloo; others, probably more fairly, speak of a cunning campaign in which all kinds of low blows were possible, not to mention wounds to self-esteem. Finally, one priest cited Plato and his praise of pairs of soldiers who always go into combat together, and who are, by virtue of this fact, the bravest and the most invincible, even unto death.

'To say that Casaroli "wanted" Silvestrini hardly corresponds to reality,' Cardinal Paul Poupard says by way of nuance. 'Casaroli had a preference, but he knew that the choice would be down to the pope. Which didn't stop him trying to push Silvestrini's candidacy and bringing out his great guns.'

In spite of the insistent pressure of Casaroli, John Paul II finally dropped Silvestrini in favour of Angelo Sodano. And since the Vatican is a fierce theocracy where, as in Silicon Valley, 'the winner takes all', Casaroli retired immediately afterwards to devote himself to helping delinquent boys in a prison in Rome. Silvestrini, hurt and depressed, would soon join the liberal opposition to Sodano and Ratzinger (the so-called 'St Gallen Group'), and would turn his attention to a school for orphans in the district of Cornelia in Rome (where I went to interview his close colleagues, particularly Archbishop Claudio Maria Celli).

Two men from the Vatican who spent time with Casaroli during the last years of his life have told me of their exchanges. These testimonies come from first hand. The former 'prime minister' to the pope did not conceal from them his liking for young men, or his bitterness towards John Paul II, or his criticisms of Sodano. These witnesses, who told me of his words and his wounds, were also surprised when they visited him in his private apartment in the Vatican, to discover photographs of naked men hanging on the walls.

'One might say that they were artistic photographs, but obviously I wasn't falling for that one,' one of Casaroli's friends confides in me.

An archbishop from the Curia also tells me that Casaroli had a work of art showing St Sebastian in that private apartment. 'There were lots of jokes about that painting, and someone even advised the former secretary of state to hide it in his bedroom.'

And the archbishop, who fears that he's gone too far, adds to reduce the tension: 'You must bear in mind that Casaroli was an aesthete ...'

According to a reliable Vatican diplomatic source, the artistic inclinations of Casaroli and his dealings with young men were used against him by the advocates of Angelo Sodano's candidacy. That of Silvestrini was torpedoed when the pope was told that he had been stopped by the police, twice, near the Valle Giulia in Rome, where there are several contemporary art museums.

'That unfounded rumour, that little piece of gossip, was the Judas kiss,' observes someone familiar with the file.

The harshness of his confrontation and this rumour-mongering had little to do with Silvestrini's eviction, according to other cardinals and Vaticanologists who I interviewed. One of them even assures me: 'It wasn't an interpersonal question for John Paul II: you have to think about these choices in terms of a political line. As soon as the Berlin Wall came down, John Paul II chose to get rid of Casaroli. It was almost automatic. And, by definition, the pope didn't intend to allow his line to perpetuate itself, which would have been the case if he had appointed Silvestrini in his place. In fact, from the outset, Silvestrini didn't have a chance. And Sodano was chosen.'

Angelo Sodano was of a different stripe altogether. He was the 'villain' of John Paul II's pontificate – and he is the 'villain' of this book. We will get to know him well. A diplomat like Casaroli, more discreet than most cardinals, with a metallic gaze, Sodano is presented by all those who know him as a Machiavellian cardinal for whom the end always justifies the means. He is the '*éminence noire*', not just '*grise*', in all the blackness and opacity of the term. For a long time he too has had the whiff of sulphur about him.

His campaign to become John Paul II's 'prime minister' was an effective one. Sodano's anti-communism won out over the moderation of Casaroli and, consequently, of Silvestrini. The fall of the Berlin Wall, which had taken place a few months earlier, probably persuaded the pope that a 'hard' line (like Sodano's) was preferable to a 'soft' one (like Casaroli's or Silvestrini's).

To ideology we must add differences in personality.

'Beginning with the pope's trip to Chile, where he was nuncio, Sodano struck him as a strong personality, even though he appeared very effeminate. He was tall, very bulky; he looked like a mountain. He had a lot of authority. And there was his great strength: he was very loyal and docile. He was the exact opposite of Casaroli,' Francesco Lepore tells me.

Federico Lombardi, who ran Radio Vatican at the time, and who would go on to become spokesman for John Paul II and Benedict XVI, completes this portrait of his character. 'Angelo Sodano was efficient. He had a systematic cast of mind. He was a good organizer. Certainly, he lacked creativity, there were no surprises up his sleeve, but that was what the pope was after.'

It appears that John Paul II's private secretary, Stanisław Dziwisz, played a part in this nomination, favouring Sodano's candidacy. According to the testimony of an influential layman in the Vatican: 'Casaroli was a very powerful secretary of state. He knew how to say "no" to the pope. Dziwisz wanted an inoffensive person in the post, a good functionary who was capable of doing the job, but who would say "yes". And everyone who, like me, lived inside the Vatican during John Paul II's pontificate knew very well that it was Dziwisz who was in charge.'

This entourage that Dziwisz and Sodano formed around the pope was far from anodyne. What a strange duo! These two characters will occupy our attention for a long time in this book.

Today Angelo Sodano lives in a very luxurious penthouse on the top floor of a place called the 'Ethiopian College' in the heart of the Vatican. He is locked up in his African ivory tower, with all his secrets. If the Garden of Eden ever existed, it must be like this little earthly paradise: when I go there, crossing a bridge, I find myself among impeccably tended lawns and fragrant magnolias. It's a Mediterranean garden, with pines and cypresses and, of course, olive trees. In the surrounding cedars I see purple-headed and moustachioed parrots, elegant and multi-coloured, whose mellifluous voices doubtless wake Cardinal Sodano from his slumbers.

Still reflecting on these beautiful long-tailed birds at the Ethiopian College, I am suddenly approached by a passing African bishop who lives there, Musie Ghebreghiorghis, a Franciscan who comes from the small town of Emdibir, 180 kilometres from Addis Ababa. The bishop shows me around his college, with Antonio Martínez Velásquez, a Mexican journalist and one of my main researchers, and talks to us at length about Angelo Sodano and his darkness. Musie is very unhappy: 'It's an abuse. Sodano shouldn't be living there. This is the Ethiopian College; so it's for Ethiopians ...'

The reason for his discontent, and that of the other Ethiopian priests living in the college: the presence of Angelo Sodano, who has privatized the top floor of the establishment. For Musie Ghebreghiorghis, Sodano should never have been given permission to live there. (Pope Benedict XVI and Cardinal Bertone will also criticize this privatization.)

We should add that the penthouse has been adapted for the cardinal's personal convenience. A lift means that Sodano, who has made good provision for his old age, doesn't have to climb the stairs. In the corridors I see photographs of the cardinal with Benedict XVI – when everyone knows that they were intractable enemies. The furniture is horrible, as it often is in the Vatican. And what isolation! As I can confirm, there is only one other Italian cardinal living on the top floor, next door to him: Giovanni Lajolo. A protégé and close friend of Sodano, Lajolo was his secretary of foreign affairs, his direct deputy at the Secretariat of State. A successful Silvestrini.

There are several sources for the dark legend, the terrible reputation of Angelo Sodano. This northern Italian, ordained priest at 23, whose father was for a long time a Christian Democrat member of parliament, is powerful and strong-willed and has used his power to make and unmake careers. His ambition was precocious. He was spotted by Paul VI when he worked on Hungary in the office of the secretary of state, and appointed nuncio to Chile in 1977. Number 2 at the Vatican for 14 years under John Paul II and dean of cardinals, he accumulated functions as few men of the Church had done before him. His achievements were generally recognized with regard to the Yugoslavian conflict, the first Gulf War, the conflicts in Kosovo and Afghanistan, and indeed the multiple tensions in the Holy Land during his mandate.

Sodano has often been compared to Cardinal Mazarin, the Italian state prelate who served both the pope and the kings of France, and whose abuses of power, number of enemies and secret amorous relationships are legendary. During the decade when John Paul II, a young and athletic pope, large and vigorous, was transformed into the 'pope of suffering', soon paralysed by Parkinson's disease, incapable of running the Curia, gradually deprived of his mobility and even of the power of speech – according to all witnesses – Sodano became the true interim pope.

Theoretically, as I have said, he formed a duo with Mgr Stanisław Dziwisz, the private secretary of John Paul II, and even a trio with Cardinal Ratzinger, prefect of the Congregation for the Doctrine of the

Faith. But the first of these, who was close to the pope, was not yet a bishop; the second, however central he might have been, was essentially packed off to doctrine and ideas. The ambition of these men would gradually be fulfilled, but in the meantime the tetrarch Sodano governed all of the internal affairs and diplomacy in the Vatican without sharing power with anyone else.

His political ideas added a fundamental hatred to personal animosities that were already well-known in Rome. Unlike Cardinal Casaroli and his scion Achille Silvestrini, who were men of compromise, Sodano was a rigid and peremptory man. He was tough and, it was said, violent, returning any blows dealt to him a hundredfold. His mode of operation: silence and rage. His ideological mainspring, the thing that animated him, was principally anti-communism. Hence his rapid proximity to John Paul II, which was formed or confirmed during the pope's controversial trip to Chile in 1987. Angelo Sodano was nuncio to Santiago at the time. And his troubled Chilean past, which no one knew in detail, would come to do a great deal of harm to the image of the cardinal secretary of state.

The history of the Vatican in the 1990s and the 2000s was thus formed ten years previously in the Chilean capital, where Sodano began his rise. I went there twice for this book and interviewed dozens of witnesses. Some of the archives of the dictatorship were starting to 'speak', even while the trial of the accomplices of General Pinochet were still going on. If there are apparently no archives from DINA, the secret services (probably destroyed), important American archives, notably those of the State Department and the CIA, were recently declassified as a result of international pressure. Copies of these original documents have been entrusted by the United States to the Chilean government and are now accessible in the Museo de la Memoria y los Derechos Humanos in Santiago. I have made intensive use of these thousands of unpublished documents for the part of this book devoted to Angelo Sodano. Many things that were still unknown a few years ago are therefore beginning to rise to the surface, like the corpses that the dictator Pinochet wanted to make disappear.

'The man of good, in those times, was close to the man of evil.' The phrase comes from Chateaubriand – but it applies equally to Sodano.

Here I am in Santiago for my investigation, and it's here that, without meaning to, I become a kind of biographer of Angelo Sodano. I wish the cardinal and his biographer could have met; in spite of letters and friendly epistolary exchanges, though, that meeting never took place. That's probably a shame. It makes me all the more aware of my responsibility. I know that the career of the cardinal secretary of state may be summed up – alas! – in the pages the follow.

Ecce homo. Angelo Sodano was the Vatican representative in Chile from March 1978 until May 1988. He arrived in Santiago in 'the time of crazy hope', shortly after the coup of Augusto Pinochet. It was a country that he knew already, having lived there between 1966 and 1968 as deputy to the nunciature. At the time, it was a crucial country for the Vatican, taking into account relationships that were considered 'specially sensitive' with the Chilean dictator.

Sodano formed a long relationship with Pinochet, which many witnesses whom I have questioned had no hesitation in calling a 'deep friendship' or even an 'intense friendship'.

'Angelo Sodano was very concerned with the rights of man. We did as much as we could. Don't forget that we had about thirty political refugees in the dependencies of the nunciature in Santiago,' argues Archbishop François Bacqué, who was Sodano's deputy in Chile.

I had several opportunities to converse and dine *tête-à-tête* with this emeritus diplomat, now retired. This was a stroke of luck: Bacqué is as chatty as Sodano is tight-lipped; as chummy and playful as the former secretary of state is silent and humourless: one wants to be loved, the other to be hated. Unlike Bacqué, Sodano always saved his kind words for his little group of cronies, enigmatic nuncios and impenetrable cardinals. And yet these two very different characters, the nuncio who succeeded and the nuncio who failed, resemble one another – mirror-image acolytes.

Most witnesses and experts that I interviewed in Santiago don't share François Bacqué positive, albeit slightly second-hand appreciation. For them, Sodano's past is in fact 'blacker than his cassock'.

Look at his way of life, first of all! According to the testimony of Osvaldo Rivera, a close adviser to Pinochet, which we collected in Chile, Angelo Sodano lived in luxury: 'One day I received a dinner invitation from the nuncio, which I accepted. When I arrived, I realized that I was the only guest. We sat down at a very elegant table covered with silver-ware. And I said to myself: "this priest wants to show you the meaning of power, of absolute power, and he wants me to understand that I am the lowest of the low". Because not only was it a luxurious environment, the display itself was ostentatious.'

Many other witnesses remember this way of life, which was far from usual for a priest, even for a nuncio. Sodano did not make modesty a virtue.

'I remember Sodano very well; he was a prince. I saw him all the time: he enjoyed the high life. He went out in his car with a police escort with a blue light. He went to all kinds of inaugurations and demanded a reserved seat in the first row. He was the exact opposite of the Church, because he was pro-Pinochet while the Chilean Church wasn't,' the writer and journalist Pablo Simonetti tells me.

An academic of some repute, for a long time Ernesto Ottone was one of the leaders of the Chilean Communist Party. He knew Sodano, and he tells me: 'In Chile, Sodano didn't give the impression of being a church-man at all. He loved good food and power. I was struck by his misogyny, which contrasted with the fact that he was very effeminate. His way of shaking hands was very unusual: he didn't shake your hand, he gave you a kind of feminine caress, like a nineteenth-century courtesan before she faints and demands smelling salts!'

Witnesses were also dumbfounded to see Sodano 'bowing all the way to the floor' when he met the dictator. With subalterns he was more friendly: 'he would slap you on the back,' a witness tells me. But women remained entirely absent from the life of the nuncio. Sometimes this loner was on his own; at other times he would appear in a crowd. Then he would arrive with his entourage, a pageant of male creatures, devoted to him body and soul. Wickedness settled in over time.

One person who worked with Sodano in the nunciature confirms this development. 'At first Sodano was prudent and reserved. He came to Chile with Rome's ideas about the dictatorship: he had a rather crit-ical vision of Pinochet, and wanted to defend the rights of man. But gradually, in contact with reality and the dictatorship, he became more pragmatic. He began to work with the regime.'

The retired nuncio François Bacqué, who was also in office with Sodano in Chile, has similar memories: 'At first, he didn't want to compromise with Pinochet. I remember a day when he was supposed to appear beside him for a military ceremony. The nuncio was traditionally present, and Sodano didn't want to go for fear of compromising the Church.'

The diplomatic archives, which are now declassified, effectively confirm that there were tensions between Sodano and Pinochet, particularly during the first few years. In 1984, in particular, when four left-wing extremists entered the apostolic nunciature asking for political asylum. But there are more documents that prove Sodano gave Pinochet his complete support: the nuncio would go so far as to close his eyes when the government ordered the arrest of priests accused of subversive activity.

In fact, Angelo Sodano inadvertently became Pinochet's guardian angel. He began minimizing his crimes, taking the approach of his predecessor in Santiago, who had, in 1973, bluntly dismissed them as 'communist propaganda' (according to documents from the American diplomatic missions revealed by WikiLeaks). He also sought to play down the systematic use of torture, which was massive and brutal, and to maintain diplomatic relations between Chile and the holy see, after several states, including Italy, had severed them.

From then on, according to numerous witness statements that I have collected (including that of the priest Cristián Precht, one of the closest colleagues of the Bishop of Santiago, Raúl Silva Henríquez), Sodano contributed to the appointment of neutral or pro-Pinochet bishops, disqualifying priests opposed to the regime. In 1984, he manoeuvred to have Silva Henríquez replaced, a moderate cardinal who criticized the violence of the dictatorship and was close to the president of the Republic, Salvador Allende. Instead, Sodano sought the appointment of Juan Francisco Fresno Larraín, a notorious ally of Pinochet and an 'insignificant' bishop according to all witnesses.

'Cardinal Fresno was essentially concerned with his passion for orange cake,' the journalist Mónica González tells me in Santiago.

It seems, however, that Cardinal Fresno was a more ambivalent figure: although a visceral anti-communist, he was said to have criticized Pinochet severely in private, and the dictator, who had been enthusiastic about him at first, soon considered him as an 'enemy' of the regime.

Pinochet was said to have complained about Fresno to Sodano, threatening to 'change religion'! Sodano then put Fresno under pressure to calm down his criticisms of the regime (according to the declassified telegrams and notes from the CIA that I have consulted).

Gradually Sodano hardened. The nuncio became colder and more rigid. He maintained his silence about the arrest and murder of four priests close to liberation theology, which explains why he was often criticized by the progressive Chilean Catholic networks (particularly by the movement También Somos Iglesia, which denounced him for his complicity with the dictatorship). He also called to order many clerics who participated in non-violent actions against Pinochet. Sodano's Church was a Church that mobilized its forces against progressive priests, against worker-priests, against the weak – not a Church that protected or defended.

Finally, with a political skill that he would become used to deploying alongside John Paul II, the nuncio locked down the Chilean Bishop's Conference, appointing at least four bishops close to Opus Dei to check it and limit its internal debates. (Most of these ultra-conservative bishops had, when they were seminarians, frequented the parish of the priest Fernando Karadima, who is central to this story, as we shall see.)

From Rome, when he became secretary of state to John Paul II, Angelo Sodano continued to pull strings in Chile and protect the dictator. In 1998, he had Francisco Javier Errázuriz appointed to the post of Archbishop of Santiago, and would then contribute to his being created cardinal. It wouldn't matter that Errázuriz would be accused of covering up cases of sexual abuse, or that he raised eyebrows in Santiago over his worldly associations and his private life: Sodano defended him against all comers.

The journalist and writer Óscar Contardo, who wrote a book about a paedophile priest who was protected by Cardinal Francisco Javier Errázuriz, had no hesitation in criticizing those who encouraged his appointment to the post. 'We find Angelo Sodano at the very heart of these scandals here in Chile. The nuncio wasn't in Santiago only for reasons of faith.'

One of the journalists I interviewed in Santiago, who has written a great deal about the crimes of the dictatorship, puts it even more strongly: 'Let's call a spade a spade: in Chile, Angelo Sodano behaved like a fascist, and he was the friend of a fascist dictator. That's the reality.'

In the Vatican, a number of people had no hesitation, in private, in comparing Sodano to the priest Pietro Tacchi Venturi. Another reactionary, this Italian Jesuit was the intermediary between Pope Pius XI and Mussolini, and we know, from the revelations of historians, that he accumulated many wrongs. He was pro-fascist, and was considered to be a great 'sexual adventurer' (with young men).

In April 1987, Sodano supervised Pope John Paul II's visit to Chile, in close cooperation with the pope's personal assistant, Stanisław Dziwisz, who was in Rome and would be travelling with the pope. According to two witnesses who took part in it, the preparatory meetings for this risky visit were 'very tense' and led to intense confrontations between the 'two camps' – the anti-Pinochet progressives and the pro-Pinochet conservatives. The other extraordinary thing about them was that they were 'chiefly composed of homosexual priests'.

The Chilean bishop who coordinated the preparation for the visit, and one of its most effective architects, was a certain Francisco Cox: this conservative would go on to play a part in the Pontifical Council for the Family in Rome, where he would present himself as very homophobic, before being denounced in the end for homosexual abuses in Chile.

Another of those behind the visit, the priest Cristián Precht, was close to the progressive cardinal of Santiago: he represented the other camp, in that violent opposition between right and left in the Chilean episcopacy. During an interview, Precht gave me detailed descriptions of those meetings, in which the nuncio Angelo Sodano participated 'three or four times', and told me on the record: 'Sodano acted, on certain subjects, like a representative of the government and of Pinochet, and not like the representative of John Paul II.' (In 2011, and then in 2018, Precht was also accused of sexual abuses of boys and suspended by Rome, before being reduced to the status of layman.)

At this time, even the United States had distanced themselves from Pinochet, whom they had initially supported. 'Now it was only the Vatican that was defending the dictatorship! No one else wanted to grant political legitimacy to Pinochet except Angelo Sodano!' I was told by Alejandra Matus, a Chilean investigative journalist and researcher who specialized in the dictatorship, and whom I met in the Starbucks at her university in Santiago.

During this trip, Sodano allowed – or, according to some versions, organized – the highly symbolic appearance of the pope and General Pinochet, together on the balcony at the Presidential Palace of La Moneda: the photograph of the two men, smiling, would be criticized all over the world, and in particular by the democratic opposition and part of the Chilean Catholic Church.

Piero Marini, John Paul II's 'master of ceremonies', was among those present. He spoke of this version of events during two interviews in Rome, in the presence of my researcher Daniele: 'Everything had been prepared in great detail, but Pinochet took it upon himself to invite the pope onto the balcony at La Moneda and take him there straight away. It wasn't part of the protocol. The pope was taken along against his will.'

The next day, at a mass in front of a million people, there were scuffles with the police, who charged the rioters during the mass; six hundred people were wounded. According to many witnesses and several investigations, Pinochet's secret services manipulated the trouble-makers. Sodano issued a communiqué holding the democratic opposition responsible, claiming the police were the victims.

That visit by John Paul II was one of the finest political stunts carried out by Pinochet and – therefore – by Sodano. The dictator heaped praises on the apostolic nuncio, offering him, a few months later, a lunch in honour of his ten years in Santiago. I have collected several witness statements about this meal, which suggest an unusual and abnormal complicity between the nuncio and the dictator. (The declassified documents of the American State Department confirm this point.)

A few weeks later, in May 1988, when a crucial referendum was being prepared for Pinochet (which he would lose in October, and which would force him to step down), Sodano was called back to Rome, where he was appointed 'minister' of foreign affairs at the Vatican. In 1990 he became the pope's 'prime minister'.

His honeymoon with Pinochet still wasn't over. As Montesquieu says: 'Any man with power is led to abuse it; he is bound to find its limits.'

Without limits, then, and at the holy see, an adventurer and extremist more than ever, and less than ever a disciple of the Gospel, Sodano continued to keep a watch over his friend the dictator, and went on supporting him even after his fall. In 1993 he insisted that Pope John Paul II bestow his 'divine grace' on General Pinochet on the occasion of his gold wedding. And when Pinochet was hospitalized in Great Britain, in 1998, and arrested because he was subject to an international arrest warrant and an extradition demand from Spain for his crimes, Sodano still kept an eye on him, supported the dictator and publicly opposed his extradition.

The first time I met Santiago Schuler was at the restaurant El Toro, which he owned. A focus of Chilean night-life, this gay restaurant is in the district of Bellavista in Santiago. We got on well, and I saw him several times, including once in 2017, during my second stay in the country, when I interviewed him in the presence of my Chilean researcher, Andrés Herrera.

Santiago Schuler is something of a special case. He is a pro-Pinochet gay. He continues to have great admiration for the dictator.

'I still have two portraits of Pinochet in my hallway,' he told me without a hint of embarrassment.

At the age of 71, the manager of El Toro told me about his career, in which Catholicism, fascism and homosexuality produced a strange cocktail. Born in Chile to a family of French wine-growers and a father of Swiss origin, he grew up in the Christian faith, and close to Opus Dei. He was married and the father of nine children. 'In the closet' for a long time, he only belatedly 'came out' after the end of the dictatorship, when he was over sixty. Since then he has tried to make up for lost time. His gay restaurant, El Toro, tiny inside, but much larger when extended into the street on a terrace under an awning, represents the heart of Santiago's gay life. And what a paradox! Chile's emblematic LGBT venue is run by a fundamentalist ex-Catholic, an old personal friend of Pinochet's!

'Homosexuals weren't very worried under Pinochet, even though the regime was indeed quite macho,' Santiago Schuler suggests.

According to Schuler and other sources, Pinochet's wife was both a practising Catholic and gay-friendly. The Pinochets even surrounded themselves with a veritable court of Catholic homosexuals. The presidential couple liked to be seen with certain local gay figures, at parties and gala dinners, just as Pinochet liked to be seen with the nuncio Angelo Sodano.

The historians and gay activists that I interviewed in Santiago don't necessarily share that analysis. Many dispute the idea that the Chilean dictatorship was conciliatory towards homosexuals. But they all acknowledge that some places were tolerated by the regime.

'I would say that the gay issue didn't exist under Pinochet,' the writer and activist Pablo Simonetti tells me. It's true that in the documents that came out after the end of the dictatorship, nobody seems have been executed or tortured for their morals. Sodomy still remained a crime, however, until the end of the 1990s, and nothing was done to combat AIDS.

In fact, in the late 1970s and early 1980s, under the Pinochet dictatorship, there was even a 'gay circuit' in private clubs, discos and bars where 'political ideas were usually left in the cloakroom'. Some bars were closed; some clubs were infiltrated by the police. There were also cases of persecution and murder, and homosexuals were tortured by the regime, but according to Óscar Contardo, Pablo Simonetti and other experts, the dictatorship didn't persecute homosexuals as such, in a special or specific way (like Castro's regime in Cuba, the previous socialist government, led by Allende, wasn't very gay-friendly either).

What is strange, on the other hand, and to some extent startling, is the very existence of a real 'gay court' in Pinochet's entourage. No one has ever described it in detail; I have to do it here, because it is at the heart of the subject of this book.

During another dinner, where he let me taste some vintage red wine of which he was the exclusive dealer in Chile, I questioned Santiago Schuler about Pinochet's 'homosexual court'. We mentioned a whole series of names and, each time, Schuler would pick up his telephone and, talking to other people who were close to Pinochet and with whom he stayed friends, reconstruct the dictator's gay or gay-friendly entourage. Six names recur systematically. All are closely connected to the apostolic nuncio Angelo Sodano.

The most illustrious of these names is that of Fernando Karadima. He was a Catholic priest who, during the 1980s, ran the parish of El Bosque in the centre of Santiago, which I visited. Located in the smart district of Providencia, it is only a few hundred metres away from the nunciature: so Angelo Sodano was Karadima's neighbour. He went to see him on foot.

It was also the church frequented by Pinochet's entourage. The dictator had good relations with Karadima, whom he protected for a long time in spite of recurring rumours, from the 1980s onwards, about the sexual abuse that went on there. According to several sources, Karadima's parish, like Sodano's nunciature, was infiltrated by the regime's security services. The homosexuality of the Chilean priest was therefore well-known by this time and by all officials, as were his sexual abuses.

'Pinochet was fascinated by the information about homosexuals brought back to him by his informers and agents. He was particularly interested in the gay Catholic hierarchy,' Schuler told me.

Ernesto Ottone, a former director of the Chilean Communist Party, and long-exiled from the country, gave me an interesting analysis when I interviewed him.

'At first, Pinochet was frowned upon by the Church. So he had to create a Church of his own from the ground up. He had to find pro-Pinochet priests, but also bishops. This recruitment and training campaign was the role of Karadima's church. Sodano defended the strategy. And since the nuncio was a notorious anti-communist, as well as being extremely vain, the attraction of power did the rest. He was on the hard right. As far as I was concerned, Sodano was pro-Pinochet.' (Another left-wing leader, Marco Enríquez-Ominami, who stood several times as a candidate in Chile's presidential election, also confirmed Sodano's 'pro-Pinochet' stance.)

The apostolic nuncio therefore became an unconditional devotee of Karadima, so much so that a room reserved for him in a wing of the vicariate of El Bosque was christened '*la sala del nuncio*' (the nuncio's drawing room). There he met many seminarians and young priests that Karadima personally introduced to him. The Chilean acted as an intermediary, a fixer, for the Italian, who was duly grateful for these kindnesses. The young men in question gravitated around the parish and its organization, the Priestly Union. This group, which consisted of five bishops and dozens of very conservative priests, was entirely devoted to Karadima, rather as the Legion of Christ would similarly be towards the priest Marcial Maciel.

'It was a kind of sect of which Karadima was the boss,' the lawyer Juan Pablo Hermosilla comments. 'Neither Opus Dei nor the Legion of Christ had really taken root in Chile, so Karadima's group assumed that role.'

Through that network of priests and his own personal homosexual connections, Karadima was kept well-informed about the Chilean clergy.

'Karadima worked hand in hand with Sodano,' Hermosilla adds.

The priest would often tell his visitors that he was able to pull strings. And thanks to the attentions of the nuncio, he claimed to have strong connections with Rome, and to be under the direct protection of John Paul II, which is probably very much of an exaggeration.

'He had the appearance of a saint, and the seminarians called him "*el santo, el santito*". He said he would be canonized after his death,' the lawyer Hermosilla adds.

Mónica González, a famous Chilean investigative journalist, agrees: 'Karadima wanted to know everything about the private lives of the priests, he listened to all the gossip, all the rumours. He was interested in progressive priests, and zealously tried to find out if they were gay. He passed on all this information to the nuncio Sodano, with a view to blocking the careers of any who were on the left.'

In all likelihood, this information, whether it was passed on by Sodano to his fascist friends or communicated directly from Karadima to Pinochet, enabled the arrest of progressive priests. Several witnesses talked of confabulations between Sodano and Sergió Rillón, Pinochet's right-hand man, and of files being swapped. So Sodano, who had Karadima's ear, and was proud of his vast knowledge, could have shared confidences with the Chilean dictatorship.

Numerous army officers, many of Pinochet's secret police and several of his personal advisers were also regular visitors to Karadima's parish. Pinochet's ministers and generals, good practising Catholics, attended mass there.

We might even say that in the 1970s and 1980s, El Bosque became the parish church of the dictatorship, and a meeting point for fascists. There were so many of them, they had so many crimes and misdeeds requiring forgiveness, that one wonders how they could go on taking communion and hope to end up in Purgatory! Except that the priest Fernando Karadima seemed to promise them paradise, with the blessing of the nuncio.

Angelo Sodano was omnipresent in El Bosque, according to all witnesses, and constantly appeared in the company of Karadima, with whom he sometimes celebrated mass. The envoy of Pope John Paul II appeared beside Pinochet at certain events. He spent the rest of his time moving in pro-fascist and furiously anti-communist circles: he was in direct contact with Sergió Rillón, who personally followed religious affairs, as well as with Francisco Javier Cuadra, the dictator's special adviser, then one of his ministers and finally his ambassador to the Vatican. (The declassified CIA archives confirm this information, as does Osvaldo Rivera, another close adviser to Pinochet, whom we interviewed.)

Sodano seemed at ease in this fascist milieu. Pinochet's personal guard adopted the archbishop as one of their own because he was ideologically reliable and never talked. And since he had a connection with John Paul II and was believed to be a future cardinal, the nuncio became a precious pawn in an overall plan. He, in return, proud of attracting such envy, ramped up his toadyism and his appetite. As Roosevelt used to say, never under-estimate a man who over-estimates himself! The vainest of nuncios, the future 'dean of cardinals' was a man of limitless pride and outsized ego.

The ambitious Sodano therefore navigated among multiple identities while trying to combine different networks and avoid making a mark. He compartmentalized his lives to the extent that it is difficult to decode his Chilean years. He took control freakery to an extreme. A reserved and even indecipherable figure in Chile, and later in Rome, he would present himself as prudent, discreet and secretive – except when he wasn't. For example, in his curious relationship with Rodrigo Serrano Bombal.

Bombal – what a name! What a pedigree! What a CV! A reserve naval officer and allegedly a member of Pinochet's secret service, he was also a regular at El Bosque. (The journalist Mónica González said that his membership in DINA, the Dirección de Inteligencia Nacional, Pinochet's secret services, is attested by his appointment record, which she was able to consult.)

How do we know that any of this information is reliable? It is all accessible now in the items in the file and the witness statements given as part of the Karadima 'affair'. Since at least 1984, Fernando Karadima had been denounced several times for sexual abuse. At the time when he was regularly visiting him, Angelo Sodano could not, in spite of his smile, have been unaware of these facts.

'Fernando Karadima spotted boys with family problems, and won their loyalty to the parish. He gradually removed and separated them from their families, and finally abused them. His system was still risky, because these boys usually belonged to the families of the Chilean elite,' I am told by the lawyer for several of the victims, Juan Pablo Hermosilla.

The priest's actions caused outrage throughout the 1980s and 1990s, but Pinochet's gay entourage and the Chilean episcopacy protected Karadima and brushed the whole case under the carpet. The Vatican, where Angelo Sodano had in the meantime become secretary of state, also covered up for Karadima, and even instructed the Chilean Church not to denounce him. (The official version is that the Vatican was not informed about the Karadima affair until 2010, when Sodano was no longer secretary of state. Only the Cardinal of Santiago, Francisco Javier Errázuriz, was said to have delayed sending the file to the holy see, keeping it to himself without acting for several years – for which he was personally indicted by the Chilean judiciary.)

The reasons that led Sodano (as well as Cardinal Errázuriz and Cardinal Bertone, who replaced Sodano as secretary of state in 2006) to protect this paedophile priest remain mysterious. Everything suggests that it was not just a matter of covering up for a priest accused of sexual abuse, but of a whole system in which the Church and Pinochet's dictatorship were closely linked, and would have had a lot to lose if the priest had begun to talk. In any case, out of loyalty to the system, Sodano would always defend priests accused of sexual abuse, to preserve the institution, defend his friends, and perhaps also to protect himself.

According to the 14 witnesses in the trial and the 50 or so complaints registered, the sexual abuse began in the late 1960s and continued until 2010. For 50 years, Karadima abused dozens of boys between the ages of 12 and 17, most of them white and blond.

It was only after the fall of the dictatorship, in 2004, that a formal inquiry was held into his activities. It would not be until 2011 that four circumstantial complaints were judged to be admissible. It was then, once Cardinal Sodano had been removed by Pope Benedict XVI, that the Vatican ordered a trial under canon law. Father Karadima was found guilty of sexual abuse of minors and punished by the pope. According to my information, he still lives in Chile today, at the age of 80, without any religious responsibilities, in a secret and isolated location. (He was finally reduced to lay status by Pope Francis in September 2018.)

Since 2010 the Chilean Church has been largely 'discredited' and 'stripped of credibility by this affair', in the words of Pablo Simonetti. The number of believers has collapsed, and the level of trust in Catholicism has dropped from 50 per cent to less than 22 per cent.

Pope Francis's visit in 2018 reopened old wounds: Francis appeared to have protected a priest close to Karadima, and we must probably see that mistake less as an error – alas – than as a desperate attempt to ensure that Karadima's entire system, and his connivances reaching all the way to Cardinals Sodano and Franciso Javier Errázuriz, did not literally collapse. After an extended investigation, the pope finally apologized in a public letter for 'committing serious errors of judgement … in [his] perception of the situation, especially due to a lack of reliable and balanced information'. He was referring explicitly to those who had kept him badly informed: according to the Chilean press, these were the nuncio Ivo Scapolo, and the cardinals Ricardo Ezzati and Francisco Javier Errázuriz – all three close to Angelo Sodano. Since then, all Chilean bishops have resigned, and the case has assumed international proportions. Several cardinals, including Ezzati and Errázuriz, have been investigated by the Chilean courts in connection with sexual abuse allegations made against other priests. Many revelations are yet to come. (In this chapter I use the evidence from the trial and witness statements, including Juan Carlos Cruz, whom I have interviewed, as well as the documents communicated to me by their chief lawyer, Juan Pablo Hermosilla, who helped me with my inquiry. A priest close to Karadima, Samuel Fernández, who repented, also agreed to speak.)

So, during his years in Chile, Angelo Sodano socialized assiduously with Pinochet and the parish of El Bosque. What did he know exactly? What were his motivations?

Here we should make clear that at no point, either during the Karadima trial, or in the course of dozens of interviews that I conducted in Santiago, was Sodano ever himself suspected of involvement in the sexual abuse of minors that was committed in El Bosque. This is clearly confirmed by Juan Pablo Hermosilla. 'We carried out an in-depth investigation, based on the relationship between Karadima and nuncio Sodano, about Sodano's personal involvement in Karadima's sexual abuse, and we found no evidence or witness statements to indicate that he took part in these crimes. I have never heard anyone say that Sodano was present when Karadima committed acts of sexual abuse. I think it didn't happen. because we would definitely know after all these years.'

But the victims' lawyer adds: 'On the other hand, it's almost impossible, taking into account the extent of Karadima's sexual crimes, their frequency and the rumours that had been circulating for a long time, and given that most of the victims were seminarians, that Sodano was unaware of what was happening.'

But one last mystery remains: the closeness of the nuncio to Pinochet's entourage. This connection, these relationships with a real gay mafia, remain strange at the very least, when we are aware of the position of the Catholic Church on homosexuality during the 1980s.

This unnatural connivance with Pinochet even meant that the nuncio was given a nickname: 'Pinochette' (according to several people I interviewed). In favour of Angelo Sodano, his defenders – who included the nuncio François Bacqué – point out to me that it was difficult for a Vatican diplomat to act as a dissident under the dictatorship. Associating with Pinochet's entourage was indispensable, and opposing him would have led to a cessation of diplomatic relations with the Vatican, the expulsion of the nuncio and perhaps to the arrest of priests. This argument holds some water.

Similarly, the cardinals I interviewed in Rome point to Sodano's major diplomatic success since his arrival in Chile in 1978. According to them he played a crucial part in mediation between Chile and Argentina during the conflict between the two Catholic countries concerning their border at the southern end of South America, near Tierra del Fuego. (But according to other reliable witnesses, Sodano was initially hostile to the mediation of the Vatican, which was initially the work of Cardinal Raúl Silva Henríquez and the Italian nuncio Antonio Samorè, whom the pope sent to the country as mediators in the conflict.)

They also stress that John Paul II wasn't shy about criticizing Pinochet, not least in a public speech that proved to be crucial. In his 1987 trip, during the mass that he celebrated, the pope allowed political opponents and dissidents to speak up beside him to criticize the regime of censorship, torture and political assassinations. This trip would have a lasting impact on the evolution of the country towards democracy from 1990 onwards.

'John Paul II put democratic pressure on Pinochet, and that paid off. A year after the pope's visit, a referendum opened the way to the democratic transition,' according to Luis Larrain, the chairman of an important LGBT association in Chile, whose father was a minister under the dictator.

Which leaves the strange role of Pinochet's political police with regard to Sodano.

'If we put ourselves in the context of the 1980s, Pinochet considered his diplomatic relations with the Vatican to be crucial. It was normal for Sodano to be hailed in public by the presidential couple, and "processed" in private by the Chilean secret services. What's stranger is the abnormal relationship that he formed, the intimate connections that he had with the dictator's agents and advisers, among the most senior-ranking in the regime,' says a Chilean journalist who wrote a great deal about the crimes of the dictatorship.

No fewer than four of Pinochet's officials 'processed' Sodano in person. First of all, Captain Sergió Rillón, a close adviser to the dictator and his 'liaison' agent for religious affairs, who had an office on the first floor of La Moneda, the presidential palace.

'He was a man of the far right and even a "national socialist". He was one of Pinochet's gurus and he represented the hard wing,' I was told by the journalist Alejandra Matus in Santiago.

He was known to be very close to Karadima and Sodano:

'Rillón was a member of Pinochet's most intimate circle. And he was a member of Sodano's most intimate circle,' Santiago Schuler tells me.

Then comes Osvaldo Rivera, a worldly self-proclaimed cultural expert working for Pinochet, who also had his entrées to the upper floors of La Moneda.

'Rivera presented himself as a "cultural tzar". But he was the one most responsible for censoring television for Pinochet. We all knew that he was operating in a milieu that was both far right and gay,' observes Pablo Simonetti. He was given the nickname 'La Puri', an ironic, feminised diminutive for 'the puritan'.

Questioned today, Osvaldo Rivera remembers Angelo Sodano very clearly. He is even loquacious on the subject. Rivera expands on Sodano's life in Chile and gives us plenty of information about his life. He recalls him 'drinking whisky, surrounded by rich and roguish friends', then going home under a close guard because he was 'quite drunk'.

Finally, Sodano was also close to Francisco Javier Cuadra, Pinochet's handyman, his spokesman, future minister and ambassador in the Vatican. He too, divorced and a father of eight, is portrayed in a *roman à clef* as having led a colourful life.

Apart from Pinochet's men whom Angelo Sodano associated with regularly, two other unsettling characters deserve a mention here, because they also gravitated around the dictator and belonged to the same 'mafia'. The first, an extravagant if closeted homosexual, Arancibia Clavel, was close to the dictator and the army, being responsible for operations involving the physical elimination of political opponents; he received a heavy sentence for his crimes before being murdered by a 'taxi boy'. The second, Jaime Guzman, was one of the theorists of the Pinochet regime: this rigid ultra-Catholic law professor was named in a DINA portfolio under the label '*homosexualismo*', according to Óscar Contardo in his book *Raro, Una historia gay de Chile*; he was murdered in 1991 by the far left. Both men knew Sodano.

The homosexual network of Pinochet has never been described – it will be a revelation for many Chileans. Researchers and journalists are currently investigating this paradoxical milieu and the financial arrangements between Pinochet and the Vatican (particularly via special funds in secret bank accounts that the dictator had at the Riggs Bank, and that might possibly have funded anti-communist offices close to Solidarność in Poland): we may expect further revelations on all these points in the years to come.

In all of these cases, the political and sexual collusions give meaning to a famous phrase attributed to Oscar Wilde and repeated in *House of Cards*: 'Everything in the world is about sex, except sex. Sex is about power.' It remains for us to understand why the apostolic nuncio Angelo Sodano took such pleasure in associating with the homosexual milieu. Why did he move in this group at the very moment when John Paul II was declaring homosexuality to be an abominable sin and an absolute evil?

In conclusion we may put forward three hypotheses. The first is to think that Angelo Sodano was manipulated by the Chilean secret services, was spied on and his nunciature infiltrated by virtue of his naiveté, his inexperience and his associations. The second would suggest that Angelo Sodano was vulnerable – for example, if he was himself homosexual – and was obliged to compromise with the regime to protect his secret. It is clear Pinochet's political police knew all the details of his professional and private life, whatever they might have been: perhaps they even blackmailed him? The third hypothesis is to assume that Angelo Sodano, that great manipulator, who shared the political ideas of Pinochet's advisers as well as their morals, moved freely in a milieu that suited him to the ground.

10

The Legion of Christ

Marcel Maciel is probably the most diabolical figure that the Catholic Church has given birth to and raised over the last 50 years. Possessing insane levels of wealth and overseeing a sustained programme of sexual violence, he was protected over several decades by John Paul II, Stanisław Dziwisz, personal secretary to the pope, and Angelo Sodano, the cardinal secretary of state, who became 'prime minister' of the Vatican.

All of the people I have interviewed in Mexico, Spain and Rome are puzzled about the support that Marcial Maciel has enjoyed from Rome, with the rare exception of Cardinal Giovanni Battista Re, the pope's 'minister of the interior' at the time, who told me during one of our discussions in his private apartment at the Vatican: 'John Paul II met Marcial Maciel during his trip to Mexico in 1979. It was the first international trip by the new pope, just after his election. John Paul II had a positive image of him. The Legion of Christ was recruiting huge numbers of new seminarians; it was a very efficient organization. But the truth about the paedophilia is that we didn't know. We started having doubts, hearing rumours, only at the end of the pontificate of John Paul II.'

For his part, Cardinal Jean-Louis Tauran, 'minister' of foreign affairs under John Paul II, also told me during four discussions at his office on Via Della Conciliazione: 'We didn't know about Marcial Maciel. We didn't know about all that. It's an extreme case. It's a truly unimaginable level of schizophrenia.'

Marciel Maciel Degollado was born in 1920 in Cotija de la Paz, in the state of Michoacán in western Mexico. He was ordained as a priest by his uncle in 1944, about the time he founded the Legion of Christ, a Catholic education charity.

This far-from-typical branch of the Mexican Church in the service of Jesus was initially treated with suspicion, both in Mexico and in the Vatican, because of its almost sectarian nature. However, within a few years, thanks to his unusually high levels of energy – though, even at this early stage, with uncertain finances – Marcial Maciel found himself at the head of countless schools, universities and charities in Mexico. In 1959 he founded Regnum Christi, the secular branch of the Legion of Christ. Several journalists (an Italian, Franca Giansoldati, a Mexican, Carmen Aristegui, and two Americans, Jason Berry and Gerald Renner) told the story of the spectacular rise and fall of Marcial Maciel; here I will pick up the broad lines from these inquiries, also drawing on dozens of interviews of my own that I undertook for this investigation during four trips to Mexico.

At the head of his 'army', whose loyalty to the pope was elevated to the level of a mantra and fanatical devotion to him as an individual, the priest Maciel recruited thousands of seminarians and harvested funds in the tens of millions, turning his system into a model of Catholic fundraising and new evangelization in line with the dreams of Paul VI and, particularly, of John Paul II.

Here we might borrow an image from the Gospel according to Saint Luke, about a person possessed by a devil, who replies to Christ when asked his name: 'My name is Legion, because we are many (demons).' Was Marcial Maciel thinking of that image when he created his demonic army?

Either way, the Mexican priest enjoyed impressive success. He was able to rely on a rigid and fanatical organization in which seminarians took a vow of chastity but also one of poverty (giving their goods, their possessions and even the money they were given for Christmas to the Legion of Christ). To that, Marciel added a commitment contrary to canon law: the 'vow of silence'. It was strictly forbidden to criticize one's superiors, particularly Father Maciel, whom the seminarians had to call '*nuestro padre*'. Even before it became a machine for sexual harassment, the Legion was an enterprise of moral harassment.

Obedience to Father Maciel was a form of sadomasochism that remains unthinkable, even before the sexual abuse. They were all willing to bend over backwards to be loved by their father, without imagining the cost.

To control his short-haired young recruits, who walked in formation, two by two – in shorts in the summer, in the winter in a double-breasted coat with double buttons and a stiff collar – the guru put in place a formidable system of internal surveillance. Their correspondence was read, their phone-calls listed, their friendships picked over. The cleverest, the most handsome, the athletes, formed the inner circle around Marcial Maciel, who loved surrounding himself with young seminarians. Their beauty was an advantage; indigenous features a handicap. If you played a nice musical instrument, that was a very much appreciated plus; if you were sickly, like the young country priest in the novel by Bernanos, that was a flaw.

Basically, physique took precedence over intellect. This was summed up for me in a fine phrase by James Alison, an English priest who spent a long time living in Mexico, and whom I interviewed in Madrid: 'The Legion of Christ are Opus Dei who don't read books.'

The double life of the legionnaire in chief was denounced very early, contrary to what the Vatican has claimed. In the 1940s, Marcial Maciel was dismissed twice from the seminary by his superiors for troubling events relating to sexuality. The first instances of sexual abuse date back to the 1940s and 1950s, and were officially signalled to the Mexican bishops and cardinals at that time. Notifications of Marcial Maciel's severe substance addiction, a dependency that accompanied his sessions of sexual abuse, also made it as far as Rome. In 1956, Maciel was suspended by the Vatican on the orders of Cardinal Valerio Valeri – evidence, if any were needed, that the file was well-known, from the 1950s onwards.

However, as happened on several occasions during the career of this brilliant liar and forger, Marcial Maciel managed to have himself pardoned: his slate was wiped clean by Cardinal Clemente Micara late in 1958. In 1965, Pope Paul VI even officially recognized the Legion of Christ in a decree linking them directly to the holy see. In 1983, John Paul II would relegitimize Marcial Maciel's sect by validating the constitutional charter of the Legion, even though it seriously contravened canon law.

It should be added that, by then the Legion of Christ had become an impressive war machine that won praise and compliments all over the place – while troubling rumours about its founder intensified. Marcial Maciel was, at this point, at the head of an empire that would, by the end of his career, include 15 universities, 50 seminaries and institutes of higher education, 177 middle schools, 34 schools for disadvantaged children, 125 religious houses, 200 educational centres and 1,200 oratories and chapels, not to mention charitable associations. Everywhere, the banner of the Legion floated on the wind and displayed its blazons.

Found innocent and relegitimized by Paul VI and John Paul II, Father Marcial Maciel ramped up his energy to develop his movement and, perversely, to assuage his hunger as a predatory priest. On the one hand, the *comprachicos* – a slang term used for people who traffic in stolen children – established privileged relations with the extremely wealthy, such as Carlos Slim, the king of Mexican telecommunication, whose wedding he officiated, and made him one of the philanthropists for his Legion. It is estimated that, through his holdings and foundations, Marcial Maciel amassed a fortune of a dozen properties in Mexico, Spain and Rome, as well as liquid assets placed in secret accounts valued at several hundred million dollars (according to the *New York Times*). Money was obviously one of the keys to the Maciel system.

On the other hand, taking advantage of exchanges made during confession, and the files he had on many young seminarians, he black-mailed those who had been identified as engaging in homosexual conduct, and abused them with impunity. All in all, the predator Maciel is said to have sexually abused dozens of children and countless seminarians: in total perhaps as many as a hundred victims.

His way of life was also highly unusual for the times – and for a priest. This father – who showed absolute humility in public, and great modesty on all occasions – lived privately in an armoured apartment, stayed in luxury hotels on his foreign travels and drove incredibly expensive sports cars. He also had false identities, kept two women by whom he would have at least four children, and had no hesitation in abusing his own sons, two of whom have since registered complaints against him.

In Rome, where he went often in the 1970s, 1980s and 1990s, he was welcomed as a humble servant of the Church by Paul VI and as a guest star by his 'personal friend' John Paul II.

It was not until 1997 that a new credible and well-founded complaint reached the pope's office. It was made by seven priests, former seminarians of the Legion, who said they had been sexually abused by Maciel.

They made their complaint under the seal of the gospel and received the support of well-known academics. The letter was filed under 'no further action' by Secretary of State Angelo Sodano and the pope's private secretary Stanisław Dziwisz. Did they pass it on to the pope? We don't know.

No surprise there: as we have seen, Angelo Sodano's approach was to always defend priests, even if they were suspected of sexual abuse. This was his view, as if he were repeating the famous Latin quote in the Raphael Rooms, which I saw in the apostolic palace: '*Dei Non Hominum Est Episcopos Iudicare*' (It is for God, not men, to judge bishops). But the cardinal went further, and during an Easter celebration he publicly denounced accusations of paedophilia as 'the latest gossip'. Later, he would be challenged, violently and by name, by another cardinal, the courageous and friendly Archbishop of Vienna, Christoph Schönborn, for covering up the sexual crimes of his predecessor, Cardinal Hans Hermann Gröer. A homosexual, Gröer was forced to resign after a noisy scandal in Austria.

'Cardinal Angelo Sodano's rule was never to abandon a priest, even when he was accused of the worst. He never deviated from that line. I think that, for him, it was a matter of avoiding divisions in the Church, and never allowing its enemies to damage it. Retrospectively, we can see this as an error, but Cardinal Sodano was a man born in the 1920s, a different age. In the case of Marcial Maciel, it is clear that this was a severe error, but it followed the same logic,' I was told by a retired archbishop who knows the cardinal well.

The fact remains that the Secretary of State Angelo Sodano was not content to be merely one of Marcial Maciel's advocates to the holy father: he was also, as nuncio and then head of the Vatican's diplomatic service, the chief 'developer' of the Legion of Christ in Latin America. The organization had no presence in Chile before Sodano's arrival; he developed contacts with Maciel and encouraged the establishment of his movement in that country, then in Argentina, and perhaps subsequently in Colombia.

Sol Prieto, an Argentinian academic and a specialist in Catholicism, whom I interviewed in Buenos Aires, tried to explain the cardinal's rational motivations. 'The whole of Angelo Sodano's logic lay in weakening the traditional religious orders, such as the Jesuits, the Dominicans, the Benedictines and the Franciscans, whom he suspected of being on the left. He preferred the lay movements or conservative congregations like

Opus Dei, Communion & Liberation, the Order of the Incarnate Word or the Legion of Christ. For him, the Church was at war and it needed soldiers, not just monks!'

Soon, new accusations of paedophilia were passed on to the Congregation of the Doctrine of the Faith in Rome, which was run at the time by Cardinal Ratzinger. Numerous rapes were reported in the late 1990s and early 2000s, and over time these came to appear not just as a series of isolated acts but as a genuine system of evil. In 1997, a complete file was opened, and the Vatican realized it had to put an end to the predator's wicked actions. In 2003, Marcial Maciel's private secretary informed the Vatican in person of the criminal behaviour of his superior, coming to Rome with evidence that he passed to John Paul II, Stanislaw Dziwisz and Angelo Sodano, who refused to listen to him (this point is confirmed by a note to Pope Benedict XVI revealed by the journalist Gianluigi Nuzzi).

These new charges led nowhere and were once again stamped 'no further action'. Cardinal Ratzinger did not launch a procedure of any kind. According to Federico Lombardi, Benedict XVI's former spokesman, the cardinal repeatedly informed Pope John Paul II of the crimes of Marcial Maciel, proposing that he be dismissed from his duties and reduced to the status of layman, but he is said to have met with a categorical refusal from Sodano or from Dziwisz.

It seems, nevertheless, that Cardinal Ratzinger took the affair seriously enough to persevere; in spite of John Paul II's obstinate position. He opened a new file on Maciel and built up a collection of evidence against him. But he was prudent man, too much so, in fact: he only moved when the lights were green. And as he tried to go into action beside John Paul II, he was forced to recognize that the lights were always red: the pope categorically refused to have his 'friend' Marcial Maciel disturbed.

To give an idea of the prevailing state of mind at this time, we might recall that Ratzinger's deputy, Tarcisio Bertone, the future secretary of state to Benedict XVI, signed – as late as 2003 – the preface to a book by Marcial Maciel, *My Life is Christ* (the Spanish 'journalist' who interviewed Maciel for that book, would be in fact an assumed identity for one of Maciel's catamites). At the same time, the *Osservatore Romano* published an article praising Maciel, an illustration of vice masquerading as virtue.

During the same period, the Slovenian Cardinal Franc Rodé likewise showed his support for the founder of the Legion, and hailed 'the example of Father Maciel in following Christ'. (When I interviewed Rodé recently, he assured me that he 'didn't know', and gave me to understand that Maciel was supported by the pope's assistant, Stanisław Dziwisz: 'When Dziwisz was created cardinal, at the same time as me, the Legion held a huge party for him – and not for me,' he told me.) As for Cardinal Marc Ouellet, who is now prefect of the Congregation of Bishops, he cleared his dicastery of blame on the grounds that Maciel was a clergyman and was not answerable to him. He also pointed out that since Maciel had never been consecrated a bishop or created a cardinal, it was proof that he was treated with suspicion …

What can we say, finally, about the final public support given by John Paul II to Maciel in November 2004? On the occasion of the sixtieth anniversary of the priest's ordination, the pope came in person, in the course of a beautiful ceremony, to say goodbye to Maciel. The photographs of the two men, affectionately embracing, while the pope was on the brink of death, went all around the world. In Mexico they were on the front page of several newspapers, prompting disbelief and unease.

It would not be until the death of John Paul II, in 2005, that the Maciel file was reopened by the newly elected pope, Benedict XVI. He authorized the opening of the archives of the Vatican so that the inquiry could be conducted, and freed the Legion from their 'vow of silence' so that they could speak.

'History will acknowledge that Benedict XVI was the first to denounce paedophilia and bring charges against Marcial Maciel, as soon as he ascended the throne of St Peter,' Federico Lombardi says to me, the former spokesman of Benedict XVI and now president of the Ratzinger Foundation.

In 2005, Marcial Maciel was stripped of all his duties by Benedict XVI, who also obliged him to retire from public life. Reduced to 'penitential silence', he was definitively suspended *a divinis*.

But under cover of official sanctions, Benedict XVI spared the priest once again. Maciel would not be able to administer the sacraments until the end of his days. His punishment was still quite lenient, however, more so than the penalty imposed on great theologians such as Leonardo Boff or Eugen Drewermann, who were punished for committing no crimes other than defending their progressive ideas. Marcial Maciel was not reported to the law by the Church; he was not excommunicated, or arrested, or imprisoned. There was not even a trial according to canon law 'because of his advanced age and frail health'.

Invited to a 'life of prayer and penitence', between 2005 and 2007 Maciel continued to travel from one house to another, from Mexico to Rome, and to take advantage of his limitless funds. He simply moved to the United States to avoid possible trials – embodying the famous phrase: 'Poor Mexico, so far from God and so close to the United States'. Suffering from pancreatic cancer, he retired in the end to a sumptuous residence in Florida, where he died in luxury in 2008, at the advanced age of 88.

It was not until the following year, in 2009, that an investigation into all organizations connected with the Legion of Christ, and its lay branch Regnum Christi, was ordered by Benedict XVI. Five bishops were put in charge of this mission of inquiry covering five continents. Their results, communicated confidentially to the pope in 2010, seem to have been so critical that the Vatican finally acknowledged in a communiqué the 'objectively immoral acts' and 'true crimes' of Marcial Maciel.

However, wittingly or not, Rome delivered a partial judgement. In denouncing the black sheep, it indirectly spared his entourage, starting with Fathers Luis Garza Medina and Álvaro Corcuera, Maciel's deputies. In 2017, the Paradise Papers would reveal that Medina and Corcuera, among about twenty Legion priests whose names were published, and who were not disturbed by Benedict XVI, enjoyed secret funds thanks to offshore financial arrangements via Bermuda, Panama and the British Virgin Islands. It would also be discovered that 35 other priests belonging to the Legion of Christ were implicated in sexual abuse scandals, not only their founder. It would be another few years before Pope Benedict XVI would put the Legion under the tutelage of the Vatican and appoint a provisional administrator (Cardinal Velasio De Paolis). Since then the file appears to have been closed and the Legionnaires have resumed their normal lives, merely taking down the countless portraits of the guru from the walls of their schools and forbidding his books – simply erasing his traces, as if nothing had happened.

New cases have burst open more recently. Óscar Turrión, the rector of the Pontifical International College of Legionnaires, called the Maria Mater Ecclesiae in Rome, where about a hundred seminarians from all over the world lived, acknowledged that he lived secretly with a woman, with whom he had two children. He had to resign.

Rumours circulate even today in Mexico, but also in Spain and Rome, about the lay branch of the Legion, Regnum Christi, and about their pontifical university, Ateneo Pontificio Regina Apostolorum, where there have been signs of deviance. The Mexican journalist Emiliano Ruiz Parra, a specialist in the Catholic Church, admitted his frustration when I interviewed him in Mexico. 'Neither Benedict XVI nor Francis grasped the extent of the phenomenon. And the problem remains: the Vatican no longer has any control over the Legion and it might have returned to its bad habits.'

Cardinal Juan Sandoval Íñiguez lives in a well-appointed Catholic residence in Tlaquepaque, a satellite town of Guadalajara in Mexico. I visit him there, on Calle Morelos, with Eliezer, a local researcher, who acts as my guide and who has managed to dig up his telephone number. The cardinal agreed to the interview without any procrastination, asking to meet us at his home that same evening.

His emeritus archbishop's residence is a little paradise luxuriating in the tropics, protected by two armed Mexican policemen. Behind a wall and some grilles, I find the cardinal's domain: three brightly coloured houses, huge, connected by a private chapel and garages where several gleaming Ford four-by-fours are parked. There are four dogs, six parrots and a marmoset. The Archbishop of Guadalajara has just retired, but his timetable doesn't seem to have dried up.

'The Catholic Church in Mexico was rich. But now it's a poor church. You must realize, for a country of 120 million inhabitants we have only 17,000 priests. We were persecuted!' the prelate insists.

Juan Sandoval Íñiguez is one of the most anti-gay cardinals in Mexico. Frequently using the word '*maricón*' (faggot) to describe homosexuals, the cardinal has radically denounced the use of condoms. He has even celebrated masses against the 'satanism' of homosexuals, and most importantly he was the inspiration behind the anti-gay-marriage movement in Mexico, marching at the head of demonstrations against the Mexican government. The Legion of Christ, to which he was close, often organized large battalions and street processions. During my stay in Mexico, I was also able to witness the big '*marcha por la familia*' against the gay-marriage plan.

'It's civil society mobilizing spontaneously,' the cardinal comments. 'I don't engage personally. But of course natural law is the Bible.'

The bird-lover is a charmer, and he keeps me for several hours to talk in French. Sometimes he takes me kindly by the hand, to emphasize his arguments, or addresses Eliezer tenderly in Spanish to ask his advice, or to ask questions about his life.

What is strange, and what strikes me straightaway is that this anti-gay archbishop is obsessed by the gay question. It's almost the only subject we talk about. Here he is, implicitly criticizing Pope Francis. He reproaches him for giving signs favourable to gays and, apparently in passing, serves me up the names of some of the bishops and cardinals in his entourage who appear to him to have similar tastes.

'You know, when Francis says the words "Who am I to judge?" he isn't defending homosexuals. He's protecting one of his colleagues; it's very different!! It's the press that tampered with everything!'

I ask the cardinal's permission to look at his library, and he gets up, keen to show me his treasures. A bluestocking prelate, he himself has written several books, which he enjoys pointing out to me.

What a surprise! Juan Sandoval Íñiguez had whole shelves devoted to the gay question. I see works about homosexual sin, the issue of lesbian and gay conversion therapies. A whole library of pro- and anti-gay texts, as if the book-burnings that the cardinal constantly advocated had no business taking place at his home. Perhaps the cardinal is enamoured of the books he would like to have burned?

Suddenly I'm startled to notice several copies, in plain view, of the famous *Liber Gomorrhianus* in English translation: *The Book of Gomorrah*. 'It's a great book, from the Middle Ages and, look, I wrote the preface to this new translation,' the cardinal says to me proudly.

What a strange book! This famous essay from 1051 written by an Italian priest who would go on to become Saint Peter Damian. In this long treatise, addressed to Pope Leo IX, the cleric denounced homosexual tendencies, which he said were very widespread, among the clergy of the time. He also pointed a finger at the bad habits of priests who confessed to each other in order to conceal their inclinations, and he even 'outed', long before the term had been coined, some senior Roman prelates of the day. The pope, however, disavowed Peter Damian, and imposed none of the sanctions that he demanded. He even confiscated his tract, according to John Boswell, who relates the story, all the more so since the College of Cardinals was very practising at the time! The book has considerable historical importance, because it was from the publication of this pamphlet in the eleventh century that the divine punishment of Sodom would come to be reinterpreted not as a problem of hospitality, as the Bible suggests, but as a sin of 'sodomy'. Homosexuality became abominable!

We are now talking to Cardinal Juan Sandoval Íñiguez about the treatments that exist to 'detoxify' homosexuals, and also paedophiles, whom he appears to consider equal to the former. There is also mention of a specialist clinic meant for the most 'incurable' paedophiles'. But the cardinal dodges the question and refuses to expand on the subject.

But I know that this residence exists. It's called 'Casa Alberione', and was founded in 1989 on the initiative, or with the support, of the cardinal in this very parish of Tlaquepaque. Foreign paedophile priests, 'sent from country to country as if they were nuclear waste', in the words of someone who knows the subject very well, were treated in this 'rehab' clinic, which enabled them to stay on as priests and to avoid getting the law involved. From the early years of the 2000s, after Pope Benedict XVI stripped paedophiles of church protection, Casa Alberione lost the reason for its existence. After an interview in the Mexican daily newspaper *El Informador*, Cardinal Juan Sandoval Íñiguez acknowledged the existence of this residence, which has received Legionnaires of Christ, but asserted that it 'had stopped taking in paedophile priests in 2001'. (A similar institution existed in Chile, 'The Club', about which Pablo Larraín made a film.)

'HOLA!' All of a sudden I've been called by a shout from behind, while the cardinal, Eliezer and I are walking in the park. I turn around in surprise, but without being as frightened as Robinson Crusoe when he first hears a parrot talking to him on his island. From its huge cage, the handsome *perico* has just begun a conversation with me. Is it going to tell me a secret? In Mexico, this kind of bird is also called '*guacamayo*', in English it can be called a '*popinjay*', but in French, it also has the name '*papegai*' (gaypope).

We walk among the peacocks and the roosters. The cardinal seems to be happy and takes his time. He is breathtakingly kind to me and Eliezer, my Mexican scout.

The dog 'Oso' (which means 'Bear') is also enjoying our company, and all of a sudden we throw ourselves into a four-man game of football, the cardinal, the dog Oso, Eliezer and me, to the amusement of five nuns who cook, clean and do the washing-up full time for the cardinal.

I question Juan Sandoval Íñiguez: 'Don't you feel a bit lonely here?'

My question seems to amuse him. He describes his rich social life. I quote Jean-Jacques Rousseau, for whom, I say, 'the vow of celibacy was unnatural'.

'Do you think there is less loneliness among married priests, or imams?' the cardinal replies: an answer in the form of a question.

'You see,' he adds, pointing to the nuns, 'I'm not alone here.'

The cardinal takes me firmly by the arm, and continues, after a long silence: 'And besides, there is also a priest here, a young priest, who joins me every afternoon.' When, late that afternoon, I'm surprised not to have seen the young priest, the cardinal adds, perhaps with some candour: 'Tonight he finishes at 10 pm.'

The kinds of protection that Marcial Maciel enjoyed in Rome are quite well-known today. Cardinal Juan Sandoval Íñiguez has been criticized by several victims of the paedophile priest for not denouncing him. He is also alleged to have placed some of his priests under 're-education' at Casa Alberione. (The cardinal denies any wrongdoing or responsibility.)

Similar criticisms were directed at the Archbishop of Mexico, Cardinal Norberto Rivera. As obsessively anti-gay as Sandoval Íñiguez, he made numerous anti-gay speeches, including statements about 'the anus which cannot serve as a sexual orifice'. In another famous remark, he acknowledged that there were many gay priests in Mexico, but that 'God had forgiven them'. More recently, he even declared that a 'child is more likely to be raped by its father if its father is homosexual'.

Specialist journalists suggest that Norberto Rivera, one of the supporters of Marcial Maciel, thoroughly denied his crimes and supposedly failed to pass on certain complaints to the Vatican. For all of these reasons, and for having publicly dismissed complainants as far-fetched, the cardinal of Mexico is now the subject of criticism for his failures and silence concerning sexual abuse. He is regularly denounced in the press, and tens of thousands of Mexicans have signed a petition to mobilize public opinion and prevent him from taking part in the conclave that elects popes. He also appears towards the top of the list of the 'dirty dozen', the 12 cardinals suspected of covering up for paedophile priests, published by the American Survivors Network of those Abused by Priests (SNAP).

Sandoval Íñiguez and Rivera were created cardinals by John Paul II, probably on the recommendation of Angelo Sodano or Stanisław Dziwisz. Both were violent opponents of liberation theology and homosexual marriage. Pope Francis, who had sharply criticized Cardinal Rivera for his homophobia, and solemnly asked the Mexican Church to cease hostilities against gays, hurried to move on from the Rivera case by making him retire in 2017, as soon as he had reached the age limit. This quiet decision was, according to a priest I interviewed in Mexico, a 'divine sanction with immediate temporal effect'.

'We know that a very significant number of clergy who supported Marcial Maciel or who are demonstrating against us and against gay marriage are homosexual themselves. It's unbelievable', the Minister of Culture, Rafael Tovar y de Teresa, tells me during an interview in his office in Mexico.

And the well-known minister adds, in the presence of my Mexican editor, Marcela González Durán: 'The religious apparatus in Mexico is gay, the hierarchy is gay, the cardinals are gay. It's incredible!'

The minister also confirms to me, when I tell him the subject of my book, that the Mexican government has precise information about these 'anti-gay gays' – of which he gives me several names among dozens. He adds that the next day he will talk about my investigation to the president of the Republic, at that time Enrique Peña Nieto, and to the Minister of the Interior, so that they can give me additional information. I would go on to have several further exchanges with Tovar y de Teresa. (I was also able to interview Marcelo Ebrard, the current Minister of Foreign Affairs, and the former mayor of Mexico, who was the main architect of plans to approve gay marriage in the country, and who knew which Catholics opposed this legal plan. Other individuals would provide me with information, including the billionaire Carlos Slim Jr, the intellectual Enrique Krauze, several directors of Televisa, the main television channel, an influential adviser to President Enrique Peña Nieto, and

José Castañeda, the former Minister of Foreign Affairs. On four visits to Mexico City, and in eight other towns and cities in the country, I received support and information from a dozen gay writers and activists, notably Guillermo Osorno, Antonio Martínez Velázquez and Felipe Restrepo. My Mexican researchers Luis Chumacero and, in Guadalajara, Eliezer Ojeda, also contributed to this story.)

The homosexual life of the Mexican clergy is a well-known and by now a well-documented phenomenon. It is estimated that over two-thirds of Mexican cardinals, archbishops and bishops are 'practising'. An important homosexual organization, FON, has even 'outed' 38 Catholic leaders, making their names public.

This proportion is said to be less significant among mere prelates and 'indigenous' bishops, among whom, according to a report officially delivered to the Vatican by Mgr Bartolomé Carrasco Briseño, 75 per cent of diocesan priests in the states of Oaxaca, Hidalgo and Chiapas, where native Americans are in the majority, live with women, either cohabiting or secretly married. In short, the Mexican clergy is said to be actively heterosexual in the countryside and practising homosexual in the cities!

Several journalists specializing in the Catholic Church confirm these tendencies. This is the case with Emiliano Ruiz Parra, author of several books on the subject and a former journalist reporting on religious questions for the daily newspaper *Reforma*: 'I would say that 50 per cent of priests are gay in Mexico, if you want a minimum figure, and 75 per cent if one is being more realistic. The seminaries are homosexual and the Mexican Catholic hierarchy is spectacularly gay.'

Ruiz Parra adds that being gay in the Church is not a problem in Mexico: it is even a rite of passage, an element of promotion and a normal 'power relation' between the novice and his master.

'There is a lot of tolerance within the Church, so much so that it is not expressed outside it. And, of course, to protect this secret, clerics must attack gays by appearing very homophobic in public. That's the key. Or the trick.'

Having investigated the Legion of Christ and Marcial Maciel, Emiliano Ruiz Parra is particularly critical about the Vatican, both in the past and in the present day, and about the many sources of support that the predator was able to rely on in Mexico. Like many others, he suggests financial arguments, corruption and bribes, as well as the homosexuality of some of his supporters, as key factors.

'If Marcial Maciel had spoken, the whole of the Mexican Church would have collapsed.'

One of Marcial Maciel's first great charitable works, the one that launched his career and overshadowed his original turpitudes, was the construction of the Church of Our Lady of Guadalupe in Rome. It is supposed to be a miniature replica of the famous basilica of the same name in Mexico, one of the most enormous in the world, which welcomes millions of pilgrims every year.

In both cases these are places of great devotion, striking for their archaic and almost sectarian rituals. The devoted and prostrated crowds strike me every time I visit the Mexican basilica. Frenchman that I am, and familiar with the rather intellectual Catholicism of my country – that of the *Pensées* of Pascal, the funeral orations of Bossuet or the *Genius of Christianity* by Chateaubriand – I have difficulty understanding this fervour and popular religiosity.

'Mexican Catholicism is inconceivable without the Virgin of Guadalupe. Love of the Virgin, like a mother's love, shines all around the world,' Mgr Monroy explains.

This former rector of the basilica in Mexico City showed me around the religious complex, which, apart from two basilicas, includes convents, museums and shops, and in the end looks to me like a real tourist industry. Mgr Monroy also showed me many pictures there presenting him in every conceivable priestly outfit (including a magnificent portrait by the gay artist Rafael Rodriguez, whom I also interviewed in Santiago de Querétaro, in the north-west of Mexico).

According to several journalists, Our Lady of Guadalupe was the site of a number of sexual scandals and, through the behaviour of some of its priests, a kind of 'gay fraternity'. In Mexico City as in Rome.

On Via Aurelia, west of the Vatican, the official Italian headquarters of the Legion of Christ was financed by young Maciel in the early 1950s. Thanks to an incredible collection of funds carried out in Mexico, Spain and Rome, the church and its parish were built beginning in 1955 and inaugurated by the Italian cardinal Clemente Micara late in 1958. At the same time, during the interregnum between Pius XII and John XXIII, the critical Vatican file on Marcial Maciel's drug addiction and homosexuality quietly disappeared.

To try to understand the Maciel phenomenon in the shadow of the purity of the Virgin of Guadalupe, we must therefore try and understand the protection that made this vast scandal possible, both in Mexico and in Rome. Several generations of Mexican bishops and cardinals, and countless cardinals in the Roman curia, closed their eyes to or knowingly supported, one of the biggest paedophiles of the twentieth century.

What can we say about the Marcial Maciel phenomenon? Was he a mythomaniac, a pathological and devilish pervert, or was he the product of a system? An isolated accidental figure or the sign of a collective shortcoming? Or, to put it another way, is this the story of a single individual, as is suggested by some to clear the institution of blame, or the product of a model of government rendered possible by the vow of chastity, the secret and endemic homosexuality within the Church, by lies and the law of silence? As with the priest Karadima in Chile, and many other cases in numerous countries in Latin America, according to the witnesses I interviewed the explanation comes down to five factors – to which I should add a sixth.

First of all, the blindness that comes from success. The dazzling successes of the Legion of Christ fascinated the Vatican for a long time, because nowhere in the world was the level of recruitment of seminarians so impressive, priestly vocations so enthusiastic and financial revenue so vast. During John Paul II's first visit to Mexico, in 1979, Marcial Maciel showed his sense of organization, the power of his political and media connections, his ability to sort out the tiniest details, with an army of assistants, while remaining humble and discreet. John Paul II was literally amazed. He went back to Mexico four times, fascinated each time by the skills of his 'dear friend' Maciel.

The second factor is the ideological proximity between John Paul II and the Legion of Christ, a far-right and violently anti-communist organization. Ultra-conservative, Marcial Maciel was the spearhead first in Mexico, then in Latin America and Spain, of the fight against Marxist regimes and the trend of liberation theology.

Obsessively anti-communist, even paranoid, Maciel anticipated the pope's expectations, and the pope duly found him a defender of his hard line against communism. By doing so, combining the psychological with the ideological, Father Maciel intelligently flattered the pride of John Paul II, a mystical pope whom witnesses privately describe as a man of great vanity and a misogynist.

The third factor, connected with the previous one, is John Paul II's need of money for his anti-communist ideological mission, particularly in Poland. It seems certain by now, in spite of the denials of the holy see, that Marcial Maciel siphoned off funds to finance the Solidarność union. According to a minister and a senior diplomat I spoke to in Mexico, these transfers of funds remained within an 'ecclesiastical' context. In Warsaw and Kraków, journalists and historians confirm to me that there were financial relationships between the Vatican and Poland. 'Money definitely circulated. It went through channels like the trade unions, churches,' I am told by the Polish Vaticanologist Jacek Moskwa, a long-time correspondent in Rome and the author of a four-volume biography of Pope John Paul II.

But during the same interview in Warsaw, Moskwa denied any direct involvement on the part of the Vatican. 'Many people have said that the Vatican Bank or the Italian Banco Ambrosiano made contributions. I think that is false.'

In the same way, the journalist Zbigniev Nosowski, head of the Catholic media service WIEZ in Warsaw, has shown himself to be quite reserved in his comments on these financial arrangements, 'I don't think that there is any possibility that money transferred from the Vatican to Solidarnosc.'

Quite apart from the principle at stake, other sources suggest the opposite. Lech Walesa, the former head of Solidarność, became President of the Polish Republic, and did in due course admit that his union received money from the Vatican. Many newspapers and books have also confirmed this: their payment came from the Legionaries of Christ of Marcial Maciel and was indeed received by Solidarność. In Latin Amercia, many even think, with no less certainty, that the Chilean dictator Auguste Pinochet made some contribution to these payments (thanks to the intervention of the Nuncio, Angelo Sodano) as well as drug traffickers from Colombia (through the offices of Cardinal Alfonso López Trujillo). At this point, all these hypotheses are possible, but they have never been confirmed beyond doubt. 'Dirty Money for Good Causes?', wonders one of those who examined the dossier: the origins of the payments may be clouded in mystery but the cause is no less just...

Through direct witnesses, we know for certain that Mgr Dziwisz, the private secretary of Pope John Paul II, had the habit of handing out to Polish visitors envelopes containing cash, whether they were clergy or members of the laity. At this time in the 1980s, the Union Solidarność was banned in Poland by law. Dziwisz used to ask his Polish visitors, 'How can I help you?'. The lack of funds was always top of the list. 'What used to happen was that this assistant of the Pope went off to a room next door and came back with a fat envelope'. This was the testimony of Adam Szostkiewicz, when I interviewed him in Warsaw. (An influential journalist on the weekly *Polityka*, Szostkiewicz has been a long-time observer of the Catholic Church in Poland. He was himself a member of Solidarność, and for six whole months was imprisoned by the Communist regime.)

According to Szostkiewicz, there were other means of access to Poland for food, medicine and maybe even suitcases of money. These means of access were essentially 'ecclesiastical': the aid came via the priests and via humanitarian convoys who came through Federal Germany. Never did the money come via the RDA nor through Bulgaria, because in these territories the inspections were extremely strict.

Catholics thus benefited from a freedom unavailable to others: the Polish authorities tolerated these activities and their inspection of goods was really quite cursory. Moreover, 'clergy were able to get visas much more easily', added Szostkiewicz. (In a recent book, *Il Caso Marcinkus*, the Italian journalist Fabio Marchese Ragona reveals that the Vatican could well have transferred more than a million dollars to Solidarność. The American Archbishop Paul Marcinkus and Stanisław Dziwisz were the essential agents in these extremely complex arrangements. The Pope's second assistant, the polish priest Mieczysław Mokrycki, known simply as Father Mietek, who is now an Archbishop in Ukraine, also played a key role in all of this, as well as the Jesuit priest Casimiro Przydatek. Both of them were close friends of Dziwisz. Journalistic investigation into all this was conducted and published in the journal *Gazeta Wyborcza*. It is entirely likely that more revelations on these matters will follow in the months and years ahead).

The suitcases of dirty money are a possible fact of John Paul II's pontificate. One might consider this all to be somewhat questionable, but the collapse of the Communist regime in Poland and subsequently the fall of the Berlin Wall and the Soviet empire, can indeed be seen to legitimise this usage of holy money.

Then there is the fourth factor, the personal bribes – because we have to use the term. Marcial Maciel gave regular handouts to prelates within the Curia. The psychopath rewarded his Roman protectors and enriched them to an unimaginable degree. He gave them luxury cars, sumptuous trips abroad and envelopes full of banknotes, both to gain influence and to win favours for his sect of 'legionnaires', and to cover up his crimes. These facts are well-established today, but none of the prelates who allowed themselves to be corrupted have been troubled by the authorities, let alone excommunicated for simony! A few of them did refuse the dirty money, and it appears that Cardinal Ratzinger, with his bachelor's austerity, was one of them. Having received an envelope of banknotes in Mexico, he is said to have returned it to the sender. Cardinal Bergoglio, it seems, was always a declared enemy of Marcial Maciel and denounced him early on, not least because Maciel hated not only the 'red priests' of liberation theology, but also the Jesuits.

Apart from the moral aspects, the financial risks taken by the Vatican are another factor – the fifth – that might explain the Church's silence. Even when it acknowledges the evidence, it doesn't want to pay the price! In the United States, cases of sexual abuse have already cost more than 3.8 billion dollars since 1980 to cover the trials, insurance and the indemnity of at least 8,600 victims. For the Vatican, to acknowledge a mistake is to accept financial responsibility. The argument concerning the cost of compensation is central in all cases of sexual abuse.

Finally – and here we are in the realm of the unthinkable – within the support that Marcial Maciel received in Mexico, Spain and the Vatican, there is something that I would modestly refer to as 'closeted clericalism'. That's the sixth factor that helps us to explain the inexplicable, probably the most painful, the deepest too, and perhaps the most important clue. Many cardinals around John Paul II in fact led a double life. Certainly, they were not, or only rarely, paedophiles; they did not necessarily commit acts of sexual abuse. On the other hand, most of them are homosexual and engaged in lives known for their duplicity. Several of these cardinals have regularly visited male prostitutes and resorted to dubious sources of finance to satisfy their inclinations. It is certain that Marcial Maciel, a dark soul, went far beyond what is tolerable, or legal, as everyone in the Vatican agrees, but to denounce his psychological models would have meant questioning their own. It would also have meant exposing themselves to the possible revelation of their own homosexuality.

Once again this could be the explanation: the culture of secrecy which has become necessary to protect the homosexuality of priests, bishops and cardinals in Mexico and in Rome – above all among high ranking priests in the Pope's immediate entourage – allowed the paedophile Maciel, thanks to the strange hijacking of the culture of clericalism, freedom to act as he wished and to be securely protected.

Once one starts equating paedophilia with homosexuality – as many cardinals have given the impression of doing, the differences blur. If everything is mixed up together, sexual abuse and sin, paedophilia, homosexuality, prostitution, and the crime differs only in its extent, not in its nature, who is to be punished? Here is where the priests get lost: What is up, what is down? Where are Good, Evil, Nature and Culture? What rules apply to me, and which to others? Can Marcial Maciel be excommunicated for his sexual crimes if, a bit like him, one is also stuck in a sexual lie, and oneself 'intrinsically disordered'? To denounce abuse is to expose oneself to no good end and, who knows, perhaps run the risk of being denounced likewise. Here we are at the heart of the secret of the Maciel case and all the paedophile crimes that have been uncovered, and that continue to be exposed, in the Vatican and among the Catholic clergy: an army of supporters, countless excuses and endless silences.

11

The Ring of Lust

'In the Vatican, he's known as Platinette, and everyone admires his daring!' I am told by Francesco Lepore. The nickname comes from a famous drag queen on Italian television who wears platinum-blond wigs.

I'm amused by these pseudonyms privately given to several cardinals and prelates. I'm not making anything up, merely pointing out what several Curia priests have revealed to me, the nastiness being even crueller inside the Church than outside it.

An influential diplomat tells me of another cardinal whose soubriquet is 'La Mongolfiera'! Why this name? He has a 'splendid appearance, nothing inside and can't carry very much weight', my source explains, stressing the supreme arrogance and vanity of the person in question – 'a piece of confetti who thinks he's a hot-air balloon'.

Cardinals Platinette and La Mongolfiera enjoyed their moment of glory under John Paul II, to whom they were reputedly close. They were part of what might be called the first 'ring of lust' around the holy father. Other lubricious circles existed, gathering together practising homosexuals at less elevated levels of the hierarchy. Heterosexual prelates were rare among those close to John Paul II; chastity was rarer still.

Before we go any further, we should look in greater detail at the cardinal vices that I am about to reveal. Who am I to judge? Once again, I am trying to be 'non-judgemental', and I am less concerned with 'outing' living priests than with describing a system – these prelates will therefore remain anonymous. In my eyes, these cardinals, bishops and priests have the right to have lovers, and to explore their inclinations, whether acquired or innate. Not being Catholic, I couldn't care less if they appear to be betraying their vow of chastity, or if they are in contravention of the rules of the Church. As for prostitution, which occurs so frequently in this group, it is legal in Italy and apparently very well-tolerated by canon law as applied in the extraterritorial zone of the holy see! The profound hypocrisy of such clergy, however, is questionable: that is the principal subject of this book, which confirms the fact that the infallibility of the pope becomes impunity when it's a matter of the morals of his entourage.

My concern here is to decode this parallel world and provide a guided tour of it during the time of John Paul II. Apart from La Mongolfiera and Platinette, to whom I shall return, I must begin with a discussion of the figure of Paul Marcinkus, the man behind the finances and secret missions of the Catholic Church, and one of those whose tasks it was to manage the Vatican City for the holy father.

A mixture of diplomat, bodyguard, translator from English, golf-player, transporter of secret funds and crook, the American archbishop Marcinkus already had a long history at the Vatican behind him when John Paul II was elected. Marcinkus was a key translator into English for Paul VI, as well as his bodyguard. He even thwarted an attempt on the life of Paul VI, and occupied several posts in the apostolic nunciatures before beginning his spectacular Roman ascent.

For mysterious reasons, Marcinkus became one of John Paul II's favourites at the beginning of his pontificate. According to several sources, the pontiff had a 'genuine affection' for this controversial Vatican figure. Marcinkus was soon appointed head of the famous Vatican Bank, which was involved in countless financial intrigues and several spectacular scandals under his auspices. The prelate was accused of corruption and found guilty by the Italian courts, but for a long time he enjoyed Vatican diplomatic immunity. He was even suspected of being behind several murders, including that of John Paul I, who died mysteriously after a month in the pontificate, but these rumours have never been proven.

Marcinkus's homosexuality is well-attested, on the other hand. About a dozen Curia prelates who associated with him confirm that he was an adventurer with a hearty appetite.

'Marcinkus was homosexual: he had a weakness for Swiss Guards. He often lent them his car, a metallic grey Peugeot 504 with a lovely leather interior. At one point I remember that he was going out with a Swiss Guard and it lasted for some time,' I am assured by one of my sources, a layman close to the archbishop who worked in the Vatican at the time, as indeed he does today.

We also know of another of Marcinkus's relationships: the one that he had with a Swiss priest, who confirmed their liaison to one of my sources. And even when he was forced to stay within the Vatican after being found guilty by the Italian courts, he went on cruising shamelessly. He then retired to the United States, taking his secrets with him: the American archbishop died in a luxury retirement home in 2006 in Sun City, Arizona. (On the two occasions when – in the presence of Daniele – I interviewed Piero Marini, Pope John Paul II's 'master of ceremonies', Marini innocently stressed Marcinkus's 'great closeness' to 'the workers'. For his part, Pierre Blanchard, a layman who was for a long time the secretary of APSA, the Administration for the Patrimony of the Holy See, and very familiar with the Vatican networks, gave me other information.)

Apart from the controversial Marcinkus, John Paul II's entourage included other homophiles among the pontiff's immediate circle of assistants and officers. The first of these was an Irish priest, Mgr John Magee, who was one of Paul VI's private secretaries, and then briefly private secretary to John Paul I, remaining in the position under John Paul II. Having been appointed bishop of the diocese of Cloyne in County Cork, he found himself at the centre of a controversy concerning his failure to act in several cases of sexual abuse that shook the country. A young seminarian witness to the Dublin Archdiocese Commission of Investigation into the Cloyne Diocese (in connection with these sexual abuse cases) said that the bishop had embraced him tightly and kissed him on the forehead; these statements were made public in the Cloyne Report published by the Commission. Mgr Magee was finally forced to resign by Benedict XVI.

One of the pope's other assistants who actively 'practised' his homosexuality was a priest who mixed the siphoning-off of funds with the seduction of young men (above consenting age to my knowledge). He also had an enthusiasm for Swiss Guards and seminarians, proclivities that he shared with one of the organizers of the pope's foreign trips.

A young seminarian from Bologna experienced this and, in the course of several interviews, gave me a detailed account of his own misadventures. During the pope's visit to that city in September 1997, two of the prelates in charge of the pontiff's travels insisted on meeting the seminarians. They immediately spotted one young man in the group who was handsome and fair, and 24 years old at the time.

'They inspected us in turn, and all of a sudden they pointed at me. They said: "You!" They asked me to come with them and wouldn't let me go. They wanted to see me all the time. It was a very insistent form of advance,' the former seminarian tells me (and he is still, when I meet him 20 years later, very charming).

During John Paul II's visit, the pope's close colleagues pushed this seminarian to the front, petting and fussing over him. They presented him to the pope in person and asked him to go up on stage with him three times.

'I worked out that they were there on the hunt. They cruised the young men and made advances to me without hesitation. At the end of the trip they invited me to come and visit them in Rome and stay with them. They told me they could put me up at the Vatican and show me the pope's office. I could see what they expected of me. I didn't respond to their advances. I failed my vocation! Otherwise,' he adds, 'I might be a bishop today!'

The recklessness of these individuals had no limits. Two other loyal colleagues of the pope's – an archbishop who advised him, as well as a very high-profile nuncio – also displayed their sexuality outrageously, to an unbelievable extent. The same was true of a Colombian cardinal whom we have not yet met, whose acquaintance we shall make shortly: this 'satanic doctor' was put in charge of the Vatican's family policy by John Paul II, but in the evening he devoted himself with astonishing regularity to male prostitutes.

In the pope's immediate entourage, there was also a trio of bishops who were quite remarkable in their way because they operated as a gang, and I must say a word on the subject here. They formed another lubricious circle around the pope. Compared with the majestic cardinals or prelates that I have mentioned, these homosexual adventurers working for his holiness were mediocre, they played it safe.

The first is an archbishop who is always presented as an angel with the face of a saint, and whose beauty has caused tongues to wag. When I meet him today, almost thirty years later, he is still a handsome man.

When he was close to Cardinal Sodano, he was also a favourite of the pontiff. His inclinations have been confirmed by many sources, and he is even said to have been removed from the Vatican diplomatic service 'after being caught in bed with a black man,' I am told by a priest in the Secretariat of State who slept with the man in question several times.

The second bishop close to John Paul II played an important role in the preparation of papal ceremonies. He also appears in photographs beside the holy father. Known for his sadomasochistic practices, he was said to have dressed all in leather when he frequented the Sphinx, a cruising club in Rome, now closed. An expression used about him became famous at the Vatican: 'Lace by day; leather by night'.

As for the third bishop in the 'gang', he is described as having been particularly perverse; he was involved in numerous suspect financial dealings and affairs involving boys. The Italian press identified him a long time ago.

So these three bishops are part of what we might call the second 'ring of lust' around John Paul II. They weren't in the first rank; they were second fiddles. Pope Francis, who has been aware of these villains for a long time, has kept them out of the way by refusing to make them cardinals. Today they are all closeted – doubly closeted, by their jobs.

These three initiates served as go-betweens and lackeys, butlers, chamberlains, masters of ceremonies, masters of celebrations, canons or heads of protocol for John Paul II. Amenable when required to be so, they sometimes offered 'services' to the most high-profile cardinals, and the rest of the time indulged in vice on their own account. (Among the entourage of Cardinal Angelo Becciu, then 'minister' of the interior under Pope Francis, I would be given confirmation of the names of these bishops in the course of a series of recorded interviews.)

I had a lengthy meeting with two of these three musketeers, accompanied by Daniele, my main Italian researcher. The first was true to his image as a gentleman and prince. For fear of outing himself, he was on his guard even though there could be no mistaking his obvious homosexuality. The second, whom we met several times in a palace at the Vatican, in the 'extraterritorial' zone, left us actually flabbergasted. In this huge building that he shared with several cardinals, the priest welcomed us wide-eyed, as if we were Tadzio in *Death in Venice*! Ugly as sin, he made advances to Daniele without any preliminaries, and gave me all sorts of compliments (when we were only meeting for the first time). He gave us contacts; we promised to visit him again (which we did). And several doors did open, giving us entrées to the pope's protocol service and the Vatican Bank, where this trio clearly had no shortage of contacts! Daniele was uncomfortable, particularly when I left him on his own for a few minutes to go to the bathroom. 'I was afraid of being molested!' he confided to me with a laugh when we left.

Among those close to John Paul II, the relationship with sexuality and cruising varies. While certain cardinals and bishops take risks, others double down on discretion. One French archbishop, later a cardinal, was, according to his former assistant, in a stable relationship, first with an Anglican priest and then with an Italian priest; another Italian cardinal lives with his companion, whom he introduced to me as 'the husband of his late sister', but everyone in the Vatican knew – starting with the Swiss Guards, who talked to me about it – the true nature of their relationship. A third, the American William Baum, whose habits have been made public, also lived in Rome with his lover, one of his assistants.

Another French-speaking cardinal whom I met several times, also close to John Paul II, is known for a slightly unusual vice: his technique consisted in inviting seminarians or trainee nuncios to lunch at his apartment, and then, claiming to be tired at the end of the meal, suggesting that they join him for a siesta. Then the cardinal would lie down on his bed without warning, and not say another word; he hoped that the young novice would join him. Drunk on reciprocity, he would wait patiently, motionless, like a spider in the middle of its web.

Another of John Paul II's cardinals was known (according to the first-hand testimony of two priests who worked with him) for cruising outside the Vatican, particularly in the parks around the Campidoglio, and had refused, as I have already mentioned, to register his official car with Vatican diplomatic plates, to give him extra freedom.

Yet another cardinal, who occupied an important position as a 'minister' to John Paul II, was brutally returned to his country after a scandal with a young Swiss Guard in which money played a part; he was later accused of having covered up cases of sexual abuse.

Other influential priests in John Paul II's entourage were homophilic but more discreet. The Dominican Mario Luigi Ciappi, one of his personal theologians, fraternally shared his life with his '*socius*' (assistant). One of the pope's confessors (according to a former assistant of Ciappi) was also prudently homophilic.

But let's return to the first 'ring of lust' in which cardinals La Mongolfiera and Platinette represent a kind of core around which the other stars gravitate. Compared with the great divas, the second rank and other peripheral cardinals are pallid indeed. Furthermore, the cardinals of this first ring are exceptional for their 'monstrous loves' and their 'hellish concert'!

I have been told of their boy-chasing escapades by their assistants and collaborators, and by their fellow cardinals, and I was even able to interrogate Platinette, whose audacity I can confirm: he grabbed my shoulder and gave my forearm a manly grip, not letting go for a moment, but not going any further either, during an interview at the holy see.

So let us step inside this parallel world where vice is rewarded in proportion to its excess. Is it for this kind of practice that the English created that beautiful phrase: 'They lived in squares and loved in triangles'? In any case, cardinals La Mongolfiera and Platinette, soon joined by a bishop whose pseudonym I shall forbear from quoting out of charity, are regular clients of the Roman male prostitutes, with whom they host foursomes.

Caught up in the whirlwinds of a dissolute life, were La Mongolfiera and Platinette taking considerable risks? We might imagine so. And yet, as cardinals, they enjoyed diplomatic immunity, and were also protected at the highest level of the Vatican as friends of the pope and his ministers. Besides, who would have talked? The Vatican had not yet been damaged by sexual scandals: the Italian press rarely covered these subjects; witnesses were silent; and the private lives of cardinals were untouchable. Social networks did not yet exist, and would only transform the media landscape later on, after the death of John Paul II: today, compromising videos and explicit photographs would probably be published on Twitter, Instagram, Facebook or YouTube. But at this time the camouflage was still fully in place.

To avoid rumours, La Mongolfiera and Platinette did take precautions: they instituted a sophisticated system of recruiting escorts via a triple filter. They themselves described their needs to a 'gentleman of His Holiness', a layman who was married and possibly heterosexual, and who, unlike his clients, had priorities other than homosexuality. He was immersed in a multitude of suspicious financial dealings, and in return for his services what he chiefly wanted was solid support at the top of the Curia and a visiting card.

In return for significant considerations, this 'gentleman of His Holiness', whose pseudonym was Negretto, a singer from Nigeria and a member of the Vatican choir, over the years constructed a fertile network of gay seminarians, Italian escorts and foreign male prostitutes. A real system of Russian dolls, each one fitting into the others, Negretto appealed to a third intermediary, whom he used as a tout and a go-between. They recruited in all directions, particularly from migrants who needed residence permits: if they proved to be 'understanding', this gentleman promised to intervene so that they would obtain their papers. (Here I am using information taken from the written records of phone-calls made by the Italian police and used in the trial to which this affair gave rise.)

The system would last for several years, under the pontificate of John Paul II and the early part of that of Benedict XVI, and supplied services not only for cardinals La Mongolfiera and Platinette and their friend the bishop, but for a fourth prelate (whose identity I have been unable to establish).

The action as such is supposed to have occurred outside the Vatican, in several residences, notably a villa with a pool, some luxury apartments in the centre of Rome and, according to two witnesses, the pope's summer residence in Castel Gandolfo. This site, which I visited with an archbishop from the Vatican, is located, opportunely enough, in the extraterritorial zone, and is the property of the holy see and not of Italy, with the consequence that the Italian police are unable to intervene (as they confirmed to me). There, far from watchful eyes, under the pretext of exercising his dogs, a prelate can also put his favourites through their paces.

According to several sources, the critical point of this network of luxury escorts was the way in which it was financed. Not only did cardinals have recourse to male prostitution to satisfy their libido; not only were they homosexuals in private while advocating severe homophobia in public; they also took care not to pay for their gigolos themselves! In fact, they dug deep into the coffers of the Vatican to pay their intermediaries, who varied over time, as did the highly expensive, if not ruinous, escorts (up to 2,000 euros an evening for luxury escorts, according to the information gathered by the Italian police working on the case). Some Vatican monsignori, broadly informed about the affair, found an ironic nickname for these thrifty prelates: 'the ATM priests'.

In the end, the Italian justice system inadvertently brought this prostitution network to an end, by having several of those behind the system arrested because of serious cases of corruption related to it. Two of the intermediaries were also arrested after being identified in telephone conversations. The prostitution network was consequently closed down by the police, who were aware of its extent, but they were unable to charge the main clients, who enjoyed Vatican immunity: Cardinals La Mongolfiera and Platinette.

In Rome, I interviewed a lieutenant colonel in the *carabinieri*. Here is his testimony.

'Apparently these cardinals were identified, but couldn't be called in for questioning, because of their diplomatic immunity. All cardinals enjoy that immunity. As soon as they were implicated in a scandal, they were automatically protected. They sought shelter behind the ramparts of the holy see. Likewise, we couldn't search their bags, even if we suspected them of drug-trafficking, for example, or take them in for questioning.'

The lieutenant colonel continues: 'In theory, the Vatican police, which does not depend on the Italian authorities, could have questioned these cardinals and prosecuted them. But the holy see would have had to ask them to do it. Yet, obviously, in this case, the backers of this trade were themselves connected to the very highest echelons of the holy see ...'

I won't go into detail about the activities of these cardinals, even though, according to the police wire-taps, their requests were highly creative. They talk about the escorts in terms of 'files' and 'situations'. The intermediaries obey, suggesting appropriate individuals that vary only in height and weight. Here are some extracts from the conversations (from the minutes of the trials):

'I won't tell you any more. He's two metres tall, such and such a weight, and he's 33.'

'I have a situation in Naples ... I don't know how to tell you, it's really not something to miss ... 32 years old, 1 metre 93, very handsome ...'

'I have a Cuban situation.'

'I've just arrived from Germany with a German.'

'I have two blacks.'

'X has a Croatian friend who wanted to see if you could find a time.'

'I've got a footballer.'

'I've got a guy from Abruzzo.'

Sometimes these exchanges revolve around both Christ and Viagra, which sums up the case very nicely.

After a long trial and several legal interventions, our 'gentleman' was sentenced for corruption; the Vatican choir was dissolved. Negretto now lives in a Catholic residence outside Italy, where people seem to satisfy his needs to buy his silence. As for the other intermediaries, whose identities I know, I haven't been able to track them down. Not only were the implicated cardinals never sentenced, or even questioned, but their real names never appeared in the records of the trial.

Pope John Paul II, if he was ever informed of the case, was unable to separate, among his inner circle, the wheat from the chaff, probably because such a detoxification process would have involved too many people. Pope Benedict XVI knew about this file, and did everything he could to marginalize the main protagonists, at first successfully, until the enterprise finally led, as we shall see, to his downfall. Francis, also well-informed, punished the implicated bishop by refusing to create him a cardinal, in spite of the promise that he had been given by a former secretary of state. For now, Platinette kept his hide. The leader of the network and master of the battlefield, La Mongolfiera, took his gilded cardinal's retirement: he still lives in luxury and, they say, with his lover. Of course, these prelates are now part of the opposition to Pope Francis; they harshly criticize any proposals he makes that are favourable to homosexuals, and demand ever greater chastity – even though they have practised it so little themselves.

The above affair would only be a minor news story were it not for the fact that it's a template for recurrent behaviour in the Roman Curia. These aren't glitches; this is a system. The prelates feel untouchable and fully enjoy their diplomatic immunity. However, we know their shortcomings and wickedness today, because witnesses have spoken. Even if attempts were made to shut them up.

Here we must return at greater length to an astonishing story closely bound up with the Mongolfiera affair. What a story it is! It's what the Poet would have called a real 'plot of genius'! The story concerns a discreet prelate, head of department at the Secretariat of State, Mgr Cesare Burgazzi, whose case was made public. (Since Burgazzi refused to answer my questions, in order to tell the story of this case I must rely on the detailed statements of two of his fellow priests, the evidence supplied by the police and the records of the resulting trials.)

One night in May 2006, Mgr Burgazzi was caught by the police, in his car, in an area of Rome well-known for cruising and male prostitution, Valle Giulia, near the Villa Borghese. His car, a Ford Focus, had been seen several times driving around the area. When they tried to take him in, the police reportedly spotted shadows moving in the darkened car, which had the seats down. They tried to apprehend – either for voyeurism or for an assault on public morals – the unfortunate prelate, who took flight at the wheel of his vehicle. There followed a 20-minute car chase across Rome which ended, as in a Hollywood film, in a big crash. Two police cars were damaged, three policemen injured. 'You don't know who I am! You don't know who you're dealing with!' Burgazzi yelled when he was arrested, sporting a black eye after playing a little too hard on the bumper-cars.

In its substance, the case is so unremarkable, and so frequent an occurrence in the Vatican, that it seems not to be of great interest. There are numerous such instances buried in police files all over the world, involving priests, prelates and even cardinals. But in this case, things aren't so simple. According to the version given by the police, who state that they showed their badges, condoms were found in Mgr Burgazzi's car, as well as his religious vestments, since the priest was arrested in plain clothes. Last of all, the police took the prelate's phone and identified a call made 'to a Brazilian transsexual named Wellington'.

For his part, Cesare Burgazzi has always claimed that the police were in plain clothes and their cars unmarked. He said he believed in good faith that they were trying to rob him, and that he even called the emergency services several times. The prelate also denied contacting the transsexual Wellington, and having condoms in his car. He claimed that several points in the police statement were false, and that their injuries were less serious than they claimed (as the court would agree on appeal). In the end, Burgazzi swore that, fearing an attempted robbery, he had only been trying to flee.

This theory of policemen disguised as highway robbers, or vice versa, seems fantastical to say the least. But the prelate repeated it so often, and the police were so incapable of proving the contrary, that the trial lasted longer than expected. At first, Burgazzi was relaxed, taking into account the vagueness of the police statements. But he appealed, and so did the prosecution: he in order to be totally exonerated; the police to have him sentenced, which was what happened on appeal when the court accepted the police version of events. Burgazzi then took the case to the court of cassation, where the affair ended, eight years after the events, with a definitive acquittal on all charges.

If the verdict was clear, the circumstances of the case remained at the very least obscure. Among other hypotheses, it is not impossible that Burgazzi fell into a trap. According to this idea, which is put forward by several people familiar with the case, it should be borne in mind that Burgazzi is a prudent man, and well-informed. Within the context of his functions at the Vatican, he is said to have discovered the scandalous financial practices and homosexual double life of several cardinals from Pope John Paul II's immediate entourage: a baffling mixture of money being siphoned off from the Vatican Bank, parallel bank accounts and prostitution networks. Cautious and, it was claimed, incorruptible, the spirited Burgazzi is even said to have made photocopies of all the documentation and put them in a safe, whose code was known only to his lawyer. Shortly afterwards, summoning up all his courage, he requested a personal meeting with the most powerful of those cardinals, with whom he shared his discoveries and asked for an explanation. We do not know the tenor of their discussions. What we do know, on the other hand, is that Burgazzi did not pass this file on to the press – proof of his loyalty to the Church and his aversion to scandal.

Did Burgazzi's threat have a connection with the incredible case at the Villa Borghese? Is it possible that the powerful cardinal implicated in the case might have taken fright and tried to neutralize the prelate? Was a trap set up for Burgazzi to compromise him and force him into silence, with the assistance of people close to the Italian police, and perhaps real police officers (a chief of police was known to be close to the cardinal in question)? Did they want to compromise him to the extent that his possible revelations would lose all credibility? All of these questions will probably go unanswered for a long time.

But we do know that Pope Benedict XVI, elected during the long judicial process that followed, insisted that Burgazzi be restored to his post at the Secretariat of State. He is even supposed to have met him during a mass and said to him: 'I know everything; keep going' (according to a witness who was told this story by Burgazzi).

This unexpected support from the pope in person is an indication of the anxiety that the affair caused in the Vatican, and lends a certain credence to the hypothesis of manipulation. Because it's hard not to be surprised by the shaky statements given by the police officers, their suspicious evidence, which the courts definitively rejected. Were they fabricated? To what end? For what possible backers? Is it possible that Cesare Burgazzi was the victim of a machination organized by one of his peers to shut him up or blackmail him? The criminal chamber of the Italian court of cassation, by finding him definitively not guilty and contesting the version given by the police officers, lent credibility to these hypotheses.

Cases involving money and morals, which are often closely linked in the Vatican, are therefore one of the keys to *The Closet*. Cardinal Raffaele Farina, one of those most familiar with these financial scandals (at Francis's request, he presided over the commission for the reform of the Vatican Bank), was the first to put me on the trail of these cross-connections. During two long interviews that he granted to me at his home in the holy see, in the presence of my Italian researcher Daniele, Farina described these unlikely collusions as being coupled like 'two yoke-devils sworn to either's purpose', in Shakespeare's words. The cardinal, of course, gave no names, but he and I both know who he was alluding to by stressing, with the confidence of one who has the evidence, that at the Vatican the love of boys goes hand in hand with the worship of the golden calf.

The explanations outlined by Farina and confirmed by several other cardinals, bishops and experts in the Vatican are in fact sociological rules. The very high percentage of homosexuals within the Roman Curia first of all explains – statistically, if we may put it that way – that several of them were at the centre of financial scandals. Added to this, there is the fact that to maintain relations in such a closed and controlled universe, framed by Swiss Guards, the police and who knows what else, one must be extremely prudent. Which offers only four alternatives: the first is monogamy, chosen by a significant proportion of prelates, who have fewer adventures than the rest. If they are not in stable couples, homosexuals engage in a more complicated life that entails one of the three remaining options: travelling to find sexual freedom (that is the royal road often taken by nuncios and assistants of the Secretariat of State, as we will see); going to specialist commercial bars; or visiting male prostitutes. In all three cases, you need money. And yet a priest's wages are usually somewhere in the region of 1,000 to 1,500 euros per month, often with pension and work accommodation thrown in – sums that are far from sufficient when it comes to satisfying complicated desires. The priests and bishops at the Vatican are not rich in funds: they are, it is said, 'minimum wage-earners who live like princes'.

In the end, the double life of a homosexual in the Vatican implies very strict control of one's private life, a culture of secrecy and financial needs: all incitements to camouflage and lies. All of this serves to explain the dangerous liaisons between money and sex, the proliferation of financial scandals and homosexual intrigues, and the rings of lust that developed under John Paul II, in a city that has become a byword for corruption.

12

The Swiss Guard

Nathanaël encountered two problems at the Vatican: girls and homosexuals. The scarcity of the former and the omnipresence of the latter.

I met this Swiss Guard by chance, when I was staying at the Vatican. I was a bit lost in the maze of stairs and he showed me the way. He wasn't shy; we fell into conversation.

At first I thought that Nathanaël was one of the contractual staff who intervened within the Vatican should anything need repair. The blue overalls that he wore that day made him look like an ordinary Italian worker. So I was surprised to see him a few days later in the red, yellow and blue 'gala' uniform: he was a Swiss Guard! A Swiss Guard with a toolbox!

I contacted Nathanaël again some time later, on another stay in Rome, and then I encountered his polite but firm refusal to see me again. I would later learn that this was one of the rules imposed on the Swiss Guard. For reasons I shall not go into here, he did agree to talk to me in the end, and we developed the habit of meeting at the Café Makasar, in the Borgo, only a few minutes' walk from the barracks of the Swiss Guard, but far from the places frequented by either monsignori or tourists, and hence discreet in a way that suited both of us.

Tall, with a long face, charming, Nathanaël was clearly very sociable. At our initial meeting, he told me his first name (altered here) and his telephone number; his surname was revealed to me only subsequently, and inadvertently, when I entered his details on my smartphone and his mobile number was automatically 'matched' with his Google + account.

However, Nathanaël isn't on Instagram or Facebook, and there is no photograph of him on Google Images, according to a strict Vatican rule that imposes extreme discretion on the Swiss Guard.

'No selfies, no profiles on social media,' Nathanaël confirms to me.

Girls and homosexuals, as stated, are the two problems that the Swiss Guard faces at the holy see. Since taking the job, he has managed to sleep 'with ten girls', he tells me, but the obligation of celibacy is a nuisance. And the rules are strict.

'We have to be at the barracks before midnight and we can never stay out. We are forbidden to be in a couple, since marriage is only authorized for senior officers, and it is strictly forbidden to bring girls back to the barracks. We are discouraged from meeting them in town, and denunciation is sometimes encouraged.'

These prudish obsessions of the old bogeymen at the Vatican bother Nathanaël, who considers that the essential questions, involving the sovereign missions of the Guard, are not taken into account – questions concerning the security of the pope, which in his view leaves much to be desired. I tell him that I have frequently returned to the Vatican via the gate called Arco delle Campare – the most magical of all, beneath the clock to the left of St Peter's in Rome – without having to show any kind of ID, and without my bag being searched, because a cardinal or an ordinary priest living inside had come out to fetch me. I showed him a key I had which allowed me to enter the Vatican, without any inspection, when I returned to the apartment in which I was staying. The Swiss Guard was troubled by my experiences.

During about a dozen secret meetings at the Café Makasar, he revealed to me what really troubled him in the Vatican: the sustained and sometimes aggressive advances of certain cardinals.

'If just one of them touches me, I'll smash his face in and resign,' he tells me in explicit terms.

Nathanaël isn't gay, or even gay-friendly: he tells me of his revulsion at several cardinals and bishops who tried it on with him (and gives me their names). He was traumatized by what he had discovered in the Vatican in terms of double lives, sexual advances and even harassment.

'I've been disgusted by what I've seen. I still haven't got over it. And to think that I took a vow to "sacrifice my life" if necessary, for the pope!'

And yet, had not the worm been in the apple from the outset? The Swiss Guard was founded in 1506 by Pope Julius II, whose bisexuality is well attested. As for the uniform of the smallest army in the world, a Renaissance rainbow-flag jacket and a two-pointed halberdier's hat decorated with heron feathers, according to legend it was designed by Michelangelo.

A police lieutenant colonel in Rome tells me that the Swiss Guard adhere to strict professional secrecy. 'There's an incredible *omertà*. They are taught to lie for the pope, for reasons of state. There are plenty of cases of harassment or sexual abuse, but they are hushed up and the Swiss Guard is always made indirectly responsible for what happened. They are given to understand that if they talk, they won't find another job. On the other hand, if they behave themselves, they will be helped to find a job when they return to civilian life in Switzerland. Their future career depends on their silence.'

In the course of my investigation, I interviewed 11 Swiss Guards. Apart from Nathanaël, whom I saw regularly in Rome, most of my contacts were made on the military pilgrimage to Lourdes or, in Switzerland, with former guardsmen whom I was able to meet during more than 30 stays in Zurich, Basel, St Gallen, Lucerne, Geneva and Lausanne. They have been reliable sources for this book, informing me about the morals of the Curia and the double lives of many cardinals who have, as might be expected, flirted with them.

I met Alexis at the Brasserie Versailles. Every year, on a large-scale pilgrimage, thousands of police officers and members of the armed forces from all over the world, all practising Catholics, meet up in Lourdes, a French city in the Pyrenees. A gathering of Swiss Guards traditionally takes place, and Alexis was among them the year when I went there. (His first name has been altered.)

'Here are the Swiss Guard at last,' exclaims Thierry, the manager of the brasserie, delighted to see the brightly coloured soldiers who attract customers and improve his turnover.

The military pilgrimage to Lourdes is a khaki and multicoloured festival in which dozens of countries are represented: you will see hats with fluorescent feathers, sharp, flashing swords, pompoms, men in kilts and all kinds of brass bands. They pray fervently and get wildly drunk, particularly on the Pont Vieux. There I see hundreds of Catholic soldiers singing, dancing and chatting people up. There are few women; homosexuals are in the closet. Binge drinking for Catholics!

In this huge booze-up, the Swiss Guards remain the number-one attraction, as I was told by the lieutenant colonel of the *carabinieri* who helped me attend the Lourdes pilgrimage.

'You will see,' he told me, 'far from Rome the Swiss Guards let themselves go a little. The pressure is less intense than it is in the Vatican, control by the officers relaxes, alcohol makes exchanges more fluid. They start talking!'

Alexis, indeed, relaxed: 'In Lourdes, we don't wear the gala uniform all the time,' the young man tells me as soon as he arrives at Brasserie Versailles. 'Last night we were in plain clothes. It's dangerous for our image if we're wearing the red, yellow and blue uniform and we're a bit tipsy!'

Alexis is no more gay-friendly than Nathanaël. He vehemently denies the received idea that the pontifical Swiss Guard has a high percentage of homosexuals. He suspects four or five of his comrades of being 'probably gay', and of course he knows the rumours about the homosexuality of one of the senior officers in the Swiss Guard of Pope Paul VI, who now lives with his partner in the Roman suburbs. He also knows, as everyone does, that several cardinals and bishops have caused a scandal within the Vatican by being in a couple with a Swiss Guard. And, of course, he knows the story of the triple murder, within the Vatican itself, when a young corporal of the Guard, Cédric Tornay, was reported to have murdered his Swiss Guard commander and his wife 'in a moment of madness'.

'That's the official version, but no one in the Guards believes it,' Alexis tells me. 'In fact Cédric's suicide was staged. He was murdered along with his commander and his wife, before a macabre scene was staged to make people believe in the theory of suicide after the double murder.' (I won't dwell here on this dramatic case, which has already been amply covered elsewhere, and about which the most esoteric hypotheses have circulated. Among these, for our subject, we need only mention that the hypothesis of a relationship between the young corporal and his commander was sometimes put forward, without really convincing anyone; their relationship, whether real or imagined, might have been used to conceal another motive for the crime. In either case, the mystery remains. For the sake of justice, Pope Francis would reopen this depressing dossier.)

Like Nathanaël, Alexis had passes made at him by dozens of cardinals and bishops, to the point that he thought of resigning from the Guard. 'The harassment is so insistent that I said to myself that I was going straight home. Many of us are exasperated by the usually rather indiscreet advances of the cardinals and bishops.'

Alexis tells me that one of his colleagues was regularly called in the middle of the night by a cardinal who said he needed him in his room. Other similar incidents were revealed by the press: from the inconsequential gift left on the bed of a Swiss Guard, along with a visiting card, to more advanced passes that could be called harassment or sexual assault.

'It took me a long time to realize that we were surrounded, at the Vatican, by frustrated men who see the Swiss Guard as fresh meat. They impose celibacy on us and refuse to let us marry because they want to keep us for themselves, it's as simple as that. They are so misogynistic, so perverse! They would like us to be like them: secret homosexuals!'

According to Alexis, Nathanaël and at least three other former Guards I interviewed in Switzerland, the internal rules are quite precise where homosexuality is concerned, even though it is barely mentioned as such during their training. The Swiss Guard are invited to demonstrate 'very great courtesy' towards cardinals, bishops 'and all the monsignori'. The ones thought of as 'newbies' are asked to be obliging and extremely polite. They must never criticize an eminence or an excellency, or refuse them anything. After all, a cardinal is the apostle of Christ on earth!

This courtesy, though, must be a façade, according to an unwritten rule of the Guard. As soon as a cardinal gives his telephone number to a young soldier, or suggests that he join him for a coffee, the Swiss Guard must thank him but politely tell him he is unavailable. If the cardinal is insistent, he must receive the same reply every time, and any rendezvous, should the Guard be intimidated into attending, must be cancelled on some pretext involving guard duty. In the most obvious cases of harassment, the Swiss Guard are invited to talk about it to their superiors, but under no circumstances should they respond to, criticize or report a prelate. The affair is almost always brushed under the carpet.

Like the other Swiss Guards, Alexis confirms the large number of homosexuals at the Vatican. He uses strong terms: 'domination', 'omnipresence', 'supremacy'. This pronounced gayitude has deeply shocked the majority of the Guards that I've interviewed. Nathanaël, when his service is over and his 'liberation' completed, never expects to set foot in the Vatican again, 'except on holiday with my wife'. Another Swiss Guard, interviewed in Basel, confirms to me that the homosexuality of the cardinals and prelates is one of the most frequently discussed subjects in the barracks, and the stories they hear from their comrades further amplify the experiences they have had themselves.

Speaking with Alexis, as with Nathanaël and the other Swiss Guards, we mention precise names, and the list of cardinals and bishops who have made passes at them is confirmed, proving to be as long as Cardinal Burke's cappa magna. Even though I know about the issue, these statements still surprise me: the number of the elect is even larger than I thought.

Why did they agree to talk to me so freely, to the extent that they are surprised by their own daring? Not out of jealousy or vanity, like some cardinals and bishops; not to help the cause, like most of my gay contacts within the Vatican. But out of disappointment, like men who have lost their illusions.

And now Alexis tells me another secret. If the officers, as I have said, are rarely homosexual, the same cannot be said of the confessors, chaplains and priests who surround the Swiss Guard.

'We are asked to go to the chapel reserved for us and confess at least once a week. And yet I've never seen as many homosexuals as I have among the chaplains of the Swiss Guard,' Alexis tells me.

The young man gives me the names of two chaplains and confessors of the Guard who he believes are homosexual (his information is confirmed by another Alemannic Swiss Guard and a Curia priest). I am also told the name of a chaplain who died of AIDS (as the Swiss journalist Michael Meier reported in an article in the *Tages-Anzeiger*, giving the man's name).

During many stays in Switzerland, where I have gone every month for several years, I met specialist lawyers and the directors of several human rights associations (such as SOS Racisme and Diskriminierung in der Schweiz). They told me of certain kinds of discrimination that affected the Swiss Guard, from the recruitment process to the code of good conduct applied to the Guards in the Vatican.

According to a Swiss lawyer, the status of the association recruiting future Swiss Guards, in the Swiss confederation, was said to be ambiguous. Is it a feature of Swiss law, or Italian law, or indeed the canon law of the holy see? The Vatican left that ambiguity in place so that it could play on all three levels. And yet since the recruitment of Swiss citizens took place in Switzerland, it should conform with that country's labour law, which applies even to foreign companies who work there. So the rules of recruitment for the Guards were deemed to be discriminatory: women were banned (although they are accepted into the Swiss army); a young married man or a man in a relationship cannot apply for a post, only bachelors are accepted; his reputation must be 'irreproachable', and he must have 'sound morals' (phrases designed to rule out not only gays, but also transsexuals); as for migrants, so dear to Pope Francis, they are also ineligible for recruitment. Last of all, it appears that people with disabilities or people of colour, black people or Asians, are also rejected during the selection process, although the texts are not explicit on this point.

According to the lawyers I consulted, the prohibition on being married was completely illegal, not to mention that it contradicts the principles of a Church that claims to encourage marriage and forbid all sexual relations outside of it.

I had the leaders of the Swiss Guard questioned in German by this lawyer about these legal anomalies, and their replies were noteworthy. They rejected the idea of discrimination, on the grounds that military constraints imposed certain rules (although these were contrary to the specific code of the Swiss army, which takes into account military specifics with regard to the age or physical condition of recruits). As regards homosexuality, they told us in writing 'that being gay is not a problem with regard to recruitment, as long as one is not too "openly gay", too visible or too feminine'. Last of all, oral rules issued during the training of the Swiss Guard and the code of conduct (the *Regolamento della Guardia Svizzera Pontificia*, which I have got hold of, and the last edition of which, with a preface by Cardinal Sodano, dates from 2006) also contain irregularities with regard to discrimination, labour law and harassment.

Anomalies that aren't merely juridical, in terms of Swiss, Italian or European law, but also moral, tell us a great deal about the peculiarities of a state that is decidedly abnormal.

13

The crusade against gays

At the same time as Pope John Paul II was protecting Marcial Maciel and part of his entourage was abandoning itself to the cruising of the Swiss Guard or lust in general, the Vatican launched its great battle against homosexuals.

There was nothing new about this war. The anti-sodomite fanaticism had existed since the Middle Ages, though this did not prevent dozens of popes from being suspected of having inclinations, including Pius XII and John XXIII – strong internal tolerance along with intense external criticism remained the rule. The Church has always been more homophobic in words than in the practices of its clergy.

However, this public discourse in Catholicism became more hardline in the late 1970s. The Catholic Church was wrong-footed by the revolution in morals that took place in the 1960s, which it had neither anticipated nor understood. Pope Paul VI, who was far from clear on the subject, reacted in 1975 with the famous 'declaration', *Persona humana*, which was part of the dynamic of the encyclical *Humanae vitae*: the celibacy of the priesthood was confirmed, value placed on chastity, sexual relations were prohibited and homosexuality was violently rejected.

To a large extent, and on the doctrinal level, the pontificate of John Paul II (1978–2005) was also part of this continuity. But the situation was aggravated by an increasingly homophobic discourse, while the pope's entourage hurled itself into a new crusade against gays (Angelo Sodano, Stanisław Dziwisz, Joseph Ratzinger, Leonardo Sandri, Alfonso López Trujillo were involved in manoeuvres, among others).

From the year of his election, the pope ensured that the debate was frozen. In a speech on 5 October 1979, delivered in Chicago to an audience of all the American bishops, he invited them to condemn acts that he called 'unnatural'. 'As compassionate pastors, you were right to say: "Homosexual activity, to be distinguished from homosexual tendencies, is morally evil." Through the clarity of this truth, you have proved the true charity of Christ; you have not betrayed those who, because of homosexuality, find themselves confronted with painful moral problems, as would have been the case if, in the name of understanding and pity, or for any other reason, you had offered false hopes to our brothers and sisters.' (Note the phrase: 'or for any other reason', which might be an allusion to the well-known morals of the American clergy.)

Why did John Paul II choose to appear, so early in his pontificate, as one of the most homophobic popes in the history of the Church? According to the American Vatican expert Robert Carl Mickens, who lives in Rome, there are two essential factors.

'He was a pope who had never known democracy, so he made all his decisions on his own, with his brilliant intuitions and his archaic Polish-Catholic prejudices, including prejudices about homosexuality. Then there was his *modus operandi*, his line throughout his pontificate was unity: he believed that a divided Church was a weak Church. He imposed great rigidity to protect that unity and the theory of the personal infallibility of the pontiff did the rest.'

John Paul II's low level of democratic culture is sometimes mentioned both in Kraków and Rome by those who knew him, along with his misogyny and his homophobia. But the pope seemed to tolerate well the omnipresence of homosexuals in his entourage. There were so many of them, and so many who were practising, among his ministers and his assistants, that he could not have been unaware of their ways of life, and not just of their 'tendency'. So why maintain such a contradictory position? Why allow such a system of hypocrisy to take root? Why such public intransigence and private tolerance? Why? Why?

The crusade that John Paul II would launch against gays, against condoms and, soon, against civil unions therefore appears in a new context, and in order to describe it we need to get inside the Vatican machine, which is the only way of understanding its violence and the profound psychological impulses behind it – the self-hatred that acts as its powerful secret motor – and finally its failure. Because it was a war that John Paul II would lose.

I shall tell this story first of all through the experience of an ex-monsignore, Krzysztof Charamsa, a simple cog in the propaganda machine, who showed us the dark side of this story by coming out. Then I will turn my attention to a cardinal in the Curia, Alfonso López Trujillo, who was one of its principal actors – and whose career in Colombia, in Latin America in general, and then in Italy, I have followed in great detail.

The first time I heard the name of Krzysztof Charamsa was in an email, from him. The prelate contacted me when he was still working for the Congregation for the Doctrine of the Faith. The Polish priest had enjoyed, he told me, my book *Global Gay*, and he asked for my help in communicating through the media his imminent coming out, though he swore me to secrecy on the subject. Not knowing at the time if he was an influential prelate as he claimed, or a charlatan, I asked my Italian friend Pasquale Quaranta, journalist with *La Repubblica*, to check his biography.

Once the authenticity of his testimony had been confirmed, I exchanged a number of emails with Mgr Charamsa, recommended the names of several journalists to him, and, in October 2015, just before the Synod on the Family, his high-profile coming out made the papers and travelled all the way around the world.

I met Krzysztof Charamsa several months later in Barcelona, the city to which he had been exiled after being stripped of his functions by the Vatican. Having become a queer and militant activist for Catalan independence, he made quite a good impression on me. We dined together with Eduard, his boyfriend, and I sensed in him, and in the looks that he gave Eduard, a certain pride, like someone who had just carried out a little revolution all by himself, his 'One-Man Stonewall'.

'You realize what he's done! Such courage! He was able to do all of that out of love. Out of love for the man he loves,' Pasquale Quaranta told me.

We saw each other again in Paris the following year and, during those various interviews, Charamsa told me his story, which he would go on to write as a book, *The First Stone*. In his interviews and his writings, the former priest always maintained a kind of restraint, of reserve, perhaps of fear if not of double-speak, which prevented him from telling the full truth. And yet, if he did *really* speak one day, his testimony would be of enormous importance, because Charamsa was at the heart of the Vatican's homophobic war machine.

For a long time, the Congregation for the Doctrine of the Faith was called the Holy Office, in charge of the sadly famous 'Inquisition' and its well-known 'Index', the list of censored or forbidden books. This Vatican 'ministry' continues, as its name suggests, to fix doctrine and define good and evil. Under John Paul II, this strategic dicastery, the second in terms of protocol after the Secretariat of State, was run by Cardinal Joseph Ratzinger. He was the one who came up with and decreed most of the texts against homosexuality, and examined most of the sexual abuse files in the Church.

Krzysztof Charamsa worked there, as adviser and deputy secretary to the International Theological Commission. I have complemented his story with those of four other internal witnesses: that of another adviser, a commission member, an expert and a cardinal who is a member of the council of that Congregation. I myself also had the chance to spend many nights, thanks to the hospitality of understanding priests, in the holy of holies: a Vatican apartment near Piazza Santa Marta, a few metres from the Palace of the Holy Office where I have met minor officials of the modern Inquisition.

The Congregation for the Doctrine of the Faith comprises about forty permanent salaried employees, known as *ufficiali, scrittori* or *ordinanze*, generally very orthodox, loyal and reliable priests (Charamsa calls them 'civil servants of the Inquisition'). Most have many degrees, often including theology, as well as canon law or philosophy. They are assisted by about thirty external *consultori*.

Generally speaking, every 'inquisitorial proceeding' (today we would say every 'point of doctrine') is studied by the functionaries, then discussed by experts and consultants before being submitted to the council of cardinals for ratification. This apparent horizontality, a source of debate, in fact conceals a verticality: only one man is authorized to interpret the texts and dictate 'the' truth. Because the prefect of the Congregation (Joseph Ratzinger under John Paul II, William Levada and then Gerhard Müller under Benedict XVI – both subject to Ratzinger) naturally has ultimate control over all the documents: he proposes them, amends them and validates them before presenting them to the pope at crucial private audiences. The holy father has the last word. Here we can see – as we have known since Nietzsche – that morality is always a tool of domination.

It is also an area highly propitious to hypocrisy. Among the 20 cardinals currently in the flow chart of the Congregation for the Doctrine of the Faith, we think that there are about a dozen homophiles or practising homosexuals. At least five live with a boyfriend. Three regularly use male prostitutes. (Mgr Viganò criticizes seven of these cardinals in his '*Testimonianza*'.)

The Congregation is therefore an interesting clinical case and the heart of Vatican hypocrisy. Charamsa: 'Since many of them are homosexual, these clergy impose a hatred of homosexuals, which is to say self-hatred, in a desperate masochistic act.'

According to Krzysztof Charamsa, as well as other internal witnesses, under prefect Ratzinger the homosexual question became an actual unhealthy obsession. The few lines of the Old Testament devoted to Sodom are read and reread; the relationship between David and Jonathan is endlessly reinterpreted, along with the phrase in the New Testament in which Paul admits his suffering at having 'a thorn in the flesh' (for Charamsa, Paul was suggesting his own homosexuality). And all of a sudden, when we have been driven mad by this dereliction, when we understand that Catholicism deserts and desolates existence, a life with no way out, perhaps one secretly begins to weep?

These erudite gayphobes in the Congregation for the Doctrine of the Faith have their own SWAG code (Secretly We Are Gay). When these priests talk among themselves in mystical jargon about the Apostle John, the 'disciple beloved of Jesus', this 'John, beloved more than the others', the one that 'Jesus, having seen him, loved', they know very well what they mean; and when they conjure the image of healing by Jesus of a young centurion's servant 'who was dear to him', according to the heavily emphasized insinuations in the Gospel according to Saint Luke, there is no doubt about the significance of this in their eyes. They know that they belong to a cursed people – and a chosen people.

During our meetings in Barcelona and Paris, Charamsa described in great detail this secret universe, this law so fully anchored in people's hearts, hypocrisy elevated to the state of a rule, double-speak, brain-washing, and he told me all of this in a tone of confession, as if giving away the ending of *The Name of the Rose*, in which the monks woo one another and exchange favours until, filled with remorse, a young monk throws himself from a tower.

'I read and worked all the time. It was all I did. I was a good theologian. That was why the directors of the Congregation were so surprised by my coming out. They expected that of everyone, except me,' the Polish priest tells me.

For a long time, the orthodox Charamsa obeyed orders without demur. He even helped to write texts of unusual vehemence against homosexuality as being 'objectively disordered'. Under John Paul II and Cardinal Ratzinger, it was quite a festival. The syllabus as a whole didn't have harsh enough words for gays. Homophobia spread ad nauseam through dozens of declarations, exhortations, letters, instructions, considerations, observations, *motu proprio* and encyclicals, so much so that it would be difficult to list all the 'papal bulls' here.

The Vatican tried to ban homosexuals from joining seminaries (not realizing that this would also mean a drop in vocations); it legitimized their exclusion from the army (when the United States wanted to suspend the 'Don't ask don't tell' rule); it suggested theologically legitimizing the discriminations to which homosexuals could be subjected in their work; and, of course, it condemned same-sex unions and marriage.

The day after World Gay Pride, which was held in Rome on 8 July 2000, John Paul II spoke during the traditional angelus prayer to denounce 'the well-known demonstrations' and to express his 'bitterness at the insult to the Great Jubilee of the year 2000'. But the faithful were few in number that weekend compared with the 200,000 people who marched in the streets of Rome.

'The Church will always say what is good and what is bad. No one can demand that it finds just something that is unjust according to natural and evangelical law,' Cardinal Angelo Sodano said on the occasion of that Gay Pride, and he did everything he could to stop the LGBT procession. We should note at the same time the attacks of Cardinal Jean-Louis Tauran, who disapproved of this demonstration 'during holy week', and those of the auxiliary bishop of Rome, Mgr Rino Fisichella, whose episcopal motto was 'I have chosen the way of truth', and who couldn't find words harsh enough to criticize World Gay Pride! A joke, incidentally, circulated inside the Vatican to explain these three pugnacious positions: cardinals were furious about the Gay Pride parade because it wouldn't let them have a float!

For 'coming out' too noisily or too late, Krzysztof Charamsa is now under twofold attack from the Curia and from the Italian gay movement. Having moved in a flash from internalized homophobia to drama queen, the prelate is found to be unsettling. I am told, for example, that at the Congregation for the Doctrine of the Faith his dismissal was linked to the fact that he didn't get the promotion he was hoping for. His homosexuality was identified, I was told by an official source, because he had lived with his boyfriend for several years.

A Curia prelate, very familiar with the case, and homosexual himself, explained: 'Charamsa was at the heart of the Vatican homophobic machine. He led a double life: he attacked gays in public, and at the same time he lived with his lover in private. For a long time he reached an accommodation with this system that he went on to condemn – just before the synod, putting the liberal wing of the Curia in difficulty. What is problematic is that he could, like myself and others, have lined up with progressive Cardinals Walter Kasper or the very friendly Schönborn. Instead of which he denounced and attacked them for years. To me, Charamsa remains a mystery.' (These severe judgements, typical of the counter-campaign waged by the Vatican, do not contradict Charamsa's story; he acknowledged that he 'dreamed of becoming a prefect of the Inquisition', and that he was involved in a real 'police department of souls').

On the other hand, Charamsa found little support among the gay Italian community, which criticized his 'pink-washing', as another activist confirms: 'In his interviews and his book, he didn't explain the system at all. He only spoke about himself, about his own little person. His confession is of no interest: when he came out in 2015 it was 50 years too late! What would really have been of interest would have been if he had told us about the system from inside, described everything, like Solzhenitsyn.'

A harsh judgement, perhaps, even though it is clear that Charamsa wasn't the gay Solzhenitsyn of the Vatican that some might have hoped for.

The crusade against gays was waged under John Paul II by another prelate, more influential than the former priest Charamsa. He was a cardinal, one of those closest to John Paul II. His name: Alfonso López Trujillo. His title: President of the Pontifical Council for the Family.

Here we are entering one of the darkest chapters in the recent history of the Vatican, and I don't want to get carried away by my story too quickly: I will need as much time as it takes to tell this absolutely extraordinary case.

Who was Alfonso López Trujillo? The specimen was born in 1946 in Villahermosa, in the region of Tolima, in Colombia. He was ordained priest in Bogotá at the age of 25, and 10 years later he became auxiliary priest of the same city, before returning to Medellín where, at the age of 43, he was made archbishop. A classical trajectory, for a priest who was born into a good family and never short of money.

The remarkable career of Alfonso López Trujillo owes a lot to Pope Paul VI, who spotted him early on during his official visit to Colombia in August 1968, and even more to John Paul II, who made him his right-hand man in Latin America at the start of his pontificate. The reason for this great friendship was simple, and identical to the one that the Polish pope formed at the same time with the nuncio Angelo Sodano or Father Marcial Maciel: anti-communism.

Alvaro Léon, now retired, was for a long time a Benedictine monk and, when he was a young seminarian, 'master of ceremonies' to Alfonso López Trujillo in Medellín. It's there that I meet this old man with a handsome, weary face, with my main Colombian 'researcher', Emmanuel Neisa. Alvaro Léon wanted to appear in my book under his real name, 'because I've waited too many years to talk,' he tells me, 'so I want to do it completely now, with courage and precision'.

We lunch together in a restaurant near Medellín cathedral, and Alvaro Léon takes his time to tell me of his life beside the archbishop, spinning out the suspense for a long while. We will stay together until the evening, exploring the city and its cafés.

'López Trujillo doesn't come from here. He studied in Medellín and his vocation came late. First of all he studied psychology, and it was only later that he became a seminarian in the city.'

Aspiring to the priesthood, the young López Trujillo was sent to Rome to complete his studies in philosophy and theology at the Angelicum. Thanks to a doctorate and a solid acquaintance with Marxism, he was able to fight on equal terms with left-wing theologians, and attack them from the right – if not the far right – as several of his books testify.

Back in Bogotá, López Trujillo was ordained a priest in 1960. For ten years he exercised his ministry in the shadows, already with great orthodoxy and not without several incidents.

'Rumours about him began circulating very quickly. When he was appointed auxiliary bishop to Bogotá in 1971, a group of laymen and priests even published a petition denouncing his extremism and demonstrated against his appointment in front of the city cathedral! It was from that moment that López Trujillo became completely paranoid,' Alvaro Léon tells me.

According to all the witnesses I questioned in Colombia, the unexpected acceleration of López Trujillo's career began with the Latin American Bishops' Council (CELAM), which regularly assembles all the Latin American bishops to define the direction of the Catholic Church in South America.

One of the founding conferences was in fact held in Medellín in 1968 (the first took place in Rio de Janeiro in 1955). That year, when campuses were erupting in Europe and the United States, the Catholic Church was in a state of great excitement following on from Vatican II. Pope Paul VI stopped off in Colombia to launch the CELAM conference.

This grand gathering proved to be decisive: it saw the emergence of a progressive current, which would soon be christened 'liberation theology', by the Peruvian priest Gustavo Gutiérrez. It was a new direction in Latin America, where large parts of the Church began to voice the need for a 'preferential option for the poor'. Many bishops defended the 'liberation of oppressed peoples' and decolonization, and denounced far-right military dictatorships. Soon a minority slipped into leftism, with pro-Guevara or pro-Castro priests, and more rare ones, like the Colombian Camilo Torres Restrepo or the Spaniard Manuel Pérez put their money where their mouth was and took up arms alongside the guerrillas.

According to the Venezuelan Rafael Luciani, a specialist in liberation theology and himself a member of CELAM and professor of theology at Boston College, 'López Trujillo genuinely emerged in reaction to the bishops' conference in Medellín'. During several meetings and dinners, Luciani brought me a great deal of information about CELAM and the part played in it by the future cardinal.

The Medellín conference, whose debates and declarations López Trujillo followed as a simple priest, was a turning point for him. He understood that the Cold War had just reached the Latin American Church. His reading was binary, and he just had to follow his nose to choose his camp.

Made a part of the administrative authorities of CELAM, the young bishop, recently elected, began – discreetly at first – lobbying internally for a militant right-wing political option against liberation theology and its preferential option for the poor. His project: to see to it that CELAM renewed its connection with conservative Catholicism. He would stay in the post for seven years.

Did he have connections with Rome, to carry out this undermining work? That much is certain, because he was appointed to CELAM thanks to the support of the Vatican and the influential Italian cardinal Sebastiano Baggio, a former nuncio to Brazil, who became director of the Congregation of Bishops. But the Colombian would only become the spearhead of John Paul II's anti-liberation theology measures after the Puebla conference in Mexico in 1979.

'In Puebla, López Trujillo was very influential, very strong. I remember very clearly,' I am told by the Brazilian Cardinal Odilo Scherer during an interview in São Paulo. 'Liberation theology was a kind of consequence of Vatican II, of the 1960s ... and also of May 1968 in France [he laughs]. It was sometimes too politicized, and had abandoned the true work of the Church.'

That year, in Puebla, López Trujillo, by now an archbishop, went into direct action. 'Prepare the bombers,' he wrote to a colleague before the conference. He organized it in great detail, apparently making 39 trips between Bogotá and Rome to prepare for the meeting. It was he who ensured that theologians like Gustavo Gutiérrez were removed from the conference hall on the grounds that they weren't bishops.

When the CELAM conference opened in Mexico with an inaugural speech by John Paul II, who had travelled there especially for the occasion, López Trujillo had a precise battle plan: his intention was to take power back from the progressive camp and make the organization turn to the right. Trained 'like a boxer before a fight', in his own words, he was ready to exchange fire with the 'leftist' priests.

This was confirmed to me by the famous Brazilian Dominican Frei Betto during an interview in Rio de Janeiro: 'At the time, most bishops were conservative. But López Trujillo wasn't just conservative: he was on the far right. He was openly on the side of big capital and the exploitation of the poor: he defended capitalism more than the doctrine of the Church. He was inclined towards cynicism. At the CELAM conference in Puebla he even slapped a cardinal.'

Alvaro Léon, López Trujillo's former colleague, continues: 'The result of Puebla was a mixed one for López Trujillo. He managed to regain power and have himself elected president of CELAM, but at the same time he didn't get rid of the liberation theology that still fascinated a large number of bishops.'

Now that he was in power, Alfonso López Trujillo was able to refine his political strategy and use iconoclastic methods to consolidate his influence. He ran CELAM with an iron fist between 1979 and 1983, and Rome was all the more appreciative of his combative attitude since it belonged, like Marcial Maciel's, to a 'local'. There was no longer any need to parachute in Italian cardinals or use apostolic nuncios to wage war against communism in Latin America: all they had to do was recruit good, subservient Latinos to 'get the job done'.

And Alfonso López Trujillo was so devoted, so passionate, that he performed his task of eradicating liberation theology with great zeal, in Medellín, in Bogotá and soon throughout the whole of Latin America. In an ironic portrait in *The Economist*, he would even be portrayed with his red cardinal's cap, like a reversal of Che Guevara in his famous beret!

The new pope, John Paul II, and his ultra-conservative entourage of cardinals, now led by their warrior López Trujillo, would make the total defeat of the liberation theology trend their priority. This was also the line taken by the US administration: the report of the Rockefeller Commission, produced at the request of President Nixon, calculated that since 1969 Liberation Theology had become more of a threat than communism: in the 1980s under Reagan, the CIA and the Department of the Secretary of State continued to investigate the subversive ideas of these 'red' Latin American priests. To achieve this, the pontiff would appoint an impressive number of right-wing and far-right bishops in Latin America during the 1980s and 1990s.

'Most of the bishops appointed in Latin America during the pontificate of John Paul II were close to Opus Dei,' the academic Rafael Luciani, a member of CELAM, confirms.

At the same time, Cardinal Joseph Ratzinger, who became the head of the Congregation for the Doctrine of the Faith, led the ideological battle against the thinkers of liberation theology, whom he accused of using 'Marxist concepts', and harshly punished several of them (López Trujillo was one of the authors of the two anti-liberation theology documents published by Ratzinger in 1984 and 1986).

In less than ten years most CELAM bishops moved to the right. Liberation theology became a minority current in the council in the 1990s, and it would only be when the fifth CELAM conference was held in Aparecida in Brazil that a new moderate current would reappear, embodied in the Argentinian Cardinal Jorge Bergoglio. An anti-López Trujillo line.

One evening in October 2017 I am in Bogotá with a former seminarian, Morgain, who worked and associated with López Trujillo for a long time in Medellín. The man is reliable; his testimony indisputable. He still works for the Colombian episcopate, which makes it difficult for him to speak out publicly (his first name has been altered). But reassured by the fact that I will quote him under a false name, he starts to tell me the scandals, first in a whisper and then in a loud voice. He too has been keeping this information secret for so long that he's eager to get it all out into the open, with countless details, over the course of a long dinner, at which my Colombian researcher is also present.

'I was working with Archbishop López Trujillo in Medellín at the time. He lived in opulent conditions and travelled about like a prince, or rather like a real "señora". When he arrived in one of his luxury cars for an episcopal visit, he asked us to put out a red carpet. Then he would get out of the car, extending his leg, of which all that could be seen at first was his ankle, and then setting a foot on the carpet, as if he was the Queen of England! We all had to kiss his rings, and he had to have clouds of incense all around him. For us, this luxury, this show, the incense, the carpet, were very shocking.'

This way of life from another era went hand in hand with a real hunt for progressive priests. According to Morgain – and his testimony has been confirmed by that of other priests – in the course of his diva tours Alfonso López Trujillo would spot priests close to liberation theology and then organize their 'removal'. Some of those priests disappeared, or were murdered by paramilitaries just after the archbishop's visit.

In the 1980s, Medellín became the world's crime capital. Drug traffickers, particularly the famous Medellín cartel of Pablo Escobar – who was believed to have been in charge of 80 per cent of the cocaine market into the United States – waged a reign of terror. In the face of the explosion of violence – the drug war, the rise in power of the guerrillas and the confrontations between rival cartels – the Colombian government declared a state of emergency (*estatuto de seguridad*). But its impotence was obvious: in 1991 alone, more than six thousand murders were recorded in Medellín.

Given this infernal spiral, paramilitary groups formed in the city to organize the defence of the populace, although it was not always possible to know if these militias – sometimes public, sometimes private – worked for the government, for the cartels or on their own account. These notorious 'paramilitaries' in turn sowed terror in the city, before themselves becoming involved in drug-trafficking to finance their own activities. For his part, Pablo Escobar reinforced his own Departamento de Orden Ciudadano (DOC), his own paramilitary militia. In the end, the boundary between the drug traffickers, the guerrillas, the military and the paramilitaries became completely blurred, throwing Medellín and the whole of Colombia into a real civil war.

We must assess López Trujillo's career in this context. According to the journalists who have investigated the Archbishop of Medellín (in particular, Hernando Salazar Palacio in his book *La Guerra secreta del cardenal López Trujillo*, and Gustavo Salazar Pineda in *El Confidente de la Mafia se Confesia*) and the research carried out for me by Emmanuel Neisa in the country, the prelate was close to certain paramilitary groups linked to the drug traffickers. He is said to have been generously financed by these groups – perhaps directly by Pablo Escobar, who presented himself as a practising Catholic – and kept them regularly informed about leftist activities within the churches of Medellín. The lawyer Gustavo Salazar Pineda, in particular, states in his book that López Trujillo received suitcases of money from Pablo Escobar, but the archbishop denied ever meeting him. (We know from a detailed investigation by Jon Lee Anderson for the *New Yorker* that Pablo Escobar was in the habit of paying the priests who supported him, many leaving with suitcases full of money.)

At that time the paramilitaries were persecuting progressive priests all the more fiercely since they believed, not without reason, that these priests close to liberation theology were allied to the three main Colombian guerrilla groups (FARC, E.L.N. and M-19).

'López Trujillo travelled with members of the paramilitary groups,' I am also told by Alvaro Léon (who accompanied him on several of his trips as master of ceremonies). 'He pointed out the priests who were carrying out social actions in the barrios and the poorer districts. The paramilitaries identified them and sometimes went back to murder them. Often they had to leave the region or the country.' (This apparently unlikely story is in fact confirmed by the information and testimonies quoted by the journalists Hernando Salazar Palacio and Gustavo Salazar Pineda in their respective books.)

One of the places where the corrupt López Trujillo was supposed to have denounced several left-wing priests is the parish known as Parroquia Santo Domingo Savio, in Santo Domingo, one of the most dangerous parts of Medellín. When I visited this church with Alvaro Léon and Emmanuel Neisa, we were given precise information about his ruthless acts. Missionaries who worked with the poor there were murdered, and a priest of the same theological current, Carlos Caldéron, was himself persecuted by López Trujillo and then by the paramilitaries, before having to flee the country for Africa.

'I took care of the trips of López Trujillo here in Santo Domingo,' Alvaro Léon tells me on the steps of the church of the Parroquia Santo Domingo Savio. 'He would usually arrive with an escort of three or four cars, with bodyguards and paramilitaries all over the place. His entourage was very impressive! Everyone was very well dressed. The church bells had to ring when he got out of his limousine, and of course he had to have a red carpet. People had to kiss his hand. He also had to have music, a choir, but we had to cut the children's hair in advance so that it was perfect, and we couldn't have any blacks. It was during these visits that the progressive priests were identified and denounced to the paramilitaries.'

Accusations brushed away with the back of the hand by Mgr Angelo Acerbi, who was nuncio in Bogotá between 1979 and 1990, when I interview him in Santa Marta, inside the Vatican, where he has retired.

'López Trujillo was a great cardinal. I can assure you that in Medellín he never had the slightest collusion either with the paramilitaries or with the guerrillas. You know, he was very threatened by the guerrillas. He was even arrested and imprisoned. He was very brave.'

Today, López Trujillo is held to be directly or indirectly responsible for the deaths of dozens of priests and bishops who were eliminated for their progressive convictions.

'It's important to tell the story of these victims, because the legitimacy of the peace process has to pass through that acknowledgement,' I am told during several conversations in Bogotá by José Antequera, the spokesman of the victims' association 'Hijos e Hijas', whose father was assassinated.

Neither must we forget the incredible wealth accumulated by the archbishop during that period. According to several witness statements, he abused his position so as to requisition all valuable objects held by the churches he visited – the jewels, the silver cups, the paintings – which he recovered for his own advantage.

'He confiscated all the valuable objects from the parishes and sold them or gave them to the cardinals or bishops of the Roman Curia, to win their favour. A minutely detailed inventory of all these thefts has since been drawn up by a priest,' Alvaro Léon tells me.

Over the last few years, testimonies have been published in Colombia by penitent mafia members or their lawyers, confirming the connections that existed between the cardinal and the drug cartels connected to the paramilitaries. These rumours were old, but according to the inquiries of several major Colombian reporters, the cardinal was financed by certain drug traffickers, which helped – along with his personal family fortune – to explain his way of life and his collection of luxury cars.

'And then one fine day, López Trujillo disappeared,' Morgain tells me. 'He evaporated. He left and never set foot in Colombia again.'

A new life began in Rome for the Archbishop of Medellín. After efficiently supporting the Colombian far right, he now set about embodying John Paul II's conservative hard line on the question of morals and the family.

Having been a cardinal since 1983, he exiled himself definitively to the Vatican on the occasion of his appointment as president of the Pontifical Council for the Family in 1990. This new 'ministry', set up by the pope shortly after his election, was one of the priorities of the pontificate.

Beginning with this period, and with the ever greater trust placed in him by Pope John Paul II – as well as his close friends Angelo Sodano, Stanisław Dziwisz and Joseph Ratzinger – the vanity of López Trujillo, already spectacular, became uncontrollable. Now he was starting to look like a figure from the Old Testament, with his rages, his excommunications and his ravings. Continuing to enjoy a way of life unimaginable for a priest, he was now a cardinal. Rumours circulated and priests sometimes told curious stories about him.

At the head of his 'ministry' of the family, which became a 'war room', López Trujillo deployed unparalleled energy to condemn abortion, defend marriage and denounce homosexuality. This man – who was frighteningly misogynistic, according to all witnesses – also devised a war against gender theory. A 'workaholic' according to several observers, he intervened on various platforms around the world to denounce pre-marital sex and gay rights. In these forums he made a name for himself with one-upmanship and verbal excesses against scientific 'interruptors of pregnancy', whom he accused of committing crimes with their test tubes or of being odious doctors who advocated the use of condoms rather than abstinence before marriage.

AIDS, now a global scourge, became López Trujillo's new obsession, and he deployed his prejudices with impunity. 'The condom is not a solution,' he repeated in Africa, exercising his authority as cardinal: it would only encourage 'sexual promiscuity', while chastity and marriage were the only proper responses to the pandemic.

Everywhere he went – in Africa, Asia and of course in Latin America – he begged governments and UN agencies not to yield to 'lies', and he urged their people to abstain from the use of condoms. In the early 2000s, in an interview with the BBC, he even declared that condoms were full of 'microscopic holes' that let through the AIDS virus, which, he claimed, were '450 times smaller than a spermatozoon'! If the subject of AIDS were not so serious, we could use as a reply the famous comment of a French minister: 'The cardinal doesn't understand condoms: he puts them on his index'.

In 1995, López Trujillo wrote a *Dictionary of Ambiguous Terms about the Family*, in which he sought to ban the expressions 'safe sex', 'gender theory' and 'family planning'. He also invented several phrases of his own, such as 'contraceptive colonialism' and the remarkable 'pan-sexualism'.

His anti-gay obsession, because it went beyond the average and the norm (which were already outrageous in the Vatican), quickly aroused suspicion. From inside, his crusade was astonishing: what was the cardinal trying to hide behind such a belligerent stance, so outrageous and so personal? Why was he so keen on provocation, on being in the spotlight? Why was he so 'black-and-white'?

Inside the Vatican some people began to mock his excesses, giving this carping cardinal the nickname 'coitus interruptus'. Outside, the association Act Up made him one of its *bêtes noires*: as soon as he was due to speak somewhere, militants disguised as giant condoms, or wearing explicit tee-shirts, a pink triangle on a black background, had fun at his expense. He condemned these blaspheming sodomites who kept him from speaking; and they in turn condemned this Old Testament prophet who wanted to crucify gays.

History will judge Alfonso López Trujillo harshly. But in Rome, this heroic fighter served as an example to John Paul II and Benedict XVI, and he was hailed to the point of caricature by Secretaries of State Angelo Sodano and Tarcisio Bertone.

He was said to be *'papabile'* – in the running for the papacy – when Pope John Paul II died. And the same pope was even said to have put him on the list of potential successors just before his death in 2005 – although this has not been proven. This sensationalist apostle cursed and raged against many left-wing Catholics, and even more against divorced couples, unnatural sexual practices and Evil. But suddenly, between the outgoing pontificate of John Paul II and the incoming pontificate of Benedict XIV, he found a platform, an echo and perhaps enthusiasts (based on a gigantic misunderstanding), and that is the poisoned gift of circumstance.

In Rome, López Trujillo remains a complex and, for many, an enigmatic figure.

'López Trujillo was opposed to Marxism and liberation theology; that was what inspired him,' Giovanni Battista Re, John Paul II's former 'minister' of the interior, tells me in the course of our interviews in his Vatican apartment.

Archbishop Vincenzo Paglia, who succeeded him as president of the Pontifical Council for the Family, is more reserved. The cardinal's rigid line on the family was no longer in vogue under Francis's pontificate, Paglia tells me, choosing his words carefully, when we speak at the Vatican. 'The dialectic between progressivism and conservatism on social questions is no longer the subject today. We must be missionaries in a radical way. I think we have to stop being self-referential. Talking about the family doesn't mean fixing rules; on the contrary, it means helping families.' (During this interview, Paglia, whose artistic leanings have often been mocked, shows me his installation representing a pop-art version of Mother Teresa: the saint of Calcutta is in striped blue plastic, perhaps latex, and Paglia switches her on. Mother Teresa lights up all of a sudden, and, in lapis-lazuli blue, starts flashing ...)

According to several sources, the influence of López Trujillo in Rome also came from his fortune. He was said to have 'rewarded' several cardinals and prelates, on the model of the Mexican Marcial Maciel.

'López Trujillo was a man of networks and money. He was violent, choleric, hard. He was one of the people who "made" Benedict XVI, on whose election he spent abundantly, with a campaign that was very well-organized and well-financed,' the Vaticanologist Robert Carl Mickens confirms.

This story would not be complete without its 'happy ending'. To reveal that apotheosis now, I return to Medellín: to the very district of the archbishopric where Alvaro Léon, López Trujillo's former master of ceremonies, guides me and Emmanuel Neisa around the alleyways surrounding the cathedral. This central district of Medellín is called Villa Nueva.

It's a strange area, where, between the Parque Bolivar and Carrera 50, around the streets called Calle 55, 56 and 57, dozens of religious shops are lined up selling Catholic articles and priestly habits, and the gay bars are decorated with pictures of gaudy transsexuals in high heels. The two worlds, sacred and profane, the plastic crucifixes and the cheap saunas, priests and prostitutes, mingle in that incredible festive spirit that is so typical of Colombia. A transsexual who looks like a sculpture by Fernando Botero accosts me enterprisingly. Around her are male prostitutes and transvestites who are clearly more fragile, more frail, far from the arty images familiar from folklore and Fellini; they are symbols of poverty and exploitation.

A little further on we visit Medellín Diversa como Vos, an LGBT centre founded by priests and seminarians. Gloria Londoño, one of the directors, welcomes us. 'We are in a strategic place, because the whole of Medellín's gay life is organized here, around the cathedral. The prostitutes, the transsexuals and transvestites are very vulnerable populations, and they are helped here by being informed of their rights. Condoms are also distributed here,' Londoño explains.

Leaving the centre, on Calle 57 we bump into a priest accompanied by his boyfriend, and Alvaro Léon, who has recognized them, points them out discreetly. We are continuing with our visit to the gay-Catholic quarter when, all of a sudden, we stop in front of a handsome building on Rue Bolivia, also known as Calle 55. Alvaro Léon points up at an apartment: 'That's where it all happened. López Trujillo had a secret apartment there, where he took seminarians, young men and prostitutes.'

The homosexuality of Cardinal Alfonso López Trujillo is an open secret that dozens of witnesses have talked to me about, and that has even been confirmed by several cardinals. His 'pan-sexualism', to quote one of the entries in his dictionary, was well known in Medellín, Bogotá, Madrid and Rome.

The man was an expert on the great gap between theory and practice, between mind and body, an absolute master of hypocrisy – which is notorious in Colombia. A man close to the cardinal, Gustavo Álvarez Gardeazábal, even went so far as to write a *roman-à-clef*, *La Misa ha terminado*, in which he denounced the double life of López Trujillo, who was, under a pseudonym, its main character. As for the many gay militants who I questioned in Bogotá during my four trips to Colombia – particularly those of the association Colombia Diversa, which includes several lawyers – they have collected a large number of witness statements, which they shared with me.

The Venezuelan academic Rafael Luciani tells me that Alfonso López Trujillo's obsessive homosexuality was 'well-known to the Latin American ecclesiastical authorities and some of the senior representatives of CELAM'. Furthermore, a book is reportedly in preparation concerning the double life and sexual violence of Cardinal López Trujillo, co-signed by several priests. As for the seminarian Morgain, one of López Trujillo's assistants, he tells me the names of several of his touts and lovers, many of whom were obliged to satisfy the archbishop's desires so as not to sabotage their careers.

'At first I didn't understand what he wanted,' Morgain tells me when we have dinner in Bogotá. 'I was innocent, and his technique of making passes escaped me completely. And then gradually I came to understand his system. He went out into the parishes, into the seminaries, the religious communities, to spot boys, whom he would then very violently waylay. He thought he was desirable. He forced the seminarians to yield to his advances. His speciality was novices. The most fragile, the youngest, the most vulnerable. But in fact he slept with anybody. He also had lots of prostitutes.'

Morgain gives me to understand that his ordination by López Trujillo was blocked because he refused to sleep with him.

López Trujillo was one of those men who seek power in order to have sex and sex in order to have power. Alvaro Léon, his former master of ceremonies, himself took a while to understand what was happening.

'Priests said to me, knowingly: "You're the kind of boy that the archbishop likes", but I didn't understand what they were insinuating. López Trujillo explained to the young seminarians that they had to be totally subject to them, and to the priests, that they had to be subject to the bishops. They had to be close-shaven, we had to dress perfectly to "please him". There were plenty of innuendos that I didn't understand at first. I was in charge of his travels and he often asked me to go with him on his outings; he used me in some way, to make contact with other seminarians. His targets were young men, white with blue eyes, particularly blonds; not the overly indigenous "Latinos", Mexican types, for example – and certainly not blacks! He hated blacks.'

The López Trujillo system was well established. Alvaro Léon goes on: 'Most of the time, the archbishop had "touts", 'M.', 'R.', 'L.' and even a bishop nicknamed "la gallina"; priests who found boys for him, cruised for them in the street and brought them back to his secret apartment. It wasn't ad hoc, it was properly organized.' (I am concealing the identity and stations of these 'tout' priests, which were confirmed to me by at least one other source. My Colombian researcher, Emmanuel Neisa, investigated each of them.)

As well as testifying to this unbridled life, these witnesses also speak of the violence of López Trujillo, who abused seminarians verbally and physically. 'He insulted them, humiliated them,' says Alvaro Léon.

All the evidence indicates that the cardinal did not live out his homosexuality quietly, like most of his colleagues in Rome. For him it was a perversion rooted in sin, which he exorcized through physical violence. Was it his vicious way of freeing himself from his 'knots of hysteria'? The archbishop had an assembly line of prostitutes: his propensity for buying bodies was notorious in Medellín.

'López Trujillo beat prostitutes; that was his relationship with sexuality. He paid them, but they had to accept his blows in return. It always happened at the end, not during the physical act. He finished his sexual relations by beating them, out of pure sadism,' Alvaro Léon goes on.

At this level of perversion, there is something strange about the violence of desire. These sexual excesses, this sadism towards prostitutes, are far from ordinary. López Trujillo had no concern for the bodies he rented out. He even had a reputation for paying his gigolos badly, negotiating hard, his eyes blank, to get the lowest price. If there is one pathetic character in this book, it's López Trujillo.

The deviations of this 'louche soul' did not stop, of course, at the borders of Colombia. The system was perpetuated in Rome, where he went cruising at Roma Termini, (according to a witness), and soon everywhere in the world, where he had a brilliant career as an anti-gay orator and millionaire john.

Travelling ceaselessly on behalf of the Curia, wearing his hat as anti-condom propagandist-in-chief, López Trujillo took advantage of these trips to find boys (according to the statements of at least two nuncios). The cardinal is said to have visited over a hundred countries, several favourites of his being in Asia, a continent that he visited frequently after discovering the sexual charms of Bangkok and Manila in particular. During those countless journeys to the other side of the world, where he was less well-known than in Colombia or Italy, the peripatetic cardinal regularly disappeared from seminaries and masses to devote himself to his trade: his 'taxi boys' and 'money boys'.

Rome, Open City. Why did you say nothing? Is it not revealing that, once again, this cosmetic life of a perverted narcissist passed itself off as holy? Like the monster Marcial Maciel, López Trujillo is said to have faked his life to an incredible degree – as everyone, or nearly everyone, in the Vatican knew.

Talking to lots of cardinals about the López Trujillo case, I never heard one of them give me an ideal portrait of him. No one said, startled by my information: 'I would have given him a clean slate in confession!' All those I met preferred instead to be silent, to frown, pull faces, raise their arms into the air or reply in coded words.

Today, tongues are looser, but the 'cover-up' in this case has worked well. Cardinal Lorenzo Baldisseri, for a long time a nuncio in Latin America before becoming one of Pope Francis's most trusted men, shared his information with me during two interviews in Rome: 'I knew López Trujillo when he was vicar general in Colombia. He was a very controversial figure. He had a split personality.'

Equally prudent, the theologian Juan Carlos Scannone, one of the men closest to Pope Francis, whom I interviewed in Argentina, wasn't surprised when I mentioned López Trujillo's double life. 'He was a plotter. Cardinal Bergoglio never liked him much. I don't even think he was ever in touch with him.' (According to my information, the future Pope Francis met López Trujillo at CELAM.)

Claudio Maria Celli, an archbishop who was one of Pope Francis's envoys to Latin America, after being one of Benedict XVI's directors of communication, knew López Trujillo well. In a carefully weighed phrase, he gives me his judgement of the man, during a discussion in Rome: 'López Trujillo was not a saint by any means.'

The nuncios knew too. Does their job not consist in making sure that a gay priest doesn't end up as a bishop, or that a bishop who likes rent boys isn't created a cardinal? And yet is it possible that those who have succeeded to the position of bishop in Bogotá since 1975 – notably Eduardo Martínez Somalo, Angelo Acerbi, Paolo Romeo, Beniamino Stella, Aldo Cavalli and Ettore Balestrero – each of them close to Angelo Sodano – could all have been unaware of this double life?

The Colombian cardinal Darío Castrillón Hoyos, prefect of the Congregation of the Clergy, shared too many secrets with López Trujillo, and probably his morals as well, so to speak! He was one of those who constantly helped him, even when he was perfectly well-informed of his moral debauchery. In the end, an Italian cardinal was equally crucial when it came to protecting López Trujillo in Rome: Sebastiano Baggio. This former national chaplain to the Italian scouts was a specialist in Latin America: he worked in nunciatures in El Salvador, Bolivia, Venezuela and Colombia. In 1964 he was appointed nuncio to Brazil, just after the coup d'état: he proved more than accommodating towards the army and the dictatorship (according to statements that I have collected in Brasilia, Rio and São Paulo; on the other hand, the Cardinal Archbishop of São Paulo, Odilo Scherer, whom I interviewed on this very subject, referred to him as a 'great nuncio who has done a lot for Brazil'). On his return to Rome, the aesthete and art collector Sebastiano Baggio was created cardinal by Paul VI and promoted to the head of the Congregation of Bishops and of the pontifical commission for Latin America – posts renewed by John Paul II, who made him one of his emissaries for the American sub-continent. The historian David Yallop describes Baggio as a 'reactionary' of the 'ultra-conservative right': this man, close to Opus Dei, supervised CELAM from Rome, and was particularly influential in the controversial conference held in Puebla in 1979, which he accompanied Pope John Paul II in attending. Witnesses describe him, along with López Trujillo, raging against the left wing of the Church, and being 'viscerally' and 'violently' anti-communist. Appointed 'camerlengo' by John Paul II, Baggio would go on wielding an extraordinary amount of power in the Vatican and protecting his 'great friend' López Trujillo, in spite of the countless rumours concerning his double life. He himself was said to have been very 'practising'. According to over ten statements collected in Brazil and Rome, Baggio was known for his special Latino friendships, and for being very hands-on with seminarians, who he liked to receive in his underpants or a jockstrap!

'López Trujillo's extravagances were much better-known than is generally accepted. Everyone knew about them – so why', Alvaro Léon wonders, 'was he appointed a bishop? Why was he put at the head of CELAM? Why was he created cardinal? Why was he appointed president of the Pontifical Council for the Family?'

A prelate in the Curia, who associated with López Trujillo, comments: 'López Trujillo was a friend of John Paul II; he was protected by Cardinal Sodano and by the pope's personal assistant, Stanisław Dziwisz. He was also very well-regarded by Cardinal Ratzinger, who appointed him to the presidency of the Pontifical Council for the Family for a new mandate, after his election in 2005. And yet everyone knew that he was homosexual. He lived with us, here, on the fourth floor of the Palazzo di San Calisto, in a 900-square-metre apartment, and he had several cars! Ferraris! He led a highly unusual life.' (López Trujillo's splendid apartment is occupied today by the African cardinal Peter Turkson, who lives in pleasant company on the same floor as the apartments of Cardinals Poupard, Etchegaray and Stafford, whom I also visited.)

Another Latin American specialist, the journalist José Manuel Vidal, who runs one of the main websites on Catholicism, in Spanish, recalls: 'López Trujillo used to come here, to Spain, very often. He was a friend of the Cardinal of Madrid, Rouco Varela. He would also come with one of his lovers; I particularly remember a handsome Pole, then a handsome Filipino. He was seen here as the "pope of Latin America", so they let him get on with it.'

Finally, I have a frank exchange with Federico Lombardi, who was spokesman to John Paul II and Benedict XVI, about the Cardinal of Medellín. Caught off guard, his response was instantaneous, almost a reflex: he raised his hands to the sky in a sign of consternation and terror.

And yet they celebrated the devil. When López Trujillo died unexpectedly in April 2008, of the consequences of a 'pulmonary infection' (according to the official communiqué), the Vatican doubled its praise

of him. Pope Benedict XVI, still seconded by Cardinal Sodano, celebrated a papal mass in honour of the memory of this caricature of a
cardinal.

On his death, however, rumours began to circulate. The first was that
he had died of the effects of AIDS; the second that he was buried in
Rome because he couldn't be buried in his homeland.

'When López Trujillo died, the decision was made to bury him here
in Rome because he couldn't be buried in Colombia,' Cardinal Lorenzo
Baldisseri tells me. 'He couldn't go back to his country, even in death!'

The reason? According to the statements I collected in Medellín, there
was a price on his head because of his proximity to the paramilitaries.
That was why it was not until 2017, or almost ten years after his death,
that Pope Francis ordered the repatriation of the body to Colombia.
Did the holy father prefer, as suggested to me by a priest involved in
this sudden repatriation, that if a scandal emerged about the cardinal's
double life, the remains of López Trujillo should not be located in Rome?
At any rate, I was able to see his tomb in a chapel in the west wing of the
transept of the huge cathedral in Medellín. The cardinal lies in this crypt,
beneath immaculately white stone, surrounded by permanently flickering candles. Behind the cross: the devil.

'As a general rule, the funeral chapel is closed by a grille. The archbishop is too afraid of vandalism. He is afraid that the tomb might be
vandalized by the family of one of the victims of López Trujillo or by a
prostitute with an axe to grind,' Alvaro Léon tells me.

And yet, strange as it may seem, in this very cathedral, situated
mysteriously in the heart of the gay area of Medellín, I see several men,
young and not so young, cruising one another. They stand there quite
openly, among the parishioners, clutching their Bibles among tourists
who have come to see the cathedral. I see them moving slowly on their
quest, between the pews of the church, or sitting against the east wall of
the cathedral – it's as if the gay street passed literally through the huge
church. And when I walk by them with Alvaro Léon and Emmanuel
Neisa, they give us sympathetic little winks – as if in final tribute to this
great transvestite in the old style, this great queen of the sacristy, this
diva of late Catholicism, this satanic doctor and antichrist: his Eminence
Alfonso López Trujillo.

To conclude, there is one last question that I'm not in a position to answer, and which seems to trouble a lot of people. Did López Trujillo, who thought that everything could be bought, even acts of violence, even sadomasochistic acts, buy penetration without condoms?

'Officially, the death of López Trujillo was connected with diabetes, but powerful and recurring rumours exist suggesting that he died of AIDS,' I am told by one of the best specialists in the Catholic Church in Latin America.

The former seminarians Alvaro Léon and Morgain had also heard the rumour, and consider it likely. Did the anti-condom cardinal die of complications related to AIDS, for which he had been treated for several years? I have often heard that rumour, but I can neither confirm nor deny it. What is certain is that his death in 2008 took place at a moment when the illness was properly treated in Rome at the Gemelli Polyclinic, the unofficial hospital of the Vatican – such treatment would surely have been made available to a cardinal who had considerable financial means, as he had. The date of his death contrasts with the state of the AIDS epidemic. Might the cardinal, perhaps, have denied his illness and refused to be treated, or, at least, only have accepted treatment when it was too late? It's possible, but unlikely. At this stage I incline towards the idea that it was a false rumour that emerged owing to the genuinely irregular life of the cardinal. Nothing I have learned allows me to say definitively that López Trujillo died of the effects of AIDS.

If he had died of that illness, however there would have been nothing exceptional about the death of Cardinal López Trujillo within Roman Catholicism. According to about ten testimonies that I collected in the Vatican and within the Italian Episcopal Conference, AIDS ravaged the holy see and the Italian episcopate during the 1980s and 1990s. A secret that was kept quiet for a long time.

A number of priests, monsignori and cardinals died of the effects of AIDS. Some patients 'admitted' their infection in confession (as one of the confessors of St Peter's confirmed to me without mentioning names). Other priests were diagnosed through their annual blood test, compulsory for Vatican staff (but this obligation does not apply to monsignori, nuncios, bishops or cardinals): this includes an AIDS test; according to my information, some priests were removed after being diagnosed positive.

The significant proportion of people with AIDS within the Catholic hierarchy is corroborated by a statistical study carried out in the United States, based on the death certificates of Catholic priests, which concluded that they had a mortality rate connected to the AIDS virus four times higher than that of the general population. Another study, based on the anonymized examination of 65 Roman seminarians in the early 1990s, showed that 38 per cent of them were seropositive. Blood transfusions, drug addiction or heterosexual relations could theoretically explain the high number of cases in these two studies – but in reality no one is falling for that.

At the Vatican, silence and denial prevail. Francesco Lepore, the former Curia priest, tells me of the death from the consequences of AIDS of a member of the Congregation for the Causes of Saints. This man, close to the Italian cardinal Giuseppe Siri, was said to have died of AIDS 'to the indifference of his superiors', and was 'buried with great discretion at dawn to avoid a scandal'. A Dutch-speaking cardinal, close to John Paul II, also died of the same virus. But, of course, never has the cause of death of a cardinal or bishop officially been given as AIDS.

'According to my internal discussions, many people in the Vatican are HIV positive or suffering from AIDS,' another monsignore confirms to me. 'At the same time, HIV-positive priests are not stupid: they don't seek treatment at the Vatican pharmacy! They go to hospitals in Rome.'

I have visited the Farmacia Vaticana several times – that unlikely institution in the east wing of the Vatican: a Dante-esque enterprise with ten tills – and, among the feeding bottles, dummies and luxury perfumes, it's hard to imagine a priest going there in search of his Truvada.

So, along with Daniele, my Roman researcher, several social workers, and members of Italian AIDS-prevention associations (particularly Progetto COROH and the old programme 'Io faccio activo'), I carried out a study in the Italian capital. We went several times to the San Gallicano Dermatological Institute (ISG), the Gemelli Polyclinic, which is connected to the Vatican, as well as the free and anonymous AIDS screening centre ASL Roma, which is on Via Catone, near St Peter's.

Professor Massimo Giuliani is one of the specialists in sexually trans-mitted diseases and AIDS at the San Gallicano Dermatological Institute. Daniele and I meet him for two interviews.

'Because we had been studying sexually transmitted diseases at San Gallicano for a long time, and particularly syphilis, we were immediately mobilized when the first cases of AIDS appeared in the 1980s. Here in Rome we became one of the first hospitals to treat patients of this kind. At the time, and until 1997, the Institute was in Trastevere, an area of Rome not very far from the Vatican. Now we're here, in this complex to the south of Rome.'

According to several sources, the San Gallicano Dermatological Institute was favoured in the 1970s by priests when they had contracted sexually transmitted diseases. For reasons of anonymity it was preferred to the Gemelli Polyclinic, which was linked to the Vatican.

When AIDS appeared, San Gallicano quite naturally became the hospital for priests, monsignori and bishops infected with the AIDS virus.

'We saw a lot of HIV-positive priests and seminarians coming here,' Professor Massimo Giuliani tells me. 'We think there is a very large AIDS problem in the Church. Here, we don't judge. The only important thing is that they come to a hospital for examination and have themselves treated. But we fear that the situation in the Church is more serious than we have seen already, because of denial.'

The question of denial among priests is well-documented: more often than the average, they refuse to be screened because they don't feel concerned; and even when they have unprotected sexual relations with men, they refuse to have themselves tested for fear of a lack of confidentiality.

'We think,' Professor Massimo Giuliani tells me, 'that the risk of being infected with AIDS when one belongs to the male Catholic community is high at present, because of denial and because of the low rate of condom use. In our terminology, priests are one of the social categories at highest risk and the most difficult to reach in terms of AIDS prevention. We have made attempts at dialogue and education, particularly in the seminaries, on the transmission and treatment of STDs and AIDS. But it's still very difficult. To talk about the risk of AIDS would mean acknowledging that priests have homosexual practices. And obviously the Church refuses to engage in that debate.'

My conversations with the male prostitutes of Roma Termini (and with the high-class escort Francesco Mangiacapra in Naples) confirm the fact that priests are among the least prudent clients where their sexual acts are concerned.

'As a rule, priests are not afraid of STDs. They feel untouchable. They are so sure of their position, of their power, that they don't take these risks into account, unlike other clients. They have no sense of reality. They live in a world without AIDS,' Francesco Mangiacapra explains.

Alberto Borghetti is a medic in the infectious diseases department of the Gemelli Polyclinic in Rome. This junior doctor and researcher receives me and Daniele at the request of the head of the service, the epidemiologist Simona Di Giambenedetto, who wanted to help us in our inquiry.

The Gemelli Polyclinic is the most Catholic of the Catholic hospitals in the world. In medical terms, it is the holy of holies! Cardinals, bishops, Vatican staff and many Roman priests go there for treatment, and they also have a priority route of access. And, of course, it is the hospital of popes. John Paul II was the most famous patient at the Gemelli, and television cameras cynically scrutinized the developments of his illness with a sepulchral buzz. Light-heartedly, the pope is said to have given a name to the Gemelli Clinic, where he was hospitalized so often: 'Vatican III'.

Visiting the hospital and its various departments, meeting various other doctors and medics, I discover a modern establishment a long way away from the image reported by gossip in Rome. Since it is a hospital attached to the Vatican, a dim view is taken of people with STDS or AIDS, I have been told.

With his professionalism and detailed knowledge of the AIDS epidemic, the junior doctor Alberto Borghetti rebuts these suspicions.

'We are one of the five most state-of-the-art Roman hospitals where AIDS is concerned. We treat all patients, and here in the scientific wing attached to the Catholic University of the Sacred Heart in Milan, is one of the main Italian centres of research into the illness. The undesirable and collateral effects of different anti-retroviral therapies are studied here; we carry out research into medical interactions and the effects of vaccinations on the HIV-positive population.'

In the infectious illnesses department that I visit, I can tell from posters and panels that patients with STDs are treated here. Borghetti confirms as much: 'We treat all STDs here, whether they are due to bacteria, like gonococci, syphilis and chlamydia, or viruses like herpes, the papilloma virus and of course hepatitis.'

According to another professor of medicine specializing in the treatment of AIDS whom I spoke to in Rome, the Gemelli Polyclinic has experienced tensions surrounding STDs and patient anonymity.

Alberto Borghetti disputes this information. 'Generally speaking, the results of examinations relating to the AIDS virus are only known to the doctor responsible for the treatment, and cannot be accessed by other health professionals at the polyclinic. At Gemelli, patients can also request anonymization of their files, which further reinforces the anonymity of HIV-positive individuals.'

According to a priest who knows the Gemelli well, this anonymization is not enough to win the trust of infected ecclesiastical patients. 'They do everything they can to guarantee anonymity, but given the bishops and priests who are treated there, it's easy to bump into people you know. The "infectious diseases department" is a clear enough title!'

A dermatologist I speak to in Rome tells me: 'Some priests tell us that they were infected by coming into contact with a syringe or an old blood transfusion: we pretend to believe them.'

Alberto Borghetti confirms that fears and denial can exist, particularly for priests: 'It's true that we sometimes receive seminarians or priests here who arrive at a very advanced stage of AIDS. Along with immigrants and homosexuals, they are probably among those who don't want to take a screening test: they are afraid, or else they are in denial. That's really a shame, because if they come into the treatment system with a late diagnosis, sometimes with aggressive illnesses, and are treated belatedly, they risk not recovering an efficient immune system.'

John Paul II was pope from 1978 until 2005. AIDS, which appeared in 1981, at the start of his pontificate, was responsible during the years that followed for over 35 million deaths. Around the world, 37 million people are still living, even today, with HIV.

The condom, which John Paul II's Vatican energetically rejected, using all his resources and the power of his diplomatic network to oppose it, remains the most efficient way of combatting the epidemic, even within an asymptomatic married couple. Every year, thanks to condoms and anti-retroviral treatments, tens of millions of lives are saved.

Since the publication of the encyclical *Humanae vitae*, the Church has condemned all prophylactic or chemical means, such as the pill or condom, that prevent the transmission of life. But, as the French Vaticanologist Henri Tincq stresses, 'must the means of preventing the transmission of death be confused with the one that prevents the transmission of life?'

Apart from John Paul II, who are the main people who defined and executed this global policy of the absolute rejection of condoms during the global pandemic of AIDS? They are a group of 12 loyal, devoted, orthodox men whose vow of chastity forbids them to have sexual relations. According to the results of my investigation, and on the basis of the hundreds of interviews conducted for this book, I can state that the great majority of these prelates are homophiles or practising homosexuals. (I have met eight out of the twelve.) What do all these men know about condoms and heterosexuality, to have been appointed judge and jury?

These 12 men, all created cardinals, were the private secretary Stanisław Dziwisz; the Secretaries of State Agostino Casaroli and Angelo Sodano; the future pope Joseph Ratzinger; the directors of the Secretariat of State: Giovanni Battista Re, Achille Silvestrini, Leonardo Sandri, Jean-Louis Tauran, Dominique Mamberti and the nuncios Renato Raffaele Martino and Roger Etchegaray. Not forgetting the last cardinal who was very influential at the time: His Eminence Alfonso López Trujillo.

14

The pope's diplomats

'Ah, you're a journalist?' Mgr Battista Ricca looks at me with unease and a hint of envy. 'I have problems with journalists,' he adds, staring me in the eye.

'He's a French journalist,' insists Archbishop François Bacqué, who has just introduced us.

'Ah,' Ricca sighs, with obvious relief. 'My problem,' he continues, 'is with Italian journalists. They have nothing in their heads. Nothing! They have zero intelligence. But if you're French, there might be a chance that you're different! It bodes well!'

It was only in the middle of my investigation, when I had already started writing this book, that I was invited to stay at the Domus Internationalis Paulus VI. Prior to that, I had been living in Rome in apartments rented on Airbnb, most of them around Roma Termini.

Archbishop François Bacqué, a retired French apostolic nuncio, suggested one day that he should book me a room at the Domus Internationalis Paulus VI, and that was how things started. His recommendation was enough for me to end up living in the holy of holies of Vatican diplomacy.

The Domus is at 70 Via della Scrofa in Rome. This official residence of the holy see is an 'extraterritorial' place, outside of Italy: the police are not permitted to enter it, and if a theft, a rape or some other crime is committed there, it is the tiny Vatican police force, and the highly incompetent legal system of the holy see, that would be in charge.

Also known as Casa del Clero (house of the clergy), the diplomatic residence is ideally located between the Piazza Navona and the Pantheon:

one of the most beautiful places in Rome; a pagan temple, a secular if not a republican one, an extraordinary symbol of 'civil' religion dedicated to all faiths and all the gods, and one that was reimagined by the LGBT emperor Hadrian, before being made the object of aggressive 'cultural appropriation' by Italian Catholicism.

Domus Internationalis Paulus VI is a place of great importance in the holy see: to stay at the heart of the Vatican machinery was therefore a great opportunity for me. Here I'm treated as a friend, no longer as someone from outside. First of all, it's a hotel for Vatican diplomats – the famous apostolic nuncios – when they stay in Rome. Sometimes foreign cardinals and bishops reside there too, rather than at Santa Marta. Cardinal Jorge Bergoglio stayed there when he passed through Rome: the pictures showing him in his white cassock, paying his own hotel bills, while travelling around the world.

Apart from cardinals and passing diplomats, the Casa del Clero is a permanent dwelling for several retired nuncios, unemployed bishops, or monsignori holding prestigious positions in the holy see. Many of them are on full board or half board. Over breakfast in the drawing rooms on the first floor or lunches taken communally in the huge restaurant, not to mention exchanges by coffee machines and long evenings in front of the television, I will get to know these nuncios, these apostolic diplomats, these assistants of the Secretariat of State or this secretary of the Congregation of Bishops. The waiters in the Casa del Clero – one of whom is a playboy worthy of a cover of *The Advocate* – have to stand their ground: the meaningful looks of nuncios and monsignori in the prime of life would be enough to make anyone panic!

The bedrooms in the Casa del Claro are on the spartan side: a weary lightbulb casts a harsh light on a single bed, generally flanked by a crucifix. The narrow beds of the priests, which I have seen so often in the Vatican apartments, display their conservatism by virtue of their size. In the drawer of the ancient and rickety bedside table lies a Bible (which I immediately replace with *A Season in Hell*). In the bathroom, a neon light dating back to the days of Pius XI gives off the light of a microwave oven. The soap is lent by the gram (and you have to give it back). Who said that Catholicism had a horror of life?

During one of my stays there, my neighbour on the fourth floor was luckier. It's an advantage to live at the Casa all year round. By dint of bumping into this eminent assistant of the Secretariat of State, one day, when he was in his boxer shorts (preparing to go to a Cher concert?), I had the chance to peer into his large corner apartment. Imagine my surprise at seeing a fabulous bright-red double bed that wouldn't have been out of place in a Fellini film. A place for a secret rendezvous? Not far from there was another famous bedroom, room 424, which was once that of Angelo Roncalli, the future Pope John XXIII.

Breakfast is meagre too. I go along to please the priests who invite me so insistently. Everything is hostile: the bread that is crucified, not toasted; the plain yoghurts bought by the dozen; the very un-Italian filter coffee on refill; the un-Catholic cornflakes. The only exception are the kiwi fruits, available in a large quantity every morning: but why kiwis? And do you peel them like a peach or cut them in two like an avocado? The question is the cause of much debate at the Casa, François Bacqué tells me. I eat four of them. Breakfasts at the Casa del Clero are like breakfasts in a retirement home where the residents are politely told to hurry up and die to make room for slightly less senile prelates – and there is no shortage in the enormous hospice that is the Vatican.

In the reading rooms of the Domus Internationalis Paulus VI, on the first floor, I made the acquaintance of Laurent Monsengwo Pasinya, an eminent Congolese cardinal from Kinshasa, a member of Francis's council of cardinals, who tells me that he likes coming to the Casa del Clero 'because one has greater freedom' than in the Vatican, before meeting with the pope.

The director of the Casa and all the Vatican residences, Mgr Battista Ricca, also lives there: his hermetic and, it seems to me, immense apartment on the left-hand side of the mezzanine is number 100. Ricca regularly lunches at the 'Casa', humbly, with two of his close friends at a table slightly away from the rest, a kind of family. And at one of our meetings, one evening, in the drawing rooms on the first floor, in front of the television, I will give Ricca the famous 'white book', for which he thanks me from the bottom of his heart.

Here you also bump into Fabián Pedacchio, private secretary to Pope Francis, who has lived in the Domus for a long time, and who is said to keep a room where he is able to work calmly with the Brazilian bishop Ilson de Jesus Montanari, secretary to the Congregation for Bishops, or with Mgr Fabio Fabene, one of the architects of the synod. Mgr Mauro Sobrino, prelate of his holiness, also lives there, and we have swapped a number of secrets. A mysterious couple of boys, dinkies and bio-queens, who listen to *Born this Way* by Lady Gaga on a loop, live here too, and I have had some lovely night-time conversations with them. A Basque priest also enjoys some delightful associations within this 'magic circle', to use his phrase.

Archbishop François Bacqué has lived here as well, since completing his diplomatic career: this fallen aristocrat is still waiting to be created cardinal. He is supposed to have asked Cardinal Jean-Louis Tauran, another Frenchman, likewise hailing from Bordeaux and very much a man of the people: 'How come you're a cardinal when you aren't an aristocrat? And why am I not, when I am from the nobility?' (This was reported to me by an assistant of Tauran's.)

Some specimens of this kind can be found in groups at the Casa del Clero, a place where ambitious young men have high hopes, and where retired clerics who have fallen from grace nurse their bruised egos. With these last offshoots of declining Catholicism, the 'Casa' mysteriously brings together this rising spiritual aristocracy with the same aristocracy in decline.

Three chapels, on the second and third floors of the Casa del Clero, mean that one can attend mass at a time of one's choice; sometimes, holy offices have been celebrated by gay groups (as I am told by a priest, in a written statement). A laundry service for the rooms means that the nuncios don't have to do their own washing. Everything is cheap, but paid for in cash. When I come to pay my bill, the Domus Internationalis Paulus VI card machine is 'unusually' out of order. And exactly the same thing will happen during each of my stays; in the end a resident will point out to me that this machine 'is out of order all the time and has been for years' (and the same unfortunate technical malfunction would occur several times while I was staying at the Domus Romana Sacerdotalis) – perhaps a way of ensuring a circulation of cash?

At the Casa del Clero people tend not to stay up late, since they get up early – but there are exceptions. On the day when I tried to sleep in,

I understood from the agitation and impatience of the cleaning women that I was close to committing a sin. Furthermore, the doors of the Casa del Clero are closed at midnight, and all the night-owl nuncios and other jet-lagged diplomats meet up to chat in the reading room until the small hours. It's the paradoxical advantage of old-fashioned curfews.

I'm fascinated by the double coach gate. There's something evocative of Gide about it; that author wrote in *If It Die* that this kind of door, the sign of an elevated social status, was a necessity for any good middle-class family. In former times, such a portal allowed you to bring a coach and horses to a door at ground level, and therefore to 'keep an equipage'. And today, at the Casa del Clero, what an equipage that would be!

At no. 19 Via di Sant'Agostino, the coach gate to the back of Domus Internationalis Paulus VI is a discreet and anonymous side door. Tan-coloured, it consists of two panels, but no steps and no threshold. In the middle: a wicket, a little panel cut from the larger panel to allow pedestrians to enter discreetly at night. The pavement is sloped in a bow, and the frame is carved from white ashlar. On the coach gate: visible nails and a plain iron handle, worn down now by so many daily entrances and so many nocturnal visitors. Oh ancient portal, such tales you could tell!

I have spent a lot of time studying this double door, spotting comings and goings, taking photographs of the beautiful porch. The door has depth. There is a kind of voyeurism in looking at closed doors, genuine urban portals, and that attraction probably explains why the art of photographing doors has become a very popular phenomenon on Instagram, where such portraits can be found under the hashtag #doortraits.

After a corridor, a grille, then an internal courtyard – another vanishing line. Via an internal staircase, which I have often taken, one reaches lift C, and from there the bedrooms of the residence, without having to pass by the concierge's lodge or reception. And if one has good keys, one can go in and out via the grille and then the coach gate, thus escaping the midnight curfew. What a blessing! It's enough to make one yearn for the days of the coach and four!

I suspect the double door of keeping a number of Vatican secrets. Will it tell them one day? Very conveniently, there is no porter on that side of the building. Another blessing! One Sunday in August 2018, I

saw a monsignore of the Secretariat of State waiting there for his handsome escort in red shorts and a blue top, hugging him sweetly in the
street and in a café, before bringing him back to the Casa! I imagine that
there are some nights when a monk, called by some pressing need, has
to take part in the office of matins at the Church of Sant'Agostino, just
opposite the coach gate, or that some travelling nuncio, feeling a sudden
urge to see Caravaggio's splendid *Madonna of the Pilgrims*, improvises a
nocturnal excursion. The Arcadia, which lives up to its name, also faces
the coach gate, as does the Biblioteca Angelica, one of the most beautiful
libraries in Rome, where a cleric might suddenly need to consult some
incunabula or the illuminated pages of the famous *Codex Angelicus*.
And then, adjacent to the Casa del Clero, to the north-west, there is the
Università della Santa Croce, better known as the university of Opus
Dei; once upon a time one could go there directly from the clergy's residence via an overhead passage, now condemned. A shame: today you
have to leave by the coach gate at night if you want to go there for a Latin
class or an ultramontane meeting with a young and hard-line seminarian of Opus Dei.

The anomaly of the Casa del Clero is to the west of the huge building,
on Piazza delle Cinque Lune: McDonald's. The Vatican, as we know, is too
poor to maintain its properties; it has had to make sacrifices and agree
to accept in return this symbol of American junk food. And according
to my information, Mgr Ricca signed the new lease agreement without
having a knife to his throat.

There have been great controversies about a McDonald's taking up
residence near the Vatican in a building which didn't belong to the holy
see, but no one batted an eyelid at this fast-food restaurant being permitted by the Vatican inside one of its own Roman residences.

'They moved a little altar dedicated to the holy virgin, which was
by the entrance used today by McDonald's, and simply brought it close to
the portal of the Casa del Clero on Via della Scrofa,' one of the tenants
of the residence tells me.

In fact I can see a kind of blue, red and yellow altar-table, to which a
poor virgin has been nailed against her will, casually shifted under the
porch of the official entrance. Did McDonald's exert pressure to ensure
that the holy virgin was moved away from its McNuggets?

The contrast is remarkable. The strait gate of constraint, with curfew and Ave Maria, at the front; a marvellous double-panelled coach gate with lots of keys to the rear: this is the raw reality of Catholicism. The pope knows all the nooks and crannies of the Casa del Clero: he has lived there for too long not to know.

On fine days, this haven of mystery moves outside; and it becomes even more intriguing. Then, the Domus Internationalis Paulus VI becomes a holiday resort. You can see young secretaries of nunciatures, having taken off their dog-collars, talking by the grille, before curfew, in tight beige t-shirts and red shorts, as well as nuncios from developing countries leaving that 'YMCA' just before midnight, for DYMK ('Does Your Mother Know') parties. They will come back in the early hours having lost their voices signing 'I will survive' or 'I am what I am', dancing with the index fingers of their left hands pointing towards the sky like St John the Baptist, in the Gay Village Fantasia festival in the EUR district of Rome, where I bumped into them.

'In my day, a priest would never have appeared in red shorts like that,' a horrified Archbishop François Bacqué tells me as we walk by those colourful specimens, who look as if they've organized some sort of Happy Hour outside the Casa del Clero.

'To travel alone is to travel with the devil!' wrote the great Catholic (and homosexual) writer Julien Green. That might be one of the rules of life of the apostolic nuncios, whose secrets I have gradually discovered.

At the start of my investigation, an ambassador to the holy see warned me: 'At the Vatican, as you will see, there are lots of gays: 50 per cent, 60 per cent, 70 per cent? No one knows. But you will see that among the nuncios the rate reaches dizzying heights! In the already gay-majority universe of the Vatican, they are the gayest of all!'

And, seeing my surprise at this revelation, the diplomat laughed in my face: 'You know, the expression "homosexual nuncio" is a kind of tautology!'

To understand this paradox, let's think of the opportunities that arise from being alone on the other side of the world. Opportunities are so lovely when one is far from home: so plentiful in Morocco and Tunisia; as easy in Bangkok as they are in Taipei. Asia and the Middle

East are missionary lands and, for nuncios of a nomadic bent, they are truly promised lands. In all these countries, I have seen them in action, surrounded by their favourites, mannered or over-excited, discovering real life far from the Vatican and ceaselessly repeating: Oh, that workman! Oh, that ferryman! Oh, that camel-driver! Oh, that rickshaw-walla!

'Fired by a masculine rage for travel', in the eloquent phrase of the poet Paul Verlaine, nuncios also draw upon their natural reserves: seminarians, first-year students, young monks, who are even more accessible in the Third World than in Rome.

'When I travel abroad, they lend me Legionnaires of Christ,' another archbishop tells me. (He isn't insinuating anything with the phrase, but it gives an idea of the status in which he holds the legionnaires when he goes to a 'former colony'.)

'The words "bar" and "holiday camp" sound good to the ears of European travellers. They set lots of priests on fire!' I was told with unusual frankness by a priest with the Foreign Missions, himself a Frenchman whom I interviewed several times in Paris. (During this investigation I met many missionary priests on the ground in Asia, in Africa, in the Maghreb and in Latin America; for this part of the discussion I am using the statements of about twenty nuncios and diplomats who have told me about the habits of their friends and co-religionists.)

In fact, this is another open secret. Priests leave traces everywhere. The managers of gay bars whom I interviewed in Taiwan, Hanoi or Hue are full of praise for this faithful and serious clientele. The waiters in the bars in the Shinjuku Ni-chōme area of Tokyo pointed out their regulars to me. Specialist gay journalists in Bangkok investigated several incidents involving 'morals' or visa questions when a prelate wanted to take an undocumented young Asian man back to Italy. Everywhere, the presence of European priests, monks and clerics is attested. The current president of the Republic of the Philippines, Rodrigo Duterte, has recognized the existence of this distinctive tourism and called for the homosexuality of ecclesiastics to be acknowledged because, as he puts it, 'approximately 90% of the clergy is gay'.

Apart from the nuncios, for whom travel is the very basis of their trade, Curia priests also use their holidays to engage in innovative sexual explorations far from the Vatican. But, of course, these monsignori rarely flaunt their professional status when they are out and about in Manila or Jakarta. They don't dress as clergymen.

'Because they have embraced principles that are stronger than their character, and because they have sublimated their desires for so long, they explode abroad,' the priest from Foreign Missions tells me.

Vietnam is particularly prized these days. The communist regime and press censorship protect ecclesiastic escapades in case of scandal, whereas in Thailand everything ends up in the press.

'Sexual tourism is migrating,' Mr Dong, the manager of two gay bars in Hue, tells me. 'It is moving from countries in the spotlight, like Thailand or Manila, towards countries with less media coverage, like Indonesia, Malaysia, Cambodia, Burma or Vietnam.' (I'm amused by the name of one of the establishments owned by Mr Dong, which I visit in Hue: it's called *Ruby*, like Berlusconi's former escort girl at his bunga bunga parties.)

Asia isn't the only destination for these priests; but it is one of the most prized for everyone excluded from standard sexuality: the anonymity and discretion that it offers are unequalled. Africa, South America (for example, the Dominican Republic, where an important network of gay priests has been described in a Polish book) and Eastern Europe also have their devotees, not to mention the United States, the template for all one-man Stonewalls. You can see them tanning themselves on the beaches of Provincetown, renting a bungalow in the 'Pines' or an Airbnb in the gaybourhoods of Hell's Kitchen, Boystown or Fort Lauderdale. One French curé tells me that after methodically visiting these bohemian and post-gay American districts, he regretted their 'excessively mixed quality' and their lack of 'gayitude'.

He's right: today the percentage of homosexuals is probably higher in the closeted Vatican than in the post-gay Castro.

Some prefer in the end to stay in Europe to do the circuit of the gay clubs in Berlin, to participate in the S&M nights at The Church in Amsterdam or not to miss the Closing Party in Ibiza, then celebrate their birthday, which becomes a 'birthweek' in Barcelona. (Here I am using actual examples concerning nuncios or priests whose sexual tourism was described to me on the ground.)

So a new rule of *The Closet* emerges, the eleventh: *Most nuncios are homosexual, but their diplomacy is essentially homophobic. They are*

*denouncing what they are themselves. As for cardinals, bishops and priests,
the more they travel, the more suspect they are!*

The nuncio La Païva, whom I have already mentioned, is no exception
to this rule. He too is a handsome specimen. And of such a species!
An archbishop, he is eternally on display. And he evangelizes. He is one
of those people who, in the compartment of an almost deserted train,
or the rows of seats of an empty bus, would go and sit down next to a
handsome young man travelling on his own, to try to bring him over to
the faith. He is also happy to trot along the street, as I have seen him do,
even though he resembles the famous nuncio by the sculptor Fernando
Botero – fat, round and very red – if it enables him to engage in conversation with a seminarian for whom he has suddenly developed a craving.

At the same time, La Païva is a winning character, in spite of his reactionary temperament. When we go out to a restaurant in Rome, he wants
me to wear a shirt and jacket, even though it's 30 degrees outside. One
evening, he even makes a scene: he doesn't like my grunge look at all,
and I need to shave! La Païva tells me off. 'I don't understand why young
people grow their beards these days.' (I'm happy for La Païva to refer to
me as if I'm a young man.)

'I'm not growing a beard, Your Excellency. And I haven't shaved badly
either. It's what you call a three-day beard.'

'Is it just laziness? Is that it?'

'I just think it's nicer. I shave every three or four days.'

'I prefer you clean-shaven, you know.'

'The Lord had a beard, didn't he?'

I'm thinking of Rembrandt's portrait of Christ (*Christuskopf*, a little
painting that I saw at the Gemäldegalerie in Berlin), perhaps the love-
liest one: his face is fine and fragile; he has long, untidy hair and a long
straggly beard. He is, in fact, a grunge Christ, and could almost have
torn jeans! Rembrandt painted him from an anonymous living model
– an idea that was new in the religious painting of the time – probably
a young man from Amsterdam's Jewish community. Hence his humanity and his simplicity. Christ's vulnerability touches me, as it touched
François Mauriac, who loved this portrait so much that, like the rest of
us, he fell in love with it.

The nuncios, diplomats and bishops with whom I rubbed shoulders at Domus Internationalis Paulus VI are the pope's soldiers around the world. Since the election of John Paul II their international engagement has been innovative, in parallel with the policy of the major countries, and particularly favourable to human rights, the abolition of the death penalty, nuclear disarmament and peace processes. More recently, Francis has made his priority the defence of the environment, attempts to bring the United States and Cuba closer together, and the pacification of FARC (the Revolutionary Armed Forces of Colombia).

'It's a diplomacy of patience. The Vatican never lets go, even when other powers do. And when everyone leaves a country, because of war for example, the nuncios stay on beneath the bombs. We've seen that in Iraq, and more recently in Syria,' stresses Pierre Morel, former French ambassador to the holy see.

Morel explains to me in detail, in the course of several interviews in Paris, the workings of this Vatican diplomacy, with the respective roles of the nuncios, the Secretariat of State, the Congregation of the Oriental Churches, the role of the 'red' pope (the cardinal in charge of the 'evangelization of the peoples', meaning the Third World), the 'black' pope (the superior general of the Jesuits), and, last of all, the 'parallel diplomacies'. The Secretariat of State coordinates the overall network and sets the general direction.

This efficient and misunderstood diplomatic apparatus has also been put at the service, under John Paul II and Benedict XVI, of an ultra-conservative and homophobic crusade. It is possible to tell this story through the careers of two emblematic nuncios who were both Vatican permanent observers at the United Nations: Archbishop Renato Martino, now a cardinal, and the nuncio Silvano Tomasi.

When I reach the home of Renato Raffaele Martino on Via Pfeiffer in Rome, a short distance from the Vatican, a Filipino – perhaps in his twenties, perhaps thirty, the quintessence of Asian beauty – opens the door to me with a broad smile. He leads me in silence to the drawing room of the cardinal, where the prelate joins me.

All of a sudden I'm not facing one Renato Martino, but about ten of them. I'm literally surrounded by portraits of the cardinal, in real size, painted in all kinds of styles, sometimes occupying entire panels, which the nuncio has arranged on every wall and in every corner of his apartment.

I can understand that, at the age of 86, the cardinal is proud of his career since his episcopal ordination by the great Agostino Casaroli, and that he should hold himself in a certain esteem. After all, he fought like the very devil to impede the battle against AIDS on five continents, with a certain degree of success, and not everybody can say that. But I can't help feeling that having so many portraits of oneself all at once, so prominent, so eye-catching, almost like so many statues, borders on the ridiculous.

The rest of our meeting is in the same vein. The old man doesn't really answer my questions, even though like most nuncios he expresses himself in impeccable French, but he takes me on a tour of the house. Martino says he has visited 195 countries during his long career as a nuncio: he has brought back countless objects from those travels, which he now shows me in his dining room, his private chapel, his interminable corridor, his ten or so rooms, and even a panoramic terrace with a wonderful view over Catholic Rome. His apartment is at least fifteen times as big as Pope Francis's.

It is a museum, a real cabinet of curiosities – a cabinet of trinkets, perhaps. The cardinal shows me, one after another, his 38 decorations, the 200 medals engraved with his name, the 14 doctorates *honoris causa* and 16 portraits of himself. I also see handkerchiefs bearing coats of arms, knick-knacks, chipped miniature elephants, a fine colonialist panama hat and, on the walls, certificates made out to 'his most reverend eminence', in the image of I don't know what weird order of chivalry (the order of St January, perhaps). And while we are wandering around these relics and jujus, I notice that the Filipino is watching us from a distance, with an expression of disappointment and restrained apathy; he must have seen processions like this so many times.

In the grand caravanserai of the apartment, a shambles, I now discover photographs of the cardinal on the back of an elephant with a handsome young man; here he is posing insouciantly with a Thai companion, there with young Laotians, Malaysians, Filipinos, Singaporeans or Thais – all fine representations of countries where he has been vice-nuncio, pro-nuncio or nuncio. Clearly Martino likes Asia. And his passion for elephants is openly on display, in every corner of his apartment.

According to two diplomatic sources, the 'creation' of Martino as a cardinal by John Paul II was long and scattered with pitfalls. Did he have enemies? A lack of 'straightness'? Was his spending too extravagant? Were there too many rumours about his conduct? Whatever the case, he was kept waiting during several consistories. Each time that the smoke didn't turn white, Martino had a burn-out. All the more so because he had bought at great expense the biretta, the calotte, the red mozzettas and the sapphire ring, even before he was made cardinal. This human comedy went on for several years, and the moiré and damask silk scarf run through with gold thread was starting to look sadly worn when the nuncio, at the age of nearly 71, was finally created cardinal. (In his '*Testimonianza*', Mgr Viganò 'outs' Martino, suspecting of him of belonging to a 'homosexual current in favour of subverting Catholic doctrine on homosexuality' in the Curia, which his friends swiftly denied in a communiqué.)

In his chapel, this time, in the middle of the portrait medallions of Martino and the amulets, carefully shielded from the sun by curtains with embroidered fringes, I discover the holy trinity of LGBT artists: Leonardo da Vinci, Michelangelo and Caravaggio. Each of these notorious homosexuals is represented by a copy of one of his works. We spend a few moments talking about his Filipino houseboy, and Martino, who doesn't seem to grasp what I'm getting at, drifts off in his imagination as he gives me an idyllic portrait of the boy, specifying that in fact he has 'two Filipinos' at his service, greatly preferring them to the more traditional nun. We understand.

The Old Testament, as everybody knows, is populated by characters more colourful, more adventurous and also more monstrous than the New. Cardinal Renato Martino is, in his way, a figure from the old scriptures. Even today he is honorary president of the Dignitatis Humanae Institute, one of the far-right Catholic associations and an ultra-conservative political lobby run by the Englishman Benjamin Harnwell. If there is a structurally homophobic organization in this book, this is it – and Renato Martino embodies its values.

In the 195 countries that he has visited, in the embassies where he has been nuncio, and as 'permanent observer' for the holy see in the United Nations for 16 years, from 1986 until 2002, Renato Martino was a great defender of human rights, a militant anti-abortionist and a violent opponent of gay rights and the wearing of condoms.

At the UN, Renato Martino was John Paul II's chief spokesman, so he had to apply the pope's line. His margin of manoeuvre was admittedly limited, as it is for all diplomats. But according to over twenty statements collected in New York, Washington and Geneva, including from three former ambassadors to the UN, Martino addressed his mission with such an anti-gay bias, such personal animosity against homosexuals, that his hatred became suspect.

'Mr Martino was not a normal diplomat,' an ambassador who was his counterpart in New York tells me. 'I've never seen anyone so binary. As a permanent observer of the holy see at the UN, he had two faces, and his political line clearly employed double standards. He had a humanist approach to human rights, which was typical of the holy see, and was always very moderate. He was a great defender of justice, of peace and, I particularly remember, the rights of Palestinians. And then, all of a sudden, when the question of the battle against AIDS, abortion or the depenalization of homosexuality arose, he became Manichean, obsessive and vindictive, as if it touched him personally. On human rights, he expressed himself a little like Switzerland or Canada; and all of a sudden, on the gay question or AIDS, he was talking like Uganda or Saudi Arabia! And what's more, the Vatican then went on to forge an unnatural alliance, in our view, with Syria and Saudi Arabia on the question of the rights of homosexuals. Martino was Dr Jekyll and Mr Hyde!'

A second diplomat at the Vatican, Silvano Tomasi, would play a similar role in Switzerland. While the prestigious permanent representation of the United Nations and its Security Council was in New York, most of the United Nations agencies intervening on the question of human rights and the fight against AIDS are in Geneva: the Human Rights Commission, the World Health Organization, UNAIDS, the Global Fund to Fight AIDS and, of course, the United Nations Human Rights Council. The Vatican is represented in all of these agencies by only one 'permanent observer' without voting rights.

When I meet Silvano Tomasi at the Vatican, where he receives me on the eve of an international meeting held in the Paul VI Audience Hall, the prelate apologizes for not having very much time to devote to me. In the end, we will speak for over an hour, and he will miss the rest of the conference – which he was supposed to be taking part in – to stay with me.

'Recently Pope Francis told us, speaking of the apostolic nuncios, that our lives should be the lives of "gypsies", Tomasi tells me, in English.

So it was as an entertainer, a nomad and perhaps a bohemian that Tomasi travelled the world, as all diplomats do. He was Vatican ambassador in Ethiopia, Eritrea and Djibouti, before being in charge of the Pontifical Council for the Pastoral Care of Migrants and Itinerant People.

'Refugees, migrants, are Pope Francis's priority. He is interested in the peripheries, in the margins of society, in displaced people. He wants to be a voice for those who have no voice,' Tomasi tells me.

Strangely, the nuncio has triple nationality: he is Italian, born north of Venice in 1940; a citizen of the Vatican State in his capacity as nuncio; and American.

'I reached New York at the age of 18. I was a Catholic student in the United States, I did my thesis at the New School in New York, and for a long time I was a priest in Greenwich Village.'

The young Silvano Tomasi was ordained as a priest in the mission of Saint Charles Borromeo, which was set up at the end of the nineteenth century, whose chief goal was to evangelize the New World. In the 1960s, he exercised his ministry in a parish dedicated to Italian immigrants living in New York: Our Lady of Pompeii, a church in the Village, at Bleecker Street and Sixth Avenue.

It's an area that I know well, having lived in Manhattan for several years. You're a five-minute walk away from the Stonewall Inn. It was there, in June 1969, when the young Silvano Tomasi moved to the area, that the American homosexual movement was born during a night of rioting. Every year, all around the world, the event is commemorated under the name of Gay Pride. During the 1970s, Greenwich Village would become the symbolic place of homosexual liberation, and it was here that the young prelate exercised his evangelical mission, among the hippies, transvestites and gay activists who took the district by storm.

During our interview we talk about the 'Village' and its LGBT fauna. Cute as a button, Silvano Tomasi expresses himself with great self-control, topped up by self-restraint. He couldn't help pulling faces as he did so.

'You see: we're having a friendly conversation – you will make me say things, and then you'll only keep in the things I've said against the Church, like all journalists,' Tomasi says to me with a laugh, but he goes on talking quite happily. (The interview was organized officially via the Vatican press service, and the prelate knew that he was being recorded, because I was using a very visible Nagra.)

After travelling a lot, Tomasi finished his career by becoming a 'permanent observer' for the holy see at the UN in Geneva. It was there, between 2003 and 2016, that he implemented the diplomacy of Popes John Paul II and Benedict XVI.

So for over ten years, the Vatican's diplomat in chief, even though he was very familiar with Greenwich Village, conducted a policy that was just as obsessively anti-gay as the one represented in New York by his colleague Renato Martino. Together, the two nuncios expended considerable energy in trying to block initiatives aimed at the international depenalization of homosexuality and the use of condoms. They intervened on numerous occasions to impede such projects by OMS, UNAIDS or the Global Fund to Fight AIDS, as several directors of those UN agencies in Geneva confirm to me, including the director general of UNAIDS, Michel Sidibé.

At the same time, these two nuncios always remained very discreet about cases of sexual abuse by priests, which amounted to thousands of cases during those years. Flexible morals, in short.

'A good diplomat is a diplomat who represents his government well. And as it happens, for the Vatican a good apostolic nuncio is one who remains loyal to the pope and the priorities he defends,' Tomasi tells me simply, to justify his actions in Geneva and his strict obedience to the line imposed by John Paul II.

In 1989, for the first time, the pope delivered a speech on the issue of AIDS to an assembly of doctors and scientists at the Vatican. He had already been seen in 1987, in Los Angeles, kissing a child sentenced to death by the virus or, during his 1988 Christmas message, calling for compassion for the victims of the epidemic, but he hadn't previously expressed himself in public on the subject. 'It seems wounding to human dignity and therefore morally illicit,' John Paul II declared this time, 'to develop AIDS prevention based on means and remedies that violate the authentically human sense of sexuality, and that are a palliative for those deep anxieties in which the responsibilities of individuals and societies are at issue.'

Certainly the pope did not mention 'condoms' as such (he never would), but this initial declaration stirred up emotions around the world. In September 1990 and again in March 1993, he would deliver another such speech, on African soil this time, in Tanzania and then in Uganda, two of the countries most touched by the pandemic, adding 'that the sexual restriction imposed by chastity is the only safe and virtuous way to put an end to the tragic wound of AIDS'. The pope never tolerated any exceptions to his rule, even in the case of asymptomatic married couples (one of whose partners is HIV positive), even though at this time one Ugandan in eight was contaminated by the virus.

This position would be hotly contested not only by the scientific and medical community, but also by influential cardinals like Carlo Maria Martini and Godfried Danneels (the Archbishop of Paris, Jean-Marie Lustiger, would, with inimitable casuistry, defend John Paul II's position while proposing exceptions as the 'lesser evil').

At the UN, Renato Martino went on to launch a virulent campaign against 'safe sex' and the use of condoms. In 1987, when a committee of American bishops published a document saying that it was necessary to inform populations about ways of protecting themselves, Martino intervened at a high level to have the text banned. He then worked to ensure that AIDS prevention did not appear in any UN documents or declarations. A little later, he used a supposedly scientific article, which was distributed on a massive scale by Cardinal López Trujillo, to denounce the dangers of 'sex without risks' and declare the existence of many infections contracted through protected sexual relations. In 2001, just before the end of his mission, when the episcopal conference in South Africa published a pastoral letter justifying the use of condoms in the case of asymptomatic married couples, Martino agitated once again to try and silence the South African bishops.

'Condoms aggravate the AIDS problem'. The phrase is one of the most famous from the pontificate of Benedict XVI. It has, admittedly, often been distorted. Let us briefly recall the context and the exact wording. On 17 March 2009, the pope was travelling to Yaoundé in Cameroon, on his first trip to Africa. On the Alitalia plane, in a press conference that had been organized in minute detail, he spoke. The question, prepared in advance, was asked by a French journalist. In his reply, after hailing the work of Catholics in the struggle against AIDS in Africa, Benedict XVI added that the illness could not be defeated only with money: 'If there is no soul,' he said, 'if Africans don't help each other, it will not be possible to defeat this scourge by distributing condoms; on the contrary, it risks increasing the problem.'

'If we are honest, we must acknowledge that the pope's response, taken as a whole, is quite coherent. What causes the problem is just one phrase: the idea that the condom is "worse", that it "aggravates" things. It is only this idea of "worse" that is wrong,' Federico Lombardi, spokes-man to Benedict XVI, admits. (Lombardi, who was with the pope on the plane, confirms to me that the question about AIDS had been cleared and prepared in advance.)

The phrase immediately caused an outcry on five continents: Benedict XVI was criticized, mocked, even ridiculed. The presidents of many countries, prime ministers and countless doctors with global reputa-tions, many of them Catholic, denounced his 'irresponsible words' for the first time. Several cardinals spoke of it as a serious 'blunder' or an 'error'. Others, such as the association Act Up, accused the pope of being quite simply 'a criminal'.

'Bishops and priests who already used anti-condom language saw themselves as being legitimated by Benedict XVI's phrase. So they deliv-ered large numbers of homilies in their churches against the anti-AIDS struggle and, of course, some of them insisted that the illness was a punishment from God to punish homosexuals,' I am told by an African priest who is also a diplomat from the holy see (and whom I met more or less by chance in a café in the Borgo in Rome).

Often these Catholic bishops and priests made common cause with homophobic American pastors, evangelicals or imams who were opposed to gay rights and condoms as a way of combatting AIDS.

According to this Vatican diplomat, the nuncios on the ground not-ably had the task of keeping an eye on the African bishops and what they had to say on homosexuality and AIDS. They had to report the slightest 'deviance' to the holy see. Under John Paul II and Benedict XVI, a priest had only to approve of the distribution of condoms, or appear favourable to homosexuality, to lose all hope of becoming a bishop.

The famous lawyer Alice Nkom explained to me that in her country, Cameroon, where I pursued investigations, there was a 'real witch-hunt against homosexuals'. And, she insists, the bishop Samuel Kéda adopted a position in favour of the criminalization of homosexuality, and sought to punish people with AIDS. In Uganda, where a gay activist was assassinated, the Catholic archbishop Cyprian Lwanga opposed the depenalization of homosexuality. In Malawi, Kenya and Nigeria, representatives of the Catholic Church distinguished themselves with homophobic and anti-condom speeches (as confirmed by a detailed report by Human Rights Watch, which was passed to Pope Francis in 2013).

A morally unjust policy with counter-productive effects, as I was told during an interview in Geneva, by the Malian Michel Sidibé, director general of the UN agency UNAIDS: 'In sub-Saharan Africa, the AIDS virus is transmitted chiefly by heterosexual relations. We can therefore assert – and we have numbers to support this – that homophobic laws, as well as being an assault on human rights, are completely useless. The more homosexuals hide, the more vulnerable they are. In the end, by reinforcing stigmatization, one runs the risk of halting the battle against AIDS, and increasing infection among vulnerable populations.'

Among many homophobic African prelates, two cardinals stand out. They have attracted attention over the past few years with their speeches against condoms and homosexuality: the South African Wilfrid Napier and the Guinean Robert Sarah, who were created cardinals by John Paul II and Benedict XVI at a time when being anti-gay was a plus on a CV. Both have since been marginalized by Francis.

Before becoming a homophobe, Wilfrid Napier was a long-time defender of human rights. His career speaks for itself: the current Archbishop of Durban was a militant in favour of the black cause and the democratic process in South Africa. At the head of the South African Episcopal Conference, he played a major role at the time of negotiations to put an end to apartheid.

And yet Napier disputed the advances suggested by Nelson Mandela about the depenalization of homosexuality, the introduction of the idea of 'sexual orientation' in the constitution of the country and, subsequently, the establishment of same-sex marriage.

Several witness statements that I collected in Johannesburg, Soweto and Pretoria identify Napier as a 'genuine homophobe' and a 'radical anti-condom militant'. In 2013, the Archbishop of Durban denounced the proposed laws in favour of gay marriage that were spreading around the world: 'It's a new form of slavery. The United States tell us, you won't have money until you distribute condoms and legalize homosexuality.' (Let's not forget that gay marriage was adopted in South Africa before the United States.)

These interventions provoked intense reactions. The Anglican archbishop Desmond Tutu, holder of the Nobel Peace Prize, opposed Napier head-on (without mentioning him by name), denouncing churches that are 'obsessed by homosexuality' when there was a serious AIDS pandemic. Tutu several times compared homophobia to racism, even saying: 'If God was homophobic, as some people claim, I would not pray to that God.'

The writer Peter Machen, director of the Durban Film Festival, also criticized Cardinal Napier, with heavy innuendo: 'Isn't it a little hard to tell, Archbishop, who is gay, when most of your colleagues wear dresses?'

Napier produced more and more anti-gay declarations; for example, denouncing 'homosexual activity' within the Church – the cause, in his view, of sexual abuse: 'Moving away from the law of God always leads to unhappiness,' he stated.

Napier's obsessive homophobia encountered resistance even in the ranks of the South African Church. The Jesuits of Johannesburg criticized the cardinal's position in their private exchanges with the apostolic nuncio (according to a first-hand source), and as far as I have been able to tell, they closed their eyes and tacitly accepted distributions of condoms.

Judge Edwin Cameron was equally critical. A friend of Nelson Mandela (who had lost a son to AIDS) Cameron is one of the most respected figures in South Africa. A militant for the black cause, he joined the ANC under apartheid, which was rare for a white person. Now a member of the South African supreme court, he publicly announced that he is HIV positive. I interviewed him several times in Johannesburg, where Cameron delivered his judgement, weighing his words carefully, on Wilfrid Napier.

'Those who tried to play down the tragedy of AIDS in Africa, or to protect LGBTI people on this continent, found themselves facing an implacable opponent in the form of Cardinal Wilfrid Napier. Listening to him, one hesitates between distress and despair. He used his considerable power as a prelate of the Roman Catholic Church to oppose the rights of women, to condemn the use of condoms and to reject all legal protection for homosexuals. He campaigned against the decriminalization of sexual relations between consenting adult men or women and, of course, against same-sex couples. In spite of this obsession, he claimed not to know any homosexuals. So he made us invisible and judged us at the same time! This sorry saga in the history of our country, and this black page for the Catholic Church in Africa, is about to come to an end, we hope, with the pontificate of Francis.'

Let us add that Cardinal Wilfrid Napier did little to counter sexual abuse within the Catholic Church, which involves dozens of priests in South Africa. The Archbishop of Durban even declared, in an interview with the BBC, that paedophiles must not be 'punished' because they are 'sick and not criminal'. In response to the scandal provoked by his words, the cardinal apologized, claiming he had been misunderstood. 'I can't be accused of homophobia,' he backtracked, 'because I don't know any homosexuals.'

Robert Sarah is a homophobe of a different kind. I talked to him informally after a lecture, but I haven't been able to interview him officially, despite several requests. On the other hand, I was able to talk several times to his collaborators, notably Nicolas Diat, the co-author of his books. Cardinal Fernando Filoni, who is in charge of African issues in the Vatican, and a priest who lived with Sarah when Sarah was secretary of the Congregation for the Evangelization of Peoples, also spoke to me.

Robert Sarah was not born Catholic; he converted. Having grown up in a Coniagui tribe, 15 hours by bush taxi from the capital of Guinea, Conakry, he shares their prejudices, their rites, their superstitions, and even their culture of sorcery and witch doctors. His family is animist, his house was made of beaten earth where he slept on the ground. The legend of Sarah, the head of the tribe, is born.

The idea of converting to Catholicism and then becoming a priest came from his contact with Missionaries of the Holy Spirit. He entered the minor seminary in the Ivory Coast, before being ordained as a priest in Conakry in 1969, at a time when the dictator in power of Guinea, Sékou Touré, was organizing a hunt of Catholics. When the city's archbishop was imprisoned in 1979, Rome appointed Sarah in his place, making him the youngest bishop in the world. A stand-off began and the prelate stood up to the new dictator, which put him on the list of people … to be poisoned.

Most of the witnesses I have questioned testify to the courage Sarah showed under the dictatorship, and his understanding of power relations. Demonstrating a modesty that conceals an extravagant ego, the prelate was able to get himself spotted by members of John Paul II's reactionary and homophilic entourage, who admired both his opposition to a pro-communist dictatorship and his rigid positions on sexual morality, the celibacy of the priesthood, homosexuality and condoms.

In 2001 John Paul II summoned Sarah, who left Africa and became 'Roman'. It was a turning point. He became secretary to the important Congregation for the Evangelization of Peoples, the ministry at the Vatican that dealt with Africa.

'I knew Robert Sarah when he arrived in Rome. He was a Bible scholar. He was humble and prudent, but also sycophantic and flattering with the cardinal prefect at the time, Crescenzio Sepe. He worked very hard,' I am told by a priest, an African specialist, who was close to Sarah at the 'Palazzo di Propaganda'.

Several observers were also surprised by the unlikely team formed by Crescenzio Sepe and Robert Sarah, an odd pair. Without batting an eyelid, the young bishop served a cardinal, known as the 'red pope', who enjoyed a colourful life and who would be dispatched far from Rome by Pope Benedict XVI.

'Sarah is a great mystic. He prays constantly, as if he's under some sort of spell. He's frightening. He's literally frightening,' a priest notes.

There are many grey areas in Robert Sarah's career, which is a bit too brilliant to be true. For example, his connection with the far-right ideas of Mgr Lefebvre, excommunicated by the pope in 1988, comes up time and again: Sarah set up a missionary school of which Lefebvre was the titular head, and he then immersed himself, in France, in a fundamentalist milieu. Is Sarah's closeness to the Catholic far right a simple venial sin of youth, or did it lastingly shape his ideas?

Another grey area concerns the liturgical and theological abilities of the cardinal, who serves mass in Latin *ad orientem* but is said not to have the requisite level of linguistic understanding. Ultra-elitist (because speaking Latin, even badly, means cutting oneself off from the ordinary people) and philistine. His writings on St Augustine and St Thomas Aquinas have come under criticism. As for his rants against the Enlightenment philosophers, they reveal 'an archaism which places superstition over reason', according to one theologian. Who adds: 'Why go back to before Vatican II when you could go all the way to the Middle Ages!'

Another French academic and theologian who lives in Rome, and who has published many important books about Catholicism, tells me, over the course of three interviews: 'Sarah is a bottom-of-the-range theologian. His theology is very puerile: "I pray, therefore I am." He abuses arguments of authority. No theologian worthy of the name could take him very seriously.'

The French journalist Nicolas Diat, close to the reactionary right, who has written several books with Sarah, comes to the cardinal's defence during the three lunches we have together in Paris.

'Cardinal Sarah isn't a "traditionalist" as people try to claim. He's a conservative. At first he was a tribal chief, we mustn't forget that. For me he's a saint with immense piety.'

A saint that some people criticize for his interpersonal skills, his way of life and his connections in Africa. An unconditional defender of the continent, in his public statements Sarah has remained discreet about the conduct of certain African prelates, such as those in the episcopal conference in Mali, or the huge sums that the Cardinal Archbishop of Bamako secretly placed in Switzerland (and which were revealed by the SwissLeaks scandal).

To this we should add a strange publishing mystery that I've discovered. The bookshop sales of books written by Cardinal Sarah barely correspond to the figures quoted. Certainly, it isn't rare for an author to 'inflate' his sales figures out of vanity. But in the circumstances, the '250,000 copies' announced in the press are almost ten times higher than the real bookshop sales. The cardinal's 'unprecedented success' is more than an exaggeration. Sales of Cardinal Sarah's books are merely average in France: at the end of 2018, *Dieu ou rien* (God or Nothing) sold 9,926 copies in the original large-format edition, and *La Force du silence* (The Strength of Silence) sold 16,325, in spite of the curious preface by the retired Pope Benedict XVI (these figures are according to the French publishing database Edistat). Sales on Amazon are equally poor. And even if we add distribution among parishes and seminaries, which are not always taken into account in publishing statistics, and the paperback format versions (only 4,608 copies sold of *La Force du silence*), we are a long way from the author's 'hundreds of thousands of copies'. Abroad, there is the same fragility, particularly since the number of translations is itself lower than some journalists may have claimed.

How can we explain this 'hiatus'? By carrying out investigations within Sarah's publishing house, I finally let the cat out of the bag. According to two people familiar with these delicate negotiations; tens, perhaps hundreds of thousands of copies of his books are said to have been bought 'in bulk' by sponsors and foundations, then distributed for free, particularly in Africa. These 'bulk sales' are entirely legal. Artificially serving to 'inflate' sales figures, they please both publishers and authors: they give the former significant profits, because they cut out distributors and bookshops; authors benefit even more because they are paid a percentage (in some cases, riders can be added to publishing contacts to renegotiate rights, if those parallel sales had not been initially envisaged). The English versions of Sarah's books are published, perhaps in similar ways, by a conservative Catholic publishing house, which falls in line with his anti-gay-marriage campaigns: Ignatius Press in San Francisco.

Diplomatic sources also confirm that copies of Sarah's books have been distributed for free in Africa; in Benin, for example. I myself have seen, in a French diplomatic cultural centre, piles of hundreds of books by the cardinal, under plastic.

Who supports Cardinal Sarah's campaign and, where appropriate, the distributions of his books? Does he enjoy financial support from Europe or America? One thing is certain: Robert Sarah maintains contacts with ultra-conservative Catholic associations, particularly the Dignitatis Humanae Institute (as confirmed to me by its director, Benjamin Harnwell). In the United States, Sarah had connections with three foundations, the Becket Fund of Religious Liberty, the Knights of Columbus and the National Catholic Prayer Breakfast, to whom he delivered a lecture. In Europe, Robert Sarah is also able to count on the support of the Knights of Columbus, particularly in France, as well as the affection of a billionaire who we have already visited in this book: Princess Gloria von Thurn und Taxis, an extremely wealthy German royalist. 'Gloria TNT' confirmed to me during a conversation at her castle in Regensburg in Bavaria: 'We've always invited the clergy here: it's part of our Catholic legacy. I receive speakers who come from Rome. I am very involved in the Catholic Church, and I love inviting speakers like Cardinal Robert Sarah. He presented his book here in Regensburg and I invited the press: we had a lovely evening. That's all part of my social life.'

In the photographs of this high-society party, we can see the princess surrounded by Robert Sarah and Nicolas Diat, as well as Cardinal Ludwig Müller, the priest Wilhelm Imkamp and Georg Ratzinger, the pope's brother (the German edition of Sarah's book has a preface by Georg Gänswein). In short: these are the main architects of what has been called 'das Regensburger Netzwerk' ('the Regensburg network').

Robert Sarah also has connections with the organisation of Marguerite Peeters, a Belgian militant extremist, homophobic and anti-feminist. Sarah wrote the preface to a little pamphlet by Peeters against gender theory, which was published almost entirely at the author's expense. In it he writes: 'Homosexuality is nonsense in terms of conjugal and family life. It is at least pernicious to recommend it in the name of Human Rights. To impose it is a crime against humanity. And it is inadmissible for western countries and UN agencies to impose on non-western countries homosexuality and all its moral deviances … To promote the diversity of "sexual orientations" even in African, Asian, Oceanian or South American territory is to lead the world towards a total anthropological and moral breakdown: towards decadence and the destruction of humanity!'

What financial support does Sarah enjoy? We don't know. In any case, Pope Francis, with certain cardinals in the Roman Curia in mind, is quoted as saying: 'There is God and there is the God of money.'

One last mystery: the cardinal's entourage never ceases to surprise observers: Sarah travels and works with gays. One of his close collaborators is a far-right gay, with a powerful reputation for being forward in his advances. And when Sarah was secretary to the Congregation for the Evangelization of Peoples, fashionable homosexual parties were organized in one of the dicastery's apartments. Within the Vatican, people still joke about this unusual time, when 'private dancers', 'chemical orgies' and 'chem-sex parties' occurred within the ministry of the 'red pope'. Did Sarah know? There is no evidence that he did.

'Was it possible that Sarah might have been unaware of the dissolute life of certain priests in the Congregation, and the risqué parties that were being held in the building where he lived and worked?' wonders a visibly shocked priest who lived with him in the ministry at the time (and whom I interviewed in Belgium).

Today, people familiar with the Curia also notice Sarah's professional proximity to a monsignore caught up in a corruption scandal which involved the procurement of male prostitutes. This prelate was mocked by the press and then accused of belonging to a gay prostitution network. Punished by the pope, the monsignore disappeared before miraculously reappearing in Sarah's team at the Vatican (his name still appears in the *Annuario Pontifico*).

'The most anti-gay cardinal in the Roman Curia is surrounded by homosexuals. He appears with them in social media. In Rome or France, which he often travels to, he is seen in the company of bustling and entirely practising gays,' a French journalist who knows him well tells me in a choked voice.

Pope Francis knows Sarah too. Because while the cardinal publicly voices admiration for the pope, he criticizes him harshly in private. When he delivers lectures, his entourage – to attract the public and sell his books – presents him as 'one of the pope's closest advisers', but in fact he is one of his most implacable enemies. Francis, who has never been taken in by obsequious courtiers or bare-faced hypocrites, regularly punishes him with brutal severity. For a long time now, Sarah has lost his odour of sanctity at the Vatican.

'The pope's technique against Sarah is what I would call Chinese water torture: you don't sack him all at once, you humiliate him little by little, depriving him of funds and taking away his collaborators, marginalizing him, denying his ideas or refusing him an audience … and then one day you make him commit hara-kiri. The technique was refined for [Raymond] Burke and [Ludwig] Müller. Sarah's turn will come in time,' a Curia priest in Cardinal Filoni's entourage tells me.

The Chinese torture is already at work. Created cardinal by Benedict XVI in 2010, Robert Sarah assumed the head of the powerful pontifical council Cor Unum, which deals with charitable Catholic organizations. He proved sectarian, and more concerned with evangelization than philanthropy. After his election, Pope Francis removed him from his post, for carrying out his charity mission in a less than charitable manner. Phase I of the Chinese torture: rather than dismissing him, the pope reorganized the Curia and entirely dissolved the pontifical council Cor Unum, thus depriving Sarah of his post. As a consolation prize, employing the famous technique of '*promoveatur ut amoveatur*' (promote to remove), the cardinal was made head of the Congregation for Divine Worship and the Discipline of the Sacraments. There again he made *faux pas* after *faux pas* and revealed himself as an unconditional militant in favour of the Latin rite and the mass *ad orientem*: the priest must celebrate the mass with his back to the congregation, facing east. The pope called him to order: stage two of the Chinese torture. Stage three: all at once Francis removed 27 of the 30 cardinals of the team advising Robert Sarah, and without even taking the trouble to consult him, appointed his own men in their place. Stage four: Francis deprived him of his assistants. In appearance, little had changed: Sarah was still in place; but the cardinal was marginalized at the very heart of his ministry.

In the shadows for a long time, it was with the Synod on the Family called by Francis that Sarah showed his true face. He had no hesitation in calling divorce a scandal and remarriage adultery. In 2015 he even delivered a hysterical speech in which he denounced, as if he were still in his animist village, the 'beast of the Apocalypse', an animal with seven heads and ten horns sent by Satan to destroy the Church. And what was this devilish beast threatening the Church? Sarah's 2015 speech is explicit on this point: it is the 'ideology of gender', homosexual unions and the gay lobby. And the cardinal went even further, comparing the LGBT lobby to Islamic terrorism: in his view, they are two sides of the same coin, the 'two beasts of the Apocalypse'. (I am quoting from the official transcript, which I have got hold of.)

In comparing homosexuals to Daesh, Sarah reached a point of no return. 'We're dealing with a fanatic,' a cardinal close to the pope says harshly, off the record. And a priest who took part in the synod tells me: 'It's no longer about religion: this is a speech typical of the far right. It's Monseigneur Lefebvre: we don't have to look any further for his sources. Sarah is re-Africanized Lefebvre.'

What is strange here is Sarah's obsession with homosexuality. What an *idée fixe*! What psychosis about this 'apocalypse'! In dozens of obscurantist interviews, the cardinal condemns homosexuals or begs them to remain chaste. Magnanimously, he even suggests for the least frugal of them 'reparative therapies' – often defended by the priest-psychoanalyst Tony Anatrella and various snake-oil salesmen – which are said to 'heal' them and allow them to become heterosexual! If a homosexual person doesn't manage to attain abstinence, reparative therapies can help them: 'in many cases, when the practice of homosexual acts has not yet been structured, [these homosexuals] can react positively to appropriate therapy'.

Against this background, the cardinal's position is not without contradictions. In France, he became one of the tutelary figures of the 'Manif pour tous' movement, without seeing that some of his 'anti-gender' supporters were also pure racists who advocated voting for the far right Marine Le Pen in the 2017 presidential election. Thus a cardinal defending an absolutist vision of the family appeared beside those seeking to reserve family allowances only for the 'native-born French', and oppose family reunification of African parents with their children.

Imprudence, or provocation? Robert Sarah even wrote the preface for a book by Daniel Mattson, *Why I Don't Call Myself Gay*. This book, with its dizzying title, is significant in that what the author proposes for homosexuals is neither 'charity' nor 'compassion' but total abstinence. Sarah suggests that being homosexual is not a sin as long as one remains continent: 'When confronted with an adulterous woman, did Jesus not say, "I do not condemn you; go and sin no more"?' This is the message of Sarah, which brings him strangely to the position of many homosexual Catholic writers and thinkers who have placed value on chastity so as not to follow their tendencies.

With this kind of statement, Sarah comes close, whether consciously or not, to the most caricatured homophiles, who have sublimated or repressed their inclinations into asceticism or mysticism. The prelate admits that he has read a great deal about this 'illness', and attended lectures in Rome addressing the homosexual question, particularly those at the pontifical university of Saint Thomas (as he reveals in his preface to the book *Why I Don't Call Myself Gay*): '[Listening to homosexuals] I sensed the loneliness, pain and unhappiness that they endured as a result of pursuing a life contrary to their true identity as God's children,' he writes. 'Only when they lived in keeping with Christ's teaching were they able to find the peace and joy for which they had been searching.'

In fact, the world of Robert Sarah is a fiction. His criticism of Western modernity as opposed to the African ideal is only credible for those who do not know Africa.

'African reality does not correspond in any way to what Sarah claims, out of pure ideology,' the African diplomat at the Vatican, who has worked with him, tells me.

The illusion is particularly palpable on three issues: the celibacy of the priesthood, AIDS and the supposed homophobia of Africa. The Canadian economist Robert Calderisi, former spokesman of the World Bank in Africa, explains to me when I interview him that most of the priests on the continent live discreetly with a woman; the others are generally homosexual and try to exile themselves to Europe. 'Africans want the priests to be like them. They like them to be married and have children,' Calderisi adds.

All the nuncios and diplomats that I have interviewed for this research, and all my contacts in the African countries – Cameroon, Kenya and South Africa – that I have visited, confirm the frequency of this double life of Catholic priests in Africa, whether they are heterosexual or homosexual.

'Sarah knows very well: a significant number of African Catholic priests live with a woman. Besides, they would lose all legitimacy in their village if they didn't demonstrate their heterosexual practice! Far from Rome, they sometimes even manage to be married in the church in their village. Sarah's current discourse on chastity and abstinence is a huge fable, when we know the lives of priests in Africa. It's a mirage,' according to a priest who specializes in Africa and who knows the cardinal well.

This prelate also confirms that homosexuality is one of the traditional rites of passage of West African tribes, particularly in Guinea. A feature of African life of which the cardinal cannot be unaware.

Today, African seminaries are also, in the image of Italian seminaries in the 1950s, homosexualized places and spaces of protection for gays. Here again, this is a sociological law or, if one might dare to say so, a kind of 'natural selection' in the Darwinian sense: by stigmatizing homosexuals in Africa, the Church forces them to hide. They take refuge in seminaries to protect themselves and not have to marry. If they can, they flee to Europe, where Italian, French and Spanish episcopates appeal to them to repopulate their parishes. And that way things come full circle.

Robert Sarah's discourse has become more hard-line since he left Africa. The bishop is more orthodox than the priest, and the cardinal more orthodox than the bishop. While he closed his eyes to many of the secrets of Africa, in Rome he was more intransigent than ever. Homosexuals then became scapegoats, along with all the things which, in his eyes, go along with it: AIDS, gender theory and the gay lobby.

Robert Sarah was one of the most vocal cardinals against the use of condoms in Africa. He rejected international development aid, which he saw as contributing to this 'propaganda', and refused the Church any social mission and punished associations, such as the Caritas network, which distributed condoms.

'There is a large gap in Africa between the ideological discourse of the Church and the work on the ground, which is often very pragmatic. I have seen nuns giving out condoms everywhere,' I am told by the Canadian economist Robert Calderisi, the former spokesman for the World Bank in West Africa.

Sarah commits another historical error on homosexuality. His template here is neo-Third-Worldist: Westerners, he says time and again, want to impose their values through human rights; in attributing rights to homosexuals they wish to deny the 'African-ness', of the peoples of that continent. Sarah, therefore, is standing up, in the name of Africa – which he left a long time ago, his detractors say – against a sick West. For him, LGBT rights can't be universal rights.

In fact, as I have discovered in India, almost all the homophobic laws currently imposed as part of the penal codes in countries in Asia and Africa were instituted around 1860 by Victorian England on the colonies and protectorates of the Commonwealth (article 377 of the Indian penal code, the initial template, and then repeated, with the same number, in Botswana, the Gambia, Kenya, Lesotho, Malawi, Nigeria, Somalia, Swaziland, Sudan, Tanzania, Zambia …). Furthermore, a comparable phenomenon also exists in North and West Africa, this time a leftover of French colonialism. The penalization of homosexuality therefore has nothing African about it – it is a leftover from colonialism. The supposedly unique quality of 'African-ness' was an injunction by the colonists to try and 'civilize' the indigenous Africans, to teach them 'good' European models and condemn homosexual practices.

Taking into account this homophobic dimension of colonial history, we can tell to what extent Cardinal Sarah's discourse is loaded. When he claims that 'Africa and Asia must absolutely protect their own cultures and values', or insists that the Church must not allow itself to have 'a western vision of the family' imposed on it, the cardinal is abusing his believers, blinded by his prejudices and his interests. His discourse here is close to that of the African dictator Robert Mugabe, former President of Zimbabwe, for whom homosexuality was an 'anti-African western practice', or that of the autocratic presidents of Kenya and Uganda, who repeat that it is 'contrary to the African tradition'.

Ultimately, if cardinals like Robert Sarah or Wilfrid Napier were consistent with themselves, they would be calling for the depenalization of homosexuality in Africa in the name of anti-colonialism, with a view to returning to a genuine African tradition.

It was not until Pope Francis that the Church's position on condoms softened, or at least became more nuanced. On his trip to Africa in 2015, the pontiff explicitly acknowledged that the condom is 'one of the [viable] methods' in the battle against AIDS. Rather than speaking about prevention, he would insist on the major role played by the Church in the treatment of the epidemic: thousands of hospitals, dispensaries and orphanages, as well as the Catholic network Caritas Internationalis, treat the sick and find anti-retroviral therapies for them. In the meantime, AIDS has led, all around the world and in Africa in particular, to over 35 million deaths.

15

Strange bedfellows

After waging the battle against the use of condoms in Africa, the cardinals and nuncios of John Paul II tried to forbid civil unions. Here we enter one of the most surprising episodes in this book: that of an army of homophiles and homosexuals going to war against gay marriage.

It was in the Netherlands that the debate began, with the surprising introduction on 1 April 2001 of marriage for same-sex couples. In Amsterdam, the gay community celebrated the event, astonished by its own daring. The resonance of this development was international. The new article of law was written as follows; quite simply: 'A marriage may be contracted by two persons of different sexes or the same sex.'

Some analysts in the holy see had spotted early warning signs, and nuncios like François Bacqué, in office in the country, had sent many diplomatic telegrams alerting Rome. But the spectacular Dutch decision was received in the Vatican like a second biblical Fall.

Pope John Paul II was out of action at that moment because of his state of health, but the secretary of state created enough agitation for two. Angelo Sodano was literally 'confused' and 'puzzled', according to a witness, and shared this confusion and puzzlement in no uncertain terms with his team, while maintaining his unshakeable placidity. Not only did he refuse to accept this precedent in Western Europe, but he feared, like the whole Curia, that the Dutch decision would open a breach that other countries would pour into.

Sodano gave the 'minister' of foreign affairs at the Vatican, the Frenchman Jean-Louis Tauran, the job of taking over the dossier, with the support of the nuncio Bacqué, who had already been his deputy in Chile. Shortly afterwards, he appointed to Geneva a bishop that he himself had consecrated, Silvano Tomasi, to follow the debate at the multilateral level. Benedict XVI's 'minister' of foreign affairs, Dominique Mamberti, would also go on to play an important part. (To tell this story, I am relying on my conversations with four key actors, Tauran, Bacqué, Tomasi and Mamberti, as well as on ten other Vatican diplomatic sources. I have also obtained copies of dozens of confidential telegrams from diplomats posted to the UN describing the positions of the Vatican. Last of all, I spoke to several foreign ambassadors, the French Minister of Foreign Affairs, Bernard Kouchner, the director of UNAIDS, Michel Sidibé, and Ambassador Jean-Maurice Ripert, who piloted the 'core group' at the UN in New York.)

Between 2001 – the Dutch 'shock' – and 2015 – the date when 'same-sex marriage' was authorized in the United States by the Supreme Court, confirming the lasting defeat of the holy see – an unprecedented battle would be played out in countless apostolic nunciatures and episcopates. Under Paul VI, there were only 73 ambassadors from the holy see, but their number reached 178 by the end of John Paul II's pontificate (there are 183 today). Everywhere, mobilization against civil unions and gay marriage would become one of the Vatican's priorities, and the louder the prelates, the more deafening the silence about their double lives.

In the Netherlands, François Bacqué was asked to mobilize bishops and Catholic associations to incite them to take to the streets and make the government go back on its decision. But the nuncio quickly realized that most of the Dutch episcopate, apart from the cardinals appointed by Rome (including the very anti-gay 'Wim' Eijk), were moderate if not liberal. The base of the Church was progressive, and had for a long time been calling for the end of the celibacy of the priesthood, the opening of communion to divorced couples and even the recognition of homosexual unions. The Dutch battle was lost in advance.

At the Human Rights Council, resistance against the 'pink wave' seemed more promising. The question of marriage had no chance of coming up for debate, given the radical opposition of the Muslim countries or several countries in Asia. However, Sodano warned the nuncio Tomasi, who had just arrived in Switzerland, that they would have to oppose with all their might the decriminalization of homosexuality, which would, here too, set a bad example and, via the snowball effect, open up the way to the acknowledgement of gay couples.

Proposals to depenalize homosexuality at the level of the United Nations already existed. Brazil, New Zealand and Norway had made some modest attempts, starting in 2003, to breach the subject, as Boris Dittrich explained during an interview in Amsterdam. 'For a long time I was a militant and a politician; and after helping to change the law of the Netherlands I thought we had to continue this fight at an international level.' This member of the Dutch parliament, a former magistrate, was the architect of gay marriage in his country.

Meanwhile, in Rome, Benedict XVI was elected and Sodano was replaced, against his will, by Tarcisio Bertone at the head of the Roman Curia. The new pope, in turn, made his opposition to homosexual marriage a priority and, perhaps, even a personal matter.

In fact, what the nuncio Tomasi did not yet understand, and what the cardinals in the Vatican under-estimated, too blinded by their prejudices, was that the state of affairs was changing in the mid-2000s. A pro-gay dynamic had taken hold in many Western countries, those of the European Union even wanting to imitate the Dutch model.

At the United Nations, the balance of power also changed when France chose to make the depenalization of homosexuality its priority, taking the head of the presidency of the European Union. Several countries in Latin America, including Argentina and Brazil, also went on the offensive. One African country, Gabon, as well as Croatia and Japan, joined this 'core group', which would bring the battle to Geneva and New York.

After months of secret inter-state negotiations, in which the Vatican was never involved, the decision was taken to present a text to the General Assembly of the United Nations, due to be held in New York in December 2008. The 'recommendation' would not be binding, unlike a 'resolution', which must be approved by the majority of voters, but the symbol would be no less powerful.

'I thought we mustn't defend a resolution if we weren't certain of obtaining the majority of votes,' Dittrich confirms. 'Otherwise we risked ending up with an official decision by the United Nations against the rights of homosexuals, and we would have lost the battle for a long time.'

To make sure that the debate did not appear strictly Western, and to avoid a gulf being created between the countries of the North and those of the South, the diplomats of the 'core group' invited Argentina to make the official declaration. So the idea would be universal, and defended on all continents.

Until 2007, Silvano Tomasi didn't take the threat seriously. But in Rome, the new 'minister' of foreign affairs of Benedict XVI, the Frenchman Dominique Mamberti, who was very familiar with the set of problems around homosexuality, got wind of the project. Apostolic nuncios are generally well-informed. Information quickly reached the holy see. Mamberti alerted the holy father and Cardinal Bertone.

Pope Benedict XVI, who made the refusal of any acknowledgement of homosexuality one of the key elements of his career, despaired of the situation. During a trip he made in person to the headquarters of the United Nations in New York on 18 April 2008, he took advantage of a private meeting with Ban Ki-moon, the secretary general of the organization, to lecture him. The pope reminded the secretary general of his absolute hostility, in muted but emphatic terms, towards any form of acceptance of the rights of homosexuals. Ban Ki-moon listened respectfully to the impassioned pope; and shortly afterwards he made the defence of gay rights one of his priorities.

Since before the summer of 2008, the Vatican had been convinced that a pro-LGBT declaration would be submitted to the United Nations. The reaction of the holy see was manifested in two directions. First of all, nuncios were called to intervene with governments to stop them doing something irreparable. But very quickly, the Vatican discovered that all the European countries, without exception, would vote for the declaration. Including Poland, dear to John Paul II's heart, and Berlusconi's Italy! The Secretary of State Tarcisio Bertone, who was now in charge of the dossier, short-circuiting the Italian Episcopal Conference, became increasingly worked up and used all his political contacts in the Palazzo Chigi and parliament, but still couldn't change the position of the Italian government.

Second, the Vatican also tested some states that looked likely to swing, but everywhere, in Australia, Israel and Japan, governments were preparing to sign the declaration. In Latin America in particular almost all Spanish and Portuguese-speaking countries went in the same direction. Cristina Kirchner's Argentina confirmed that they were ready to make the text public, and there were also rumours that Cardinal Jorge Bergoglio, at the head of the Argentinian Episcopal Conference, was hostile to any form of discrimination.

The Vatican came up with a sophisticated, if not a sophistical position, built on specious if not fallacious arguments: 'No one is for the penalization of homosexuality or its criminalization,' the holy see insisted, going on to explain that existing texts on human rights were 'enough'. Creating new ones would mean running the risk, under the pretext of battling injustice, of creating 'new forms of discrimination'. The diplomats of the Vatican finally fought against the expressions 'sexual orientation' and 'gender identity', which in their view had no value in international law. To acknowledge them might lead to the legitimation of polygamy or sexual abuse. (Here I am quoting the terms that appeared in diplomatic telegrams.)

'The Vatican dared to stir up a fear of paedophilia to prevent the depenalization of homosexuality! It was incredible! The argument was very specious given what we know of the number of cases involving paedophile priests,' a French diplomat who took part in the negotiations stresses.

In opposing the extension of human rights to homosexuals, Benedict XVI's Vatican reconnected with the old Catholic suspicion of international law. For Joseph Ratzinger, the norms that he turned into a dogma were divine in essence: they were therefore imposed on states because they were superior to them. This ultramontanism soon came to seem anachronistic. Francis, after his election, would prove deeply hostile to 'clericalism', and would do his best to bring the Church back into the world order, forgetting the outdated notions of Benedict XVI.

When this Ratzingerian strategy failed, the holy see changed its method. Because it was no longer possible to convince the 'rich' countries of its stance, the time had come to mobilize the 'poor' ones. In Geneva, Silvano Tomasi tried to block the UN process, raising awareness among his colleagues from Muslim, Asian and particularly African countries (which he was well-informed about from having been an observer with the African Union in Addis Ababa). His fellow nuncio at the United

Nations in New York, Celestino Migliore, who replaced Renato Martino, did likewise. Pope Benedict, from Rome, agitated as well, somewhat overcome in every sense of the word.

'The line of our diplomacy was along the lines of what I would call the voice of reason and common sense. We are in favour of the universal and not of particular interests,' Silvano Tomasi told me simply, to explain the Catholic Church's opposition to the UN declaration.

It was then that the Vatican committed an error that many Western diplomats considered a historic mistake. In its new crusade, the holy see sealed agreements with several Muslim dictatorships or theocracies. In diplomacy, this is called a 'reversal of alliance'.

The Vatican thus joined a disparate contingency coalition, approaching Iran, Syria, Egypt, the Organization of the Islamic Conference and even Saudi Arabia, with which it didn't even have diplomatic relations! According to corroborative sources, apostolic nuncios engaged in numerous dialogues with the heads of states in which they were otherwise in conflict on the issues of the death penalty, religious freedom and human rights in general.

On 18 December 2008, as planned, Argentina defended the 'Declaration on Sexual Orientation and Gender Identity' before the General Assembly of the United Nations. The initiative received the support of 66 countries: all the states of the European Union signed it, without exception, as well as 6 African countries, 4 Asian countries, 13 in Latin America, as well as Israel, Australia and Canada. For the first time in the history of the UN, states of all continents spoke out against human rights violations based on sexual orientation.

'It was a very moving historical session. I admit I was on the brink of tears,' Jean-Maurice Ripert, the French ambassador at the UN who piloted the 'core group', admitted when I interviewed him in Paris.

As was also predicted, a counter-declaration, 'Supposed Notions of Sexual Orientation and Gender Identity', was read out in parallel by Syria, in the name of 59 other countries. This text was based on the defence of the family as a 'natural and fundamental element of society', and criticized the creation of 'new rights' and 'new standards' that betray the spirit of the UN. In particular, the text condemned the expression 'sexual orientation', which was criticized for having no basis in international law, and because it would open the way to a legitimation of 'numerous deplorable acts, including paedophilia'. Almost all the Arab countries supported this counter-declaration, as well as 31 African countries, several countries in Asia, and of course Iran. Among the signatories was Benedict XVI's Vatican.

'The Vatican aligned itself inadmissibly with Iran and Saudi Arabia. It could at least have abstained,' says Sergio Rovasio, the president of the gay association Certi Diritti, close to the Italian Radical Party, during our interview in Florence.

All the more so, since 68 'neutral' countries like China, Turkey, India, South Africa or Russia, refused to associate themselves with the text presented by Argentina or the counter-declaration from Syria. The Vatican, in the end, could have imitated them.

When I questioned the nuncio Silvano Tomasi on the Vatican's position, he regretted that this declaration marked 'the beginning of a movement in the international community and the United Nations to integrate gay rights within the overall agenda of human rights'. The remark is fairly accurate. Between 2001, the date of the adoption of marriage for homosexual couples in the Netherlands, and the end of the pontificate of Benedict XVI in 2013, international 'momentum' had developed on gay issues.

The American Secretary of State Hillary Clinton said precisely this when she declared to the United Nations in Geneva, in December 2011: 'Some have suggested that gay rights and human rights are separate and distinct; but, in fact, they are one and the same. (…) Gay rights are human rights, and human rights are gay rights.'

The diplomats of the Vatican listened in silence to this message, adopted today by most Western and Latin American governments: either you embrace human rights completely, or not at all.

And yet, until the end of his pontificate, Benedict XVI refused to let go. On the contrary, he would also take up the fight against civil unions and gay marriage. In fact, yet again, the pope made it a question of principle. But did he realize that this battle was, like the previous one, lost in advance?

'For a man like Benedict XVI, the battle against homosexuality had always been a great cause of his life. He couldn't even imagine gay marriage being legalized,' a Curia priest confirms to me.

At this dark moment, there was no question of retreating, even if it meant losing out! So he launched himself blindly, thrown into the lions' den like the first Christians, come what may!

The irrational and dizzying history of this crazed commitment against gay marriage is a crucial chapter in this book, since it reveals an army of homophilic priests and closeted homosexual prelates who, day after day, would mobilize against another army of 'openly gay' activists. The war over gay marriage was, more than ever, a battle between homosexuals.

Before dealing at length with Spain and Italy in the next few chapters, I will start by telling the story of this battle on the basis of my interviews on the ground in three countries: Peru, Portugal and Colombia.

With a little white goatee, a big watch and a brown suede jacket, Carlos Bruce is an unmissable figure in Latin America's LGBT community. I met this MP, twice a minister in moderate right-wing governments, several times in Lima, in 2014 and 2015. He described to me a context that was generally favourable to gay rights on the continent, although specific national characteristics might rein in that dynamic, as they do in Peru. There is an active gay scene in Lima, as I have been able to observe, and tolerance is on the rise. But the recognition of the rights of gay couples, civil unions and gay marriage bumped up against the Catholic Church, which prevented any progress, in spite of the Church's moral failure evidenced by the increasing number of cases of paedophilia.

'Here, Cardinal Juan Luis Cipriani is viscerally homophobic. He talks about homosexuals as "adulterated and damaged goods", and for him gay marriage is comparable, in his words, to the Holocaust. And yet, when a bishop was accused of sexual abuse in the region of Ayacucho, Cipriani came to his defence!' Carlos Bruce remarks, visibly disgusted.

A member of Opus Dei, Cipriani was created cardinal by John Paul II thanks to the active support of Vatican Secretary of State Angelo Sodano, and, like him, he has been criticized for his links with the far right and his animosity towards liberation theology. It is true that certain priests close to this current of thought have been able to take up arms alongside Maoist guerrillas like Shining Path or, more Guevarist, the MRTA – which terrorized the conservative clergy.

Apart from these local peculiarities, the cardinal has succeeded like so many of his co-religionists in squaring the circle: being both violently hostile to marriage between people of the same sex (even civil unions still don't exist in Peru) and failing to denounce paedophile priests.

During the 2000s, Cardinal Cipriani delivered so many anti-gay speeches that he was contradicted and publicly called to account by the new mayor of Lima, Susana Villarán, even though she is a convinced Catholic. She was so exasperated by the double standards of Cardinal Cipriani, who is opposed to gay rights but remains discreet about paedophile priests, that she waged war against him. She appeared at Gay Pride and mocked the bogeyman cardinal.

'Here, the chief resistance to gay rights,' Carlos Bruce adds, 'is the Catholic Church, as it is everywhere in Latin America, but I think the homophobes are busy losing ground. People are very clear on the subject of the protection of gay couples.'

This is a judgement also shared by the journalist Alberto Servat, an influential cultural critic whom I met several times in Lima: 'These repeated sexual scandals in the Church are very shocking to public opinion. And Cardinal Cipriani gave the impression of doing nothing to limit sexual abuse. One of the accused priests is now a refugee in the Vatican ...'

And Carlos Bruce concluded, making concrete suggestions that would mean a definitive repudiation of Cipriani: 'I think the Church must accept all the consequences of moral failure: it must stop criticizing homosexual relations between consenting adults, and authorize marriage; then it must abandon its silence about sexual abuse and completely abandon its general and institutionalized cover-up strategy. Finally, because this is the key to the problem, it must end the celibacy of the priesthood.'

In Portugal, where I went twice for this investigation, in 2016 and 2017, the debate on gay marriage was the reverse of the one in Peru or the rest of Europe, because the Catholic hierarchy didn't follow Rome's instructions. Whereas in France, Spain and Italy, for example, cardinals anticipated and supported the position of Benedict XVI, the Portuguese episcopate, on the contrary, weakened prejudices. The cardinal at that time, in 2009–10, was the Archbishop of Lisbon: José Policarpo.

'Policarpo was a moderate. He never did what Rome told him to. He calmly voiced his disagreement with the planned law on gay marriage, but refused to let the bishops take to the streets,' the journalist António Marujo, a religious specialist who co-wrote a book with Policarpo, explains to me.

It has to be said that the Portuguese Church, compromised under the dictatorship before 1974, now keeps its distance from the Catholic far right. It doesn't seek to become involved in political matters, and stays out of parliamentary debates. This is confirmed to me by José Manuel Pureza, the vice-president of the Portuguese parliament, an MP with the left bloc (Bloco de Esquerda) and a practising Catholic, who was one of the chief architects of the law on homosexual marriage.

'Cardinal Policarpo, known for having been favourable to democracy under the dictatorship, chose a form of neutrality on marriage. At the level of principles and family morality, he was against the planned law, but he was very measured. The Church had the same moderate attitude on abortion and adoption by same-sex couples.' (This analysis joins that of three other major political figures who supported gay marriage, and whom I interviewed in Lisbon: the intellectual Francisco Louçá; Caterina Martins, the speaker for Bloco de Esquerda; and Ana Catarina Mendes, spokeswoman for the prime minister António Costa.)

During my travels in this little Catholic country, I have been struck by its political moderation: social questions are discussed politely and homosexuality seems to be discreetly becoming an uncontentious issue even in churches. Sometimes women even take some of the functions of priests in Portugal, because of the crisis in vocations, taking on all tasks except the sacraments. Many Catholic priests are also married, particularly Anglican converts who were already in an established relationship before joining the Roman Church. I have also met several homosexual priests and monks, who seem to live out their unique lives quite peacefully, particularly in monasteries. The parish of Santa Isabel, in the heart of Lisbon, welcomes all couples and all genders. As for the chief translator of the Bible into Portuguese, Frederico Lourenço, he is publicly married to his partner.

This soft liberalism has not escaped the attention of Rome: the neutrality of the Lisbon episcopate on social questions – such as its low level of mobilization against the law on marriage – has caused consternation. Rome was waiting to put its foot down; Cardinal Policarpo supplied the pretext for them to take action.

Following an interview that was judged to be too liberal (especially on the question of the ordination of women), Policarpo was summoned to Rome at the request of Pope Benedict XVI, by the Secretary of State Tarcisio Bertone. There, according to corroborative sources (and a detailed inquiry into the subject by the journalist António Marujo in *Público*), Bertone gave the cardinal a dressing-down, and he had to publish a communiqué, publicly moderating his moderation. The pope hoped to turn the Policarpo page as soon as possible.

At this time, Benedict XVI's key man in Portugal was the auxiliary bishop of Lisbon and vice-rector of the Catholic University, Carlos Azevedo. The organizer of the pope's trip in 2010, which was aimed specifically at attempting to block the law on marriage, Azevedo became a rising figure in the Portuguese Church. Pope Benedict XVI had big ambitions for his protégé: he planned to create him cardinal and appoint him Patriarch of Lisbon in place of the uncontrollable Policarpo. For a long time a hospital chaplain, Azevedo was neither really liberal nor entirely conservative; he was intellectually respected by everybody, and his rise seemed to be unstoppable, once he had caught the pope's eye.

'Bishop Carlos Azevedo was a voice who was very much listened to, highly respected,' stresses the former minister Guilherme d'Oliveira Martins.

But Benedict XVI had once again found himself a 'closeted' cleric! We could even mock the virtuosity of a man who is an expert, in spite of himself, in the art of surrounding himself with homosexuals who go on to be 'outed' for their double life. Rumours of Azevedo's homosexuality were rife, and fed by another closeted prelate who gossiped to the four winds, out of jealousy, in a kind of ecclesiastical 'revenge porn' at which Catholic bishoprics seem to excel. The rumours were such that Azevedo's career was compromised.

Apparently magnanimous towards prelates who have tendencies, whether active or not, the clerics close to Ratzinger extracted Azevedo to Rome to release him from the noose in which he had inadvertently trapped himself. A post was created, made to measure, and a title found for the unfortunate prelate, thanks to the great understanding of Cardinal Gianfranco Ravasi, who knows the tune: the exiled bishop was appointed '*delegato*' to the Pontifical Council for Culture in Rome. Shortly after this successful and creative extraction, the main Portuguese weekly *Visão* published a detailed investigation into Azevedo's homosexuality back when he lived in Porto. For the first time in the recent history of Portugal, the possible homosexuality of a bishop came out into the open, which was enough to cause a scandal – and to lead to the poor prelate's definitive ostracism. Azevedo was abandoned by all his Portuguese friends, rejected by the nuncio and abandoned to his fate by Cardinal Policarpo, because supporting him would have entailed the risk of falling under suspicion himself.

If there was, in fact, an Azevedo 'scandal', it wasn't in the place where one might have expected to find it: not so much in the possible homosexuality of a bishop, but in the blackmail to which he was subject, and his abandonment by several prelates who shared his inclinations.

'Azevedo was the victim of blackmail or revenge. But he wasn't defended by the episcopate as one might have imagined,' confirms Jorge Wemans, the founder of the daily newspaper *Público*.

I have interviewed the Portuguese bishop in Rome several times, and he told me about his life, his mistakes and his unhappy exile. He now spends his days at the Pontifical Council for Culture and afternoons at the Vatican library, researching ancient Portuguese religious figures. He is moderate, tolerant and an expert in ecumenism: he is an intellectual – there aren't many of those in the Vatican.

Writing these lines, I think of this intelligent bishop whose career has been broken. He couldn't defend himself. He couldn't plead his case before the Italian nuncio in office in Lisbon, a rigid pretentiously arty conservative whose hypocrisy about the case beggars belief. Very dignified, Azevedo has never spoken publicly about his tragedy, made all the more poignant since he was, he tells me, the 'spiritual director' of the man in question. 'The "boy" was an adult,' he adds, 'and there was never any sexual abuse.'

All in all, shouldn't the Church of Rome have defended the bishop, who was a victim? And in the end, if there is any morality in Pope Francis's church, shouldn't Carlos Azevedo now be Patriarch of Lisbon and a cardinal, as most of the Catholic priests and journalists that I met in Portugal believe he should be – a country where gay marriage was adopted once and for all in 2010?

A third example of the battle against gay marriage is Colombia. We are already familiar with this country through the figure of Cardinal Alfonso López Trujillo. In Bogotá, the anti-gay obsession of the Catholic Church didn't fade away with the death of its most homophobic homosexual cardinal; a fact that caused unexpected discord and put Pope Francis in difficulties.

Back in 2015–16 the Vatican was at the centre of a large-scale diplomatic dance trying to put an end to the armed conflict with the FARC guerrillas, which had been going on for over fifty years. Seven million people were displaced, and at least 250,000 murdered during what we must call a civil war.

Along with Venezuela and Norway, the Vatican was involved in the lengthy Colombian peace negotiations that were carried out in Cuba. FARC representatives were accommodated in a Jesuit seminary. Cardinal Ortega in Havana and the Cuban episcopate, the nuncios in office in Colombia, Venezuela and Cuba, as well as the diplomats of the Secretariat of State, took part in negotiations between the government and the guerrillas. Pope Francis was active behind the scenes and received the main participants in the peace process, signed in Cartagena, in September 2016.

And yet, a few days later, the popular referendum that was to confirm the peace agreement was rejected. And it was discovered that the Colombian episcopate, with the cardinals and bishops at their head, had rallied to the 'no' camp and to former president Uribe, a virulent ultra-Catholic and anti-communist, who campaigned with the slogan: 'We want peace, but not this peace.'

The reasons for the rejection by the Catholic authorities have nothing to do with the peace process, which they had nonetheless derailed: for them, the important thing was to denounce gay marriage and abortion. In fact, since the Colombian supreme court had legalized adoption and marriage between people of the same sex, the Catholic Church claimed that the referendum concerning the peace process, if it was favourable to the powers currently in place, would definitively legitimate that policy. Out of pure electoral opportunism, the Church therefore sabotaged the referendum to defend its conservative positions.

As a cherry on the cake, the Colombian Minister of Education, Gina Parody, openly lesbian, at the same time suggested introducing anti-discriminatory policies with regard to LGBT people in schools. This announcement was interpreted by the Colombian Church as an attempt to introduce 'gender theory' into classes. If the peace referendum was adopted, the defence of homosexuality would be too, the representatives essentially said, calling for abstentions or a 'no' vote.

'The Colombian Church has always been allied with the darkest forces in the country, particularly the paramilitaries. This was true in the days of Cardinal Alfonso López Trujillo and it remains true today. Gay marriage and gender theory were only a pretext. They called for the "no" vote because neither the paramilitaries nor the Colombian Church really wanted to contribute to peace. And they went so far as to disavow the pope for that reason,' a Jesuit priest I met in Bogotá rages.

Double-speak and a double game that would reach abyssal depths in crucial European countries – Spain and Italy – to which we will now turn our attention.

16

Rouco

The battle against 'gay marriage' was not played out only in faraway terri-tories such as South Africa or Latin America. It was not confined to the countries of northern Europe, which were often – small consolation for the Vatican – predominantly Protestant. What was more worrying for Rome was that, at the end of John Paul II's pontificate, the debate touched the hard core of Catholicism: Spain, so important in Christian history; and lastly Italy itself, the heart of the papacy, its navel, its centre.

At the end of his interminable pontificate, John Paul II, who was ill by now, impotently witnessed the transformation in public opinion and the debate that was beginning in Spain about same-sex marriage. At the end of his own pontificate, in 2013, Benedict XVI could not help but observe, even more impotently, that France was preparing to adopt the law on gay marriage before Italy did the same for civil unions, shortly after his departure. Same-sex marriage would also come to Italy shortly after.

Between those two dates, homosexual unions became accepted in most of Europe – if not legally in all places, then at least in people's minds.

'¡No pasarán!' The message from Rome was clear. Cardinal Rouco received it loud and clear. In fact, he didn't need much asking. When his friend Angelo Sodano, secretary of state to John Paul II, who had become a second pope in many respects since the holy father's illness, asked to block 'gay marriage' whatever it took, Rouco was already at the head of the 'resistance'. For Rome, It was imperative that Spain not yield. If gay marriage were to be legalized there, the symbol would be so powerful, the effects so considerable, that the whole of Latin America could fall very soon.

'*¡No pasarán!*' is not, in fact, really Rouco's language. This Catholic neo-nationalist was closer to the ideas of the dictator Franco than to those of the Spanish Republicans. But he understood the message, which he would repeat and amplify as intensely as did Cardinal Bertone when he came to replace Sodano.

I went to Spain five times – before, during and after the battle over gay marriage. In 2017, when I came back to Madrid and Barcelona for my last interviews, I found myself at the heart of the election of the president of the Spanish Episcopal Conference. More than ten years had passed since the battle over gay marriage; but the wound didn't seem to have healed. The players were the same; so were the violence, the rigidity, the double lives. As if Catholic Spain were jogging on the spot. And still there, still pulling the strings: Cardinal Rouco. In Spanish, the word is '*titiritero*' – the puppet-master.

Antonio María Rouco Varela was born on the 'camino' of Santiago de Compostela: he grew up in Villalba, in Galicia, in the north-west of Spain, a staging town on the great pilgrimage taken even today by hundreds of thousands of believers. When he was born, in August 1936, the civil war was just beginning in Spain. His authoritarian career, over the decades that followed, was in line with that of many priests at the time, who supported Franco's dictatorship.

From a modest family, with a sick mother and a father who would leave him an orphan prematurely, young Rouco enjoyed a social rise that was far from typical. His education at the minor seminary was strict and conservative – even 'medieval', according to a priest who knows him well. He adds: 'At that time, in Spanish Catholic schools, young boys were told that masturbation, by itself, was an abominable sin. Rouco grew up with this Old Testament mythology, which believed in the flames of hell, where homosexuals would be burned!'

Ordained a priest in 1959, at the age of 22, *hidalgo* Rouco already dreamed of being a knight fighting the infidel, his shield emblazoned with the purple cross and the blood-red sword of the military order of St James – which can be seen even today in the Prado, on the chest of Velázquez himself, in one of the finest paintings in the world: *Las Meninas*.

His biographers know little about the ten years that Rouco then spent in Germany, during the 1960s, where he studied philosophy and theology, particularly with the liberal Jesuit Karl Rahner. During this time he is described as having been a rather moderate priest, socially ill at ease, of a frail constitution, effeminate, depressed, questioning; some even think he was progressive.

Back in Spain, Rouco spent seven years in Salamanca; he was elected bishop under Paul VI. During the 1980s he became close to the Archbishop of Madrid, Ángel Suquía Goicoechea, a conservative chosen by John Paul II to succeed the liberal and anti-Franco Vicente Tarancón. Perhaps for strategic reasons more than out of conviction, he joined the new line in Madrid and the Vatican. And it paid off. He was consecrated Archbishop of Santiago de Compostela at the age of 47 – his dream. Ten years later, he was appointed Archbishop of Madrid and then created cardinal by John Paul II.

I have a meeting with José Manuel Vidal at Robin Hood restaurant in Madrid. The name is written in English, not in Spanish. This free-trade canteen is run by the social centre of Padre Ángel's church of San Antón, which receives the homeless and the '*niños de la calle*'. Vidal, a former priest himself for 13 years, has his meals there to support the association. It's there that we will meet several times.

'Here, at lunchtime, it's a restaurant like any other. In the evening, on the other hand, it's free for the poor. They eat the same things as we do: we pay at lunchtime so they can eat for free in the evening,' Vidal explains.

A child of Vatican II, a Jesuit who became a curé, José Manuel Vidal is also part of this big family, a long, unquiet river that runs unnoticed by many through the 1970s and 1980s: that of priests who left the church to get married. I admire Vidal for his openness in a country where it is generally estimated that one priest in five lives out of wedlock with a woman.

'In my youth, in the 1950s, the Church was the only upward route for the son of a peasant like me,' he says.

The defrocked curé knows the Spanish Church from the inside; he can decode its intrigues, he knows it from every angle, and behind the 'murderous purity' he can spot its tiniest secrets, as in the film *Bad Education* by Almodóvar. Having become a journalist at *El Mundo*, then director of the important online media company Religion Digital – the foremost Catholic website in Spanish around the world – Vidal published a biography of Cardinal Antonio María Rouco Varela. Its title, in large capital letters, as if it were about a character as famous as John Paul II or Franco, is simply: 'ROUCO'.

'My past as a priest granted me access to internal information; my current secularization gives me a liberty that is rare among Spanish ecclesiastics,' Vidal tells me, expertly summing up the situation.

In 626 pages, José Manuel Vidal's investigation is a fascinating snapshot of Catholic Spain from the 1940s until the present day: the collaboration with the fascist dictatorship; the battle against communism; the domination of money and the corruption that infected the clergy; the ravages of celibacy and sexual abuse. And yet Vidal maintains a kindly vision of these priests – of whom he was one – who still believe in God and love their fellow man.

Cardinal Rouco was the most powerful man in the Spanish Catholic Church over a period of 20 years, from his appointment as Archbishop of Madrid in 1994 until his retirement at the behest of Pope Francis in 2014.

'Rouco is a deeply Machiavellian man. He has dedicated his life to the control of the Church in Spain. He had a real court at his disposal; he had money, a lot of money; he had soldiers, troops, a genuine army,' Vidal explains, charting his unusual ascent.

A figure of the '*ancien régime*', in the words of his biographer, Rouco Varela is a deeply anachronistic figure in Spain. Unlike his predecessors, such as Cardinal Vicente Enrique y Tarancón, who was the man of Vatican II and the democratic transition in Spain, he does not seem to have 'made a clean break with Francoism' according to Father Pedro Miguel, a Jesuit that I interviewed in Madrid.

Rouco is a 'rigid-minded opportunist' who chose Rome over Spain', Vidal tells me. He had no scruples about getting Catholics engaged in the political arena: he mobilized the episcopate and soon the whole of the Spanish Church, behind the most sectarian fringe of the Partido Popular – the right wing of the party of José María Azar.

The cornerstone of Rouco's power comes from a combination of four networks: Opus Dei, the Legion of Christ, the Kikos, and finally the organization Communion and Liberation.

Opus Dei has always played an important part in Spain, where this secret fraternity was created in 1928. According to several corroborative testimonies, Rouco is probably not himself a member of Opus Dei, even though he has manipulated 'the Work'. As concerns the Legion, who are more easily influenced because less literate, they formed Rouco's inner circle (the cardinal was a supporter of Marcial Maciel, even after the first revelations of his rapes and paedophilia).

Rouco's third network is known in Spain under the name of 'Los Kikos' (and also under the name of the movement The Neocatechumenate). This is a Catholic youth movement that seeks to return to the sources of ancient Christianity and contests the secularization that is spreading around the world. Finally, the sizeable conservative Catholic movement Communion and Liberation, which was created in Italy, has a strong presence in Spain (its president has been Spanish since 2005).

'These four right-wing movements form the social base of Rouco's power: they constitute his army. Whenever he wanted, "General" Rouco could send them into the street, and the four of them could fill the big squares in Madrid. That was his modus operandi. We worked that out when he launched his battle against gay marriage,' Vidal explains to me.

After the gay marriage debate, Rouco demonstrated his gifts as an organizer during the World Youth Days in 1989, which were held, in fact, in the city of Santiago de Compostela. There, the archbishop did his utmost, and his efficiency impressed Pope John Paul II, who congratulated him publicly in his first address. At the age of 52, Rouco enjoyed his hour of glory and a privilege for which others have waited a lifetime. (Rouco would repeat this charm offensive with Benedict XVI in 2011, for the World Youth Days in Madrid.)

Intellectually, Rouco's way of thinking was based on that of Pope John Paul II, who went on to create him cardinal. Catholicism is besieged by enemies; it must be defended. According to several witnesses, this rock-hard vision of a fortress Church explains the cardinal's rigidity, his authoritarian streak, the mobilization of the troops that involved themselves in street battles on his orders, and his taste for extravagant power and control.

On the question of homosexuality, his genuine obsession, Rouco was in the same line as the Polish pope: homosexuals are not condemned if they choose continence; and if they don't, they should be offered 'reparative therapies' to allow them to attain absolute chastity.

Elected and then re-elected four times to the head of the Spanish Episcopal Conference, Rouco would stay there for 12 years, not counting those when he would continue to pull strings, as a '*titiritero*', without officially having any power (which remains the case today). Still flanked by his secretary, from whom he is inseparable, and his hairdresser, who doesn't leave him alone for a second – '*una bellíssima persona*', as Rouco acknowledged – the archbishop developed a big head. Rouco became a Sodano!

The power of Rouco Varela is Spanish, but it is also Roman. For reasons of ideological inclinations and inclinations pure and simple, Rouco has always held an odour of sanctity at the Vatican. Close to John Paul II and Benedict XVI, who defended him in all circumstances, he was also very close to the cardinals Angelo Sodano and Tarcisio Bertone. Since power attracts power, Rouco had tight control over all the Spanish appointments, and in return the priests and bishops owed their careers to him. The nuncios attended to his every need. And since, as in Spain, the Church measured its power entirely in terms of the relationship between Rome and Madrid, he was now called the 'vice-pope'.

'Rouco governed through fear and the trade in influences. He was always spoken of as a "*traficante de influencias*", a priest in Madrid tells me.

Rouco set out his pieces and deployed his power. He had his '*hombres de placer*' ("men of pleasure"), as the jesters who made the king laugh were known at the court of Spain. His sister's son, Alfonso Carrasco Rouco, was appointed bishop, prompting controversy about nepotism. People started talking about this Rouco as the 'cardinal nephew', which brought back unhappy memories.

And oh, so much money! Like Cardinal López Trujillo, like the Secretaries of State Angelo Sodano and Tarcisio Bertone, Rouco was, in his way, a plutocrat. Thanks to this wealth (and perhaps that of the Spanish Episcopal Conference), he was able to cultivate his power in Rome.

In Spain itself, the Archbishop of Madrid lived like a prince in an 'ático' restored in 2004 for several million euros. This penthouse flat, with its old master paintings, is on the upper storey of the somewhat inappropriately named Palacio de San Justo, an eighteenth-century town house, magnificent admittedly, and beguiling with its late-baroque, rococo style (I saw this palace when I visited Cardinal Osoro, Rouco's successor).

'It's impossible to gauge from abroad what a shock Francis's election has been for the Spanish episcopate,' Vidal explains to me. 'The bishops lived here like princes, beyond good and evil. All dioceses here are grandiose palaces, and the Spanish Church has an unimaginable property portfolio everywhere, in Madrid, Toledo, Seville, Segovia, Granada, Santiago de Compostela … And there was Francis asking them to become poor, to leave their palaces, to return to pastoral values and to humility. What matters to them here, with this new Latino pope, isn't so much doctrine, because they've always been very accommodating in that respect; no, what matters to them is having to remove themselves from luxury, to stop being princes, to leave their palaces, and, horror of horrors, having to start to serve the poor!'

If the election of Francis was a shock for the Spanish Church, for Rouco it was a tragedy. A friend of Ratzinger's, he was startled by his renunciation of the papacy, which he had never imagined in his worst nightmares. And from the election of the new pope, the Cardinal Archbishop of Madrid is said to have uttered this dramatic line, as reported by the press: 'The conclave escaped us.'

He probably knew what to expect! Within a few months Pope Francis had ordered Rouco's retirement. He began by removing him from the Congregation of Bishops, a choice position that allowed him to decide on the appointment of all the Spanish prelates. Marginalized in the Vatican, Rouco was also asked to leave his post as Archbishop of Madrid, which he had been clinging on to in spite of the age limit. Then, furiously accusing all those who had betrayed him, he imperiously demanded to be able to choose his successor and suggested three names *sine qua non* to the nuncio in Spain. The list came back from Rome with four names, none of which Rouco had suggested!

But the hardest thing was still to come. The most unthinkable punishment for this prince of the Church was to follow from the highest echelons, from Rome itself: he was asked to leave his Madrid penthouse. Like Angelo Sodano and Tarcisio Bertone in Rome, in similar circumstances, he refused categorically, and let things drift. Pressed by the nuncio, Rouco suggested that his successor should live on the floor below his, which would allow him to stay where he lived, in his palace. Once again the holy see refused: Rouco had to get out and leave his luxury apartment in the Palacio de San Justo to the new Archbishop of Madrid, Carlos Osoro.

Was Cardinal Rouco an exception, an extreme case, as some people in Spain claim today, to clear him, and try and make people forget about his escapades and his sumptuous lifestyle? It would be nice to think so. And yet this evil genius is rather the product of a system produced by the pontificate of John Paul II, where men were intoxicated by power and bad habits, without any opposing force to halt their deviations. In this, Rouco was not very different from a López Trujillo or an Angelo Sodano. Opportunism and Machiavellianism, of which he was a master, were tolerated, if not encouraged, by Rome.

The frame of reference here is threefold once again: ideological, financial and homophilic. For a long time, Rouco had been in step with the Vatican of John Paul II and Benedict XVI. He adhered without hesitation to the war on communism and the struggle against liberation theology as decreed by Wojtyła; he espoused the anti-gay ideas of Ratzinger's pontificate; he associated with Stanisław Dziwisz and Georg Gänswein, the famous private secretaries to the popes. Rouco was the essential link for their policies in Spain, their ally, their servant and their host at a luxury chalet in Tortosa, south of Barcelona (according to three first-hand testimonies).

His entourage was homophilic and his friendships particular. Here, again, we find a template also seen in Italy and many countries around the world. In the 1950s and 1960s, Spanish homosexuals frequently chose the seminary to escape their condition or persecution. Around Rouco, there were many crypto-gays who had found refuge in the Church.

'Under Franco, who was in appearance a very pious, very Catholic dictator, homosexuality was a crime, There were arrests, prison sentences, homosexuals sent to labour camps. So for many young homosexuals, the priesthood seemed like the only solution against persecution. Many became priests. That was the key, the rule, the model,' Vidal explains.

Another Jesuit priest I interviewed in Barcelona said to me: 'Everyone who had been called a "*maricón*" in the streets of their village ended up in the seminary.'

Was this case of the Stations of the Cross along the road of Santiago de Compostela taken by Rouco himself? The way of sublimated homophilia in the style of Maritain or internalized homophobia in the style of Alfonso López Trujillo (a close friend of Rouco, who came to see him often in Madrid)? We don't know.

'I investigated the subject at length,' Vidal goes on. 'Rouco was never interested in girls: women were always invisible to him. His misogyny was disturbing. So the vow of chastity with women wasn't a problem for him. As regards men, there were a lot of troubling things, a lot of gay people around him, but no traces of real inclinations. My hypothesis is that Rouco was completely asexual.'

It was in this context, between 2004 and 2005, at the end of John Paul II's pontificate, that Rouco launched himself into the Spanish battle against gay marriage.

'We would have to see that for Sodano, and then for Ratzinger and Bertone, the proposed law in favour of marriage in Spain immediately appeared as an unspeakable peril,' Vidal observes. 'They feared a snowball effect on the whole of Latin America. For them, gay marriage had to be stopped here, in Spain, before the contagion spread everywhere. They were terrified by the risk of a domino effect. The man of the moment, as far as they were concerned, was Rouco. He was the only man capable of stopping gay marriage once and for all.'

Rouco wouldn't disappoint them. No sooner had Prime Minister Zapatero spoken up in favour of gay marriage in 2004 (he had put it in his election programme without imagining that he could be elected, and didn't really believe in same-sex marriage himself) than he found Rouco Varela in his way. And he made his first demonstration of strength, without a word of warning. With his 'Kikos', his Legion of Christ and the help of Opus Dei, the cardinal incited the common people to stage protests. Hundreds of thousands of Spaniards turned up in the streets of Madrid in the name of '*la familia sí importa*'. Twenty bishops would march with the crowds against gay marriage during this period.

With his first successes, Rouco felt that his strategy had been vindicated. Rome applauded loudly. There were more demonstrations in 2004, and doubts began to take hold in public opinion. Pope Ratzinger congratulated Rouco via his personal secretary Georg Gänswein. Rouco had won his bet: the Zapatero government was at a dead end.

'Rouco really became our *bête noire* at that moment. He had brought the bishops into the street; this was something unthinkable for us,' I am told by Jesús Generelo, the president of the main federation of LGBT associations in Spain, a man close to the political left.

But in spring 2005, the situation changed. Did the bishops go too far in speaking out? Were the banners in the street too over the top? Did the religious mobilization remind them of the Francoism that had also claimed to fight in favour of the family and Catholic values?

'Rouco's main mistake was to bring the bishops into the street. Franco had done that too. The Spaniards immediately interpreted the message: it was the return of fascism. The image was devastating, and public opinion turned,' according to José Manuel Vidal.

After a curious war lasting several months, the media opted in favour of gay marriage. The newspapers, some of which were connected to the episcopate, began to criticize the demonstrations and caricature their leaders.

Cardinal Rouco himself became the favoured target. His vehemence on the issue won him the unlikely nickname of 'Rouco Siffredi' (after the Italian pornographic actor Rocco Siffredi), even among priests (according to the testimony of one of them). On the internet, the cardinal was endlessly caricatured: he became 'Rouco Clavel', queen of the day, an allusion to the actor Paco Clavel, queen of the night, a famous singer of La Movida, an occasional transvestite and always extravagantly dressed. 'He's Rouco Varela by day and Paco Clavel by night' became a fashionable slogan. The Church was losing the support of the young and the big cities; the elite of the country and the business classes were also switching, to avoid seeming uncool. Soon, polls showed that two-thirds of Spaniards supported the proposed law (the figure is now about 80 per cent).

Rome, following the debates day by day, was starting to become alarmed by the turn that things were taking. Rouco was accused of going too far, and of letting the furious bishops overstep the mark. The new secretary of state, Tarcisio Bertone, who travelled to Madrid as a matter of urgency, met Zapatero and asked Rouco to 'calm down'. That the new strong man in the Vatican, the closest collaborator of Pope Benedict XVI, himself very homophobic, wanted to moderate Rouco was a highly unusual situation.

It has to be said that behind the bellicose slogans and violently anti-gay-marriage banners, the Spanish episcopate was in fact more divided than it admitted. Rouco lost the support of his own Church. So the new cardinal, Carlos Amigo, and the Bishop of Bilbao, Ricardo Blázquez (who would be created cardinal by Francis in 2015), disputed his line. Fernando Sebastián, the Archbishop of Pamplona (whom Francis would also make a cardinal in 2014) – a left-wing prelate and serious theologian, and a former scribe to Cardinal Tarancón – even attacked Rouco's strategy head-on, comparing it to a return to the old regime – meaning Francoism.

Of course Sebastián, Amigo and Blázquez disapproved of same-sex marriage, which Zapatero supported, but they also contested the mobilization of bishops in the street. They thought that the Church should stay out of politics, even if it could give its ethical point of view on social issues.

Cardinal Rouco engaged in a power struggle within the Spanish Episcopal Conference, supported by two of his lieutenants. Let's linger for a moment on the case of these two men, major figures in the Spanish Church who would both be removed from their posts by Francis. Because nowhere but in Spain could the battle be so fierce between the Ratzingerians and the pro-Francis faction, and nowhere else would it be so dependent on the 'rigid men who lead a double life'.

The first is Antonio Cañizares, Archbishop of Toledo and Primate of Spain. This friend of Rouco's was also close to Cardinal Ratzinger, so much so that in Spain he was known as 'little Ratzinger' (Benedict XVI would create him cardinal in 2006). Like the American Cardinal Burke, Cañizares liked to wear the cappa magna, the cardinals' bridal dress which, worn with veils flying, could measure up to several metres long and on major occasions is held by choirboys and handsome seminarians.

'Since Cañizares is very small, seeing him in his long dress makes him look even more ridiculous. It makes him look like Mari Bárbola!' a renowned journalist tells me (referring to the dwarf in *Las Meninas*; a bad joke that several others repeated to me).

There were many statements critical of Cañizares and rumours about the make-up of his entourage. Several complaints were made against him by MPs and LGBT associations for his homophobic remarks and 'incitement to hatred'. One struggles to understand whether such a cardinal served the Christian cause or caricatured it. In any case, shortly after his election, Francis chose to remove him from Rome, where he was prefect of the Congregation for Divine Worship and the Discipline of the Sacraments, and sent him back to Spain. He loudly demanded that he be appointed to the archbishopric of Madrid; Francis crossed him off the list and appointed him to Valencia.

The cardinal's right-hand man was even more of a caricature, and more extremist if that's possible. Bishop Juan Antonio Reig Pla waged the anti-gay-marriage battle in his own way: with the subtlety of a drag queen barging into the changing room at Barça.

Outraged by gay marriage and 'gender ideology', Reig Pla denounced homosexuals with apocalyptic violence. He published testimonies from people who had been 'cured' thanks to 'reparative therapies'. He compared homosexuality to paedophilia. Later, he would even claim, on prime-time television, prompting a national scandal, that 'homosexuals will go to hell'.

'Bishop Reig Pla is his own caricature. He was the best ally of the gay movement during the battle for gay marriage. Every time he opened his mouth he won us supporters. We were lucky to have adversaries like him!' one of the directors of a Madrid gay association tells me.

The spiritual battle and the battle of men that was fought in the country between these six cardinals and prelates, Rouco-Cañizares-Reig versus Amigo-Blázquez-Sebastián, profoundly marked Catholic Spain in the 2000s. It also exposed the fault line between Benedict XVI and Francis, and even today it remains so powerful that it explains most of the tensions that exist within the Spanish episcopate. (During the last election of the Spanish Episcopal Conference, when I was back in Madrid, Blázquez was once again re-elected president and Cañizares vice-president, a way of preserving the balance between the pro- and anti-Francis forces.)

Despite the exceptional mobilization conducted by Cardinal Rouco Varela, on 2 July 2005 Spain became the third country in the world, after the Netherlands and Belgium, to open marriage up to all same-sex couples. On 11 July, the first marriage was celebrated, and almost five thousand couples would marry over the next year. It was a shattering defeat for the conservative wing of the Spanish episcopate. (A constitutional submission originating in the Partido Popular and supported by the Church would be subsequently presented: the decision of the supreme court judges, by eight votes to three, was incontrovertible, and a definitive victory for the supporters of gay marriage.)

Since that date the question of gay marriage has remained the main dividing line in the Spanish Church. In order to understand it, however, we need to think about it counter-intuitively: not believe that 'gay' bishops are necessary in the clan of defenders of gay marriage, and that 'hetero' prelates would be hostile to it. The rule, as always, is rather the reverse: it is the noisiest and the most anti-gay who are usually the most suspect.

The Spanish episcopate is, like all the rest, highly homosexualized. Among the thirteen cardinals that the country currently has (four are electors and nine non-electors of over 80), people who know the field estimate that most of them are homophile, at least five being practising. As for the battle that has been played out over gay marriage between the camps Rouco-Cañizares-Reig on the one hand and Amigo-Blázquez-Sebastián on the other, at least four of the six key players are homophilic. (Apart from about a hundred interviews that I carried out in Madrid and Barcelona, here I am using the testimony of someone close to Cardinal Osoro, as well as information from within the Spanish Episcopal Conference communicated by one of its directors.)

Still, Pope Francis was very familiar with the Spanish episcopate, its frenzies, its charlatans and its sweethearts, and had decrypted its codes. So, from his election in 2013, he would undertake a major house-cleaning in Spain.

The three moderate cardinals that he created (Osoro, Blázquez and Omella) confirm that he brought it under control. The apostolic nuncio Fratino Renzo, whose way of life, golf parties and associations dismayed Francis, was totally bypassed (and his departure already planned). As for the pedlar of bogus 'reparative' therapies bishop Reig Pla, who was waiting to be made cardinal, he went on waiting.

'We're at the start of a new transition!' José Beltrán Aragoneses, editor-in-chief of *Vida Nueva*, the journal of the Spanish Episcopal Conference, tells me.

The new Archbishop of Barcelona, Juan José Omella y Omella – using prudent, diplomatic and slightly coded tones – confirms the change of line to me when he receives me in his beautiful office beside the Catalan cathedral.

'Since the council, the Spanish episcopate has learned its lesson: we aren't politicians. We don't want to intervene in political life, even if we can express our thought from a moral point of view … [But] I think we must be sensitive to people's concerns. Not engage on the political level, or at least respectfully. Respect, not a belligerent attitude, not a warlike attitude. [On the contrary] we need an attitude of welcome, of dialogue, not one of judgement, as Francis has reminded us [with his 'Who am I to judge?']. We have to help to build a better society and resolve problems, always bearing the poorest in mind.'

His words are skilful, surgical. The Rouco page has turned. Omella, formerly a missionary in Zaire, was the new strong man in Spanish Catholicism. The one who refused to go into the street to demonstrate against homosexual marriage was made a cardinal by Francis. He would be based at the Congregation of Bishops, in place of the conservative

Cañizares, who had been transferred from the office. Intransigent against sexual abuse by priests, more suspicious about double lives, Omella is also more tolerant of gays.

During one of my trips to Madrid, when the bishops were tearing themselves apart over the election of their new president within the Spanish Episcopal Conference (CEE), an important LGBT association threatened to publish a list of the Spanish *'obispos rosa'* (pink bishops). The promised 'outing' barely elicited a reaction; everyone in the local media had long known what to expect! And no matter what happened, it was largely assumed that one of them would be elected at the episcopal conference!

One evening I was present at a live broadcast in the studios of COPE, a popular radio station owned by the Spanish Episcopal Conference. I was surprised that the election of the new president of the CEE appeared to be an event in Spain (when it didn't provoke the slightest interest in France). Faustino Catalina Salvador, the editor-in-chief of religious programmes at COPE, predicted victory for Cardinal Blázquez, the pro-Francis camp; other participants – the Ratzingerian and pro-Rouco wing – forecast that it would be Cañizares.

After the broadcast, I continued the conversation with some of the journalists on the talk show that I had just witnessed. I was surprised to hear people saying of one Spanish cardinal or another that he was *'en el armario'* or *'enclosetado'* (in the closet). Everyone was aware of it, and spoke almost openly about the homosexuality of certain prelates. The gay question even appeared to be one of the underlying themes, one of the issues, in the election of the new president of the episcopal conference!

'People think that Francis's man in Spain is Osoro. That's not the case. Francis's man is Omella y Omella,' says an important executive in the CEE, himself homosexual, with whom I also spend several evenings talking.

Slightly apart from all these debates, and keeping his own counsel, the Archbishop of Madrid, Carlos Osoro, was the great loser in this CEE election. When I meet him for an interview, I understand that this complicated man, who comes from the 'right' wing but is allied with

Francis, is trying to find his feet. Like all the new converts to Pope Francis, who created him cardinal, he wants to establish his credentials. And to show signs of goodwill to Rome on the subject of pastoral care, he went to see Padre Ángel's church of the 'poor' in the gay quarter of Chueca. The day when I went there, it was filled with homeless people, happy to find a place where they had access to toilets, hot coffee, Wi-Fi, biscuits for their dogs, all for free. 'A red carpet for the poor', said the CEE priest who accompanied me. 'Homosexuals also attend this church. It's the only one that treats them well', he tells me.

Before, the church of San Antón was closed, abandoned, like many small isolated Catholic churches in Spain. The crisis in priestly vocations is alarming; there are fewer and fewer parishioners everywhere (fewer than 12 per cent of Spaniards are still practising, according to the demographers); the churches are empty; and the many cases of sexual abuse are eating into the episcopacy. Spanish Catholicism is in dangerous decline in one of the countries in the world where it was once most influential.

'Rather than leaving the church closed, Cardinal Osoro gave it to Padre Ángel. That was a brilliant idea. It's come back to life since then. There are gays all the time, gay priests, mixed with the homeless and the poor of Madrid. Padre Ángel told the gays and the transgender people that they were welcome, that this church was their house, so they came!' the priest goes on.

Here we have the 'peripheries' dear to Pope Francis reintegrated into a city-centre church that is called '*la casa de todos*'. Cardinal Osoro, now gay-friendly, even shook hands with members of the Crismhom association who gather there (masses for homosexuals are currently celebrated in Madrid by a gay priest, as I have been able to confirm). The cardinal was a bit tense but he 'did the job', according to several witnesses.

'We swapped a few words and a few phone numbers,' a regular member of the church confirms.

Osoro's assistant also told me he was worried about the fact that 'the cardinal was giving his number to everybody: half the people in Madrid have his mobile and Osoro gave it to me too', when we met.

'Padre Ángel even held the funeral of Pedro Zerolo in his church. It was very moving. The whole of the gay community, the whole quarter of Chueca, a stone's throw away, came with rainbow flags,' the Spanish priest from the CEE goes on.

Zerolo, whose photograph I have often seen in the offices of the LGBT associations in Madrid, is considered to be the icon of the Spanish gay movement. He was one of the architects of gay marriage and married his partner a few months before he died of cancer. And the priest adds: 'His funeral was magnificent and very moving. But that day, Cardinal Osoro, rather annoyed, told Padre Ángel that he was perhaps going too far.'

17

CEI

All of a sudden, the Italian cardinal Angelo Bagnasco takes his ring off his right ring finger and spontaneously gives it to me. With a jeweller's precision, this crumpled little man holds out the ring in the palm of his hand, and I take the ring in the hollow of mine. I admire it. The scene is played out at the end of our conversation, while we are talking about cardinals' outfits and the cardinal's ring. For a bishop, it isn't the 'Fisherman's Ring', which is reserved for the pope, but the mark of a privileged relationship with the faithful. It replaces the wedding ring, perhaps to indicate that they have married their flock. At that precise moment, without his attributes and the symbol of his episcopal responsibilities, does the cardinal feel as if he's laid bare and under scrutiny?

If his watch is a luxury one, and his bishop's chain – with its equally luxurious precious metal pectoral cross – Angelo Bagnasco's ring is simpler than I would ever have dreamed. On the ring fingers of many cardinals and archbishops whom I've visited, I have seen stones so precious, so daring in their amethyst green, yellow ruby and violet emerald colours, that I wondered if they weren't just bits of transparent quartz painted in Marrakesh. I've seen rings on twisted fingers, homophilic cardinals wearing a garnet ring which, they said, kept devils at bay, and, on the hands of closeted cardinals, bezel set rings with goldstones. And what bezels! They all know that it would be a mistake to put the rings on their thumbs. Or on their index fingers!

It has to be said that all dog-collars and all clerical attire look the same. And even if Maria, one of the saleswomen in De Ritis, a renowned shop selling priestly garments near the Pantheon in Rome, struggled to explain to me the difference in cut and form, to the eye of a layman like me there is little difference between these frowsty garments. There isn't much variety in their outfits – not all cardinals are as daring as His Eminence Raymond Burke – so the senior prelates compensate for this shortcoming with jewels. And what jewels! A real 'rain of the wind of diamonds' as a Poet writes! What elegance, what style, what taste in the choice of sizes, assortments and colours. This sapphire, this amethyst, this Balay ruby, these stones are so fine, so well-worked, that they fit their equally precious wearers like a glove. And how much value is concentrated here, turning these men, guilty as they are of such gentle larceny, into veritable safes? Sometimes I have seen strait-laced prelates wearing spectacular pectoral crosses, with their diamonds, and twisting or interlaced biblical creatures, making them look as if they've come out of a drawing by Tom of Finland. And such variety too, in the cuff-links, so conspicuous that the prelates, surprised by their own audacity, are reluctant to wear them for fear of giving themselves away.

Angelo Bagnasco's ring is simple and beautiful. It isn't a dazzling rectangle, or gold enclosing a diamond like some that Pope Benedict XVI wore. Such simplicity is surprising when we know our man.

'Cardinals spend a lot of time choosing their rings. Often they have them made to measure. It's an important step and sometimes a considerable financial investment,' says one of the salesmen at Barbiconi, a famous merchant of ecclesiastical habits, pectoral crosses and rings, on Via Santa Caterina da Siena in Rome. And he adds, like a shopkeeper: 'You don't have to be a priest to buy a ring!'

When I visited him, Cardinal Jean-Louis Tauran wore not only a Cartier ring and an ecumenical cross given to him by his close friend, an Anglican priest, but also a sublime solitaire ring, green and gold, on his right ring finger.

'I attach very great sentimental value to this ring that you see there,' Tauran said to me. 'I had it made from the wedding rings of my father and mother, fused together. From this material, the jeweller made my cardinal's ring.'

As I discovered in the course of my investigation, some prelates have only one ring. With humility, they engrave on the obverse the figure of

Christ, a saint or an apostle, for example; sometimes they prefer to have a crucifix or the cross of their religious order; on the reverse, you can see their episcopal coat of arms or, for a cardinal, under his ligature, the arms of the pope who created him cardinal. Other cardinals have several rings, a veritable panoply; they change them according to the occasion, as they change their cassocks.

This eccentricity is easily understood. Bishops who wear such beautiful pearls remind me of the veiled women I have seen in Iran, Qatar, the United Arab Emirates or Saudi Arabia. The strictness of Islam, which extends not only to hair, and to the thickness and wideness of the hijab, but also to the length of shirt-sleeves or dresses, transfers female elegance to the veil, whose brilliant colours, enticing shapes and the expensiveness of cashmere, pure silk or angora fabrics are the paradoxical consequence. The same is true of these Catholic bishops: constrained by their Playmobil vestments, dog-collar and black shoes, they let their imagination run riot with rings, watches and cuff-links.

Dressed to the nines, his hair perfectly combed, Cardinal Bagnasco receives me in his private residence at Via Pio VIII, a cul-de-sac located behind the Vatican that takes me a good twenty minutes to get to on foot from St Peter's Square in Rome. The road was steep and sunlit, delaying my arrival; besides, the cardinal has set the time of our meeting, rather imperiously, as prelates often do, not suggesting any alternative, but imposing his own timetable, with no room for discussion – even Italian ministers are more accommodating and hospitable! For these reasons, I arrive late for our meeting, having worked up a slight sweat. The cardinal invites me to use his bathroom. And it's at that moment that I am submerged in a cloud of scent.

He is refined and flirtatious, well-pomaded. I had been told of the perfumes of Cardinal Bagnasco – woody, amber, cypress or citric – and now I understand why. Is it Egoiste by Chanel, La Nuit de L'homme by Yves Saint-Laurent, or Vétiver by Guerlain? Anyway, the cardinal likes to swathe himself in perfume. Rabelais used to mock the flatulence of Italian prelates! He would never have imagined that we would one day mock them for smelling like divas!

Essentially, perfumes fulfil more or less the same function as rings. They allow uniqueness when clerical attire imposes uniformity. Amber, violet, musk, champaca – all these I have discovered in the Vatican. How many oils! How many scents! What a riot of perfumes! But doesn't anointing yourself with Opium immediately constitute a discreet admission of addiction?

For a long time Angelo Bagnasco was the most powerful and most senior dignitary in the Italian Church. More than any other bishop in his country, he was the grand vizier of 'Spaghetti Catholicism' (a term sometimes used for Italian Catholicism to distinguish it from the Catholicism of the holy see). He has made and unmade careers; has co-created cardinals.

In 2003, he was appointed archbishop for the armed forces, a post which, he says, filled him 'with trepidation' because it was a 'huge diocese', which consisted in evangelizing 'soldiers everywhere in Italy and even beyond with the military missions abroad'. Appointed Archbishop of Genoa in 2006, replacing Tarcisio Bertone when he became secretary of state to Benedict XVI, Bagnasco was then created cardinal by the pope, to whom he is said to have been close. Most importantly, for ten years, between 2007 and 2017, he presided over the Italian Episcopal Conference – the famous 'CEI'. Until he was removed from it by Pope Francis.

His heart is warmed by the fact that a French writer and journalist should come to see him after this forced retirement, even though he is proscribed and banished. He doesn't speak French, or English, or Spanish, or any foreign language, unlike the majority of cardinals, but he does his best to explain himself, translated by Daniele, my Italian researcher.

Cardinal Bagnasco is a man in a hurry, one of those people who throw sugar lumps into their coffee without bothering to take off the paper, just to save some time. Those who know him but don't like him have described him to me as an irascible and vindictive man, a man of great cunning, a 'passive authoritarian', according to a priest who knew him well at the CEI, where he alternated carrot and stick to impose his views. But he is courteous and patient with us. Bagnasco constantly taps his foot, faster and faster. Out of boredom or because he would like to speak ill of the pope but is holding himself back?

Since his fall, Bagnasco has been seeking a new paradise. Having been a cynical ally of Benedict XVI and Cardinal Bertone, he now rebukes them for hurling the Church into a venture into the unknown with Francis. It is no compliment for either.

Of course, the ringed and cuff-linked cardinal barely criticizes his co-religionists, let alone the pope, when speaking to us. But his facial expressions betray his thoughts. So when I mention the name of Cardinal Walter Kasper and his geopolitical ideas, Bagnasco cuts me off, his face contorted with disdain. The name of the most progressive of his opponents provokes such an explicit grimace that, inadvertently, Bagnasco is living proof that men and monkeys have a common ancestry.

'He isn't someone who knows diplomacy,' Bagnasco says, simply and succinctly.

And when we start talking about the tensions within the Italian Episcopal Conference, and Cardinal Bertone's attempts to regain control of the CEI, Bagnasco turns towards Daniele and says about me, in Italian, while uneasily testing the atmosphere: '*Il ragazzo è ben informato!*' (The boy is well-informed.)

Bagnasco darts me a meaningful look. One of those looks that are strange, decisive and completely different. It's one of those moments when a cardinal's eyes meet mine, as has happened to me several times. They stare at me, study me, penetrate me. It takes only an instant, a second, but something happens. Cardinal Bagnasco wonders, looks at me, hesitates.

The cardinal lowers his eyes and measures his words: 'Cardinal Bertone wanted to deal with relations between the Church and the Italian government. But I continued on my way. The Italian Episcopal Conference (CEI) is in charge of the questions related to the Italian government and it is not the business of the Vatican!' (This point has been confirmed to me by Cardinal Giuseppe Betori, former secretary general of the CEI, whom I interviewed in Florence.)

And after a pause, the cardinal who dreamed of being '*papabile*', but had to lower his ambitions, specifically targeting Bertone, adds: 'When you're in the Curia, when you're in the Vatican, you're no longer in the CEI. And when you've been in the Curia, and when you've finished your mission, you can't go back to the CEI. It's over.'

Now we talk about homosexual civil unions, of which I know Cardinal Bagnasco was the chief opponent in Italy. And, playing at being daring, I ask if the Church's position has evolved with Pope Francis.

'Our position on civil unions was the same ten years ago as it is today,' the cardinal sharply declares.

Now Bagnasco is trying to convince me of the sound foundation of his position. He launches into a long exposition to justify the discrimination against homosexuality encouraged by the Italian Church, as if the CEI were independent of the Vatican. A passable theologian but a poor philosopher, he quotes the Gospels and the Catholic Catechism to support his thesis (with some pertinence) and relies on the thought of the philosophers Habermas and John Rawls (whom he paraphrases shamelessly). As with most cardinals – Kasper being an exception – I am struck by the philosophical mediocrity of his thought: he instrumentalizes authors, has read the texts at a slant and, for ideological reasons, retains only a few arguments from a complex and anachronistic reasoning; so much so that I feel as if Bagnasco is about to quote from *The Origin of Species*, a book that I saw in the library of his waiting room, in a bid to prohibit gay marriage on the basis of evolution!

Slightly hunched, cunning in my own way, I now question Cardinal Bagnasco, leading him gently away from the topic at hand, to talk about Francis's appointments and his personal situation. What does he think of the fact that in order to be created cardinal under Benedict XVI you had to be anti-gay, while under Francis you have to be gay-friendly?

The great paymaster of anti-gay demonstrations in Italy looks at me: he smiles through gritted teeth. Bagnasco seems startled by my question but doesn't give himself away. His body language speaks for him. We leave on good terms with a promise to see each other again. Always a man in a hurry, he takes our email addresses and, twice, Daniele's mobile number.

The Italian Episcopal Conference (CEI) is an empire in an empire. For a long time, it was even the kingdom itself. Since the election of the Pole Wojtyła, followed by that of the German Ratzinger and then the Argentinian Bergoglio, after the Italians had run out of popes, the CEI has remained the antechamber of power of the outdated theocracy that is the Vatican. A matter of geopolitics and global balance.

Unless, that is, the cardinals of the CEI have been chased from power after exercising it too imprudently, with Angelo Sodano and Tarcisio Bertone? Or are they now being made to pay for their hypocritical life-styles and their murderous settling of scores, which perverted Italian Catholicism and perhaps cost John Paul I his life and Benedict XVI his crown?

It remains the case that the CEI is no longer producing popes, and is yielding fewer and fewer cardinals. That may change one day, but for now the Italian episcopate is restricted to the country itself. Almost inconsolable, these cardinals and bishops nevertheless draw consolation from the amount of work that remains to be accomplished at home. There is so much to do. To begin with: fighting against gay marriage.

Since Bagnasco was elected to the presidency of the CEI, shortly after the election of Benedict XVI, civil unions have become one of the main concerns of the Italian episcopate. Like Rouco in Spain, like Barbarin in France, Bagnasco chose a power struggle: he wanted to go into the street and mobilize the crowd. He is cleverer than Rouco and more rigid than Barbarin, but he has steered a steady course.

It has to be said that the CEI, with its properties, its media, its soft power, its moral ascendancy, and its thousands of bishops and priests installed in even the tiniest villages, enjoys an extraordinary amount of power in Italy. It also carries a crucial amount of political weight, which often goes hand in hand with all the abuse and insider influence in that country.

'The CEI has always intervened in Italian political life. It is rich, it is powerful. The priest and the politician walk side by side in Italy, where they're still stuck in *Don Camillo!*' Pierre Morel, former French ambassador to the holy see, says ironically.

All the witnesses I have interviewed – in the episcopate, the Italian parliament and the cabinet of the prime minister – confirm this crucial influence in Italian public life. This was notably the case, under John Paul II, when Cardinal Camillo Ruini, Bagnasco's predecessor, was president of the episcopal conference: the golden age of the CEI.

'Cardinal Ruini was the Italian voice of John Paul II and he held the Italian parliament in his hands. Those were the great years of the CEI. Since Bagnasco, under Benedict XVI, that power has diminished. Under

Francis, it has vanished completely,' I am told by a prelate who lives in the Vatican and knows the two former presidents of the CEI.

Archbishop Rino Fisichella, who was also one of the directors of the CEI, confirms this point to me in the course of two interviews: 'Cardinal Ruini was a pastor. He had a profound intelligence and a clear political vision. John Paul II trusted him. Ruini was the chief collaborator with John Paul II when it came to Italian affairs.'

A diplomat in office in Rome, who is well acquainted with the Vatican machine, confirms in turn: 'At the start of the pontificate, Cardinal Ruini broadly said to John Paul II: "I'll relieve you of Italian affairs, but I want all of them, the lot." Having got what he wanted, he did the job. And he even did it very well.'

From Cardinal Camillo Ruini's dining room, the view of the Vatican gardens is as spectacular as it is strategic. We are on the first floor of the Pontificio Seminario Romano Minore, a luxury penthouse on the edge of the Vatican.

'It's a fabulous place for me. You can look down on the Vatican, but you're not inside it. You're right next to it, you're very close, but you're outside it,' Ruini says, straight-faced.

To meet the 88-year-old cardinal, I had to send countless letters and make numerous phone-calls – all in vain. Somewhat disconcerted by the constant lack of response, which is rather unusual in the Church, in the end I left the 'white book' as a present for the retired cardinal with the porter, and added a short note. Eventually, his assistant arranged a meeting for me, adding that 'his eminence has agreed to receive you because of the beauty of your writing in blue fountain pen.' So the cardinal was an aesthete!

'I was at the head of the CEI for 21 years,' Ruini tells me in excellent French. 'It's true that, thanks to me, and thanks to favourable circumstances, I was able to turn the CEI into an important organization. John Paul II trusted me. He always trusted me. He was a father to me, a grandfather. He was an example of strength, wisdom and love of God.'

Visibly happy to engage in conversation with a French writer, the old cardinal takes his time (and when I leave at the end of our interview he will write down his private telephone number on a little piece of paper, encouraging me to come back and see him).

In the meantime, Ruini tells me the story of his career: how he was a young theologian; his passion for Jacques Maritain and the French thinkers; the importance of John Paul II, whose death, as cardinal vicar of Rome, as tradition decrees, he was the first to announce by a 'special declaration' (before the substitute Leonardo Sandri made the official announcement in St Peter's); the history of the CEI and his 'cultural project'; but also the deconfessionalization and the secularization that considerably weakened the influence of the Italian Church. Without acrimony, but with a certain melancholy, he talked about the glorious past and the decline of Catholicism today. 'The times have changed,' he adds, not without some sadness.

I question the cardinal on the influence of the CEI and on his own role.

'I think my ability lay in the art of government. I was always capable of making decisions, or taking a direction and going ahead. That was my strength.'

We talked often about the money of the CEI, the key to its influence.

'The CEI is money,' a senior figure in the Vatican confirms to me.

Which Ruini acknowledges without hesitation: 'The Concordat between the Italian state and the Church gave a lot of money to the CEI.'

We also talk about politics, and the cardinal insists on his connections with Christian Democracy, as well as with Romano Prodi and Silvio Berlusconi. For several decades he has known all the heads of the Italian parliament!

'There was a real interpenetration between the Italian Church and Italian politics; that's the problem, that's what perverted everything,' one of the Italian priests, Ménalque (his name has been changed), who was at the heart of the CEI, explains to me.

Ménalque was one of the most interesting people I met whilst preparing this book. This priest was at the centre of the CEI machine during the years when Cardinal Camillo Ruini, then Cardinal Angelo Bagnasco, were presidents. He had a front-row seat. Today, Ménalque is a priest who has become bitter, if not anti-clerical, a complex and unexpected figure of the kind that the Vatican produces with disconcerting regularity. He chose to talk to me and describe in detail, from the inside, at first hand, the working of the CEI. Why did he talk? For several reasons, as with several of those who speak in this book: first of all, because of his homosexuality, now accepted, post-coming out, which makes 'the homophobia of the CEI' intolerable to him; then, to denounce the hypocrisy of many prelates and cardinals in the CEI, whom he knows better than anyone, anti-gay in public and homosexual in private. Lots of them have made passes at him, and he knows the opaque codes and rules concerning *droits de seigneur* within the CEI. Ménalque is speaking like this for the first time because he has lost his faith, and because, having paid a heavy price for that loss – unemployment, friends who turn their back on you, isolation – he felt betrayed. I interviewed him for over ten hours, three times, at an interval of several months, far from Rome, and became attached to this unhappy priest. He was the first to reveal to me a secret that I would never have imagined. And here is the secret: in his view, the CEI is intrinsically an organization that is predominantly gay.

'Like many Italian priests, like the majority of them, I entered the seminary because I had a problem with my sexuality,' Ménalque tells me during one of our lunches. 'I didn't know what it was, and it took me a long time to find out. Of course it was repressed homosexuality, an internal repression so powerful that it wasn't just inexpressible, it was incomprehensible, even to me. And like most priests, not having to chat up girls, not having to get married, was a real relief to me. Homosexuality was one of the springboards of my vocation. Priestly celibacy is a problem for a heterosexual priest; for the young gay that I was, it was a blessing. It was a liberation.'

The priest has hardly ever told the story of this part of his life, its dark side, and he tells me that the dialogue has brought him relief.

'It was about a year after I was ordained a priest that the problem really arose. I was 25. I tried to forget. I said to myself that I wasn't effeminate, that I didn't correspond to the stereotype, that I couldn't be homosexual. So I struggled.'

It was an uneven struggle. Painful, unjust, stormy. It could have led to suicide, but crystallized instead into self-hatred, the classic template for the internalized homophobia of the Catholic clergy.

The young priest then had two solutions, like most of his co-religionists: accepting his homosexuality and leaving the Church (but all he had then were his theology degrees, which aren't much use in the workplace); or to start a hidden double life. It's basically the door or the closet.

The rigidity of the Catechism on celibacy and heterosexual chastity has always had as a corollary in Italy a great tolerance towards the 'inclination'. All witnesses questioned confirmed that homosexuality was for a long time a real rite of passage in Italian seminaries, in churches and in the CEI, as long as it remained discreet and confined to the private sphere. The sexual act with a person of the same sex does not jeopardize the sacrosanct rule of heterosexual celibacy – in letter, at least, if not spirit. And long before Bill Clinton invented the phrase, the rule of Italian Catholicism on homosexuality, the template of the Vatican closet, was: 'Don't ask, don't tell.'

Following a long tradition, and one that applies to most of the directors of the CEI, Ménalque became a priest *and* gay. A hybrid.

'The great strength of the Church is that it deals with everything. You feel safe and protected; it's difficult to leave. So I stayed. I started living a double life. I chose to cruise outside and not inside the Church, to avoid rumours. It's a choice that I made prematurely, while lots of people favour the opposite option and cruise only within the Church. My life as a gay priest wasn't simple. It was a battle against myself. When I see myself today in the middle of this battle, isolated and lonely, I feel desperate. I cried in front of my bishop, who made me believe that he couldn't understand why. I was afraid. I was terrified. I was trapped.'

It was then that the priest discovered the main secret of the Italian Church: homosexuality was so general, so omnipresent, that most careers depend on it. If you choose your bishop, if you move along the right lines, if you form good friendships, if you play the 'closet game', you rise rapidly through the echelons of the hierarchy.

Ménalque gave me the name of bishops who have 'helped' him, cardinals who wooed him shamelessly. We talk about the elections to the CEI, 'a worldly battle', he says; about the power of the empires that Cardinals Camillo Ruini and Angelo Bagnasco have constructed; about the sly part played in the Vatican by the Secretaries of State Angelo Sodano and Tarcisio Bertone; about the equally extravagant role of the apostolic nuncio in charge of Italy, Paolo Romeo, an intimate colleague of Sodano, future Archbishop of Palermo and created cardinal by Benedict

XVI. We also talk about the appointments of Cardinals Crescenzo Sepe in Naples, Agostino Vallini in Rome or Giuseppe Betori in Florence, said to correspond to the clan logics of the CEI.

In contrast, Ménalque decodes for me the 'negative' appointments of Pope Francis, those influential bishops in the CEI who didn't become cardinals, the 'non-nominations' that are equally revealing as far as he is concerned. So, whether out of punishment or penitence, some major figures in the CEI are still waiting to be 'raised to the purple': neither Archbishop Cesare Nosiglia of Turin, nor Archbishop Rino Fisichella, have been created cardinals. On the other hand, Corrado Lorefice and Matteo Zuppi (known affectionately as 'Don Matteo' in the heart of the community of Sant'Egidio, which he comes from) were respectively appointed Archbishop of Palermo and of Bologna, and seem to embody Francis's line by being close to the poor, the excluded, prostitutes and migrants.

'People here call me "Your Eminence", even though I'm not a cardinal! It's out of habit, because all the archbishops of Bologna have always been cardinals,' Matteo Zuppi says when he receives me in his office in Bologna. Gay-friendly, relaxed, warm and voluble, he hugs his visitors, avoids double-talk and agrees to engage in regular dialogue with LGBT associations. Whether it's sincere or strategic, he appears as the opposite of his predecessor, the hypocritical Cardinal Carlo Caffarra, a control freak, a virulent homophobe and, of course, closeted.

Ménalque is calm and precise. He talks to me about the anti-gay tendencies of the Italian Cardinal Salvatore de Giorgi, whom he knows well, of the deep secrets of Communion and Liberation, and of the famous Progetto Culturale of the CEI. One scandal emerges in the course of the discussion: the Boffo affair, which I will discuss shortly.

Ménalque left the CEI without causing a scandal and without coming out. He felt the need to leave and find his freedom. 'I left one day, and that was it. My friends liked me a lot when I was a priest, but when I stopped being one they abandoned me without any regrets. They never called me. I never got a single telephone call.'

In fact, the directors of the CEI did everything they could to keep Ménalque inside the system; to let him go when he knew so many things was too risky. They made him offers that some would find difficult to refuse, but the priest held his ground and didn't go back on his decision.

Leaving the Church is a one-way journey. When you make that choice, you burn your bridges. You leave once and for all. For this former abbot, the cost was extremely high.

'I had no more friends, no more money. They all abandoned me. Is that what the Church teaches? I'm sad for them. If I could go back in time, I would definitely choose to become something other than a priest.'

'Why do they stay?'

'Why do they stay? Because they're afraid. Because they have nowhere else to go. The more time passes, the harder it is to leave. Today I feel sorry for my friends who stayed.'

'Are you still a Catholic?'

'Please, don't ask me that question. The way the Church treated me, the way those people treated me, you can't call that "Catholic". I am so happy to have left and to be "out"! "Out" of the Church and also publicly gay. Now I can breathe. It's a daily battle to earn my living, to live, to reconstruct myself, but I'm free. I AM FREE.'

An organization that is predominantly gay by virtue of its membership, the CEI is firstly a power structure. It cultivates power reltions spasmodically. The homosexual issue is crucial to that, because it is at the heart of the networks confronting one another, the careers that are being made and unmade, and because it can be used as a weapon to pressure, but the key to its structural working remains power first and foremost.

'Like all priests, I'm a big fan of Pasolini. And I would say that the CEI resembles, in some respects, *Salò or the 120 days of Sodom*, the Pasolini film based on the Marquis de Sade not only in terms of sex but also the instrumentalization of power. The higher you get up the hierarchy, the more struck you are by the fact that the violence of power has no limits,' Ménalque explains.

Apart from a brief attempt by Cardinal Bertone, Benedict XVI's secretary of state, to regain control of it in the late 2000s, the CEI has always jealously protected its autonomy. It seeks to manage itself without the mediation of the Vatican, and deals directly with relations between the Catholic Church and the Italian political milieu. This 'interpenetration', to borrow ex-abbot Ménalque's word, gave rise to the semi-'agreements' of the government, the many compromises, high levels of tension and numerous intrigues.

'We have always been very autonomous. Cardinal Bertone tried to get the CEI back, but it was a disaster. The conflict between Bertone and Bagnasco was very painful. It caused extremely serious damage. But Bagnasco resisted,' Cardinal Camillo Ruini explains. (He does not mention to me the fact that the disaster in question was the Boffo affair, which revolved around the gay question.)

For a long time, the CEI was close to the Christian Democrats, the centre-right Italian political party based around a kind of social Christianity and a powerful level of anti-communism. But out of opportunism, it always managed to be close to the powers that be. When Silvio Berlusconi became, for the first time in 1994, the president of the Italian Council, a large part of the CEI began flirting with his party Forza Italia, to anchor itself more strongly to the right.

Officially, of course, the CEI would not lower itself to do 'political' politics, and places itself above the fray. But as over sixty interviews carried out in Rome and in about fifteen Italian towns and cities make clear, the CEI's flirtation with Berlusconi was an open secret. These unnatural relations, which lasted at least from 1994 until 2011, under John Paul II and Benedict XVI, during Berlusconi's three terms of office, were accompanied by frequent discussions, including about the appointment of cardinals.

The Cardinal Archbishop of Florence, Giuseppe Betori, who received me in his huge palace on Piazza del Duomo, was at the time close to Cardinal Ruini, as secretary general of the CEI. During that conversation, recorded with his permission, and in the presence of my researcher Daniele, this pleasant cardinal, with his round face, gave me a detailed account of the story of the CEI.

'We might say that the CEI was created with Paul VI; before him, it didn't exist. The first informal meeting took place here, in Florence, in 1952, in this very office, where the Italian cardinals at the head of a diocese were meeting. It was still quite modest.'

Betori insists on the 'Maritainian' nature of the CEI, after the French philosopher Jacques Maritain, which might be interpreted as the Church's democratic choice, and a desire to break with Mussolini's fascism and anti-Semitism. It may, however, have to do with a desire to organize the separation of the political and religious spheres, a kind of Italian version of French *laïcité* (which was, it is true, never the idea of the CEI). It can also be read in another manner: that of a Catholic Freemasonry with codes and co-options.

'Since the beginning, the CEI has considered that everything to do with Italy, and relations with the Italian government, must go through it and not through the Vatican,' the cardinal adds.

As secretary general of the CEI, Betori was in a position to gauge the power of Italian Catholicism: he was one of the main driving forces behind the demonstrations against civil unions in 2007, and incited the bishops to take to the streets.

Two structures were essential at the time to facilitate this anti-gay mobilization. The first was intellectual; the second more political. The president of the CEI, Camillo Ruini, who was close, as I have said, to Pope John Paul II and Cardinal Sodano, anticipated the battles to come about sexual morality. With a sure political sense, Ruini imagined the famous Progetto Culturale of the CEI. This ideological laboratory defined the CEI's line on the family, AIDS and, shortly afterwards, homosexual unions. To prepare for it, confidential meetings were held around Cardinal Ruini, his secretary general Giuseppe Betori, the editor of the CEI's journal, Dino Boffo, and a lay director, one Vittorio Sozzi.

'We were a group of bishops and priests, with laymen, literary men, scientists and philosophers. We wanted to rethink the whole presence of Catholicism in Italian culture. My idea was to win back the elites, to get culture back. We did this with the Bishops [Giuseppe] Betori, Fisichella, Scola, and the journalist Boffo too', Camillo Ruini explains to me. (I have had exchanges with Boffo on Facebook and Sozzi on the telephone, but they refused formal interviews, unlike Mgr Betori, Fisichella and Ruini. Finally, the entourage of Mauro Parmeggiani, the former private secretary to Cardinal Ruini, now Bishop of Tivoli, was crucial to this story about the CEI).

'It was there, in this curious circle, that the anti-gay-marriage strategy of the CEI was dreamed up. Ruini came up with it, influenced by Boffo, with a deeply Gramscian logic: to win back the Catholic masses through culture,' I am told by a source who was present at several of these meetings.

The template of this veritable 'culture war' recalls the one put in place by the American 'new right' in the 1980s, with the addition of political Gramscianism. According to Ruini, the Church, if it is to assert its influence, must recreate a 'cultural hegemony', relying on civil society, its intellectuals and its cultural representatives. This 'Gramscianism for dummies' can be summed up in one phrase: it's through the battle of ideas that the political battle will be won. But what a strange source of ideas! The conservative wing of the Italian Church laying claim to the ideas of a Marxist thinker, and caricaturing him in this way, always had something suspicious about it. (During two interviews, Archbishop Rino Fisichella, a central figure in the CEI, confirmed to me the neo-Gramscian nature of the 'cultural project', but felt that it shouldn't be over-estimated.)

Cardinal Ruini, flanked by Betori, Boffo, Parmeggiani and Sozzi, therefore imagined, with cynicism and hypocrisy, that it was possible to give faith back to the Italians by waging the battle of ideas. Sincerity is a different matter.

'The CEI's Progetto Culturale was not a cultural project, contrary to what its name might suggest, but an ideological project. It was Ruini's idea and it finished with him, leading nowhere, when he left,' I am told by Father Pasquale Iacobone, an Italian priest who is now one of the directors of the 'ministry' of culture at the holy see.

So not very cultural, and not very intellectual either, judging by Ménalque's testimony: 'Cultural? Intellectual? It was all mostly ideological, and all about jobs. The president of the CEI – first of all Ruini, who had three mandates, then Bagnasco, who had two – decided which priests were to become bishops, and which bishops would be made cardinals. They transmitted their list to the secretary of state at the Vatican, they talked about it, and it was done.'

The second body that played a part in this anti-gay mobilization was the movement Communion and Liberation. Unlike the CEI or its Progetto Culturale, which are elitist and religious structures, 'CL', as it is known, is a lay organization that has tens of thousands of members. Founded in Italy in 1954, this conservative movement now has branches in Spain, Latin America and many other countries. During the 1970s and 1980s, CL became close to Giulio Andreotti's Christian Democratic

Party, and then formed links with the Italian Socialist Party out of pure anti-communism. In the 1990s, after the Socialist Party and the Christian Democratic Party ran out of steam, the directors of the movement started making pacts with Silvio Berlusconi's right-wing party. It was an opportunistic choice for which Communion and Liberation would pay dearly, and which would begin its decline. At the same time, CL approached Italian employers' associations and the most conservative fringes of society, cutting itself off from its base and its original ideas. The man behind this hardening of attitudes was Angelo Scola, the future Cardinal of Milan, who also became one of the organizers of the battle against civil unions in 2007.

After the left came to power, the new head of government, Romano Prodi, announced his intention to create a legal status for same-sex couples, a kind of civil union. In order to Italianize it, and not to take the American term 'civil union', the project was given a strange new name: DICO (for *DIritti e doveri delle persone stabilmente COnviventi*).

With the announcement of Romano Prodi's official commitment, and the adoption of the planned law by the Italian government, in 2007 the CEI and Communion and Liberation mobilized. Cardinal Ruini first of all (even though he was a friend of Prodi), followed by his successor Bagnasco, set the Italian Church in motion. Cardinal Scola, a cynical ally of Berlusconi, did the same. Despite lacking their versatility, Berlusconi shared the anti-gay sentiment of the Italian cardinals: had he not said 'it's better to be excited by beautiful women than gay'? It was a good omen. And he made a reliable ally.

'Prodi was my friend, that's true. But not on civil unions! The project was called off. I brought down his government! I brought down Prodi! Civil unions: that was my battlefield,' Cardinal Camillo Ruini tells me enthusiastically.

A multitude of texts, of pastoral notes and interviews with prelates, would thus rain down on the Prodi government. Catholic associations were created, sometimes artificially; pro-Berlusconi groups became agitated. The Church, in fact, barely needed to be pressured: it mobilized itself on its own, conscientiously, but also for internal reasons.

'The bishops and cardinals most active against DICO were homosexual prelates who were all the noisier in that they hoped to prove that they were no longer suspect. It's very classic,' comments another priest with the CEI whom I interviewed in Rome.

This explanation is obviously partial. An unfortunate chain of events explains the unprecedented mobilization of bishops and their misdemeanours. In fact, just as the first discussions were being held about the DICO project, the process for the appointment of the new president of the CEI was under way. So there was furious competition among several potential candidates. Ruini, the outgoing representative, and two archbishops, Carlo Caffarra in Bologna and Angelo Bagnasco in Genoa, fought for the post.

There was also an additional Italian incongruity. Unlike other episcopal conferences, the president of the CEI is traditionally appointed by the pope from a list of names put forward by the Italian bishops. Ruini was appointed by John Paul II, but in 2007 Benedict XVI was the king-maker. This partly explains the incredible barrage of homophobia to which Prodi's legal project would be subjected.

At around this time, Cardinal Ruini wrote such a violent text against gay couples that the Vatican asked him to moderate the tone (according to two internal circles within the CEI). The very 'closeted' Caffarra spoke out in the media against gays, denouncing their lobby in parliament, because 'it is impossible to consider [an MP] as Catholic if he accepts homosexual marriage' (Caffarra would moderate his tone when he was definitively barred from the presidency of the CEI). As for Bagnasco, more intransigent than ever, he cranked up the pressure and became the head of the anti-DICO crusade to please Benedict XVI, who finally appointed him, in March 2007, in the middle of this controversy, to the presidency of the CEI.

A fourth man became active on the Roman scene: he too imagined that he was on the short list of Pope Benedict XVI and his secretary of state Tarcisio Bertone, who was eagerly following the case. Was he making a gesture? Had someone incited him to wage a campaign? Did he launch himself into the fray out of vanity? Rino Fisichella, a well-known Italian bishop, close to Angelo Sodano, was the rector of the Pontifical Lateran University (he would later be appointed president of the Academy for life by Benedict XVI before becoming president of the Pontifical Council for the Promotion of the New Evangelization).

'You can't be a believer and live as a pagan. Above all, you have to put your lifestyle first. If the lifestyle of believers is not coherent with their profession of faith, there is a problem,' Rino Fisichella told me without stammering or blushing when I interviewed him, in the presence of Daniele, in his office. (He too was recorded with his agreement.)

Then, to align his faith and his lifestyle, Fisichella launched his own campaign. One of the ideologues of the CEI, at the head of its commission for the 'doctrine of faith', he doubled-down on his rigid approach to the homosexual issue, as displayed by his presence at the head of the marches against civil unions.

'For 15 years I was chaplain to the Italian parliament, so I know the MPs,' Fisichella confirmed to me.

This guerrilla fighter of the Italian Church would have an important political impact. The Prodi government, technocratic and politically weak, would soon be divided on the issue of gay marriage, and on several others, rapidly weakening into disunity and finally falling, less than two years after it formed. Berlusconi would be back for a third time, in 2008.

The CEI had won the battle. DICO was dead and buried. But mightn't the Church have gone too far? Voices began to wonder, particularly after a homily, now famous, by Archbishop Angelo Bagnasco – who had in the meantime been created cardinal by Pope Benedict XVI in return for his mobilization. That day, Bagnasco even compared the recognition of homosexual couples to the legitimization of incest and paedophilia. His words sparked fury among laypeople and in Italian political ranks. It also brought him death threats; and even though the police in Genoa did not take these very seriously, he would ask for, and be given, after applying a certain amount of pressure, a beefy bodyguard.

The 'left' wing of the episcopate had been embodied during this period, in Italy, by Cardinal Carlo Maria Martini, who would break silence to express his disagreement with the Ruini, Scola, Fisichella and Bagnasco line. A former Archbishop of Milan, Martini may be considered one of the most 'gay-friendly' figures in the Italian Church; one of the most marginalized too, under John Paul II. A liberal Jesuit, born in Turin, he had written several open works about social questions, and given a much-noticed interview with the former mayor of Rome in which he showed himself to be favourable to homosexuals. In other texts, he defended the idea of a 'Vatican III' which would undertake deep reform of the Church with regard to questions of sexual morality, and he was open to a debate around homosexual unions, but without encouraging them. He defended the use of condoms under certain circumstances, in explicit disagreement with the thoughts of Benedict XVI, whom he opposed head-on. Finally, he wrote a regular column in the newspaper *Corriere della Sera* in which he was quite forthright about opening up the debate concerning women priests or the ordination of married men: the famous *viri probati*.

'The Italian Church has a debt towards Martini. His intuitions, his way of being a bishop, the depth of his choices, his willingness to engage in dialogue with everybody, his courage, quite simply, were the sign of a modern approach towards Catholicism,' I am told by Archbishop Matteo Zuppi, a man close to Pope Francis, during an interview in his office in Bologna.

On the margins of the Council of European Episcopal Conferences, of which he was president from 1986 until 1993, Carlo Maria Martini was part of the 'St Gallen Group', named after the Swiss city where several moderate cardinals met privately for a few years, between 1995 and 2006, around the Germans Walter Kasper and Karl Lehmann, the Italian Achille Silvestrini, the Belgian Godfried Danneels and the British cardinal Cormac Murphy-O'Connor, with the deliberate desire to suggest a progressive successor to John Paul II: Carlo Maria Martini, in fact.

'The group's initiative was down to Martini. The first meeting was held in Germany, in my diocese, then all the meetings took place in St Gallen,' Cardinal Walter Kasper tells me during several conversations. 'Silvestrini came every time, and he was one of its main figures. But it wasn't a "mafia", as Cardinal Danneels suggested. That was never the case! We never revealed names at the time. We never acted with a view to a conclave. We were a group of pastors and friends, not a group of plotters.' (In fact the term 'mafia' could be interpreted as 'gay mafia' according to the usage of Danneels, himself closeted, to indicate the homophilia of the members of this informal group.)

After the election of Joseph Ratzinger and the illness of Martini, the group lost its *raison d'être* and gradually dissolved. We might imagine, however, that its members anticipated, if they didn't prepare for, the election of Francis. The Bishop of St Gallen, Ivo Fürer, who was also secretary general of the Council of European Episcopal Conferences, based in fact in St Gallen, was its kingpin. (The story of this informal group is beyond the scope of this book, but it is interesting to note that the gay question was regularly discussed there. Mgr Ivo Fürer, 88 and Cardinal Danneels, 85, are both very ill these days; but I managed to interview their colleagues in St Gallen and Brussels: they confirmed that the network was clearly an anti-Ratzinger group of which some members were homophilic.)

Opposed to the conservative line of John Paul II and the repressive policies of Benedict XVI, Carlo Martini embodied, until his death in 2012 at the age of 85, an open and moderate face of the Church that would, a few months later, find its best spokesman with the election of Francis. (The votes of Martini's supporters had already gone, in vain, to Bergoglio during the 2005 conclave to block the election of Benedict XVI.)

While the CEI attempted to block civil unions and to neutralize the heretic Martini, another farcical battle, to which it had the key, was being played out. Would this episcopal organization, which was tilting resolutely to the right, be revealed in fact to have a number of gay members?

A militant with Catholic Action and the Communion and Liberation movement, the layman Dino Boffo had been a close colleague of Camillo Ruini, future cardinal and president of the CEI since the early 1980s. Confidant, intimate colleague, ghost-writer and mentor to Ruini, he became a journalist on the CEI's newspaper, *Avvenire*, before being promoted to deputy director in the early 1990s, then director, in 1994. After the election of Bagnasco to the head of the CEI, Boffo became close to the new cardinal, according to several sources. (For this investigation I engaged in dialogue with Boffo on Facebook, where he was immediately talkative, concluding his messages with an unforgettable '*ciaoooo*', but he refused to talk to me on the record; on the other hand, a journalist with whom I worked in Rome met him in a park and was able to have a conversation with him in which Boffo rather imprudently confirmed some of the information in this book.)

For reasons of political differences within the CEI and revelations of call-girl scandals involving the president of the Council, Silvio Berlusconi, Dino Boffo began to attack him just before 2009. Was he acting on his own, or to order? Was he still dependent on Ruini, or was he now a man of the new president of the CEI, Bagnasco, who was the head of the editorial board of *Avvenire*? Did other actors seek to compromise Cardinals Ruini and Bagnasco through Boffo, who was close to them? We know that Boffo associated every day with Stanisław Dziwisz, private secretary to Pope John Paul II, from whom he took his orders, and with whom he was close friends. Did his protector incite him to write this article?

Either way, Boffo published, perhaps naively, a series of highly charged articles accusing Berlusconi of sexual misdeeds. Obviously the attack did not go unnoticed, coming as it did from the official journal of the Italian bishops. It could even be interpreted as a declaration of war against Berlusconi; what diplomats call a reversal of allegiances.

The response from the 'president of the council' was not long in coming. At the end of the summer of 2009, the daily newspaper *Il Giornale*, which belongs to the Berlusconi family, published an article in which Boffo was violently attacked for delivering a moral lecture to Berlusconi, when he himself had been 'sentenced for harassment', and for being homosexual (a copy of his police record was made public).

The Boffo affair would last several years, and be the subject of a number of trials. In the meantime, Boffo would be fired from *Avvenire* by the CEI, on the orders of the entourage of Pope Benedict XVI, before being partly re-employed by the Italian episcopate when it was proven that the published police record was a forgery, and that he had not been sentenced for harassment. Dino Boffo was compensated for false dismissal, and he is now supposed to be an employee of the CEI or one of its departments. In the end, several people were sentenced in this case: the article in *Il Giornale* was found to be defamatory.

According to those familiar with the dizzying Boffo case, it is said to be a succession of political scores being settled among homosexual factions in the Vatican and the CEI over the Berlusconi issue, with an uneasy role being played by the Communion and Liberation movement, which had become the interface between the party of the prime minister and the Italian Church. Pope John Paul II's personal secretary, Stanisław Dziwisz, and Cardinal Ruini, were at the heart of this battle, as were Cardinals Angelo Sodano and Leonardo Sandri and Secretary of State Tarcisio Bertone, but not necessarily on the same side – the misalliances ran so deep.

'In the Vatican they wanted to put an end to Ruini's influence, or at least weaken it, and decided to do so specifically over the gay question,' the ex-CEI priest, Ménalque, observes. (According to the revelations in the book *Sua Santità*, by Gianluigi Nuzzi, Boffo accused Bertone by name of having been behind the attack on him, in secret letters to Georg Gänswein, which have now been published. But because it does not clearly address the homosexual question, the book remains opaque for those who do not understand these networks.)

In the end, Boffo is said to have been caught up in a tangle of contrary Machiavellian allegiances and serial denunciations. His supposed homosexuality is said to have been leaked to the Berlusconi press by the Vatican, perhaps by the teams of Secretary of State Tarcisio Bertone, the Vatican police, or the director of l'*Osservatore romano*, Giovanni Maria Vian. All suggestions that were, of course, firmly denied in a communiqué from the holy see in February 2010, joined on this occasion by the CEI. (When I interviewed him five times, recording our conversations with his agreement, Giovanni Maria Vian, who was close to Bertone and an enemy of both Ruini and Boffo, firmly denied having been the 'mole' in this case, but he gave me clues that proved to be very enlightening. As for Cardinal Ruini, whom I also interviewed, he defended Boffo and Dziwisz.)

'The Boffo affair was a settling of scores among gays, among several gay factions of the CEI and the Vatican,' confirms an expert in Roman Catholicism who was an adviser to the Italian prime minister, at the Palazzo Chigi.

And here we find another rule of *The Closet* – the twelfth: *Rumours peddled about the homosexuality of a cardinal or a prelate are often leaked by homosexuals, themselves closeted, attacking their liberal opponents. They are essential weapons used in the Vatican against gays by gays.*

Ten years after the failure of the first proposed law, Act II of the battle of civil unions was played out in parliament at the end of 2015. Some people predicted the same circus as in 2007 – but in fact times had changed.

The new prime minister, Matteo Renzi, who had opposed the proposition of the law ten years previously, even taking to the street against the project, had also changed his mind. He even promised a law on civil unions in his investiture speech in 2014. Conviction? Calculation? Opportunism? Probably for all those reasons at once and, first and foremost, to satisfy the left wing of the Democratic Party and his majority, a hybrid catch-all that brought together former communists, the traditional left and moderates from the old Christian Democratic Party. One of Matteo Renzi's centre-right ministers, Maurizio Lupi, was himself close to the conservative Catholic Communion and Liberation movement. (To tell the story of this new battle, I am drawing on interviews that I had with several Italian deputies and senators, and with five of the main advisers to Prime Minister Matteo Renzi – Filippo Sensi, Benedetto Zacchiroli, Francesco Nicodemo, Roberta Maggio and Alessio De Giorgi.)

The question of civil unions was taken seriously by Matteo Renzi, and it deserved to be. It was the hot topic of the moment, which troubled the fine running of his government. He could even have lost his majority over this proposed law, which the prime minister himself did not initiate, but which, he said in essence, he would be prepared to defend if parliament could agree on a text.

In 2014, Italy was still one of the few Western countries without a law protecting '*coppie di fatto*', couples living out of wedlock, whether they were heterosexual or not. The country was lagging behind in Western Europe, universally mocked and regularly condemned by the European Court of Human Rights. In Italy itself, the constitutional court asked parliament to produce a law. Matteo Renzi put the question in his three-year diary, promising a text for September 2014; before forgetting his promise.

On the ground, however, pressure was mounting. The mayor of Rome, Ignazio Marino, soon acknowledged that 16 homosexual marriages had been contracted abroad, and he had them transcribed into Italian civil law, causing a lively debate among the majority. The mayors of Milan, Turin, Bologna, Florence, Naples and about fifteen other cities did the same. Hoping to put an end to the movement, Angelino Alfano, Renzi's interior minister (belonging to the new centre right), decreed that these 'documents' were illegal and of no legal effect: the mayors had given gay couples, he joked, an 'autograph'.

In Bologna, where I went at the end of 2014, the atmosphere was electric. The mayor of Bologna, Virginio Merola, had just told the minister of the interior: '*Io non obbedisco*' (I will not obey). And in a tweet, he even announced: 'Bologna in pole position to support civil rights!' The gay community, particularly well-organized, stood behind their mayor.

In Palermo, where I met Mirko Antonino Pace, the president of the Arcigay Association, at around the same time, he described to me an unprecedented mobilization in Sicily, a region that was considered highly conservative in terms of morals.

'During the primaries,' he told me, 'Matteo Renzi was the most timid of candidates on LGBT rights; he opposed a firm "no" to gay marriage. But unlike previous prime ministers, he seemed to want to do something.'

During meetings with gay Italian militants in the spring of 2015, when I went to Naples, Florence and Rome this time, I had a sense that the LGBT movement was a real pressure cooker on the brink of exploding. Everywhere, militants were meeting, demonstrating and mobilizing.

'Italy is gradually changing. Something happened after the referendum in Ireland. Italy isn't moving on its own: it is being forced, incited to change. How can we justify the fact that there is no law in favour of homosexual couples in Italy? Everyone realizes that we can't justify it any longer. We have to believe in change if we want it to happen!' I am told by Gianluca Grimaldi, a journalist I met in Naples in March 2015.

What still worried the prime minister was the calendar, and he confided in his team around this time: 'We risk losing the Catholic vote.' Then he prevaricated and tried to gain some time. The pope, in fact, called a second Synod on the Family, at the Vatican, for October 2015: it was impossible to launch a debate on civil unions before that date. So they told the impatient parliamentarians, beginning with Monica Cirinnà, that they would have to wait a little longer.

When I interviewed senator Cirinnà, the first mover behind the text in favour of civil unions, she subtly summed up the internal tensions provoked by the proposed law: 'I knew it would be a difficult law, and that it would divide the country. A law that would cause a problem within the Democratic Party, that would profoundly divide conservatives and progressives in Italy. But the debate was never between laypeople and Catholics; that would be an incorrect analysis. The conflict divided both conservatives and progressives, whether they were on the right or the left.'

The Church, which had not said its final word, continued to influence the elected politicians, even those on the left. Still at the head of the CEI, Cardinal Bagnasco promised to send the bishops and politicians into the street and bring down the government again.

'We knew that the Italian bishops, mobilized by Cardinal Bagnasco, well-known for his ultra-conservative ideas, were preparing to use all their representatives inside and outside parliament to derail the law,' Monica Cirinnà confirms.

Matteo Renzi, a former Catholic scout, was well-informed of the situation within the Church and of the personal issues that concerned certain prelates. At the Palazzo Chigi, the seat of the Italian prime minister, his head of cabinet, Benedetto Zacchiroli, a former seminarian and deacon, is openly homosexual: he was unofficially in charge of relations with the CEI, and had been following the case very closely. Several times, the conservative right had attacked Matteo Renzi over the fact that the person in charge of relations with the Catholics was gay!

The left-wing politicians fought back, for example in Bologna and Naples. According to two first-hand witnesses, both of whom took part in the 'negotiation', Cardinal Carlo Caffarra, Archbishop of Bologna, was said to have been 'approached' because of his legendary homophobia: he was told, at a tense meeting, that rumours were circulating about his double life and his gay entourage, and that if he mobilized against civil unions, it was likely that gay activists would spread their information this time … The cardinal listened, flabbergasted. Over the weeks that followed, he seemed to lower his guard for the first time, and softened his homophobic ardour. (Now that Carlo Caffarra is dead, I have talked about him to local MPs, a senior police officer, the prime minister's cabinet and his successor in Bologna, Archbishop Matteo Zuppi.)

A pact of a different kind had been made in Naples with Cardinal Crescenzio Sepe. This former prefect of the Congregation for the Evangelization of Peoples was known for the cleverness of his gossip, the gaiety of his heart and his love of lace. A man close to John Paul II, he distinguished himself by violent attacks on Gay Pride in Naples, where he was appointed archbishop in 2006. When the debate on civil unions arose, homosexual militants discreetly contacted him, asking him to moderate his words. Since rumours concerning his financial management and the goings-on in his entourage could have injured his reputation and cost him his post in Rome, Sepe proved to be less rigid. Having been very anti-gay in 2007, he became almost gay-friendly in 2016. Perhaps fearing a scandal, the cardinal even offered invitations to gay activists to let them meet the pope! (Mgr Sepe did not want to see me, even though I sent several requests; two gay militants, a Neapolitan journalist and a diplomat based in Naples, confirmed this information.)

At this stage of the debate, Matteo Renzi had no intention of abandoning his proposed law to satisfy bishops who were also a bit too fond of lace; or to oppose the Church. So, late in 2015, he decided to make a pact with the moderate wing of the CEI, which now has its 'hawks' and its 'doves'. Yesterday, under John Paul II and Benedict XVI, the CEI was a Brezhnevian monolith; now, under Francis, a Gorbachevian pope, it is a place of debate. An agreement is possible.

High-level dialogues were conducted with Mgr Nunzio Galantino, the new secretary of the CEI, friendly and close to Francis. According to my information, there was never any question of blackmail, although it is possible that the bishop might have panicked at the idea of a rosary of cardinals being outed in the Italian press. The parliamentarians mobilized and, supported by the Palazzo Chigi, presented the 'doves' of the CEI, in a classic dialectic within the left, with a simple alternative. It is the usual language of the left, which raises the threat and spectre of the extreme left to have its reforms passed. The deal was clear: it would be civil unions with the government in place, without right of adoption; or else, soon, gay marriage, and adoption, with the hard left, gay activists and the supreme court. Your choice.

As well as these meetings between the senior representatives of the majority party and the CEI, there were – as I am able to reveal here – secret meetings between Matteo Renzi and the pope himself, in which the question of civil unions is supposed to have been discussed frankly and at length. Traditionally, Italian prime ministers have always engaged in dialogue 'on the other side of the Tiber', according to a famous expression which means that they informally seek the advice of the Vatican. But this time, Matteo Renzi met the pope in person to resolve the problem at first hand. Several ultra-confidential meetings were held, always at night, between Francis and the prime minister, *tête-à-têtes* without the presence of the two men's advisers (these secret meetings, of which there were at least two, have been confirmed to me by one of Matteo Renzi's chief advisers).

It is impossible to know the exact tenor of these confidential exchanges. But three things remain certain: the pope proved favourable to civil unions in the early 2000s, in Argentina, and was then opposed to marriage: so a possible agreement with Matteo Renzi along the same lines appears coherent. Then, Francis did not speak out against civil unions in 2015–16 and did not get involved in the Italian political debate: he remained silent. And we know that with Jesuits, silence is also the adoption of a position! Most importantly: the CEI did not really mobilize against civil unions in 2016, as it had done in 2007. According to my information, the pope asked the loyal Mgr Nunzio, whom he put in charge of the CEI, to keep a low profile.

In fact, they had worked out, at the Palazzo Chigi, that the Church could be 'nominalist', using a term employed by the popes in Avignon and the Franciscan friars and their novices in *The Name of the Rose* by Umberto Eco.

'The CEI became nominalist. I mean that it was prepared to let us get on with it, without saying anything, as long as we didn't mention the word "marriage" or the sacraments,' another adviser to Renzi tells me.

At the Palazzo Chigi they were carefully following the internal battle within the CEI that followed on from this secret agreement, and were amused by the harsh confrontation between hetero, crypto-gay, unstraight and closeted factions. The pope's instructions, which seem to have been to let civil unions go ahead, immediately passed on by Nunzio Galantino, provoked a fierce reaction in the conservative wing of the CEI. Galantino had been imposed as secretary general by Francis as soon as he was elected, but he did not have full powers. Cardinal Angelo Bagnasco was still president from 2014 to 2016, even though his days were numbered (the pope would remove him in 2017).

'We mobilized against the proposed law in 2016 in exactly the same way as we had in 2007,' Bagnasco insisted over and over again during my conversation with him.

The supporter of a fighting form of Catholicism, Cardinal Bagnasco mobilized all his contacts in the press and in parliament, and of course among the Italian bishops. So the journal *Avvenire*, bellicose on the subject, issued multiple statements against civil unions. Similarly, in July 2015 a long article was addressed to all members of parliament to 'make them see reason'. Bagnasco was active on all fronts, as he had been in the heady days of 2007.

And yet the spirit of the age had changed. 'Family Day' did not enjoy the same success in June 2015 as it had done in February 2007, when more than five hundred associations, encouraged by the CEI, had mobilized against the first proposed law on civil unions.

'This time it was a universal flop,' Senator Monica Cirinnà tells me.

The movement was running out of steam. In fact, Francis's line had come out on top: the argument for civil unions as a bulwark against gay marriage was crucial. Not to mention the fact that since the pope appointed cardinals and bishops, standing up to him meant compromising one's future. Homophobia was a condition of consecration under John Paul II and Benedict XVI; under Francis, the 'rigid' clerics who led a double life no longer had the odour of sanctity.

'Bagnasco was already in decline. He was seriously weakened, and he was no longer supported by either the pope or the Curia. He himself had understood that if he raised his voice too loudly against the proposed law, he would hasten his fall,' an adviser to Matteo Renzi confided in me.

'The parishes aren't mobilized,' a conservative cardinal observed with regret.

The final option chosen by the CEI can be summed up in a single phrase: 'make a sacrifice for the greater good'. The CEI confirmed its opposition to the planned law, but in contrast to 2017 it moderated its troops. The hawks of 2007 became the doves of 2016. It didn't, though, yield on adoption. It even engaged in a secret lobbying campaign for this right offered to homosexual couples to be withdrawn from the planned law (a line that might also be that of the pope).

The CEI would find an unexpected ally in this umpteenth battle: the Five Star Movement of Beppe Grillo. According to the Italian press and my own sources, the populist party, which includes several closeted homosexuals among its leaders, was said to have negotiated a Machiavellian pact with the Vatican and the CEI: abstention on adoption by its members of parliament in return for support from the Church for its candidate in Rome's council elections (Virginia Raggi did indeed become mayor in June 2016). Several meetings were held on this subject, including one at the Vatican, with three senior figures from the Five Star Movement, in the presence of Mgr Becciu, the pope's 'minister' of the interior, and perhaps of Mgr Fisichella, a bishop who had long been very influential within the CEI. (These meetings were made public in a report in *La Stampa*, and have also been confirmed by an internal source in the CEI; they might indicate a certain duplicity on the part of Pope Francis. When asked about it, Mgr Fisichella denied having taken part in any such meeting.)

The cautious calculation of Matteo Renzi and the secret pact of the Five Star movement translated into a new compromise: the right to adoption was withdrawn from the proposed law. Thanks to this considerable concession, the debate calmed down. The 5,000 opposition amendments were reduced to a few hundred, and the 'Cirinnà' law, named after the senator who put it forward, was adopted this time.

'This law really changed Italian society. The first unions were celebrated with parties, sometimes organized by the mayors of the big cities themselves, inviting the population to come and congratulate the couples. In the first eight months after the adoption of the law, over three thousand civil unions have been celebrated in Italy,' I am told by Monica Cirinnà, the senator of the Democratic Party who has become, for fighting for the law, one of the icons of Italian gays.

So Pope Francis performed a big clear-out in the CEI. At first, with a certain Jesuit perversity, he asked Cardinal Bagnasco in person to do the cleaning-up work on the financial misdemeanours and abuses of power of the Italian Episcopal Conference. The holy father no longer wanted a 'self-referential' (one of the secret codes to talk about practising homosexuals) Italian Church consisting of local potentates and careerist corporatism. Wherever the pope carried out surveys, in the large Italian cities, he often discovered homophiles and 'closeted homosexuals' at the head of the main archbishoprics. There are now more 'practising' homosexuals in the CEI than there are at San Francisco City Hall.

Most importantly, the pope asked Bagnasco to take radical measures with regard to sexual abuse, whereas the CEI had often refused in principle to denounce suspect priests to the police and the courts. In fact, on this point, Pope Francis was removed from reality: we know from the revelation of an internal document of 2014 that the CEI of Cardinals Ruini and Bagnasco organized a genuine protection system, exonerating bishops of any obligation to pass their information to the law and even refusing to listen to the victims. There were many cases of paedophilia in Italy during the 1990s and 2000s, and they were always played down by the CEI. (The case of Alessandro Maggiolini, former Bishop of Como, is symptomatic: this prelate, both ultra-homophobic and 'closeted', was supported by the CEI when he was suspected of protecting a paedophile priest.)

After asking Bagnasco to do this unpleasant job, and imposing a deputy on him that he didn't want (Bishop Nunzio Galantino), the pope finally removed the cardinal.

'It's a classic Jesuit technique. Francis appoints a deputy, Galantino, who starts making all the decisions in place of the boss, Bagnasco, and then one day he replaces the boss for never making any decisions and becoming useless,' a French Vatican expert tells me. And she adds: 'The pope applied the same Machiavellian technique to Cardinal Sarah, to Cardinal Müller, to Burke, and with Pell!'

Relations became a bit tenser when Bagnasco, perhaps understanding the trap he had fallen into, sparred with the pope when he suggested that Italian churches should be sold to help the poor: 'It's a joke,' Bagnasco carped.

Francis punished him initially by excluding him from the plenary session of the important Congregation of Bishops, which plays a central role in the appointment of all prelates; in his place, contrary to all traditions, he appointed the number 2 in the CEI. As the cardinal continued to put off making reforms, playing down the importance of paedophilia and denigrating him in private, Francis bided his time. And, at the normal term of the end of his mandate, the pope imposed Bagnasco's successor, without even giving him the hope of being a candidate for his own succession. So in 2014, Gualtiero Bassetti, a Bergoglian bishop who was rather in favour of homosexual civil unions, was created cardinal by Francis (one of the few Italians to have been made a cardinal in this pontificate) before being appointed, in 2017, president of the CEI.

Other heads would fall. The Curia bishop Rino Fisichella, an influential operator within the CEI who was expecting to be created cardinal, was removed from the list of potential candidates. Angelo Scola, the powerful Cardinal Archbishop of Milan and a tutelary figure within the conservative Communion and Liberation movement, was in turn given early retirement by Francis, who made this representative of the Ratzingerian wing pay for his political manoeuvres, his cynical alliance with Berlusconi and his silences on sexual abuse by priests.

At the same time, Francis put a stop to the Progetto Culturale of the CEI, a homophobic structure within the organization, specifically removed Vittorio Sozzi and marginalized Dino Boffo.

Francis's line was clear. He wanted to normalize and re-Italianize the CEI, as though saying to his bishops: 'After all, you only represent Italy.'

For a long time in the Vatican, the rule of evictions bore the decorous euphemism '*promoveatur ut amoveatur*': promoted in order to be removed. A prelate was appointed to a new mission to remove him from the one where he was no longer wanted. Now Francis took his gloves off. He fired people without warning, and without anywhere for them to go.

'Francis really does have a cunning perversity. He appointed to an Italian city a bishop known for fighting against prostitution, in replacement of one known for his use of male prostitutes!' one archbishop tells me.

A priest in the Curia, one of the best informed, gives me this analysis shared by several prelates and close collaborators of the pope: 'I think that Francis, who is not naïve and who knew what to expect, was flabbergasted by the homosexualization of the Italian episcopate. Also, if he perhaps initially imagined that he would be able to "cleanse" the Vatican and the CEI of their homophilic cardinals, bishops and prelates, now he is obliged to make do with them. For want of heterosexual candidates, he has been forced to surround himself with cardinals that he knows to be gay. He no longer has the illusion that he can change the existing state of affairs. He can only "contain" the phenomenon. What he is trying to do is a policy of "containment".'

Still progress, of a kind.

18

Seminarians

For several months, Daniele had been investigating the seminaries and universities of Rome. Together we managed over the years to identify 'informers' who were capable of helping us with each of the 'major' Roman seminaries. We now had contacts in about twelve of these pontifical establishments: in the Dominican University of St Thomas Aquinas (called the Angelicum), at the University Urbaniana, the Lateran University, the PNAC (the American college), the Gregorian University (Jesuit), the Ethiopian College, the French seminary and the Germanicum, the Pontifical University of St Anselm (Benedictine), the University of the Holy Cross (Opus Dei), and even at the Pontifical Athenaeum Regina Apostolorum of the Legionaries of Christ.

Thanks to these 'representatives', we were able to approach over fifty gay seminarians in Rome and, by osmosis, dozens more in several other countries, particularly France, Spain, Switzerland and Latin America. This way, I was able to investigate the homosexual 'problem' at the heart of the Church: in the *alma mater* of the priests.

My first two seminarians were introduced to me in Rome by Mauro Angelozzi, one of the directors of the LGBT Mario Mieli association. We met confidentially, at the headquarters of this cultural centre. I then saw the seminarians again and, thanks to them, was able to extend my initial network. And when I was spending an evening with Mauro, who organizes the famous gay parties known as the Muccassassina ('The Murderous Cow') every Friday evening in Rome, he introduced me to one of his colleagues, who worked with him in organizing the

Muccassassina. It was then that Mauro told me, while finishing the introductions, 'He's a seminarian too!'

'I've changed, haven't I?'

The boy saying this to me is the waiter in one of my favourite restaurants in Rome, the Trattoria Monti, near the Church of Santa Maria Maggiore.

'You see, I'm not as young as I used to be!' adds the waiter, who posed in a famous calendar of handsome seminarians.

For a few months, in fact, I'd been intrigued by this calendar, on sale in the streets of Rome and even at the gates of the Vatican. Price: 10 euros. Every year, 12 seminarians and young priests have their photographs taken. The black-and-white pictures, of handsome young men in dog-collars, are, of course, enticing, and several of these young clerics are so sexy that one might suggest the Church had assembled a line-up worthy of the cast of *Glee*. Some cardinals, it is said, never fail to buy the calendar every year; but for my part I've never seen it hanging in a single office in the Vatican.

It was then that I discovered the truth. The waiter in front of me had indeed posed in the famous *Calendario Romano*. He is undoubtedly gay. But he has never been a seminarian!

A dream shattered. Robert Mickens, a Vaticanologist who has already looked into this mysterious calendar and with whom I have dinner at the Trattoria Monti, confirms this mean trick. In fact, the calendar is a fake. However hot they might be, the young men posing in front of the lens of the Venetian photographer Piero Pazzi are neither seminarians nor young priests, but models selected by a gay-friendly company that came up with this little business idea. And it works! A new edition has been published every year since 2003, often with the same photos. It allegedly sells 100,000 copies annually (according to the publisher; the figures are impossible to check).

One of the models is the manager of a gay bar; another is the waiter I'm talking to, who adds: 'No, I'm not a seminarian. I never have been. I posed a long time ago. I got paid for it.'

He, at least, has never dreamed of becoming a priest. The Church, he confirms, laughing 'is much too homophobic for me'.

False lead. To investigate the gay seminarians of Rome, we had to find another way in.

In 2005, Pope Benedict XVI approved an important instruction, published by the Congregation for Catholic Education, asking that no more candidates with 'deep homosexual tendencies' be ordained. The text was confirmed in 2016 by the Congregation of the Clergy: to be ordained as a priest one first had to put one's emotional life in order!

The Church was thus re-emphasizing the obligation of sexual absti-nence, and stipulating that access to the priesthood is forbidden to 'those who practise homosexuality, show deep-seated homosexual tendencies or maintain what is called gay culture'. Out of prudence, the document adds an 'exception' for people with 'homosexual tendencies which are the expression of a *transitory* problem such as, for example, that of an unfinished adolescence'. Finally, the document reminds us that it would be 'seriously imprudent' to admit to the seminary someone 'who had not attained a mature, settled and free emotional state, chaste and faithful in celibacy'.

Inspired and approved by Benedict XVI, this text from 2005 was written by the Polish cardinal Zenon Grocholewski, prefect of the Congregation for Catholic Education. He further insisted in a note to the bishops all over the world (which I have managed to get hold of) that the rule was limited to future priests: 'The instruction does not call into question the validity of the ordination and situation of priests who are already ordained and who have homosexual tendencies.'

Grocholewski knows the subject very well – and not only because he bears the first name of the bisexual hero of *The Abyss* by Marguerite Yourcenar. His friends warned him that calling into question the or-dination of homosexual priests would lead to such a bloodbath that the Church would probably never recover: there would hardly be any car-dinals left in Rome, none in the Curia and perhaps not even a pope! The former Italian member of parliament and gay activist Franco Grillini often repeated: 'If all the gays in the Catholic Church were to leave at once – something which we would like very much – they would cause it serious operational problems.'

In the Vatican, this Polish cardinal had taken a great interest in the sex lives of priests and bishops, out of personal inclination and professional obsession. According to two sources, including a priest who worked with him, Grocholewski is even supposed to have assembled files on the inclinations of several cardinals and bishops. One of them, a bishop from the famous ring of corruption around John Paul II, where the misappropriation of funds, and prostitution went together like a coach and horses, is still waiting for the cardinal's hat!

Aside from the precise guidelines issued by Cardinal Ratzinger, as the situation deteriorated Grocholewski was led to formulate instructions designed to banish the evil. Homosexuality had literally run 'out of control' in the seminaries. All over the world, scandal followed hard upon scandal, abuse upon abuse. But these outrages were as nothing compared to another, still more pressing reality: the files emerging from the nunciatures and archbishoprics testified to a *de facto* normalisation of homosexuality. Seminarians lived almost normally as couples, pro-LGBT meetings were held in Catholic establishments, and going out in the evening to gay bars in the city had become, if not accepted practice, then at least a possibility.

In 2005, when he wrote his circular, Grocholewski received a request for help from the United States to deal with the homosexualization of the seminaries. Some were said to be 'almost specialists in the recruitment of homosexuals'. The same was true in Austria, where the seminary of Sankt-Polten had become a model of the genre: photographs shown in the press show the director of the Catholic institution, as well as the deputy director, kissing student priests (the seminary has since been closed).

'It was a very big scandal in the Vatican,' confirms the former priest Francesco Lepore. The photographs were really shocking. But it was an extreme case, most unusual. The fact that the director of the seminary was himself involved in this misbehaviour is, to my knowledge, unique. On the other hand, the fact that seminaries have a large majority of young gays has become quite banal: they experience their homosexuality as perfectly normal, and go out discreetly to gay clubs without too much difficulty.

Given scandals of this kind, the American episcopate ordered an inspection of 56 seminarians. It was entrusted to the archbishop of the armed forces, the American Edwin O'Brien. It was a choice that seemed odd to some; O'Brien would later be identified as being part of a 'homosexual current' in Mgr Viganò's 'Testimonianza'.

Another symptomatic case that Grocholewski knew well was that of the seminaries in the country of his birth: the Archbishop of Poznań, one Juliusz Paetz, was accused of sexual harassment of seminarians; he denied it but had to resign from his post. We might also cite numerous affairs of 'disorderly conduct', which were much talked about in Jesuit seminaries in Germany, Dominican ones in France, Benedictine ones in Italy and England ... As for Brazil, hundreds of seminarians, priests and even bishops were filmed chatting up a top model on their webcam, and even masturbating in front of the camera (for what would become the famous documentary Amores Santos, directed by Dener Giovanini).

All of these scandals – and other less notorious ones, which the Church claimed it was totally powerless to deal with – led the Vatican to take measures. According to the cardinals that I interviewed, no one ever believed in the efficacy of these, for three reasons. The first was that they inevitably deprived the Church of vocations, at a time when it badly needed them, homosexuality having supplied a recruitment base for decades. We might even think that the crisis in vocations in Europe was connected with this phenomenon: gay liberation hardly encourages homosexuals to become priests, especially when they feel increasingly rejected by a Church that has become homophobic to the point of caricature.

The second reason was that the measures forced homosexual seminarians who had stayed in the religious institution to hide even more: they would lead a yet more 'closeted' double life than before. The psychological effects of such repression and internalized homophobia in seminaries obviously cause great confusion, which can lead to serious existential unease, suicides and future perversion. So the Grocholewski circular only made the problem worse, rather than containing it.

The third reason is a legal one: forbidding entry to seminaries on the grounds of a candidate's supposed sexual orientation has become discriminatory. Of course, such discrimination is illegal in many countries. Pope

Francis said the following in December 2018, 'Homosexuality among the clergy is a very serious issue which should be the subject of discernment among candidates for the priesthood or the religious life'. However he insists: 'Homosexuality is nonetheless a reality which it is impossible to deny. This is what is causing me much concern'. For this the Pope was heavily criticised.

One of the people who inspired Grocholewski's circular deserves a mention here: he is the French priest-psychoanalyst Tony Anatrella, an adviser to the pontifical councils on the family and health. A theorist close to Cardinal Ratzinger and whose influence in Rome was significant at the time, Anatrella stated in 2005: 'We must free ourselves from the belief that insofar as a homosexual respects his commitment to continence lived in chastity he will pose no problems, and could therefore be ordained a priest'. Anatrella argued insistently that not only practising homosexuals should be got rid of, but also those with 'inclinations' and tendencies who don't necessarily act upon them.

Several sources indicated that Mgr Anatrella did not only inspire, but also participated in the writing of Grocholewski's circular: Grocholewski is said to have consulted him and met him several times. According to his entourage, Grocholewski was impressed by the arguments of the priest-psychoanalyst, and his denunciations of the 'narcissistic goals' of gay priests and their obsession with 'seduction'. Pope Benedict XVI, himself eventually convinced by Anatrella's analyses of chastity, is said to have applauded him, making him a model to be followed and a Catholic intellectual to be listened to. What does Mgr Anatrella really want? He has attracted a great deal of attention in France.

I must return for a few moments to this thinker. A poster-boy for demonstrators against gay marriage and a close colleague of Cardinal Ratzinger, Tony Anatrella was appointed as a consultant to the Vatican for the pontifical councils in charge of the family and health. Thanks to this Roman recognition he then became the quasi-official voice of the Church on the gay question, even when he was becoming increasingly fundamentalist.

From the mid-2000s, Anatrella was given the task by the French Conference of Bishops to draft their policy document against gay marriage. His notes and articles and, soon, his books, became increasingly violent, not only against marriage, but also more broadly against homosexuals. With all his strength, and on every media stage, this priest-therapist even rejected 'the legal recognition of homosexuality' (even though it had been decriminalized in France since Napoleon). He denounced the homosexualisation of the seminaries and therefore demanded that individuals with homosexual inclinations be excluded from them. Indulgently, Anatrella also appointed himself the spokesman of 'reparatory therapies' which in his view gave homosexuals a solution for ceasing to be so.

Since the priest was also a psychoanalyst – although he did not belong to any psychoanalytic association – he offered 'conversion' sessions to his patients, preferably male, in a specialist consultancy. There he received young seminarians who were filled with doubt, and boys of middle-class Catholic families who had problems with their sexual identity. However, Dr Anatrella hid his intentions, as we understand from the fact that in order to correct this 'evil', his patients had to undress and be masturbated by him! This charlatan worked for many years until three of his patients decided to lodge a complaint against him for sexual assault and repeated molestation. The media scandal became international, particularly as Anatrella was close to Rome, to Popes John Paul II and Benedict XVI. (Mgr Anatrella has denied these accusations. Even if the case was eventually dropped because of statutory limitation periods, it nonetheless established the facts: Mgr Anatrella was suspended from his duties and a canonical trial was launched by the cardinal of Paris; in July 2018, at the end of this religious trial, the priest was sanctioned and suspended once and for all from any public priestly practices by the new archbishop of Paris, Mgr Aupetit.)

Ydier and Axel are the two seminarians whom I meet at the Mario Mieli cultural centre (their names have been changed).

'There are about twenty of us in my seminary. Seven are clearly gay. About six others have, we might say, tendencies. That agrees more or less with the usual percentage: between 60 and 70 per cent of seminarians are gay. Sometimes I think it's as many as 75 per cent,' Axel tells me.

The young man would like to join the Rota, one of the three tribunals in the holy see and the initial reason for his attending the seminary.

Ydier, for his part, wants to become a teacher. He wears a white cross on his shirt, and has dazzling blond hair. I mention this.

'Fake blond! It's fake! I have brown hair,' he tells me.

The seminarian goes on: 'The atmosphere at my seminary is also very homosexual. But there are important nuances. There are students who really live out their homosexuality; others who don't, or not yet. There are homosexuals who are really chaste; there are also heterosexuals who are practising for want of women, out of substitution, one might say. And there are others who only live it out secretly. It's a very unique atmosphere.'

The two seminarians share more or less the same analysis: in their view, the celibacy rule and the prospect of living together prompts young men who are undecided about their inclinations to join Catholic establishments. They are far from their village for the first time, without their family, and in a strictly masculine context and strongly homosexual universe, they begin to understand their uniqueness. Often, the ordinands – even the older ones – are still virgins when they reach the seminary: in contact with other boys, their tendencies are revealed or come into focus. Then the seminaries become the context for future priests 'coming out' and having their first experiences. It's a real rite of passage.

The story of the former American seminarian Robert Mickens sums up a path taken by many.

'What was the solution when you discovered that you had a different "sensibility" in an American city like Toledo, Ohio, where I come from? What were the options? For me, going to the seminary was a way of dealing with my homosexuality. I was in conflict with myself. I didn't want to confront that question in the United States. I left for Rome in 1986, and I studied at the Pontifical North American College. During my third year at the seminary, when I was 25, I fell in love with a boy.' (Mickens was never ordained as a priest: he became a journalist at Radio Vatican, where he stayed for 11 years, and then for *The Tablet*, and he is now editor-in-chief of *La Croix International*. He lives in Rome, where I met him several times.)

Another seminarian, a Portuguese I met in Lisbon, tells me a story quite similar to that of Mickens. He had the courage to come out to his parents. His mother replied: 'At least we'll have a priest in the family.' (He joined the seminary.)

Another example: that of Lafcadio, a Latin American priest of about thirty who now teaches in a Roman seminary (his name has been changed). I met him at the Propaganda restaurant after he became the lover of one of my translators. No longer able to conceal his homosexuality, he chose to talk to me frankly, and we've met up again for dinner five times during this investigation.

Like Ydier, Axel and Robert, Lafcadio linked his career path to his homosexuality. After a difficult adolescence in the depths of Latin America, but with no initial doubts about his sexuality, he chose to join the seminary 'out of a sincere vocation', he tells me, even though an emotional laziness and boundless ennui – the cause of which he didn't know at the time – may have played a part in his decision. Gradually, he managed to put a name to his malaise: homosexuality. And then, suddenly, a chance event: on a bus, a boy put his hand on his thigh. Lafcadio tells me: 'I suddenly froze. I didn't know what to do. As soon as the bus stopped, I fled. But that evening I was obsessed by that trivial gesture. I thought about it constantly. It seemed terribly good, and I hoped it would happen again.'

He gradually discovered and accepted his homosexuality, and left for Italy, since the Roman seminaries were 'traditionally', he tells me, the place 'where the sensitive boys of Latin America are sent'. In the capital, he started living a well-compartmentalized life, without ever allowing himself to spend the night away from the seminary where he stayed, and where he now had important responsibilities.

With me, he is 'openly gay', and he talks about his obsessions and intense sexual desires. 'I'm often horny', he says. 'So many nights spent in random beds – and still this promise to return to the seminary, before curfew, even when there were so many things to do!'

In accepting his homosexuality, Lafcadio also started seeing the Church in another light.

'Since then, I've got better at decoding things. Sometimes I find monsignori, archbishops and cardinals making passes at me in the Vatican. Before, I wasn't aware of what they wanted from me. And now I know!' (Lafcadio became one of my precious informers because, young and good-looking, with close connections inside the Roman Curia, he was subjected to sustained affectionate solicitations and recurrent flirtations on the part of several cardinals, bishops and even a 'liturgy queen' in the pope's entourage – several of which encounters he described to me.)

Like a number of seminarians I have interviewed, Lafcadio describes to me another phenomenon that is particularly widespread in the Church, so much so that it has a name: *crimen sollicitationis* (solicitation in confession). In confessing their homosexuality to their priest or spiritual director, the seminarians leave themselves exposed.

'A number of priests to whom I have confessed my doubts or attractions have made advances to me,' he tells me.

Often these solicitations are fruitless: at other times they receive consent and lead to a relationship; sometimes couples form. At yet other times, these confessions – even though this is a sacrament – lead to touching, harassment, blackmail or sexual aggression. When a seminarian confesses that he has attractions or tendencies, he takes risks. In some cases, the young man is denounced by his superior, as the former priest Francesco Lepore experienced at the Pontifical University of the Holy Cross.

'In the course of a confession, I mentioned my internal conflicts to one of the chaplains of Opus Dei. I was open and a bit naïve. What I didn't know was that he would betray me and tell everyone around him.'

Other seminarians have been trapped into having their confessions used against them to exclude them from the seminary; something that is strictly illegal under canon law because the secrets of the confessional are absolute, and betraying them should mean excommunication.

'Here again, the Church demonstrates double standards. It puts up with the denunciation of homosexuals, whose admissions have been elicited in confession, but it forbids priests who are made aware of sexual abuse in confession to betray that secret,' one seminarian laments.

According to several witnesses, cruising in confession occurs particularly frequently during the first few months of a seminarian's training, during the year of 'discernment' or 'propaedeutic', more rarely at the level of the diaconate. Among the regular clergy, Dominicans, Franciscans and Benedictines have confirmed to me that they underwent this 'rite of passage' as novices. Advances made, whether consented to or not, are justified by a kind of biblical excuse: in the book of Job, the guilty party is the one who yields to temptation, not the tempter themselves; in a seminary, then, the guilty party is ultimately always the seminarian, and not the predatory superior – and here we encounter the whole inversion of the values of Good and Evil that the Church constantly maintains.

To achieve some kind of understanding of the Catholic system, of which the seminaries are only the antechamber, we must decrypt another code of *The Closet*: that of friendships, protections and protectors. Most of the cardinals and bishops I have interviewed have talked to me about their 'assistants' or their 'deputies' – meaning: their 'protégés'. Achille Silvestrini was the protégé of Cardinal Agostino Casaroli; the layman Dino Boffo of Stanisław Dziwisz; Paolo Romeo and Giovanni Lajolo of Cardinal Angelo Sodano; Gianpaolo Rizzotti of Cardinal Re; Don Lech Piechota of Cardinal Tarcisio Bertone; Don Ermes Viale of Cardinal Fernando Filoni; Archbishop Jean-Louis Bruguès of Cardinal Jean-Louis Tauran; the future cardinals Pietro Parolin and Dominique Mamberti, also the protégés of Cardinal Tauran; nuncio Ettore Balestrero of Cardinal Mauro Piacenza and then Cresenzio Sepe; Fabrice Rivet of Cardinal Giovanni Angelo Becciu, etc. One could take hundreds of examples of this kind, which dramatize the idea of the 'guardian angel' and the 'favourite' – and sometimes the 'wicked angel'. These 'special friendships' can turn into homosexual relationships, but in most cases they aren't. In general they are a system of highly compart-mentalized hierarchical alliances, which can lead to clans, factions and sometimes *camarillas*. And as in any living body, there are reversals, turnarounds and inversions of allegiance. Sometimes these binomials, in which both parties are 'bound together', become genuine associa-tions of lawbreakers – and the key to understanding certain financial scandals or VatiLeaks affairs.

This model of 'protector' and 'protégé', which recalls some indigenous tribes studied by Claude Lévi-Strauss, can be found at all levels of the Church, from the seminaries to the College of Cardinals, and gener-ally makes appointments unintelligible and hierarchies opaque to the outsider who cannot decrypt their codes. It would take an anthropolo-gist to grasp their complexity!

A Benedictine monk, who was one of the directors of the Saint Anselm University in Rome, explains the implicit rule to me. 'Overall, you can do what you like in a religious house as long as you are not discovered. And even when you are caught red-handed, the superiors turn a blind eye, particularly if you let them believe that you're ready to correct yourself. In a pontifical university like St Anselm, you would also have to bear in mind that the majority of the teaching body is homosexual!'

In 'A Heart Beneath a Cassock', Rimbaud described, from the visionary heights of his 15 years, the 'intimacies of seminarians', their sexual desires which revealed themselves 'clad in the holy robe', their genitals beating under their 'seminarian caps', the 'imprudence' of a 'confidence' betrayed and, perhaps, the abuses by the father superior whose 'eyes emerge from his fat'. The poet would sum up the subject later in his own way: 'I was very young. Christ sullied my breath.'

'The confessional is not a torture chamber,' Pope Francis has said. The holy father could have added: 'And neither should it be a place of sexual abuse.'

Most of the seminarians I interviewed helped me to understand something that I hadn't grasped, and that is very nicely summed up by a young German I met by chance in the streets of Rome: 'I don't see that as a double life. A double life would be something secret and hidden. But my homosexuality is well-known within the seminary. It isn't noisy, it isn't militant, but it is known. What is truly forbidden, however, is to be militantly in favour, to assert oneself. But as long as one remains discreet, everything is fine.'

The 'don't ask, don't tell' rule does outstanding work, as it does elsewhere in the Church. Homosexual practice is better tolerated in the seminaries when it is not displayed. But woe to him who causes a scandal!

'The only thing that is really banned is to be heterosexual. Having a girl, bringing a girl back, would mean immediate exclusion. Chastity and celibacy apply mostly to women,' the German seminarian adds with a broad smile.

A former seminarian who lives in Zurich explains his point of view. 'Essentially, the Church has always preferred gay priests to heterosexual priests. With its anti-gay circulars, it claims to be changing things a little, but you can't change a reality with a circular! While the celibacy of priests remains in place, a gay priest will always receive a better welcome in the Church than a straight priest. That's a reality, and there's nothing the Church can do about it.'

The seminarians I have interviewed agree on another point: a heterosexual cannot feel completely at ease in a Catholic seminary, because – and I'm quoting the expressions they used – of 'the looks', the 'special friendships', the 'bromances' the 'boy-chasing', and the 'sensitivity', 'fluidity', 'tenderness' and 'generalized homoerotic atmosphere' that emanates from it. Anyone who wasn't a confirmed bachelor would be flummoxed.

'Everything is homoerotic. The liturgy is homoerotic, the habits are homoerotic, the boys are homoerotic, not to mention Michelangelo!' the former seminarian Robert Mickens tells me.

And another seminarian adds, repeating a mantra that I have heard several times: 'Jesus never once mentions homosexuality. If it's such a terrible thing, why does Jesus not talk about it?'

After a pause, he observes: 'Being in a seminary is a bit like being in *Blade Runner*: no one knows who is a human and who is a replicant. It's an ambiguity that straights usually take a dim view of.' The seminarian suddenly continues, as if thinking about his own fate: 'Let's not forget that lots of people give it up!'

The journalist Pasquale Quaranta is one of those. He, too, tells me about his time as a seminarian. Now an editor at *La Repubblica*, Quaranta was, with the publisher Carlo Feltrinelli and a young Italian writer, one of the three people who persuaded me to undertake the project of this book. Over several dozen dinners and evenings in Rome, but also travelling to Perugia or Ostia, where we traced Pasolini's last moments, he told me his history.

The son of a Franciscan friar who left the Church to marry his mother, Pasquale initially chose the path of a priest. He spent eight years with the Stigmatines, a clerical congregation dedicated to teaching and the Catechism.

'I must say, I had a good education. I'm very grateful to my parents for sending me to the seminary. They passed on a passion for *The Divine Comedy*!'

Was homosexuality one of the secret drivers of this vocation? Pasquale doesn't think so: he entered the minor seminary at too young an age for it to have an influence. But maybe that's why he abandoned his vocation.

When he discovered his homosexuality, and talked about it to his father, their extremely good relations broke down instantly. 'My father didn't talk to me again. We stopped seeing one another. He was traumatized. At first he thought the problem was me; then that the problem was him. Gradually, over a long period of dialogue, which lasted several years, we were reconciled. In the meantime, I had renounced the priesthood and, on his deathbed, my father corrected the proofs of a book that I was preparing to publish about homosexuality, written with a priest who helped me to accept myself more fully.'

Aren't gay seminarians who haven't yet renounced their sexuality still happy and blossoming? When I ask them about this point, their faces close, their smiles fade, doubt creeps in. Apart from the South American Lafcadio, who tells me that he 'loves his life', the others insist on the unease of always being 'in a grey area', slightly hidden, slightly silent, and the risks that they take for their future career in the Church.

For many people, the seminary is an opportunity to 'come out', but it's also a place where they become aware of an impasse. Most struggle with their homosexuality, which had become oppressive in this context. As the Poet writes: 'laden with my vice, the vice that has spread its roots of suffering in my side since the age of reason – which rises to heaven, beats me, knocks me over, drags me along'.

They are all afraid of missing out on their lives, of becoming fossils among people who resemble them all too closely. At the seminary, life clouds over: they discover what their lives as priests will be, surrounded by lies and fantasies, the harsh life of a lonely and insincere Jansenist, a life flickering like a candle flame. As far as the eye can see, there is only suffering, silence, acts of tenderness prevented as soon as they are imagined, 'false sentiments', 'captive beauties' and most of all, 'the deserts of love'; time passing, youth fading, the spectre of being prematurely old. All around, a 'paradise of sadness', as, again, the Poet writes.

Seminarians are obsessed with the idea of exhausting their 'nocturnal capital' before they have even made use of it a first time. In the gay community, people generally speak of 'gay death'; the 'expiry date' for a homosexual is said to be fixed at 30, the age that marks the end of easy cruising! Better to be married off before the axe falls. And yet, not having been able to give free rein to their passion before this, it is often at that age, when their 'sexual market value' declines, that many priests start going out. Hence the obsessive anxiety of seminarians who remain afraid to make up for time lost in the mist, the chem-sex and spanking parties. Hidden away in their seminaries, will they have to wait to be 30 years old to grow up in back rooms?

This dilemma, which has been described to me so often by Catholic priests, has increased tenfold. Before the 1970s, the Church was a refuge for those who suffered discrimination outside it; since then, it has become a prison for those who have come and those who have stayed – they all feel cramped and confined, while gays outside are free. The Poet again: 'Oh Christ! eternal theft of energies.'

Unlike other, older seminarians, who have talked to me about flagellations, self-punishment or physical abuse, Ydier, Axel and Lafcadio have not endured such extreme torment; but they too have had their share of tears. They have cursed life and that suffering that feeds on itself, as though consenting and masochistic. They so wish they had been different, in the end repeating the terrible cry of André Gide: 'I'm not like the others! I'm not like the others!'

Which leaves masturbation. The Church's obsession with it has reached its apogee in present-day seminaries, according to my interviewees, though the priests themselves know from experience that it doesn't make you blind. Of course, such exaggerated attempts to control and constrain behaviour barely have any effect these days: we are a long way from the time when seminarians 'who had yielded to temporary onanism' could fear for their health and be 'persuaded to smell the sulphur' (in Angelo Rinaldi's memorable phrase).

Masturbation, which was once a taboo subject in is now a major subject that is frequently mentioned by teachers. This vain obsession is not aimed at the rejection of any form of sexuality without the purpose of procreation (the official reason for the prohibition) but, primarily, at the totalitarian control of the individual, deprived of their family and their bodies; a genuine depersonalization in service of the collective.

An *idée fixe*, repeated so frequently, so manically today, that onanism becomes a kind of 'closet' within a 'closet', a double-locked form of homosexual identity. While priests engage in it furiously, dreaming of the 'sweet burn' of freedom.

'To think they still teach seminarians that masturbation is a sin – it's medieval! And the fact that it's more discussed and targeted than paedophilia tells us a lot about the Catholic Church,' Robert Mickens tells me.

Another day, when I'm coming back from the Vatican, a young man stares hard at me near the Ottaviano Metro station. Wearing a big wooden cross on his tee-shirt, he is accompanied by an old priest (as he will tell me later), and, after an awkward moment, he comes over to me. His name is Andrea, and he shyly asks for my telephone number. Under his arm he has a copy of *AsSaggi biblici*, a theological manual edited by Franco Manzi – which gives him away and also makes him interesting in my eyes. I spark up a conversation.

At the end of that evening, we have a coffee in a bar in Rome, and he quickly admits to me that he gave me a false name and that he is a seminarian. We will talk again several times and, like the other future priests, Andrea describes his universe to me.

Contrary to expectations, Andrea, openly homosexual with me, is a devotee of Benedict XVI. 'I preferred Benedetto. I don't like Francis. I don't like this pope. What I'd really like to do is re-establish contact with the Church from before Vatican II.'

How does he reconcile his gay life with his life as a seminarian? Andrea shakes his head, visibly distressed and regretting that ambivalence. Between pride and flagellation, he was hesitant in his reply. 'You see, I'm not as good a Christian as that. I've tried. And yet I can't do it. The flesh, you know. And I reassure myself by telling myself that most of the seminarians I associate with are like me.'

'Did you choose the seminary because you were gay?'

'I don't see things that way. The seminary was primarily a temporary solution. I wanted to see if homosexuality was a lasting thing for me. Afterwards, the seminary became a compromise solution. My parents want to believe that I'm not a homosexual; they like the fact that I'm in the seminary. And in a way it lets me live according to my tastes. It isn't easy, but it's better that way. If you have any doubts about your sexuality, if you don't want people around you to know you're gay, if you don't want to hurt your mother: then you go to the seminary! To return to my own reasons, the predominant one is clearly homosexuality, even if I wasn't originally completely aware of it. I only really had confirmation of my homosexuality once I entered the seminary.'

And Andrea adds, in a sociological vein: 'I think it's a kind of rule: a large majority of priests have discovered that they were attracted by boys in the homoerotic and strictly masculine universe of the seminaries. When you're at your school in the Italian provinces, you have only a very small chance of meeting homosexuals that you like. It's always quite risky. And then you get to Rome, to the seminary, and there are almost only boys, and almost everyone is homosexual, and young, and handsome, and you understand that you too are like them.'

During our discussions, the young seminarian gives me a detailed description of the atmosphere in the seminary. He tells me he often uses two apps: Grindr and ibreviary.com – the gay networking tool, and a Catholic breviary in five languages available free on smart phones. A perfect summary of his life!

At the age of 20, Andrea has already had many lovers, about fifty.

'I meet them on Grindr or among the seminarians.'

Blaming himself for this double life, and to ease his disappointment at not being a saint, he has made up little rules to give himself a good conscience. So, for example, he tells me that he won't allow himself to have sexual relations at a first meeting on Grindr: he always waits for at least the third!

'That's my method, my Ratzinger side,' he tells me ironically.

I press him on his reasons for going on wanting to become a priest. The alluring young man hesitates. He doesn't really know. He thinks for a moment, then says: 'Only God knows.'

According to lots of statements I have collected in the Roman pontifical universities, the double life of seminarians has evolved considerably over the last few years because of the internet and smart phones. A large proportion of those who went out at the dead of night looking for chance encounters or, in Rome, in clubs like Diabolo 23, K-Men's Gay, the Bunker or the Vicious Club, can now cruise from the comfort of their own home. Thanks to apps like Grindr, Tinder or Hornet, and hook-up sites like GayRomeo (now PlanetRomeo), Scruff (for more mature men and 'bears'), Daddyhunt (for those who like 'daddies'), or Recon (for fetishists and 'extreme' sexualities), they no longer need to move, or to take too many risks.

Along with my researchers in Rome, I also discover the homosexuality of several seminarians, priests or curia bishops thanks to the magic of the internet. Often they gave us their email addresses or mobile numbers out of politeness or complicity, when we met in the Vatican. After we went on to record the information, quite innocently, in our Gmail address books or on our smart phones, different accounts and names associated with them appeared automatically on WhatsApp, Google+, LinkedIn or Facebook. Often pseudonyms! Starting with these borrowed names, the double life of these seminarians, priests or curia bishops – certainly very discreet, but not geeky enough – emerged from these networking sites, as if through the intervention of the Holy Spirit! (Here I am thinking of a dozen precise cases, and especially several monsignori whom we have already encountered in the course of this book.)

Today, lots of them spend their evenings on GayRomeo, Tinder, Scruff or Venerabilis – but mostly on Grindr. As for me, I have never liked this dehumanizing and repetitive app, but I understand its logic: using geolocation and in real time, it points you to all the nearby available gays. It's diabolical!

According to several priests, Grindr has become a very widespread phenomenon in seminaries and priests' meetings. So troublesome has the use of the app become for the Church that it has led to the eruption of several major scandals (for example, in the Irish seminary). Often priests spot each other without meaning to, having discovered that another gay cleric is a few metres away. And my team and I have also managed to prove that Grindr does its job every evening inside the Vatican State.

All it took was two smart phones positioned on either side of the little Catholic state to discover that there is a very low margin of error in identifying the presence of gays. When we carried out the experiment, twice, not very many were connected in the Vatican, but according to several internal contacts, Vatican exchanges on Grindr are frequently intense.

The site Venerabilis deserves a story all to itself. Created in 2007, it was an online platform dedicated entirely to 'homosensitive' priests, who posted advertisements or exchanged messages in chatrooms. A place of exchange and support, it led to the creation of real-life discussion groups: for a while, these groups even met at the café in the famous Feltrinelli bookshop at Largo Torre Argentina, at different times according to their university schedule. One of the site administrators, who was close to Tarcisio Bertone, Mgr Tommaso Stenico, was known within the Curia to be homosexual, but practising outside the Vatican (he was dismissed from his Vatican functions after being outed in an Italian television programme). Over time, Venerabilis developed into an ecclesiastical cruising site and, after being denounced by the conservative Catholic press, it was closed down. We have traces of it in web archives and on the 'deep web', but it is no longer accessible or indexed by search engines.

On Facebook, another site used a lot for cruising, because of the diversity of its members, it is easy to spot gay priests or seminarians. This is true, for example, of several prelates that we followed in Rome: most of them were unfamiliar with the confidentiality protocols of the social network, and left their list of friends visible. You only had to look at the account of a Roman gay well-connected in the homosexual community of the city, to determine from 'friends in common' whether a priest was gay or not. A timeline need not contain a single gay message: the way Facebook works almost automatically gives gays away.

On Twitter, Instagram, Google+ or LinkedIn, by cross-connecting them with Facebook, you can do the same kind of research quite legally. Thanks to professional tools like Maltego, Brandwath, or KB Crawl, one can analyse all the social contacts of a priest, his friends, the contents that he has liked, shared or posted, and even see his different connected accounts (often under different identities). I have had the opportunity to use this kind of high-performance software that allows you to chart all of a person's interactions on social networks on the basis of public information that he has left on the web. The result is impressive, because the person's complete profile emerges from thousands of bits of data that he himself has communicated on these networks without even remembering: in most cases, if that person is homosexual, the information appears with a low margin of uncertainty. To escape this kind of tool you need to have compartmentalized your life – using separate networks and never having shared the slightest personal information – to such an extent that it is almost impossible.

Smart phones and the internet are therefore busy changing the lives of seminarians and priests for better or for worse. In the course of this investigation, I too have made considerable use of new digital tools, renting flats on Airbnb, using Waze and driving around in Ubers, contacting priests on LinkedIn or Facebook, keeping important documents or recordings on Pocket, Wunderlist or Voice Record, and having secret exchanges with many sources on Skype, Signal, WhatsApp or Telegram. Today journalists are truly digital and I'm indeed a digital writer.

In this book, I'm not trying to reduce the lives of seminarians and priests to homosexuality, orgies, masturbation or online pornography. There are, of course, certain clerics who might be called 'ascetic', who aren't interested in sex and who accept their chastity with equanimity. But, according to witnesses, priests who are faithful to the vow of celibacy are in a minority.

In fact, revelations about the homosexuality of priests and double lives in the Vatican are only beginning. With the proliferation of smart phones, which mean that everything can be filmed and recorded, and with the growth of social networks in which everything is known, the secrets of the Vatican will become harder and harder to keep. The word has been liberated. Now, brave journalists all over the world are investigating the generalized hypocrisy of the clergy, and witnesses are starting to talk. Some cardinals I have spoken to think that 'these questions aren't essential', that 'too much has been made of them', and that 'sexual controversies are behind us'. They want to turn the page.

I think exactly the opposite. I believe we've barely touched the subject. And that everything I talk about in this book is only the first page in a long story that is being written. I even suspect that I'm falling short of reality. The revelation, the exposure, the narrative of the secret and almost unexplored world of *The Closet*, is only just starting.

Part IV

Benedict

BENEDICT XVI

2005–2013

WILLIAM LEVADA
Congregation for the Doctrine of Faith

GEORG GÄNSWEIN
Personal Secretary

TARCISIO BERTONE
Secretary of State

FERNANDO FILONI
Secretary for Internal Affairs

DOMINIQUE MAMBERTI
Secretary for Relations with States

**GABRIELE CACCIA
PETER WELLS**
Assessor

ETTORE BALESTRERO
Under Secretary

19

Passivo e bianco

At the headquarters of the Ratzinger Foundation, in Rome, the war is over. Now, history alone will judge – and God, in his mercy. On the walls: a number of photographs and paintings showing Benedict XVI. Here, he is still a cardinal; and there, he has already retired, pope 'emeritus'.

Between those two images, I am struck by a huge portrait, prominently exhibited: the pontiff, still in office, sitting in great pomp on a very high papal chair, red and golden, smiling, majestic in his white robes with their gold embroidery. His topaz-yellow mitre, with its haughty appearance, amplifies him still further, making him truly larger than life. Curly-haired cherubs, fauns, psyches or cupids, are carved into the wooden arms of the chair. The pope's scarlet complexion, *ex cathedra*, predominates in a rainbow of colours and a firework display of lace. Benedict XVI sits enthroned like a king. At the peak of his glory.

Looking at this timeless portrait from close up, I find a resemblance with Pope Innocent X as painted by Velázquez, sitting in majesty like Benedict, with his tawny robes and his frills and furbelows, the scarlet cap on his head and his gleaming ring (the magnificent *Portrait of Innocent X* is in the Galeria Doria Pamphilj in Rome). Looking again more closely, the change, the radical transformations, become more obvious. Now I can see the face of the holy father as reproduced by Francis Bacon for his *Study of a Pope II, after Velázquez*, a version of which is shown in the Vatican museums.

Innocent X's Cubist face is completely distorted: it looks like a mask, the nose is twisted, almost erased; the eyes are piercing. Is the holy father furious, or is he hiding a secret? Is he a perverse narcissist or an incarnation of the purity of the world? Is he torn by desire, or thinking about his lost youth? Is he crying? Why is he crying? As the philosopher Gilles Deleuze has observed, Francis Bacon leaves out the causes of the pope's anxiety, depriving us of a rational explanation. As in the paintings of Velázquez and Bacon, although executed with a far lesser degree of talent, the Ratzinger mystery is displayed in this large portrait that no one looks at, in the headquarters of a foundation that no one visits any more, and which is now deserted. A pontiff in all his ineffable simplicity and indecipherable complexity.

Benedict XVI is the first modern pope to have retired from his role. It was said that it was for reasons of health; it was an element that counted, of course, among others – one of the 14 long stations of the cross that constituted his brief pontificate. Benedict wasn't the victim of a gay lobby, as has been suggested. However, nine of the fourteen stages of this Via Dolorosa that would seal his fate and precipitate his fall concern homosexuality.

When I visit the Ratzinger Foundation, nobody is there. Every time I've gone to these ghost offices, the official places of work of the Vatican on Via Conciliazione in Rome, to meet Father Federico Lombardi, he was alone. No secretary; no assistant; not a living soul. And when you show up at the entrance, the fat and inebriated doorman doesn't even filter the visitors: there are so few of them.

I ring, and Federico Lombardi himself opens the door.

Loyal, meticulous, soft-spoken and always available, Lombardi is a mystery. He was one of the closest colleagues of three popes, and he lingers in the memory of journalists as the spokesman of Benedict XVI during his long trek to Golgotha. Who is he? He has spoken so often, but we don't know anything about him.

On the one hand, he's a Jesuit of great humility, who is generally admired and loved. His life of austerity and reading, marked by a certain detachment, and his self-abnegation, contrasts with some of the entourages of the popes he has served; they lived beyond their means, surrounded by luxury, money-laundering and sex scandals; he chose to live below his means. And even today, when I meet him, he comes on foot from the Jesuit headquarters in the Borgo, where he lives in a Spartan bedroom. He is probably one of the few people in the Vatican who really respects the three vows of the religious life (poverty, chastity, obedience to God), to which, like all the members of his Congregation, he added a fourth vow of special obedience to the pope.

On the other hand, Father Federico is a '*papimane*' (pope-maniac), as Rabelais so nicely puts it to describe prelates who live in blessed adoration of the pope. This Loyola has turned obedience to the pope into an absolute, a value placed far above the truth. The adage applies to him as it does to all Jesuits: 'I will believe that black is white, if that's what the Church says.' Having become colour-blind under Ratzinger, Lombardi has often seen the black smoke as white. So much so that journalists have frequently rebuked him for his double-speak: a spokesman who side-stepped truths, downplaying the number of paedophilia scandals that rained down unpredictably on the pontificate, and thus winning himself the nickname of 'Pravda'. As Pascal, who didn't like the Jesuits, wrote: 'We can say things that are false and believe that they are true, but the term "liar" includes the intention of lying.'

During five long meetings with Lombardi, this priest, with his winning manner, calmly answered my questions and tactfully corrected my interpretations.

'I don't think there's a contradiction between truth and obedience to the pope. As a Jesuit, I am of course at the service of a positive interpretation of the holy father's message. That is where I have put my passion. But I have always said what I thought.'

The American Vaticanologist Robert Carl Mickens is hardly convinced by this rewriting of events, which he severely criticizes. 'The Catholic Church is certainly the organisation that talks most about the truth. The word is always on its lips. It is forever brandishing "truth" around. And at the same time it is an organisation more given to lying than any other in the world. The spokesman for John Paul II, Joaquín Navarro-Valls, and the spokesman for Benedict XVI, Federico Lombardi, never told the truth.'

During the pontificate of Benedict XVI – an almost uninterrupted sequence of failures, errors, scandals, issues and controversies – the soldier Lombardi was obliged to step up to the front on very many occasions. Required to perform innumerable contorted acts of diplomacy, to defend the indefensible, the elderly priest is now starting a well-deserved retirement.

Federico Lombardi came to the Vatican under John Paul II, more than twenty-five years ago, where he was put in charge of Radio Vatican, a post traditionally reserved for Jesuits. And yet, according to his friends and former colleagues, whom I have interviewed, Lombardi never took the hard line of John Paul II or Benedict XVI. He is rather on the left, close to the sensibility of Italian social Catholicism. In fact, Father Lombardi has always played against type: he has served popes who were very dissimilar to him, and in the end he was discharged by a Jesuit, Francis, whose ideas he shared, and who should, had things turned out better, have been 'his' pope.

'For me, the priority was to be at the service of the reigning pope. A Jesuit supports and identifies with the pontifical line. And since I studied in Germany, I had great admiration for Ratzinger's theology, for his equilibrium,' he says.

Climbing the steps of the holy see, like other members of the nunciatures, Lombardi was promoted under John Paul II: he was appointed head of the Vatican press office (the general office of communication), before becoming spokesman to the pope shortly after the election of Benedict XVI.

In this job, he succeeded the Spaniard Joaquín Navarro-Valls, whose links with Opus Dei are well-established. When he was young, everyone thought he was sexy: 'Why would the Lord only call ugly people?' Pope John Paul II is supposed to have said of him when he was complimented on his entourage! Strangely, Navarro-Valls was a celibate layman who had taken a vow of heterosexual chastity without being forced to, as Jacques Maritain and Jean Guitton did in their day.

I have always been amused by these chaste, 'numerary' laymen in the Vatican who are not keen on 'members of the fair sex', and have only one fear: having to get married! Why do they take a vow of celibacy that no one expects them to take? If they aren't married, doubts grow; and if they are not known to have a woman in their lives, no doubts remain permissible. Federico Lombardi, however, is a priest.

And now the spokesman for the three last popes launches, over the course of our various discussions, into a number of comparisons. He is subtle, almost always discerning.

'John Paul II was the man of the people. Francis is the man of proximity. Benedict XVI was the man of ideas. I remember first and foremost: the clarity of his thought. Benedict XVI was not a popular communicator like John Paul II was able to be, or as Francis is today. He didn't like the applause, for example, while Wojtyła loved it. Benedict XVI was an intellectual, a great intellectual,' Lombardi tells me.

An intellectual, then. Among the many cardinals that I have interviewed, they all acknowledge that if John Paul II was spiritual and mystical, Benedict XVI was above all a great theologian. Some put forward this argument to add contritely that he wasn't really made to be a pope.

'For me he's the greatest theologian of our time,' Cardinal Giovanni Battista Re explains to me.

Cardinal Paul Poupard, goes further. 'I was a colleague of Ratzinger's for 25 years. And, how can I put it, governing wasn't his forte.'

When he stepped down, the pope himself laid claim to the power of his theological work, but acknowledged his administrative weakness. 'Practical government is not really my speciality, which does, I would say, amount to a certain weakness,' Benedict XVI wrote in his book *Last Testament*.

Ratzinger, an egghead? Without a doubt. The theologian left behind him impressive intellectual work for the Catholic Church, even if it is now chiefly discussed by people who tend to value him too highly, speaking of him as a 'cardinal thinker', and those who play down its importance – a good teacher, no more.

The purpose of my book is not to retrace the life, or even the intellectual life, of the future Pope Benedict XVI. For my subject, I need only to focus on a few dates and some salient points. First of all, the Bavarian childhood of the young Ratzinger, in a modest, loving, rural family, where everyday life was made up of faith, German classical music and books. In photographs from the time, Joseph already has that chubby, pink face, the effeminate smile, the rigidity, the stiffness of body, that we would later see in him when he became pope.

A curious detail: when he was a child, he says, he 'liked playing at priests' (as others play with dolls). Another: his mother was possessive and a love-child. A third: he was the son of a police inspector, with all that that implies in terms of authority and rigour; but his father was anti-Hitler. Joseph Ratzinger would later be accused of being a member of the Hitler Youth in Germany and some would even insultingly call him Pope 'Adolf II', who would bless you 'in the name of the Father, the Son and the Third Reich'.

His membership of the Hitlerjugend is well-attested, and the pope has explained himself at length on the subject. He joined the Hitler Youth at the age of 14, like the great majority of young Germans in the mid-1930s, and his enlistment does not necessarily reflect his ideological proximity to Nazism. Joseph Ratzinger would subsequently desert from the Wehrmacht, in which, as he has frequently repeated, he was enlisted against his will (the biography of Benedict XVI was minutely studied in Israel when he was elected, and the pope was exonerated of his alleged Nazi past).

A devotee of Goethe and the Latin and Greek classics, with a love of the paintings of Rembrandt, the young Ratzinger wrote poems and learned the piano. Early on, he fed on German philosophy, Heidegger and Nietzsche – the kind of food that often leads to anti-humanism, and Ratzinger is, in fact, very 'anti-Enlightenment'. He also read the French thinkers, starting with the poet Paul Claudel, and even (Cardinal Poupard tells me) learned the language to be able to read Claudel in the original. Ratzinger was so moved by the author of *The Satin Slipper* that he would reread his profession of faith through Claudel's conversion, glossing over the fact that Claudel's conversion was inspired by his passionate reading of *A Season in Hell* by a young anti-clerical and homosexual 'mystic in the savage state': Arthur Rimbaud. Ratzinger also read Jacques Maritain, and several serious studies have shown how close some of Ratzinger's theses are to those of Maritain, particularly on chastity, love and the couple. But the future pope could also be naïve and fragile: he was a keen reader of *The Little Prince*.

We have little information, apart from anecdotes and an autobiography so controlled that it conceals shadowy areas and essential tangles, about the ecclesiastical vocation of the young seminarian Ratzinger, or about his powerful inspirations, even if the choice of the priesthood, and its corollary, celibacy, is well-matched with the speculative character of the future pope. The photograph of his ordination, on 29 June 1961, shows him happy and proud, all dressed in lace. He is a rather handsome man. He is still nicknamed 'the choirboy'.

'Collaborator with truth': this was the motto that Joseph Ratzinger chose when he was made a bishop in 1977. But was he driven by the truth? And why did he become a priest? Must we follow and believe him? Benedict XVI often lies, as we all do; sometimes you have to let him lie. And we surmise – we are told – that in making the case of the priesthood and celibacy, there may have been 'complications', as the complex mechanisms of a Swiss watch are called, in the life of the young Ratzinger.

For him, puberty was a parenthesis, a time of doubts, disorder, perhaps a dizziness that he wanted to forget, a time of sleepless nights. According to his biographers, it appears that this boy with the thin voice, muffled like that of François Mauriac, was confused during his youth, and that he encountered emotional difficulties. Was he the kind of little prodigy who fills his teachers with wonder but doesn't know how to talk to a girl in a bar? Did he discover a wound cauterised by chastity, in which he sought refuge? We don't know. Let us not forget how hard it was for an adolescent immediately after the war (Ratzinger was 20 in 1947) to guess his possible 'tendencies' or to know that he was 'homophilic'. By way of comparison, so precocious and courageous a person as the Italian film-maker Pier Paolo Pasolini, who belonged to the same generation as Joseph Ratzinger, was able to write in his youth, in a letter of 1950: 'I was born to be serene, balanced, natural: my homosexuality was an extra, it was outside and had nothing to do with me. I always saw it by my side as an enemy.'

Homophilia as an internal 'enemy': is that the personal experience of this troubled and 'insecure' pope who has always spoken of his 'great weakness', his 'holy anxiety', his fundamental 'inadequacy' and his secret loves 'in different dimensions and different forms', even though, of course, he adds: 'going into intimate details would be out of the question'? How can we tell?

In any case, Joseph Ratzinger played the shy virgin; he was never attracted by the other sex, unlike John Paul II or Francis. There is no mention in his life of any girl or woman; his mother and sister are the only ones who counted; and furthermore, Maria was essentially and lastingly in charge of the house. Several witnesses confirm that his misogyny hardened with the years. We might also note that, very belatedly, a single carnal impulse for a woman, before his time in the seminary, was miraculously discovered in 2016 by the pope's official interviewer, Peter Seewald, during conversations for the holy father's farewell book. This 'great love' is said to have troubled the young Ratzinger a great deal, and complicated his decision to take a vow of celibacy. However, Seewald seems so unconvinced by this information that it was not published in his book of interviews with the pope emeritus – 'for lack of space', Ratzinger would say. In the end, it would be revealed by Seewald in the newspaper *Die Zeit*, and therefore prudently confined to a German readership. At the age of almost 90, the pope suddenly invented an 'affair'! Between the lines, and at no one's prompting, he suddenly revealed that he was once (before the vow of chastity, of course) in love with a woman! A heart beneath the cassock! Who would have believed it?

And in fact nobody did. The last confession was so incredible that it was immediately decoded as a failed attempt to silence the rumours, by then almost universal in the German press, about the pope's supposed homosexuality. To be counter-intuitive, this secret love may perhaps even have been a confession. Might this be one of Virgil's shepherdesses who were really shepherds? Was she Albertine, the famous character in *In Search of Lost Time*, behind whom was hidden Proust's moustachioed chauffeur? The anecdote appeared so manufactured, and artificial, that it had the paradoxical effect of rousing people's suspicion still further. 'One only leaves ambiguity to one's detriment', Cardinal de Retz liked to say – a phrase that applies to everyone in the Vatican.

One thing is certain: Joseph Ratzinger only half-chose the priesthood: as a priest, he would also be a professor; as pope, he would go on spending his holidays in Castel Gandolfo writing for whole days at a time. Which didn't stop him from moving quickly, thanks to a peerless intelligence and capacity for hard work: as soon as he was ordained, he became a teacher; as soon as he became a bishop, he was created cardinal. His election to Peter's throne was in the order of things, as soon as John Paul II died.

Was he progressive or conservative? It seems a strange question, since Joseph Ratzinger has always been associated with the right wing of the Church. Obvious in the context of the present day, the answer was more difficult at the time. Contrary to the nicknames imposed on him in the meantime – 'Panzer-Kardinal', 'God's Rottweiler', 'German Shepherd' – the young Ratzinger began his career on the left of the Church as an exegete of Vatican II (in which he participated as 'peritus' or expert). Cardinals who knew him at the time and witnesses that I have questioned in Berlin, Munich and Regensburg, have talked to me about him as a progressive whose thought was complex and far from intransigent. Joseph Ratzinger was quite open and benevolent. He didn't assume that every expression of dissent was down to Lutherans or atheists. In debate, he often seemed hesitant, almost shy. 'The Ratzingers are not very exuberant,' he would say in one interview. He was said never to impose his point of view.

And yet, contrary to the path taken by his former theologian friend Hans Küng, or his fellow cardinal Walter Kasper, Joseph Ratzinger would gradually undertake an increasingly restrictive reading of Vatican II. A man of the council, and therefore a progressive, he became its demanding and orthodox guardian, so much so that he could no longer accept any interpretation other than his own. A man who had grasped the importance of Vatican II and saluted its modernity would go on to try and control its effects. By then the sixties and May 1968 had happened – and Joseph Ratzinger had taken fright.

'Ratzinger is a theologian who got scared. He was afraid of the Second Vatican Council, afraid of liberation theology, afraid of Marxism, afraid of the "sixties", afraid of homosexuals,' I am told by Professor Arnd Bünker, an influential German theologian I interviewed in St Gallen.

More than any pope before or after him, Joseph Ratzinger was filled with 'sad passions'. So serene in general, he was the enemy of the 'sexual liberationists': he was haunted by the fear that someone, somewhere, might be having pleasure. He turned his obsessions with 'nihilist deviations' (meaning May 1968) into encyclicals. His guilt became papal bulls.

The pontificate of Benedict XVI, during which a strict orthodoxy settled in, seemed like a 'restoration' to his opponents: Benedict XVI himself used the word, synonymous with the return to divine-right monarchy, prompting controversy.

'It's true, he put Vatican II in the freezer,' a cardinal who was close to the former pope concedes.

What did he think, at this time, about social questions and, among them, of homosexuality? Joseph Ratzinger knew about the issues from his reading, at least. Several of the Catholic authors that he venerated – Jacques Maritain, François Mauriac – were obsessed by it, and the subject also terrified Paul Claudel.

The future Pope Benedict XVI used the following significant expression, in the form of a kind of self-censorship which is still a sign of the times: he claimed to read only 'respectable writers'. Never in his career did he mention the name of Rimbaud, Verlaine, André Gide or Julien Green, authors that he must have encountered, and probably read, but who ruled themselves out precisely because of their confessions. On the other hand, he was able to display his passion for François Mauriac and Jacques Maritain, writers who were 'respectable' at the time because their inclinations were only revealed later.

Finally, where his culture is concerned, we would have to admit that Joseph Ratzinger adopted one part of Nietzsche's philosophy: 'Without music, life would be a mistake.' We might even say that the future pope was a 'fabulous opera' all by himself: he was wild about German music from Bach to Beethoven, overlooking the homophile Handel. And most importantly: Mozart, whom he had already played on the piano as a child with his brother. ('When the Kyrie began, it was as if heaven was opening up', Ratzinger said, looking back on his youth.) The operas of Mozart enchanted him, while Italian opera – which was often summed up, according to a famous phrase, as 'the efforts of a baritone to stop the tenor and the soprano from sleeping together' – bored him. Joseph Ratzinger's inclination was not Mediterranean but Teutonic: the subtlety of *Cosí*, the ambiguous erotomania of *Don Giovanni* and, of course, the quintessential androgyny of *Apollo et Hyacinthus*. Mozart is the most 'gender theory' of all operatic composers. Some monsignori I have interviewed called Ratzinger a 'liturgy queen' or an 'opera queen'.

Benedict XVI is also a style. He is a veritable gender theory all by himself. *Sua cuique persona* (to each his mask), as the Latin expression has it.

As soon as he was elected, this eccentric pope became the heart-throb of Italian magazines: a fashionable figure, seen wearing all the fashion houses of Milan, as once Grace Kelly, Jacqueline Kennedy Onassis and Elizabeth II had done.

It has to be said that Benedict XVI liked to flirt. At first, like all popes, his robes were made to measure for him by Gammarelli, the famous 'clerical tailor' right next to the Pantheon. There, in that little dark, discreet and expensive shop, one can buy a mitre, a biretta, a mozzetta, a rochet or a simple dog-collar, all kinds of cassocks and curial scarves, as well as the famous Gammarelli red socks.

'We're an ecclesiastical tailor's, and at the service of the whole clergy, from seminarians to cardinals, via priests, bishops, and of course the holy father, who is our most precious customer,' Lorenzo Gammarelli, the manager of the shop, tells me during an interview. Adding: 'But, of course, when it's the pope we go to the Vatican, to his apartments.'

During our conversation, I still feel that we're missing something. Paul VI, John Paul II and Francis are venerated here, but the name of Benedict XVI remains difficult to pronounce. As if it's in brackets.

The insult to Gammarelli has not been forgotten: Benedict XVI did his shopping at Euroclero, a rival, whose shop is near St Peter's. Its by now famous director, Alessandro Cattaneo, made his fortune thanks to this pope. Criticized on this essential element in the liturgy, Pope Benedict XVI would make a much-noticed return visit to the official tailor, but without abandoning Euroclero: 'You can't do without Gammarelli!' he would admit. Two tailors are better than one.

Only two? Benedict XVI was so keen on haute couture that he had a flock of tailors, hatters and cobblers hanging on his heels. Soon it was Valentino Garavani making his new red cape; then Renato Balestra sewing his big blue chasuble. In March 2007, on a visit to a boys' prison, the pope appeared in full sail in an extravagant long bonbon-pink robe!

On another sunny day, Italians were startled to see their pope wearing Ray-Bans; and soon he would also wear a pair of Geox shoes made by the Venetian shoemaker Mario Moretti Polegato.

This was a strange choice for such a chaste pope: some of these tailors and boot-makers are well-known for their 'intrinsically disordered' morals. Criticized for the Ray-Bans, Christ's representative on earth opted instead for Serengeti-Bushnell sunglasses, which are slightly more discreet; criticized for his Geoxes, he opted instead for a sublime pair of sparkling Prada moccasins in brilliant lipstick red. Much ink was spilt about the Prada loafers – hundreds of articles at the very least. So much so that deeper investigations and a report by CNN star Christiane Amanpour showed that they weren't, perhaps, Prada shoes after all. While the devil might wear Prada, the same wasn't necessarily true of the pope!

Benedict XVI had a marked liking for accessories. More than any pope before him, he provided his chamberlain, the man who prepared his outfits, with plenty of work. And the odd scare. In one photograph, Ratzinger appears with the smile of a teenager who has just done something very silly. This time, did the pope hide his new madness from his tailor? Because here he was looking terribly cheerful in a red ermine-lined bonnet. Admittedly it was what is known in ecclesiastical language as a 'camauro', a winter hat, but popes stopped wearing those with John XXIII. This time, the press mocked Papa Ratzinger for wearing a silly Santa Claus hat!

Full alert in the holy see! Incident in the Vatican! Benedict XVI was asked to explain himself. And he did, in this admission, known as the Santa hat confession: 'I only wore it once. I was just cold, and my head is sensitive. And I said, since we've already got the camauro, let's wear it. I haven't worn it again since them. To avoid any superfluous interpretations.'

Frustrated by these grouches and miseries, the pope returned to his chasubles and mozzettas. But let's not misunderstand our queenie: here he is again, taking out of the cupboard a fluorescent red mozzetta with ermine edging, abandoned by Francis since then. A consummate show-girl, the pope also added to the fashion of the day the medieval chasuble in the shape of a violin!

And of course, hats. Let's linger for a moment on his laughable choice of headgear, whose audacity surpasses understanding. For a non-pope to wear such bicorn hats, such outlandish headgear, would mean if not purgatory then at least an identity check by the police. The most famous was a cowboy hat (think *Brokeback Mountain*) but in bright red. In 2007, *Esquire* magazine put the pope first in its list of personalities, under the heading 'Accessory of the year'.

Let us add an old gold watch of the German Junghans brand, an iPod Nano, a fringed leotard, and the famous cuff-links which, by his own account, 'made his life difficult' – and the caped portrait of Benedict XVI is painted. Even Fellini, in the ecclesiastical fashion show in his film *Roma*, which did not stint on ermine and pink shoes, would never had dared go quite so far. And if one dared, one might have quoted the inverted rhymes of a famous sonnet by Michelangelo: '*Un uomo in una donna, anzi un dio*' (A man in a woman, or rather a god).

We owe the most faithful portrait of Cardinal Ratzinger to Oscar Wilde. He provided a masterly description of the future pope in the famous chapter in *The Picture of Dorian Gray*, when his hero is transformed into a homosexualized dandy and develops an enthusiasm for the priestly vestments of Roman Catholicism: devotion mingled with sacrifice; the cardinal virtues and the bright young men; pride 'that is half the fascination of sin'; a passion for perfume, jewels, gold cuff-links, embroidery, scarlet clothing and German music. It's all there. And Wilde concludes: 'In the mystic offices to which such things were put, there was something that quickened his imagination.' And again: 'Is insincerity really such a terrible thing? I think not. It is merely a method by which we can multiply our personalities.'

I imagine Joseph Ratzinger exclaiming, like the dandy Dorian Gray, after trying out all those jewels, all those perfumes, all those embroideries, and of course all those operas: 'How exquisite life had once been!'

And then there is Georg. Apart from the habits and hats, Joseph Ratzinger's relationship with Georg Gänswein was so much discussed, and prompted so many rumours, that we must approach it with greater caution than the polemicists did.

The German monsignore was not the cardinal's first protégé. Before Georg, we know of at last two other special friendships that Ratzinger had with young assistants. Each time, these dizzying relationships were genuine osmoses, and their ambiguities provoked recurring rumours. All of these boys were remarkable for their angelic beauty.

The German priest Josef Clemens was Cardinal Ratzinger's faithful assistant for a long time. With a pleasing physique (but ten years older than Georg), Clemens is said to have had a real intellectual *coup de foudre* for the young priest Gänswein, and subsequently recruited him as his own assistant. In line with a well-trodden scenario in Italian opera, rather less so in the German variety, Gänswein, the assistant's assistant, soon managed to take Clemens's place, once Clemens had been promoted and elected bishop. This '*capo del suo capo*' – getting closer to his boss's boss – would become celebrated in the annals of the Vatican.

Two first-hand witnesses within the Congregation for the Doctrine of the Faith told me the plot of this soap opera, its seasons and episodes, and even its 'cliff-hangers'. They mentioned a failed 'transfiliation' – a word I loved.

For want of room here, I'll go straight to the season finale: the conclusion of this episode is marked, as it must be, by the defeat of Clemens, who was imprudent in his treatment of the ambitious trainee prelate. Georg triumphs! It's amoral, I know, but that's what's in the script.

In the meantime, the psychological divorce turned into a dramatic quarrel: domestic disputes in public; low blows by drama queens; back-and-forth dithering by the paranoid pope, who was finally reluctant to leave his 'great and beloved soul' before following his natural inclinations; Georg's refusal to give his new phone number to Joseph; and, finally, the remake and the public scandal, in a modern version of *Gunfight at the O.K. Corral*, via the first episode of the series *VatiLeaks*.

Being averse to conflict, and even less fond of scandal (the affair was being talked about in the Italian press), Ratzinger consoled the spurned son by promoting him *promoveatur ut amoveatur*. And Georg became the true assistant. The Primus.

Before getting to him, I need to quote a second assistant who also quickened the imagination of Benedict XVI and enjoyed a rapid rise: this was the Maltese Alfred Xuereb. He was the pope's second private secretary, deputy to Georg Gänswein – and one who didn't try to take the caliph's place. Benedict XVI maintained excellent relations with him and, when he left office, took him to Castel Gandolfo. Shortly afterwards, he was supposed to have been entrusted to Francis, and stayed with him briefly. The new pope – who had heard the rumours about his wickedness and Machiavellianism – quickly got rid of him on the pretext that he needed a Hispanic assistant: in his place he would choose the Argentinian prelate Fabián Pedacchio, whom he had known for a long time. Alfred Xuereb was finally reassigned to Cardinal George Pell, to oversee the morals and finances of the Vatican Bank.

Georg is Marlboro Man. Gänswein has the athletic physique of a movie star or a fashion model. His Luciferian beauty is an extra. When people talked to me about him in the Vatican, they often mentioned the charm of actors in Visconti films. For some, Georg is Tadzio in *Death in Venice* (for a long time he too had long curly hair); for others, he is Helmut Berger in *The Damned*. We might add Tonio from *Tonio Kröger*, perhaps, because of his heartbreakingly blue eyes (and because Ratzinger has read Thomas Mann, who writes so cogently about repressed or thwarted inclinations).

Apart from these aesthetic and, in the end, superficial criteria, there are at least four fundamental factors underlying the perfect accord between the young monsignore and the old cardinal. First of all, Georg was 30 years younger than Ratzinger (almost the same as the age gap between Michelangelo and Tommaso Cavalieri), and had an unparalleled humility and tenderness towards the pope. He was also a German from Bavaria, born in the Black Forest, which reminded Ratzinger of his own youth. Georg was as virtuous as a Teutonic knight and human, too human, like Wagner's Siegfried, always in search of friendships. Like the future pope, Georg also liked sacred music and played the clarinet (Benedict XVI's favourite piece is Mozart's Clarinet Quintet).

Finally, the fourth key to this very intimate friendship: Georg Gänswein was a severe conservative, a traditionalist and anti-gay, who liked power. Several articles, which have not been challenged, suggest that he was close, in Écône in Switzerland, to the Saint Pius X Fraternity of Mgr Lefebvre, the far-right dissident who was finally excommunicated. Others, particularly in Spain, where I interviewed a large number of people, and where Georg spent his holidays near ultra-conservative circles, thought he was a member of Opus Dei; he also taught at the University of Santa Croce in Rome, which belongs to that institution. But his allegiance to 'The Work' has never been confirmed or proven. This fiery man's inclinations are nevertheless clear.

In Germany and in German-speaking Switzerland, where I carried out investigations over more than fifteen stays, visiting Georg Gänswein's friends and enemies, his past is still the subject of rumours. Thick dossiers, which have circulated widely, are kept by several journalists I have met in Berlin, Munich, Frankfurt and Zurich, concerning his supposed links with the far-right fringe of Germanic Catholicism. Is he really the poisonous dandy that people say he is?

The fact remains that Gänswein is at the heart of what is known in Bavaria as the 'Regensburg network'. This is a movement of the radical right in which Cardinal Joseph Ratzinger, his brother Georg Ratzinger (who still lives in Regensburg) and Cardinal Gerhard Müller have long shone brightly. The royalist billionaire Princess Gloria von Thurn und Taxis, whom I interviewed in her castle in Regensburg, seems to have been the patron of this group for a long time. This counter-intuitive network also includes the German priest Wilhelm Imkamp (who is now put up by Princess 'Gloria TNT' in her palace), and the 'luxury bishop' of Limburg, Franz-Peter Tebartz-van Elst, who received me in Rome (he was, perhaps thanks to the support of Cardinal Müller and Bishop Georg Gänswein, brought back into the Pontifical Council for the Promotion of the New Evangelization, run by Archbishop Rino Fisichella, in spite of a financial scandal: Tebartz-van Elst, known as 'Mgr Bling Bling' had had his bishop's residence restored for 31 million euros, causing great controversy and later earning him severe punishment from Pope Francis).

Not far from Bavaria, a major offshoot of this 'Regensburg network' is located in Coire, in German-speaking Switzerland, around Bishop Vitus Huonder and his deputy, the priest Martin Grichting. According to over fifty priests, journalists and experts in Swiss Catholicism that I have spoken to in Zurich, Illnau-Effretikon, Geneva, Lausanne, St Gallen, Lucerne, Basel and, of course, Coire, the bishop of the town has surrounded himself with far-right homophobes, as well as with homophiles who are sometimes very 'practising'. This hybrid and versatile entourage is the subject of much gossip in Switzerland.

So Georg was, for Joseph, what we might call a good match. He and Ratzinger formed a fine spiritual alliance. Gänswein's ultra-conservatism, even in its contradictions, resembles that of the old cardinal. The two singletons, having met one another, would not part. They would live together in the Apostolic palace: the pope on the third floor; Georg on the fourth. The Italian press went completely wild for the couple, and found a nickname for Georg: 'Bel Giorgio'.

The power relations between the two men of the Church are not, however, easy to decode. Some people have written that Georg, knowing that the pope was old and frail, had started dreaming of the same kind of role as Stanisław Dziwisz, the famous personal assistant to John Paul II, whose influence would grow as the pope declined. Gänswein's taste for power can no longer be in doubt once we read the secret documents in VatiLeaks. Others have guessed that Benedict XVI was only second fiddle, and went along with his assistant. A typical relationship of reverse domination, they concluded, not entirely convincingly. With a certain degree of humour, as if making fun of all this gossip, Georg came up with this snowy metaphor: 'My role is to protect His Holiness from the avalanche of letters that he receives'. Adding: 'In a sense I'm his snow-plough.' The title of a famous profile of Georg in *Vanity Fair*, which made the front page, is a quotation from him: 'Being handsome isn't a sin.'

Was he overdoing it? This thwarted Narcissus loved to appear by the side of the holy father. There are hundreds of photographs: Don Giorgio holding the pope's hand; whispering in his ear; helping him to walk; holding him a bouquet of flowers; delicately putting a hat back on his head when it has blown off. Some of these snaps are even more unexpected, like the ones in which, in the style of Jack and Jackie Kennedy, Georg appears above the pope with a large bright-red cape, his jacket floating in the wind, putting it delicately over the shoulders of the great man, in the manner of a masculine guardian angel protecting him from the cold, before embracing him tenderly and fastening his habit. In this series of images, Benedict XVI is dressed entirely in white; Georg wears a black cassock, with a discreet purple silk hem and 86 magenta buttons. No private assistant to a pope has ever appeared like this – not Pasquale Macchi with Paul VI, nor Stanisław Dziwisz with John Paul II, nor Fabián Pedacchio with Francis.

One last detail. The reader may not attach too much importance to this, and will say that it happens all the time; that it's a very widespread practice and doesn't mean anything. But the writer thinks otherwise;

nothing is too small to have a meaning and, in a flash, details sometimes give away a truth that people have tried to hide for a long time. The devil, as we know, is in the detail.

It is this: I have learned that the pope has given a new name to Georg: he calls him 'Ciorcio', pronounced in a strong Italian accent. This is not a nickname used in the Curia, but an affectionate diminutive that the pope has chosen, and that he alone uses. A way, of course, of distinguishing him from his older brother, who has the same first name; a way of saying that this professional relationship is also a friendship, or what we might call a 'loving friendship'.

What we must not under-estimate is the jealousies that the presence of this literate Antinoüs beside Cardinal Ratzinger has provoked in the holy see. All of Georg's enemies within the Curia would, in fact, come out of the woodwork with the first 'VatiLeaks' affair. When one questions priests, confessors, bishops or cardinals within the Vatican, this jealousy explodes, barely veiled: Georg is alternately described as 'a beautiful person', 'nice to look at', 'George Clooney at the Vatican' or a prelate 'for paparazzis' (a vicious pun on 'Papa Ratzi'). Some people have pointed out to me that the relationship with Ratzinger 'made tongues wag' inside the Vatican, and that when photographs of Georg, in hiking gear or tight shorts, appeared in the mainstream Italian press, 'the awkwardness became unbearable'. Not to mention the collection of men's fashion for autumn–winter 2007 launched by Donatella Versace and called 'clergyman': the fashion designer admitted that she was inspired by 'Beau Georg'.

In the face of all this extravagance, clearly tolerated by the holy father, several repressed cardinals and closeted monsignori were shocked. Their resentment, their jealousy, was intense and played a part in the failure of the pontificate. Georg Gänswein was accused of casting a spell on the pope and, under cover of humility, concealing what he was genuinely up to: the German prelate was said to have had a streak of ruthless ambition. He already saw himself as a cardinal, or indeed '*papabile*'!

These rumours and gossip, which were regularly passed on to me at the Vatican without ever being proven, all focus on the same thing: an emotional relationship.

This is also the thesis of a book by David Berger, published in Germany: *Der Heilige Schein* (The Holy Imposture). A first-hand witness, Berger was a young neo-Thomist theologian from Bavaria, who rose rapidly through the Vatican when he became a member of the Pontifical Academy of St Thomas Aquinas in Rome and a contributor to several journals published by the holy see. Cardinals and prelates alike flattered – and sometimes made passes at – this closeted homosexual, even though he had never been ordained a priest. The young man responded to their attentions.

For somewhat mysterious reasons, this consultor with a boundless ego suddenly adopted a militantly pro-homosexual position, becoming editor-in-chief of one of the main gay German newspapers. Hardly surprisingly, the Vatican immediately withdrew his accreditation as a theologian.

In his book, apart from his own experiences, he describes in great detail the liturgical homoerotic aesthetic of Catholicism and the subliminal homosexuality of Benedict XVI. Revealing confidences unearthed by him as a gay theologian in the heart of the Vatican, he estimated the number of homosexuals in the Church at 'over 50 per cent'.

Towards the middle of his book, he goes further, talking about the erotic photographs and sexual scandal at the seminary of Sankt Pölten in Austria, which even implicated the entourage of the pope. Shortly afterwards, in a television interview on ZDF, David Berger denounced Benedict XVI's sex life, referring to accounts he had heard from priests and theologians.

This 'outing' operation provoked an intense scandal in Germany, but barely at all outside the German-speaking world (the book has not been translated into other languages). The reason may be the slenderness of the thesis.

When I met him in Berlin, David Berger replied frankly to my questions, and gave me his *mea culpa*. We lunched together, in a Greek restaurant, which was somewhat ironic, given that he is often criticized for his anti-immigrant views.

'I come from a left-wing, hippie-style family. I acknowledge that I had a lot of trouble admitting my homosexuality in my adolescence, and that there was a lot of tension between becoming a priest and becoming gay. I was a seminarian and fell in love with a boy. I was 19. More than thirty years later, I still live with him,' Berger tells me.

When he went to Rome, and mixed quite naturally with the gay networks in the Vatican, Berger began to live a double life, with his lover regularly visiting him.

'The Church has always been a place where homosexuals felt safe. That's the key. For a gay, the Church is "safe".'

In his book, which is filled with his Roman adventures, David Berger describes the homoerotic universe of the Vatican. And yet, when he accuses the pope and his secretary, this high-powered witness who toppled into gay militancy supplies no proof. In the end, he even had to apologize for going too far in the ZDF interview.

'I have never disavowed my book, contrary to what people may have said. I just regretted stating on television that Benedict XVI was homosexual, when I had no proof. I apologized.'

After our lunch, David Berger suggests that we go and have a coffee at his place, a few blocks away, in the heart of the historic gay district of Schöneberg. There he lives surrounded by books and paintings in a large Berlin apartment with a lovely classic fireplace. We pursue the conversation about the 'Regensburg network', which he discusses at length in his book under the name of the 'Gänswein network'. According to him, Bishop Georg Gänswein, Cardinal Müller, the priest Wilhelm Imkamp and Princess Gloria von Thurn und Taxi belong to this same hard-right 'network'.

Strangely, David Berger shares several points in common with his detractors. Like them, he has moved towards some of the views of the German far right (AfD), as he acknowledges during our conversation, justifying himself with reference to two major problems in Europe: immigration and Islam.

'David Berger lost a lot of credibility when he became close to the German far right and the ultra-nationalist AfD party. He also became obsessively anti-Muslim,' the former German MP Volker Beck tells me when I meet him in Berlin.

David Berger's theory of Joseph Ratzinger and Georg's active homosexuality is largely discredited today. We have to acknowledge that we know nothing about the particular relationship between Pope Benedict XVI and his private secretary. No one, even in the Vatican, has been able to establish the truth. It's all speculation. Even though Georg goes to see the holy father twice a week when he 'wakes up' (the pope has siestas), and lunches and dines with him *tête-à-tête*, this isn't anything even close to proof.

From a distance, the limits of the bromance appear vague; from close up, let's suggest the most likely hypothesis: that of 'loving friendship' in the great tradition of the Middle Ages, chaste and purely beautiful. This idealization of Platonic love, this dream of a fusion of souls in chastity, corresponds to Ratzinger's psychology. And perhaps he drew his passion and his bursts of energy from that 'loving friendship'.

If this hypothesis is true – and how can we know? – it may be that Ratzinger was more sincere than LGBT activists believed when they rebuked him so often for being 'in the closet'. According to this view, Benedict XVI had no other ambition than to impose his own virtues on others and, faithful to his own vow of chastity, he was only asking homosexuals to do as he did. So, Ratzinger 'would be a man to be hunted from the human race had he not shared and surpassed the rigours that he imposed on others': these memorable words are Chateaubriand's, referring to the Abbé de Rancé, but they are also perfectly applicable to Ratzinger.

If the intimate life of Joseph Ratzinger is a mystery to us, contrary to what some people have claimed, the private life of Georg is much less so. I have interviewed priests who he lived with at Sancta Martha, an assistant who worked with him, and contacts who knew him in Spain, Germany and Switzerland. All of these sources describe with yearning a very agreeable priest, 'sinuously handsome', always very nicely turned out, an 'obviously irresistible creature', but sometimes 'moody', 'mercurial' and 'capricious'; no one has a bad word to say about him, but I'm told that in his youth, this young blond liked to enjoy wild nights and, like all priests, spent evenings among other young men.

One thing is certain: Gänswein was interested in the double lives of cardinals, bishops and priests. Always secretive, this 'control freak' was said, according to several sources, to ask for information about certain prelates. In the Vatican closet, everyone keeps an eye on everyone else – and homosexuality is at the heart of many intrigues.

This handsome young man also regularly travelled, to avoid the constraints of the Vatican, to visit other parishes and to forge new friendships. Very handsome, he likes to surround himself with men, rather than feed rumours – which are numerous but unfounded – about his relationships with women.

'He's very endearing,' a priest I interviewed in Switzerland tells me. 'He's very affable,' I am told by a priest I meet in Madrid. He has 'worldly' associations, a third tells me, in Berlin. Less of a courtier now, more courted, given his prestigious titles, he enjoys advantageous associations in which his narcissism can only be of benefit.

Despite rumours and gossip, Pope Benedict XVI never got rid of his favourite: on the contrary, he promoted him. After the VatiLeaks scandal, in which Georg was both a victim, and at the same time partly responsible (if only by virtue of trusting the mole responsible for the leaks), the pontiff renewed his trust in him, appointing him both Director of the Pontifical Palace (essentially, head of protocol) and making him an archbishop. The official act took place on Epiphany, 6 January 2013 – a month before the startling resignation of the holy father – and we can date the unofficial end of the pontificate from that extravagant mass.

'Benedict XVI was daring!' The phrase comes from a Curia priest who was stunned by the event he had witnessed, 'the finest in his life'. No other modern pope had had the audacity to hold such a coronation mass, such an extravagant gesture, such an act of folly for his handsome protégé. On the day of Georg Gänswein's consecration as archbishop, Benedict XVI presided over one of the most beautiful liturgical celebrations of all time. (Five people who were present described the scene to me, including two cardinals, and the ceremony – lasting almost three hours – can be seen on YouTube. I also managed to get hold of the original libretto of the mass, and its musical score, which is 106 pages long! Details of the ceremony were related to me at length by dazzled Vaticanologists. Archbishop Piero Marini, the master of ceremonies to Pope John Paul II and Benedict XVI, and Pierre Blanchard, who was for a long time the director of APSA – two men, then, very familiar with the unshakeable protocol of the Vatican – explained its hieratic rules to me as well.)

Below Michelangelo's magnificent dome and the gilded stucco baroque pillars of Bernini's baldaquin, the pope consecrated Georg in St Peter's Basilica in Rome. Stubborn, with his legendary *hostinato rigore* ('obstinate rigour' is the motto of Leonardo da Vinci), the pope did not try to conceal what he was doing, as so many cardinals do when they promote their protégés; he went completely public with it. That's what I've always admired about him.

Benedict XVI insisted on giving the pastoral ring to his Bavarian excellency Georg Gänswein in person, in a Fellini-esque ceremony engraved forever on the memory of the 450 statues, 500 columns and 50 altars of the basilica. First comes the procession, slow, superb, and choreographed to perfection; the pope with his huge topaz-yellow mitre, standing in a little indoor popemobile, a throne on wheels, travels like a giant the full 200-metre length of the nave to the sound of triumphant brass, beautiful organ sounds and the children's choir of St Peter's, straight as unlit candles. The chalices are encrusted with precious stones; the censers smoke. In the front rows of this new style of episcopal organization, dozens of cardinals and hundreds of bishops and priests in their finest robes provide a palette of red, white and ox-blood. There are flowers everywhere, as if at a wedding.

Then the ceremony proper begins. Flanked by Secretary of State Tarcisio Bertone and the incorrigible Cardinal Zenon Grocholewski, co-consecrators, the pope, twinkling with pride and contentment, speaks in a voice that is faint but still beautiful. In front of him, where the nave and the transept meet, four prelates, including Georg, lie with their bellies to the ground, as tradition decrees. In a flash, a ceremonial priest rearranges Georg's robe when he doesn't do himself up properly. The pope, motionless and imperturbable on his throne, concentrates on his great work, his 'sacred aromas' and his flame. Above his head, a host of cherubs looks admiringly at the scene, while even Bernini's kneeling angels are stirred with emotion. It is the coronation of Charlemagne! It is Hadrian moving heaven and earth, building cities and mausolea to pay tribute to Antinous! And Hadrian even makes a whole audience of Roman dignitaries, cardinals, ambassadors, several politicians and former ministers, and even the prime minister Mario Monti, become a blur of genuflections.

Suddenly the pope takes Georg's head in his hands: the emotion has reached its peak. Georg gives a Leonardo smile before plunging his hair into the pontifical hands, the cameras freeze, the cardinals – I recognize Angelo Sodano, Raymond Burke and Robert Sarah in the pictures – hold their breath; the chubby cherubs holding the fonts are open-mouthed. 'Time is out of joint.' Between the Kyrie, Gloria, Credo, Sanctus and Benedictus, the music is lovely in St Peter's, calculated down to the last diapason by several 'liturgy queens'. The pope spends a long time (19 seconds) stroking the salt-and-pepper curls of his George Clooney, with infinite delicacy along with infinite prudence. But 'the body doesn't lie', as the great choreographer Martha Graham used to put it.

The pope was, of course, informed about the rumours that are going around, and about the name of the lover attributed to him. Wicked? Uranist? He laughs. And makes things worse! What panache! What glamour! Ratzinger had the grandeur of Oscar Wilde who, when warned of the danger he ran in associating with young Bosie, appeared in public with him more often; or of a Verlaine, whose family insistently asked him to get rid of the young Rimbaud, but who went off to live with him instead – actions that cost both Oscar Wilde and Verlaine two years in prison respectively. 'The insults of men / What do they matter? / Well, our heart alone / Knows what we are.'

In his way, Joseph Ratzinger remained loyal to his singleton, in spite of the frantic warnings of the Curia. This high mass was a magnificent statement. And that day, he was radiant. His restrained smile was a marvel. Having drained the chalice to the dregs, he was not afraid of taking another drink from it. He is handsome. He is proud. Magnetized by his own daring, he has won. Seeing him again in the video, so superbly dramatic, I have perhaps never loved him as much as in that moment.

Georg had been consecrated as an archbishop by the holy father, and no one yet knew that Benedict XVI had taken the most spectacular decision that a pope has ever taken: he would announce his resignation shortly afterwards. Was Georg already aware of it? It's probable, but not definite. Whatever the case, for the pope, the coronation mass dedicated that day to 'Ciorcio' would be his historical testament.

For now, the carnival continues. The mass is endless, so much so that the pope will be over twenty minutes late for the angelus, and will have to apologize to the impatient crowd in St Peter's Square.

'It was a celebratory liturgy! A spectacle! A mistake! The liturgy cannot be a spectacle,' says an outraged Piero Marini, former master of ceremonies to John Paul II and Benedict XVI, during our interview.

More generous, one of his successors, Mgr Vincenzo Peroni, master of liturgy to Pope Francis, who also contributed at the time to the preparation of the mass, explains to me when we have a one-on-one dinner together: 'Such a ceremony illustrated the beauty that reveals the face and the glory of God: nothing is beautiful enough for God.'

At the end, amid sustained applause – which is rare – and the flashes of the photographers, I can make out Bach's *Art of Fugue*, played by a chamber orchestra in the upper floors of the basilica, and one of the favourite 'music for the eyes' of Joseph Ratzinger. To the sustained rhythm and rigour of Bach, the huge cortège sets off back down the nave, framed by the multicoloured Swiss Guard and the black-suited bodyguards.

An extravaganza! When it passes in front of the *Pietà*, one of the most beautiful sculptures in the world, it is not unthinkable that Michelangelo's statue is dumbstruck by the departed procession.

Just as unusually, the church ceremony was followed by another at the town hall. After the mass, over two hundred guests were invited to take part in a prestigious reception in the big Paul VI Audience Hall, Finally, in the evening, a more intimate gala dinner organized in the Vatican museums by the audacious pope, who would take part in person, surrounded for the occasion by Leonard da Vinci, Michelangelo, Caravaggio and Il Sodoma.

Pope Francis confirmed the dual function of the great chamberlain Georg Gänswein, after the resignation of Benedict XVI and his own election. An unusual situation, and an unusual title: Georg is now both personal secretary to the retired pope and prefect of the pontifical house of the acting pope.

This double hat has the advantage of allowing daring comparisons. How many times have I heard a phrase attributed to Georg Gänswein, that he works 'for an active pope and a passive pope'? It was immediately picked up in newspaper offices and syndicated! Gay militants still delight in it! I found the phrase in question in the original speech, and the version handed down is sadly apocryphal. During a talk in 2016, Georg briefly compared the two popes and said: 'Since the election of Francis, there are not two popes but, in fact, an expanded ministry with an active member and a contemplative member [*un membro attivo e un membro contemplativo*]. That's why Benedict XVI has not given up his name or his white cassock.' Inevitably, the phrase was removed from its context, travestied on lots of gay websites and repeated endlessly by dozens of bloggers. Even though Georg never actually mentioned an 'active pope' and a 'passive pope'!

Between the two holy fathers, Georg is a link, a messenger. He was one of the first to be informed by Benedict XVI of his plan to resign. Georg is said to have replied: 'No, holy father, it's not possible.' When Benedict finally did step down, in 2013, Georg was seen with the pope flying by helicopter to Castel Gandolfo, an image mocked as suggesting that the pope was ascending into the heavens while he was still alive! Georg then moved with the pontiff and his two felines into the monastery of Mater Ecclesiae, behind a guarded gate and high grilles – unlike any other building inside the Vatican.

I am told that Francis appreciates the intelligence of Georg, who is more than just a handsome face. He is a man of great culture, very Teutonic, and so different from the Hispanic culture of the pope that he opens up new perspectives to him. A profile of Gänswein published by *Vanity Fair* quoted the man who wanted to be Benedict XVI's *éminence grise* expressing the wish 'that people don't stop at his looks but go beyond to what lies under his cassock'.

Ecce Homo. While we're looking at the personality of Benedict XVI, let's look also at a hypothesis that I shall borrow in part from Freud's subtle and daring analysis of Leonardo da Vinci's homosexuality. I'm not a psychoanalyst, but I'm surprised, like many others, by the fact that homosexuality was one of the cardinal questions, if I may put it like that, of Joseph Ratzinger's life and thought. He's one of the theologians who have studied this matter in depth. In a way, the gay question lends substance to his life, and that makes him very interesting.

With Freud, we might think that there is no human life without sexual desire in the broadest sense, a libido that inevitably persists among the priesthood, even in sublimated or repressed forms. For Leonardo da Vinci it is, Freud tells us, about homosexuality repressed into knowledge, experiment, art and the non-consummated beauty of boys (even if recent research has starkly contradicted Freud, since the painter was indeed a practising homosexual). Leonardo da Vinci also wrote in his notebooks this much-discussed phrase: 'intellectual passion drives out sensuality'.

For Joseph Ratzinger, it appears that one can put forward a similar hypothesis, with all necessary prudence: has a certain latent homosexuality been sublimated into vocation and repressed into research? Might a literary and musical aesthetic, effeminacy, extravagant clothing, the cult of the beauty of boys, provide some clues? Is it just a matter of 'bovaryism', living one's life through the lives of fictional characters to avoid confronting reality?

Ratzinger's life lies entirely within the horizon of his reading and writing. Did he have to build up his strength around a secret inner rigidity? That intellectual or aesthetic activity derives from desire is a well-known psychosexual process in artistic and literary lives, as well as in the religious life. If we wish to follow Freud, we might talk about an Oedipus complex sublimated into an 'obsessional neurosis': a Prometheus complex, perhaps?

What we know about Benedict XVI's emotional life is limited, but the little we do know is already more than significant: his emotional tendency points in a single direction. From the musicians Joseph Ratzinger likes, the androgynous figures he highlights in the operas that enchant him, the writers he reads, the friends he surrounds himself with, the cardinals he appoints, the countless decisions he has made against homosexuals, and even his final fall, partly wrapped up in the gay question, we might hypothesize that homophilia was the thorn in Joseph Ratzinger's flesh.

There can hardly be any doubt that he was the most tormented of men, overwhelmed by sin or, at least, by the sense of sin: in this, he is a tragic figure. The idea that this repression might explain his 'internalized homophobia' is one that has often been put forward by countless psychoanalysts, psychiatrists, priests and progressive theologians, and, of course, by gay militants, Some, like the journalist Pasquale Quaranta, have even suggested to me the expression 'Ratzinger syndrome' to define this archetypal model of 'internalized homophobia'.

Rarely has a man so argued against his 'parish' – and this obstinacy became suspicious in the end. Benedict XVI is believed by some to have made others pay for his own doubts. And yet it seems to me that this psychological explanation is frail, because if we subject Joseph Ratzinger's writings to close analysis, we discover his most cherished secret. I would maintain another hypothesis, which is that he is not in fact a homophobic homosexual, as many have said, if we extend the term to include a profound and general aversion to homosexuals. In fact, Cardinal Ratzinger has always been careful, as no prelate has so clearly been before him, to distinguish between two forms of homosexuality. The first of these, homosexuality lived and emphasized, gay identity and culture, is intrinsically disordered. What Ratzinger rejects is the homosexual act. The weakness of the flesh, sexuality between men – that's the sin.

On the other hand, and this point seems to me to have been neglected, there is a homosexuality that Ratzinger has never rejected, even elevating it into an indispensable model, far superior in his eyes to carnal love between a man and a woman This is ascetic homosexuality, which has been corrected by 'superhuman legislations': this struggle against the self – energetic, incessant and truly diabolical – which in the end opens up into abstinence. This triumph over the senses is the model towards which the whole of Ratzinger's personality and work has tended. Nietzsche warned us in *Twilight of the Idols*, when he turned the eunuch into the ideal model of the Church: 'The saint pleasing to God is the ideal castrato.'

In the end, we might say that if he rejects 'LGBT' individuals, Ratzinger does not reserve the same harsh treatment for those who hesitate, those who seek, those sexual agnostics, those who are 'questioning', the 'Qs' in the American terminology, who appear in the new formulation LGBTQ! By and large, among the despised gays, the pope is said to be disposed to save those who renounce, those who do not indulge in 'acts of homosexuality', who remain chaste.

Ratzinger forged this ideal of the abstinent homosexual saint and repeated it in his encyclicals, *motu proprio*, apostolic exhortations, letters, books and interviews. We could go back to the most elaborate text, which is of great importance: the key articles in the *New Catechism of the Catholic Church* (1992). We know that Cardinal Ratzinger was its editor-in-chief, assisted by a talented German-speaking bishop whom Professor Ratzinger had as a pupil and took under his wing – Christoph

Schönborn. While the enterprise was collective, the work of the hands of about fifteen prelates, based on the work of a thousand bishops, it was Ratzinger who coordinated the project as a whole and personally wrote, along with Schönborn and the French bishop Jean-Louis Bruguès, the three key articles concerning homosexuality (§ 2357ff.). The section in which they are collected is entitled – giving a sense of the tone – 'Chastity and homosexuality'.

In the first article, the *Catechism* merely affirms that 'homosexual acts are intrinsically disordered. They are contrary to the natural law. They close the sexual act to the gift of life. They do not proceed from a genuine affective and sexual complementarity. Under no circumstances can they be approved.' After signalling that the number of people who have 'deep-seated homosexual tendencies' is 'not negligible', that it is a 'trial' for them, and that they must be 'accepted with respect, compassion and delicacy', the *Catechism* opens up on to Ratzinger's grand theory. 'Homosexual persons are called to chastity. By the virtues of self-mastery that teach them inner freedom, at times by the support of disinterested friendship, by prayer and sacramental grace, they can and should gradually and resolutely approach Christian perfection.'

Christian perfection! Homosexuals weren't asking for that much! It is possible that the true author of the text, Ratzinger, reveals himself marvellously here, by over-estimating 'abstinent' homosexuals after condemning 'practising' homosexuals (the two other authors, more 'friendly', Schönborn and Bruguès, are more progressive in this respect).

This is the binary proposition: a rejection of the practices and 'exercise' of homosexuality; the idealization of chastity and 'non-consummated' homosexuality. The practising homosexual is blamed; the non-practising praised. A completely self-contradictory position, if one thinks about it. Here we are at the heart, the very quintessence, of the Ratzingerian system.

Pope Benedict XVI would come back to this like a demon. In several books and interviews he would repeat his phrases amid the most colourful formulations. For example, in *Light of the World*, a book of official interviews: 'If someone has deep homosexual tendencies – even today we do not know if they are truly innate or whether they appear in early childhood – in any case, if those tendencies hold that person in their power, it is a great trial for that person ... But that still does not mean that homosexuality is just.' The interviewer, normally less reckless, adds that there are many homosexuals in the Church. And Benedict XVI replies: 'That is also one of the difficulties of the Church. And the people concerned must at least try not to yield to that tendency actively so that they may remain faithful to the mission inherent in their ministry.'

We are familiar with this 'mastered' homosexuality: it's Plato and Platonic love rather than Socrates and Socratic love; it is Saint Augustine being fickly heterosexual, but struggling against himself and attaining sanctity by becoming chaste; it is Handel, Schubert, Chopin and perhaps Mozart; it is Jacques Maritain and the young André Gide; it is François Mauriac and the young Julien Green; it is Rimbaud as dreamed of by Claudel, who imagined him as abstinent; it is Leonardo da Vinci and Michelangelo before they put their desires into practice. In other words: all the intellectual and artistic passions of Joseph Ratzinger.

Accepting the homosexual as long as he renounces his sexuality. It's a daring wager on Ratzinger's part. And what heroic man, by means of self-flagellation, can achieve such a feat? Perhaps a Ratzinger or, by making sacrifices, a replicant or a Jedi! For everyone else, the 'normal people' who know that abstinence is unnatural, Benedict XVI's thought leads inevitably to a double life, and as the Poet puts it, 'the old lying loves' and 'lying couples'. In principle, the Ratzingerian project was doomed to failure and hypocrisy – around the world and within the pontifical house itself.

Did he go too far in this praise of abstinence that condemns the practice more than the idea? Did he not gullibly open the door to countless hypocrisies in a Church that was becoming homosexualized at a great rate? In fact, Cardinal Ratzinger saw the trap and the limits of his grand theory. So, in 1986, with the help of the American episcopate, which surreptitiously suggested a form of words to him, he summed things up in his famous *Letter to the Bishops of the Catholic Church on the Pastoral Care of Homosexual Persons* – the first document in the whole history of Christianity devoted solely to the question. Bearing in mind that a distinction must be made between the homosexual 'condition' and 'tendency' on the one hand, and homosexual 'acts' on the other, Cardinal Ratzinger confirmed that only the latter, homosexual acts, are 'intrinsically disordered'. But he immediately added a caveat: taking into account the 'excessively benevolent' interpretations that he had noticed being made, he need only point out that the 'inclination itself' is bad, even if it is not a sin. Indulgence has its limits.

More perhaps than another man of his generation, Joseph Ratzinger has run counter to history – and to his own life. His reasoning, which is absolutely perverse, would soon lead him to justify discrimination against homosexuals, encouraging their dismissal from workplaces or the army, encouraging the refusal of employment or access to housing for them. By legitimizing institutional homophobia in this way, the cardinal and then the pope would inadvertently confirm that his theological power was not without its prejudices.

Perhaps that was how it had to be? Because let us not forget that Joseph Ratzinger was born in 1927, and that he was 42 when the gay 'liberation' of Stonewall happened. He became pope at 78 – already an old man. His thinking is that of a man who has remained locked in the homophobic ideas of his time.

In the end, and more than when I began this investigation, I feel a certain tenderness towards this introverted, locked-up, thwarted man, for this tragic figure whose anachronism haunts me. This serious intellectual has thought of everything – but failed to deal honestly with the issue that is most essential for him: a man of another age, for whom a lifetime has not been enough to resolve his own inner conflict, while today, tens of millions of teenagers all over the world, less literate or intelligent than he, are able to decode the same puzzle within a few months, before they turn 18.

Then I wonder how, perhaps, in other places or other times, some Michelangelo might have helped to reveal his identity, hidden away in a block of marble, and revealed this 'closeted' man, this Atlas, this Slave, this young or bearded Prisoner, like those one can see so splendidly emerging from the stone in the Galleria dell'Accademia in Florence. Shouldn't we, in the end, have a certain respect for this man who loved beauty and who struggled against himself all his life – an illusory combat, certainly; tragic in its way; but ultimately sincere?

Whatever the truth of this question – a truth that we will probably never know – I prefer to fall back on this generous hypothesis of a priesthood that he chose to protect himself from himself, a conjecture that gives a humanity and a tenderness to one of the most enduring homophobes of the twentieth century.

'*Naturam expellas furca, tamen usque recurret*', Horace writes (Drive away nature with a fork, it comes back at a gallop). Can one conceal one's true nature in the long run? One of the most revealing phrases in Benedict XVI's pontificate, and one of the most extraordinary, appears – albeit anecdotally – in his book of official interviews, *Light of the World*, published in 2010. In one long interview, the pope returns at length to the huge global controversy provoked by his obscurantist words about AIDS (on his first trip to Africa, he had declared that the distribution of condoms was 'aggravating' the epidemic). So the pope set about correcting his words, to make himself more easily understood. And all of a sudden, in his reply, he says: 'There may be individual cases, for example when a [male] prostitute uses a condom, when that may become a first step towards moralisation … But it is not the true way of responding to the evil of the HIV virus. The correct response lies necessarily in the humanisation of sexuality.'

Freud would have loved this phrase, which he would doubtless have dissected as meticulously as he did Leonardo da Vinci's childhood memory. What is absolutely extraordinary here is not the pope's formulation on AIDS, but his *lapsus linguae* doubled by a *lapsus calami*. Uttered verbally and reread when written down, the phrase has been validated twice as such (I have checked the original, and it is written with a masculine article, '*ein Prostituierter*', pp. 146–7 in the German edition). In Africa, where the very great majority of cases of AIDS involve heterosexuals, the only concession that Benedict will agree to make concerns a male prostitute. Not even a female sex worker. When he thinks about prostitutes in Africa, Benedict, whatever the cost, imagines them as masculine! Never has a slip been so revealing. And I have lost count of the number of priests, bishops, journalists or gay militants who have quoted this phrase to me, whether embarrassed or radiant, sometimes indeed bursting out laughing. This double slip is probably one of the most revealing confessions in the whole history of Catholicism.

20

The vice-pope

The photo is so unreal that it looks as if it's photoshopped. The Cardinal Secretary of State Tarcisio Bertone appears enthroned in majesty: he is sitting on a chair elevated on a blue rostrum, wearing his red-lined yellow mitre. This triply-staged subterfuge – the rostrum, the throne, the mitre – makes him look like a slightly scary giant. He sits stiffly like an emperor during a sacred rite, unless it's just an excess of calcium.

On his right, Cardinal Jorge Bergoglio is very small: sitting on a plain metal chair, off the rostrum, he is dressed simply in white. Bertone wears black aviator sunglasses; Bergoglio his big spectacles. Bertone's gold-coloured chasuble ends in white lace that reminds me of my grandmother's doilies; on his wrist a watch glitters: a Rolex, it has been established. The tension between the two men is palpable: Bertone stares straight ahead with an inquisitorial expression, frozen like a mummy; Bergoglio's mouth is open with alarm, perhaps at the sight of this pedantic Caesar.

This photograph, which is easy to find on Google and Instagram, dates from November 2007: it was taken during a trip by the secretary of state to Argentina for a beatification ceremony. At the time, Bertone was the most powerful figure in the Catholic Church, after Benedict XVI: he was known as 'the vice-pope'. A few years later, he would be moved aside; Bergoglio would be elected pontiff under the name of Francis.

Tarcisio Bertone was born in Piedmont in 1934. He shares this place of origin – Northern Italy – with Angelo Sodano, his predecessor at the Secretariat of State. After Sodano, he is the second villain of this book.

And of course, in the great Shakespearean theatre that the Roman Curia has always been, these two giants of vanity and rigidity would become 'complementary enemies'.

The son of mountain peasants, Bertone is a Salesian, a member of a Catholic congregation founded in Italy that places education at the heart of its mission. For a long time, his career was quite tranquil. For 30 years he was seldom mentioned: he was a priest, and he taught. Of course, discreetly, he was networking; and in the end he was appointed, at the age of 56, Archbishop of Vercelli in the Piedmont of his birth.

One of the men who knew him well at this time was Cardinal Raffaele Farina, who is also a Salesian, and who welcomes Daniele and me into his apartment in the Vatican. From his window we can see the pope's apartments a few metres away and, a little further off, the spectacular terraces of Cardinals Giovanni Battista Re and Bertone. And even further off, the penthouse terrace of Angelo Sodano. All of these octogenarians observe one another fixedly, with envy and animosity, from their respective windows. Terrace warfare.

'I was in charge of the Salesian University when Bertone joined us,' Farina explains. 'He was my deputy. I know him well, and I would never have appointed him secretary of state of the Vatican. He liked travelling and looking after his own business. He talks a lot, particularly in Italian and sometimes in French; he has a lot of international contacts but he failed at the Salesian University before failing at everything in the Vatican.'

And Cardinal Farina adds, as if by way of digression: 'Bertone always moved his hands around. He's a northern Italian who talks with his hands like a man of the South!'

Farina knows all the secrets of the Vatican. Created cardinal by Benedict XVI, to whom he was close, he was appointed by Francis to the presidency of the important commission for the reform of the Vatican Bank. Between finance, corruption and homosexuality, he knows everything, and we talk at length about these subjects with astonishing freedom over the course of several conversations.

At the end of one of our meetings, we accompany Farina to his next destination. We get into his little car, a Volkswagen Up!, and end our conversation in this Vatican diplomatic vehicle, which he drives himself at the age of 85. We pass in front of the apartment building where Tarcisio Bertone lives, then in front of Angelo Sodano's. We drive along the steep streets of the Vatican, among the blossoming cherry trees, beneath the vigilant eye of the police who know from experience that Cardinal Farina is no longer as keen-eyed as he was. Here he's just ignored a stop sign; now he's going the wrong way down a one-way street; each time, the police wave at him and politely point him in the right direction. Safe and sound, though after a few hair-raising moments, we reach the Porta Santa Anna, complete with a marvellous memory of a discussion with a cardinal who has told us a lot. My goodness, how much!

Is Bertone an idiot? That's what everybody tells me at the Vatican today. It's hard to find a prelate or a nuncio to defend him, even if those outraged criticisms, now coming from the same people who carried him to his pinnacle only yesterday, forget Bertone's rare qualities. Among which are: his great capacity for work; his loyalty to his colleagues; his sense of networking in the Italian episcopate; his Ratzingerian dogmatism. But for want of natural authority he has, like many an incompetent before him, become authoritarian. People who knew him in Genoa describe him as a formalist; as someone who was very arrogant and who surrounded himself with young celibates and old bachelors in the palace where he received his guests.

'He kept us waiting as if we were having an audience with the pope,' the former French ambassador to the Vatican, Pierre Morel, tells me, describing one such occasion.

One of Bertone's former students, when he was teaching law and French, a priest who I meet in London, tells me on the other hand that 'he was a very good teacher and very funny'. Bertone liked to quote, the same source tells me, Claudel, Bernanos and Jacques Maritain. In a written exchange, Bertone confirms that he has read these authors, apologizes for his slightly rusty French, and thanks me for 'refreshing' it by giving him a book – the famous little white book.

For many, Tarcisio Bertone reached his level of incompetence at the Secretariat of State. Cardinal Giovanni Battista Re, former 'minister' of the interior to John Paul II and an enemy of Bertone, weighs his words carefully: 'Bertone was very good at the Congregation for the Doctrine of the Faith, but he wasn't ready for the post of secretary of state.'

Don Julius, the confessor at St Peter's, who associated with Bertone and may have taken his confession, adds: 'He was presumptuous; he was a bad teacher of canon law.'

The confessors at St Peter's, most of whom are homophilic at the least, are an interesting source of information within the Vatican. Lodged in an ancient building on Piazza Santa Marta, they live in individual cells and lovely collective refectories. I often had my meetings there, in the parlatorio which, even though it is located at the nerve centre of the holy see, is as discreet a place as one might wish for: no one disturbs a confessor who is taking confession – or confessing himself.

From this observation post between the Palace of Justice and the offices of the Vatican police, a stone's throw from Pope Francis's residence and facing Bertone's apartment, the confessors see and know everything. It was here that Paolo Gabriele was placed in detention after the VatiLeaks affair: for the first time, their cells became a genuine prison.

With a guarantee of anonymity, the confessors of St Peter's tell me everything. They know which cardinal is implicated in which corruption scandal; who is sleeping with whom; which handsome assistant joins his boss in his luxury apartment in the evening; who likes the Swiss Guards, or who prefers the more manly policemen.

One of the priests, preserving the secrets of the confessional, tells me: 'No corrupt cardinal has ever told us in confession that he is corrupt! No homophilic cardinal has confessed his inclinations! They talk to us about stupid things, about unimportant details. And yet we know they are so corrupt that they no longer have any idea what corruption is. They even lie in confession.'

Bertone's career really took off when Joseph Ratzinger appointed him number two at the important Congregation for the Doctrine of Faith This was in 1995; he was 60.

For a rigid man, being appointed to the most doctrinaire post in the whole of the Church was a blessing. 'Rigidity squared', a Curia priest tells me. It was here that Bertone acquired a bad reputation as a member of the thought police.

Mgr Krzysztof Charamsa, who has worked at the Palace of the Holy Office for many years, compares it to a 'branch of the KGB', a real oppressive totalitarian system that 'controlled souls and bedrooms'. Did Bertone exert psychological pressure on certain homosexual bishops? Did he tell a particular cardinal that there was a file about him and that he should keep his nose clean? Charamsa remains evasive when I ask him.

The fact remains that this way of working at the Congregation for the Doctrine of Faith earned Bertone the nickname of Hoover.

'He was a less intelligent Hoover, though,' the archbishop who revealed this nickname to me adds by way of correction.

J. Edgar Hoover, who ran the US Bureau of Investigation and its successor, the FBI, for almost fifty years, combined an intelligent understanding of people and situations with a strict organization of his cloistered existence. Fighting ceaselessly and demonically against himself, he drew up very thorough secret files of the private lives of countless public figures and American politicians. We know now that this extraordinary capacity for work, this perverse taste for power, this anti-communist obsession, coexisted with a secret: he was also homosexual, or at least a homophile. He lived a large part of his contradiction-filled life with his chief deputy Clyde Tolson, whom he appointed deputy director of the FBI before making him his heir.

The comparison with Bertone breaks down on certain points, the copy might be different from the model, but the psychology is there. Bertone is a failed Hoover.

In 2002, Tarcisio Bertone was made Archbishop of Genoa by John Paul II then created cardinal on Ratzinger's insistence. A few months after his election, Benedict XVI called for him to replace Angelo Sodano as seceretary of state: Bertone became the pope's 'prime minister'.

The successful arriviste now had all the powers. Just as Sodano had really been the vice-pope for the last ten years of John Paul II's pontificate because of the holy father's long illness, Bertone became vice-pope thanks to Benedict XVI's lack of interest in the management of affairs of state.

According to several sources, Bertone put in place a system of internal controls consisting of signals, alerts and 'monitoring', a whole chain of command that came back to him, to protect the secrets of the Vatican. This system should have allowed him to stay in power for a long time, if he hadn't encountered two unexpected complications in his otherwise faultless career: the VatiLeaks affair, first of all, and then, still more unexpectedly, Benedict XVI's 'abdication'.

Less organized than Hoover, Bertone knew, like him, how to correct his shortcomings in his choice of men. So he became close to a certain Domenico Giani, whom he appointed to the head of the Corpo della gendarmeria of the Vatican, in spite of the fierce opposition of Cardinal Angelo Sodano, who hoped that he himself would be able to go on pulling the strings. At the head of a hundred gendarmes, inspectors and police officers, this former officer of the Italian Guardia di Finanza became Bertone's shadow in all secret affairs and missions.

'The Italian chiefs of police were very critical towards the Vatican gendarmerie, which refused to cooperate with us and used zones of extraterritoriality and diplomatic immunity to cover up certain scandals. Relations became increasingly tense,' a senior Italian policeman tells me.

In a book that is controversial but that contains information provided by Georg Gänswein and an assistant of Bertone's, the essayist Nicolas Diat suggests that Domenico Giani was subject to external influences, without stating whether this might have come from Freemasonry, the gay lobby or the Italian secret service. A cardinal he quotes considered that he was 'guilty of high treason', and that this was one of the 'most serious examples of infiltration in the holy see'. (These serious insinuations have never been proven; they have been firmly denied by the spokesman for Benedict XVI; and Pope Francis renewed his trust in Giani.)

With the help of Domenico Giani and the technical services of the Vatican, Bertone kept the Curia under surveillance. Hundreds of cameras were installed everywhere; communications were screened. There was even a plan to authorize just a single, particularly secure model of mobile phone. Uproar among the bishops! They refused to be monitored! The attempt to harmonize smartphones failed, but checks took place nonetheless. (Cardinal Jean-Louis Tauran confirmed this point.)

'Means of communication, telephones and computers, were closely screened and checked by the Vatican. That way they knew everything that happened in the holy see and, if need be, they had proof against anyone who might cause problems. But generally speaking they kept it all to themselves,' I am told by the former priest Francesco Lepore, who was himself subject to reinforced surveillance before his dismissal.

John Paul II's former 'minister' of the interior, Giovanni Battista Re, whom I spoke to on this subject, in the presence of Daniele, still doubts that the Vatican would have been capable of surveillance at this level. 'By definition, at the Vatican, the secretary of state knows everything and, of course, has files on everybody. But I don't think Bertone was as organized as that, or that he had files on everyone.'

Like most surveillance systems, that of Bertone and Giani prompted strategies of avoidance on the part of the curia prelates. Most of them started using secure applications like Signal or Telegram; they also bought themselves second private mobile phones, using which they could safely speak ill of the secretary of state, discuss rumours about their co-religionists or hook up on Grindr. Inside the Vatican, where use of the internet was particularly monitored and screened, that second telephone allowed them to get through the firewall to forbidden addresses, such as erotic sites.

One day, when I was in the private apartment of a priest I was staying with inside the Vatican, we carried out an experiment. We tested several erotic sites and were blocked by a message: 'If you want to unblock this site, please call the internal number 181, formerly 83511, or 90500.' Talk about 'parental control'!

I carried out the same experiment again a few months later from the apartment of a bishop, still inside the Vatican, and this time I read on the screen that 'access to the web page requested' is blocked on the initiative of 'the security police' of the Vatican. One reason was given: 'Adult content'. I just had to tap 'send' to ask for it to be unblocked.

'Senior Vatican figures think they can escape this supervision. They are allowed to get on with it; but if one day they become an "obstacle", what is known can be used to control them,' Francesco Lepore explains.

Pornography, essentially gay pornography, is such a frequent phenomenon in the Vatican that my sources speak of 'serious addiction problems among the Curia prelates'. Some priests have even resorted to dedicated services to battle these addictions, like NoFap, a specialist site based in a Catholic church in Pennsylvania.

This internal surveillance was stepped up during the pontificate of Benedict XVI, as scandals, rumours and, of course, the first VatiLeaks affair proliferated. Tarcisio Bertone was himself caught up in these leaks, and his paranoia redoubled. He started looking for microphones in his private apartments, suspecting colleagues, and even dismissed his chauffeur, whom he suspected of informing Cardinal Sodano.

Meanwhile, the Vatican machine seized up. In charge of international relations, but poor at speaking foreign languages, Bertone became isolated from the local episcopates and started making mistake after mistake. A poor diplomat, he concentrated on what he knew best, namely Italian politics and relations with the country's rulers, whom he had hoped to be able to control directly (this point was confirmed to me by two presidents of the CEI, Cardinals Ruini and Bagnasco).

Benedict XVI's secretary of state also surrounded himself with undistinguished colleagues, prompting a number of rumours. These included the famous Lech Piechota, Bertone's favourite assistant, from whom he seems to have been inseparable, like Ratzinger with Georg Gänswein or John Paul II with Stanisław Dziwisz.

I tried to interview Piechota, but without success. Since the end of the pontificate of Benedict XVI, this Polish priest has been transferred, I was informed, to the Pontifical Council of Culture. During one of my many visits to that ministry, I asked after Piechota and tried to find out by what miracle – he having never had the slightest interest in the arts – he had fetched up there. Did he have some hidden artistic talent? Had he been shunted aside? I tried innocently to understand.

So I interviewed the directors of the Ministry of Culture twice about Piechota. Was he there? The reply was categorical: 'I don't know who you're talking about. He isn't here.'

A strange denial. Lech Piechota appears in the *Annuario Pontificio* as being a policy officer for the Pontifical Council of Culture, alongside the names of Father Laurent Mazas, the priest Pasquale Iacobone and Bishop Carlos Azevedo, all three of whom I have interviewed. And when I call the switchboard of that ministry, I am put through to Piechota. We speak briefly, but, strangely, the former assistant to the 'prime minister', a man who used to talk every day with dozens of cardinals and heads of government from all over the world, speaks neither French nor English nor Spanish.

So Piechota is a policy officer in the Ministry of Culture, but they seem to have forgotten that he's there. Has he got into trouble since his name was leaked in the VatiLeaks scandal? Does this personal private secretary of Cardinal Bertone need to be protected? Why does this Polish priest Piechota keep himself so much to himself? Why does he sometimes leave his office at the Pontifical Council of Culture when Bertone tells him to (according to two witnesses)? Why do we see him driving about in a big official car: a luxury Audi A6, with tinted windows and back windscreen and a diplomatic Vatican plate? Why does Piechota still live in the Palace of the Holy Office, where I have bumped into him several times, and where this big car is parked in a privileged parking place where no one else is allowed to park? And when I asked these questions to members of the Curia, why did they smile? Why? Why?

It has to be said that Tarcisio Bertone has lots of enemies. Among them, there is Angelo Sodano, who remained on the inside at the start of the pontificate of Benedict XVI. From his Ethiopian College, which he has had restored at great expense, the former secretary of state has been caught in an ambush. He has certainly been stripped of his responsibilities, but he remains a *decano* (dean) in the College of Cardinals: this title gives him even greater authority over the electors in the conclave, who still see him as a pope-maker. Since Sodano has exercised power for such a long time, he too has his bad habits: from his gilded closet, he shuffles men and files about those men as if he were still in charge. Bertone understood too late that Sodano was one of the dynamiters-in-chief of the pontificate of Benedict XVI.

It all began, as so often, with a humiliation. The former cardinal secretary of state of John Paul II did everything he could to stay in the court. For the first year of his reign, the pope kept Sodano in his post for form's sake, and for another more significant reason: there was no one else to appeal to! Joseph Ratzinger had never been a political cardinal: he had no gang, no team, no one to place or promote but Georg, his personal assistant. But Ratzinger had always been highly suspicious of Sodano, about whom he, like everyone else, had received shocking information.

He was flabbergasted by what he was told about his Chilean past, so much so that he didn't want to believe the rumours.

Taking advantage of his canonical age of 79, Benedict XVI finally parted company with Sodano. According to his memoirs, it happened as follows: 'He was the same age as me. If the pope is old, because he was elected when elderly, the secretary of state, at least, has to be in top form.'

Making a cardinal of almost eighty retire: Sodano couldn't bear it. Without waiting, he reared up, rebelled, started casting aspersions. He resisted. When he understood that the game was up, he demanded to be able to choose his successor (his protégé and deputy Giovanni Lajolo, a former member of the APSA who was a nuncio in Germany), but without success. And when at last he learned the name of his replacement, the Archbishop of Genoa Tarcisio Bertone, he was horrified: 'He could have been my deputy! He isn't even a nuncio! He doesn't even speak English! He isn't part of the cassocked aristocracy!' (In his defence, Bertone speaks quite good French and Spanish, as well as Italian, as I have been able to check.)

Now begins an episode of slander, gossip and revenge of a kind unknown in Italy since the time of Julius Caesar, when the general punished his soldiers for outing him by calling him 'Queen'!

Of course gossip has always played a large part in the history of the holy see. It is the 'gay poison' that the Poet speaks of, and the 'sickness of rumours, slander and gossip' denounced by Pope Francis. This kind of gossip was typical of homosexual life before 'gay liberation'. It consists of the same allusions, the same jokes, the same slanders that cardinals use today to hurt and wound – in the hope of hiding their own double lives.

'The Vatican is a court with a monarch. And as with the clergy, there is no separation between private and public life, no family, everyone lives in a community, everything is known, everything is mixed-up. That's how rumours, gossip and slander become a system,' the Vaticanologist Romilda Ferrauto, who was for a long time one of the directors of Radio Vatican, tells me.

Rabelais, a former monk himself, had been aware of this tendency among prelates of the pontifical court to 'curse everyone' while 'fornicating like mad'. As for 'outing', the terrible weapon of homophobes, it has always been highly prized by homosexuals themselves, in the gay clubs of the 1950s, as it is in the principality of the Vatican today.

Pope Francis, a shrewd observer of 'his' Curia, was not mistaken when he mentioned in his speech, among the '15 curial diseases': existential schizophrenia; courtiers who 'murder in cold blood' the reputation of their fellow cardinals; the 'terrorism of gossip' and those prelates who 'create a parallel world for themselves, where they set aside all that they severely teach others, and begin to live a hidden and often dissolute life'. Could it be clearer? The connection between slander and double lives is now established by the most irrefutable witness there is: the pope.

Be that as it may, the former secretary of state, Angelo Sodano, organized his revenge on Bertone in great detail: having trained in Pinochet's Chile, he knew the score, the murderous rumours and the ruthless methods. First of all, he refused to leave his luxury apartment, which Bertone had to recover from him. After all, the new secretary of state had to make do with a *pied-à-terre* while Sodano's new penthouse was being restored and polished.

On the side of the resistance, the bad-tempered Sodano stirred up his networks within the College of Cardinals and the rumour machine. Bertone was slow in taking the exact measure of the battle of celestial egos. By the time he did, after VatiLeaks, it would be too late. By that time, everyone had already been given early retirement, along with the pope!

One of Sodano's close accomplices was an Argentinian archbishop who was a nuncio in Venezuela and Mexico: Leonardo Sandri, whom we have already mentioned. The new pope, who was as suspicious of him as he was of Sodano, chose to part company with this troublesome Argentinian as well. He did respect conventions: he made Sandri a cardinal in 2007 and put him in charge of the Eastern Churches. But that wasn't enough for this egoistic macho man, who couldn't bear the idea of being stripped of his post as 'minister' of the interior to the pope. In turn, he joined Sodano in the resistance, a foot soldier in a small guerrilla force in the Sierra Maestra of the Vatican.

The holy see has never been spared scenes of domestic discord and family feuds. In the Vatican ocean of ambitions, perversions and slander, many popes have managed to navigate dangerous cross-winds. Another secretary of state could probably have steered the Vatican ship to a safe harbour – even with Benedict XVI; another pope, if he had taken care of the Curia, would have been able to float the ship again – even with Bertone. But the association between an ideologically-driven pope and a cardinal who was incapable of managing the Curia, so full of himself and so craving recognition, could not work. The pontifical couple had been a shaky team from the beginning, and its failure was swiftly confirmed. 'We trusted each other, we got on well, so I didn't let him go,' the pope emeritus would later confirm with good will and generosity, speaking of Bertone.

Controversies erupted one after the other, and with startling speed and violence: during his speech in Regensburg, the pope provoked an international scandal by suggesting that Islam was intrinsically violent, thus undoing all the Vatican's efforts of interreligious dialogue (the speech had not been read through, and in the end the pope had to apologize); by swiftly and unconditionally rehabilitating the Lefebvrist ultra-fundamentalists, including a notorious anti-Semite and revisionist, the pope was accused of supporting the far right and entered a huge controversy with the Jews. These grave and fundamental errors in communication quickly weakened the holy father. And, inevitably, his past in the Hitler Youth rose to the surface.

Cardinal Bertone would soon be at the centre of a huge property scandal. The press, drawing on information from VatiLeaks, accused him of having grabbed himself a penthouse, like Sodano – 350 square metres in the Palazzo San Carlo, created by knocking together two previous apartments – and of adding a vast terrace, itself measuring 300 square metres. The restoration work on his palazzo, costing 200,000 euros, was said to have been financed by the foundation of the Bambino Gesù Paediatric Hospital. (Pope Francis would ask Bertone to return this sum, and a trial by the Vatican was announced against the extravagant cardinal.)

Little is known about it, but in the background a gay camarilla was stirring up plots and intrigues like mad. Among them, cardinals and bishops, all practising, were on manoeuvres. A real war of nerves began, aimed at Bertone and of course, through him, the pope. The backdrop to these plots consisted of so many reheated hatreds, slander, rumours, relationships, old break-ups and sometimes romances that it is hard to disentangle the interpersonal problems from the real underlying questions. (In his '*Testimonianza*', Archbishop Viganò suspected Cardinal Bertone 'of being notoriously in favour of the promotion of homosexuals to positions of responsibility'.)

In this ill-tempered context, new and serious revelations of sexual abuse scandals reached the holy see from several countries. Already on the brink of exploding, the Vatican would be swept away by this great groundswell from which, over ten years later, it still has not recovered.

As homophobic as Sodano, Bertone had his own theory about the paedophile question, which he finally delivered to the public and the press during a trip to Chile, where he arrived looking in great spirits and flanked by his favourite assistant. The secretary of state expressed himself officially here, in April 2010, concerning the psychology of paedophile priests. A new global controversy was about to erupt.

This is what Cardinal Bertone said: 'Many psychologists, many psychiatrists, have shown that there is no connection between celibacy [of priests] and paedophilia; but many others have shown, I have been told recently, that there is a connection between homosexuality and paedophilia. That is true. That is the problem.'

The official intervention, made by the number two at the Vatican, did not go unnoticed. These words, uttered vaguely, prompted international outrage: hundreds of personalities, including LGBT militants but also European ministers and Catholic theologians, denounced the prelate's irresponsible words. For the first time, his declaration brought a prudent denial from the Vatican press service, validated by the pope. For Benedict XVI to emerge from the shadows to express a hint of disagreement with his excessively homophobic 'prime minister': it was not without a certain irony. This was a serious moment.

How could Bertone come out with such absurd language? I have interviewed several cardinals and prelates about this point: they pleaded error of communication or clumsiness; only one gave me an interesting explanation. According to this curia priest who worked at the Vatican under Benedict XVI, Bertone's position on homosexuality was strategic, but also reflected the essentials of his thought. Strategic, primarily, because it was a tried and tested technique for casting the blame on the lost sheep that had no business being in the Church rather than calling the celibacy of the priesthood into question. The secretary of state's statement also reflects his underlying thoughts because, according to the same source, it reflected the thinking of theorists to whom Bertone was close, such as Cardinal Alfonso López Trujillo or the priest-psychoanalyst Tony Anatrella. Two highly practising homosexuals!.

To this we would also have to add some context that I discovered during my trips to Chile. The first is that the congregation most affected by sexual abuse in Chile is the very one from which Bertone himself emerged: the Salesians of Don Bosco.

Then, and this caused much mirth: when Bertone spoke in public to denounce homosexuality as a template for paedophilia he was surrounded in hundreds of photographs by at least two notorious homosexual priests. His declaration 'lost credibility' as a result of that simple fact, several sources indicate.

Finally, Juan Pablo Hermosilla, one of the main Chilean lawyers in the Church's sexual abuse scandals, particularly that of the paedophile priest Fernando Karadima, gave me the following explanation about the links between homosexuality and paedophilia, which strikes me as pertinent.

'My theory is that paedophile priests use information that the Catholic hierarchy has at its disposal in order to protect themselves. It is a form of pressure or blackmail. Bishops who had homosexual relations themselves were obliged to say nothing. This explains why Karadima was protected by bishops and archbishops: not because they were paedophiles themselves, and most of them are not, but to avoid the discovery of their own homosexuality. That, for me, is the true source of the Church's corruption and institutionalized cover-up.'

We could go further still. Many of the excesses of the Church, many silences, many mysteries are explained by this simple rule of *The Closet*: 'everybody looks out for each other'. Why do the cardinals say nothing? Why do they all close their eyes? Why was Pope Benedict XVI, who knew about many sexual scandals, never brought to justice? Why did Cardinal Bertone, ruined by the attacks of Angelo Sodano, not bring out the intelligence that he had about his enemy? Talking about others means that they may talk about you. That is the key to the *omertà* and the general lies of the Church. The Vatican and the Vatican closet are like Fight Club – and the first rule of Fight Club is, you don't talk about Fight Club.

Bertone's homophobia didn't stop him buying a gay sauna in Rome city centre. It was in such terms, at least, that the press presented this incredible news.

In order to understand this new scandal, I went to the place in question, no. 40 Via Aureliana, the sauna Europa Multiclub. One of the most popular gay establishments in Rome, it is a sports club-cum-cruising spot with saunas and hammams. Frolicking is possible and legal there, because the club is considered 'private'. You need a membership card to get in, as in most gay places in Italy – a national peculiarity. For a long time, the card was distributed by the association Arcigay; now it is sold for 15 euros by Anddos, a kind of lobby group for the patrons of gay establishments.

'The membership card is compulsory to get in to the sauna, because the law forbids sexual relations in a public place. We're a private place,' Mario Marco Canale, the manager of the Europa Multiclub, says by way of self-justification.

He is both the manager of the Europa Multiclub and the president of the Anddos association. He receives me wearing both hats at the very site of the controversy.

He goes on, this time wearing the hat of his association: 'We have almost 200,000 members in Italy because a large number of bars, clubs and saunas require the Anddos card for entrance.'

This membership-card system for gay venues is unique in Europe. Originally, in the anti-gay, macho Italy of the 1980s, it was designed to make homosexual places safe, keep their clientele loyal and legalize sexuality on-site. Today, it persists for less essential reasons, under the pressure of the managers of the 70 clubs that form the Anddos association, and perhaps also because it allows the association to wage its struggle against AIDS and receive public subventions.

For several gay militants I have spoken to, 'this card is an archaic remnant and it's high time it was got rid of'. Apart from the possible surveillance of homosexuals in Italy (which Anddos firmly denies), according to an activist, this card is the symbol of a 'homosexuality that is closeted and shameful, and which seeks to be a private affair'.

I interviewed Marco Canale about the controversy and the many press articles that presented the Europa Multiclub as a place run by the Vatican, indeed by Cardinal Bertone himself.

'In Rome, you have to bear in mind that hundreds of buildings belong to the holy see,' Canale tells me, without clearly denying the information.

In fact, the building on the corner of Via Aureliana and Via Carducci, in which the sauna is located, was bought by the Vatican for 20 million euros in May 2008. Cardinal Bertone, at the time 'prime minister' to Pope Benedict XVI, supervised and rubber-stamped the financial operation. According to my information, the sauna only represents part of a vast property complex, also including about twenty priests' apartments and even one cardinal's apartment. This was how the press managed to put two and two together and get the eye-catching headline: 'Cardinal Tarcisio Bertone has bought the biggest gay sauna in Italy!'

But the scandal remained disconcertingly amateurish, because the secretary of state and his office had indeed given the green light to this huge property purchase without anyone noticing that it contained the biggest gay sauna in Italy, visible and known to everybody and opening on to the street. As for the price paid by the Vatican, it seems unusual: according to a survey by the Italian newspaper *La Repubblica*, the building had previously been sold for 9 million euros, and therefore the Vatican had been diddled out of 11 million for this financial operation!

When we met, Marco Canale was amused by the controversy, even though he revealed another secret motivation behind it: 'At the Europa Multiclub we receive lots of priests and even cardinals. And every time there's a jubilee, a synod or a conclave, we realize immediately: the sauna is fuller than usual. Thanks to all the visiting priests!'

According to another source, the number of priests who are members of the Anddos gay association is equally high. It is possible to find out, because to become a member you have to supply a valid identification document; and the person's profession appears on an Italian ID even if it is immediately anonymized by the computer system.

'But we're not the police. We don't keep tabs on anybody. We have lots of members who are priests, that's all!' Canale concludes.

Another affair that was played out under Benedict XVI and Bertone, but that would only be revealed under Francis, concerns 'chem-sex parties'. I had heard for a long time that parties like this were happening inside the Vatican itself, real collective orgies in which sex and drugs combined in a sometimes dangerous cocktail ('chem' here means 'chemicals' for synthetic drugs, often MDMA, GHB, DOM, DOB and DiPT).

For a while I thought these were rumours, of which there are so many in the Vatican. And then, all of a sudden, in the summer of 2017, the Italian press revealed that a monsignore, the priest Luigi Capozzi, who had been one of the chief assistants to Cardinal Francesco Coccopalmerio, had been arrested by the Vatican police for organizing 'chem-sex parties' in his private apartment in the Vatican. (On this matter I questioned a Curia priest who knew Capozzi well, and I also met Cardinal Coccopalmerio.)

Close to Tarcisio Bertone, and greatly appreciated by Cardinal Ratzinger, Capozzi lived in an apartment in the Palace of the Holy Office, surrounded by four cardinals, several archbishops and numerous prelates, including Lech Piechota, assistant to Cardinal Bertone, and Josef Clemens, the former private secretary to Cardinal Ratzinger.

I know this building well, because I have had the opportunity to dine there dozens of times: one of its entrances is on Italian territory, the other inside the Vatican. Capozzi had an apartment ideally located for organizing those startling orgies, because he was able to have it both ways: the Italian police couldn't search his apartment or his diplomatic vehicle, because he lived inside the Vatican; but he was able to leave his home with impunity, without passing through checks made by the holy see or being searched by the Swiss Guard, because of the door that opens directly on to Italy. A whole ritual was acted out inside: the 'chem-sex parties' took place in a muted red light, with the consumption of large quantities of hard drugs, glasses of cannabis vodka and very lubricious guests. Real 'nights in hell'!

According to the witnesses I have interviewed, Capozzi's homosexuality was common knowledge – and was therefore probably known to his superiors, to Cardinal Coccopalmerio and Tarcisio Bertone – all the more so given that the priest had no hesitation in going out to Rome's gay clubs or, in the summer, attending the big LGBT parties held at the Fantasia Gay Village in the south of the capital.

'During those chem-sex parties, there were also priests and Vatican employees,' one witness adds, a monsignore who took part in these parties.

Since these revelations, Luigi Capozzi has been hospitalized in the Pius XI Clinic, and hasn't communicated with the outside world. (He is still presumed innocent, since his trial for the use and possession of drugs has not taken place.)

So Benedict XVI's pontificate hit the ground running and developed with a swift and unbridled proliferation of scandals. On the gay question, the war against homosexuals resumed unabated, as in the time of John Paul II, and hypocrisy was more than ever at the heart of the system. A hatred of homosexuals on the outside; homophilia and the double life on the inside. The circus went on.

'The gayest pontificate in history': the expression comes from the former prelate Krzysztof Charamsa. When I interviewed him in Barcelona, and then in Paris, this priest who had worked beside Joseph Ratzinger for a long time repeated this expression about the Benedict XVI years several times: 'the gayest pontificate in history'. The Curia priest Don Julius, who notes that it was 'difficult to be heterosexual under Benedict XVI', even if there were some rare exceptions, uses a potent expression to describe the pope's entourage: 'fifty shades of gay'.

Francis himself, unmistakably more direct than his predecessor, stresses the paradoxes of this incongruous entourage, using a cutting phrase to attack the Ratzingerians: 'theological narcissism'. Another code that he uses to imply homosexuality is 'self-referential'. Rigidity, as we know, often conceals double lives.

'I feel deep sadness when I think about Benedict's pontificate, one of the darkest moments for the Church, in which homophobia represented a constant and desperate attempt to conceal the very existence of homosexuality among us,' Charamsa tells me.

During the pontificate of Benedict XVI, the higher up the Vatican hierarchy you went, the more homosexuals you found. The majority of the cardinals that the pope created are said to be homophile at least, and some are even very 'practising'.

'Under Benedict XVI, a homosexual bishop who gave the appearance of being chaste had more chance of becoming a cardinal than a heterosexual bishop,' I am told by a well-known Dominican friar, a keen connoisseur of Ratzingerian thought, who held the Benedict XVI Chair in Regensburg.

Every time he travelled, the pope was accompanied by some of his closest collaborators. Among them was the famous prelate nicknamed Mgr Jessica by the press, which claimed he took advantage of the holy father's regular visits to the church of Saint Sabina in Rome, the headquarters of the Dominicans, to give his visiting card to the younger friars. His 'pickup line' was discussed by the whole world when it was revealed in a report by *Vanity Fair*: he tried to proposition seminarians by suggesting that they go and see John XXIII's bed!

'He was very "touchy" and very intimate with the seminarians,' admits the priest Urien, who witnessed him in action.

Two other extremely gay bishops assigned to the pope, who surrounded Ratzinger with their affection and were close to Secretary of State Bertone, also enjoyed pursuing boys: having honed their techniques under John Paul II, they went on perfecting them under Ratzinger. (I met both of them with Daniele, and one of them came on to us with perseverence.)

In the Vatican, all this became so dominant a subject of gossip that some priests became annoyed. So, for example, the archbishop and nuncio Angelo Mottola, who held posts in Iran and Montenegro, addressed Cardinal Tauran during one of his visits to Rome and said (according to an eye-witness): 'I don't understand why this pope [Benedict XVI] condemns homosexuals when he surrounds himself with all these "*ricchioni*"' (the Italian word is hard to translate: 'faggots' would be the closest meaning).

The pope paid no heed to rumours, and pursued his own course. When Leonardo da Vinci's *Saint John the Baptist* was shown at the Palazzo Venezia in Rome, during the long tour organized by the Louvre after its restoration, he decided to go there in majesty. Benedict XVI, surrounded by his entourage, made a special trip. Was it the androgyne with curly Venetian-blond hair that attracted him, or the index finger of the left hand of this 'son of thunder' pointing towards heaven? Restored and sublime, *Saint John the Baptist* had just had his coming out, and the pope didn't want to miss the event. (The model for *Saint John the Baptist* is believed to have been Salai, a poor and delinquent boy with an intense angelic and androgynous beauty, whom Leonardo da Vinci met by chance in the streets of Milan in 1490: this 'little devil' with the long curls remained his lover for a long time.)

Another time, in 2010, during a general audience, the pope witnessed a brief dance display in the Paul VI Hall: four sexy acrobats came on stage and, before the holy father's admiring eyes, suddenly undressed, removing their tee-shirts. Bare-chested, bursting with youth and beauty, they then performed a cheerful number that can be found on YouTube. Sitting on his huge white papal throne, the holy father got spontaneously to his feet, overwhelmed, to salute them. Behind him, Cardinal Bertone and Georg Gänswein applauded enthusiastically. It was later learned that the little troupe had had the same success at Gay Pride in Barcelona. Might a member of the pope's entourage have spotted them there?

None of this stopped the pope, once again, from redoubling his attacks against gays. Recently elected, and taking into account the fact that 'homosexual culture was constantly advancing', Benedict XVI had, at the end of 2005, already asked the Congregation for the Doctrine of the Faith to write a new text condemning homosexuality even more severely. There was a lively debate among his entourage to decide whether it should be an encyclical or a mere 'document'. The text was eventually finalized in a highly polished version, which was circulated for commentary, as is the rule, among the members of the Council of the Congregation for the Doctrine of the Faith (one of the priests who assisted Cardinal Jean-Louis Tauran had access to this document and described it to me in detail). The viciousness of the text was shocking, according to this priest, who had also read the opinions of the consultants and members of the Congregation, Tauran among them, concerning the file (including those of the bishops and future cardinals Albert Vanhoye and Giovanni Lajolo, and of the bishop Enrico Dal Covolo, all three of whom were very homophobic in their commentaries.) The priest remembers medieval phrases about 'unnatural sin', the 'baseness' of homosexuals and, indeed, the 'power of the international gay lobby'.

'Some of the people consulted argued for a powerful intervention in the form of an encyclical; others recommended producing a less significant document; still others advised, given the risk of counter-productive consequences, not to return to this question,' the priest remembers.

The option of an encyclical would finally be abandoned, the pope's entourage having once again dissuaded him from returning to the subject – once too often? But the spirit of the text would live on.

In a context that was already that of the end of an era, after fewer than five years of the pontificate, the Vatican machine came to an almost complete standstill. Benedict XVI retreated into shyness and began weeping often. The vice-pope, Bertone, suspicious by nature, became totally paranoid. He saw plots everywhere, machinations, cabals! In reaction to this he is said to have intensified his checks, the rumour factory worked overtime, the files filled up and there were increasing numbers of wire-taps by the Vatican police.

In the ministries and congregations of the Vatican, there were multiple resignations, whether voluntary or imposed. In the Secretariat of State, the nerve centre of power, Bertone took personal charge of the spring-cleaning process, so suspicious was he of traitors and even more of clever characters who might have outshone him. So various Judases, Peters and Johns, all living under the same roof, were asked to leave the Last Supper.

Tarcisio Bertone got rid of two of the most experienced nuncios in the Secretariat of State: Mgr Gabriele Caccia, exiled to Lebanon (where I met him); Pietro Parolin was sent to Venezuela.

'When Caccia and Parolin departed, Bertone was left on his own. The system, which was seriously dysfunctional, violently collapsed,' the American Vaticanologist Robert Carl Mickens observes.

Many people began requesting audiences with the pope without having to go through the troublesome secretary of state. Sodano said everything that he had on his heart to the pope; and Georg Gänswein, who was approached directly in order to short-circuit Bertone, received all the malcontents, who formed a lengthy queue outside his office. And while the pontificate was in its death-throes, four important cardinals – Schönborn, Scola, Bagnasco and Ruini – suddenly emerged to ask for an audience with Benedict XVI. These experts in Vatican intrigues, keen connoisseurs of the bad habits of the curia, proposed that Bertone be replaced immediately. And as if by chance, their action was leaked immediately to the press. The pope wouldn't hear a word of it, and cut them short. 'Bertone's staying, *basta!*'

It is beyond doubt that homosexuality has been at the heart of numerous intrigues and several scandals within the pontificate. But it would be a mistake here to oppose two camps, as some have done: one 'friendly' and the other homophobic, or one 'closeted' by contrast with chaste heterosexuals. The pontificate of Benedict XVI, whose scandals were, to a certain degree, the product of the 'rings of lust' that began to gleam under John Paul II, in fact opposed several homosexual clans who all shared the same homophobia. Under this pontificate, all, or nearly all, were chips off the same block.

War was unleashed against gays, condoms and civil partnerships. While in 2005, at the time of Joseph Ratzinger's election, gay marriage was still a very limited phenomenon, eight years later, by the time of Benedict XVI's resignation, it was becoming almost universal throughout Europe and Latin America. This abbreviated pontificate can be summed up in an incredible sequence of battles lost in advance. No pope in modern history has been so anti-gay; and no pope has impotently witnessed such momentum in favour of the rights of gays and lesbians. Soon, almost thirty countries would recognize marriage between people of the same sex, including the Germany of the pope's birth, which would in 2017, by a very large parliamentary majority, adopt the law against which Joseph Ratzinger had fought throughout his life.

However, Benedict XVI never stopped fighting. The list of bulls and briefs, his speeches, his letters, his messages against gay marriage, is endless. In open contempt of the separation between Church and State, he intervened frequently in the public debate and, in the background, the Vatican manipulated all the anti-gay-marriage demonstrations.

It was the same failure every time. But what is very revealing, here again, is that many of those involved in the battle were themselves homophilic, 'in the closet' or practising. They were often 'of the parish'.

The guerrilla war against gay marriage was waged, under the pope's authority, by nine men: Tarcisio Bertone, the secretary of state, assisted by his deputies Leonardo Sandri, as substitute or 'minister' of the interior, Fernando Filoni, and Dominique Mamberti, as 'minister' of foreign affairs, as well as by William Levada and then Gerhard Müller, at the head of the Congregation for the Doctrine of the Faith. Giovanni Battista Re and Marc Ouellet played the same role within the Congregation for Bishops. And, of course, Cardinal Alfonso López Trujillo, at the head of the Pontifical Council for the Family, blustered against gay marriage.

Let's take for example another Ratzingerian, the Swiss cardinal Kurt Koch, a bishop from Basel, whom the pope called to his Curia in 2010. At the same time, the journalist Michael Meier, a specialist in religious matters at the *Tages-Anzeiger*, the main German-speaking Swiss daily newspaper, published a long report about Koch based on several firsthand eye-witness statements and original documents. In it, Meier reveals the existence of a book published by Koch, but one that has strangely disappeared from his bibliography, *Lebensspiel der Freundschaft, Meditativer Brief an meine Freund* (literally: The Game of Friendship: A Meditative Letter to My Friend). This book, of which I have a copy, reads like a real love letter to a young theologian. Meier also describes the cardinal's sensitive entourage. He reveals a secret apartment that Koch is supposed to have shared with another priest, and implies that Koch was leading a double life.

'Everyone understood that Koch was uncomfortable in his skin,' Michael Meier told me at several interviews in his Zurich apartment. To my knowledge Meier's article has never been criticized by Koch; he never made use of his right to reply.

Was Koch the victim of slanderous denunciations by his entourage? The fact remains that Ratzinger brought Koch to his Curia. By creating him cardinal and making him his minister of 'ecumenism', he gently exfiltrated him from Basel. (Cardinal Koch refused to answer my questions, but in Rome I questioned one of his deputies, Father Hyacinthe Destivelle, who described to me at length the 'Schülerkreis', the circle of Ratzinger's disciples of which Koch was in charge. We also had a discussion about Tchaikovsky's homosexuality.)

In Italy, however, Benedict XVI's morbid homophobia was beginning to exasperate his gay-friendly milieu. It was falling increasingly out of line with public opinion (the Italians had understood its logic!) and LGBT activists were fighting back. The times were changing. The pope would find this out at his expense.

By tragically fighting the wrong battle – he was essentially attacking homosexuality, while facing up to paedophilia barely at all – the holy father first lost the moral campaign. He would be attacked on a personal level more than any other pope who had come before him. Today it is hard to imagine the criticism to which Pope Benedict XVI was subjected during his pontificate. Nicknamed, in an incredible phrase, 'Passivo e Bianco' by Italian homosexual circles, he was regularly denounced as being 'in the closet', and turned into a symbol of internalized homophobia. He was effectively crucified by LGBT activists and the media.

In the archives of Italian gay associations, on the internet and on the deep web, I have found countless articles, tracts and photographs that illustrate this guerrilla war. In all likelihood no pope has ever been so hated in the modern history of the Vatican.

'I have never seen anything like it. It was literally a continuous flood of highly-charged articles, rumours, attacks from all sides, violent articles by bloggers, insulting letters, in every language, from all countries. Hypocrisy, duplicity, insincerity, double-dealing, internalized homophobia, he was accused of all of these *ad nauseam*,' I am told by a priest who worked in the Vatican press office during that time.

At demonstrations in favour of civil partnerships in Italy in 2007, I saw placards that bore these words: '*Joseph e Georg, Lottiamo anche per voi*' (Joseph and Georg, we're fighting for you too). And this one: '*Il Papa è Gay come Noi*' (The Pope is gay like us).

In a little book that enjoyed modest success, but that struck people with its audacity, the anarchist journalist and well-known figure on the Italian underground scene, Angelo Quattrocchi, literally outed Benedict XVI. Entitled *The Pope is NOT Gay*, his ironic book brought together many girly and sissy photographs of the pope and his protégé Georg. The text itself is mediocre and crammed with factual errors, and includes neither proof of what it suggests nor any new information; but the photographs depict their bromance and are very funny. Nicknamed 'the Pink Pope', Ratzinger is shown from every angle.

At the same time, Benedict XVI's nicknames proliferated, each one crueller than the last: one of the worst, along with 'Passivo e bianco', was 'La Maledetta' ('the cursed one', and a play on 'Benedetto').

Former classmates or students who knew the pope also started talking, like the German author Uta Ranke-Heinemann, who studied with him at Munich University. At the age of 84 she stated that, in her view, the pope was gay. (She supplied no proof beyond her own testimony.)

Everyone in the world, dozens of LGBT associations, gay media outlets, as well as the tabloid press in Britain and elsewhere, hurled themselves into a crazed campaign against Ratzinger. And how skilled the celebrity columnists were at using innuendo and allusion, veiled phrases and clever wordplay, to say things without actually saying them!

The famous British-born American blogger Andrew Sullivan – a noted conservative polemicist and long-time gay activist – attacked the pope in turn, in an article that enjoyed considerable success. The impact of his attack was all the greater for Sullivan, himself, being Catholic. For Sullivan there was no doubt that the pope was gay, even though he advanced no proof beyond Benedict XVI's extravagant accoutrements and his 'bromance' with Georg.

Every time, these campaigns specifically targeted Georg Gänswein, generally described as Ratzinger's 'favourite' secretary, 'rumoured boyfriend' and 'the holy father's life partner'. In Germany, Georg was nicknamed, in a play on the pronunciation of his first name: 'gay.org'.

So outrageous did things become that one gay priest was said to have developed the habit of cruising in the parks of Rome and introducing himself as 'Georg Gänswein, personal secretary to the pope'. This was a total fabrication, of course, but it may have helped to amplify the rumour. The story recalls the technique of the great writer André Gide, who, after making love with beautiful boys in North Africa, told them (according to one of his biographers): 'Remember that you've slept with one of the greatest French writers: François Mauriac!'

How can we explain such dogged persecution? First of all, there was the anti-homosexual discourse of Benedict XVI, who was naturally preparing for the attack, since, as the expression goes, he had created a rod for his own back.

It's a fact: the pope had forgotten the Gospel of Luke: 'Do not judge, and you will not be judged. Do not condemn, and you will not be condemned.'

The former Curia priest Francesco Lepore, one of whose books had a foreword written by Joseph Ratzinger, explained to me: 'It's obvious that a pope who was so refined, so effeminate and so close to his magnificent private secretary, was an easy target for gay activists. But it was primarily because of his very homophobic positions that these attacks were directed at him. Many people said that he was a closeted homosexual, but no one supplied any proof. Personally I think that he's homophilic, because there are so many clues in that direction, but at the same time I think he never practised.'

Another Italian priest who works at the Vatican puts this point of view in perspective. 'Those images exist, and it's true that any gay looking at photographs of Benedict XVI, his smile, his gait, his manners, might think that he is homosexual. All the denials in the world will not shake that deep conviction people have. Besides – and this is the trap that he fell into – as a priest he can't deny these rumours, because he couldn't have wives or mistresses. A priest will never be able to prove that he was heterosexual!'

Federico Lombardi, Benedict XVI's spokesman and the current director of the Ratzinger Foundation, is unmoved by this wave of criticism that continues even today. 'You know, I lived through the Irish crisis, the German crisis, the Mexican crisis … I think that history will pay tribute to Benedict XVI on the question of paedophilia, where he clarified the positions of the Church and denounced sexual abuse. He was braver than anyone else.'

There remains the question of the 'gay lobby', which poisoned the pontificate and was a genuine obsession of Ratzinger's. Real or imagined, Benedict XVI still felt that he was put in a difficult situation by this 'lobby', which, in his *Last Testament*, he would brashly congratulate himself for 'dissolving'! Francis, too, denounced a 'gay lobby' in his famous reply: 'Who am I to judge?' (and in his first conversation with the Jesuit Antonio Spadaro).

On the basis of hundreds of interviews carried out for this book, I reached the conclusion that such a lobby does not exist in the precise sense of the term. If it did, this kind of secret Freemasonry would have to work for a cause, in this instance the promotion of homosexuals. There is no such thing in the Vatican; if a gay lobby did exist there, it would not live up to its name, since most of the homosexual cardinals and prelates in the holy see generally act against the interests of gays.

'I think that talking about a gay lobby in the Vatican is a mistake,' the former Curia priest Francesco Lepore confirms. A lobby would imply a power structure aimed secretly at achieving a goal. That's impossible and absurd. The reality is that in the Vatican there is a majority of homosexuals with power. Out of shame, out of power, but also out of careerism, these cardinals, these archbishops, these priests want to protect their power and their secret lives. These people have no intention of doing anything at all for homosexuals. They lie to everyone else, and sometimes they lie to themselves. But there is no lobby.'

Here I would put forward another concept that seems to me to provide a better image, not so much of a 'lobby' but of gay life in the Vatican: the 'rhizome'. In botany, a rhizome is a plant that doesn't just have an underground root but also vegetation that is rich in horizontal and vertical ramifications, multiplying everywhere, to the point that one no longer knows whether the plant is under or above ground, or what is root and what is aerial stem. On a social level, the 'rhizome' (an image that I have borrowed from the book *A Thousand Plateaux* by the philosophers Gilles Deleuze and Félix Guattari) is a network of entirely decentralized, disordered relationships and connections, with no beginnings or limits; each branch of the rhizome can connect with any other, without hierarchy or logic, without a centre.

Homosexual life in the Vatican and more broadly in the Catholic Church, taking the form of clandestine companionship, seems to me to be structured as a rhizome. With its own internal dynamic, whose energy derives both from desire and from secrecy, homosexuality links hundreds of prelates and cardinals in a way that escapes hierarchies and codes. By virtue of this fact – involving multiplicity, acceleration, derivation – it creates countless multidirectional connections: loving relationships, sexual liaisons, emotional break-ups, friendships, reciprocal arrangements, situations of dependency and professional promotions, abuses of dominant positions and *droits de seigneur*; nevertheless the lines of causation, the ramifications and the relationships cannot be clearly established or decoded from outside. Each 'branch' of the rhizome, each 'fragment' of the Great Work, is often ignorant of the sexuality of the other branches: it's homosexuality at different levels, isolated 'drawers' of the same closet (the American theologian Mark Jordan chose a different image, comparing the Vatican to a hive with its 'honeycomb of closets': constructed from so many tiny closets, each homosexual priest is, to an extent, isolated in his own cell). So you mustn't underestimate the opacity of individuals and the isolation they feel, even when they are part of the rhizome. It is an aggregation of weak creatures whose unity does not bring strength, a network in which everyone is vulnerable and often unhappy. And in this way, we can explain why some bishops and cardinals whom I have interviewed, even when they are themselves gay, seemed sincerely startled by the extent of homosexuality within the Vatican.

In the end, the thousand-strong homosexual contingent in the Vatican, this extraordinarily dense and secret rhizome, is more than a simple 'lobby'. It is a system. It's the template of the Vatican closet.

Did Cardinal Ratzinger understand that system? Impossible to say. On the other hand, it is clear that Pope Francis discovered the resources and extent of the rhizome when he reached St Peter's throne. And we cannot understand VatiLeaks, the war on Francis, the culture of silence about thousands of sex-abuse cases, the recurrent homophobia of the cardinals, or indeed the resignation of Benedict XVI, if we fail to measure the extent and the depth of the rhizome.

So there is no 'gay lobby'; there is something else in the Vatican: a network of homophilic or homosexualized, polymorphic relations, without a centre, but dominated by secrecy, double lives and lies, constructed as a 'rhizome'. Which we might just as well call: *The Closet*.

21

Dissidents

'I fear he won't make it through the winter,' Radcliffe says to me in a whisper.

The priest takes a coin from his pocket. He gives it to an old man sitting in the street. He strikes up a conversation with him, and then we continue on our way along the streets of Oxford. It is freezing.

'Every year I think he ages by five years.'

Timothy Radcliffe knows the homeless people in his district, and tries to help them with whatever he has to hand. It's a small and inconspicuous gesture, banal in its simplicity, and one that has become rare in a 'self-referential' Church that has tended to distance itself from the poor.

This Dominican friar isn't a rebel as such; he is an English priest and theologian with an international reputation, and one of the great figures of the Church, since his tenure as 'master' of the Dominican order between 1992 and 2001. Still, Radcliffe is one of those who hold a critical view.

While the Vatican of Benedict XVI was already in a state of siege, Secretary of State Tarcisio Bertone was losing his footing and opposition was getting more intense in the Roman Curia, other fronts appeared. Around the world, 'dissidents' were beginning to rebel against the intransigence and rigidity of the pope. Timothy Radcliffe is one of those who opposed the conservative drift of the pontificate.

'I hated Ratzinger for a long time; it was stronger than me. I even wrote an article against him. And then, when I got to Rome, as master of the Dominicans, and met him, my judgement evolved. He was a cardinal at the time and I could talk to him with confidence, because I represented one of the important orders of the Church. I talked to him a lot. And I would have to say that you could always argue with Ratzinger. In the end, I had respect and even affection for him.'

After a first interview with Radcliffe in Blackfriars Hall at Oxford University, where he lives, we continue the discussion in a French restaurant in the city. Radcliffe has time: now an international speaker, he isn't taking the plane until the next morning. We talk all evening, and I spend the night at the Blackfriars' so that I don't have to get the last train back to London.

When the Dominican order elected as its head, in 1992, the very liberal and gay-friendly Timothy Radcliffe, the Vatican was startled. How could such an error have occurred? Had the Dominicans all gone mad? Scandalized, Cardinals Angelo Sodano and Giovanni Battista Re tried to come up with a stratagem to contest the choice. The cardinal in charge of religious orders, Jean Jérôme Hamer, a Belgian, was prompted to take retaliatory measures.

'Hamer, who was a Dominican himself, boycotted me! After I was elected, he only came to visit the order when I wasn't there! And then we talked. He was more accepting of me. Then he only came when I was there!' Radcliffe tells me.

It has to be said that Timothy Radcliffe is a rare species in Roman Catholicism: an openly pro-gay theologian. He has always defended LGBT people and made significant gestures to include them in the Church. In particular, he declared that homosexuals could be faithful to Christ, and that relationships between men could be as 'generous, vulnerable, tender or mutual' as heterosexual relations. He also published a book on the question of AIDS and adopted courageous positions on the question of condoms.

'It doesn't matter if you're gay or heterosexual: the essential thing is to love,' Radcliffe tells me during our interview, speaking very freely, perhaps under the influence of a very robust Côtes du Rhône.

Few prelates at this level talk straight. About the homosexuality and homophobia of the Church, Radcliffe has no taboos. He never campaigns: he states the facts. Calmly, serenely. He preaches.

He is a man of immense culture, theological, of course, but also philosophical, geopolitical and artistic. He is capable of writing long articles about Rembrandt, or of making a thrilling comparison between *Jurassic Park* and Leonardo da Vinci's *Last Supper*.

During his years in Rome, the Dominican made close connections with the moderate wing of the Church, becoming a friend of the great liberal cardinals Carlo Maria Martini and Achille Silvestrini. He tells me of their shared outings in the capital in Silvestrini's little car.

His long period in the Vatican was marked, at the end of the pontificate of John Paul II, when the church of Cardinals Sodano and Ratzinger became ultra-conservative, by a need to protect dissident theologians who were often threatened. Radcliffe defended numerous key figures, in the first rank of whom was the liberation theologian Gustavo Gutiérrez, who in fact became a Dominican …

'When you join the order, you're protected. Of course the Dominicans protect their friars,' Radcliffe comments simply.

The priest is discreet about these battles, but, according to other sources, Timothy Radcliffe defended priests who risked being excommunicated; he wrote large numbers of letters and, in the most difficult cases, he went to see Cardinal Ratzinger in person to plead a case, avoid a punishment or request a period of grace. Faced with the cardinal's 'Tipp-Ex technique', which consisted of deleting the names of the dissidents he didn't like, the Dominican chose to argue.

Dissident? Radcliffe is just a believer, and a demanding one. He adds, insisting forcefully on this point, when we say goodbye: 'I love my Church. Yes, I love it.'

James Alison is one of those dissidents who needed protecting. An Englishman, like Timothy Radcliffe, and also trained by the Dominicans, this priest is one of the bravest figures I have met in the Church. An openly gay theologian and priest, Alison is a specialist in Latin America, where he spent many years, particularly in Mexico and Brazil. He also spent a long time in the United States, before moving to Madrid.

We are in a vinoteca in the gay district of Chueca, and Alison is with his dog Nicholas, a French bulldog he adopted in Brazil. The priest tells me about his career and his passion for travel. This 'travelling preacher' goes round the world to give talks and colloquia, and has no hesitation along the way in celebrating masses for LGBT groups. In Madrid, for example, I see him officiating within the Crismhom association, a group of gay Christians with more than two hundred members who meet in a little bar in Chueca, which is where I go to see them.

Having been a priest in Latin America for a long time, Alison tells me of the battles between Joseph Ratzinger and the liberation theologians. For several decades, the cardinal obsessively pursued the Peruvian Gustavo Gutiérrez, who was summoned to explain himself before the great German professor, called to Rome and humiliated. The Brazilian Leonardo Boff, a highly respected figure in Latin America, was silenced by Ratzinger for his controversial views, before choosing to leave the Franciscan order for personal reasons. The Jesuit priest and theologian Jon Sobrino, an advocate of left-wing theology, was attacked by Alfonso López Trujillo and Joseph Ratzinger for many years. The Marxist Frei Betto, a Brazilian progressive theologian, who spent several years in prison under the dictatorship, was given a dressing-down by the pope.

What is paradoxical about this rearguard action is that the great figures of liberation theology – especially Gutiérrez, Boff, Sobrino, Betto – were the manifestly non-gay clerics, whereas most of the cardinals or bishops who attacked them, both in Latin America and in the Vatican, and accused them of 'deviance' from the norm, were homophilic or practising homosexuals! We need only think of Cardinals Alfonso López Trujillo or Sebastiano Baggio, among others … The world turned upside down, in short.

'I have always had a lot of respect for the theology of Benedict XVI. I only regret that Ratzinger accentuated the intellectual winter decreed by John Paul II. And I am very happy that Pope Francis has rehabilitated several of those thinkers who were marginalized for too long,' Alison says prudently.

Cardinal Walter Kasper, a major figure in the liberal wing of the Curia, and one of those who inspired Pope Francis's project, qualifies the situation. 'These figures from liberation theology are very different. Gustavo Gutiérrez, for example, was sincerely committed to the poor. He wasn't aggressive, he was thinking of the Church. To me, he was credible. Boff, on the other hand, could be very naïve about Marxism, for example; he was more aggressive. Others made the choice of joining guerrilla organizations and taking up arms. That couldn't be tolerated.'

On the gay question, liberation theology was relatively slow and divided, before becoming the avant-garde of 'queer theology'. Prisoners of the Marxist vulgate, few of the thinkers in this 'liberationist' movement understood the importance of race, sex or sexual orientation in relation to exclusion or poverty, at least at first. Frei Betto, one of the key figures in the movement, acknowledged this when I interviewed him in Rio de Janeiro: 'Liberation theology evolved according to its context. At first, in the 1960s and 1970s, the discovery of Marxism was crucial as a frame of reference. Even today, Marx remains essential for the analysis of capitalism. At the same time, as new questions emerged, liberation theology adapted. On ecology, for example, Leonardo Boff is known today as one of the fathers of eco-theology, and he had a great influence on Pope Francis's encyclical on integral ecology: *Laudato si'*. And, thanks to the women involved in the base communities, and to feminist theologians, questions like sexuality and gender arose. I myself have just published a little manual on questions of gender and sexual orientation. No subject is taboo to us.'

For his part, the Cardinal Archbishop of São Paulo, Paulo Evaristo Arns, who was close to liberation theology, dared to encourage the use of condoms and criticized John Paul II for forbidding the debate on the celibacy of priests, which did not, in his view, have any serious foundation (he also went to Rome to defend Boff against Ratzinger). Mannered and effeminate, Evaristo Arns was so strangely gay-friendly that certain Brazilian theologians who were among his friends suspected him of having tendencies, which in their view explained his liberalism. But this hypothesis, which I heard often during my investigation in Rio, Brasília and São Paulo, does not seem to be based on any precise evidence and has never been confirmed; on the other hand, it is clear that he was an opponent of the dictatorship in Brazil, and that he 'celebrated masses for the victims of military power' (according to the testimony of André Fischer, one of the main figures in the Brazilian gay movement, whom I met in São Paulo).

In any case, it was in the liberation theology movement, and much later (from the 1990s), that an actively pro-gay movement appeared, of which James Alison was one of the theorists: a veritable 'gay theology'.

'Alison was one of those who anticipated and accompanied this movement of liberation theology towards feminism, towards minorities, towards gays,' Timothy Radcliffe confirms.

In this somewhat unexpected intellectual evolution, liberation theology began thinking of poverty and exclusion no longer in terms of social class and groups, but in terms of individuals. This idea was summed up by the German theologian Michael Brinkschröder when I met him in Munich: 'We developed an interest in the individual, with his or her origins, race, sex, sexual orientation. Marxist references were increasingly ineffective. Instead, we turned to "French theory" (the philosophers Michel Foucault, Gilles Deleuze, Jacques Derrida) and radical feminist thought (Judith Butler). That's how we moved from liberation theology to "gay theology" and soon to "queer theology"'.

Theologians like the American Robert Goss (an openly gay former Jesuit), the radical feminist Marcela Althaus Reid in Argentina, the Brazilians Paulo Suess and André Musskopf (a Lutheran), and even the Dominican friar Carlos Mendoza-Alvarez in Mexico, helped to define or nurture this 'queer theology'. We might also cite the name of the Brazilian Luiz Carlos Susin, a Capuchin friar who was, he told me, 'the organizer of a "side event" on liberation theology, in 2005, during one of the first meetings of the World Social Forum in Porto Alegre'. This workshop on questions of gender contributed to the expansion of 'queer theology' in Latin America.

Today, many 'queer' Bible reading groups still keep this current alive, even though it has tended to run out of steam for lack of academic recognition, or because it has broken down into various chapels and LGBTIQ+ undercurrents, the natural direction of 'deconstruction' a little 'in the style of Protestantism' (in Michael Brinkschröder's phrase).

It is no surprise that 'queer theology' also came under violent criticism from the Vatican under Benedict XVI. Some priests suffered sanctions; some theologians lost their accreditation. In Mexico, Angel Méndez of the Jesuit Universidad Iberoamericana was even punished severely for teaching 'queer theology'. 'Openly gay, HIV positive and living with my boyfriend', as he confirmed to me, Méndez was fired in contravention of Mexican law forbidding discrimination in the workplace. He paid a high price for his sincerity and his LGBT theological teachings. More recently, the new rector, a gay-friendly Jesuit, David Fernández Dávalos, has hired him back.

The same logic inspires priests as different as Timothy Radcliffe, Paulo Evaristo Arns, James Alison, Carlos Mendoza-Alvarez, Angel Méndez, Luiz Carlos Susin, and many other 'gay' or 'queer' theologians: sincerity, authenticity and the rejection of hypocrisy on homosexuality. Without necessarily being gay themselves, they know that the percentage of homosexuals in the Church is very high.

A down-to-earth man who has travelled widely in Latin America, James Alison has observed that most priests there lead a double life. 'In Bolivia and Peru, for example, priests generally have a female concubine. The ones who are celibate are often homosexual. Basically, I would say that the rural diocesan clergy are largely practising and straight, and the urban religious clergy tend to be practising homosexuals,' Alison tells me.

As for the war waged against gays under John Paul II, of which Father Alison himself was a victim, because he has been stripped of any official title, many think that it was very counter-productive.

'For the Church, it's a desperate waste of energy,' Alison adds.

But times are changing. Most liberation theologians and pro-gay priests now have peaceful relations with the holy see. Pope Francis has good relations with Gustavo Gutiérrez and Frei Betto whom he received at the Vatican, and Leonardo Boff, who is now one of its key intellectuals. As for James Alison, the priest without a parish who was subjected to an irregular trial under canon law, he has just had a call from the Vatican, in which the man at the other end wanted to know how he was. He still hasn't got over it! Alison refused to comment on that private conversation, or to tell me the identity of the person who called him. But information circulated at the Curia, and I learned the name of the person who called Alison from the Vatican switchboard: it was Pope Francis.

During the 1980s, 1990s and 2000s, Popes John Paul II and Benedict XVI didn't pick up the phone: they sent their guard dogs. The Secretariat of State, the Congregation for the Doctrine of the Faith and the Congregation for Religious were put in charge of these inquisitions. Files were drawn up on Timothy Radcliffe and James Alison, among many others. There was no shortage of calls to order, bullying, punishments and 'examinations'.

For 30 years, Joseph Ratzinger was the grand inquisitor. As prefect of the Congregation for the Doctrine of the Faith, then as pontiff, he put in place a sophisticated system of sanctions, seconded for a long time by his wicked imp Tarcisio Bertone. What is striking is not so much the violence or the excommunications, which were rare in the end, as Ratzinger's perversity and his liking for 'martyric' humiliations. No *autos-da-fé*: examinations of conscience! Ratzinger used and abused a whole palette of gradual punishments. And he used such imagination in his sanctions!

His opponents, often homosexual or gay-friendly, were marginalized or banished, blamed or mortified, reduced to the state of laymen, 'placed under examination', forced into 'penitential silence' or stripped of their *missio canonica* (meaning that their work no longer had any value in the eyes of the Church). The famous theologian Eugen Drewermann, who dynamited the Vatican ideology of John Paul II in his *The Cleric: A Psychoanalytic Study of Clergymen and Religious Orders*, was severely punished. The list of those excluded, sanctioned or turned into pariahs is a long one: Father Charles E. Curran (an American who was too open to divorce, the pill and homosexuality); Father Matthew Fox (a heterosexual Dominican who aspired to marry); the American priest Robert Nugent (favourable towards gays); the Belgian Jesuit Jacques Dupuis (a specialist in religion in India); the nun and theologian Lavinia Byrne (an Englishwoman in favour of women's ordination); the Brazilian nun and theologian Ivone Gebara (considered too liberal on sexual morality and abortion); or indeed the Italian Father Franco Barbero (who, in a book written with the journalist Pasquale Quaranta, defended the idea that love between persons of the same sex did not contradict the Gospels). Even the dead weren't spared: ten years after his death, attention was paid to the writings of the Indian Jesuit Anthony de Mello, famous for his pro-gay teachings of the Bible, which encouraged manifestations of affection between members of religious orders according to a 'third way' that was neither sexuality nor celibacy – and he was declared non-compliant.

Demonstrating a kind of individual fanaticism, Benedict XVI also suspended priests and nuns who distributed condoms in Africa. Not to forget the unusual treatment by John Paul II and Joseph Ratzinger of the French bishop Jacques Gaillot, who defended homosexuals and condoms as a means of fighting AIDS: he was in the end appointed Bishop *in partibus* of Parténia, an episcopal seat in the Algerian desert, with no parish or congregations, since the town disappeared under the sand at the end of the fifth century.

Joseph Ratzinger summoned recalcitrant clerics countless times to make them justify themselves for whole days, he made them confess, comment repeatedly on a failing, describe an error, justify a simple 'tone'. Convinced that the Church itself escaped his criticism because it embodied morality within itself, this doctrinaire pope often used arguments of authority. His positions are described by his detractors as arbitrary and peremptory, 'justified by the absence of justification' (in the phrase from Albert Camus' *The Rebel*). A rigidity that is all the more artificial since Pope Francis would have no difficulty altering or reversing most of his diktats.

All of those who were excluded, punished or reduced to silence suffered severe after-effects and stigmas: deracination; the idea of losing a family; financial stalemate because it was difficult for them to find work; the feeling of failure after the end of 'voluntary servitude'; and finally, and perhaps most importantly, the indefinable lack of what I would call 'fraternity'.

Whether they were excluded or left voluntarily, defrocked priests only accelerated the great crisis in vocations, a silent and lasting movement that began in the 1970s. Some lost their faith after Paul VI's rigid encyclical on sexual morality, *Humanae vitae*; thousands of priests threw their cassocks to the winds to marry in the 1970s and 1980s; others left the Church during the systematic liquidation of the advances of Vatican II under John Paul II; others finally abandoned their parishes as right-wing theologians and homophobia came to dominate the Roman Curia.

At the same time, tens of millions of the faithful moved away from the Church because of its distance from the spirit of the age, its ultra-conservative positions on marriage, women's rights, the rights of homosexuals, or condoms and AIDS; many believers were also shocked by revelations of sexual abuse and the protection enjoyed by predatory priests. Cardinal Ratzinger's insistence on putting books in the Index cut the Church off from its intellectuals; finally, artists also moved away from a Church that had lost a taste for the beauty of things.

'Joseph Ratzinger created a theological desert around him. He silenced everyone. He was the only theologian who was allowed to speak. He would not tolerate contradiction. Ratzinger was responsible for the suffocation of freedom of thought and the spectacular impoverishment of Catholic theological thought over the last four years,' Father Bento Domingues tells me.

This renowned Dominican theologian, whom I interviewed in Lisbon, has greater freedom to speak since, at the age of 84, he is no longer intimidated by authoritarianism. He adds angrily: 'Ratzinger was unimaginably cruel towards his opponents. He even held a canonical trial against a theologian who he knew was dying of cancer.'

During this investigation, everywhere in the world – in Portugal and Japan, in the United States and Hong Kong, or in the missions of Africa and Asia – I have met liberal or gay-friendly priests who are trying to move their Church to focus on those at its 'periphery'. They have all been at war with Joseph Ratzinger or his local conservative representative.

Strangely, one of the places where that opposition to Joseph Ratzinger was the most powerful as well as the most intransigent was the Middle East. During my stays in eight Arab countries for this inquiry, I met 'Eastern Christians' as well as European missionaries who are, in many cases, still 'evangelizing' the Middle East, sometimes forgetting that colonialism belongs in the past.

In Rome, the Vatican 'brain' in charge of the Eastern Christians is Cardinal Leonardo Sandri. We have already met this prelate: he is a figure of the kind that rarely exists outside of the pages of the Old Testament, which is populated by eminent figures of similar calibre, colourful and seemingly, at times, considering themselves to be above good and evil, which makes them more interesting, with their diabolical contradictions and their long beards, than the smooth characters of the aseptic block-busters that are the Gospels.

The Argentinian, as we know, was John Paul II's 'minister' of the interior; ostracized under Benedict XVI, he was given a consolation prize: the Congregation for the Eastern Christians. When I visited this 'minister' in his spectacular office on Via della Conciliazione in Rome, I first came across a crazed *camarilla* of assistants, secretaries, second-in-commands, ushers and butlers, who took care of me and left me hugely impressed. Some of them could have been André Gide's travelling companions in the East!

Here, more than elsewhere, protocol remains a serious matter. And I discover the importance for the Italians of the 'ante-room'. Waiting for Cardinal Sandri, I am asked to sit first in a huge waiting room; eventually, from this large room, an usher guides me towards a little vestibule, then from that ante-room a butler leads me towards a sort of boudoir, his Eminence's private secretarial office, before at last I am delicately introduced, perhaps so as not to wake the beast, into the big office of the bogeyman, which I finally enter.

Cardinal Sandri is imposing: he has a large, stubborn-looking forehead and a rugged style. Contrary to the official Vatican instructions that oblige all prelates to receive visitors, for reasons of confidentiality, in private drawing rooms, he receives them in his office. Rebellious and scornful of the norms, Sandri invites me to take a seat on his sofa. He speaks impeccable French, like many cardinals, and he is both charming and sympathetic towards me. He takes my hand to show me, from his window, the office of the 'Equestrian Order of the Knights of Jerusalem' (you couldn't make this up), and gives me a welcome present: a gold (or gold-plate) medal with a picture of Pope Francis.

'Are you a believer?' Sandri asks me during our interview (which is recorded, with the cardinal's agreement).

I reply that, after the Enlightenment, after Spinoza, Nietzsche and Darwin, after Voltaire and Rousseau, after Rimbaud, it has become difficult, particularly for a Frenchman ...

'Ah yes, secularization! I know!' Sandri says, with a penetrating look, his voice exaggeratedly loud, and with a wide, grouchy gesture.

Like many people in the Vatican, and in the Catholic world, Leonardo Sandri has a passion for the East. This Latin with the Leonardo smile likes long caravan trails and the clear separation of the sexes.

Thanks to his new post, Sandri has discovered a new direction for his life, about which he talks to me at length: a connoisseur of the Chaldeans,

Syriacs and Melkites, he describes to me the Byzantine subtleties of the Eastern Churches. He recommends some places to go for a trip that I'm taking to Lebanon and the United Arab Emirates, and suggests contacts who I can go and see on his behalf. Sandri knows the area like the pockets of his cassock. A cardinal, a former diplomat, a nuncio, he is one of the greatest Vatican specialists in the subtleties of the Middle East, with its Aladdins, its whirling dervishes with their Qamar, its Ali Babas and their 40 thieves.

He and I share this passion for the East. It is that of the Crusades and the Catholicism of conquest, of the Mount of Olives, of St Louis and Napoleon. But the 'journey to the East' was also a genre very popular among homosexual writers (Rimbaud in Aden, Lawrence in Arabia, André Gide in Tunisia, Oscar Wilde in the Maghreb, Pierre Herbart in Africa, Henry de Montherlant in Algeria and Morocco, Pierre Loti in Galilee, Jean Genet in Palestine, William Burroughs and Allen Ginsberg in Tangier ...). The Poet writes: 'The East, the primitive homeland'.

'Several of the writers who wanted to take that "journey to the East", a great literary motif, were homosexual. The name of Sodom has always contained a formidable symbolic charge,' observes Benny Ziffer, the chief literary editor of *Haaretz*, over dinner in Tel Aviv.

So the East is also a gay passion! A great delusion: the primitive homeland for Catholics; a new Sodom for gays. An escape that proves to be a trick, a market for fools; only sexual miseries are acquired there.

In the Near East and the Middle East, in the Levant or the Maghreb, I have come across 'hummus queens', as they are known in the Lebanon: those who, unable to satisfy their inclinations in the Roman Curia, their diocese or their monastery, go to the lands of their Christian ancestors and their lovers. How fascinated I was by those Knights of the Equestrian Order of Jerusalem, those Knights of the Order of Malta, those missionary-philanthropists of l'Œuvre d'Orient who sometimes show a double allegiance to the Church and to the beauties of Arabia. How strange are those pilgrims who are terrified by Islam, but are unafraid in the arms of a Muslim. In Morocco, Algeria and Tunisia, where I have often encountered them, those priests who like to be whistled at in the street, as if they were princesses, have told me guardedly about the gay-friendly places they went to, the 'obliging' hotels and the luxury riads. For example,

European Catholic clergy once frequented the former Benedictine monastery of Toumliline, isolated in the Atlas Mountains (according to the testimony of diplomats, senior military officers and people close to the royal family whom I interviewed in Morocco). In Egypt, I was also told of the gay-friendly atmosphere of the Dominican Institute of Oriental Studies in Cairo.

This passion for the East has ramifications even inside the Vatican. According to the testimony of a Curia priest and a confessor at St Peter's, in the Vatican there is considerable consumption of Arab porn videos on YouPorn, as well as of the Italian version of the video platform citebeur. com and a website that offers Arab escorts in Rome.

In Lebanon, on the kind recommendation of Cardinal Sandri, I meet the apostolic nuncio Gabriele Caccia. This diplomat was Sandri's young deputy under Ratzinger, in the post of 'assessor', or a kind of number two to the 'minister' of the interior at the Vatican. Removed from office by Tarcisio Bertone, he was exiled to Beirut, where he agreed to see me. One of the heads that rolled under Ratzinger, he seems to be in seventh heaven and the archbishop tells me that he adores Lebanon. (Francis recently moved him to the Philippines.)

The nunciature is far from the centre of Beirut, in Bkerké, north of the Lebanese capital. It is a bastion of Christianity: Our Lady of Lebanon is a stone's throw away, as is the headquarters of the Patriarchate of the Maronites, one of the main Eastern-rite Catholic communities. Caccia lives and works there, protected by the soldiers of the Lebanese army, in a small house below the nunciature (which was being restored when I visited). The view of Beirut and the surrounding valley is spectacular.

Like all Vatican diplomats, Caccia is not allowed to speak without authorization, so our conversation is off the record. But I'm impressed by his knowledge of the country and his courage: he goes everywhere, at his own risk wearing his archbishop's robes and the scarlet moiré silk biretta of apostolic nuncios. Here, war is not far away: there is no gender theory, no racy parties. Caccia doesn't give me a jewel by way of a welcome present: but the Gospel of St Luke, translated into Arabic.

The Eastern-rite Catholic Churches are faithful to Rome, but their priests can be ordained when they are married. Here we are at the heart of the great contradiction of the Vatican, which, despite the cost, has been obliged to recognize such practising heterosexuality.

'Priestly celibacy is a relatively recent decision. Even in Rome, priests got married into the eleventh century! Here we are faithful to tradition: priests are often married. On the other hand, once one has been ordained, marriage is no longer possible, and bishops are always chosen from among celibate priests,' I am told by Bishop Samir Mazloum, the spokesman for the Maronite patriarch, when I interview him in Beirut.

Popes John Paul II and Benedict XVI were very angry about this Eastern exception, which they considered abnormal, and did everything they could to hold it back. So, for a long time, they were opposed to Eastern Catholic priests being able to serve in European churches when they were married – a solution that would, on the other hand, have eased the crisis of vocations in Europe. But the precedent of Anglican or Lutheran converts led them to tolerate exceptions, later universalized by Pope Francis: now many Catholic priests serving in French, Spanish or Italian churches are married. On the subject of the celibacy and marriage of priests, the Eastern Christians therefore represent an opposition to the rules issued by the Vatican.

The Maronite priest Fadi Daou, a professor of theology and president of the important Adyan Foundation, whom I interviewed in Beirut with my Arab researcher Hady elHady, sums up the situation like this: 'We are Eastern Christians affiliated to Rome, but independent. An estimated 55 per cent of Maronite priests are married; we choose our bishops freely. We are more liberal on certain subjects, like the celibacy of the priesthood; and more conservative on others, like the status of women or homosexuality. Pope Francis recognized the uniqueness of our churches, authorizing our married priests to serve in Western Europe.' (With the same prudence, Mgr Pascal Gollnish of the Œuvre d'Orient and Cardinal Raphael Sako, the so-called Patriarch of Babylon, who represents the Catholic Chaldean Church, confirmed this information during interviews in Paris.)

Some priests, journalists or academics who I met in the region told me that 'Catholics were very much under threat in the East, like homosexuals'. These two 'minorities' even had the same enemies in the

Arab world. A Lebanese priest confirms: 'The map of persecutions of Catholics matches up strangely, and almost perfectly, with the map of persecutions against homosexuals.'

In the Far East – far beyond the 'Near East' favoured by the French and the 'Middle East' of the English – the situation is also very different. The most distant 'peripheries' experience a more liberal form of Catholicism, dissidents in their own way. The Church of Rome is usually very much in the minority there, except in the Philippines and East Timor, and, to a lesser extent, in South Korea and Vietnam.

In the holy see, the man in charge of the 'evangelization' of Asia and Africa is Cardinal Fernando Filoni. Nicknamed the 'red' pope, he is at the head of one of the strategic ministries for the future of Catholicism. Himself a nuncio, close to Cardinal Sodano, Filoni was in office in Iraq in the early 2000s, when he showed true courage at a time when most Western diplomats had fled the country even before the American military intervention against Saddam Hussein.

I meet him in the historic office of Propaganda Fide, the Congregation for the Evangelization of Peoples, a famous building designed by Bernini, on the Piazza di Spagna in Rome.

'The name "red pope" is a deliberate contrast to the name of the holy father, who is the "white pope", or the superior of the Jesuits, who is the "black pope",' Filoni explains to me in perfect French.

During about twenty trips to around ten countries in Asia, particularly Japan, Hong Kong, Taiwan, Singapore and China, I was able to gauge the extent to which Asian Catholicism tends to soften some of the rigidities imposed by Rome. In contact with local churches and Foreign Missions, I observed a great contrast between rules and practices: the celibacy of heterosexual priests, contrary to the local culture, is not generally respected to any great extent, and there is a particularly large number of homosexual Catholic European missionaries.

In China, where Roman Catholicism is clandestine, the private lives of Catholic priests and bishops is subjected to active surveillance on the part of the regime, which has no hesitation in 'using' the possible double lives of clerics (often actively heterosexual) to control them or to 'buy' their cooperation (according to several first-hand testimonies I collected in Beijing, Shanghai, Canton, Shenzhen, Hong Kong and Taiwan). The work of local priests in China, such as the Jesuit Father Benoît Vermander, whom I met, is no less exemplary in view of the risks involved; that of the foreign missionaries, called 'parachutists' here, because they land in foreign parts to spread the word and remain isolated for a long time, is in many cases courageous.

In Japan, in the entourage of an influential bishop, I am told that the Japanese Church is very liberal and that its bishops, for that specific reason, have had their disagreements with Benedict XVI. 'The episcopate prefers to avoid conflicts. We are loyal to the principles of tolerance, equanimity and consensus that prevail on the island. We receive injunctions from Rome with good will; but we still go on doing what we think is right for Japan, without worrying too much about the Vatican,' a priest close to the Japanese Episcopal Conference explains.

During the 2014 synod, the Japanese Catholic Church also produced, as Father Pierre Charignon confirmed, a chaplain sent to Tokyo by the Foreign Missions in Paris, a 15-page official document deploring the positions of Rome: they criticized its 'lack of hospitality' and its 'artificial' standards on contraception, condoms and divorced couples.

'We prefer Francis,' Noriko Hiruma, one of the directors of the Justice and Peace committee of the Japanese Bishops Conference, tells me.

During my stay, I visit a Catholic pro-LGBT church in the gay quarter of Shinjuku Ni-chome. There, a priest openly campaigns in favour of same-sex couples, and distributes condoms to the young people in the gaybourhood.

The opposition to Joseph Ratzinger is less discreet in the spiritual 'peripheries' of Western Europe. In Germany, Austria, the Netherlands, Belgium and Switzerland, but also in the Scandinavian countries and Ireland, the pope's rigidity was universally denounced. Entire divisions of the Church have even become dissident.

'Here, you are in a Catholic parish like any other,' Monica Schmid tells me.

And in fact I go with her to visit the stripped-down modern church of Effretikon in Switzerland, where everything seems to be in line with

Catholic doctrine. Except that this generous woman, Monica Schmid, is the curé here.

Schmid describes her church to me at length and with passion, the great panoply of sacraments and rituals available, and I guess that she is much better-versed in theology and liturgy than most priests. 'Her' church is modern and open: many parishioners are faithful to it (according to Meinrad Furrer, a Catholic pastoral assistant who comes with me on several trips to Switzerland).

On a number of stays in Illnau-Effretikon, Zurich, Geneva, Lausanne, Coire, St Gallen, Lucerne and Basel, I can see that more and more women and laypeople are officiating in Switzerland. Many members of religious orders are publicly accepting their homosexuality and getting organized. Some, in a grey area, are still authorized to celebrate mass; others are limited to preaching without consecration. There are associations, like Network in Zurich, which brings together LGBT Catholics. Sometimes, priests that I have met celebrate blessings of homosexual couples. They were all openly in rebellion against Joseph Ratzinger and now demand that the 'Kirche von Unten' (Church from below) finally be listened to.

Of course, Rome and, in particular, Pope Benedict XVI, did all they could to bring these dissident parishes into line, asking the Swiss bishops to sanction them. The latter, who are sometimes zealots, tried to apply the 'unfriendly' rule of Rome – often before being 'outed' by the press for their double lives! With the result that a ceasefire was decreed. And the pro-gay Swiss dissidents are now left in peace.

In Germany, opposition was even more head-on. Within the heart of the Church, the German episcopate had been overtaken by the people, in deep rebellion against the Vatican. While the Germans had at first welcomed his election, Benedict XVI quickly disappointed them. His pontificate soon started an unprecedented wave of protest, Benedict becoming *persona non grata* in his own country. His moral positions, which were held to be reactionary, were rejected even by Catholics: during his trip to Berlin, dozens of family, feminist, lay and homosexual associations demonstrated in the streets. At the same time, over a hundred MPs announced that they were boycotting his speech to the Bundestag, while even the president of the parliament asked the pope to change his line on the celibacy of the priesthood. In the end, the president of the Republic of Germany, himself remarried, publicly criticized the moral position of the holy father on divorced couples.

'Here, the majority of German theologians are hostile to Ratzinger,' I am told in Berlin by the former member of parliament Volker Beck, who was one of those who boycotted the pope.

In his own country Joseph Ratzinger's point of view has become inaudible. Almost 90 per cent of Germans are questioning the celibacy of the priesthood and the prohibition on the ordination of women. Movements of homosexual priests and associations of LGBT believers have also proliferated to the extent that they can seem like one of the most dynamic components of the Church, and are sometimes supported by the local clergy. Cardinal Reinhard Marx, Archbishop of Munich and president of the German Episcopal Conference, is one of the few Ratzingerians who have been open on the gay question: in 2018, weighing his words carefully, he let it be understood that Catholic priests could in certain cases organize 'blessing ceremonies for homosexual couples'. Better than anyone else, this prelate knows that whole sections of German-speaking Catholicism are in disagreement with the Vatican, that gay priests are in the majority in churches in German-speaking Europe, and even more numerous among German Jesuits, Franciscans and Dominicans.

The case of the Cardinal Archbishop of Vienna, Hans Groër, helped to open people's minds: rigid, homophobic and a practising homosexual, the cardinal led a double life until his old demons caught up with him. Accused by young priests of unwanted touching and sexual abuse, he was subject to numerous complaints. And as the list of victims lengthened – more than a thousand among the boys and young men of the diocese – the Groër affair became a scandal throughout the German-speaking world.

During the trial, the protections that the cardinal enjoyed at a high level exploded into broad daylight. In the case file, the new Archbishop of Vienna, Christoph Schönborn, bravely criticized the role of Pope John Paul II and his deputy Angelo Sodano who, according to him, protected the paedophile cardinal.

Let's pause for a moment on the figure of Schönborn. The successor to Groër in Vienna is one of the most gay-friendly cardinals in the present-day Church. An enthusiastic reader of Jacques Maritain and Julien Green (who is buried in Austria), a lover of the East and a regular visitor to the Austrian Hospice in Jerusalem, Schönborn privately claims to be attentive to the concerns of homosexuals. At the end of the 1990s, for example, the Archbishop of Vienna encouraged the creation of the journal *Dialog*, published by the diocese, and distributed in several hundred thousands of copies to Austrian Catholics. The debate on the celibacy of the priesthood or the granting of the sacraments to divorced couples was played out in its pages.

'We launched that journal under the auspices of and with funding from the diocese, with the constant support of Archbishop Schönborn and his vicar general, Helmut Schüller. We were loyal to the Church, but at the same time, the debate was opened up more and more ...' Martin Zimper, its editor-in-chief, tells me during several meetings in Lucerne, where he now lives with his partner Peter.

Openness has its limits: Schönborn put an end to the experiment when the homosexual prism of the magazine became too much of a presence, but the impact of the publication on Austrian Catholicism has been impressive.

It was also in the immediate entourage of the Archbishop of Vienna that the Pfarrer Initiative (Pastors' Initiative), co-founded by Father Helmut Schüller, was launched in 2006. This very influential movement sought to give a structure to groups of priests who were in a state of rupture with the Church. In 2011, Schüller issued an 'appeal to disobedience', signed by almost four hundred priests and deacons, to demand an end to celibacy and the ordination of women. Meanwhile the group 'Wir sind Kirche' (We are Church), born in the time of Groër scandal, was also intended to reform the Austrian Church, collecting over five hundred thousand signatures in support of this liberal line.

Most of these movements and groups were severely rebuked by Cardinal Joseph Ratzinger and then by Benedict XVI.

'The pope was much more critical about pro-gay Catholic associations than about the multi-recidivist paedophile cardinal Hans Groër. He wasn't even reduced to layman status!' I am told by a German-speaking theologian.

In this context, Christoph Schönborn navigates cautiously, in a kind of benevolently unspoken response, to the many gay priests and bishops in his country: a kind of 'don't ask, don't tell', which is very much his style according to one of his former colleagues. He resists asking questions of his entourage, for fear of the answers they might give him. That way he continues to involve gays in initiatives by the archbishopric of Vienna, and he says he was impressed by the solidarity that he has witnessed among homosexual couples in the face of the AIDS crisis: 'It was exemplary. Full stop,' he said. On many stays in France, the travelling cardinal meets up with his gay-friendly co-religionists, particularly at the Dominican convent in Toulouse, where I met them. Schönborn also wrote a highly complimentary letter, which I have been able to consult, to a gay Austrian couple who had just entered into a civil partnership. And on 1 December 2017, Schönborn even celebrated a gay-friendly mass in Vienna in the course of which he paid tribute to people with AIDS. Of course, today, Schönborn is close to Pope Francis.

22

VatiLeaks

An overly curious butler: that is more or less the official explanation given for the affair known today under the name of 'VatiLeaks'. This thesis, concocted by the holy see, has been repeated by the more naïve Vaticanologists. The expression 'VatiLeaks' was also dreamed up by the pope's immediate entourage (Federico Lombardi claimed authorship when I interviewed him). Clearly, the reality is a little more complex.

The guilty party, who of course acted 'on his own', is one Paolo Gabriele: he was the pope's 'majordomo', or 'butler'. This rascal is said to have photocopied hundreds of confidential documents, 'borrowed' from Pope Benedict XVI's private secretariat which made their way into the press in 2012. The scandal was clearly a huge one. Handwritten internal letters meant for the pope, secret notes that had been handed to Georg Gänswein in person, and even the copies of coded diplomatic cables between the nunciatures and the Vatican, suddenly found themselves in the public eye. The culprit was a layman, 48-years-old, married and the father of three children: an Italian charmer, a handsome man with a liking for secret networks. A chamberlain! A butler! A fall guy!

In fact, nobody could believe that the butler had acted on his own: the affair was a campaign, if not a plot, organized at the highest level of the Vatican. It was designed to destabilize the Secretary of State Tarcisio Bertone and, through him, Pope Benedict XVI. A computer expert was even accused of involvement in VatiLeaks, which confirms that the butler had at least one accomplice. The main victim of VatiLeaks, Cardinal Bertone, spoke of a 'nest of vipers and secret letter-writers': the phrase is in the plural. A lot more than just one butler.

Once the official version is eliminated, the case that shook the pontificate of Benedict XVI and led to his fall remains very opaque. A lot of questions are still unanswered even today: who were the people who first recruited Paolo Gabriele to this strategic post with the pope? To which cardinals was 'Paoletto', as he was nicknamed, secretly close? Why did Gänswein leave Paolo Gabriele so much room for manoeuvre in his own office, where the documents were pilfered, and what was the precise nature of their relationship? Did Paolo himself choose which documents to photocopy or did he initially photocopy them for Georg before making doubles behind his back? What was the role of the former private secretary to Joseph Ratzinger, Josef Clemens, who notoriously had a tenacious hostility to Gänswein and was in contact with Paolo Gabriele? Finally, why did the Vatican cover up for most of the high-level protagonists of this plot, charging only the butler, which made him look like the ideal scapegoat?

One thing is certain: VatiLeaks would lead to the fall of Benedict XVI and bring to light a degree of unimagined viciousness within the Vatican. Most importantly, a second affair, perhaps best called VatiLeaks II, would soon follow.

Several senior dignitaries in the Church have been linked to the first episode of VatiLeaks: the American cardinal James Harvey, who was among those who had recruited the butler, and seemed to be close to him; the Italian cardinal Mauro Piacenza, who also played Pygmalion with Paolo Gabriele; Archbishop Carlo Maria Viganò, who was secretary general to the governorate of the Vatican City; Archbishop Paolo Romeo, the future nuncio Ettore Balestrero, or even the former private secretary to Cardinal Ratzinger, Josef Clemens. All of these prelates were suspected (in the press and several books) of involvement in the affair one way or another, and, even though their role has not been established, the very fact that they were transferred, marginalized or dismissed by Benedict XVI or Francis might suggest a link with the case.

As for the butler, though he did not name possible backers in his expeditious trial, he did repeat that he had acted out of duty: 'What I feel most strongly is the conviction that I acted out of exclusive, I would even say visceral, love of the Church of Christ and for [the pope] ... I don't consider myself a thief,' Gabriele insisted. He believed that the Vatican was the 'kingdom of hypocrisy', that there was an '*omertà*' about the reality of what happened there. So he acted as he did to bring the truth to light, and to protect 'the holy father, who had not been correctly informed'. In an interview conducted by the television channel La Sette, Paolo Gabriele added: 'Seeing evil and corruption everywhere in the Church, I had reached a point of no return, my brakes failed. I was convinced that a shock, even one that happened through the media, would help to put the Church back on track'. Gabriele, who discreetly alludes to hypocrisy and gay corruption, never accepted full responsibility for the crime, and still refuses to express remorse.

So it is likely that Paolo Gabriele acted under instructions, even though he was the only one to be sentenced to 18 months in prison for aggravated theft. Finally, Pope Benedict XVI, who considered the butler 'his own son', pardoned Gabriele. The pope, who met him before giving clemence, even suggested that he might have been manipulated: 'I don't want to analyse his personality. It's a curious mixture of things, by which someone convinced him or he convinced himself. He has understood that he shouldn't have done it,' Benedict XVI said in his *Last Testament*.

'Most of those involved in VatiLeaks I and II are homosexuals,' an archbishop in the Roman Curia confirms to me. 'This point explains both affairs, but it was systematically concealed by the Vatican and played down by the press. It isn't a lobby, as one might say. It is simply a matter of gay relationships and the interpersonal acts of revenge that followed on from it. Francis, who knew the file intimately, punished the culprits.'

The second VatiLeaks affair began in Madrid. While it erupted under Francis, it started under Ratzinger. This time the villain of the story is Lucio Ángel Vallejo Balda, a very different kettle of fish from Paolo Gabriele.

During an in-depth investigation that I carried out in Spain, Vallejo Balda's career appeared as crystal-clear as his actions would be opaque.

The journalist José Manuel Vidal, himself a former priest, described this character to me over several interviews in Madrid: 'Vallejo Balda's is the story of a little country pastor who got too big for his boots. He is handsome and attractive, he has climbed swiftly through the ranks of the Spanish episcopate. He is close to Opus Dei, so he is rewarded by ultra-conservative circles. Here, in Madrid, he became close to Cardinal Rouco Varela, a homophobe who likes to be surrounded by boys like this, both uptight and louche, that move in gay-friendly Spanish Catholic circles.'

When Pope Benedict XVI and Cardinal Bertone asked Rouco to recommend a reliable priest to look after financial matters, the Spanish cardinal sent them Balda. The young priest's financial competence and morals were questionable at best, but for Rouco it was an unexpected opportunity to place one of his own pawns within the pope's entourage. Except that Balda turned out to be a disruptive character, resembling the hero of Pasolini's film *Theorem* or the Christ-like character in Dostoyevsky's *Idiot*: he would turn heads, and explode like a bomb inside the Vatican.

Ordained a priest at 26, Lucio Ángel Vallejo Balda, a 'small-town boy' who had become a Madrileño, was 'irresistible', I am told by people who knew him at the time. Now 55, and back serving in the countryside once more, he is still a handsome man.

'He was a provincial who had just fetched up from the sticks. He was an angel, as his first name suggests. He had a charm that was both rural and arriviste. He quickly made a big impression on Cardinal Rouco Varela, all the more so since he was close to Opus Dei,' another priest I meet in Madrid tells me.

His promotion, which was desired by his inventor Rouco, and his spectacular ascent through Rome, notably with the support of the Spanish cardinal Antonio Cañizarès, were treated with some reservation in Spain, within the Bishops Conference. Now that tongues have loosened, I learn that certain Spanish bishops and cardinals publicly criticized the appointment of Balda to Rome, seeing him as a 'little *guapo*' leading a 'dissolute' life of 'a reprobate'.

'The directors of the Spanish Bishops Conference [CEE] considered this choice illegitimate and dangerous to the pope. There was even a minor revolt against Rouco on the subject, here in Madrid,' another priest close to the CEE tells me.

Still, Balda, who came from a poor rural family, became a real devil in Rome, where this exiled angel began to lead *la dolce vita*: luxury hotels, smart restaurants, boys' nights out and the VIP lifestyle. He made something of a name for himself on the other side of the Tiber.

'In Rome the young man went berserk,' a Roman priest who knew him well tells me.

Without any particular intelligence, but with the kind of daring that can accomplish anything, Vallejo Balda became number two at APSA, the Administration of the Patrimony of the Apostolic See, which looks after the properties and the money of the Vatican. Also placed in charge of the bank of the holy see, the young Spaniard now knew everything. Become full of himself, he had access to contacts and to money. Bertone trusted him so blindly that he inadvertently created a free-for-all.

When VatiLeaks II exploded, the Hispanic angel with the boundless ambition and wild lifestyle was the first suspect. Highly sensitive documents about the Vatican Bank were published in books by two Italian journalists, Gianluigi Nuzzi and Emiliano Fittipaldi. The world was stunned to discover the countless illegal bank accounts, the unlawful money transfers and the opacity of the Vatican Bank, with no shortage of evidence to back them up. Cardinal Tarcisio Bertone himself came under scrutiny for having his luxury apartment in the Vatican renovated with money from the Bambino Gesù Paediatric Hospital.

Also at the heart of the affair was a woman – so rare in the Vatican – Francesca Immacolata Chaouqui, an Italian-Egyptian aged 31. A laywoman, charming and communicative, she was liked by the conservatives of the Curia because she was close to Opus Dei; she threw the day-to-day business of the Vatican into confusion with managerial methods she had adopted at Ernst & Young; most importantly, she drove the few heterosexuals in the Curia mad with her ample bosom and luxuriant hair. Oddly for a woman, she had received excellent references for her post in the Vatican, and was appointed as an expert to the Commission on the Reform of the Finances and Economy of the Holy See. Did this *femme fatale* have a secret relationship with the *prêtre fatal* Vallejo Balda? That was the theory implicitly defended by the Vatican.

'The Vatican invented the story of the relationship between Vallejo Balda and Francesca Immacolata Chaouqui. That storytelling was aimed at making sense of an affair that didn't really make sense, unless Balda had other relationships that had to be covered up,' a Curia priest explains to me.

A confessor at St Peter's confirms: 'When he was arrested, Vallejo Balda was placed in residence in our house, here, between the Palace of Justice and the gendarmeria, on Piazza Santa Marta. He was able to get hold of a telephone and a computer, and he lunched with us every day. I know for a fact that he was never Chaouqui's lover.'

In all likelihood, the ambition of VatiLeaks II was to destabilize Francis, just as Vatileaks I had been intended to dethrone Benedict XVI. The operation may have been organized by cardinals from Ratzinger's Curia who were opposed to the political line of the new pope, and put into action by Balda.

One of them, rigid and living a double life, is central to this affair: he was in charge of one of the 'ministries' of the Vatican. The priest Don Julius, who associated with him inside the Vatican, talks of him as an 'old-fashioned old-school gay lady' who lived only to denigrate others. The Vaticanologist Robert Carl Mickens said of him: 'He's a nasty queen.'

Benedict XVI was naturally aware of the unnatural sexuality of the cardinal and his unusual extravagances. But according to several witnesses, he liked him, because he thought for a long time that his homosexuality was not practising, but chaste or 'questioning'. On the other hand, Francis, who is not good at spotting the nuances of 'gayness', but was well-informed about the 'case', removed him from the Curia. A felon, a homophobe and ultra-gay, this cardinal is in any case the link between the two VatiLeaks. Without the homosexual key, these affairs would remain opaque; with that key, they start to become clear.

During the trial, five people were accused by the Vatican of criminal association: Vallejo Balda, his private secretary, the consultant Francesca Immacolata Chaouqui and the two journalists who divulged the documents. Balda would be sentenced to 18 months in prison; after serving only half of his sentence, he would be given a conditional release and sent back to his original diocese in north-west Spain, where he remains today. The cardinals who may have been behind the affair or accomplices of Balda have not been troubled by the Vatican courts.

The two VatiLeaks affairs are like episodes one and two of a single television series to which Catholic Italy knows the secret. They both revolve around the question of homosexuality, so much so that a well-informed Vaticanologist describes them ironically as 'the affair of the butler and the hustler', although the tangle of motivations behind these two cases is so intricate that it is difficult to tell who is being aimed at behind these less than flattering terms.

One mystery remains to be solved. Among the motives that might explain why a man would turn against his own side, what was the one that led Paolo Gabriele and Lucio Ángel Vallejo Balda to speak? If we believe the MICE code, the famous expression used by secret services all over the world, there are essentially four reasons that can lead somebody to turn against his own people: Money; Ideology (ideas); Corruption (particularly sexual blackmail); and Ego. Given the extent of the betrayal and the degree of felony, we might think that the different perpetrators of these two psychodramas were inspired by the four MICE codes simultaneously.

On the desk of Cardinal Jozef Tomko: the book by Francesca Immacolata Chaouqui. The Slovakian cardinal picks up the book, which he is clearly reading, and shows it to me.

The old man, cheerful and sympathetic, receives Daniele and me in his private apartment. We talk about his career as 'red pope', the name given to the cardinal in charge of the evangelization of peoples; we talk about his reading, apart from Chaouqui: Jean Daniélou, Jacques Maritain and Verlaine, about whom the perfectly francophone cardinal talks to me passionately. On the shelves of the drawing room where he receives us, I see a fine photograph of Pope Benedict XVI, enveloped in his red cloak, affectionately holding Jozef Tomko's hands in his.

This proximity to Joseph Ratzinger made Tomko one of the three cardinals with the task of investigating the Roman Curia after VatiLeaks. Along with his colleagues, the Spaniard Julián Herranz and the Italian Salvatore De Giorgi, he was put in charge of a top-secret internal inquiry. The result – a very closely-guarded report, two volumes of 300 pages – was an explosive document about wrongdoing in the Curia and the financial and homosexual scandals of the Vatican. Some commentators and journalists even thought that the report might ultimately have led to the pope's resignation.

'Herranz, De Giorgi and I listened to everyone. We tried to understand. It was brotherly. It wasn't a trial at all, as some people said afterwards,' Jozef Tomko tells me.

And the old cardinal adds, about the report, in an enigmatic observation: 'We don't understand the Curia. No one understand the Curia.'

The three cardinals, then aged 87, 88 and 94 respectively, were conservatives. They had spent most of their careers in Rome and knew the Vatican inside out. De Giorgi was the only Italian who had been bishop and archbishop in several cities in the country – he was the most rigid of the three. Tomko was a more 'friendly' missionary, who had travelled all over the world. The third, Herranz, was a member of Opus Dei. He was in charge of the coordination and running of the mission.

When I visit Herranz in his apartment, near St Peter's Square, he shows me an old photograph of himself as a young Spanish priest standing beside the founder of the Order, Josemaría Escrivá de Balaguer, arm in arm.

In the photograph, at the age of 27, the young Herranz is astonishingly alluring; the old man looks at this picture, which speaks of a time very long ago, irretrievable, as if the young soldier for Opus Dei had become a stranger to him. He pauses. How sad it is! The photograph has stayed eternally young, and he has aged terribly. Herranz is silent for a few seconds, and perhaps he begins to dream of another world, reversed – in which this photograph has aged and he has remained eternally young?

According to the testimony of priests or assistants who worked with Tomko, Herranz and de Giorgi, the three cardinals were literally 'obsessed' by the homosexual question. De Giorgi was known for observing power relations within the Curia through the prism of gay networks, and he is accused, like Herranz, of often confusing paedophilia and homosexuality.

'De Giorgi is orthodox. He's also a flirt who likes to be talked about. His aim in life seemed to be for the *Osservatore Romano* to write positively about him! He kept begging us to do so,' a journalist on the

Vatican's official press organ tells me. (In spite of several requests, De Giorgi is the only one of the three cardinals who refused to see me, a refusal that he expressed in complicated terms, full of animosity and reproach, and with such irrational homophobia that it ended up making him suspect in my eyes.)

It took Herranz, Tomko and De Giorgi eight months to carry out their inquiry. A hundred priests working in the Vatican were interviewed. Only five people had official access to the report, which was so sensitive that a copy was even supposed to have been locked in Pope Francis's safe.

What the three reporters discovered was the extent of corruption in the Vatican. Two people who have read this report – among the cardinals, their assistants, the entourage of Benedict XVI and other cardinals or prelates from the Curia – described it in broad outline, as well as certain passages in greater detail. Pope Benedict XVI himself, in his *Last Testament*, revealed the elements of the report, which concerned, he suggested, a 'homosexual coterie' and a 'gay lobby'.

'We know that homosexual scandals are one of the central elements in the report by the three cardinals,' a Curia priest who worked for one of the cardinals tells me under cover of anonymity.

The most striking conclusion in the report is the connection between financial affairs and homosexuality – the hidden gay life that went hand in hand with financial impropriety. This articulation between sex and money is one of the keys that help us understand the closet of the Vatican.

The report also reveals that a group of gay cardinals, at the highest level of the Curia, wanted to bring down Cardinal Bertone. It also addresses the 'rings of lust' in the Vatican, and tries to describe the network that made the leak and scandal of VatiLeaks I possible. Several names are mentioned in the report, such as those of Cardinals James Harvey, Mauro Piacenza and Angelo Sodano. Senior prelates were also reported to have been subjected to blackmail. Although I don't know everything in detail, I am told that the names of Georg Gänswein and the pope's brother, Georg Ratzinger, also appear in the report.

As serious as it seeks to be, this report is, according to a person who had access to it, a 'masquerade' and even a '*tartufferie*'. The three homophobic cardinals were claiming to decrypt the reality of the closet, but they missed the overall system because they didn't understand its reach nor its codes. Sometimes, they identify the plotters and settle their own scores. They lambaste some lost sheep, as always, and draw up some 'sexual histories' on the basis of rumours, gossip and hearsay, without subjecting them to the process of analysis that is elementary for any kind of judgement. These schizophrenic prelates, who are by no means above the suspicions they denounce, strangely act as judge and jury.

The main conclusion of the report is therefore the revelation of a major 'gay lobby' in the Vatican (the expression appears several times in the report, according to two sources). But the three cardinals, who were in the end fairly incompetent, struggled to decrypt realities they only touched upon. They over-estimate here, they under-estimate there – the only true problem in the Vatican: its intrinsically homosexual template. In the end, the opacity of the report is all the greater for having failed to understand, or even to try and describe, what the Vatican closet really is.

In any case, Benedict XVI and Francis publicly repeated the most powerful expression in the report, its alleged 'gay lobby', confirming in fact that it occupies a central position in the document. At the time of the passing of power from Benedict XVI to Francis, photographs of Castel Gandolfo show a box and well-sealed files on a low table. According to several sources, this is the famous report.

We can understand Benedict XVI's horrified response when reading this secret document. In the face of such lust, so many double lives, so much hypocrisy, so many closeted homosexuals everywhere, in the very heart of the Vatican, did all this sensitive pope's beliefs about 'his' Church collapse? Some have said as much. I am also told that he wept when he read the report.

For Benedict XVI, it was too much. Would this torment never end? He didn't want to fight any more. Reading the report by the three cardinals, his decision was made – he would leave St Peter's boat.

But the stations of the cross of Benedict XVI, that tragic figure, were not yet over. He had a few more to go before his 'renunciation'.

Well before the submission of the secret report, paedophilia scandals had stained the nascent pontificate of Benedict XVI. From 2010, they became endemic. These were not isolated cases or false steps, as he had claimed for a long time, while he was a cardinal, to protect the Church: it was a system. And it was now in the spotlight.

'Booze, boys or broads?' – the question arose in English-speaking newspaper offices with each new case, an incessant flood of revelations of abuse of all kinds under Ratzinger's papacy. (Although it was rarely girls!) Tens of thousands of priests (5,948 in the United States, 1,880 in Australia, 1,670 in Germany, 800 in the Netherlands, 500 in Belgium, etc.) were denounced during those years, the biggest series of scandals in the whole history of modern Christianity. Tens, maybe hundreds of thousands of victims are listed (4,444 in Australia alone, 3,677 minors in Germany …). Dozens of cardinals and hundreds of bishops were implicated. Episcopates were in pieces, dioceses ruined. With the resignation of Benedict XVI, the Catholic Church would be a wasteland. In the meantime, the Ratzinger system would literally have collapsed.

It isn't the intention of this book to cover these thousands of paedophilia scandals in detail. Instead, it is to understand why Benedict XVI, so prolix and obsessive in his war against legal homosexual acts, seemed powerless in the face of sexual abuse of minors. Certainly, he was very quick to denounce the 'filth in the Church' and, addressing the Lord, to declare: 'the dirty clothes and face of your Church frighten us!' He also published several texts of great severity.

But between denial and shock, amateurism and panic, and still with little or no empathy for the victims, the response of the pontificate to the subject remains disastrous.

'The sexual abuses of the Church are not a dark page in the pontificate of Benedict XVI: it is the greatest tragedy, the greatest disaster in the history of Catholicism since the Reformation,' a French priest tells me.

There were two opposing theories on the subject. The first (the one, for example, of Federico Lombardi, former spokesman of the pope, and of the holy see in general): 'Benedict XVI acted with dexterity, and he was the first pope to take the question of sexual abuse by priests seriously.' During five interviews, Lombardi reminds me that the pope 'laicized' – meaning reduced to the state of layman – 'more than 800 priests' who were recognized as being guilty of sexual abuse. The figure is impossible to check and, according to other witnesses, it was grossly exaggerated and there were no more than a few dozen (in the preface to

Last Testament, an official book by Benedict XVI published in 2016, the figure of 400 is quoted – half Lombardi's number). A system of universalized lying in the Vatican having been established, it is at least possible to doubt the reality of these figures.

The second theory (which is generally that espoused in the courts of law in the concerned countries, and in the press): the Church of Benedict XVI was responsible, and perhaps culpable, for all of these cases. We know, in fact, that from the 1980s onwards, all sexual abuse scandals, at Joseph Ratzinger's request, were brought before the Congregation for the Doctrine of the Faith in Rome, where they were dealt with. Since Joseph Ratzinger was the prefect of this 'ministry', and then pope, he was therefore in charge of that file between 1981 and 2013, over a period of more than thirty years. Historians will probably prove very harsh in their assessment of the ambiguities of this pope and his actions: some think that he will consequently never be canonized.

To this we must add the breakdown of justice in the Vatican. At the holy see – a genuine theocracy rather than a state governed by law – there is not, in fact, a separation of powers. According to all the witnesses I have interviewed, including high-ranking cardinals, Vatican justice leaves much to be desired. Canon law is constantly distorted, apostolic constitutions are incomplete, magistrates are inexperienced and courts lack procedure and are not treated seriously. I have spoken with Cardinal Dominique Mamberti, prefect of the Supreme Court of the Apostolic Signature, and with Cardinal Francesco Coccopalmerio, president of the Pontifical Council for Legislative Texts, and it seemed to me that these prelates would not be able to judge cases of this kind independently.

'There is no true justice system in the Vatican. The procedures aren't reliable, investigations aren't credible, there is a serious shortage of funds, people are incompetent. There isn't even a prison! It's a parody of justice,' an archbishop close to the Congregation for the Doctrine of the Faith confirms to me.

Giovanni Maria Vian, director of the *Osservatore Romano*, who was close to Secretary of State Tarcisio Bertone, and a central player in this system, confessed to me during one of our conversations (all recorded with his agreement) that he refused to publish the records of hearings and trials in the official journal of the Vatican, because it risked discrediting the institution …

This parody of Vatican justice is denounced by numerous legal specialists, including a former ambassador to the holy see who, a lawyer himself, confirms: 'These cases of sexual abuse are of great legal and technical complexity: they need inquiries over several months, a large number of hearings, as is apparent at present from the trial of Cardinal George Pell in Australia, which mobilized dozens of magistrates and lawyers and thousands of hours of legal process. Imagining that the Vatican can judge one of these cases is nonsense. It isn't prepared for that: it doesn't have the texts, or the procedures, or the lawyers, or the magistrates, or the means of investigation, or the law to deal with it. There is no other solution for the Vatican but to acknowledge its fundamental incompetence, and let the national legal systems deal with the issues.'

This severe judgement might be nuanced by the serious work carried out by certain cardinals or bishops, for example the work done by Charles Scicluna, Archbishop of Malta, on the cases of Marcial Maciel in Mexico and Fernando Karadima in Chile. However, even the Vatican's anti-paedophile commission, created by Pope Francis, has prompted criticisms: in spite of the good will of Cardinal Sean O'Malley, Archbishop of Boston, who presided over it, three of its members resigned to protest against the slowness of procedures and the double game of the dicasteries involved. (At the age of 74, O'Malley is from another era, and seems barely capable of dealing with cases of this kind: in his 'Testimonianza', Mgr Viganò challenges his impartiality; and during a stay in the United States in the summer of 2018, when I asked the cardinal for an interview, his secretary, embarrassed, admitted that 'he doesn't read his emails, he doesn't know how to use the internet and he has no mobile phone'. She suggested sending him a fax.)

Finally, it is difficult not to mention here the case concerning the brother of Benedict XVI himself. In Germany, Georg Ratzinger found himself at the centre of a huge scandal of physical and sexual abuse against minors when running the famous boys' choir at Regensburg Cathedral between 1964 and 1994. Since 2010, the German courts and an internal report by the diocese revealed that over 547 children from the school to which that prestigious choir is affiliated were victims of violence, and 67 of them of sexual abuse and rape. Forty-nine priests and laymen are now suspected of this violence, including nine for sexual assault. In spite of his denials, it is hard to believe that Georg Ratzinger was not aware of the situation. Besides, as we have since learned, the scandal was taken so seriously by the holy see that it was followed at the highest level by the Congregation for the Doctrine of the Faith, and the immediate entourage of the pontiff is said to have defended Georg Ratzinger. (Three cardinals are cited in numerous judicial procedures currently under way in Germany.)

Voices are raised today, even among priests and theologians, to consider that the Catholic Church's failure on this case affects the very top level of the governance and the ideas of Joseph Ratzinger. Among these, some said to me:

'This is a man who has devoted his life to denouncing homosexuality. He makes it one of the greatest evils of humanity. At the same time, he has said very little about paedophilia, and was very late in becoming aware of the scale of the problem. He has never really differentiated on the theological level between freely consenting relations between adults and the sexual abuse of minors below the age of 15.'

Another theologian who I met in Latin America told me: 'Ratzinger's problem is his value system. It was completely perverted from the outset. He has severely sanctioned the liberation theologians and punished priests who distributed condoms in Africa, but he has found excuses for paedophile priests. He ruled that the Mexican multi-recidivist and paedophile criminal Marcial Maciel was too old to be reduced to layman status!'

Still, for Pope Benedict XVI, the uninterrupted sequence of revelations about sexual abuse in the Church was more than a 'season in hell'. It struck at the heart of the Ratzinger system and its theology. Whatever the public denials and positions of principle might have been, Benedict was well-aware deep inside, I would dare to say from experience, that celibacy, abstinence and the failure to acknowledge the homosexuality of priests were at the heart of the whole scandal. His thought, minutely elaborated at the Vatican for four decades, exploded into pieces. This intellectual failure must have contributed to his resignation.

A German-speaking bishop sums up the situation: 'What will be left of Joseph Ratzinger's thought when the balance is truly drawn up? I would say his sexual morality and his positions on the celibacy of priests, abstinence, homosexuality and gay marriage. That is his only true novelty and originality. And yet sexual abuse destroyed all that, once and for all. His prohibitions, his rules, his fantasies, none of that holds any more. Nothing remains today of his sexual morality. And even if no one dares to admit it publicly in the Church, everyone knows that it won't be possible to put an end to sexual abuse by priests until celibacy has been abolished, until homosexuality is acknowledged by the Church, allowing priests to be able to denounce abuse, and until women are ordained as priests. All other measures concerning sexual abuse are in vain. Overall, the Ratzingerian perspective needs to be completely overturned. Everyone knows. And everyone who says the opposite is now an accomplice.'

This judgement is stark, but many within the Church share if not these words at least these ideas.

In March 2012, Benedict XVI flew to Mexico and Cuba. His 'seasons in hell' flew with him: after a winter marked by new revelations of paedophilia, here was a springtime of scandals. Joseph Ratzinger would discover in Havana a diabolical world whose existence he had not suspected, even in his worst nightmares – a new station of the cross. It was on his return from his trip to Cuba that he made the decision to resign. And here is why.

23

The abdication

When I knock at Jaime Ortega's door in Cuba, Alejandro, a charming young man, opens up. I tell him I would like to talk to the cardinal. Kind and sympathetic, and trilingual, Alejandro asks me to wait for a moment. He closes the door and leaves me alone on the landing. Two or three minutes pass and the door opens again. Suddenly in front of me: Jaime Ortega y Alamino. He is there, in person: an old gentleman looking me up and down, with a quizzical gaze, dubious and playful at the same time. He is a plump little man, so small that the giant cross on his paunch looks even bigger than it is.

He brings me into his corner offices and apologizes for not answering my earlier requests. 'My usual assistant, Nelson, is in Spain at the moment. He's doing a degree. Everything has been a bit disorganized since he went away,' Ortega explains.

We talk about rain and fine weather – a hurricane has just struck Martinique, and is due to reach Cuba in a few hours. The cardinal is worried about my return journey to France if the planes don't take off.

Jaime expresses himself in impeccable French. Without warning, he starts addressing me informally, in the Cuban style. And all of a sudden, without ceremony, based on an impression gained over only a few minutes, staring at me, he says: 'If you like, we could have dinner together tomorrow night.'

Getting to meet the cardinal of Cuba, one of the most famous prelates in Latin America, took infinite patience. I travelled to Havana five times for this investigation, and every time the cardinal was out of the country or unavailable, or else he didn't reply to my requests.

At the archbishop's palace I was told that he never received journalists; at reception in the Centro Cultural Félix Varela, where he resides discreetly, they swore blind that he didn't live there; his spokesman, Orlando Márquez, answered my questions because, he warned me, the cardinal wouldn't have time to see me personally. Luckily, one morning, in the archbishop's palace, I happened upon a kind contact who showed me the most hidden places of Cuban Catholicism, let me in on some essential secrets and finally gave me the exact address of Cardinal Ortega. 'Ortega lives there, on the third floor, but no one will tell you, because he wants to be discreet,' my source tells me.

Like Rouco Varela in Madrid, Tarcisio Bertone and Angelo Sodano in the Vatican, Ortega has requisitioned the top two floors of a kind of magnificent *palacio colonial* in the Bay of Havana, to turn it into his private residence. The location is superb, in the middle of exotic flowers, palm trees and fig trees ideally situated on Calle Tacón, in the old city, just behind the baroque cathedral and not far from the headquarters of the Cuban episcopate.

Boasting a cloister with a beautiful patio, this urban hacienda was for a long time the headquarters of the Jesuits, then the headquarters of the diocese, before finally becoming the Centro Cultural Félix Varela.

Here, the Cuban Church gives language classes and awards general degrees that are recognized by the Vatican if not by the Cuban government. I spend several days hanging around in the library, which is open to researchers, before discovering, hidden in the right wing, a private lift that goes up to the third floor. I reach a door that says '*No Pase. Privado*' (No entry. Private), with no other clues. I go in.

The first time Benedict XVI went to Cuba, in March 2012, he was aware of sexual abuse in Latin America, but he still under-estimated the extent of it. This pope, who wasn't very familiar with the Hispanic world, didn't know that paedophilia had become endemic there, particularly in Mexico, Chile, Peru, Colombia and Brazil. Most importantly, like everyone else, he thought that Cuba had been spared.

Who described the situation in the Cuban Church in detail to the holy father? Was he told on the plane, or when he stepped out in Havana? What I have been assured of by two different Vatican diplomatic sources is that Benedict XVI swiftly started to discover the extent of sexual corruption in the local Church. Three foreign diplomats in Havana have also described this situation in detail to me, as have several Cuban dissidents who have stayed on the island. Catholics from Little Havana in Miami, the Protestant pastor Tony Ramos (of Cuban origin), as well as journalists from WPLG Local 10, one of the main local television channels, also gave me precious information during several trips to Florida.

If it is generally difficult to investigate sexual matters within the Church, talking about abuse committed by Cuban priests is almost mission impossible. The press is completely controlled; censorship on the island is total; access to the internet is restricted, and it is slow and prohibitively expensive. And yet everything is known in Cuba, as I was gradually going to discover.

'In the Church here in Cuba, exactly the same thing is happening in terms of sexual abuse as is going on in the United States, Mexico and the Vatican,' Roberto Veiga warns me. 'Black masses on Sundays, orgies, cases of paedophilia and prostitution: the Cuban Church is very compromised.'

For a long time Veiga was director of the Catholic journal *Espacio Laical*. In this capacity, he worked officially and directly for ten years with Cardinal Jaime Ortega, so he knows the Catholic system from the inside. Since then, he has left the Church to join Cuba Posible, a group of dissident intellectuals who have distanced themselves from the Church as well as from the Castro regime. I meet Veiga at the Hotel Plaza, in the company of Ignacio González, my Cuban 'fixer'. And we talk for a long time about the tense relations between the Church and the communist regime of the Castro brothers.

'We experienced a regular civil war between the government and the Church in the 1960s,' Roberto Veiga goes on. 'The Castro brothers and Che Guevara thought the bishops were in opposition to the regime and they kept on hacking away at Catholicism: a lot of churches were closed; the private schools were nationalized; priests were harassed, kept under surveillance or deported. Jaime Ortega was arrested himself, as he has often said, but strangely, he was sent to the UMAP camps right from the start, when he had just been ordained as a priest.'

The UMAP (Military Units to Aid Production) camps of unhappy memory were re-education and forced labour camps, dreamed up by the Castro regime to take everybody who didn't want to do their regular military service (Servicio Militar Obligatorio). Among them, the vast majority were therefore conscientious objectors, and about 10 per cent were dissidents, political opponents, peasants who had refused the expropriation of their land, Jehovah's Witnesses, and homosexuals or Catholic priests. If the Church was mistreated by the Cuban revolutionaries in 1969, it appears that few seminarians and ordinary priests were deported to the UMAP camps, unless they were also conscientious objectors, political dissidents or homosexuals.

In his famous memoirs, the homosexual Cuban writer Reinaldo Arenas related how between 1964 and 1969 the Castro regime had opened camps to 'treat' homosexuals. Obsessed with virility and prejudices, Fidel Castro saw homosexuality as a petit-bourgeois, capitalist and imperialist phenomenon. So homosexuals had to be 're-educated' and set on the right path. The technique deployed is described at length by Arenas, who was interned in such a camp himself: they projected photographs of naked men to the 'patients', who were given electric shocks at the same time. These 'reparative' therapies were supposed to correct their sexual orientation little by little.

After being freed from one of these camps, Jaime Ortega, who had been ordained as a priest at the age of 28, began a long and discreet career in the Cuban Church. He wanted to turn that dark page and be forgotten. He had a flair for organization and dialogue, and most importantly he was ready to compromise with the regime in many respects to avoid a return to prison and the marginalization of Catholicism in Cuba. Was it a good strategy?

'It was the only possible option. Ortega understood that resistance was not the solution, and that only dialogue could work,' Roberto Veiga stresses.

At the archbishop's palace in Havana, where I interview him, Mgr Ramón Suárez Polcari, the spokesman for the current archbishop, makes the same analysis. 'Cardinal Ortega was deeply marked by the difficult experience of the UMAP camps. That was where he opted for dialogue rather than confrontation. The Church was no longer to appear as an opposition party. It was a braver choice than people said; it meant that he had to stay where he was, not go into exile, not give up the Catholic presence in Cuba. That too was a form of resistance.'

On the walls of the palace, a grand residence in yellow and blue in the centre of Havana, I see large portraits of Cardinal Ortega, put up to celebrate the 50 years of his priesthood. In these photographs he can be seen as a child, a young priest, a young bishop and finally an archbishop – a veritable cult of personality.

The director of the Centro Cultural Félix Varela, a layman by the name of Andura, also confirms the pertinence of this choice of collaboration with the communist regime: 'The Cuban Church wasn't stocked with weapons, as people have said, but it's true that it was clearly in opposition during the 1960s. Those were dark years for us Catholics. We absolutely had to start up a dialogue again. But that doesn't mean that we're a branch of government!'

Spotted by the new Pope John Paul II's apostolic nuncio, Ortega was appointed Bishop of Pinar del Río in 1979, then Archbishop of Havana in 1981. He was 45.

Jaime Ortega then began a meticulous job of rapprochement with the regime, with the aim of achieving the full recognition of the Catholic Church in Cuba. Between 1986 and 1987 he discreetly led negotiations at the highest level of state. They ended in a kind of non-aggression pact: the Church recognized communist power; and the communists recognized Catholicism.

From that date, the Church regained a form of legitimacy in Cuba, a condition of its development. Catechism classes were timidly re-authorized, the episcopate began republishing journals that had been forbidden until then, and appointments of bishops were made prudently, with the appearance of independence, but with subtle government vetoes. Meetings took place, at first informally, then officially, between Fidel Castro and Jaime Ortega. The possibility of a visit from the pope was mooted. For this effective strategy, and for his courage, the Archbishop of Havana was elevated to the status of cardinal by John Paul II in 1994.

Despite his having been ordained comparatively late, he became one of the youngest cardinals of the age.

'Jaime Ortega is a man of great intelligence. He has always had a long-term vision. He has a rare political flair, and he anticipated very early on that the regime would need to establish peaceful relations with the Church. He believes in taking his time,' Roberto Veiga adds.

Mgr Ramón Suárez Polcari also stresses the cardinal's talents: 'Ortega is a man of God. But at the same time he has a great facility of communication. He is also a man of ideas and culture. He is very close to artists, to writers, to dancers ...'

Since then, with a great sense of diplomacy, Ortega organized the trips of three popes to Cuba, including the historic visit of John Paul II in January 1998, followed by that of Benedict XVI in March 2012, and two trips by Francis in 2015 and 2016. He also played an important part in the secret negotiations that enabled the rapprochement between Cuba and the United States (for which he met President Obama in Washington), and was involved in the peace negotiations between the Colombian government and FARC guerrillas in Havana, before retiring in 2016.

The Brazilian intellectual Frei Betto, who knows Cuba well, and who published a book of interviews with Fidel Castro about religion, sums up the role of the cardinal during a conversation in Rio de Janeiro. 'I know Ortega well. He is a man of dialogue who brought about a rapprochement between the Church and the Cuban revolution. He played a crucial part in that. I respect him a lot, even though he has always had reservations about liberation theology. He was the one who supervised the trips to Cuba by three popes, and Francis even came twice. And I would say, although I'm joking, that these days it's easier to find Francis in Havana than in Rome!'

This remarkable career has been pursued at the inevitable cost of compromises with the regime.

'Ortega has not had fluid relations with the opposition and with dissidents since the 1980s. His relations are better with the government,' Roberto Veiga matter-of-factly observes.

At the Vatican, some diplomats share this judgement. One of these is Archbishop François Bacqué, who was for a long time a nuncio in

Latin America: 'He was thought to be a bit too accommodating with the regime,' Bacqué tells me.

Others in Rome are even more critical: one nuncio wonders if Ortega wasn't serving 'two masters at once': the pope and Fidel. Another diplomat considers that the Cuban Church is not independent of the state, and that Ortega has played a double game: according to this view, he told the Vatican one thing and the Castro brothers something else. Perhaps. But it seems that Pope Francis, who knows the Cuban political situation well, went on trusting Jaime Ortega.

During another trip to Cuba, on which I was accompanied by the Colombian Emmanuel Neisa, one of my Latin American researchers (changing passports and, several times, lodgings so as not to attract attention), we met many Cuban dissidents in Havana, including Bertha Soler, the spokeswoman for the famous Damas de Blanco, the courageous activist Antonio Rodiles, the artist Gorki and the writer Leonardo Padura (as well as several others whom I can't name here). Points of view vary, but most of them were highly critical concerning Ortega's role, even if these dissidents accept that he played a positive part in the liberation of certain political prisoners.

'I would say that Cardinal Ortega is defending the regime. He never criticizes their human rights record or the political situation. And when the pope came to Havana, Francis criticized the Mexican and the American regimes on the question of immigration, but he never said anything about the total absence of freedom of the press, freedom of association, freedom of thought in Cuba,' Antonio Rodiles explained when I interviewed him four times at his home in Havana.

On the other hand, Bertha Soler, whom I also interviewed, is more indulgent about Jaime Ortega's record: her husband, Angel Moya Acosta, a political opponent whom I met with her, was freed after eight years in jail, like hundreds of other dissidents, thanks to an agreement that the cardinal negotiated between the Cuban regime, the Spanish government and the Catholic Church.

Balance was inevitably difficult to maintain between, on the right, Ortega, the anti-communist hard line of John Paul II and Cardinal Angelo Sodano – to whom he is close – and the need for compromise, on the left, with the Castro brothers. Particularly when, in the early

1980s, Fidel developed an enthusiasm for liberation theology: the *leader maximo* read Gustavo Gutiérrez and Leonardo Boff and published a book of interviews with Frei Betto about religion. Also, as a versatile diplomat, Ortega began moderately denouncing, at the same time, the excesses of capitalism and of communism. In place of liberation theology, endorsed by Castro but fought against everywhere in Latin America by John Paul II and Joseph Ratzinger, he subtly advocated a 'theology of reconciliation' between Cubans.

'In his youth, Ortega was close to liberation theology, but he moved away from it,' I am told by Tony Ramos, a pastor of Cuban origin in Miami who knew Ortega in Havana when he was 18, and was at one point in the same seminary as the future cardinal.

Ramos adds, in a enigmatic phrase (and wishing to keep the rest of our conversation off the record): 'Ortega has always lived in conflict, like many priests.'

It is certain, as several contacts I interviewed in Havana observed, that the regime was perfectly aware of the relationship, the encounters, the travels, the private life, the sexual morality – whatever it might be – of Jaime Ortega. Given his role in the hierarchy, and his frequent connections with the Vatican, it is clear that the cardinal was under 24-hour surveillance by the Cuban political police. One of its specialities is to compromise sensitive personalities by filming them *in flagrante*, at home or in hotels.

'Cardinal Ortega is a puppet who is completely in the power of the Castro regime. He is in the hands of Raúl Castro. Let's not forget that Cuba is the most monitored society in the world,' Michael Putney, one of the most respected journalists in Florida, tells me when I interview him at the offices of WPLG Local 10 in northern Miami.

Was Ortega blackmailed, as some suggest? Was he himself, or his entourage, so vulnerable that they didn't have any room for manoeuvre to criticize the regime? One of the best English-speaking specialists in Cuban intelligence tells me over lunch in Paris that Cardinal Ortega and his entourage were placed under direct surveillance by Alejandro Castro Espín, the son of the former president Raúl Castro. The unofficial head of the Cuban secret services is even said over the years to have drawn up a complete dossier, using very sophisticated surveillance technology, on

the leaders of the Catholic Church in Cuba, and Jaime Ortega in particular. In other words, Ortega is 'atendido', protected at a very high level. A
secretive person, Alejandro Castro Espín occupies the role of coordinator
of the defence council and national security, which covers all of Cuban
intelligence and counter-espionage: he is said to be Cardinal Ortega's liaison officer. This would involve looking into all exchanges with the Vatican,
and while there are hardly any photographs of him (we know that he lost
an eye while fighting in Angola), he has recently appeared in one picture,
in the company of his Father Raúl, standing next to Pope Francis.

'The Castro regime has a long history of compromising sensitive
individuals and opponents to the regime, based on their sexuality. And
homosexuality is one of the most powerful blackmailing tools when you
are in the closet, particularly if you are a priest or a bishop,' the same
source tells me. (This information coincides with the startling revelations
about the wire-taps and sexual blackmail of the regime, by Fidel Castro's
personal bodyguard, Lieutenant Colonel Juan Reinaldo Sánchez, in his
book *The Hidden Life of Fidel Castro*, published after his exile.)

A few years ago, the televised testimony of a former colonel in the
Cuban Fuerzas Armadas Revolucionarias, Roberto Ortega, also caused
a stir in Cuban circles. This army officer, exiled to the United States,
claimed that Archbishop Jaime Ortega led a double life: he had had intimate relations with a Cuban secret service agent described as a 'big
black guy six foot tall'. The Cuban government, according to this ex-colonel, had videos and concrete proof against Jaime Ortega. This evidence
could be useful to put pressure on or blackmail the cardinal to guarantee
his total support for the Castro regime. While this televised interview
provoked numerous press articles, which can be found online, and while
it has not been denied by Cardinal Ortega himself, it does not constitute
concrete proof. As for the statements by this ex-colonel, while they are
held to be credible by experts that I have interviewed, they may also have
been fed by rumours or a desire for revenge inherent in political exile.

One thing is certain, in any case: the sexual scandals within the Church
in Cuba have proliferated for several decades, both within the archbishop's palace and the episcopate and in several dioceses in the country.

'Here in Cuba there have been lots of paedophilia scandals, a lot of sexual corruption, a real moral failure of the Church. But obviously the press has never mentioned it. The government knows everything; it has all the evidence, but it has never used it against the Church. It is keeping it to use when it needs to. It's the regime's usual blackmail technique,' Veiga tells me.

Rumours of the homosexuality of numerous priests and bishops in the Cuban episcopate are so common in Havana that they have been passed on to me with many details and names by almost all the people I have interviewed on the island – more than a hundred witnesses, including the main dissidents, foreign diplomats, artists, writers and even priests of Havana.

'We have to pay attention to rumours. They can come from anywhere. We must not under-estimate the fact that there are always enemies of the Church within government, even if Fidel and Raúl Castro have evolved over the past few years,' cautions Mr Andura, the director of the Centro Cultural Félix Varela.

And he adds, seeming to deny what he has just said: 'It should also be pointed out that homosexuality hasn't been a crime in Cuba for a long time. If the boys are over 16, which is the age of sexual majority here, and if they are consenting, and there are no money or power relations involved, there is no problem as such.'

Orlando Márquez, editor of the newspaper of the Cuban episcopate, *Palabra Nueva*, and spokesman for Cardinal Ortega, with whom he has worked for 20 years, also agrees to see me. A good communicator, skilful and friendly, Márquez doesn't avoid any questions. Was it necessary to reach a compromise with the communist regime?

'If the cardinal hadn't chosen the path of dialogue, there would be no bishops in Cuba, it's as simple as that.'

What does he think about talk of Cardinal Ortega's homosexuality?

'It's a very old rumour. I've heard it very often. It's because he was sent to the UMAP camps; that's where the rumours began. Sometimes people even say that I'm gay, because I'm close to Ortega!' Orlando Márquez adds, bursting out laughing.

Was Cardinal Ortega informed about sexual abuse in the archbishopric of Havana, as several diplomats in Cuba suggest? Were they covered up? What exactly happened in the Cuban Catholic hierarchy? Four first-hand testimonies confirm the considerable number of sexual scandals stretching out over many years: first of all, that of a priest I met on the recommendation of a Western diplomat; a director of the Mesa de Diálogo de la Juventud Cubana (an NGO specializing in human rights and youth); a pair of Christian activists; and finally, a fourth Cuban dissident. This information has also been confirmed in Madrid, by people very familiar with Cuba. In Santiago de Chile, two people close to Fidel Castro whom I interviewed also gave me useful information (Ernesto Ottone, the former leader of the Chilean Communist Party, and Gloria Gaitán, the daughter of the famous murdered Colombian leader). In the Vatican itself, three diplomats in the holy see confirmed that there were serious problems of sexual abuse in Cuba. The file in the Secretariat of State is highly confidential, but it is well-known to Pope Francis's diplomats, two of whom – the 'minister' of the interior, Giovanni Angelo Becciu, and the diplomat, Mgr Fabrice Rivet – were in office in Havana.

I have also been given to understand that Pope Francis asked Cardinal Ortega to leave the archbishopric of Havana due to his passivity over and covering up of these scandals. This isn't exactly true. As I am told by Guzmán Carriquiry, who runs the Pontifical Commission for Latin America in the Vatican, Jaime Ortega was almost eighty-years-old when he resigned, and since the pope had already kept him on beyond the age limit, it was normal for him to be replaced.

Mgr Fabrice Rivet, who was number two in the Vatican embassy in Havana and was present with Benedict XVI when the pope met Fidel Castro in the nunciature, refuses to express himself 'on the record', even though he receives me five times at the Secretariat of State. With regard to Ortega, of whom he has nothing bad to say, he only says enigmatically: 'He is very controversial.' (Cardinals Pietro Parolin and Beniamino Stella, who were respectively nuncios in Caracas and Cuba, are also well-informed about the situation; the same is true of Tarcisio Bertone, who went to Cuba five times, and one of whose private secretaries, the future nuncio Nicolas Thévenin, held office in Cuba. Plainly well-informed, Thévenin would also give me, via the journalist Nicolas

Diat, one day when I was having lunch with him, some information about Ortega, Cuba, homosexuality and communists. Georg Gänswein, for whom Thévenin was once an assistant, is also aware of the file's contents.)

Interviewed twice at his home in Rome, Cardinal Etchegaray, who was John Paul II's 'flying' ambassador, and who knows Cuba intimately, is more favourable towards Ortega, as is Cardinal Jean-Louis Tauran, former 'minister' of foreign affairs to John Paul II, with whom I have discussed these sexual scandals in detail, and who claims that they are 'pure speculation'.

But others in Rome and Havana are less restrained. And sometimes all it takes is a honeyed question, with promises of keeping things off the record, for tongues to loosen about the sexual morals of the archbishopric.

First of all, there is the impressive number of homosexuals among the priests and bishops of Cuba. Protected at the level of the episcopate, this genuine Freemasonry has become very visible, spilling out of the closet. They are also very 'practising'. So I am given lengthy descriptions of the famous Sunday evening mass in Havana Cathedral which, in the 1990s, became a very popular hook-up spot in the capital.

Then there are the priests and prelates of the Vatican who go regularly to Cuba as sexual tourists, with the blessing of the Cuban Catholic hierarchy. I have visited clubs and specialist parties in Havana for which European priests make the trip. So Cuba became, at least from the mid-1980s, a destination of choice for those who are both 'of the parish' and 'in the closet'.

'In a way, members of religious orders think they're exempt from man-made laws, in Cuba more than anywhere else. In their eyes, their unique status justifies and legitimizes them in exempting themselves from common law,' Roberto Veiga suggests prudently.

Within the Cuban episcopate, I am also told about instances of 'internal' sexual abuse, perpetrated by prelates on seminarians or young priests. A certain number of monsignori are also reputed to use escorts, abusing these young men while paying them modest sums. Often, according to a first-hand witness, prostitutes are invited in groups to salacious parties where vulgar language is used – *pinga* (cock), *friqui friqui* (fucking), *maricones* (queers) – and humiliations inflicted. Should they refuse to take part in these sensual banquets, they are denounced to the police, who systematically arrest the escorts and leave the prelates be.

Male prostitution is massive in Cuba, in particular thanks to a network of specialist clubs and bars. It also occurs on the pavements close to more mainstream places such as the Las Vegas, Humboldt 52 (which is now closed), La Gruta, and Café Cantante. Around the Parque Central, there are countless male prostitutes, as there are in the evening on Calle 23 or along the famous Malecón. In a country where corruption is universal, and where there are no journalistic or legal safeguards, it is hardly astonishing that the Catholic Church should have developed bad habits here more than elsewhere.

'Cardinal Ortega is aware of everything that happens in the archbishopric: he checks everything. But if he said anything at all about sexual abuse within the Church, carried out by people close to him, carried out by bishops, his career would have been cut short. So he closed his eyes,' a dissident I interview in Havana tells me.

This cowardice, these silences, this *omertà*, these scandals are so extraordinary that it must have taken Benedict XVI's entourage a lot of courage to inform the pope before or during his stay in Havana. When he found out about it all, and more importantly when he discovered the scale of the problem of the archbishopric in Havana, this pope who was able to gauge the breadth of the 'filth' in the Church (in his own words), was now seized with disgust. According to one witness, the pope, listening to this story, wept once again.

After this, there was a lot of tension between Benedict XVI and Ortega, who previously had 'very special relations' with the pope (according to someone who witnessed their meeting). This time, Joseph Ratzinger had had enough. He cracked. Intransigent and shy, he had spent his whole life trying to thwart evil, and here he was literally surrounded, encircled by homosexual priests and cases of paedophilia. Was there not a single virtuous prelate?

'Benedict XVI's trip to Cuba was chaotic. The pope was in an altered state, saddened and deeply overwhelmed by what he had just learned about the extent of sexual abuse in the Cuban Church. Why he continued with his trip I don't know. Only one thing is certain: he would decide to resign barely a week after his return from Cuba,' Roberto Veiga tells me in the presence of one of my other researchers, Nathan Marcel-Millet.

In Mexico, during the same trip, the pope had been disenchanted. But Cuba! Even in Cuba! This wasn't a matter of missteps or accidents: it was a whole system. The Church was full of 'filth', he said it himself; but this time he discovered that the Church everywhere was corrupt. Wearied by jetlag and by the Mexican stage of his tour, where he was slightly injured during a fall, the holy father was in physical pain; in Cuba, he suffered moral pain as well. All witnesses agree: the trip was 'terrible'. It was even a 'genuine Calvary'.

On the paradise island of Cuba, the pope discovered the extent of sin in the Church. 'The net also contains some bad fish,' he would say afterwards, in a state of despair. The trip to Cuba was the fall of the old Adam.

'Yes, it was at the time of his trip to Mexico and Cuba that Pope Benedict XVI began to consider the idea of stepping down,' Federico Lombardi confirms during one of our five conversations at the offices of the Ratzinger Foundation (Lombardi accompanied the pope to Latin America).

'Why did the Castro regime, which knew all the details of these scandals implicating the Cuban episcopate, not act?' I ask Roberto Veiga.

'It's a powerful way of keeping the Church under control,' he replies. 'Not denouncing prostitution or paedophilia scandals is a way of covering them up. But it is also a way of guaranteeing that the Church, one of the main opposition forces on the island, will never turn against the regime.'

On his return from Havana, Benedict XVI was a man in pieces. Part of him had broken. He was a 'great soul asphyxiated'. All around him, the columns of the temple were cracked.

A few days later, the pope decided to resign (but he would only announce his decision publicly six months later). In his book *Last Testament*, Benedict twice identified the trip to Cuba as the crucial moment; and while he mentioned only the physical fatigue and the 'burden' of his papal mission, different sources allow me to assert that he was 'overwhelmed' by what he learned about sexual abuse during his visit. Cuba would prove to be one of the last stops along the stations of the cross of Benedict XVI's pontificate.

'Fall? What fall? It was an act of liberation', I am told by a grumpy Cardinal Poupard when I interview him about Benedict XVI's last days as pope.

Renunciation, abdication, act of liberation? Whatever the truth, on 11 February 2013, during a routine consistory, Benedict XVI abdicated. In the inaugural mass of the pontificate, eight years earlier, he had declared: 'Pray for me, so that I may love the flock more and more. Pray for me, so that I don't shy away from the wolves.' The wolves had just got the better of him. It was the first time in the modern age that a pope had stepped down, and also the first time since the Avignon papacy that two popes had coexisted.

For us, today, it is hard to imagine the clap of thunder in the Vatican sky. Secretly prepared for several months, Benedict XVI's resignation seemed very sudden. At the moment of the announcement, the Curia, calm and unconcerned, instantly became Leonardo da Vinci's *Last Supper*, as if Christ had just said again: 'Verily I tell you that one of you will betray me.' Time was once again out of joint. The terrified and speechless cardinals now formed a dislocated community, then protested amid the chaos of their love and truth: 'Lord, is it me?' And the pope, serene in his choice, bringing his internalized tragedy to a close, peaceful now that he had finished 'fighting with himself', was now barely concerned with this agitated Curia, so mean and perverse, so closeted, or with those intrigues featuring so many rigid men leading double lives, in which the wolves had got the better of him; for the first time, he was triumphant. His abdication – a flash of light, a historic gesture that made him great at last – was the first good decision, perhaps the only one, of his brief pontificate.

The event was so inconceivable that the Church is still trying to tame the waves and aftershocks. Because nothing will be as it was: by abdicating, the pope 'came down from the Cross', in the perfidious words of Stanisław Dziwisz, former private secretary to John Paul II. Roman Catholicism had reached its low point. Henceforth, the pope's job is a pontificate of limited duration, almost a temporary contract; an age limit would be imposed; the pope had become a man like any other, and his power had shrunk, becoming temporal.

Everyone also understood that his illness was only one of the reasons for his resignation, among those invoked to explain such a spectacular gesture. Benedict XVI's spokesman, Federico Lombardi, made frequent appearances to insist that it was only the state of the holy father's health, his physical fragility, that explained his historically unique gesture. His insistence raised smiles.

The pope's state of health was a factor. Joseph Ratzinger fell victim to a stroke in 1991, the consequence of which, as he himself revealed, was to make him slightly blind in his left eye. He also wore a pacemaker to combat chronic atrial fibrillation. But I am not convinced that there was a new element in the pope's health around 2012 to 2013 sufficient to explain his decision. The pope was not close to death; he has gone on to live past the age of 90. The narrative has been repeated too often to be true.

'The Vatican explained the pope's resignation with reference to his problems of health: it was obviously a lie, as is so often the case,' Francesco Lepore states.

Nowadays, few journalists, theologians or even members of the Roman Curia whom I have met consider Benedict XVI's resignation to have been linked to his health. After the false denial, in the most perfect Stalinist tradition, even the cardinals I have spoken to acknowledge that there were 'other factors'.

In the course of his long stations of the cross, Pope Benedict XVI – we can assert here – threw in the sponge for a number of combined or inter-linked reasons, in which homosexuality occupied a central place. Among the 14 stations of that Via Dolorosa, I would list: the state of his health; his age; his ineptitude for government; the failure of Cardinal Bertone to reform the Curia; religious controversies and his disastrous attempts at communication; the cover-up of thousands of paedophile scandals; the collapse of his theology on celibacy and the chastity of priests because of sexual abuse; the trip to Cuba; VatiLeaks I; the report by the three cardinals; the methodical attacks on his pontificate by Cardinal Sodano; rumours or possible threats relating to Georg Gänswein or his brother Georg Ratzinger; internalized homophobia or 'Ratzinger syndrome'; and finally Mozart, because this pope who didn't like noise preferred to return to his piano and his classical music, which he missed terribly.

Here I would leave open the question concerning which of these 14 Stations of the Cross were crucial in bringing Benedict XVI's pontificate to a close. Each of us can bring our own arguments to bear, revise the order or ponder each station in relation to the others. All that I can affirm here is that among the 14 stations of his walk to Calvary, which lasted eight years, the fact is that at least ten of them are connected directly or indirectly to the homosexual question – a question that was also his personal tragedy.

Epilogue

'I don't love women. Love needs reinventing.' These standard-bearing phrases, these famous words from the manifesto of the young Poet of *A Season in Hell*, drenched in a mixture of Christ-like and homosexual impulses, can guide us through this epilogue. The reinvention of love may even be the most surprising revelation of this book – the finest and the most optimistic too – and the one with which I would like to conclude this long investigation.

At the heart of the Church, in a highly restricted universe, priests are living out their amorous passions while at the same time renewing gender and imagining new kinds of family.

This is an even better-kept secret than the homosexuality of a large part of the College of Cardinals and the clergy. Beyond the lies and the universal hypocrisy, the Vatican is also an unexpected place of experimentation: new ways of living as a couple are constructed there; new emotional relationships are tried out; new models of the family of the future are explored; preparations are made for the retirement of elderly homosexuals.

At the end of this investigation, five main profiles of priests take shape, encompassing most of our protagonists: the 'mad virgin'; the 'infernal husband'; the model of the 'queen of hearts'; the 'distorted Don Juan'; and finally the 'La Mongolfiera'. In this book we have rubbed shoulders with all of these archetypes, whether we have loved or hated them.

The model of the 'mad virgin', all asceticism and sublimation, is the one that characterizes Jacques Maritain, François Mauriac, Jean Guitton and perhaps also some recent popes. 'Thwarted' homophiles, they have chosen religion in order not to yield to the flesh, and the cassock to escape their inclinations. 'Loving friendship' is their natural inclination. We may assume that they have barely moved into action, even though François Mauriac, as we know, knew other men intimately.

The model of the 'infernal husband' is more practising: the 'closeted' or 'questioning' priest is aware of his homosexuality, but is afraid of experiencing it, constantly oscillating between sin and expiation, in a state of great emotional confusion. Sometimes his special friendships lead to action, in turn producing deep crises of conscience. This model of the individual who takes no pleasure in life, who never ceases to worry, is that of many cardinals whom we have met in this book. In these first two models, homosexuality may be a practice, but it is not an identity. The priests in question do not accept or recognize themselves as gay; they even tend, on the contrary, to prove homophobic.

The model of the 'queen of hearts' is one of those most frequently encountered: unlike the two previous models, this is a characteristic identity, as indeed it was for Julian Green; it is shared by numerous cardinals and countless Curia priests that I have met. If they can, these priests favour monogamy, often idealized, with the gratifications that go with being faithful to one another. They have long-term relationships and lead a double life, not without a 'perpetual balance between boys whose beauty damns them, and God, whose goodness absolves them'. They are hybrid creatures, both arch-priests and arch-gays.

The 'distorted Don Juan' chases after young men, not skirts – 'men of pleasure'. Some cardinals and bishops that we have mentioned are perfect examples of this category: they burn their candles at both ends and are happy to make passes at all and sundry, with the impenitent courtier's famous list of 'one thousand and three' in proper form – and sometimes off the beaten track. (The types 'mad virgin', 'infernal husband' and 'queen of hearts' are borrowed from the Poet Rimbaud; 'distorted Don Juan' from the poem 'Don Juan Pipé', by his lover, Verlaine.)

Finally, the model 'La Mongolfiera' is that of perversion or prostitution networks: it is the model, par excellence, of the appalling Cardinal La Mongolfiera, but also of Cardinal Platinette and several other cardinals and Curia bishops. (Here I am leaving aside the few rare cardinals who are truly asexual and chaste; and those heterosexuals who have relationships according to one of the previous models, but with a woman – who are also large in number, but are not the subject of this book. It should also be said that there is the category of sexual predators, such as Father Marcial Maciel, who elude any objective classification.)

So we can see: homosexual profiles vary greatly within the Catholic Church, even though the great majority of prelates in the Vatican and the characters in this book may be placed in one or another of these groups. I notice two constants. On the one hand, the majority of these priests have nothing to do with 'ordinary love'; their sex life can be restrained or exaggerated, closeted or dissolute, and sometimes all of these things at once, but it is rarely banal. On the other hand, a certain fluidity remains: the categories are not as hermetic as I have described them; they represent a whole spectrum, a continuum, and some gender-fluid priests move from one group to the other in the course of their lives, between two worlds, as if in limbo. However, several categories are missing or rare in the Vatican: true transsexuals are as good as non-existent, and bisexuals seem to be unrepresented. In the 'LGBT' world of the Vatican, there are hardly any 'B's or 'T's, only 'L's and a huge crowd of 'G's. (I haven't mentioned lesbianism in this book, because I wasn't able to carry out my inquiry in a very discreet world where you probably have to be female to have good access, but I would suggest, on the basis of several statements, that female religious life in the closet is as dominated by the prism of lesbianism as the life of the male clergy is by the gay question.)

If homosexuality is the rule and heterosexuality is the exception in the Catholic priesthood, that doesn't mean that it is accepted as a collective identity. Even though it is the norm 'by default', it seems like a very individualized 'practice', so hidden and 'closeted' that it translates neither into a way of life nor into a culture. The homosexuals in the Vatican and the clergy are innumerable, but they do not form a community, and therefore they cannot have a lobby. They are not 'gays' in the proper sense of the word, if we understand that to mean accepted homosexuality, lived collectively. But they have common codes and references. Those of *The Closet*.

In the course of my investigation, I have discovered genuine loving relationships within the clergy which, according to age and circumstance, can take the form of paternal, filial or fraternal love – and those loving friendships comforted me. Old fellows together? Confirmed bachelors? Many, in fact, live out their homosexuality stubbornly, and practise it assiduously, according to the fine model described by Paul Verlaine: 'The story of two men living together / Better than non-model husbands.'

It's a fact: the constraints of the Church have forced those priests to come up with extraordinary detours to experience wonderful love affairs, like classical dramatists who attained perfect literary perfection while being obliged to respect the very strict rule of the three unities: time, place and action.

Experiencing love under the Vatican constraint: some people manage to do so at the cost of unimaginable pieces of play-acting. I'm thinking of one famous cardinal, among the most highly-ranked of the holy see, who lives with his lover. During a conversation I had with him, in his magnificent apartment in the Vatican, while we were sitting out on a sun-drenched terrace, the cardinal's companion arrived. Had the conversation gone on for too long, or had the boyfriend come home early? In any case, I sensed the embarrassment of the cardinal, who looked at his watch and quickly put an end to our dialogue, after having unburdened himself to us for several hours previously. As he walked Daniele and me to the entrance of his penthouse, he was forced to introduce his companion with a highly convoluted explanation.

'He's my late sister's husband,' the old cardinal stammered, probably believing that I would fall for his lie.

But I'd been warned. At the Vatican, everybody knows this cleric's secret. The Swiss Guards talked to me about his tender companion; the priests of the Secretariat of State joked about the unusual length, by the cardinal's standard, of this particular relationship. I left the couple in peace, amused by their attempts to pretend that there was nothing between them, and now imagined them starting their little dinner à deux, taking a ready meal out of the fridge, watching television in their slippers and stroking their little dog – a (nearly) bourgeois couple like any other.

We encounter a similar kind of innovative relationship at the home of another cardinal emeritus who also lives with his assistant, which again creates several advantages. The lovers can spend a long time together, without arousing too much suspicion; they can also travel and go on holidays as lovers, because they have a ready-made alibi. No one can question their closeness, given the fact that they are working together. Sometimes the assistants live in the cardinals' homes, which is even more practical. Once again, no one is surprised. The Swiss Guard have confirmed to me that they have to turn a blind eye 'whatever company the cardinals took'. They have absorbed the rule 'Don't ask, don't tell', which remains mantra number one at the Vatican.

Sleeping with one's private secretary is an omnipresent model in the history of the Vatican. It's a great classic of the holy see: there are so many secretary-lovers, the tendency is so deeply anchored, that it could even be turned into a new sociological rule: the thirteenth of *The Closet*: *Do not ask who the companions of cardinals and bishops are; ask their secretaries, their assistants or their protégés, and you will be able to tell the truth by their reaction.*

Did Nietzsche not state that 'marriage must be considered as a long conversation'? By hitching themselves to an assistant, prelates finally construct lasting relationships based more on work than on emotion. That may explain their longevity. Because power relations are also at work here, some of these cardinals owe their sexual success to their position: they have been able to feed and encourage the ambition of their favourites.

These 'arrangements' remain vulnerable. Making one's lover one's assistant is a bit like a straight couple having a baby to save a marriage. What happens in the event of a break-up, of jealousy, of cheating? The cost of separation is multiplied ten times over compared with a 'normal' couple. To leave one's assistant is to risk embarrassing situations: rumours; betrayal; sometimes blackmail. Not to mention 'transfiliation', to use a religious image: an assistant close to a cardinal can't start serving another cardinal, a transfer of allegiance which often provokes jealousy and sometimes ends up in violence. Many Vatican affairs and scandals can be explained by these emotional break-ups between an eminence and his protégé.

A variant of this model has been dreamed up by a cardinal who, after paying for his young men, seems to have settled down. He has developed a charade: every time he goes out, every time he travels, he is accompanied by his lover, whom he introduces as his bodyguard! (An anecdote confirmed to me by two prelates, as well as by the former priest Francesco Lepore.) A cardinal with a bodyguard! In the Vatican, everybody smiles at such extravagance. Not to mention the jealousy that the relationship provokes, because the companion in question is, I am told, 'a knockout'.

Many cardinals and priests in the Vatican have invented their own *Amoris laetitia*, a form of love between men of a new kind. It's no longer 'coming out', a sacrilegious admission on papal territory, but 'coming home' – which consists in bringing one's lover to one's own apartment. And this takes us to the heart of gay households in the world today. Have priests anticipated new LGBT ways of life? Are they now inventing what sociologists call affective fluidity and 'liquid love'?

A French cardinal with whom I struck up a friendship lived for a long time with an Anglican priest; an Italian archbishop with a Scotsman; one African cardinal also has a long-distance relationship with a Jesuit at Boston College and another with his boyfriend in Long Beach.

Love? Bromance? Boyfriend? Significant other? Hook-up? Sugar daddy? Friends with benefits? Best friends for ever? Everything is possible and forbidden at the same time. We get lost in words, even in English; we struggle to decode the precise nature of these relationships, which are constantly renegotiating the clauses of the contract that relate to those who are or were 'practising'. This is a logic already analysed by Marcel Proust, in terms of homosexual love, and this will be the last rule in this book, the fourteenth of *The Closet*: *We are often mistaken about the loves of priests, and about the number of people with whom they have liaisons: because one wrongly interprets friendships as liaisons, which is an error of addition; but also because we fail to imagine friendships as liaisons, which is another kind of error, this time by subtraction.*

Another model of love within the Catholic hierarchy involves 'adoptions'. I know of a good dozen of cases in which a cardinal, an archbishop or a priest has 'adopted' his boyfriend. It is true, for example, of a francophone cardinal who adopted a migrant of whom he was particularly fond, prompting great surprise among the police, who discovered, when they examined this undocumented individual, that the cleric intended to legalize his companion!

One Hispanic cardinal has adopted his '*amigo*', who became his son (and remained his lover). Another elderly cardinal whom I visited lives with his young 'brother'; the nuns who live with them quickly worked out that he was his lover, and give themselves away by calling him his 'new' brother.

A renowned priest also told me how he 'adopted a young Latin American, an orphan, who was selling his body in the street'. At first his client, the relationship 'rapidly became paternal, by common agreement, and it is no longer sexual,' the priest tells me. The young man is wild and elusive, and his protector talks to me about him as if he is his son, which in the eyes of the law he is.

'This relationship has humanized me,' the priest tells me.

The boy was very unsocialized, very insecure: the path of the relationship was therefore strewn with pitfalls, drug addiction not being the least of them. He too had been legalized after countless administrative obstructions, which the priest described to me during several interviews at their shared home. He supports his young friend; he is teaching him his new language and helping him get his foot on the ladder to get some training that might help him get a job. A crazy, noble dream, wanting to offer a better life to a stranger!

Luckily, the former sex worker, who owns nothing but the story of his life, is busy changing for the good. Rather than a 'coming out', the priest is offering his protégé a 'coming of age'. The priest takes his time; he exerts no pressure on his friend, even though the latter has caused all sorts of trouble, even threatening to burn down their shared apartment. Both know that he will never abandon his son, whose love-turned-friendship is the product not of blood ties but of elective fatherhood.

This generous and inventive relationship is based on sacrifices and a genuine love that one can't help but admire.

'Even my sister had difficulties, at first, imagining that this was a real father–son relationship, but her daughters had no trouble welcoming their new cousin,' the priest tells me.

And he adds that he has learned a lot and changed for the better in contact with his friend – and I can tell from his expression, from the look in his beautiful eyes when he talks about his companion, that this relationship has given a meaning to the priest's life which it hadn't had before.

These post-gay friendships elude all classification. In a way they correspond to what Michel Foucault recognized in his famous essay 'Friendship as a Way of Life'. The homosexual philosopher wondered: 'How is it possible for men to be together? To live together, to share their time, their meals, their bedroom, their leisure, their sorrows, their knowledge, their confidences? What does it mean to be among men, "laid bare" outside of institutional relationships, outside of family, profession, forced camaraderie?' As surprising as it might seem, priests and clerics are busy inventing these new ways of life, these new families, these new forms of post-gay love, as imagined by the homosexual philosopher who died of AIDS over thirty years ago.

Priests who generally, and prematurely, leave their parents must learn to live among men from adolescence onwards: in that way, they create a new 'family' for themselves. Without relatives, without children, these new structures of reconstituted solidarity are an unusual mixture of friends, protégés, lovers, colleagues, ex-lovers, to which we might add an elderly mother or a passing sister; here loves and friendships are mixed in a way that is not lacking in originality.

One priest told me his own story when I met him in a city on the Atlantic Ocean. Italian Catholics know him well because he was the anonymous character in *La Confessione* (republished under the title *Io, prete gay*), the story of the life of a homosexual in the Vatican published in 2000 by the journalist Marco Politi.

Now 74, this priest wanted to speak again for the first time since *La Confessione*. His simplicity, his faith, his generosity, his love of life all touched me. When he tells me about the men he has loved – and not only desired – I don't feel at any point that his faith is diminished. On the contrary, I find him loyal to his commitments and, at any rate, more sincere than many Roman monsignori and cardinals who preach chastity by day and cavort with rent boys at night.

The priest had some fine relationships, and he talks to me about the three men who mattered to him, in particular Rodolfo, an Argentinian architect. 'Rodolfo changed the course of my life,' the priest tells me simply.

The two men lived together in Rome for five years, while the priest had put his priesthood in parentheses so as not to betray his vow of chastity, after asking for a kind of extended leave, even though he went on working in the Vatican every day. Their relationship was based not so much on sexuality, as one might have thought, as on intellectual and cultural dialogue, generosity and tenderness, the attuning of their personalities – all of that mattered as much as the physical dimension.

'I thank God for letting me meet Rodolfo. With him, I really learned what it means to love. I learned to let go of all those fine words that have nothing to do with the facts,' the priest tells me.

And he also confirms that while he lived that long relationship discreetly, he didn't hide it: he talked about it to his confessors and his spiritual director. He chose honesty, which is rare in the Vatican, and rejected 'dishonest loves'. His career, of course, suffered; but it made him a better person, and a more confident one.

We walk together along a stretch of sea, near the Atlantic, and the priest, who took the afternoon to show me around the city where he lives, talks endlessly to me about Rodolfo, the love of his life, fragile and distant, and I gauge the extent of the feelings which the priest attributes to the relationship. He will later write me long letters explaining points that he didn't have time to communicate to me, to correct a particular impression, to add a particular element. He is so worried about being misunderstood.

When Rodolfo died in Rome, after a long illness, the priest went to his funeral. On the plane carrying him towards his ex-lover, he was tormented, even paralysed, by the question of knowing whether he would 'have to' or 'be able to' or 'want to' celebrate the ceremony.

'At the appointed hour, the priest in charge of the funeral didn't turn up,' he remembers. 'It was a sign from heaven. As time was passing, I was asked to replace him. And that was how a little text that I had scribbled down on the journey taking me to Rodolfo became the homily at his funeral.'

I will keep the text that the priest sent me confidential, because it is so simple and so touching that it would inevitably misrepresent this beautiful loving relationship. An intimacy that was for a long time inexpressible and yet revealed, and even hailed in the open, in front of everyone, in the very heart of this church in Rome, at the funeral mass.

In the very heart of the Vatican, two legendary homosexual couples still shine in the memory of those who knew them, and I would like to end this book with them. They both worked at Vatican Radio, the central media organization of the holy see, and the pope's broadcaster.

'Bernard Decottignies was a journalist at Vatican Radio. Almost all of his colleagues were aware of his relationship with Dominique Lomré, who was a painter. They were both Belgian. They were incredibly close. Bernard helped Dominique with all his exhibitions; he was always there to reassure him, help him and love him. He always gave priority to Dominique. He had dedicated his life to him,' Romilda Ferrauto, the former editor of the French section at Vatican Radio, tells me.

Father José Maria Pacheco, who was also a friend of the couple, and for a long time a journalist in the Portuguese section of the station, confirmed the beauty of this relationship during a conversation in Portugal: 'I remember Bernard's serenity and professionalism. What strikes me even today is the "normality" with which he lived out, day by day, his professional life and his emotional relationship with Dominique. I remember Bernard as someone who experienced his homosexual condition and his life as a couple without anxiety or militancy. He didn't need to tell people he was gay, or hide it – just because there was nothing to hide. It was simple and, in a way, "normal". He lived out his homosexuality peacefully, calmly, in the dignity and beauty of a stable loving relationship.'

In 2014, Dominique died, apparently of a respiratory illness.

'From that moment,' Romilda Ferrauto tells me, 'Bernard wasn't the same. His life lost its meaning. He was on sick leave, but he remained depressed. One day he came to see me and said, "You don't understand: my life stopped with the death of Dominique."'

'With the loss of Dominique,' Father José Maria Pacheco tells me, 'something irreversible happened. For example, Bernard stopped shaving and his long beard was in a way a sign of his distress. When I bumped into him, Bernard was broken, inwardly devoured by pain.'

In November 2015 Bernard committed suicide, plunging the Vatican once again into a state of sorrow and alarm.

'We were all devastated. Their love was so strong. Bernard committed suicide because he couldn't live without Dominique,' Ferrauto adds.

The American journalist Robert Carl Mickens, who worked at Vatican Radio for a long time, also remembers Dominique's death: 'Father Federico Lombardi, the pope's spokesman wanted to celebrate Bernard's funeral in the Church of Santa Maria in Traspontina. At the end of the ceremony, he came to hug me because I was very close to Bernard. That very powerful homosexual loving relationship was well known to everybody, including Father Lombardi.'

Romilda Ferrauto adds: 'Bernard tried as much as possible not to hide his homosexuality. In that he was honest and brave. Most of the people who knew accepted his homosexuality and, at the French office, we knew his partner.'

Another male couple, Henry McConnachie and Speer Brian Ogle, were also well known in Vatican Radio. They both worked in the English service of the station. When they died of old age, the Vatican paid tribute to them.

'Henry and Speer had lived together in Rome since the 1960s,' Mickens, who was a close friend of Henry's, tells me. 'As a couple they were very "colourful", but not openly gay. They belonged to a different generation for which a certain discretion prevailed. They were, let's say, "gentlemen".'

Cardinal Jean-Louis Tauran wanted to celebrate, in person, the funeral of Henry McConnachie, whom he had known for a long time, just as he had known about his sexuality.

'Almost everyone was aware of the homosexuality of those two couples and they had lots of friends at Vatican Radio. And they are still remembered with great tenderness,' Romilda Ferrauto concludes.

*

The world that I have described in this book isn't mine. I'm not Catholic. I'm not even a believer, although I measure the importance of Catholic culture in my life and in the history of my country, a little as Chateaubriand talks about the 'genius of Christianity'. Neither am I anti-clerical, and this book isn't opposed to Catholicism but primarily, whatever one might think, it is a critique of a very special gay community – a critique of my own community.

That is why I think it's useful to mention, by way of epilogue, the story of a priest who had an important influence on me during my youth. I don't often talk about my own life in my books, but here, given the subject, everyone will understand why it's necessary. I owe this truth to the reader.

To tell the truth, I was a Christian until the age of 13. At that time, in France, Catholicism was, as they say, 'everyone's religion'. It was an almost banal cultural fact. My priest's name was Louis. He was called, quite simply, 'Abbot Louis' or 'Father Louis'. Like a figure by El Greco, exaggeratedly bearded, he turned up one morning in our parish near Avignon, in the South of France. Where did he come from? I didn't know at the time. Like all the inhabitants of our town, we welcomed this 'missionary' to Provence; we adopted him and we loved him. He was a simple priest, not a curé – a vicar, not a prelate. He was young and likeable. He presented a fine image of the Church.

He was also paradoxical. An aristocrat, originally from Belgium – as far as we could tell – an intellectual, but one who also spoke the simple language of the poor. He called us by our first names, smoking his pipe. He saw us in a way as his family.

I didn't have a Catholic education: I went to secular public schools which, luckily in France, keep religion at a distance; for which I thank my parents. We seldom went to mass, which seemed incredibly tedious to us. Between my first communion and my second, I became one of the favourite pupils of Father Louis, perhaps his absolute favourite, so much so that my parents asked him to become my confirmation sponsor. Becoming the friend of a priest, which is an unusual kind of friendship, was a significant experience, when my natural bent would have been towards the criticism of religion, along the lines of the young Poet: 'How stupid they are, those village churches', where the children listen to 'the divine babble'.

I was Catholic by tradition. I was never 'a slave of my baptism'. But Father Louis was brilliant. I was too unruly to be a choirboy, and I think

I was expelled from Sunday school for lack of discipline. My priest wasn't offended – on the contrary. Teaching the Catechism to the children of the parish? Living around the sacristy and hosting the village fair? I was a young Rimbaud, seeking new horizons! The abbot, like us, aspired to wide spaces. He encouraged me to join the chaplaincy that he ran, and we went on field trips for five or six years. It was a working-class chaplaincy, unlike the more bourgeois movements like the pioneers or the scouts. He gave me a passion for travelling and he taught me rock-climbing, roped to him. Under the pretext of 'spiritual retreats', we left for a youth camp, by bike or on foot, in the Provençal Alpilles, in the Calanques range in Marseille, near the mountain of Lure in the Alpes-de-Haute-Provence, or in the high mountains, with our tents and tent-pegs, sleeping in refuges, climbing the Dôme de Neige des Écrins. And in the evening, on trips far away from my family, I started reading books which, sometimes, without pressing the point, this widely read priest recommended to us, perhaps for evangelizing purposes.

Why did he become a priest? At the time we didn't know much about Louis', life 'before'. What had he done before reaching our parish near Avignon? Writing this book, with the help of his closest friends, I tried to find his traces. I researched in the archives of the diocese, and I was able to reconstruct his itinerary quite precisely from Lusambo, in Zaire (then the Belgian Congo), where he was born in 1941, to Avignon.

I remember the cultural proselytism and 'leisure catechism' of Abbé Louis. In this respect, he was both modern and traditional. A man of art and literature, he liked Gregorian chant and arthouse cinema. He took us to see 'issue' movies to engage with us in tendentious discussions of suicide, abortion, the death penalty or world peace (never, that I can remember, homosexuality). As far as he was concerned, everything was up for discussion, without taboos, without prejudices. But as a graduate in philosophy and theology – Louis topped off his religious education with a degree in canon law at the Pontifical Gregorian University in Rome – he was a formidable debater. He was both a product of Vatican II, of its modernity, and the inheritor of a conservative conception of the Church that made him nostalgic for Latin and traditional robes. He was a passionate admirer of Paul VI, less so of John Paul II. He was in favour of a renewed catechism, shaking up tradition, but he also insisted on the unshakeable links of marriage, so much so that he rejected communion for certain divorced couples. *In fact, in Avignon, with his contradictions and his free spirit, he baffled his parishioners.*

Worker-priest for some (irritated, the local bourgeoisie accused him of being a communist); a country priest for others, who revered him; he was a literate priest for yet others, both admired and envied, because rural people are always suspicious of city-dwellers who read books.

He was reproached for being 'haughty', meaning intelligent. His ironic joie de vivre worried people. His anti-bourgeois culture, which made him despise money, vanity and ostentation, didn't sit well with the practising Catholics who, not knowing what to think, found him too 'spiritual' for their tastes. They were suspicious of the (excessively numerous) travels he had taken, and the new ideas he had brought back. They said he was 'ambitious'; it was predicted that he would one day be a bishop or even a cardinal, and, in our parish, this character out of Balzac – Lucien de Rubempré more than Rastignac – was mistaken for a social climber. I remember that, unlike many priests, he wasn't a misogynist and he enjoyed the company of women. For that reason, he was rumoured to have a mistress in the person of a local militant socialist. I interviewed her for this book and the story still makes her laugh. He was also reproached – why would you do such a thing? – for his hospitality, which was his main business, because he provided lodging for the poor, young people on the margins and passing strangers in the parish. There were also rumours, although I didn't know it at the time, of unnatural encounters with the sailors in the port of Toulon; they said that he travelled the world in search of adventures. He laughed all of this off, and greeted his supposed mother-in-law in the parish with a thunderous: 'Belle-maman'.

To paraphrase Chateaubriand, in his fine portrait of the Abbé de Rancé, I would write that 'this whole family of religion around [Father Louis] had the tenderness of the natural family and something more'.

For me, the dialogue with God – and with Father Louis – stopped at the door of my lycée in Avignon. I never hated Catholicism, I just forgot about it. The pages of the gospel, which I had never really read, were replaced by Rimbaud, Rousseau and Voltaire (less the Voltaire of Écrasez l'infâme than that of Candide, in which the Jesuits are all gay). I believe less in the Bible than in literature – it strikes me as more trustworthy, its pages are infinitely more beautiful and in the end less fantastical.

So in Avignon I went on assiduously attending the Chapelle des Pénitents Gris, the Cloître des Carmes, the Chapelle des Pénitents Blancs, the Jardin Urbain V, the Cloître des Célestins and, most importantly, the Cour d'Honneur at the Palais des Papes, but not to take Christian instruction: I had seen pagan spectacles there. Avignon was, as we know, the capital of Christendom and the seat of the papacy in the fourteenth century, with nine popes living there (and my second Christian name, according to a popular tradition in Avignon, is Clément, like three of those popes, including an anti-pope!). However, for most French people today, Avignon represents something else: the capital of public secular theatre. Henceforth, my gospels were called Hamlet and Angels in America, and I am not afraid to write that Molière's Dom Juan means more to me than the Gospel of John. I would even give the whole of the Bible in exchange for the whole of Shakespeare, and one single page of Rimbaud means more to me than the complete works of Joseph Ratzinger! And besides, I have never put a Bible in the drawer of my bedside table, but instead A Season in Hell, in the Pléiade edition which, with its Bible-like paper, looks like a prayer book. I have only a few books in this lovely collection but the Complete Works of Rimbaud are always within reach, placed near my bed, in case of insomnia or bad dreams. It's become a rule of life.

Some traces remain of that religious training, which has now dissipated. In Paris, I continue the Provençal tradition, which consists of making a crib scene every year with little figurines bought at the santon fair in Marseille (we also eat at Christmas the famous '13 desserts'). I worked for several years on the journal Esprit; my cinematic tastes were shaped by the thought of the Catholic critic André Bazin. If, as a reader of Kant, Nietzsche and Darwin, and a son of Rousseau and Descartes more than Pascal – I'm French, after all! – I can no longer be a believer today, not even a 'cultural Christian', I respect Christian culture and therefore the '(cultural) genius of Christianity'. And I like that phrase from a French prime minister who said: 'I'm a Protestant atheist.' Let's say, then, that I'm a 'Catholic atheist', an atheist of Catholic culture. Or, to put it another way, I'm a 'Rimbaldien'.

In my parish near Avignon (which Louis also left after being appointed curé to another town in Provence in 1981), Catholicism has declined. The curé, the Poet writes, 'has taken away the key of the church'. A church which didn't know how to move with its times: it relied on the celibacy of the priesthood, which is, as we can tell today, deeply unnatural, and forbade the sacraments to divorced people, even though most of the families in my village are now stepfamilies. Whereas there were three masses every Sunday with three priests in my church, there is now only one, every third Sunday, the travelling curé who has come from Africa, running from one parish to another, in this suburb of Avignon, which is now a Catholic desert. In France, about 800 priests die every year; fewer than a hundred are ordained ... Catholicism is gradually fading away.

For me too, Catholicism is a page that has been turned, without resentment or rancour, without animosity or anticlericalism. And soon Father Louis moved away too.

I learned of his death when I was living in Paris, and the loss of my priest at the age of 53 made me terribly sad. I wanted to pay tribute to him, so I wrote a little piece for the local pages of the daily paper Le Provençal (now La Provence), published anonymously under the title 'The Death of Father Louis'. Now I am rereading this article, which I have just rediscovered, and at the end of it I refer slightly naively to the Italian film Cinema Paradiso and its old Sicilian projectionist Alfredo, who taught the hero, Totò, a choirboy, to live; he was later able to free himself from the parish cinema and become a film director in Rome. And with those words, I said farewell to Louis.

And yet I would find him again almost twenty-five years later.

When I was finishing this book, and when I had lost trace of Father Louis for many years, he re-entered my life unexpectedly. One of Louis's female friends, a progressive parishioner with whom I had stayed in contact, told me about the end of his life. Far from Avignon, living in Paris, I had known nothing about it; and nobody in the parish had known his secrets. Louis was homosexual. He lived a double life which, retrospectively, made sense of his paradoxes, his ambiguities. Like so many priests, he tried to marry his faith and his sexual orientation. It seems to me, as I remember this atypical priest whom we loved so much, that he was troubled by a pain within, a sadness. But it is possible that this reading is merely retrospective.

I have also learned of the conditions of his death. In his biography, which the diocese gave me when I did my research, the end of his life is discreetly set out: 'Retired Priests' Hostel in Aix-en-Provence from 1992 until 1994'. But speaking to his friends, another reality appeared: Louis died of AIDS.

During those years when the illness was almost always fatal, and just before – alas – he was able to benefit from anti-retroviral drugs, Louis was first treated at the Institut Paoli-Calmette in Marseille, a hospital that specialized in the treatment of AIDS early on, before being moved to a clinic in Villeneuve d'Aix-en-Provence, run by the Sisters of the Chapel of St Thomas. That was where he died 'desperately waiting', I was told, for a treatment that did not arrive in time. He never really talked about his homosexuality and denied the nature of his illness. Most of his religious colleagues, probably informed about the nature of his condition, abandoned him. Demonstrating solidarity would have meant, here again, supporting a gay priest and perhaps running the risk of being suspected. The authorities of the diocese preferred to hide the causes of his death and most of the priests who had worked alongside him, frightened now, vanished as soon as he was bedridden. He contacted them, but none of them replied. Hardly anyone visited him. (One of the few priests who stayed with him until the end wondered, when I interviewed him, whether it wasn't Louis who wanted to put distance between himself and his co-religionists; Cardinal Jean-Pierre Ricard, currently archbishop of Bordeaux, who was at the time an auxiliary vicar in Marseille, whom I questioned over lunch in Bordeaux, remembered Father Louis but told me he had forgotten the details of his death.)

'He died on his own, abandoned by almost everyone, in terrible pain. He didn't want to die. He rebelled against death,' says one of the women, a left-wing Christian, who was with him at the end of his life.

Today, I think of the suffering of that man on his own, rejected by the Church – his only family – denied by his diocese and kept at arm's length by his bishop. That all happened under the pontificate of John Paul II.

AIDS? A priest with AIDS? 'I simply had to frown as if someone had set out a difficult problem. It took me a long time to understand that I was going to die of a disease that is found rarely among people of my age.' That was the reaction of the young country priest, learning that he has contracted stomach cancer, in that fine novel by Georges Bernanos and the even more magnificent film by Robert Bresson. The young man also says: 'I did repeat to myself that nothing had changed in me, but still the thought of going home with this thing made me ashamed.' I don't know if Louis thought the same thing during his own martyrdom. I don't know whether, in his fragility and his distress, he believed and thought, like Bernanos's priest: 'God withdrew from me'.

In fact, Louis was never a 'country priest', as the subtitle of the collection of his homilies reveals. The comparison with Bernanos's curé, looking for the help of grace, is therefore slightly deceptive. Louis never had an ordinary, modest life. He was an aristocratic priest who, taking the path opposite to the one adopted by many official prelates, who are born poor and end up in lust and luxury in the Vatican; he began his life in the aristocracy and ended it in contact with simple people, and I know that in that reversal, for him and for them, homosexuality played its part.

It is incomprehensible to me that the Church could have been insensitive to his Via Dolorosa. That his Christ-like suffering, bad blood, filth and fainting received no response from the diocese was for a long time a scandal to me – a mystery. It makes me shiver to think of it.

Only the nuns of the Chapel of Saint Thomas, magnificently devoted, surrounded him with their anonymous affection until his death in early summer 1994. A bishop finally agreed to preside over the ceremony. Louis was then cremated in Manosque in the Alpes-de-Haute-Provence (burials of AIDS patients were forbidden at the time and cremation was mandatory). Some days later, in line with his wishes, his ashes were scattered in the sea, very discreetly, by four women, two of whom told me of the scene, from a little boat that he had bought at the end of his life, a few kilometres from Marseille, off the 'Calanques', where we had sometimes gone together. And in that region, that magnificent 'country', the 'South' of France – which we call 'the Midi' – they say that the only events are the storms.

ACKNOWLEDGEMENTS

The Closet is the account of an investigation carried out for over four years, in Italy and in over thirty countries. In all, 1,500 interviews were conducted for the book: among them were 41 cardinals, 52 bishops and monsignori, 45 apostolic nuncios, secretaries of nunciatures or foreign ambassadors, 11 Swiss Guards and over 200 Catholic priests and seminarians. Most of the information included here is first-hand, collected by the author in person and on the ground (no interviews have been carried out by phone or email).

Most of the 41 cardinals I have met in the course of over 130 interviews are members of the Roman Curia. Here is the list: Angelo Bagnasco, Lorenzo Baldisseri, Giuseppe Betori, the late Dario Castrillón Hoyos, Francesco Coccopalmerio, Stanisław Dziwisz, Roger Etchegaray, Raffaele Farina, Fernando Filoni, Julián Herranz, Juan Sandoval Íñiguez, Walter Kasper, Dominique Mamberti, Renato Raffaele Martino, Laurent Monsengwo, Gerhard Ludwig Müller, Juan José Omella, Jaime Ortega, Carlos Osoro, Marc Ouellet, George Pell, Paul Poupard, Giovanni Battista Re, Jean-Pierre Ricard, Franc Rodé, Camillo Ruini, Louis Raphaël Sako, Leonardo Sandri, Odilo Scherer, Achille Silvestrini, James Francis Stafford, Daniel Sturla, the late Jean-Louis Tauran, Jozef Tomko (seven other cardinals I interviewed do not appear here and remain anonymous because they explicitly asked to remain 'off the record').

To carry out this investigation, I lived regularly in Rome, for an average of a week a month, between 2015 and 2018. I was also able to stay several times within the Vatican and was given lodgings in two other extraterritorial residences in the holy see, including, for a long time, the Domus International Paulus VI (or Casa del Clero) and Domus Romana Sacerdotalis. I also carried out investigations in about fifty Italian cities, including, several times, Milan, Florence, Bologna, Naples and Venice, as well as Castel Gandolfo, Cortona, Genoa, Ostia, Palermo, Perugia, Pisa, Pordenone, Spoleto, Tivoli, Trento, Trieste and Turin.

Apart from the Vatican City and Italy, I have carried out investigations in about thirty other countries to which I travelled for the purposes of research: Argentina (Buenos Aires, San Miguel; 2014, 2017), Belgium (Brussels, Mons; several stays between 2015 and 2018), Bolivia (La Paz; 2015), Brazil (Belém, Brasilia, Porto Alegre, Recife, Rio de Janeiro, São Paulo; 2014, 2015, 2016, 2018), Chile (Salvador; 2014, 2017), Colombia (Bogotá, Cartagena, Medellin; 2014, 2015, 2017), Cuba (Havana; 2014, 2015, 2016), Ecuador (Quito; 2015), Egypt (Alexandria, Cairo; 2014, 2015),Germany (several visits to Berlin, Frankfurt, Munich and Regensburg; 2015–18), Hong Kong (2014, 2015), India (New Delhi; 2015), Israel (Tel Aviv, Jerusalem, Dead Sea; 2015, 2016), Japan (Tokyo; 2016), Jordan (Amman; 2016), Lebanon (Beirut, Bkerké; 2015, 2017), Mexico (Guadalajara, Mexico City, Monterrey, Puebla,Veracruz, Xalapa; 2014, 2016, 2018), Palestine (Gaza, Ramallah; 2015, 2016), the Netherlands (Amsterdam; several visits between 2015 and 2018), Peru (Arequipa, Lima; 2014, 2015), Poland (Krakow, Warsaw; 2013, 2018), Portugal (Lisbon, Porto; 2016, 2017), Saudi Arabia (Riyadh; 2018), Spain (Barcelona, Madrid; many visits between 2015 and 2018), Switzerland (Basel, Coire, Geneva, Illnau-Effretikon, Lausanne, Lucerne, St Gallen and Zurich; several visits between 2015 and 2018), Tunisia (Tunis; 2018), United Arab Emirates (Dubai; 2016), United Kingdom (London; several visits between 2014 and 2018), Uruguay (Montevideo; 2017) United States (Boston, Chicago, New York, Philadelphia, San Francisco, Washington; 2015, 2016, 2017, 2018). Also before the beginning of this investigation I travelled to about twenty other countries, including Algeria, Canada, Cameroon, China, Denmark, Indonesia, Iran, Kenya, Russia, South Africa, South Korea, Taiwan, Thailand, Venezuela, Vietnam etc., which also provided useful information.

The Closet is based on rigorously precise quotations and sources. Most of the interviews were recorded, with the agreement of my interlocutors, or carried out in the presence of a researcher or translator, who was witness to them; all in all, I have almost four hundred hours of recordings. The quotations, in line with typical journalistic practice, have been reproduced verbatim.

As we might guess, the private testimonies of cardinals and prelates are infinitely more interesting than their public statements. Since my intention was not to 'out' living priests, I have chosen to protect my sources. And even though I am, on principle, quite reserved about unattributed statements, this book would not have been possible without this anonymization. I have however tried to limit their number to a minimum, preferring instead to use in the text the information communicated by the people I have interviewed. Similarly, in a few rare cases, and at their request, I have agreed to change the names of certain priests (the pseudonyms used have been clearly indicated throughout the book, and all come from characters created by André Gide). As for the cardinals Platinette and La Mongolfiera, the archbishop La Païva, or the famous monsignori Jessica and Negretto, they are 'authentic pseudonyms', if I can put it like that, used secretly at the Vatican. Any reader trying to make a connection between a pseudonym and a real name, or who comes across anonymized sources, would inevitably get lost.

An investigation of this kind could never have been conducted by one author working alone. To complete it, I have benefited from a team including over 80 collaborators, translators, advisers and researchers around the world. Among them, I should like to cite and thank here my main researchers who have accompanied me over this long adventure. The Italian journalist Daniele Particelli worked with me for three years and accompanied me constantly in Rome and Italy. In Argentina and Chile, Andrés Herrera carried out lengthy investigations for me on my various Hispanic visits. In Colombia, Emmanuel Neisa was a constant help. In Paris, the Mexican Luis Chumacero, who was able to translate to and from six languages, was my assistant. I also had the constant help of: René Buonocore, Fabricio Sorbara and the soldiers, police officers and carabinieri of the LGBT association 'Polis Aperta' in Italy; Enrique Anartelazo in Spain; Guilherme Altmayer, Tom Avendaño and Andrei Netto in Brazil; Pablo Simonetti in Chile; Miroslaw Wlekły, Marcin Wójcik and Jerzy Szczesny in Poland; Vassily Klimentov in Russia; Antonio Martínez Velázquez, Guillermo Osorno, Marcela Gonzáles Durán and Eliezer Ojedo Felix in Mexico; Jürg Koller, Meinrad Furrer and Martin Zimper in Switzerland; Michael Brinkschröder, Sergey Lagodinsky and Volker

Beck in Germany; Michael Denneny in the US; Hady ElHady in Egypt, Dubai and Lebanon; Abbas Saad in Lebanon and Jordan; Benny and Irit Ziffer in Israel; Louis de Strycker and Bruno Selun in Belgium; Erwin Cameron in South Africa; Nathan Marcel-Millet and Ignacio González in Cuba; Julian Gorodischer and David Jacobson in Argentina; Julia Mitsubizaya and Jonas Pulver in Japan; Alberto Servat in Peru; Martin Peake in Australia. (The complete list of this team of over 80 researchers in this book is available online.)

During my research for this book, I made four broadcasts about the Vatican for national radio on France Culture, several articles for *Slate* and the journal *Esprit*, and organized a colloquium about the diplomacy of Pope Francis at the University Sciences-Po-Paris. These parallel projects fed into this book, and afforded the opportunity for fruitful encounters.

I am infinitely grateful to my translators for their work – and their speed – particularly Matteo Schianchi (for the Italian), who has already translated three of my books, and Shaun Whiteside (for English).

My main editor, Jean-Luc Barré (at Robert Laffont/Editis), has believed in this book from early on: he was an attentive editor and a vigilant proofreader, without whom the book wouldn't exist. At Robert Laffont, Cécile Boyer-Runge has actively defended the project. At Feltrinelli, in Milan, I also owe a great deal to my Italian editors: my loyal friend Carlo Feltrinelli – who has believed in this book since 2015 – and of course Gianluca Foglia, who coordinated its publication; but also my editors Alessia Dimitri and Camilla Cottafavi. Robin Baird-Smith (Bloomsbury) was the vital editor of this book for the Anglo-Saxon world, along with his colleague Jamie Birkett. I also thank Blanca Rosa Roca, Carlos Ramos and Enrique Murillo and Pawel Gozlinski. I would also like to thank my Italian literary agent Valeria Frasca, as well as, for the Hispanic world, my adviser Marcela González Durán, and for the rest of the world, Benita Edzard.

For their proofreading and fact-checking, I would like to thank my friends Stéphane Foin, Andrés Herrera, Emmanuel Paquette, Daniele Particelli, Marie-Laure Defretin and three priests, an archbishop and a renowned Vaticanologist who must remain anonymous. The journalist Pasquale Quaranta has constantly helped me in Rome over the past four years. I also thank Sophie Berlin and Reinier Bullain Escobar. I should also like to thank my 28 'sources' within the Roman Curia – monsignori, priests, religious and lay people – all openly gay with me, who work or live in the Vatican every day: they were regular informants over four years, sometimes my 'hosts' in the Vatican, and without them this book would not have seen the light of day. Understandably, they have all remained anonymous in this book.

This book is accompanied and defended by a consortium of about fifteen lawyers, coordinated by the Frenchman Maître William Bourdon, the author's lawyer: Maître Appoline Cagnat (Bourdon & Associés) in France; Massimiliano Magistretti in Italy; Scott R. Wilson, Esq., in the United States; Maya Abu-Deeb (of Bloomsbury) and Felicity McMahon (of 5RB) in the United Kingdom; Juan Garcés in Spain; Juan Pablo Hermosilla in Chile; Antonio Martínez in Mexico; the legal office of Teixeira, Martis & Advogados in Brazil; Jürg Koller in Switzerland; Katharina Winter in Germany. Valérie Robe was my legal adviser for the French edition.

Finally, this book relies on a very large number of written sources, footnotes and a wide-ranging bibliography containing over a thousand references to books and articles. Since the format of this book does not allow us to cite them here, interested researchers and readers will find, free online, in a document of 300 pages, all of these sources as well as several unpublished chapters (my journey to the real Sodom in Israel-Palestine-Jordan; a chapter on France; a part about Brazil; and a text on the art and culture of the Vatican). All quotations are also given here with their references as well as 23 fragments from Rimbaud, 'the Poet' in this book.

For more: see the site www.sodoma.fr; updates will also be published under the hashtag #sodoma on the author's Facebook page: @fredericmartel as well as on his Instagram account: @martelfrederic and the Twitter feed: @martelf

A NOTE ON THE TYPE

The text of this book is set in Minion, a digital typeface designed by Robert Slimbach in 1990 for Adobe Systems. The name comes from the traditional naming system for type sizes, in which minion is between nonpareil and brevier. It is inspired by late Renaissance-era type.